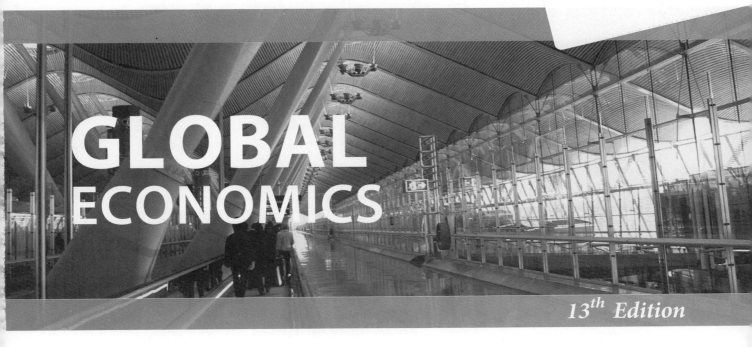

GLOBAL ECONOMICS

13ᵗʰ Edition

Robert J. Carbaugh

Professor of Economics
Central Washington University

SOUTH-WESTERN
CENGAGE Learning™

Australia • Brazil • Japan • Korea • Mexico • Singapore • Spain • United Kingdom • United States

SOUTH-WESTERN
CENGAGE Learning™

Global Economics, 13ᵗʰ Edition
Robert J. Carbaugh

Vice President of Editorial, Business:
Jack W. Calhoun

Vice President/Marketing: Bill Hendee

Publisher: Joe Sabatino

Executive Editor: Michael Worls

Supervising Developmental Editor:
Katie Yanos

Executive Marketing Manager:
Keri Witman

Associate Marketing Manager: Betty Jung

Content Project Management:
PreMediaGlobal

Manager of Technology, Editorial:
Emily Gross

Media Editor: Deepak Kumar

Senior Manufacturing Coordinator:
Sandee Milewski

Print Buyer: Arethea Thomas

Production Service: PreMediaGlobal

Copyeditor: Jonathan Moore

Senior Art Director: Michelle Kunkler

Cover Designer: Patti Hudepohl

Cover Image: © Shuterstock

Photo Credits:
B/W Image: Comstock Images

Cover Image: © 2010 Photos.com,
a division of Getty Images. All rights
reserved.

Permissions Acquisitions Manager, Text:
Mardell Glinski Schultz

Permissions Acquisitions Manager, Images:
Deanna Ettinger

Exam_View_® is a registered trademark of eInstruction Corp. Windows is a registered trademark of the Microsoft Corporation used herein under license. Macintosh and Power Macintosh are registered trademarks of Apple Computer, Inc. used herein under license.
© 2008 Cengage Learning. All Rights Reserved.
Cengage Learning WebTutor™ is a trademark of Cengage Learning.
Library of Congress Control Number: 2010933655
International Edition:
ISBN 13: 978-1-4390-4044-7
ISBN 10: 1-4390-4044-3

Cengage Learning International Offices

Asia
www.cengageasia.com
tel: (65) 6410 1200

Australia/New Zealand
www.cengage.com.au
tel: (61) 3 9685 4111

Brazil
www.cengage.com.br
tel: (55) 11 3665 9900

India
www.cengage.co.in
tel: (91) 11 4364 1111

Latin America
www.cengage.com.mx
tel: (52) 55 1500 6000

UK/Europe/Middle East/Africa
www.cengage.co.uk
tel: (44) 0 1264 332 424

Represented in Canada by
Nelson Education, Ltd.
tel: (416) 752 9100 / (800) 668 0671
www.nelson.com

Cengage Learning is a leading provider of customized learning solutions with office locations around the globe, including Singapore, the United Kingdom, Australia, Mexico, Brazil, and Japan. Locate your local office at:
cengage.com/global

For product information: **www.cengage.com/international**
Visit your local office: **www.cengage.com/global**
Visit our corporate website: **www.cengage.com**

Printed in Canada
1 2 3 4 5 6 7 14 13 12 11 10

AVAILABILITY OF RESOURCES MAY DIFFER BY REGION. Check with your local Cengage Learning representative for details.

Contents in Brief

Contents

v

CHAPTER 3

Sources of Comparative Advantage 79

CHAPTER **4**

Tariffs **123**

CHAPTER **5**

Nontariff Trade Barriers **169**

CHAPTER 6

Trade Regulations and Industrial Policies 207

CHAPTER 7

Trade Policies for the Developing Nations 255

CHAPTER 8

Regional Trading Arrangements 295

CHAPTER 9

International Factor Movements and Multinational Enterprises 339

CHAPTER 12

Exchange-Rate Determination 443

CHAPTER 13

Mechanisms of International Adjustment 473

CHAPTER 14

Exchange-Rate Adjustments and the Balance of Payments 485

CHAPTER 15

Exchange-Rate Systems and Currency Crises 507

Preface

My belief is that the best way to motivate students to learn a subject is to demonstrate how it is used in practice. The first twelve editions of *Global Economics* reflected this belief and were written to provide a serious presentation of international economic theory with an emphasis on current applications. Adopters of these editions strongly supported the integration of economic theory with current events.

The thirteenth edition has been revised with an eye toward improving this presentation and updating the applications as well as toward including the latest theoretical developments. Like its predecessors, this edition is intended for use in a one-quarter or one-semester course for students who have no more of a background than the principles of economics. This book's strengths are its clarity, organization, and applications, which demonstrate the usefulness of theory to students. The revised and updated material in this edition emphasizes current applications of economic theory and incorporates recent theoretical and policy developments in international trade and finance.

International Economics Themes

This edition highlights six current themes that are at the forefront of international economics:

- The Global Economic Downturn of 2007–2009
  - Anatomy of the economic crisis—Ch. 1
  - Trade protectionism intensifies as economies fall into recession—Ch. 4
  - U.S. fiscal stimulus and "Buy American" legislation—Ch. 5
  - Do government subsidies to automakers weaken the World Trade Organization?—Ch. 6
  - Falling commodity prices squeeze the economies of developing nations—Ch. 7
  - Does the U.S. tax code send American jobs offshore?—Ch. 9
  - The paradox of capital flows from developing countries to advanced countries—Ch. 10
- Globalization of economic activity
  - Waves of globalization—Ch. 1
  - Has globalization gone too far?—Ch. 1
  - Putting the H-P Pavilion together—Ch. 1
  - Soaring transportation costs hinder globalization—Ch. 3
  - Constraints imposed by capital flows on the choice of an exchange rate system—Ch. 15

- Free trade and the quality of life issues
  - Does the principle of comparative advantage apply in the face of job outsourcing?—Ch. 2
  - Boeing outsources work, but protects its secrets—Ch. 2
  - Does trade make the poor even poorer?—Ch. 3
  - Does wage insurance make free trade more acceptable to workers?—Ch. 6
  - The environment and free trade—Ch. 6
- Trade conflicts between developing and advanced nations
  - Is international trade a substitute for migration?—Ch. 3
  - Economic growth strategies—import substitution versus export-led growth—Ch. 7
  - Does foreign aid promote the growth of developing countries?—Ch. 7
  - How to bring developing countries in from the cold—Ch. 7
  - The Doha Round of multilateral trade negotiations—Ch. 6
  - China's export boom comes at a cost: how to make factories play fair—Ch. 7
  - Do U.S. multinationals exploit foreign workers?—Ch. 9
- Liberalizing trade: the WTO versus regional trading arrangements
  - Does the WTO reduce national sovereignty?—Ch. 6
  - Regional integration versus multilateralism—Ch. 8
  - Is Europe really a common market?—Ch. 8
  - French and Dutch Voters Sidetrack European Integration—Ch. 8
  - From NAFTA to CAFTA—Ch. 8
  - Will the Euro Fail?—Ch. 8
- The dollar as a reserve currency
  - Paradox of foreign debt: how the United states has borrowed without cost—Ch. 10
  - Why a dollar depreciation may not close the U.S. trade deficit—Ch. 14
  - Preventing currency crises: currency boards versus dollarization—Ch. 15
  - China lets Yuan rise against dollar—Ch. 15
  - Should the Special Drawing Right replace the dollar as the world's reserve currency?—Ch. 17

Besides emphasizing current economic themes, the thirteenth edition of this text contains many new contemporary topics such as outsourcing and the U.S. auto industry, U.S. safeguards limit imports of textiles from China, bailout fund for the Eurozone, bike imports force Schwinn to downshift, and currency markets draw day traders. Faculty and students will appreciate how this edition provides a contemporary approach to international economics.

Organizational Framework: Exploring Further Sections

Although instructors generally agree on the basic content of an international economics course, opinions vary widely about which arrangement of material is appropriate. This book is structured to provide considerable organizational flexibility. The topic of international trade relations is presented before international monetary relations, but the order can be reversed by instructors who choose to start with monetary theory. Instructors can begin with Chapters 10–17 and conclude with Chapters 2–9. Those who do not wish to cover all the material in the book can easily omit all or parts of Chapters 6–9 and Chapter 13, and Chapters 15–17 without loss of continuity.

The thirteenth edition streamlines its presentation of theory so as to provide greater flexibility for instructors. This edition uses *Exploring Further* sections at the end of certain chapters to discuss more advanced topics. The *Exploring Further* sections consist of the following:

- Comparative advantage in money terms—Ch. 2
- Indifference curves and trade—Ch. 2
- Offer curves and the equilibrium terms of trade—Ch. 2
- The specific-factors theory—Ch. 3
- WTO Makes Ruling on Boeing-Airbus Aircraft Subsidy Dispute—Ch. 3
- Offer curves and tariffs—Ch. 4
- Tariff-rate quota welfare effects—Ch. 5
- Export quota welfare effects—Ch. 5
- Welfare effects of strategic trade policy—Ch. 6
- Government procurement policy and the European Union—Ch. 8
- Economies of scale and NAFTA—Ch. 8
- Can the Euro Survive?—Ch. 8
- Techniques of foreign-exchange market speculation—Ch. 11
- A primer on foreign-exchange trading—Ch. 11
- Fundamental forecasting—regression analysis—Ch. 12
- Income adjustment mechanism—Ch. 13
- Exchange rate pass-through—Ch. 14

Supplementary Materials

Global Economics Web Site (www.cengage.com/international)

In this age of technology, no text package would be complete without Web-based resources. An international economics website is offered with the thirteenth edition. This site, **www.cengage.com/international**, contains many useful pedagogical enrichment features including NetLink Exercises, which draw upon the expanded NetLinks feature at the end of each chapter. While the NetLinks direct the student to an appropriate international economics website to gather data and other relevant information, the NetLink Exercises allow students to access these Web sites to answer pertinent and practical questions that relate to international economics. As an added enrichment feature, a Virtual Scavenger Hunt engages and encourages students to search for international economics answers at various Internet Web sites.

PowerPoint Slides

The thirteenth edition also includes PowerPoint slides created by Andreea Chiritescu of Eastern Illinois University. These slides can be easily downloaded from the Carbaugh Web site (**www.cengage.com/international**). The slides offer professors flexibility in enhancing classroom lectures. Slides may be edited to meet individual needs.

Instructor's Manual

To assist instructors in the teaching of international economics, I have written an *Instructor's Manual with Test Bank* that accompanies the thirteenth edition. It contains: (1) brief answers to end-of-chapter study questions; (2) multiple-choice questions for each chapter; and (3) true-false questions for each chapter. The *Instructor's Manual with Test Bank* is available for download for qualified instructors from the Carbaugh Web site (**www.cengage.com/international**).

Study Guide

To accompany the thirteenth edition of the international economics text, Professor Jim Hanson of Willamette University has prepared an online *Study Guide* for students. This guide reinforces key concepts by providing a review of the text's main topics and offering practice problems, true-false and multiple-choice questions, and short-answer questions. Contact your local Cengage representative for details.

Acknowledgments

I am pleased to acknowledge those who aided me in preparing the current and past editions of this textbook. Helpful suggestions and often detailed reviews were provided by:

- Burton Abrams, University of Delaware
- Richard Adkisson, New Mexico State University
- Richard Anderson, Texas A&M
- Brad Andrew, Juniata College
- Richard Ault, Auburn University
- Mohsen Bahmani-Oskooee, University of Wisconsin—Milwaukee
- Kevin Balsam, Hunter College
- Kelvin Bentley, Baker College Online
- Robert Blecker, Stanford University
- Scott Brunger, Maryville College
- Jeff W. Bruns, Bacone College
- Roman Cech, Longwood University
- John Charalambakis, Asbury College
- Mitch Charkiewicz, Central Connecticut State University
- Xiujian Chen, California State University, Fullerton
- Miao Chi, University of Wisconsin—Milwaukee
- Howard Cochran, Jr., Belmont University
- Charles Chittle, Bowling Green University
- Christopher Cornell, Fordham University
- Elanor Craig, University of Delaware
- Manjira Datta, Arizona State University
- Ann Davis, Marist College
- Firat Demir, University of Oklahoma
- Gopal Dorai, William Paterson College
- Veda Doss, Wingate University
- Seymour Douglas, Emory University
- G. Rod Erfani, Transylvania University
- Carolyn Fabian Stumph, Indiana University-Purdue University Fort Wayne

- Farideh Farazmand, Lynn University
- Daniel Falkowski, Canisius College
- Patrice Franko, Colby College
- Emanuel Frenkel, University of California—Davis
- Norman Gharrity, Ohio Wesleyan University
- Sucharita Ghosh, University of Akron
- Jean-Ellen Giblin, Fashion Institute of Technology (SUNY)
- Leka Gjolaj, Baker College
- Thomas Grennes, North Carolina State University
- Darrin Gulla, University of Kentucky
- Li Guoqiang, University of Macau (China)
- William Hallagan, Washington State University
- Jim Hanson, Willamette University
- Bassam Harik, Western Michigan University
- John Harter, Eastern Kentucky University
- Seid Hassan, Murray State University
- Phyllis Herdendorf, Empire State College (SUNY)
- Pershing Hill, University of Alaska-Anchorage
- David Hudgins, University of Oklahoma
- Ralph Husby, University of Illinois-Urbana/Champaign
- Robert Jerome, James Madison University
- Mohamad Khalil, Fairmont State College
- Wahhab Khandker, University of Wisconsin—La Crosse
- Robin Klay, Hope College
- William Kleiner, Western Illinois University
- Anthony Koo, Michigan State University
- Faik Koray, Louisiana State University
- Peter Karl Kresl, Bucknell University
- Fyodor Kushnirsky, Temple University
- Edhut Lehrer, Northwestern University
- Jim Levinsohn, University of Michigan
- Benjamin Liebman, St. Joseph's University
- Susan Linz, Michigan State University
- Andy Liu, Youngstown State University
- Alyson Ma, University of San Diego
- Mike Marks, Georgia College School of Business
- John Muth, Regis University
- Al Maury, Texas A&I University
- Jose Mendez, Arizona State University
- Mary Norris, Southern Illinois University
- John Olienyk, Colorado State University
- Shawn Osell, Minnesota State University—Mankato
- Terutomo Ozawa, Colorado State University
- Peter Petrick, University of Texas at Dallas
- Gary Pickersgill, California State University, Fullerton
- William Phillips, University of South Carolina
- John Polimeni, Albany College of Pharmacy and Health Sciences
- Rahim Quazi, Prairie View A&M University
- Chuck Rambeck, St. John's University

- James Richard, Regis University
- Daniel Ryan, Temple University
- Manabu Saeki, Jacksonville State University
- Nindy Sandhu, Claifornia State University, Fullerton
- Jeff Sarbaum, University of North Carolina, Greensboro
- Anthony Scaperlanda, Northern Illinois University
- Juha Seppälä, University of Illinois
- Ben Slay, Middlebury College (now at PlanEcon)
- Gordon Smith, Anderson University
- Robert Stern, University of Michigan
- Paul Stock, University of Mary Hardin-Baylor
- Laurie Strangman, University of Wisconsin—La Crosse
- Manjuri Talukdar, Northern Illinois University
- Nalitra Thaiprasert, Ball State University
- William Urban, University of South Florida
- Jorge Vidal, The University of Texas Pan American
- Adis M. Vila, Esq., Winter Park Institute Rollins College
- Jonathan Warshay, Baker College
- Darwin Wassink, University of Wisconsin—Eau Claire
- Peter Wilamoski, Seattle University
- Harold Williams, Kent State University
- Chong Xiang, Purdue University
- Hamid Zangeneh, Widener University

I would like to thank my colleagues at Central Washington University—Tim Dittmer, David Hedrick, Koushik Ghosh, Tyler Prante, Peter Saunders, Thomas Tenerelli, Chad Wassell—for their advice and help while I was preparing the manuscript. I am also indebted to Shirley Hood who provided advice in the manuscript's preparation.

It has been a pleasure to work with the staff of South-Western—Mike Worls, Katie Yanos and Lena Mortis—who provided many valuable suggestions and assistance in seeing this edition to its completion. Thanks also go to Jennifer Ziegler and Jean Buttrom, who orchestrated the production of this book in conjunction with Mary Stone, project manager at PreMediaGlobal. I also appreciate the meticulous efforts that Jonathan Moore did in the copyediting of this textbook. Moreover, Keri Witman and Betty Jung did a fine job in advertising and marketing the thirteenth edition. Finally, I am grateful to my students, as well as the faculty and students at other universities, who provided helpful comments on the material contained in this new edition.

I would appreciate any comments, corrections, or suggestions that faculty or students wish to make so I can continue to improve this text in the years ahead. Please contact me! Thank you for permitting this text to evolve to a thirteenth edition.

Bob Carbaugh
Department of Economics
Central Washington University
Ellensburg, Washington 98926
Phone: (509) 963–3443
Fax: (509) 963–1992
Email: Carbaugh@cwu.edu

The International Economy and Globalization

In today's world, no nation exists in economic isolation. All aspects of a nation's economy—its industries, service sectors, levels of income and employment, and living standard—are linked to the economies of its trading partners. This linkage takes the form of international movements of goods and services, labor, business enterprise, investment funds, and technology. Indeed, national economic policies cannot be formulated without evaluating their probable impacts on the economies of other countries.

The high degree of **economic interdependence** among today's economies reflects the historical evolution of the world's economic and political order. At the end of World War II, the United States was economically and politically the most powerful nation in the world, a situation expressed in the saying, "When the United States sneezes, the economies of other nations catch a cold." But with the passage of time, the U.S. economy has become increasingly integrated into the economic activities of foreign countries. The formation in the 1950s of the European Community (now known as the European Union), the rising importance in the 1960s of multinational corporations, the market power in the 1970s enjoyed by the Organization of Petroleum Exporting Countries (OPEC), and the creation of the euro at the turn of the twenty-first century have all resulted in the evolution of the world community into a complicated system based on a growing interdependence among nations.

Recognizing that world economic interdependence is complex and its effects uneven, the economic community has taken steps toward international cooperation. Conferences devoted to global economic issues have explored the avenues through which cooperation could be fostered between industrial and developing nations. The efforts of developing nations to reap larger gains from international trade and to participate more fully in international institutions have been hastened by the impact of the global recession, industrial inflation, and the burdens of high-priced energy.

Over the past 50 years, the world's market economies have become increasingly interdependent. Exports and imports as a share of national output have risen for most industrial nations, while foreign investment and international lending have expanded. This closer linkage of economies can be mutually advantageous for trading nations. It permits producers in each nation to take advantage of the specialization and efficiencies of large scale production. A nation can consume a wider variety of products at a cost less than that which could be achieved in the absence of trade. Despite these advantages, demands have grown for protection against imports. Protectionist pressures have been strongest during periods of rising unemployment caused by economic recession. Moreover, developing nations often maintain that the so-called liberalized trading system called for by industrial nations serves to keep the developing nations in poverty.

Economic interdependence also has direct consequences for a student taking an introductory course in international economics. As consumers, we can be affected by changes in the international values of currencies. Should the Japanese yen or British pound appreciate against the U.S. dollar, it would cost us more to purchase Japanese television sets or British automobiles. As investors, we might prefer to purchase Swiss securities if Swiss interest rates rise above U.S. levels. As members of the labor force, we might want to know whether the president plans to protect U.S. steelworkers and autoworkers from foreign competition.

In short, economic interdependence has become a complex issue in recent times, often resulting in strong and uneven impacts among nations and among sectors within a given nation. Business, labor, investors, and consumers all feel the repercussions of changing economic conditions and trade policies in other nations. Today's global economy requires cooperation on an international level to cope with the myriad issues and problems.

Globalization of Economic Activity

When listening to the news, we often hear about globalization. What does this term mean? **Globalization** is the process of greater interdependence among countries and their citizens. It consists of the increased interaction of product and resource markets across nations via trade, immigration, and foreign investment—that is, via international flows of goods and services, of people, and of investments in equipment, factories, stocks, and bonds. It also includes non-economic elements such as culture and the environment. Simply put, globalization is political, technological, and cultural, as well as economic.

In terms of people's daily lives, globalization means that the residents of one country are more likely now than they were 50 years ago to consume the products of another country, to invest in another country, to earn income from other countries, to talk by telephone to people in other countries, to visit other countries, to know that they are being affected by economic developments in other countries, and to know about developments in other countries.

What forces are driving globalization?[1] The first and perhaps most profound influence is technological change. Since the industrial revolution of the late 1700s, technical innovations have led to an explosion in productivity and slashed transportation costs. The steam engine preceded the arrival of railways and the mechanization of a growing number of activities hitherto reliant on muscle power. Later discoveries

---

[1]World Trade Organization, *Annual Report*, 1998, pp. 33–36.

and inventions such as electricity, the telephone, the automobile, container ships, and pipelines altered production, communication, and transportation in ways unimagined by earlier generations. More recently, rapid developments in computer information and communications technology have further shrunk the influence of time and geography on the capacity of individuals and enterprises to interact and transact around the world. For services, the rise of the Internet has been a major factor in falling communication costs and increased trade. As technical progress has extended the scope of what can be produced and where it can be produced, and advances in transport technology have continued to bring people and enterprises closer together, the boundary of tradable goods and services has been greatly extended.

Also, continuing liberalization of trade and investment has resulted from multilateral trade negotiations. For example, tariffs in industrial countries have come down from high double digits in the 1940s to about five percent in the early 2000s. At the same time, most quotas on trade, except for those imposed for health, safety, or other public policy reasons, have been removed. Globalization has also been promoted through the widespread liberalization of investment transactions and the development of international financial markets. These factors have facilitated international trade through the greater availability and affordability of financing.

Lower trade barriers and financial liberalization have allowed more and more companies to globalize production structures through investment abroad, which in turn has provided a further stimulus to trade. On the technology side, increased information flows and the greater tradability of goods and services have profoundly influenced production location decisions. Businesses are increasingly able to locate different components of their production processes in various countries and regions and still maintain a single corporate identity. As firms subcontract part of their production processes to their affiliates or other enterprises abroad, they transfer jobs, technologies, capital, and skills around the globe.

How significant is production sharing in world trade? Researchers have estimated production sharing levels by calculating the share of components and parts in world trade. They have concluded that global production sharing accounts for about 30 percent of the world trade in manufactured goods. Moreover, the trade in components and parts is growing significantly faster than the trade in finished products, highlighting the increasing interdependence of countries through production and trade.[2]

Waves of Globalization

In the past two decades, there has been pronounced global economic interdependence. Economic interdependence occurs through trade, labor migration, and capital (investment) flows such as corporation stocks and government securities. Let us consider the major waves of globalization that have occurred in recent history.[3]

---

[2]A. Yeats, *Just How Big Is Global Production Sharing?* World Bank, Policy Research Working Paper No. 1871, 1998, Washington, DC.

[3]This section draws from World Bank, *Globalization, Growth and Poverty: Building an Inclusive World Economy,* 2001.

First Wave of Globalization: 1870–1914

The first wave of global interdependence occurred from 1870 to 1914. It was sparked by decreases in tariff barriers and new technologies that resulted in declining transportation costs, such as the shift from sail to steamships and the advent of railways. The main agent that drove the process of globalization was how much muscle, horsepower, wind power, or later on, steam power a country had and how creatively it could deploy that power. This wave of globalization was largely driven by European and American businesses and individuals. Therefore, exports as a share of world income nearly doubled to about eight percent while per capita incomes, which had risen by 0.5 percent per year in the previous 50 years, rose by an annual average of 1.3 percent. The countries that actively participated in globalization, such as the United States, became the richest countries in the world.

However, the first wave of globalization was brought to an end by World War I. Also, during the Great Depression of the 1930s, governments responded by practicing protectionism: a futile attempt to enact tariffs on imports to shift demand into their domestic markets, thus promoting sales for domestic companies and jobs for domestic workers. For the world economy, increasing protectionism caused exports as a share of national income to fall to about five percent, thereby undoing 80 years of technological progress in transportation.

Second Wave of Globalization: 1945–1980

The horrors of the retreat into nationalism provided renewed incentive for internationalism following World War II. The result was a second wave of globalization that took place from 1945 to 1980. Falling transportation costs continued to foster increased trade. Also, nations persuaded governments to cooperate to decrease previously established trade barriers.

However, trade liberalization discriminated both in terms of which countries participated and which products were included. By 1980, trade between developed countries in manufactured goods had been largely freed of barriers. However, barriers facing developing countries had been eliminated for only those agricultural products that did not compete with agriculture in developed countries. For manufactured goods, developing countries faced sizable barriers. However, for developed countries, the slashing of trade barriers between them greatly increased the exchange of manufactured goods, thus helping to raise the incomes of developed countries relative to the rest.

The second wave of globalization introduced a new kind of trade: rich country specialization in manufacturing niches that gained productivity through **agglomeration economies**. Increasingly, firms clustered together, some clusters produced the same product, and others were connected by vertical linkages. Japanese auto companies, for example, became famous for insisting that their parts manufacturers locate within a short distance of the main assembly plant. For companies such as Toyota and Honda, this decision decreased the costs of transport, coordination, monitoring, and contracting. Although agglomeration economies benefit those in the clusters, they are bad news for those who are left out. A region can be uncompetitive simply because not enough firms have chosen to locate there. Thus, a divided world can emerge, in which a network of manufacturing firms is clustered in some high-wage region, while wages in the remaining regions stay low. Firms will not shift to a new location until the discrepancy in production costs becomes sufficiently large to compensate for the loss of agglomeration economies.

During the second wave of globalization, most developing countries did not participate in the growth of global trade in manufacturing and services. The combination of continuing trade barriers in developed countries, and unfavorable investment climates and antitrade policies in developing countries, confined them to dependence on agricultural and natural-resource products.

Although the second globalization wave succeeded in increasing per capita incomes within the developed countries, developing countries as a group were being left behind. World inequality fueled the developing countries' distrust of the existing international trading system, which seemed to favor developed countries. Therefore, developing countries became increasingly vocal in their desire to be granted better access to developed-country markets for manufactured goods and services, thus fostering additional jobs and rising incomes for their people.

Latest Wave of Globalization

The latest wave of globalization, which began in about 1980, is distinctive. First, a large number of developing countries, such as China, India, and Brazil, broke into the world markets for manufacturers. Second, other developing countries became increasingly marginalized in the world economy and realized decreasing incomes and increasing poverty. Third, international capital movements, which were modest during the second wave of globalization, again became significant.

Of major significance for this wave of globalization is that some developing countries succeeded for the first time in harnessing their labor abundance to provide them with a competitive advantage in labor-intensive manufacturing. Examples of developing countries that have shifted into manufacturing trade include Bangladesh, Malaysia, Turkey, Mexico, Hungary, Indonesia, Sri Lanka, Thailand, and the Philippines. This shift is partly due to tariff cuts that developed countries have made on imports of manufactured goods. Also, many developing countries liberalized barriers to foreign investment, which encouraged firms such as Ford Motor Company to locate assembly plants within their borders. Moreover, technological progress in transportation and communications permitted developing countries to participate in international production networks. However, the dramatic increase in manufactured exports from developing countries has contributed to protectionist policies in developed countries. With so many developing countries emerging as important trading countries, reaching further agreements on multilateral trade liberalization has become more complicated.

Although the world has become more globalized in terms of international trade and capital flows compared to 100 years ago, there is less globalization in the world when it comes to labor flows. The United States, for example, had a very liberal immigration policy in the late 1800s and early 1900s, and large numbers of people flowed into the country, primarily from Europe. As a large country with abundant room to absorb newcomers, the United States also attracted foreign investment throughout much of this period, which meant that high levels of migration went hand in hand with high and rising wages. However, since World War I, immigration has been a disputed topic in the United States, and restrictions on immigration have tightened. In contrast to the largely European immigration in the 1870–1914 globalization wave, contemporary immigration into the United States comes largely from Asia and Latin America.

TABLE 1.1

MANUFACTURING AN HP PAVILION, ZD8000
LAPTOP COMPUTER

Component	Major Manufacturing Country
Hard-disk drives	Singapore, China, Japan, United States
Power supplies	China
Magnesium casings	China
Memory chips	Germany, Taiwan, South Korea, Taiwan, United States
Liquid-crystal display	Japan, Taiwan, South Korea, China
Microprocessors	United States
Graphics processors	Designed in United States and Canada; produced in Taiwan

Source: From "The Laptop Trail," *The Wall Street Journal*, June 9, 2005, pp. B1 and B8.

Another aspect of the most recent wave of globalization is foreign outsourcing, in which certain aspects of a product's manufacture are performed in more than one country. As travel and communication became easier in the 1970s and 1980s, manufacturing increasingly moved to wherever costs were the lowest. For example, U.S. companies shifted the assembly of autos and the production of shoes, electronics, and toys to low-wage developing countries. This shift resulted in job losses for blue-collar workers producing these goods and cries for the passage of laws to restrict outsourcing.

When an American customer places an order online for a Hewlett-Packard (HP) laptop, the order is transmitted to Quanta Computer Inc. in Taiwan. To reduce labor costs, the company farms out production to workers in Shanghai, China. They combine parts from all over the world to assemble the laptop which is flown as freight to the United States, and then sent to the customer. About 95 percent of the HP laptop is outsourced to other countries. The outsourcing ratio is close to 100 percent for other U.S. computer producers including Dell, Apple, and Gateway. Table 1.1 shows how the HP laptop is put together by workers in many different countries.

By the 2000s, the Information Age resulted in the foreign outsourcing of white-collar work. Today, many companies' locations hardly matter. Work is connected through digitization, the Internet, and high-speed data networks around the world. Companies can now send office work anywhere, and that means places like India, Ireland, and the Philippines, where for a $1.50 to $2 per hour companies can hire college graduates to do the jobs that go for $12 to $18 per hour in the United States. Simply put, a new round of globalization is sending upscale jobs offshore, including accounting, chip design, engineering, basic research, and financial analysis, as seen in Table 1.2. Analysts estimate that foreign outsourcing can allow companies to reduce costs of a given service from 30 to 50 percent.

For example, Boeing uses aeronautics specialists in Russia to design luggage bins and wing parts for its jetliners. Having a master's degree or doctorate in math or aeronautics, these specialists are paid $650 per month in contrast to a monthly salary of $6,000 for an American counterpart. Similarly, engineers in China and India, earning $1,000 a month, develop chips for Texas Instruments and Intel; their American counterparts are paid $7,000 a month. However, companies are likely to keep crucial research and development and the bulk of office operations close to home. Many jobs cannot go anywhere because they require face-to-face contact with customers. Economists note that the vast majority of jobs in the United States consist of services such as retail, restaurants and hotels, personal care services, and the like. These services are necessarily produced and consumed locally, and thus cannot be sent off-shore.

Besides saving money, foreign outsourcing can enable companies to do things they simply couldn't do before. For example, a consumer products company in the United States found it impractical to chase down tardy customers buying less than

TABLE 1.2

GLOBALIZATION GOES WHITE COLLAR

U.S.Company	Country	Type of Work Moving
Accenture	Philippines	Accounting, software, office work
Conseco	India	Insurance claim processing
Delta Air Lines	India, Philippines	Airline reservations, customer service
Fluor	Philippines	Architectural blueprints
General Electric	India	Finance, information technology
Intel	India	Chip design, tech support
Microsoft	China, India	Software design
Philips	China	Consumer electronics, R&D
Procter & Gamble	Philippines, China	Accounting, tech support

Source: From "Is Your Job Next?" *Business Week*, February 3, 2003, pp. 50–60.

$1,000 worth of goods. When this service was run in India, however, the cost dropped so much the company could profitably follow up on bills as low as $100.

Although the Internet makes it easier for U.S. companies to remain competitive in an increasingly brutal global marketplace, is foreign outsourcing good for white-collar workers? A case can be made that Americans benefit from this process. In the 1990s, U.S. companies had to import hundreds of thousands of immigrants to ease engineering shortages. Now, by sending routine service and engineering tasks to nations with a surplus of educated workers, U.S. labor and capital can be shifted to higher-value industries and cutting-edge research and development.

However, a question remains: What happens if displaced white-collar workers cannot find greener pastures? The truth is that the rise of the global knowledge industry is so recent that most economists have not begun to figure out the implications. But people in developing nations like India see foreign outsourcing as a bonus because it helps spread wealth from rich nations to poor nations. Among its many other virtues, the Internet might turn out to be a great equalizer. Outsourcing will be further discussed at the end of Chapter 2.

The United States as an Open Economy

It is generally agreed that the U.S. economy has become increasingly integrated into the world economy (become an open economy) in recent decades. Such integration involves a number of dimensions that include the trade of goods and services, financial markets, the labor force, ownership of production facilities, and the dependence on imported materials.

Trade Patterns

To appreciate the globalization of the U.S. economy, go to a local supermarket. Almost any supermarket doubles as an international food bazaar. Alongside potatoes from Idaho and beef from Texas, stores display melons from Mexico, olive oil from Italy, coffee from Colombia, cinnamon from Sri Lanka, wine and cheese from France,

TABLE 1.3

THE FRUITS OF FREE TRADE: A GLOBAL FRUIT BASKET

On a trip to the grocery store, consumers can find goods from all over the globe.

Apples	New Zealand	Limes	El Salvador
Apricots	China	Oranges	Australia
Bananas	Ecuador	Pears	South Korea
Blackberries	Canada	Pineapples	Costa Rica
Blueberries	Chile	Plums	Guatemala
Coconuts	Philippines	Raspberries	Mexico
Grapefruit	Bahamas	Strawberries	Poland
Grapes	Peru	Tangerines	South Africa
Kiwifruit	Italy	Watermelons	Honduras
Lemons	Argentina		

Source: From "The Fruits of Free Trade," *Annual Report*, Federal Reserve Bank of Dallas, 2002, p. 3.

and bananas from Costa Rica. Table 1.3 shows a global fruit basket that is available for American consumers.

The grocery store isn't the only place Americans indulge their taste for foreign-made products. We buy cameras and cars from Japan, shirts from Bangladesh, DVD players from South Korea, paper products from Canada, and fresh flowers from Ecuador. We get oil from Kuwait, steel from China, computer programs from India, and semiconductors from Taiwan. Most Americans are well aware of our desire to import, but they may not realize that the United States ranks as the world's greatest exporter by selling personal computers, bulldozers, jetliners, financial services, movies, and thousands of other products to just about all parts of the globe. Simply put, international trade and investment are facts of everyday life.

As a rough measure of the importance of international trade in a nation's economy, we can look at the nation's exports and imports as a percentage of its gross domestic product (GDP). This ratio is known as **openness**.

$$Openness = \frac{(Exports + Imports)}{GDP}$$

Table 1.4 shows measures of openness for selected nations as of 2007. In that year, the United States exported 11 percent of its GDP while imports were 16 percent of GDP; the openness of the U.S. economy to trade thus equaled 27 percent. Although the U.S. economy is significantly tied to international trade, this tendency is even more striking for many smaller nations, as seen in the table. Simply put, large countries tend to be less reliant on international trade because many of their companies can attain an optimal production size without having to export to foreign nations. Therefore, small countries tend to have higher measures of openness than do large ones.

Figure 1.1 shows the openness of the U.S. economy from 1890 to 2007. One significant trend is that the United States became less open to international trade between 1890 and 1950. Openness was relatively high in the late 1800s due to the rise in world trade resulting from technological improvements in transportation (steamships) and communications (trans-Atlantic telegraph cable). However, two

TABLE 1.4

EXPORTS AND IMPORTS OF GOODS AND SERVICES AS A PERCENTAGE OF GROSS DOMESTIC PRODUCT GDP), 2007

Country	Exports as a Percentage of GDP	Imports as a Percentage of GDP	Exports Plus Imports as a Percentage of GDP
Netherlands	74	66	140
South Korea	46	45	91
Germany	45	40	85
Norway	46	29	75
Canada	38	34	72
United Kingdom	29	33	62
France	27	28	55
United States	11	16	27
Japan	14	13	27

Source: From The World Bank Group, *Data and Statistics: Country Profiles, 2008* available at **http://www.worldbank.org/data.**

world wars and the Great Depression of the 1930s caused the United States to reduce its dependence on trade, partly for national security reasons and partly to protect its home industries from import competition. Following World War II, the United States and other countries negotiated reductions in trade barriers, which contributed to rising world trade. Technological improvements in shipping and communications also bolstered trade and the increasing openness of the U.S. economy.

The relative importance of international trade for the United States has increased by about 50 percent during the past century, as seen in Figure 1.1. But a significant fact is hidden by these data. In 1890, most U.S. trade was in raw materials and

FIGURE 1.1

OPENNESS OF THE U.S. ECONOMY, 1890–2007

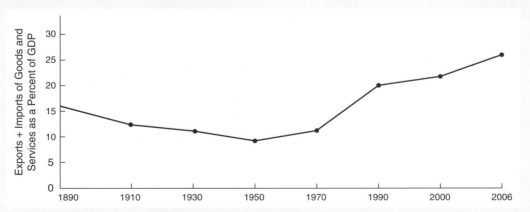

The figure shows that for the United States the importance of international trade has increased by more than 50 percent from 1890 to the early 2000s.

Source: Data from U.S. Census Bureau, Foreign Trade Division, *U.S. Trade in Goods and Services*, at **http://www.census.gov/foreign-trade/statistics.**

agricultural products, today, manufactured goods and services dominate U.S. trade flows. Therefore, American producers of manufactured products are more affected by foreign competition than they were a hundred years ago.

The significance of international trade for the U.S. economy is even more noticeable when specific products are considered. For example, we would have fewer personal computers without imported components, no aluminum if we did not import bauxite, no tin cans without imported tin, and no chrome bumpers if we did not import chromium. Students taking a 9 a.m. course in international economics might sleep through the class (do you really believe this?) if we did not import coffee or tea. Moreover, many of the products we buy from foreigners would be much more costly if we were dependent on our domestic production.

With which nations does the United States conduct trade? Canada, China, Mexico, and Japan head the list, as seen in Table 1.5.

Labor and Capital

Besides the trade of goods and services, movements in factors of production are a measure of economic interdependence. As nations become more interdependent, labor and capital should move more freely across nations.

However, during the past 100 years, labor mobility has not risen for the United States. In 1900, about 14 percent of the U.S. population was foreign born. But from the 1920s to the 1960s, the United States sharply curtailed immigration. This curtailment resulted in the foreign-born U.S. population declining to 6 percent of the total population. During the 1960s, the United States liberalized restrictions and the flow of immigrants increased. By 2009, about 12 percent of the U.S. population was foreign born while foreigners made up about 14 percent of the labor force. People from Latin America accounted for about half of this figure while Asians accounted for another quarter. These immigrants contributed to economic growth in the United States by taking jobs in labor-scarce regions and filling the types of jobs native workers often shun.

TABLE 1.5

LEADING TRADE PARTNERS OF THE UNITED STATES, 2008

Country	Value of U.S. Exports of Goods (in billions of dollars)	Value of U.S. Imports of Goods (in billions of dollars)	Total Value of Trade (in billions of dollars)
Canada	260.9	335.6	596.5
China	71.5	337.8	409.3
Mexico	151.5	215.9	367.4
Japan	66.6	139.2	205.8
Germany	54.7	97.6	152.3
United Kingdom	53.8	58.6	112.4
South Korea	34.8	48.1	82.9
France	29.2	44.0	73.2
Taiwan	25.3	36.3	61.6
Malaysia	13.0	30.7	43.7

Source: From U.S. Census Bureau, "Foreign Trade Statistics," at **http://www.census.gov/foreign-trade/statistics**. See also U.S. Department of Commerce, Bureau of Economic Analysis, *U.S. Transactions by Area*, available at **http://www.bea.gov/**.

Although labor mobility has not risen for the United States in recent decades, the country has become increasingly tied to the rest of the world through capital (investment) flows. Foreign ownership of U.S. financial assets has risen since the 1960s. During the 1970s, OPEC recycled many of their oil dollars by making investments in U.S. financial markets. The 1980s also witnessed major flows of investment funds to the United States as Japan and other nations, with dollars accumulated from trade surpluses with the United States, acquired U.S. financial assets, businesses, and real estate. By the late 1980s, the United States was consuming more than it produced, and became a net borrower from the rest of the world to pay for the difference. Increasing concerns were raised about the interest cost of this debt to the U.S. economy and about the impact of this debt burden on the living standards of future U.S. generations. As a major lender to the United States, China openly criticized the United States in 2009 for being irresponsible in its financial affairs.

Globalization has also increased in international banking. The average daily turnover in today's foreign-exchange market (where currencies are bought and sold) is estimated at almost $2 trillion, compared to $205 billion in 1986. The global trading day begins in Tokyo and Sydney and, in a virtually unbroken 24-hour cycle, moves around the world through Singapore and Hong Kong to Europe and finally across the United States before being picked up again in Japan and Australia. London remains the largest center for foreign-exchange trading, followed by the United States; significant volumes of currencies are also traded in Asia, Germany, France, Scandinavia, Canada, and elsewhere.

In commercial banking, U.S. banks developed worldwide branch networks in the 1960s and 1970s for loans, payments, and foreign-exchange trading. Foreign banks also increased their presence in the United States throughout the 1980s and 1990s, reflecting the multinational population base of the United States, the size and importance of U.S. markets, and the role of the U.S. dollar as an international medium of exchange and reserve currency. Today, more than 250 foreign banks operate in the United States; in particular, Japanese banks have been the dominant group of foreign banks operating in the United States. Like commercial banks, securities firms have also globalized their operations.

By the 1980s, U.S. government securities were traded on virtually a 24-hour basis. Foreign investors purchased U.S. treasury bills, notes, and bonds, and many desired to trade during their own working hours rather than those of the United States. Primary dealers of U.S. government securities opened offices in such locations as Tokyo and London. Stock markets became increasingly internationalized, with companies listing their stocks on different exchanges throughout the world. Financial futures markets also spread throughout the world.

Why Is Globalization Important?

Because of trade, individuals, firms, regions, and nations can specialize in the production of things they do well and use the earnings from these activities to purchase from others those items for which they are high-cost producers. Therefore, trading partners can produce a larger joint output and achieve a higher standard of living than would otherwise be possible. Economists refer to this as the law of comparative advantage, which will be further discussed in Chapter 2.

GLOBALIZATION   THE GLOBAL RECESSION OF 2007–2009

Although globalization has provided benefits to many countries, when economic problems arise in a country such as the United States, they can easily be transmitted abroad. Let us consider the global economic crisis of 2007–2009.

In 2007, the global financial system resembled a patient in intensive care. The body was attempting to fight off a disease that was spreading, and as it did so, the body convulsed, stabilized for a time, and then convulsed again. The doctors in charge resorted to ever-more invasive treatment and experimented with remedies that have never been tried before. How did the global economy suffer its worst crisis since the 1930s?

The immediate cause of the global economic crisis was the collapse of the U.S. housing market and the resulting surge in mortgage loan defaults. Hundreds of billions of dollars in losses on these mortgages undermined the financial institutions that originated and invested in them. The implications for creditors and bond investors were clear: RUN from all financial institutions that might fail! Therefore, creditors and uninsured depositors pulled their funds and cashed out of securities issued by risky institutions and invested in U.S. Treasury securities that were considered to have no risk of default. Many institutions failed, such as Washington Mutual and Wachovia, and others struggled to survive. Banks were fearful about making loans to one another, let alone to businesses and households. As the credit spigot closed, the global economy withered. Global stock investors dumped their holdings in expectations of declining corporate earnings. The result was a self-reinforcing adverse economic downturn.

ROOTS OF THE PROBLEM

The roots of the problem stemmed from a lack of fear in the booming housing market of 2006. Traditionally, banks accepted deposits and made loans, eking out profits under the burden of heavy bank regulations designed to protect depositors. The banks took all the risk, but that created an incentive to know the borrower and lend money only to people who could actually pay it back. However, beginning in the 1970s, government-sponsored credit agencies like Fannie Mae and Freddie Mac began purchasing huge amounts of mortgage loans from banks and packaging them into mortgage-backed securities (MBS) which were sold to investors. Banks were thus replenished with funds that could then be used for additional mortgage loans. The MBS removed the risk of default from banks and shifted it to investors and the federal government, which implicitly guaranteed the investments. This system greatly reduced the fear of bankers in making mortgage loans. Also, bankers had no fear of making mortgage loans in a booming market because the expected appreciation of house prices would increase the value of the collateral if borrowers could not or would not pay. Moreover, households had little fear of purchasing a house with little or no down payment, because they were confident that housing prices would only go up.

Government also contributed to the financial crisis by pressuring banks to serve poor borrowers and poor regions of the country. Beginning in 1992, Congress pushed Fannie Mae and Freddie Mac to increase their purchases of mortgages going to low-income borrowers. The Community Reinvestment Act did the same thing with traditional banks. This approach resulted in mortgages being made to many households who were unable to repay their loans. Also, poorly designed capital requirements resulted in banks not having sufficient safety cushions during periods of economic downturn.

According to the **law of comparative advantage**, the citizens of each nation can gain by spending more of their time and resources doing those things in which they have a relative advantage. If a good or service can be obtained more economically through trade, it makes sense to trade for it instead of producing it domestically. It is a mistake to focus on whether a good is going to be produced domestically or abroad. The central issue is how the available resources can be used to obtain each

History shows that asset bubbles tend to occur when money is plentiful and inexpensive: Cheap money encourages leverage that boosts asset prices and encourages additional leverage. And money was very abundant and cheap in the United States in the early 2000s. That was partly due to low inflation and economic stability that decreased investors' perceptions of risk, and thus interest rates. Also, a flood of capital swept into U.S. financial instruments from high-saving emerging countries such as China. This flood was reinforced by the easy money policy of the Federal Reserve.

The Crisis Goes Global

The financial crisis that started in the United States soon spread to Europe. European banks were drawn into the financial crisis in part due to their exposure to defaulted mortgages in the United States. As these banks had to write off losses, fear and uncertainty spread regarding which banks had bad loans and whether they had enough capital to pay off their debt obligations. As banks became reluctant to lend money to each other, the interest rates on interbank loans increased. A number of European banks failed and stock market indexes declined worldwide. Investors transferred vast capital resources into stronger currencies such as the U.S. dollar, the yen, and the Swiss franc, leading many emerging nations to seek aid from the International Monetary Fund.

The financial crisis also spread to emerging economies that generally lacked the resources to restore confidence in their financial systems. Highly leveraged countries, such as Iceland, were vulnerable to the flight of capital. Countries that got rich during the commodities boom, such as oil-abundant Russia, were vulnerable to the global recession. Extremely poor countries suffered from decreases in foreign aid by wealthy countries. Even China experienced a substantial slowdown in growth as the global recession depressed its export markets.

Simply put, the global economic crisis of 2008–2009 was essentially a crisis of confidence. It started with bad real estate loans and highly leveraged bets on those loans. Then it froze credit markets in which banks would not lend to each other and businesses and households could not get the short-term loans needed to finance day-to-day operations.

One way to combat a crisis in confidence is to bolster the balance sheet of institutions that appear to be at risk, making it clear to creditors that they can once again safely lend to those institutions. This method should restore confidence and lessen the impact on the real economy. After some delay and confusion, the governments of the United States and Europe announced plans to pump liquidity into troubled financial institutions and to provide increased or unlimited deposit insurance to prevent runs on banks. Also, central banks in these countries engineered coordinated interest-rate reductions and purchased commercial paper and other money market instruments directly from corporate issuers and money market funds. Moreover, governments initiated large fiscal stimulus packages in the form of tax cuts and increased government spending. Finally, the International Monetary Fund provided financial aid to Iceland, Ukraine, Hungary, and other emerging countries. At the writing of this book in December 2009, it appeared that the recession was ending in the United States. Other aspects of the global economic downturn will be discussed in subsequent chapters of this book.

good at the lowest possible cost. When trading partners use more of their time and resources producing things they do best, they are able to produce a larger joint output, which provides the source for mutual gain.

International trade also results in gains from the competitive process. Competition is essential to both innovation and efficient production. International competition helps keep domestic producers on their toes and provides them with a strong incentive to improve the quality of their products. Also, international trade usually weakens monopolies. As countries open their markets, their monopoly producers face competition from foreign firms.

With globalization and import competition, U.S. prices have decreased for many products, like TV sets, toys, dishes, clothing, and so on. However, prices increased for many products untouched by globalization, such as cable TV, hospital services, sports tickets, rent, car repair, and others. From 1987 to 2003, faster growing import competition wrung inflationary pressures from domestic producer prices in a large range of industries, as seen in Figure 1.2. The gains from global markets are not restricted to goods traded internationally. They extend to such non-traded goods as houses, which contain carpeting, wiring, and other inputs now facing greater international competition.

FIGURE 1.2

GLOBAL COMPETITION LOWERS INFLATION

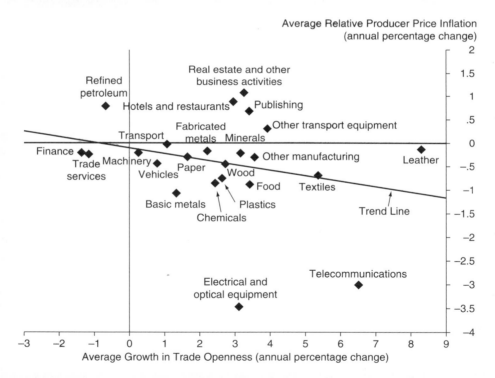

World imports relative to U.S. consumption have doubled over the past four decades, making more of what consumers purchase subject to increased competition inherent in international trade. This added competition tends to hold down the cost of goods and services as seen for the period 1987 to 2003.

Source: Drawn from "The Best of All Worlds: Globalizing the Knowledge Economy," *2006 Annual Report*, Federal Reserve Bank of Dallas, p. 12.

For example, during the 1950s General Motors (GM) was responsible for about 60 percent of all passenger cars produced in the United States. Although GM officials praised the firm's immense size for providing economies of scale in individual plant operations, skeptics were concerned about the monopoly power resulting from GM's dominance of the auto market. Some argued that GM should be broken up into several independent companies to inject more competition into the market. Today, however, stiff foreign competition has resulted in GM's current share of the market to stand at less than 24 percent.

Not only do open economies have more competition, but they also have more firm turnover. Being exposed to competition around the globe can result in high-cost domestic producers exiting the market. If these firms are less productive than the remaining firms, then their exit represents productivity improvements for the industry. The increase in exits is only part of the adjustment. The other part is new firms entering the market, unless there are significant barriers. With these new firms comes more labor market churning as workers formerly employed by obsolete firms must now find jobs in emerging ones. However, inadequate education and training can make some workers unemployable for emerging firms creating new jobs that we often cannot yet imagine. This is probably the key reason why workers find globalization to be controversial. Simply put, the higher turnover of firms is an important source of the dynamic benefits of globalization. In general, dying firms have falling productivity, and new firms tend to increase their productivity over time.

Also, economists have generally found that economic growth rates have a close relation to openness to trade, education, and communications infrastructure. For example, countries that open their economies to international trade tend to benefit from new technologies and other sources of economic growth. As Figure 1.3 shows, there appears to be some evidence of an inverse relation between the level of trade barriers and the economic growth of nations. That is, nations that maintain high barriers to trade tend to realize a low level of economic growth.

International trade can also provide stability for producers, as seen in the case of Invacare Corporation, an Ohio-based manufacturer of wheelchairs and other health care equipment. For the wheelchairs it sells in Germany, the electronic controllers come from the firm's New Zealand factories; the design is largely American; and the final assembly is done in Germany, with parts shipped from the United States, France, and the United Kingdom. By purchasing parts and components worldwide, Invacare can resist suppliers' efforts to increase prices for aluminum, steel, rubber, and other materials. By selling its products in 80 nations, Invacare can maintain a more stable workforce in Ohio than if it was completely dependent on the U.S. market. If sales decline anytime in the United States, Invacare has an ace up its sleeve—exports.

FIGURE 1.3

TARIFF BARRIERS VERSUS ECONOMIC GROWTH

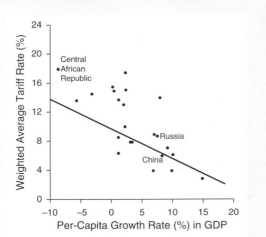

The figure shows the weighted average tariff rate and per-capita growth rate in GDP for 23 nations in 2002. According to the figure, there is evidence of an inverse relationship between the level of tariff barriers and the economic growth of nations.

Source: Data taken from The World Bank Group, *2005 World Development Indicators*, available at **http://www.worldbank.org/data/**.

On the other hand, rapid growth in countries like China and India has helped to increase the demand for commodities like crude oil, copper, and steel. Thus, American consumers and companies pay higher prices for items like gasoline. Rising gasoline prices, in turn, have spurred governmental and private-sector initiatives to increase the supply of gasoline substitutes like biodiesel or ethanol. Increased demand for these alternative forms of energy has helped to increase the price of soybeans, and corn, which are key inputs in the production of chicken, pork, beef, and other foodstuffs.

Moreover, globalization can make the domestic economy vulnerable to disturbances initiated overseas, as seen in the case of India. In response to India's agricultural crisis, some 1,200 Indian cotton farmers committed suicide during 2005–2007 to escape debts to money lenders. The farmers borrowed money at exorbitant rates, so they could sink wells and purchase expensive biotech cotton seeds. But the seeds proved inadequate for small plots, resulting in crop failures. Moreover, farmers suffered from the low world price of their cotton crop, which fell by more than a third from 1994–2007. Prices were low partly because cotton was heavily subsidized by wealthy countries, mainly the United States. According to the World Bank, cotton prices would have risen about 13 percent if the subsidies had been eliminated.

Although India's government could impose a tariff on imported cotton to offset the foreign subsidy, its textile manufacturers, who desired to keep production costs low, welcomed cheap fibers. Thus, India's cotton tariff was only 10 percent, much lower than its tariffs on most other commodities.

The simple solution to the problem of India's farmers would be to move them from growing cotton to weaving it in factories. But India's restrictive labor laws discourage industrial employment, and the lack of a safety net resulted in farmers clinging to their marginal plots of land.

There is great irony in the plight of India's cotton farmers. The British developed India's long-fiber cotton in the 1800s to supply British cotton mills. As their inexpensive cloth drove India's weavers out of business, the weavers were forced to work the soil. By the early 2000s, India's textile-makers were enjoying a revival, but its farmers could not leave the soil to work in factories.[4]

Globalization: Increased Competition From Abroad

Although economists recognize that globalization and free trade can provide benefits to many firms, workers, and consumers they can inflict burdens on others. Consider the cases of the Schwinn Bicycle Company and the Dell Computer Corporation.

Bicycle Imports Force Schwinn to Downshift

The Schwinn Bicycle Company illustrates the notion of globalization and how producers react to foreign competitive pressure. Founded in Chicago in 1895, Schwinn grew to produce bicycles that became the standard of the industry. Although the Great Depression drove most bicycle companies out of business, Schwinn survived by producing durable and stylish bikes; sold by dealerships that were run by people who understood bicycles and were anxious to promote the brand. Schwinn emphasized continuous innovation that resulted in features such as built-in kickstands, bal-

---

[4]"Cotton Suicides: The Great Unraveling," *The Economist*, January 20, 2007, p. 34.

loon tires, chrome fenders, head and taillights, and more. By the 1960s, the Schwinn Sting-Ray became the bicycle that virtually every child wanted. Celebrities such as Captain Kangaroo and Ronald Reagan pitched ads claiming that "Schwinn bikes are the best."

Although Schwinn dominated the U.S. bicycle industry, the nature of the bicycle market was changing. Cyclists wanted features other than heavy, durable bicycles that had been the mainstay of Schwinn for decades. Competitors emerged such as Trek, which built mountain bikes, and Mongoose, which produced bikes for BMX racing.

Moreover, falling tariffs on imported bicycles encouraged Americans to import from companies in Japan, South Korea, Taiwan, and eventually China. These companies supplied Americans with everything ranging from parts and entire bicycles under U.S. brand names, or their own brands. Using production techniques initially developed by Schwinn, foreign companies hired low-wage workers to manufacture competitive bicycles at a fraction of Schwinn's cost.

As foreign competition intensified, Schwinn moved production to a plant in Greenville, Mississippi in 1981. The location was strategic. Like other U.S. manufacturers, Schwinn relocated production to the South in order to hire nonunion workers at lower wages. Schwinn also obtained parts produced by low-wage workers in foreign countries. However, the Greenville plant suffered from uneven quality and low efficiency, and it produced bicycles no better than the ones imported from the Far East. As losses mounted for Schwinn, the firm declared bankruptcy in 1993.

Eventually Schwinn was purchased by the Pacific Cycle Company which farmed the production of Schwinn bicycles out to low-wage workers in China. Most Schwinn bicycles today are built in Chinese factories and are sold by Wal-Mart and other discount merchants. And cyclists do pay less for a new Schwinn under Pacific's ownership. It may not be the industry standard that was the old Schwinn, but it sells at Wal-Mart for approximately $180, about a third of the original price in today's dollars. Although cyclists lament that a Schwinn is no longer the bike it used to be, Pacific Cycle officials note that it is not as expensive as in the past either.[5]

Dell Sells Factories in Effort to Slash Costs

The personal computer (PC) business is full of rags-to-riches stories. But perhaps none is more dramatic than the rise (and fall) of Dell Computer Corporation.

In 1984, as a nineteen year old student at the University of Texas, Michael Dell started a computer company from a dorm room with a $1,000 in capital and built it into an industry powerhouse with a market capitalization of more than $100 billion. Initially, Dell Computer produced PCs in its own factories for a market that was dominated by business customers purchasing large quantities of desktop PCs. The firm pioneered an innovative strategy of selling computers directly to customers, only manufacturing them after they were ordered. After a customer placed an order over the phone or through the Web, the firm's factories assembled the needed components, installed PCs with software, and shipped them in a matter of hours.

---

[5]Judith Crown and Glenn Coleman, *No Hands: The Rise and Fall of the Schwinn Bicycle Company, an American Institution.* (New York, Henry Holt and Co., 1996) and Jay Pridmore, *Schwinn Bicycles.* (Osceola, WI, Motorbooks International, 2002). See also Griff Wittee, "A Rough Ride for Schwinn Bicycle," *The Washington Post*, December 3, 2004.

This system slashed idle inventory and allowed the firm to avoid marketing expenses associated with selling through retail channels. By 1999, Dell overtook Compaq to become the largest seller of PCs in the United States.

Although Dell has been highly efficient in producing desktop PCs, the firm has not been a low-cost manufacturer of laptops. Years ago, competitors such as Hewlett-Packard (HP) and Apple realized cost savings by entering into agreements with other firms to produce their laptops; many of these manufacturers are in low-wage countries such as Malaysia and China. Moreover, by the early 2000s, growth had switched to laptops sold to consumers at retail stores such as Best Buy and Office Max. However, Dell continued to lag behind its competitors in developing an efficient system to manufacture laptops. This lack of development resulted in a fall in Dell's sales and earnings and the replacement of the firm by HP as the world's biggest PC maker.

These adversities have forced Dell to sell many of its factories in an attempt to cut costs. Rather than producing PCs itself, the firm has increasingly contracted with foreign companies to manufacture them. In 2008, analysts estimated that Dell had reduced production costs for each computer by 15 to 20 percent by shifting manufacturing from the United States to China. It remains to be seen if Dell can chop its production costs further so as to regain its market leadership.

These two examples highlight how international trade is dynamic in nature as producers gain and lose competitiveness in response to changing market conditions.[6]

Common Fallacies of International Trade

Despite the gains derived from international trade, fallacies abound.[7] One fallacy is that trade is a zero-sum activity—if one trading party gains, the other must lose. In fact, just the opposite occurs—both partners gain from trade. Consider the case of trade between Brazil and the United States. These countries are able to produce a larger joint output when Brazilians supply coffee and Americans supply wheat. The larger production makes it possible for Brazilians to gain by using revenues from their coffee sales to purchase American wheat. At the same time, Americans gain by doing the opposite, by using revenues from their wheat sales to purchase Brazilian coffee. In turn, the larger joint output provides the basis for the mutual gains achieved by both. By definition, if countries specialize in what they are comparatively best at producing, they must import goods and services that other countries produce best. The notion that imports are "bad" but exports are "good"—popular among politicians and the media—is incorrect.

Another fallacy is that imports reduce employment and act as a drag on the economy, while exports promote growth and employment. This fallacy stems from a failure to consider the link between imports and exports. For example, American imports of German machinery provide Germans with the purchasing power to buy our computer software. If Germans are unable to sell as much to Americans, then they will have fewer dollars with which to buy from Americans. Thus, when the vol-

---

[6]Michael Dell, *Direct From Dell: Strategies that Revolutionized an Industry*, 2006, New York, Harper-Collins Publishers, Steven Holzner, *How Dell Does It*, 2006, McGraw Hill and Justin Scheck, "Dell Plans to Sell Factories in Effort to Cut Costs," *The Wall Street Journal*, September 5, 2008.

[7]*Twelve Myths of International Trade*, U.S. Senate, Joint Economic Committee, June 1999, pp. 2–4.

ume of U.S. imports decreases, the automatic secondary effect is that Germans have fewer dollars with which to purchase American goods. Therefore, sales, production, and employment will decrease in the U.S. export industries.

Also, people often feel that tariffs, quotas, and other import restrictions will save jobs and promote a higher level of employment. Like the previous fallacy, this one also stems from the failure to recognize that a reduction in imports does not occur in isolation. When we restrict foreigners from selling to us, we are also restricting their ability to obtain the dollars needed to buy from us. Thus, trade restrictions that reduce the volume of imports will also reduce exports. As a result, jobs saved by the restrictions tend to be offset by jobs lost due to a reduction in exports.

Why don't we use tariffs and quotas to restrict trade among the 50 states? After all, think of all the jobs that are lost when, for example, Michigan "imports" oranges from Florida, apples from Washington, wheat from Kansas, and cotton from Georgia. All of these products could be produced in Michigan. However, the residents of Michigan generally find it cheaper to "import" these commodities. Michigan gains by using its resources to produce and "export" automobiles, and other goods it can produce economically. Indeed, most people recognize that free trade among the 50 states is a major source of prosperity for each of the states. Similarly, most recognize that "imports" from other states do not destroy jobs—at least not for long.

The implications are identical for trade among nations. Free trade among the 50 states promotes prosperity; so, too, does free trade among nations. Of course, the sudden removal of trade barriers might harm producers and workers in protected industries. It can be costly to quickly transfer the protected resources to other, more productive activities. Gradual removal of the barriers would minimize this shock effect and the accompanying cost of relocation.

Does Free Trade Apply to Cigarettes?

When President George W. Bush pressured South Korea in 2001 to stop imposing a 40 percent tariff on foreign cigarettes, administration officials said the case had nothing to do with public health. Instead, it was a case against protecting the domestic industry from foreign competition. However, critics maintained that nothing is that simple with tobacco. They recognized that free trade, as a rule, increases competition, lowers prices, and makes better products available to consumers, leading to higher consumption. Usually, that's a good thing. However, with cigarettes, the result can be more smoking, disease, and death.

Globally, about 4 million people die each year from lung cancer, emphysema, and other smoking-related diseases, making cigarettes the largest single cause of preventable death. By 2030, the annual number of fatalities could hit 10 million, according to the World Health Organization. That has antismoking activists and even some economists arguing that cigarettes are not normal goods but are, in fact, "bads" that require their own set of regulations. They contend that the benefits of free trade do not apply to cigarettes and that they should be treated as an exception to trade rules.

This view is finding favor with some governments, as well. In recent talks of the World Health Organization, dealing with a global tobacco-control treaty, a range of nations expressed support for provisions to emphasize antismoking measures over free-trade rules. However, the United States opposed such measures. In fact, the

United States, which at home has sued tobacco companies for falsifying cigarettes' health risks, has promoted freer trade in cigarettes. For example, President Bill Clinton demanded a sharp reduction in Chinese tariffs, including those on tobacco, in return for U.S. support of China's entry into the World Trade Organization. Those moves, combined with free-trade pacts that have decreased tariffs and other barriers to trade, have helped stimulate the international sales of cigarettes.

The United States, first under President Clinton and then President Bush, has only challenged rules imposed to aid local cigarette makers, not nondiscriminatory measures to protect public health. The United States opposed South Korea's decision to impose a 40-percent tariff on imported cigarettes because it was discriminatory and aimed at protecting domestic producers and not at protecting the health and safety of the Korean people, according to U.S. trade officials. However, antismoking activists maintain that this is a false distinction and that anything that makes cigarettes more widely available at a lower price is harmful to public health. However, cigarette makers oppose limiting trade in tobacco. They maintain that there is no basis for creating new regulations that weaken the principle of open trade protected by the World Trade Organization.

Current trade rules permit countries to enact measures to protect the health and safety of their citizens, as long as all goods are treated equally, tobacco companies argue. For example, a trade-dispute panel notified Thailand that, although it could not prohibit foreign cigarettes, it could ban advertisements for both domestic and foreign-made smokes. But tobacco-control activists worry that the rules could be used to stop governments from imposing antismoking measures. They contend that special products need special rules, pointing to hazardous chemicals and weapons as goods already exempt from regular trade policies. Cigarettes kill more people every year than AIDS. Anti-tobacco activists think it's time for health concerns to be of primary importance in the case of smoking, too.

Is International Trade an Opportunity or a Threat to Workers?

- Tom lives in Chippewa Falls, Wisconsin. His former job as a bookkeeper for a shoe company, which employed him for many years, was insecure. Although he earns $100 a day, promises of promotion never panned out, and the company eventually went bankrupt as cheap imports from Mexico forced shoe prices down. Tom then went to a local university, earned a degree in management information systems, and was hired by a new machine-tool firm that exports to Mexico. He now enjoys a more comfortable living even after making the monthly payments on his government-subsidized student loan.

- Rosa and her family recently moved from a farm in southern Mexico to the country's northern border, where she works for a U.S.-owned electronics firm that exports to the United States. Her husband, Jose, operates a janitorial service and sometimes crosses the border to work illegally in California. Rosa, Jose, and their daughter have improved their standard of living since moving out of subsistence agriculture. However, Rosa's wage has not increased in the past year; she still earns about $2.25 per hour with no future gains in sight.

Workers around the globe are living increasingly intertwined lives. Most of the world's population now lives in countries that either are integrated into world markets for goods and finance or are rapidly becoming so. Are workers better off as a result of these globalizing trends? Stories about losers from international trade are often featured in newspapers: how Tom lost his job because of competition from poor Mexicans. But Tom currently has a better job, and the U.S. economy benefits from his company's exports to Mexico. Producing goods for export has led to an improvement in Rosa's living standard, and her daughter can hope for a better future. Jose is looking forward to the day when he will no longer have to travel illegally to California.

International trade benefits many workers. It enables them to shop for the cheapest consumption goods and permits employers to purchase the technologies and equipment that best complement their workers' skills. Trade also allows workers to become more productive as the goods they produce increase in value. Moreover, producing goods for export generates jobs and income for domestic workers. Workers in exporting industries appreciate the benefits of an open trading system.

But not all workers gain from international trade. The world trading system, for example, has come under attack by some in industrial countries in which rising unemployment and wage inequality have made people feel apprehensive about the future. Cheap exports produced by lower-cost, foreign workers threatens to eliminate jobs for some workers in industrial countries. Others worry that firms are relocating abroad in search of low wages and lax environmental standards or fear that masses of poor immigrants will be at their company's door, offering to work for lower wages. Trade with low-wage developing countries is particularly threatening to unskilled workers in the import-competing sectors of industrial countries.

As an economy opens up to international trade, domestic prices become more aligned with international prices; wages tend to increase for workers whose skills are more scarce internationally than at home and to decrease for workers who face increased competition from foreign workers. As the economies of foreign nations open up to trade, the relative scarcity of various skills in the world marketplace changes still further, harming those countries with an abundance of workers who have the skills that are becoming less scarce. Increased competition also suggests that unless countries match the productivity gains of their competitors, the wages of their workers will deteriorate. It is no wonder that workers in import-competing industries often lobby for restrictions on the importation of goods so as to neutralize the threat of foreign competition. Slogans such as "Buy American" and "American goods create American jobs" have become rallying cries among many U.S. workers.

However, keep in mind that what is true for the part is not necessarily true for the whole. It is certainly true that imports of steel or automobiles can eliminate American jobs. But it is not true that imports decrease the total number of jobs in a nation. A large increase in U.S. imports will inevitably lead to a rise in U.S. exports or foreign investment in the United States. In other words, if Americans suddenly wanted more European autos, eventually American exports would have to increase to pay for these products. The jobs lost in one industry are replaced by jobs gained in another industry. The long-run effect of trade barriers is thus not to increase total domestic employment, but at best to reallocate workers away from export industries and toward less efficient, import-competing industries. This reallocation leads to a less efficient utilization of resources.

Simply put, international trade is just another kind of technology. Think of it as a machine that adds value to its inputs. In the United States, trade is the machine that turns computer software, which the United States makes very well, into CD players, baseballs, and other things that it also wants, but does not make quite so well. International trade does this at a net gain to the economy as a whole. If somebody invented a device that could do this, it would be considered a miracle. Fortunately, international trade has been developed.

If international trade is squeezing the wages of the less skilled, so are other kinds of advancing technology, only more so. Yes, you might say, but to tax technological progress or put restrictions on labor-saving investment would be idiotic: that would only make everybody worse off. Indeed it would, and exactly the same goes for international trade—whether this superior technology is taxed (through tariffs) or overregulated (in the form of international efforts to harmonize labor standards).

This is not an easy thing to explain to American textile workers who compete with low-wage workers in China, Malaysia, etc. However, free-trade agreements will be more easily reached if those who might lose by new trade are helped by all of the rest of us who gain.

Backlash Against Globalization

Proponents of free trade and globalization note how it has helped the United States and other countries prosper. Open borders permit new ideas and technology to flow freely around the world, fueling productivity growth and increasing living standards. Moreover, increased trade helps restrain consumer prices, so inflation becomes less likely to disrupt economic growth. Estimates of the net benefits that flow from free trade are substantial: International trade has increased the real income of U.S. households by between $7,000 and $13,000 since the end of World War II. It also has increased the variety of goods and services available to American consumers by a factor of four between 1972 and 2001.[8] Without trade, coffee drinkers in the United States would pay much higher prices because the nation's supply would depend solely on Hawaiian or Puerto Rican sources.

In spite of the advantages of globalization, critics maintain that U.S. policies primarily benefit large corporations rather than average citizens—of the United States or any other country. Environmentalists argue that elitist trade organizations, such as the World Trade Organization, make undemocratic decisions that undermine national sovereignty on environmental regulation. Also, unions maintain that unfettered trade permits unfair competition from countries that lack labor standards. Moreover, human rights activists contend that the World Bank and International Monetary Fund support governments that allow sweatshops and pursue policies that bail out governmental officials at the expense of local economies. Put simply, a gnawing sense of unfairness and frustration has emerged about trade policies that ignore the concerns of the environment, American workers, and international labor standards.

The noneconomic aspects of globalization are at least as important in shaping the international debate as are the economic aspects. Many of those who object to globalization resent the political and military dominance of the United States, and they also resent the influence of foreign (mainly American) culture, as they see it, at the expense of national and local cultures.

---

[8]Scott Bradford, Paul Grieco, and Gary Hufbauer, "The Payoff to America from Globalization," *The World Economy*, July 2006, pp. 893–916.

The World Trade Organization's summit meeting in Seattle, Washington, in 1999 attests to a globalization backlash in opposition to continued liberalization of trade, foreign investment, and foreign immigration. About 100,000 anti-globalization demonstrators swamped Seattle to vocalize their opposition. The meeting was characterized by shattered storefront windows, looting, tear gas, pepper spray, rubber bullets, shock grenades, and a midnight-to-dawn curfew. Police in riot gear and the National Guard were called in to help restore order.

Such backlash reflects concerns about globalization, and these appear to be closely related to the labor-market pressures that globalization might be imparting to American workers. Public opinion surveys note that many Americans are aware of both the benefits and costs of interdependence with the world economy, but they consider the costs to be more than the benefits. In particular, less-skilled workers are much more likely to oppose freer trade and immigration than their more-skilled counterparts who have more job mobility. While concerns about the effect of globalization on the environment, human rights, and other issues are an important part of the politics of globalization, it is the tie between policy liberalization and worker interests that forms the foundation for the backlash against liberalization in the United States.[9] Table 1.6 summarizes some of the pros and cons of globalization.

The way to ease the fear of globalization is to help people to move to different jobs as comparative advantage shifts rapidly from one activity to the next. This process implies a more flexible labor market and a regulatory system that fosters investment. It implies an education system that provides people with the skills that make them mobile. It also implies removing health care and pensions from employment,

TABLE 1.6

ADVANTAGES AND DISADVANTAGES OF GLOBALIZATION

Advantages	Disadvantages
Productivity increases faster when countries produce goods and services in which they have a comparative advantage. Living standards can increase more rapidly.	Millions of Americans have lost jobs because of imports or shifts in production abroad. Most find new jobs that pay less.
Global competition and cheap imports keep a constraint on prices, so inflation is less likely to disrupt economic growth.	Millions of other Americans fear getting laid off, especially at those firms operating in import-competing industries.
An open economy promotes technological development and innovation, with fresh ideas from abroad.	Workers face demands of wage concessions from their employers, which often threaten to export jobs abroad if wage concessions are not accepted.
Jobs in export industries tend to pay about 15 percent more than jobs in import-competing industries.	Besides blue-collar jobs, service and white-collar jobs are increasingly vulnerable to operations being sent overseas.
Unfettered capital movements provide the United States access to foreign investment and maintain low interest rates.	American employees can lose their competitiveness when companies build state-of-the-art factories in low-wage countries, making them as productive as those in the United States.

Source: "Backlash Behind the Anxiety over Globalization," *Business Week*, April 24, 2000, p. 41.

---

[9]Kevin Kliesen, "Trading Barbs: A Primer on the Globalization Debate," *The Regional Economist*, Federal Reserve Bank of St. Louis, October 2007, pp. 5–9.

so that when you move to a new job, you are not risking an awful lot besides. And for those who lose their jobs, it implies strengthening training policies to help them find work. Indeed, these activities are expensive, and they may take years to work. But an economy that finds its national income increasing because of globalization can more easily find the money to pay for it.

Terrorism Jolts the Global Economy

Some critics point to the terrorist attack on the United States on September 11, 2001, as what can occur when globalization ignores the poor people of the world. The terrorist attack resulted in the tragic loss of life for thousands of innocent Americans. It also jolted America's golden age of prosperity, and the promise it held for global growth, that existed throughout the 1990s. Because of the threat of terrorism, Americans have become increasingly concerned about their safety and their livelihoods.

As the United States retaliated against Osama bin Laden and his band of terrorists, analysts were concerned that this conflict might undo a decades-long global progression toward tighter economic, political, and social interdependence—the process known as globalization. Fueled by trade, globalization has advanced the ambitions, and boosted the profits, of some of the world's largest corporations, many of them based in the United States, Europe, and Japan. Indeed, companies such as General Electric, Ford Motor Company, Toyota, Honda, and Coca-Cola have been major beneficiaries of globalization. Also, globalization has provided developing countries a chance to be included in the growing global economy and share in the wealth. In many developing countries, it has succeeded: life expectancies and per capita income have increased, and local economies have flourished.

But the path to globalization has been rocky. Critics argue that it has excluded many of the world's poor, and that the move toward prosperity has often come at the expense of human rights and the quality of the environment. For many Islamic fundamentalists, globalization represents an intolerable secularization of society, and must be prevented. This view contrasts with much of the Western criticism, which calls for the reform of globalization, not its undoing.

Globalization certainly isn't going to disintegrate—the world's markets are too interdependent to roll back now. But globalization could well become slower and more costly. With continuing terrorism, companies will likely have to pay more to insure and provide security for overseas staff and property. Heightened border inspections could slow shipments of cargo, forcing companies to stock more inventory. Tighter immigration policies could reduce the liberal inflows of skilled and blue-collar laborers that have permitted companies to expand while keeping wages in check. Moreover, a greater preoccupation with political risk has companies greatly narrowing their horizons when making new investments. Put simply, the rapid expansion in trade and capital flows in the past has been driven by the idea that the world is becoming a seamless, frictionless place. Continuing terrorism imperils all of these and puts sand in the gears of globalization.

Many economists view international trade to be a weapon in the war against terrorism in the long-run. They maintain that expanded trade wraps the world more tightly in a web of commerce, lifting living standards in impoverished regions and eliminating an important cause of war and terror. For example, following the 2001 terrorist attack against the United States, the U.S. government negotiated

COMPETITION IN THE WORLD STEEL INDUSTRY

TRADE CONFLICTS

During the 1960s and 1970s, the relatively low production costs of foreign steelmakers encouraged their participation in the U.S. market. In 1982, the average cost per ton of steel for integrated U.S. producers was $685 per ton—52 percent higher than for Japanese producers, the highest of the Pacific Rim steelmakers. This cost differential was largely due to a strong U.S. dollar and higher domestic costs of labor and raw materials, which accounted for 25 and 45 percent, respectively, of total cost. Moreover, domestic operating rates were relatively low, resulting in high fixed costs of production for each ton of steel.

This cost disadvantage encouraged U.S. steelmakers to initiate measures to reduce production costs and regain competitiveness. Many steel companies closed obsolete and costly steel mills, coking facilities, and ore mines. They also negotiated long-term contracts permitting materials, electricity, and natural gas to be obtained at lower prices. Labor contracts were also renegotiated, with a 20 to 40 percent improvement in labor productivity. However, U.S. steel companies were burdened with large unfunded pension obligations and healthcare costs for hundreds of thousands of retirees, while their employee base was shrinking.

By the turn of the century, the U.S. steel industry had substantially reduced its cost of producing a ton of steel. The productivity of the U.S. steelworker was estimated to be higher than that of most foreign competitors, a factor that enhanced U.S. competitiveness. But

semi-industrialized nations, such as South Korea, Brazil, and China, had labor-cost advantages because of lower wages and other employee costs. Overall, the cost disadvantage of U.S. steel companies narrowed considerably from the 1980s to the early in the first decade of the 2000s. Table 1.7 shows the average costs of producing a ton of steel for selected nations in 2009. At that time, Russia's average cost was the lowest at $424 per ton.

TABLE 1.7

WORLD STEEL COST COMPARISONS: COST PER TON OF STEEL, 2009

Country	Average Cost Per Ton
Japan	$634
United States	
Integrated mills	613
Mini mills	466
Western Europe	602
China	579
Eastern Europe	557
India	500
Brazil	480
Russia	424
Global average	563

Source: From Peter F. Marcus and Karlis M. Kirsis, *World Steel Dynamics*, *Steel Strategist #35*, September 2009.

trade deals with Jordan, Vietnam, Chili, and various Central American countries. Put simply, trade cannot make peace, but trade can help. If you look at history, strong trading relations have rarely led to conflict. Of course, trade needs to be accompanied by other factors, such as strong commitments to universal education and well-run governments, to promote world peace.

However, these economists note that a trade-based strategy to unite the world would require a far greater investment of money and political capital than the United States and Europe have demonstrated. Moreover, they argue that the United States and Europe must push for massive debt relief for impoverished nations. They also recommend that industrial countries slash tariffs and quotas for the steel, textiles, clothing, and crops produced by poor nations, even though increased imports could harm U.S. and European producers. Indeed, these recommendations invite much debate concerning the political and economic stability of the world.

The Plan of this Text

This text is an examination of the functioning of the international economy. Although the emphasis is on the theoretical principles that govern international trade, there also is considerable coverage of the empirical evidence of world trade patterns and trade policies of the industrial and developing nations. The book is divided into two major parts. Part One deals with international trade and commercial policy; Part Two stresses the balance of payments and the adjustment in the balance of payments.

Chapters 2 and 3 deal with the theory of comparative advantage, as well as theoretical extensions and empirical tests of this model. This topic is followed by a treatment of tariffs, nontariff trade barriers, and contemporary trade policies of the United States in Chapters 4 through 6. Discussions of trade policies for the developing nations, regional trading arrangements, and international factor movements in Chapters 7 through 9 complete the first part of the text.

The treatment of international financial relations begins with an overview of the balance of payments, the foreign-exchange market, and the exchange-rate determination in Chapters 10 through 12. The balance-of-payments adjustment under alternate exchange rate regimes is discussed in Chapters 13 through 15. Chapter 16 considers macroeconomic policy in an open economy, and Chapter 17 analyzes the international banking system.

Summary

1. Throughout the post-World War II era, the world's economies have become increasingly interdependent in terms of the movement of goods and services, business enterprise, capital, and technology.

2. The United States has seen growing interdependence with the rest of the world in its trade sector, financial markets, ownership of production facilities, and labor force.

3. Largely owing to the vastness and wide diversity of its economy, the United States remains among the countries for which exports constitute a small fraction of national output.

4. Proponents of an open trading system contend that international trade results in higher levels of consumption and investment, lower prices of commodities, and a wider range of product choices for consumers. Arguments against free trade tend to be voiced during periods of excess production capacity and high unemployment.

5. International competitiveness can be analyzed in terms of a firm, an industry, and a nation. Key to the concept of competitiveness is productivity, or output per worker hour.

6. Researchers have shown that exposure to competition with the world leader in an industry improves a firm's performance in that industry. Global competitiveness is a bit like sports: You get better by playing against folks who are better than you.

7. Although international trade helps workers in export industries, workers in import-competing industries feel the threat of foreign competition. They often see their jobs and wage levels undermined by cheap foreign labor.

8. Among the challenges that the international trading system faces are dealing with fair labor standards and concerns about the environment.

Key Concepts & Terms

- Agglomeration economies (p. 4)
- Economic interdependence (p. 1)
- Globalization (p. 2)
- Law of comparative advantage (p. 12)
- Openness (p. 8)

Study Questions

1. Identify the major fallacies of international trade.
2. What problems does terrorism pose for globalization?
3. What factors influence the rate of growth in the volume of world trade?
4. Identify some of the major challenges confronting the international trading system.
5. What significance does growing economic interdependence have for a country like the United States?
6. When is international trade an opportunity for workers? When is it a threat to workers?
7. What are some of the major arguments for and against an open trading system?
8. What do researchers have to say about the relation between a firm's productivity and exposure to global competition?
9. What factors explain why the world's trading nations have become increasingly interdependent, from an economic and political viewpoint, during the post-World War II era?
10. What is meant by international competitiveness? How does this concept apply to a firm, an industry, and a nation?

PART 1

International Trade Relations

CHAPTER 2

Foundations of Modern Trade Theory: Comparative Advantage

The previous chapter discussed the importance of international trade. This chapter answers the following questions: (1) What constitutes the **basis for trade**—that is, why do nations export and import certain products? (2) At what **terms of trade** are products exchanged in the world market? (3) What are the **gains from international trade** in terms of production and consumption? This chapter addresses these questions, first by summarizing the historical development of modern trade theory and next by presenting the contemporary theoretical principles used in analyzing the effects of international trade.

Historical Development of Modern Trade Theory

Modern trade theory is the product of an evolution of ideas in economic thought. In particular, the writings of the mercantilists, and later those of the classical economists—Adam Smith, David Ricardo, and John Stuart Mill—have been instrumental in providing the framework for modern trade theory.

The Mercantilists

During the period 1500–1800, a group of writers appeared in Europe, which was concerned with the process of nation building. According to the **mercantilists**, the central question was how a nation could regulate its domestic and international affairs so as to promote its own interests. The solution lay in a strong foreign-trade sector. If a country could achieve a *favorable trade balance* (a surplus of exports over imports), it would realize net payments received from the rest of the world in the form of gold and silver. Such revenues would contribute to increased spending and a rise in domestic output and employment. To promote a favorable trade balance, the mercantilists advocated government regulation of trade. Tariffs, quotas, and other commercial policies were proposed by the mercantilists to minimize imports in order to protect a nation's trade position.[1]

By the eighteenth century, the economic policies of the mercantilists were under strong attack. According to David Hume's **price-specie-flow doctrine**, a favorable trade balance is possible only in the short run, for over time it would automatically be eliminated. To illustrate, suppose England achieve a trade surplus that results in an inflow of gold and silver. Because these precious metals constitute part of England's money supply, their inflow increases the amount of money in circulation. This increase leads to a rise in England's price level relative to that of its trading partners. English residents would therefore be encouraged to purchase foreign-produced goods, while England's exports would decline. As a result, the country's trade surplus would eventually be eliminated. The price-specie-flow mechanism thus shows that mercantilist policies could provide at best only short-term economic advantages.[2]

The mercantilists were also attacked for their *static view* of the world economy. To the mercantilists, the world's wealth was fixed. This view meant that one nation's gains from trade came at the expense of its trading partners; not all nations could simultaneously enjoy the benefits of international trade. This view was challenged with the publication in 1776 of Adam Smith's *The Wealth of Nations*. According to Smith (1723–1790), the world's wealth is not a fixed quantity. International trade permits nations to take advantage of specialization and the division of labor, which increase the general level of productivity within a country and thus increase world output (wealth). Smith's dynamic view of trade suggested that *both* trading partners could simultaneously enjoy higher levels of production and consumption with trade. Smith's trade theory is further explained in the next section.

Although the foundations of mercantilism have been refuted, mercantilism is alive today. However, it now emphasizes employment rather than holdings of gold and silver. Neo-mercantilists contend that exports are beneficial because they result in jobs for domestic workers, while imports are bad because they take jobs away from domestic workers and transfer them to foreign workers. Thus, trade is considered a zero-sum activity in which one country must lose for the other to win. There is no acknowledgment that trade can provide benefits to all countries, including mutual benefits in employment as prosperity increases throughout the world.

Why Nations Trade: Absolute Advantage

Adam Smith, a classical economist, was a leading advocate of **free trade** (open markets) on the grounds that it promoted the international division of labor. With free trade, nations could concentrate their production on the goods that they could make the most cheaply, with all the consequent benefits from this division of labor.

Accepting the idea that *cost differences* govern the international movement of goods, Smith sought to explain why costs differ among nations. Smith maintained that *productivities* of factor inputs represent the major determinant of production cost. Such productivities are based on natural and acquired advantages. The former include factors relating to climate, soil, and mineral wealth, whereas the latter include

---

[1]See E. A. J. Johnson, *Predecessors of Adam Smith* (New York: Prentice-Hall, 1937).

[2]David Hume, "Of Money," *Essays, Vol. 1*, (London: Green and Co., 1912), p. 319. Hume's writings are also available in Eugene Rotwein, *The Economic Writings of David Hume* (Edinburgh: Nelson, 1955).

TABLE 2.1

A Case of Absolute Advantage when Each Nation is More Efficient in the Production of One Good

World output possibilities in the absence of specialization

	OUTPUT PER LABOR HOUR	
Nation	Wine	Cloth
United States	5 bottles	20 yards
United Kingdom	15 bottles	10 yards

special skills and techniques. Given a natural or acquired advantage in the production of a good, Smith reasoned that a nation would produce that good at a lower cost and thus become more competitive than its trading partner. Smith viewed the determination of competitiveness from the *supply side* of the market.[3]

Smith founded his concept of cost on the **labor theory of value** that assumes that, within each nation, labor is the only factor of production and is homogeneous (of one quality) and the cost or price of a good depends exclusively on the amount of labor required to produce it. For example, if the United States uses less labor to manufacture a yard of cloth than the United Kingdom, the U.S. production cost will be lower.

Smith's trading principle was the **principle of absolute advantage**: in a two-nation, two-product world, international specialization and trade will be beneficial when one nation has an absolute cost advantage (that is, uses less labor to produce a unit of output) in one good and the other nation has an absolute cost advantage in the other good. For the world to benefit from specialization, each nation must have a good that it is absolutely more efficient in producing than its trading partner. A nation will *import* those goods in which it has an absolute cost *disadvantage*; it will *export* those goods in which it has an absolute cost *advantage*.

An arithmetic example helps illustrate the principle of absolute advantage. Referring to Table 2.1, suppose workers in the United States can produce 5 bottles of wine or 20 yards of cloth in an hour's time, while workers in the United Kingdom can produce 15 bottles of wine or 10 yards of cloth in an hour's time. Clearly, the United States has an absolute advantage in cloth production; its cloth workers' productivity (output per worker hour) is higher than that of the United Kingdom, which leads to lower costs (less labor required to produce a yard of cloth). In like manner, the United Kingdom has an absolute advantage in wine production.

According to Smith, each nation benefits by specializing in the production of the good that it produces at a lower cost than the other nation, while importing the good that it produces at a higher cost. Because the world uses its resources more efficiently as the result of specializing, an increase in world output occurs that is distributed to the two nations through trade. All nations can benefit from trade, according to Smith.

The writings of Smith established the case for free trade, which is still influential today. According to Smith, free trade would increase competition in the home market and reduce the market power of domestic companies by lessening their ability to take advantage of consumers by charging high prices and providing poor service. Also, the country would benefit by exporting goods that are dear on the world market for imports of goods that are cheap on the world market. Smith maintained that the wealth of a nation depends on this division of labor, which is limited by the extent of the market. Smaller and more isolated economies cannot support the degree of specialization that is needed to significantly increase productivity and reduce cost, and thus tend to be relatively poor. Free trade allows countries, especially smaller countries, to more fully take advantage of the division of labor, thus attaining higher levels of productivity and real income.

[3] Adam Smith, *The Wealth of Nations* (New York: Modern Library, 1937), pp. 424–426.

TABLE 2.2	

EXAMPLES OF COMPARATIVE ADVANTAGES IN INTERNATIONAL TRADE

Country	Product
Canada	Lumber
Israel	Citrus fruit
Italy	Wine
Jamaica	Aluminum ore
Mexico	Tomatoes
Saudi Arabia	Oil
China	Textiles
Japan	Automobiles
South Korea	Steel, ships
Switzerland	Watches
United Kingdom	Financial services

Why Nations Trade: Comparative Advantage

In 1800, a wealthy London businessman named David Ricardo (1772–1823) came across *The Wealth of Nations* while on vacation and was intrigued. Although Ricardo appreciated the persuasive flair of Smith's argument for free trade, he thought that some of Smith's analysis needed improvement. According to Smith, mutually beneficial trade requires each nation to be the *least-cost producer* of at least one good that it can export to its trading partner. But what if a nation is more efficient than its trading partner in the production of *all* goods? Dissatisfied with this looseness in Smith's theory, Ricardo developed a principle to show that mutually beneficial trade can occur whether or not countries have any absolute advantage. Ricardo's theory became known as the **principle of comparative advantage**.[4]

Like Smith, Ricardo emphasized the supply side of the market. The immediate basis for trade stemmed from the cost differences between nations, which their natural and acquired advantages supported. Unlike Smith, who emphasized the importance of absolute cost differences among nations, Ricardo emphasized *comparative* (relative) cost differences. Indeed, countries often develop comparative advantages, as shown in Table 2.2.

According to the principle of comparative advantage, even if a nation has an absolute cost disadvantage in the production of *both* goods, a basis for mutually beneficial trade may still exist. The *less efficient* nation should specialize in and export the good in which it is relatively less inefficient (where its absolute disadvantage is least). The *more efficient* nation should specialize in and export that good in which it is relatively more efficient (where its absolute advantage is greatest).

To demonstrate the principle of comparative advantage, Ricardo formulated a simplified model based on the following *assumptions*:

1. The world consists of two nations, each using a single input to produce two commodities.
2. In each nation, labor is the only input (the labor theory of value). Each nation has a fixed endowment of labor, and labor is fully employed and homogeneous.
3. Labor can move freely among industries within a nation but is incapable of moving between nations.
4. The level of technology is fixed for both nations. Different nations may use different technologies, but all firms within each nation utilize a common production method for each commodity.
5. Costs do not vary with the level of production and are proportional to the amount of labor used.
6. Perfect competition prevails in all markets. Because no single producer or consumer is large enough to influence the market, all are price takers. Product quality does not vary among nations, implying that all units of each product are identical.

---

[4]David Ricardo, *The Principles of Political Economy and Taxation* (London: Cambridge University Press, 1966), Chapter 7. Originally published in 1817.

There is free entry to and exit from an industry, and the price of each product equals the product's marginal cost of production.

7. Free trade occurs between nations; that is, no government barriers to trade exist.

8. Transportation costs are zero. Consumers will thus be indifferent between domestically produced and imported versions of a product if the domestic prices of the two products are identical.

9. Firms make production decisions in an attempt to maximize profits, whereas consumers maximize satisfaction through their consumption decisions.

10. There is no money illusion; that is, when consumers make their consumption choices and firms make their production decisions, they take into account the behavior of all prices.

11. Trade is balanced (exports must pay for imports), thus ruling out flows of money between nations.

Table 2.3 illustrates Ricardo's principle of comparative advantage when one nation has an absolute advantage in the production of both goods. Assume that in one hour's time, U.S. workers can produce 40 bottles of wine or 40 yards of cloth, while U.K. workers can produce 20 bottles of wine or 10 yards of cloth. According to Smith's principle of absolute advantage, there is no basis for mutually beneficial specialization and trade, because the U.S. workers are more efficient in the production of both goods.

However, the principle of comparative advantage recognizes that U.S. workers are four times as efficient in cloth production ($40/10 = 4$) but only twice as efficient in wine production ($40/20 = 2$). The United States thus has a *greater absolute advantage* in cloth than in wine, while the United Kingdom has a *smaller absolute disadvantage* in wine than in cloth. Each nation specializes in and exports that good in which it has a *comparative* advantage—the United States in cloth, the United Kingdom in wine. Therefore, through the process of trade, the two nations receive the output gains from specialization. Like Smith, Ricardo asserted that both nations can gain from trade.

Simply put, Ricardo's principle of comparative advantage maintains that international trade is solely due to international differences in the productivity of labor. The basic prediction of Ricardo's principle is that countries will tend to export those goods in which their labor productivity is relatively high.

In recent years, the United States has realized large trade deficits (imports exceed exports) with countries such as China and Japan. Some of those who have witnessed the flood of imports coming into the United States seem to suggest that the United States does not have a comparative advantage in anything. It is possible for a nation not to have an absolute advantage in anything; but it is not possible for one nation to have a comparative advantage in everything and the other nation to have a comparative advantage in nothing. That's because comparative advantage depends on *relative* costs. As we have seen, a nation having an absolute disadvantage in all goods would find it advantageous to specialize in the production of the good in which its absolute disadvantage is *least*. There is no reason for the United States to surrender and let China produce all of

TABLE 2.3

A CASE OF COMPARATIVE ADVANTAGE WHEN THE UNITED STATES HAS AN ABSOLUTE ADVANTAGE IN THE PRODUCTION OF BOTH GOODS

World output possibilities in the absence of specialization

Nation	OUTPUT PER LABOR HOUR	
	Wine	Cloth
United States	40 bottles	40 yards
United Kingdom	20 bottles	10 yards

TRADE CONFLICTS   DAVID RICARDO

David Ricardo (1772–1823) was the leading British econo-mist of the early 1800s. He helped develop the theories of *classical economics*, which emphasize economic freedom through free trade and competition. Ricardo was a suc-cessful businessman, financier, and speculator, and he accumulated a sizable fortune.

Being the third of 17 children, Ricardo was born into a wealthy Jewish family. His father was a merchant banker. They initially lived in the Netherlands and then moved to London. Having little formal education and never attend-ing college, Ricardo went to work for his father at the age of 14. When he was 21, Ricardo married a Quaker despite his parents' preferences. After his family disinherited him for marrying outside the Jewish faith, Ricardo became a stockbroker and a loan broker. He was highly successful in business and was able to retire at 42, accumulating an estate that was worth more than $100 million in today's dollars. Upon retirement, Ricardo bought a country estate and established himself as a country gentleman. In 1819, Ricardo purchased a seat in the British parliament and held the post until the year of his death in 1823. As a member of parliament, Ricardo advocated the repeal of the Corn Laws which established trade barriers to protect British landowners from foreign competition. However, he was unable to get parliament to abolish the law, which lasted until its repeal in 1846.

Ricardo's interest in economics was inspired by a chance reading of Adam Smith's *The Wealth of Nations*

when he was in his late twenties. Upon the urging of his friends, Ricardo began writing newspaper articles on eco-nomic questions. In 1817 Ricardo published his ground-breaking *The Principles of Political Economy and Taxation* which laid out the theory of comparative advantage as discussed in this chapter.

Like Adam Smith, Ricardo was an advocate of free trade and an opponent of protectionism. He believed that protectionism led countries toward economic stagnation. However, Ricardo was less confident than Smith about the ability of a market economy's potential to benefit society. Instead, Ricardo felt that the economy tends to move toward a standstill. Yet Ricardo contended that if govern-ment meddled with the economy, the result would be only further economic stagnation.

Ricardo's ideas have greatly affected other econo-mists. His theory of comparative advantage has been a cornerstone of international trade theory for almost 200 years and has influenced generations of economists in the belief that protectionism is bad for an economy.

Sources: Mark Blaug, *Ricardian Economics*. (New Haven, CT: Yale University Press, 1958), Samuel Hollander, *The Economics of David Ricardo*, (Cambridge: Cambridge University Press, 1993), and Robert Heilbronner, *The Worldly Philosophers*, (New York: Simon and Schuster, 1961).

everything. The United States would lose and so would China, because world output would be reduced if U.S. resources were left idle. The idea that a nation has nothing to offer confuses absolute advantage and comparative advantage.

Although the principle of comparative advantage is used to explain international trade patterns, people are not generally concerned with which nation has a compar-ative advantage when they purchase something. A person in a candy store does not look at Swiss chocolate and U.S. chocolate and say, "I wonder which nation has the comparative advantage in chocolate production?" The buyer relies on price, after allowing for quality differences, to tell which nation has the comparative advantage. It is helpful, then, to illustrate how the principle of comparative advantage works in terms of money prices, as seen in *Exploring Further 2.1.*

Production Possibilities Schedules

Ricardo's law of comparative advantage suggested that specialization and trade can lead to gains for both nations. His theory, however, depended on the restrictive assumption of the labor theory of value, in which labor was assumed to be the only factor input. However, in practice, labor is only one of several factor inputs.

Recognizing the shortcomings of the labor theory of value, modern trade theory provides a more generalized theory of comparative advantage. It explains the theory using a **production possibilities schedule**, also called a transformation schedule. This schedule shows various alternative combinations of two goods that a nation can produce when *all* of its factor inputs (land, labor, capital, entrepreneurship) are used in their most efficient manner. The production possibilities schedule thus illustrates the maximum output possibilities of a nation. Note that we are no longer assuming labor to be the only factor input, as Ricardo did.

Figure 2.1 illustrates hypothetical production possibilities schedules for the United States and Canada. By fully using all available inputs with the best available technology during a given time period, the United States can produce either 60 bushels of wheat, or 120 autos, or certain combinations of the two products. Similarly, Canada can produce either 160 bushels of wheat, or 80 autos, or certain combinations of the two products.

FIGURE 2.1

TRADING UNDER CONSTANT OPPORTUNITY COSTS

With constant opportunity costs, a nation will specialize in the product of its comparative advantage. The principle of comparative advantage implies that with specialization and free trade, a nation enjoys production gains and consumption gains. A nation's trade triangle denotes its exports, imports, and terms of trade. In a two nation, two product world, the trade triangle of one nation equals that of the other nation; one nation's exports equal the other nation's imports, and there is one equilibrium terms of trade.

Just how does a production possibilities schedule illustrate the concept of comparative cost? The answer lies in the slope of the production possibilities schedule, which is referred to as the **marginal rate of transformation** (*MRT*). The *MRT* shows the amount of one product a nation must sacrifice to get one additional unit of the other product:

$$MRT = \frac{\Delta Wheat}{\Delta Autos}.$$

This rate of sacrifice is sometimes called the *opportunity cost* of a product. Because this formula also refers to the slope of the production possibilities schedule, the *MRT* equals the absolute value of the production possibilities schedule's slope.

In Figure 2.1, the *MRT* of wheat into autos gives the amount of wheat that must be sacrificed for each additional auto produced. Concerning the United States, movement from the top endpoint on its production possibilities schedule to the bottom endpoint shows that the relative cost of producing 120 additional autos is the sacrifice of 60 bushels of wheat. This sacrifice means that the relative cost of each auto produced is 0.5 bushels of wheat sacrificed (60/120 = 0.5); that is, the *MRT* = 0.5. Similarly, Canada's relative cost of each auto produced is 2 bushels of wheat; that is, Canada's *MRT* = 2.0.

Trading Under Constant-Cost Conditions

This section illustrates the principle of comparative advantage under **constant opportunity costs**. Although the constant-cost case may be of limited relevance to the real world, it serves as a useful pedagogical tool for analyzing international trade. The discussion focuses on two questions. First, what are the *basis for trade* and the *direction of trade*? Second, what are the potential *gains from trade*, for a single nation and for the world as a whole?

Referring to Figure 2.1, notice that the production possibilities schedules for the United States and Canada are drawn as straight lines. The fact that these schedules are linear indicates that the relative costs of the two products do not change as the economy shifts its production from all wheat to all autos, or anywhere in between. For the United States, the relative cost of an auto is 0.5 bushels of wheat as output expands or contracts; for Canada, the relative cost of an auto is 2 bushels of wheat as output expands or contracts.

There are *two reasons* for constant costs. First, the factors of production are perfect substitutes for each other. Second, all units of a given factor are of the same quality. As a country transfers resources from the production of wheat into the production of autos, or vice versa, the country will not have to resort to resources that are inadequate for the production of the good. Therefore, the country must sacrifice exactly the same amount of wheat for each additional auto produced, regardless of how many autos it is already producing.

Basis for Trade and Direction of Trade

Let us now examine trade under constant-cost conditions. Referring to Figure 2.1, assume that in **autarky** (the absence of trade) the United States prefers to produce and consume at point *A* on its production possibilities schedule, with 40 autos and

40 bushels of wheat. Assume also that Canada produces and consumes at point A' on its production possibilities schedule, with 40 autos and 80 bushels of wheat.

The *slopes* of the two countries' production possibilities schedules give the *relative cost* of one product in terms of the other. The relative cost of producing an additional auto is only 0.5 bushels of wheat for the United States but it is 2 bushels of wheat for Canada. According to the principle of comparative advantage, this situation provides a basis for mutually favorable specialization and trade owing to the differences in the countries' relative costs. As for the direction of trade, we find the United States specializing in and exporting autos and Canada specializing in and exporting wheat.

Production Gains from Specialization

The law of comparative advantage asserts that with trade each country will find it favorable to specialize in the production of the good of its comparative advantage and will trade part of this for the good of its comparative disadvantage. In Figure 2.1, the United States moves from production point A to production point B, totally specializing in auto production. Canada totally specializes in wheat production by moving from production point A' to production point B' in the figure. Taking advantage of specialization can result in **production gains** for both countries.

We find that prior to specialization, the United States produces 40 autos and 40 bushels of wheat. But with complete specialization, the United States produces 120 autos and no wheat. As for Canada, its production point in the absence of specialization is at 40 autos and 80 bushels of wheat, whereas its production point under complete specialization is at 160 bushels of wheat and no autos. Combining these results, we find that both nations together have experienced a net production gain of 40 autos and 40 bushels of wheat under conditions of complete specialization. Table 2.4(*a*) summarizes these production gains. Because these production gains

TABLE 2.4

GAINS FROM SPECIALIZATION AND TRADE: CONSTANT OPPORTUNITY COSTS

(a) Production Gains from Specialization

	BEFORE SPECIALIZATION		AFTER SPECIALIZATION		NET GAIN (LOSS)	
	Autos	Wheat	Autos	Wheat	Autos	Wheat
United States	40	40	120	0	80	−40
Canada	40	80	0	160	−40	80
World	80	120	120	160	40	40

(b) Consumption Gains from Trade

	BEFORE TRADE		AFTER TRADE		NET GAIN (LOSS)	
	Autos	Wheat	Autos	Wheat	Autos	Wheat
United States	40	40	60	60	20	20
Canada	40	80	60	100	20	20
World	80	120	120	160	40	40

arise from the reallocation of *existing* resources, they are also called the *static gains* from specialization: through specialization, a country can use its current supply of resources more efficiently and thus achieve a higher level of output than it could without specialization.

Japan's opening to the global economy is an example of the static gains from comparative advantage. Responding to pressure from the United States, in 1859 Japan opened its ports to international trade after more than two hundred years of self-imposed economic isolation. In autarky, Japan found that it had a comparative advantage in some products and a comparative disadvantage in others. For example, the price of tea and silk was much higher on world markets than in Japan prior to the opening of trade, while the price of woolen goods and cotton was much lower on world markets. Japan responded according to the principle of comparative advantage: it exported tea and silk in exchange for imports of clothing. By using its resources more efficiently and trading with the rest of the world, Japan was able to realize static gains from specialization that equaled eight to nine percent of its gross domestic product at that time. Of course the long-run gains to Japan of improving its productivity and acquiring better technology were several times this figure.[5]

However, when a country initially opens to trade and then trade is eliminated, it suffers static losses, as seen in the case of the United States. In the early 1800s, Britain and France were at war. As part of the conflict, the countries attempted to prevent the shipping of goods to each other by neutral countries, notably the United States. This policy resulted in the British and French navies confiscating American ships and cargo. To discourage this harassment, in 1807 President Thomas Jefferson ordered the closure of America's ports to international trade: American ships were prevented from taking goods to foreign ports and foreign ships were prevented from taking on any cargo in the United States. The intent of the embargo was to inflict hardship on the British and French, and thus discourage them from meddling in America's affairs. Although the embargo did not completely eliminate trade, the United States was as close to autarky as it had ever been in its history. Therefore, Americans shifted production away from previously exported agricultural goods (the goods of comparative advantage) and increased production of import-replacement manufactured goods (the goods of comparative disadvantage). The result was a less efficient utilization of America's resources. Overall, the embargo cost about eight percent of America's gross national product in 1807. It is no surprise that the embargo was highly unpopular among Americans and, therefore, terminated in 1809.[6]

Consumption Gains from Trade

In the absence of trade, the consumption alternatives of the United States and Canada are limited to points *along* their domestic production possibilities schedules. The exact consumption point for each nation will be determined by the tastes and preferences in each country. But with specialization and trade, the two nations can achieve post-trade consumption points *outside* their domestic production possibilities schedules; that is, they can thus consume more wheat and more autos than they could

---

[5]D. Bernhofen and J. Brown, "An Empirical Assessment of the Comparative Advantage Gains from Trade: Evidence from Japan," *The American Economic Review*, March 2005, pp. 208–225.

[6]D. Irwin, *The Welfare Cost of Autarky: Evidence from the Jeffersonian Trade Embargo, 1807–1809* (Cambridge, MA) Working Paper No. W8692, December 2001.

consume in the absence of trade. Thus, trade can result in **consumption gains** for both countries.

The set of post-trade consumption points that a nation can achieve is determined by the rate at which its export product is traded for the other country's export product. This rate is known as the **terms of trade**. The terms of trade define the relative prices at which two products trade in the marketplace.

Under constant-cost conditions, the slope of the production possibilities schedule defines the domestic rate of transformation (domestic terms of trade), which represents the relative prices that two commodities can be exchanged at home. For a country to consume at some point *outside* its production possibilities schedule, it must be able to exchange its export good internationally at a terms of trade more favorable than the domestic terms of trade.

Assume that the United States and Canada achieve a terms-of-trade ratio that permits both trading partners to consume at some point outside their respective production possibilities schedules (Figure 2.1). Suppose that the terms of trade agreed on is a 1:1 ratio, whereby 1 auto is exchanged for 1 bushel of wheat. Based on these conditions, let line *tt* represent the international terms of trade for both countries. This line is referred to as the **trading possibilities line** (note that it is drawn with a slope having an absolute value of one).

Suppose now that the United States decides to export, say, 60 autos to Canada. Starting at post-specialization production point *B* in the figure, the United States will slide along its trading possibilities line until point *C* is reached. At point *C*, 60 autos will have been exchanged for 60 bushels of wheat, at the terms-of-trade ratio of 1:1. Point *C* then represents the U.S. *post-trade consumption point*. Compared with consumption point *A*, point *C* results in a consumption gain for the United States of 20 autos and 20 bushels of wheat. The triangle *BCD* that shows the U.S. exports (along the horizontal axis), imports (along the vertical axis), and terms of trade (the slope) is referred to as the **trade triangle**.

Does this trading situation provide favorable results for Canada? Starting at post-specialization production point *B'* in the figure, Canada can import 60 autos from the United States by giving up 60 bushels of wheat. Canada would slide along its trading possibilities line until it reaches point *C'*. Clearly, this is a more favorable consumption point than point *A'*. With trade, Canada experiences a consumption gain of 20 autos and 20 bushels of wheat. Canada's trade triangle is denoted by *B'C'D'*. Note that in our two country model, the trade triangles of the United States and Canada are identical; one country's exports equal the other country's imports, which exchange at the equilibrium terms of trade. Table 2.4(*b*) summarizes the consumption gains from trade for each country and the world as a whole.

One implication of the foregoing trading example is that the United States produced only autos, whereas Canada produced only wheat; that is, **complete specialization** occurs. As the United States increases and Canada decreases the production of autos, both countries' unit production costs remain constant. Because the relative costs never become equal, the United States does not lose its comparative advantage, nor does Canada lose its comparative disadvantage. The United States therefore produces only autos. Similarly, as Canada produces more wheat and the United States reduces its wheat production, both nations' production costs remain the same. Canada produces only wheat without losing its advantage to the United States.

The only exception to complete specialization would occur if one of the countries, say Canada, is too small to supply the United States with all of the U.S. needs for wheat. Then Canada would be completely specialized in its export product, wheat, while the United States (large country) would produce both goods; however, the United States would still export autos and import wheat.

Distributing the Gains from Trade

Our trading example assumes that the terms of trade agreed to by the United States and Canada will result in both benefiting from trade. But where will this terms of trade actually lie?

A shortcoming of Ricardo's principle of comparative advantage is its inability to determine the actual terms of trade. The best description that Ricardo could provide was only the *outer limits* within which the terms of trade would fall. This is because the Ricardian theory relied solely on domestic cost ratios (supply conditions) in explaining trade patterns; it ignored the role of demand.

To visualize Ricardo's analysis of the terms of trade, recall our trading example of Figure 2.1. We assumed that for the United States the relative cost of producing an additional auto was 0.5 bushels of wheat, whereas for Canada the relative cost of producing an additional auto was 2 bushels of wheat. Thus, the United States has a comparative advantage in autos, whereas Canada has a comparative advantage in wheat. Figure 2.2 illustrates these domestic cost conditions for the two countries. However, for each country, we have translated the domestic cost ratio, given by the negatively sloped production possibilities schedule, into a *positively sloped* cost-ratio line.

According to Ricardo, the domestic cost ratios set the **outer limits for the equilibrium terms of trade**. If the United States is to export autos, it should not accept any terms of trade less than a ratio of 0.5:1, indicated by its domestic cost-ratio line. Otherwise, the U.S. post-trade consumption point would lie inside its production possibilities schedule. The United States would clearly be better off without trade than with trade. The U.S. domestic cost-ratio line therefore becomes its **no-trade boundary**. Similarly, Canada would require a minimum of 1 auto for every 2 bushels of wheat exported, as indicated by its domestic cost-ratio line; any terms of trade less than this rate would be unacceptable to Canada. Thus, its domestic cost-ratio line defines the no-trade boundary line for Canada.

For gainful international trade to exist, a nation must achieve a post-trade consumption location at least equivalent to its point along its domestic production possibilities schedule. Any acceptable international terms of trade has to be more favorable than or equal to the rate defined by the domestic price line. Thus, the **region of mutually beneficial trade** is bounded by the cost ratios of the two countries.

FIGURE 2.2

EQUILIBRIUM TERMS-OF-TRADE LIMITS

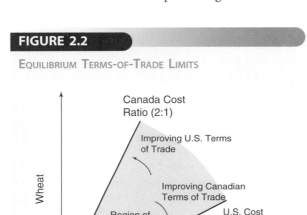

The supply-side analysis of Ricardo describes the outer limits within which the equilibrium terms of trade must fall. The domestic cost ratios set the outer limits for the equilibrium terms of trade. Mutually beneficial trade for both nations occurs if the equilibrium terms of trade lies between the two nations' domestic cost ratios. According to the theory of reciprocal demand, the actual exchange ratio at which trade occurs depends on the trading partners' interacting demands.

Equilibrium Terms of Trade

As noted, Ricardo did not explain how the actual terms of trade would be determined in international trade. This gap was filled by another classical economist, John Stuart Mill (1806–1873). By bringing into the picture the intensity of the trading partners' demands, Mill could determine the actual terms of trade for Figure 2.2. Mill's theory is known as the **theory of reciprocal demand**.[7] It asserts that within the outer limits of the terms of trade, the actual terms of trade are determined by the relative strength of each country's demand for the other country's product. Simply put, production costs determine the outer limits of the terms of trade, while reciprocal demand determines what the actual terms of trade will be within those limits.

Referring to Figure 2.2, if Canadians are more eager for U.S. autos than Americans are for Canadian wheat, the terms of trade would end up close to the Canadian cost ratio of 2:1. Thus, the terms of trade would improve for the United States. However, if Americans are more eager for Canadian wheat than Canadians are for U.S. autos, the terms of trade would fall close to the U.S. cost ratio of 0.5:1, and the terms of trade would improve for Canadians.

The reciprocal-demand theory best applies when both nations are of equal economic size, so that the demand of each nation has a noticeable effect on market price. However, if two nations are of unequal economic size, it is possible that the relative demand strength of the smaller nation will be dwarfed by that of the larger nation. In this case, the domestic exchange ratio of the larger nation will prevail. Assuming the absence of monopoly elements working in the markets, the small nation can export as much of the commodity as it desires, enjoying large gains from trade.

Consider trade in crude oil and autos between Venezuela and the United States before the rise of the Organization of Petroleum Exporting Countries (OPEC). Venezuela, as a small nation, accounted for only a very small share of the U.S.-Venezuelan market, whereas the U.S. market share was overwhelmingly large. Because Venezuelan consumers and producers had no influence on market price levels, they were in effect price takers. In trading with the United States, no matter what the Venezuelan demand was for crude oil and autos, it was not strong enough to affect U.S. price levels. As a result, Venezuela traded according to the U.S. domestic price ratio, buying and selling autos and crude oil at the price levels that existed within the United States.

The example just given implies the following generalization: If two nations of approximately the *same size* and with similar taste patterns participate in international trade, the gains from trade will be shared about *equally* between them. However, if one nation is significantly larger than the other, the *larger* nation attains *fewer* gains from trade while the *smaller* nation attains *most* of the gains from trade. This situation is characterized as the **importance of being unimportant**. What's more, when nations are very dissimilar in size, there is a strong possibility that the larger nation will continue to produce its comparative-disadvantage good because the smaller nation is unable to supply all of the world's demand for this product. *Exploring Further 2.3* helps further explain equilibrium terms of trade using offer curves.

---

[7]John Stuart Mill, *Principles of Political Economy* (New York: Longmans, Green, 1921), pp. 584–585.

TRADE CONFLICTS — BABE RUTH AND THE PRINCIPLE OF COMPARATIVE ADVANTAGE

Babe Ruth was the first great home-run hitter in baseball history. His batting talent and vivacious personality attracted huge crowds wherever he played. He made baseball more exciting by establishing home runs as a common part of the game. Ruth set many major league records, including 2,056 career walks and 72 games in which he hit two or more home runs. He had a .342 lifetime batting average and 714 career home runs.

George Herman Ruth (1895–1948) was born in Baltimore. After playing baseball in the minor leagues, Ruth started his major league career as a left-handed pitcher with the Boston Red Sox in 1914. In 158 games for Boston, he compiled a pitching record of 89 wins and 46 losses, including two 20-win seasons—23 victories in 1916 and 24 victories in 1917.

On January 2, 1920, a little more than a year after Babe Ruth had pitched two victories in the Red Sox World Series victory over Chicago, he became violently ill. Most suspected that Ruth, known for his partying excesses, simply had a major league hangover from his New Year's celebrations. The truth was, though, that Ruth had ingested several bad frankfurters while entertaining youngsters the day before, and his symptoms were misdiagnosed as being life-threatening. The Red Sox management, already strapped for cash, thus sold its ailing player to the Yankees the very next day for $125,000 and a $300,000 loan to the owner of the Red Sox.

Ruth eventually added five more wins as a hurler for the New York Yankees and ended his pitching career with a 2.28 earned run average. Ruth also had three wins against no losses in World Series competition, including one stretch of 29 2/3 consecutive scoreless innings. At the time, Ruth was one of the best left-handed pitchers in the American league.

Although Ruth had an absolute advantage in pitching, he had even greater talent at the plate. Simply put, Ruth's comparative advantage was in hitting. As a pitcher, Ruth had to rest his arm between appearances, and thus could not bat in every game. To ensure his daily presence in the lineup, Ruth gave up pitching to play exclusively in the outfield.

In his 15 years with the Yankees, Ruth dominated professional baseball. He teamed with Lou Gehrig to form what became the greatest one-two hitting punch in baseball. Ruth was the heart of the 1927 Yankees, a team regarded by some baseball experts as the best in baseball history. That year, Ruth set a record of 60 home runs; at that time, a season had 154 games as compared to 162 games of today. He attracted so many fans that Yankee Stadium, which opened in 1923, was nicknamed "The House That Ruth Built." The Yankees released Ruth after the 1934 season, and he ended his playing career in 1935 with the Boston Braves. In the final game he played, Ruth hit three home runs.

The advantages to having Ruth switch from pitching to batting were enormous. Not only did the Yankees win four World Series during Ruth's tenure, but they also became baseball's most renowned franchise. Ruth was elected to the Baseball Hall of Fame in Cooperstown, New York, in 1936.

Sources: Edward Scahill, "Did Babe Ruth Have a Comparative Advantage as a Pitcher?" *Journal of Economic Education*, Vol. 21, 1990. See also, Paul Rosenthal, "America at Bat: Baseball Stuff and Stories," *National Geographic*, 2002, Geoffrey Ward and Ken Burns, *Baseball: An Illustrated History*, (Knopf, 1994), and Keith Brandt, *Babe Ruth: Home Run Hero*, (Troll, 1986).

Terms-of-Trade Estimates

As we have seen, the terms of trade affect a country's gains from trade. How are the terms of trade actually measured?

The **commodity terms of trade** (also referred to as the *barter terms of trade*) is a frequently used measure of the international exchange ratio. It measures the relation between the prices a nation gets for its exports and the prices it pays for its imports.

TABLE 2.5

Commodity Terms of Trade, 2008 (2000 = 100)

Country	Export Price Index	Import Price Index	Terms of Trade
Australia	273	149	183
Canada	185	146	127
United States	167	147	114
Denmark	189	182	104
Switzerland	194	194	100
Germany	174	192	91
China	102	159	64
Japan	103	182	57

Source: From International Monetary Fund, *IMF Financial Statistics*, Washington, DC., March 2009.

This is calculated by dividing a nation's export price index by its import price index, multiplied by 100 to express the terms of trade in percentages:

$$Terms\ of\ Trade = \frac{Export\ Price\ Index}{Import\ Price\ Index} \times 100$$

An *improvement* in a nation's terms of trade requires that the prices of its exports rise relative to the prices of its imports over the given time period. A smaller quantity of export goods sold abroad is required to obtain a given quantity of imports. Conversely, a *deterioration* in a nation's terms of trade is due to a rise in its import prices relative to its export prices over a time period. The purchase of a given quantity of imports would require the sacrifice of a greater quantity of exports.

Table 2.5 gives the commodity terms of trade for selected countries. With 2000 as the base year (equal to 100), the table shows that by 2008 the U.S. index of export prices rose to 167, an increase of 67 percent. During the same period, the index of U.S. import prices rose by 47 percent, to a level of 147. Using the terms-of-trade formula, we find that the U.S. terms of trade *improved* by 14 percent [(167/147) × 100 = 114] over the period 2000–2008. This means that to purchase a given quantity of imports, the United States had to sacrifice 14 percent *fewer* exports; conversely, for a given number of exports, the United States could obtain 14 percent *more* imports.

Although changes in the commodity terms of trade indicate the direction of movement of the gains from trade, their implications must be interpreted with caution. Suppose there occurs an increase in the foreign demand for U.S. exports, leading to higher prices and revenues for U.S. exporters. In this case, an improving terms of trade implies that the U.S. gains from trade have increased. However, suppose that the cause of the rise in export prices and terms of trade is the falling *productivity* of U.S. workers. If this results in reduced export sales and less revenue earned from exports, we could hardly say that U.S. welfare has improved. Despite its limitations, however, the commodity terms of trade is a useful concept. Over a long period, it illustrates how a country's share of the world gains from trade changes and gives a rough measure of the fortunes of a nation in the world market.

Dynamic Gains From Trade

The previous analysis of the gains from international trade stressed specialization and reallocation of *existing* resources—the so-called static gains from specialization. However, these gains can be dwarfed by the effect of trade on the country's growth rate and thus on the volume of additional resources made available to, or utilized by, the trading country. These are known as the **dynamic gains from international trade** as opposed to the static effects of reallocating a fixed quantity of resources.

We have learned that international trade tends to bring about a more efficient use of an economy's resources, which leads to higher output and income. Over time, increased income tends to result in more saving and, thus, more investment in equipment and manufacturing plants. This additional investment generally results in a higher rate of economic growth. Moreover, opening an economy to trade can lead to imported investment goods, such as machinery, which fosters higher productivity and economic growth. In a roundabout manner, the gains from international trade grow larger over time. Empirical evidence shows that countries that are more open to international trade tend to grow faster than closed economies.[8]

Free trade also increases the possibility that a firm importing a capital good will be able to locate a supplier who will provide a good that more nearly meets its specifications. The better the match, the larger is the increase in the firm's productivity, which promotes economic growth.

Economies of large-scale production represent another dynamic gain from trade. International trade allows small and moderately sized countries to establish and operate many plants of efficient size, which would be impossible if production were limited to the domestic market. For example, the free access that Mexican and Canadian firms have to the U.S. market under the North American Free Trade Agreement (NAFTA) allows them to expand their production and employ more specialized labor and equipment. These improvements have led to increased efficiency and lower unit costs for these countries.

Also, increased competition can be a source of dynamic gains in trade. For example, when Chile opened its economy to global competition in the 1970s, its exiting producers with comparative disadvantage were about eight percent less efficient than producers that continued to operate. The efficiency of plants competing against imports increased three to ten percent more than in the domestic economy where goods were not subject to foreign competition. A closed economy shields companies from international competition and permits them to pull down overall efficiency within an industry. However, open trade forces inefficient firms to exit the industry and allows more productive firms to grow. Therefore, trade results in adjustments that raise the average industry efficiency in both exporting and import-competing industries.[9]

Simply put, besides providing static gains rising from the reallocation of existing productive resources, trade can also generate dynamic gains by stimulating economic growth. Proponents of free trade note the many success stories of growth through trade. However, the effect of trade on growth is not the same for all countries. In general, the gains tend to be less for a large country such as the United States than for a small country such as Belgium.

How Global Competition Led to Productivity Gains for U.S. Iron Ore Workers

The dynamic gains from international trade can be seen in the U.S. iron ore industry, located in the Midwest. Because iron ore is heavy and costly to transport, U.S. producers supply ore only to U.S. steel producers located in the Great Lakes region. During the early 1980s, depressed economic conditions in most of the industrial

---

[8]D. Dollar and A. Kraay, "Trade, Growth, and Poverty," *Finance and Development*, September 2001, pp. 16–19 and S. Edwards, "Openness, Trade Liberalization, and Growth in Developing Countries," *Journal of Economic Literature*, September 1993, pp. 1358–1393.

[9]Nina Pavcnik, "Trade Liberalization, Exit, and Productivity Improvements: Evidence from Chilean Plants," *Review of Economic Studies*, Vol. 69, January 2002, pp. 245–276.

world resulted in a decline in the demand for steel and thus falling demand for iron ore. Ore producers throughout the world scrambled to find new customers. Despite the huge distances and the transportation costs involved, mines in Brazil began shipping iron ore to steel producers in the Chicago area.

The appearance of foreign competition led to increased competitive pressure on U.S. iron ore producers. To help keep domestic iron mines operating, American workers agreed to changes in work rules that increased labor productivity. In most cases, these changes involved an expansion in the set of tasks a worker was required to perform. For example, the changes required equipment handlers to perform routine maintenance on their equipment. Before, this maintenance was the responsibility of repairmen. Also, new work rules resulted in a flexible assignment of work that required a worker to occasionally do tasks assigned to another worker. In both cases, the new work rules led to the better use of a worker's time.

Prior to the advent of foreign competition, labor productivity in the U.S. iron ore industry was stagnant. Because of the rise of foreign competition, labor productivity began to increase rapidly in the early 1980s; by the late 1980s, the productivity of U.S. iron ore producers had doubled. Simply put, the increase in foreign competitive pressure resulted in American workers adopting new work rules that enhanced their productivity.[10]

Changing Comparative Advantage

Although international trade can promote dynamic gains in terms of increased productivity, patterns of comparative advantage can and do change over time. In the early 1800s, for example, the United Kingdom had a comparative advantage in textile manufacturing. Then that advantage shifted to the New England states of the United States. Then the comparative advantage shifted once again to North Carolina and South Carolina. Now the comparative advantage resides in China and other low-wage countries. Let us see how changing comparative advantage relates to our trade model.

Figure 2.3 illustrates the production possibilities schedules, for computers and automobiles, of the United States and Japan under conditions of constant opportunity cost. Note that the *MRT* of automobiles into computers initially equals 1.0 for the United States and 2.0 for Japan. The United States thus has a comparative advantage in the production of computers and a comparative disadvantage in auto production.

Suppose both nations experience productivity increases in manufacturing computers but no productivity change in manufacturing automobiles. Assume that the United States increases its computer-manufacturing productivity by 50 percent (from 100 to 150 computers) but that Japan increases its computer-manufacturing productivity by 300 percent (from 40 to 160 computers).

Because of these productivity gains, the production possibilities schedule of each country rotates outward and becomes flatter. More output can now be produced in each country with the same amount of resources. Referring to the new production possibilities schedules, the *MRT* of automobiles into computers equals 0.67 for the United States and 0.5 for Japan. The comparative cost of a computer in Japan has

---

[10]Satuajit Chatterjee, "Ores and Scores: Two Cases of How Competition Led to Productivity Miracles," *Business Review*, Federal Reserve Bank of Philadelphia, Quarter 1, 2005, pp. 7–15.

FIGURE 2.3

CHANGING COMPARATIVE ADVANTAGE

If productivity in the Japanese computer industry grows faster than it does in the U.S. computer industry, the opportunity cost of each computer produced in the United States increases relative to the opportunity cost of the Japanese. For the United States, comparative advantage shifts from computers to autos.

thus fallen below that in the United States. For the United States, the consequence of lagging productivity growth is that it loses its comparative advantage in computer production. But even after Japan achieves comparative advantage in computers, the United States still has a comparative advantage in autos; the change in manufacturing productivity thus results in a change in the direction of trade. The lesson of this example is that producers who fall behind in research and development, technology, and equipment tend to find their competitiveness dwindling.

It should be noted, however, that all countries realize a comparative advantage in some product or service. For the United States, the growth of international competition in industries such as steel may make it easy to forget that the United States continues to be a major exporter of aircraft, paper, instruments, plastics, and chemicals.

To cope with changing comparative advantages, producers are under constant pressure to reinvent themselves. Consider how the U.S. semiconductor industry responded to competition from Japan in the late 1980s. Japanese companies quickly became dominant in sectors such as memory chips. This dominance forced the big U.S. chip makers to reinvent themselves. Firms such as Intel, Motorola, and Texas Instruments abandoned the dynamic-random-access-memory (DRAM) business and invested more heavily in manufacturing microprocessors and logic products, the next wave of growth in semiconductors. Intel became an even more dominant player in microprocessors, while Texas Instruments developed a strong position in digital signal processors, the "brain" in mobile telephones. Motorola gained strength in microcontrollers and automotive semiconductors. A fact of economic life is that no producer can remain the world's low-cost producer forever. As comparative advantages change, producers need to hone their skills to compete in more profitable areas.

Trading Under Increasing-Cost Conditions

The preceding section illustrated the comparative-advantage principle under constant-cost conditions. But in the real world, a good's opportunity cost may *increase* as more of it is produced. Based on studies of many industries, economists think the opportunity costs of production increase with output rather than remain constant for most goods. The principle of comparative advantage must be illustrated in a modified form.

Increasing opportunity costs give rise to a production possibilities schedule that appears *concave*, or bowed outward from the diagram's origin. In Figure 2.4, with movement along the production possibilities schedule from *A* to *B*, the opportunity cost of producing autos becomes larger and larger in terms of wheat sacrificed. Increasing costs mean that the *MRT* of wheat into autos *rises* as more autos are produced. Remember that the *MRT* is measured by the absolute slope of the production possibilities schedule at a given point. With movement from production point *A* to production point *B*, the respective tangent lines become *steeper*—their slopes increase in absolute value. The *MRT* of wheat into autos rises, indicating that each additional auto produced requires the sacrifice of increasing amounts of wheat.

Increasing costs represent the typical case in the real world. In the overall economy, increasing costs result when inputs are imperfect substitutes for each other. As auto production rises and wheat production falls in Figure 2.4, inputs that are less and less adaptable to autos are introduced into that line of production. To produce more autos requires more and more of such resources and thus an increasingly greater sacrifice of wheat. For a *particular product*, such as autos, increasing-cost is explained by the principle of diminishing marginal productivity. The addition of successive units of labor (variable input) to capital (fixed input) beyond some point results in decreases in the marginal production of autos that is attributable to each additional unit of labor. Unit production costs thus rise as more autos are produced.

Under increasing costs, the slope of the concave production possibilities schedule varies as a nation locates at different points on the schedule. Because the *MRT* equals the production possibilities schedule's slope, it will also be different for each point on the schedule. In addition to considering the *supply factors* underlying the production possibilities schedule's slope, we must also take into account the demand factors (tastes and preferences), for they will determine the point along the production possibilities schedule at which a country chooses to consume.

FIGURE 2.4

PRODUCTION POSSIBILITIES SCHEDULE UNDER
INCREASING-COST CONDITIONS

Increasing opportunity costs lead to a production possibilities schedule that is concave, viewed from the diagram's origin. The marginal rate of transformation equals the (absolute) slope of the production possibilities schedule at a particular point along the schedule.

Increasing-Cost Trading Case

Figure 2.5 shows the production possibilities schedules of the United States and Canada under conditions of increasing costs. In Figure 2.5(a), assume that in the absence of trade the United States is located at point A along its production possibilities schedule; it produces and consumes 5 autos and 18 bushels of wheat. In Figure 2.5(b), assume that in the absence of trade Canada is located at point A' along its production possibilities schedule, producing and consuming 17 autos and 6 bushels of wheat. For the United States, the relative cost of wheat into autos is indicated by the slope of line $t_{U.S.}$, tangent to the production possibilities schedule at point A (1 auto = 0.33 bushels of wheat). In like manner, Canada's relative cost of wheat into autos is indicated by the slope of line t_C (1 auto = 3 bushels of wheat). Because line $t_{U.S.}$ is *flatter* than line t_C, autos are relatively cheaper in the United States and wheat is relatively cheaper in Canada. According to the law of comparative advantage, the United States will export autos and Canada will export wheat.

As the United States specializes in auto production, it slides downward along its production possibilities schedule from point A toward point B. The relative cost of autos (in terms of wheat) rises, as implied by the increase in the (absolute) slope of the production possibilities schedule. At the same time, Canada specializes in wheat. As Canada moves upward along its production possibilities schedule from point A' toward point B', the relative cost of autos (in terms of wheat) decreases, as evidenced by the decrease in the (absolute) slope of its production possibilities schedule.

The process of specialization continues in both nations until the relative cost of autos is identical in both nations and U.S. exports of autos are precisely equal to Canada's imports of autos, and conversely for wheat. Assume that this situation occurs when the domestic rates of transformation (domestic terms of trade) of both

FIGURE 2.5

TRADING UNDER INCREASING OPPORTUNITY COSTS

With increasing opportunity costs, comparative product prices in each country are determined by both supply and demand factors. A country tends to partially specialize in the product of its comparative advantage under increasing-cost conditions.

nations converge at the rate given by line *tt*. At this point of convergence, the United States produces at point *B*, while Canada produces at point *B'*. Line *tt* becomes the international terms-of-trade line for the United States and Canada; it coincides with each nation's domestic terms of trade. The international terms of trade are favorable to both nations because *tt* is steeper than $t_{U.S.}$ and flatter than t_C.

What are the *production gains* from specialization for the United States and Canada? Comparing the amount of autos and wheat produced by the two nations at their points prior to specialization with the amount produced at their post-specialization production points, we see that there are gains of 3 autos and 3 bushels of wheat. The production gains from specialization are shown in Table 2.6(*a*).

What are the *consumption gains* from trade for the two nations? With trade, the United States can choose a consumption point along international terms-of-trade line *tt*. Assume that the United States prefers to consume the same number of autos as it did in the absence of trade. It will export 7 autos for 7 bushels of wheat, achieving a post-trade consumption point at *C*. The U.S. consumption gains from trade are 3 bushels of wheat, as shown in Figure 2.5(*a*) and also in Table 2.6(*b*). The U.S. *trade triangle*, showing its exports, imports, and terms of trade, is denoted by triangle *BCD*.

In like manner, Canada can choose to consume at some point along international terms-of-trade line *tt*. Assuming that Canada holds constant its consumption of wheat, it will export 7 bushels of wheat for 7 autos and wind up at post-trade consumption point *C'*. Its consumption gain of 3 autos is also shown in Table 2.6(*b*). Canada's *trade triangle* is depicted in Figure 2.5(*b*) by triangle *B'C'D'*. Note that Canada's trade triangle is identical to that of the United States.

In this chapter, we discussed the autarky points and post-trade consumption points for the United States and Canada by assuming "given" tastes and preferences (demand conditions) of the consumers in both countries. In *Exploring Further 2.2*,

TABLE 2.6

GAINS FROM SPECIALIZATION AND TRADE: INCREASING OPPORTUNITY COSTS

(a) Production Gains from Specialization

	BEFORE SPECIALIZATION		AFTER SPECIALIZATION		NET GAIN (LOSS)	
	Autos	**Wheat**	**Autos**	**Wheat**	**Autos**	**Wheat**
United States	5	18	12	14	7	−4
Canada	17	6	13	13	−4	7
World	22	24	25	27	3	3

(b) Consumption Gains from Trade

	BEFORE TRADE		AFTER TRADE		NET GAIN (LOSS)	
	Autos	**Wheat**	**Autos**	**Wheat**	**Autos**	**Wheat**
United States	5	18	5	21	0	3
Canada	17	6	20	6	3	0
World	22	24	25	27	3	3

we introduce indifference curves to show the role of each country's tastes and preferences in determining the autarky points and how gains from trade are distributed.

Partial Specialization

One feature of the increasing-cost model analyzed here is that trade generally leads each country to specialize only partially in the production of the good in which it has a comparative advantage. The reason for **partial specialization** is that increasing costs constitute a mechanism that forces costs in two trading nations to converge. When cost differentials are eliminated, the basis for further specialization ceases to exist.

Figure 2.5 assumes that prior to specialization the United States has a comparative cost advantage in producing autos, whereas Canada is relatively more efficient at producing wheat. With specialization, each country produces more of the commodity of its comparative advantage and less of the commodity of its comparative disadvantage. Given increasing-cost conditions, unit costs rise as both nations produce more of their export commodities. Eventually, the cost differentials are eliminated, at which point the basis for further specialization ceases to exist.

When the basis for specialization is eliminated, there exists a strong probability that both nations will produce some of each good. This is because costs often rise so rapidly that a country loses its comparative advantage vis-à-vis the other country before it reaches the endpoint of its production possibilities schedule. In the real world of increasing-cost conditions, partial specialization is a likely result of trade.

Another reason for partial specialization is that not all goods and services are traded internationally. For example, even if Germany has a comparative advantage in medical services, it would be hard for Germany to completely specialize in medical services and export them. It would be very difficult for American patients who require back surgeries to receive them from surgeons in Germany.

Differing tastes for products also result in partial specialization. Most products are differentiated. Compact disc players, digital music players, automobiles, and other products entail a variety of features. When purchasing automobiles, some people desire capacity to transport seven passengers while others desire good gas mileage and attractive styling. Thus, some buyers prefer Ford Expeditions and others prefer Honda CRVs. Simply put, the United States and Japan have comparative advantages in manufacturing different types of automobiles.

The Impact of Trade on Jobs

As Americans watch the evening news on television and see Chinese workers producing goods that they used to produce, they might conclude that international trade results in an overall loss of jobs for Americans. Is this true?

Standard trade theory suggests that the extent to which an economy is open influences the *mix* of jobs within an economy and can cause dislocation in certain areas or industries, but has little effect on the *overall* level of employment. The main determinants of total employment are factors such as the available workforce, the total spending in the economy, and the regulations that govern the labor market.

According to the principle of comparative advantage, trade tends to lead a country to specialize in producing goods and services at which it excels. Trade influences

FIGURE 2.6

THE IMPACT OF TRADE ON JOBS

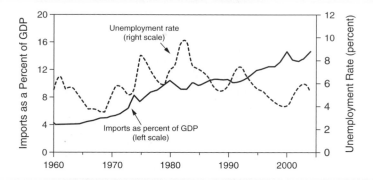

Increased international trade tends to neither inhibit overall job creation nor contribute to an increase in the overall rate of unemployment. As seen in the figure, the increase in U.S. imports as a percentage of GDP over the past several decades has not led to any significant trend in the overall unemployment for Americans.

the mix of jobs because workers and capital are expected to shift away from industries in which they are less productive relative to foreign producers and toward industries having a comparative advantage.

The conclusion that international trade has little impact on the overall number of jobs is supported by data on the U.S. economy. If trade is a major determinant on the nation's ability to maintain full employment, measures of the amount of trade and unemployment would move in unison, but in fact, they generally do not. As seen in Figure 2.6, the increase in U.S. imports as a percentage of GDP over the past several decades has not led to any significant trend in the overall unemployment rate for Americans. Indeed, the United States has been able to achieve relatively low unemployment while imports have grown considerably.

Simply put, increased trade has neither inhibited overall job creation nor contributed to an increase in the overall rate of unemployment. This topic will be further examined in Chapter 10 in the essay entitled "Do Current Account Deficits Cost Americans Jobs?"

Comparative Advantage Extended to Many Products and Countries

In our discussion so far, we have used trading models in which only two goods are produced and consumed and in which trade is confined to two countries. This simplified approach has permitted us to analyze many essential points about comparative advantage and trade. But the real world of international trade involves more than two products and two countries; each country produces thousands of products and trades with many countries. To move in the direction of realism, it is necessary to understand how comparative advantage functions in a world of many products and many countries. As we will see, the conclusions of comparative advantage hold when more realistic situations are encountered.

More Than Two Products

When two countries produce a large number of goods, the operation of comparative advantage requires that the goods be ranked by the degree of comparative cost. Each country exports the product(s) in which it has the greatest comparative advantage. Conversely, each country imports the product(s) in which it has greatest comparative disadvantage.

Figure 2.7 illustrates the hypothetical arrangement of six products—chemicals, jet planes, computers, autos, steel, and semiconductors—in rank order of the comparative advantage of the United States and Japan. The arrangement implies that chemical costs are lowest in the United States relative to Japan, whereas the U.S. cost advantage in jet planes is somewhat less. Conversely, Japan enjoys its greatest comparative advantage in semiconductors.

This product arrangement clearly indicates that, with trade, the United States will produce and export chemicals and that Japan will produce and export semiconductors. But where will the cutoff point lie between what is exported and what is imported? Between computers and autos? Or will Japan produce computers and the United States produce only chemicals and jet planes? Or will the cutoff point fall along one of the products rather than between them—so that computers, for example, might be produced in both Japan and the United States?

The cutoff point between what is exported and what is imported depends on the relative strength of international demand for the various products. One can visualize the products as beads arranged along a string according to comparative advantage. The strength of demand and supply will determine the cutoff point between U.S. and Japanese production. A rise in the demand for steel and semiconductors, for example, leads to price increases that move in favor of Japan. These increases lead to rising production in the Japanese steel and semiconductor industries.

FIGURE 2.7

HYPOTHETICAL SPECTRUM OF COMPARATIVE ADVANTAGES FOR THE UNITED STATES AND JAPAN

When a large number of goods is produced by two countries, operation of the comparative-advantage principle requires the goods to be ranked by the degree of comparative cost. Each country exports the product(s) in which its comparative advantage is strongest. Each country imports the product(s) in which its comparative advantage is weakest.

More Than Two Countries

When a trading example includes many countries, the United States will find it advantageous to enter into *multilateral trading relations*. Figure 2.8 illustrates the process of multilateral trade for the United States, Japan, and OPEC. The arrows in the figure denote the directions of exports. The United States exports jet planes to OPEC, Japan imports oil from OPEC, and Japan exports semiconductors to the United States. The real world of international trade involves trading relations even more complex than this triangular example.

This example casts doubt upon the idea that *bilateral balance* should pertain to any two trading partners. Indeed, there is no more reason to expect bilateral trade to balance between nations than between individuals. The predictable result is that a nation will realize a trade surplus (exports of goods exceed imports of goods) with trading partners that buy a lot of the things that it supplies at low cost. Also, a nation will realize a trade deficit (imports of goods exceed exports of goods) with trading partners that are low-cost suppliers of goods that it imports intensely.

FIGURE 2.8

MULTILATERAL TRADE AMONG THE UNITED STATES, JAPAN, AND OPEC

When many countries are involved in international trade, the home country will likely find it advantageous to enter into multilateral trading relations with a number of countries. This figure illustrates the process of multilateral trade for the United States, Japan, and OPEC.

Consider the trade "deficits" and "surpluses" of a dentist who likes to snow ski. The dentist can be expected to run a trade deficit with ski resorts, sporting goods stores, and favorite suppliers of items like shoe repair, carpentry, and suppliers of essential services like garbage collection and medical care. Why? The dentist is highly likely to buy these items from others. On the other hand, the dentist can be expected to run trade surpluses with his patients and medical insurers. These trading partners are major purchasers of the services provided by the dentist. Moreover, if the dentist has a high rate of saving, the surpluses will substantially exceed the deficits.

The same principles are at work across nations. A country can expect to run sizable surpluses with trading partners that buy a lot of the things the country exports, while trade deficits will be present with trading partners that are low-cost suppliers of the items imported.

What would be the effect if all countries entered into bilateral trade agreements that balanced exports and imports between each pair of countries? The volume of trade and specialization would be greatly reduced, and resources would be hindered from moving to their highest productivity. Although exports would be brought into balance with imports, the gains from trade would be lessened.

Exit Barriers

According to the principle of comparative advantage, an open trading system results in a channeling of resources from uses of low productivity to those of high productivity. Competition forces high cost plants to exit, leaving the low cost plants to operate in the long run. In practice, the restructuring of inefficient companies can take a long time because they often cling to capacity by nursing along antiquated plants. Why do companies delay plant closing when profits are subnormal and over-capacity exists? Part of the answer lies in the existence of **exit barriers**, various cost conditions that make lengthy exit a rational response by companies.

Consider the case of the U.S. steel industry. Throughout the past three decades, industry analysts maintained that overcapacity has been a key problem facing U.S. steel companies. Overcapacity has been caused by factors such as imports, reduced demand for steel, and installation of modern technology that allows greater productivity and increases the output of steel with fewer inputs of capital and labor.

Traditional economic theory envisions hourly labor as a *variable* cost of production. However, the U.S. steel companies' contracts with the United Steelworkers of America, their labor union, make hourly labor a *fixed* cost instead of a variable cost, at least in part. The contracts call for many employee benefits such as health and life insurance, pensions, and severance pay when a plant is shut down as well as unemployment benefits.

Besides employee benefits, other exit costs tend to delay the closing of antiquated steel plants. These costs include penalties for terminating contracts to supply raw materials and expenses associated with the writing off of undepreciated plant assets. Steel companies also face environmental costs when they close plants. They are potentially liable for cleanup costs at their abandoned facilities for treatment, storage, and disposal costs that can easily amount to hundreds of millions of dollars. Furthermore, steel companies cannot realize much by selling their plants' assets. The equipment is unique to the steel industry and is of little value for any purpose other than producing steel. What's more, the equipment in a closed plant is generally in need of major renovation because the former owner allowed the plant to become antiquated prior to closing.

Simply put, exit barriers hinder the market adjustments that occur according to the principle of comparative advantage.

Empirical Evidence on Comparative Advantage

We have learned that Ricardo's theory of comparative advantage implies that each country will export goods for which its labor is relatively productive compared with that of its trading partners. Does his theory accurately predict trade patterns? A number of economists have put Ricardo's theory to empirical tests.

The first test of the Ricardian model was made by the British economist G.D.A. MacDougall in 1951. Comparing the export patterns of 25 separate industries for the United States and the United Kingdom for the year 1937, MacDougall tested the Ricardian prediction that nations tend to export goods in which their labor productivity is relatively high. Of the 25 industries studied, 20 fit the predicted pattern. The MacDougall investigation thus supported the Ricardian theory of comparative advantage. Using different sets of data, subsequent studies by Balassa and Stern also supported Ricardo's conclusions.[11]

---

[11]G.D.A. MacDougall, "British and American Exports: A Study Suggested by the Theory of Comparative Costs," *Economic Journal* 61, 1951. See also B. Balassa, "An Empirical Demonstration of Classical Comparative Cost Theory," *Review of Economics and Statistics*, August 1963, pp. 231–238 and R. Stern, "British and American Productivity and Comparative Costs in International Trade," *Oxford Economic Papers*, October 1962.

A more recent test of the Ricardian model comes from Stephen Golub, who examined the relation between relative unit labor costs (the ratio of wages to productivity) and trade for the United States vis-a-vis the United Kingdom, Japan, Germany, Canada, and Australia. He found that relative unit labor cost helps to explain trade patterns for these nations. The U.S. and Japanese results lend particularly strong support for the Ricardian model, as shown in Figure 2.9. The figure displays a scatter plot of U.S.-Japan trade data showing a clear, negative correlation between relative exports and relative unit labor costs for the 33 industries investigated.

Although there is empirical support for the Ricardian model, it is not without limitations. Labor is not the only factor input. Allowance should be made where appropriate for production and distribution costs other than direct labor. Differences in product quality also explain trade patterns in industries such as automobiles and footwear. We should therefore proceed with caution in explaining a nation's competitiveness solely on the basis of labor productivity and wage levels. The next chapter will further discuss this topic.

FIGURE 2.9

RELATIVE EXPORTS AND RELATIVE UNIT LABOR COSTS: U.S./JAPAN, 1990

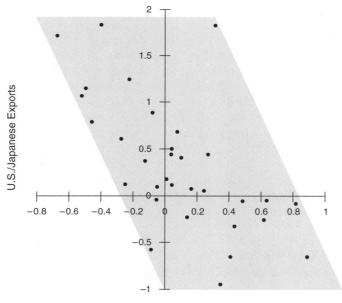

The figure displays a scatter plot of U.S./Japan export data for 33 industries. It shows a clear negative correlation between relative exports and relative unit labor costs. A rightward movement along the figure's horizontal axis indicates a rise in U.S. unit labor costs relative to Japanese unit labor costs; this correlates with a decline in U.S. exports relative to Japanese exports, a downward movement along the figure's vertical axis.

Source: Stephen Golub, *Comparative and Absolute Advantage in the Asia-Pacific Region*, Center for Pacific Basin Monetary and Economic Studies, Economic Research Department, Federal Reserve Bank of San Francisco, October 1995, p. 46.

Does Comparative Advantage Apply in the Face of Job Outsourcing?

For decades, most economists have insisted that countries, on balance, gain from free trade. Their optimism is founded on the theory of comparative advantage developed by David Ricardo. It states that if each country produces what it does best and allows trade, all will realize lower prices and higher levels of output, income, and consumption than could be achieved in isolation. However, is the theory of comparative advantage relevant in the 2000s when we see white-collar jobs shifting to low-wage countries? Does the fact that engineering, programming, and other high-skilled jobs are moving to places such as India and China conflict with Ricardo's principle?

When Ricardo formulated his theory, major factors of production—climate, soil, geography, and even most workers—could not move to other nations. However, critics of Ricardo note that in today's world, important resources—technology, capital, and ideas—can easily shift around the globe. Comparative advantage is weakened if resources can move to wherever they are most productive—in today's case, to a relatively few nations with abundant cheap labor. In this case, there are no longer shared gains—some nations win and others lose.[12]

Critics see a major change in the world economy caused by three developments. First, strong educational systems produce millions of skilled workers in developing nations, especially in China and India, who are as capable as the most highly educated workers in advanced nations but can work at a much lower cost. Second, inexpensive Internet technology allows many workers to be located anywhere. Third, new political stability permits technology and capital to move more freely around the globe. Table 2.7 identifies those U.S. occupations most likely to go offshore.

Critics fear that the United States may be entering a new phase in which American workers will encounter direct world competition at almost every job category—from the machinist to the software engineer to the medical analyst. Anyone whose job does not entail daily face-to-face interaction may now be replaced by a lower-paid, equally skilled worker across the globe. American jobs are being sacrificed not because of competition from foreign firms, but because of multinational companies, often headquartered in America, that are slashing expenses by locating operations in low-wage nations.

Advantages of Outsourcing

However, not everyone agrees with the claim that free trade based on comparative advantage no longer applies in today's world. They note that it is technology, not the movement of labor, that is creating new opportunities for trade in services, and this does not negate the case for free trade.[13]

---

[12]Charles Schumer and Paul Craig Roberts, "Second Thoughts on Free Trade," *The New York Times*, January 6, 2004, op ed. See also Paul Samuelson, "Where Ricardo and Mill Rebut and Confirm Arguments of Mainstream Economists Supporting Globalization," *Journal of Economic Perspectives*, Summer 2004, pp. 135–146.

[13]Jagdish Bhagwati, et. al., "The Muddles Over Outsourcing," *Journal of Economic Perspectives*, Fall 2004, pp. 93–114. See also McKinsey Global Institute, *Offshoring: Is It a Win-Win Game?* (Washington, D.C: McKinsey Global Institute, 2003).

TABLE 2.7

U.S. OCCUPATIONS REGARDED AS HIGHLY LIKELY
TO GO OFFSHORE

Occupation	Number of U.S. Workers, 2007
Computer programmers	389,090
Data entry keyers	296,700
Actuaries	15,770
Film and video editors	15,200
Mathematicians	2,930
Medical transcriptionists	90,380
Interpreters and translators	21,930
Economists	12,470
Graphic designers	178,530
Bookkeeping and accounting clerks	1,815,340

Source: Data drawn from AlanBlinder, "Offshoring: The Next Industrial Revolution?" *Foreign Affairs*, March/April, 2006 and "Pain From Free Trade Spurs Second Thoughts," *The Wall Street Journal*, March 28, 2007.

Technologies such as the Internet have made the U.S. service sector a candidate for outsourcing on a global scale. High-tech companies such as IBM can easily outsource software programming to India, and American medical centers are relying on Indian doctors to process data. Indeed, it seems that policymakers have few options to slow down this process of rapid technological change.

Proponents of outsourcing maintain that it can create a win-win situation for the global economy. Obviously, outsourcing benefits a recipient country, say India. Some of its people work for, say, a subsidiary of Southwestern Airlines of the United States and make telephone reservations for Southwestern's travelers. Moreover, incomes increase for Indian vendors supplying goods and services to the subsidiary, and the Indian government receives additional tax revenue. The United States, also benefits from outsourcing in several ways:

- *Reduced costs and increased competitiveness for Southwestern, which hires low-wage workers in India to make airline reservations.* In the United States, many offshore jobs are viewed as relatively undesirable or of low prestige; whereas in India, they are often considered attractive. Thus, Indian workers may have higher motivation and out produce their U.S. counterparts. The higher productivity of Indian workers leads to falling unit costs for Southwestern.
- *New exports.* As business expands, Southwestern's Indian subsidiary may purchase additional goods from the United States, such as computers and telecommunications equipment. These purchases result in increased earnings for U.S. companies such as Dell and AT&T and additional jobs for American workers.
- *Repatriated earnings.* Southwestern's Indian subsidiary returns its earnings to the parent company; these earnings are plowed back into the U.S. economy. Many offshore providers are, in fact, U.S. companies that repatriate earnings.

Catherine Mann of the Institute for International Economics analyzed the outsourcing of manufactured components by U.S. telecommunications and computer firms in the 1990s. She found that outsourcing reduced the prices of computers and communications equipment by 10 to 30 percent. This stimulated the investment boom in information technology and fostered the rapid expansion of information technology jobs. Also, she contends that taking information technology services offshore will have a similar effect, creating jobs for American workers to design and implement information technology packages for a range of industries and companies.[14]

Simply put, proponents of outsourcing contend that if U.S. companies cannot locate work abroad they will become less competitive in the global economy as

---

[14]Catherine Mann, *Globalization of IT Services and White-Collar Jobs: The Next Wave of Productivity Growth*, International Economics Policy Briefs, (Washington, D.C: Institute for International Economics, December 2003).

OUTSOURCING OF BOEING 787 DREAMLINER TRIGGERS MACHINIST'S STRIKE

TABLE 2.8

PRODUCING THE BOEING 787: EXAMPLES OF HOW BOEING OUTSOURCES ITS WORK

Country	Part/Activity
Japan	Wing, mid-fuselage section, fixed trailing edge, wing box
China	Rudder, vertical fin, fairing panels
South Korea	Wing tip, tail cone
Australia	Inboard flap, movable trailing edge
Canada	Engine pylon fairing, main landing gear door
Italy	Horizontal stabilizer
United Kingdom	Main landing gear, nose landing gear

Source: "Boeing 787: Parts From Around the World Will Be Swiftly Integrated," *The Seattle Times*, September 11, 2005, "Boeing Shares Work, But Guards Its Secrets," *The Seattle Times*, May 15, 2007, and "Outsourcing at Crux of Boeing Strike," *The Wall Street Journal*, September 8, 2008.

In 2007, the first wings for Boeing's new $150 million jetliner, the 787 Dreamliner, landed in Seattle, Washington, ready-made in Japan. Boeing assigned to three Japanese firms 35 percent of the design and manufacturing work for the 787, with Boeing performing final assembly in only three-day's time. Other nations, such as Italy, China, and Australia, were also involved in supplying sections of the 787, as seen in Table 2.8. Boeing maintained that by having contractors across the world build large sections of its airplanes, the firm could decrease the time required to build its jets by more than 50 percent.

To decrease costs, Boeing required foreign suppliers to absorb some of the costs of developing the plane. In return for receiving contracts to make sections of the 787, foreign suppliers invested billions of dollars, drawing from whatever subsidies were available. For example, Japan's government provided loans of up to $2 billion to the three Japanese suppliers of Boeing, and Italy provided regional infrastructure for its supplier company. This spreading of risk allowed Boeing to decrease its developmental costs and thus be a more effective competitor against Airbus.

The need to find engineering talent and technical capacity was another motive behind Boeing's globalization strategy. According to Boeing executives, the complexity of designing and producing the 787 requires that people's talents and capabilities are brought together from all over the world. Also, sharing work with foreigners helps Boeing maintain close relationships with its

customers. For example, Japan has spent more money buying Boeing jetliners than any other country: Boeing shares its work with the Japanese, and the firm in turn secures a virtual monopoly in jetliner sales to Japan.

But the strategy backfired when Boeing's suppliers fell behind in getting their jobs done, which resulted in the 787's production being more than a year behind schedule. The suppliers' problems ranged from language barriers to snarls that erupted when some contractors themselves outsourced chunks of work. Boeing was forced to turn to its own union workforce to piece together the first few airplanes after their sections arrived at the firm's factory in Seattle, with thousands of missing parts. That action resulted in anger and anxiety among union workers who maintained that if Boeing had let them build the 787 in the first place, they would have achieved the production goal. Boeing workers also feared that the firm would eventually attempt to allow foreign contractors to go one step further and install their components directly in the 787. Although Boeing officials insisted that they had no intentions to do this, they refused to give union workers assurances in writing.

In 2008, nearly 27,000 machinists walked off their jobs at Boeing. While wages and health-care costs were important issues, job security emerged as the most crucial topic. When the strike was settled, Boeing agreed to minor restrictions being placed on the outsourcing of Boeing work to external vendors. The firm also agreed to increase the wages of its workers by four percent per year during the duration of the new contract.

their competitors reduce costs by outsourcing, thus weakening the U.S. economy and threatening more American jobs. They also note that job losses tend to be temporary and that the creation of new industries and new products in the United States will result in more lucrative jobs for Americans. As long as the U.S. workforce retains its high level of skills and remains flexible as companies position themselves to improve their productivity, high-value jobs will not disappear in the United States.

Outsourcing and the U.S. Automobile Industry

Developments in the U.S. automobile industry over the past century illustrate the underlying forces behind outsourcing. In the early 1900s, it took only 700 parts for workers at Ford Motor Company to produce a Model T. With this relatively small number of parts, Ford blended the gains of large-scale mass production with the gains of a high degree of specialization within a single plant. Workers were highly specialized and usually performed one single task along an automated assembly line, while the plant was vertically integrated and manufactured the vehicle starting from raw materials.

As consumers became wealthier and insisted on more luxurious vehicles, and competitors to Ford emerged, Ford was forced to develop a family of models, each fitted with comfortable seats, radios, and numerous devices to improve safety and performance. As cars became more sophisticated, Ford could no longer efficiently produce them within a single plant. As the number of tasks outgrew the number of operations that could be efficiently conducted within a plant, Ford began to outsource production. The firm has attempted to keep strategically important tasks and production in-house while noncore tasks are purchased from external suppliers. As time has passed, increasing numbers of parts and services have come to be considered noncore, and Ford has farmed out production to a growing number of external suppliers, many of which are outside the United States. Today, about 70 percent of a typical Ford vehicle comes from parts, components, and services purchased from external suppliers. Clearly, without the development toward increased specialization and outsourcing, today's cars would be either closer to Model T technology in quality or they would be beyond the budgets of ordinary people. By the first decade of the 2000s, service industries, such as information technology and bill processing, were undergoing similar developments as the automobile industry had in the past.[15]

Burdens of Outsourcing

Of course, the benefits of outsourcing to the United States do not eliminate the burden on Americans who lose their jobs or find lower-wage ones due to foreign outsourcing. American labor unions often lobby Congress to prevent outsourcing, and several U.S. states have considered legislation to severely restrict their governments from contracting with companies that move jobs to low-wage developing countries.

So far, the debate about the benefits and costs of outsourcing has emphasized jobs rather than wages. However, the risks to the latter may be more significant. Over the past three decades, the wages of low-skilled American workers, those with a high school education or less, decreased both in real terms and relative to the wages of

---

[15]World Trade Organization, *World Trade Report 2005* (Geneva, Switzerland), pp. 268–274.

skilled workers, especially those with a college education or higher. Technological change and outsourcing caused the demand for low-skilled American workers to decline. Now the outsourcing of high-skilled jobs threatens to shift demand to cheaper substitutes in Asia. Like the assembly line revolution that reduced demand for skilled artisan workers during England's industrial revolution, the new wave of outsourcing may prove to be a technical change that decreases demand for many U.S. skilled workers. Although the outsourcing of high-skilled American jobs may yield economic benefits for the nation, there may be a sizable number of losers as well.

Many observers feel that the plight of the displaced worker must be increasingly addressed if free trade based on comparative advantage is to be widely accepted by the American public. Generous severance packages, accompanied by insurance programs, are among the measures that could lessen the adverse effects of people suffering job losses due to outsourcing. Also, the U.S. education system must be revamped so it prepares workers for jobs that cannot easily go overseas. Moreover, the tax code should be revised so as to reward firms that produce jobs that stay in the United States.

Some U.S. Manufacturers Prosper by Keeping Production in the United States

Do U.S. companies have to conduct foreign outsourcing to be competitive? It has long been an axiom that American-manufactured goods such as kitchen appliances and TV sets cannot compete in a world where cheaper labor can be found elsewhere. Is this necessarily true? If companies could increase the skill level for such work and perform the task more efficiently, the advantages from moving production would decline. Simply put, if work can be upgraded, it's not so obvious which countries should do the exporting.

Let us first consider the case of Fortune Brands, a company that produces such diverse products as Titleist golf clubs, Swingline staplers, Jim Beam whiskey, and Master Lock padlocks. At the turn of the century, Fortune was implementing a cost-cutting program to improve its competitiveness. The firm expanded its manufacturing industrial park in Nogales, Mexico, which employed more than 3,000 people, most of them performing work Fortune used to do in the United States. For example, it brought Master Lock padlocks down from Milwaukee, Wisconsin, and Acco Industries' Swingline staplers from Queens, New York.

Locating in the Mexican industrial park was an effort to slash costs. It wasn't just a matter of taking advantage of low wages in Mexico—although that was a major factor—but of squeezing every possible cent out of costs. By constructing its own industrial park, Fortune reduced costs by obtaining its land all at once and lowered energy expenses by installing its own electric substation. Efficiencies were also gained by contracting single suppliers of packaging materials and components and having one waste-hauler for all of the park's plants.

According to Fortune, buyers like Wal-Mart, Lowe's, and Home Depot put great pressure on it to hold its costs down. Simply put, Fortune justified its move to Nogales on the grounds that if it didn't move abroad, its customers would find someone else who would.

However, not all companies choose to leave the United States. This fact often applies to manufacturers of high-end goods that appeal to affluent consumers.

This business is often better done when it is close to the American customer. By producing in the United States, firms can better manage manufacturing processes and make changes to products on short notice. If the product being sold to Americans is locally customized, delicate, or very large, the odds are high that it is manufactured in the United States.

For example, consider Sony Corp., of Japan, which manufactures top-of-the line $6,000 Sony Grand WEGA TV sets at a factory near Pittsburgh, Pennsylvania. The TV sets utilize state-of-the-art technology and tend to be large, with screens ranging from 42 to 70 inches. Their size and electronic sophistication make proximity to the consumer an advantage, as does the ability to react quickly to changes in preferences for high-end equipment. Simply put, proximity gives Sony a distinct advantage with its retail partners throughout the United States, as the firm has the ability to quickly meet consumer demand with specific products.[16]

Summary

1. To the mercantilists, stocks of precious metals represented the wealth of a nation. The mercantilists contended that the government should adopt trade controls to limit imports and promote exports. One nation could gain from trade only at the expense of its trading partners because the stock of world wealth was fixed at a given moment in time and because not all nations could simultaneously have a favorable trade balance.

2. Smith challenged the mercantilist views on trade by arguing that, with free trade, international specialization of factor inputs could increase world output, which could be shared by trading nations. All nations could simultaneously enjoy gains from trade. Smith maintained that each nation would find it advantageous to specialize in the production of those goods in which it had an absolute advantage.

3. Ricardo argued that mutually gainful trade is possible even if one nation has an absolute disadvantage in the production of both commodities compared with the other nation. The less productive nation should specialize in the production and export of the commodity in which it has a comparative advantage.

4. Comparative costs can be illustrated with the production possibilities schedule. This schedule indicates the maximum amount of any two products an economy can produce, assuming that all resources are used in their most efficient manner. The slope of the production possibilities schedule measures the marginal rate of transformation, which indicates the amount of one product that must be sacrificed per unit increase of another product.

5. Under constant-cost conditions, the production possibilities schedule is a straight line. Domestic relative prices are determined exclusively by a nation's supply conditions. Complete specialization of a country in the production of a single commodity may occur in the case of constant costs.

6. Because Ricardian trade theory relied solely on supply analysis, it was not able to determine actual terms of trade. This limitation was addressed by Mill in his theory of reciprocal demand. This theory asserts that within the limits to the terms of trade, the actual terms of trade are determined by the intensity of each country's demand for the other country's product.

---

[16]"Fortune Brands Moves Units to Mexico to Lower Costs," *The Wall Street Journal*, August 7, 2000, p. B2, and "New Balance Stays a Step Ahead," *U.S. News & World Report*, July 2, 2001, p. 34; and " Low-Skilled Jobs: Do They Have to Move?" *Business Week*, February 26, 2001, pp. 94–95, "For Some Manufacturers, There Are Benefits to Keeping Production at Home," *The Wall Street Journal*, January 22, 2007, p. A2.

7. The comparative advantage accruing to manufacturers of a particular product in a particular country can vanish over time when productivity growth falls behind that of foreign competitors. Lost comparative advantages in foreign markets reduce the sales and profits of domestic companies as well as the jobs and wages of domestic workers.

8. In the real world, nations tend to experience increasing-cost conditions. Thus, production possibilities schedules are drawn concave to the diagram's origin. Relative product prices in each country are determined by both supply and demand factors. Complete specialization in production is improbable in the case of increasing costs.

9. According to the comparative-advantage principle, competition forces high cost producers to exit from the industry. In practice, the restructuring of an industry can take a long time because high cost producers often cling to capacity by nursing along antiquated plants. Exit barriers refer to various cost conditions that make lengthy exit a rational response for high cost producers.

10. The first empirical test of Ricardo's theory of comparative advantage was made by MacDougall. Comparing the export patterns of the United States and the United Kingdom, MacDougall found that wage rates and labor productivity were important determinants of international trade patterns. A more recent test of the Ricardian model, conducted by Golub, also supports Ricardo.

Key Concepts & Terms

- Autarky (p. 38)
- Basis for trade (p. 31)
- Commodity terms of trade (p. 44)
- Complete specialization (p. 41)
- Constant opportunity costs (p. 38)
- Consumption gains (p. 41)
- Dynamic gains from international trade (p. 45)
- Exit barriers (p. 56)
- Free trade (p. 32)
- Gains from international trade (p. 31)
- Importance of being unimportant (p. 43)
- Increasing opportunity costs (p. 49)
- Labor theory of value (p. 33)
- Marginal rate of transformation (p. 38)
- Mercantilists (p. 31)
- No-trade boundary (p. 42)
- Outer limits for the equilibrium terms of trade (p. 42)
- Partial specialization (p. 52)
- Price-specie-flow doctrine (p. 32)
- Principle of absolute advantage (p. 33)
- Principle of comparative advantage (p. 34)
- Production gains (p. 39)
- Production possibilities schedule (p. 37)
- Region of mutually beneficial trade (p. 42)
- Terms of trade (p. 31)
- Theory of reciprocal demand (p. 43)
- Trade triangle (p. 41)
- Trading possibilities line (p. 41)

Study Questions

1. The gains from specialization and trade are discussed in terms of *production gains* and *consumption gains*. What do these terms mean?

2. How does the commodity terms-of-trade concept attempt to measure the direction of trade gains?

3. What factors underlie whether specialization in production will be partial or complete on an international basis?

4. What is meant by the theory of reciprocal demand? How does it provide a meaningful explanation of the international terms of trade?

5. Why is it that the pre-trade production points have a bearing on comparative costs under increasing-cost conditions but not under conditions of constant costs?

6. Why is it that the gains from trade could not be determined precisely under the Ricardian trade model?

7. What is meant by constant opportunity costs and increasing opportunity costs? Under what conditions will a country experience constant or increasing costs?

8. Table 2.9 gives hypothetical export price indexes and import price indexes (1990 = 100) for Japan, Canada, and Ireland. Compute the commodity terms of trade for each country for the period 1990–2006. Which country's terms of trade improved, worsened, or showed no change?

TABLE 2.9

Export Price and Import Price Indexes

Country	EXPORT PRICE INDEX		IMPORT PRICE INDEX	
	1990	2006	1990	2006
Japan	100	150	100	140
Canada	100	175	100	175
Ireland	100	167	100	190

9. How does the comparative-cost concept relate to a nation's production possibilities schedule? Illustrate how differently shaped production possibilities schedules give rise to different opportunity costs.

10. The maximum amount of steel or aluminum that Canada and France can produce if they fully use all the factors of production at their disposal with the best technology available to them is shown (hypothetically) in Table 2.10.

    Assume that production occurs under constant-cost conditions. On graph paper, draw the production possibilities schedules for Canada and France; locate aluminum on the horizontal axis and steel on the vertical axis of each country's graph. In the absence of trade, assume that Canada produces and consumes 600 tons of aluminum and 300 tons of steel

and that France produces and consumes 400 tons of aluminum and 600 tons of steel. Denote these autarky points on each nation's production possibilities schedule.

TABLE 2.10

Steel and Aluminum Production

	Canada	France
Steel (tons)	500	1200
Aluminum (tons)	1500	800

a. Determine the *MRT* of steel into aluminum for each nation. According to the principle of comparative advantage, should the two nations specialize? If so, which product should each country produce? Will the extent of specialization be complete or partial? Denote each nation's specialization point on its production possibilities schedule. Compared to the output of steel and aluminum that occurs in the absence of trade, does specialization yield increases in output? If so, by how much?

b. Within what limits will the terms of trade lie if specialization and trade occur? Suppose Canada and France agree to a terms-of-trade ratio of 1:1 (1 ton of steel = 1 ton of aluminum). Draw the terms-of-trade line in the diagram of each nation. Assuming that 500 tons of steel are traded for 500 tons of aluminum, are Canadian consumers better off as the result of trade? If so, by how much? How about French consumers?

c. Describe the trade triangles for Canada and France.

11. Both Smith and Ricardo contended that the pattern of world trade is determined solely by supply conditions. Explain.

12. The hypothetical figures in Table 2.11 give five alternate combinations of steel and autos that Japan and South Korea can produce if they fully use all factors of production at their disposal with the best technology available to them. On graph paper, sketch the production possibilities schedules of Japan and South Korea. Locate steel on the vertical axis and autos on the horizontal axis of each nation's graph.

TABLE 2.11

Steel and Auto Production

JAPAN		SOUTH KOREA	
Steel (tons)	**Autos**	**Steel (tons)**	**Autos**
520	0	1200	0
500	600	900	400
350	1100	600	650
200	1300	200	800
0	1430	0	810

a. The production possibilities schedules of the two countries appear concave, or bowed out, from the origin. Why?

b. In autarky, Japan's production and consumption points along its production possibilities schedule are assumed to be 500 tons of steel and 600 autos. Draw a line tangent to Japan's autarky point and from it calculate Japan's *MRT* of steel into autos. In autarky, South Korea's production and consumption points along its production possibilities schedule are assumed to be 200 tons of steel and 800 autos. Draw a line tangent to South Korea's autarky point and from it calculate South Korea's *MRT* of steel into autos.

c. Based on the *MRT* of each nation, should the two nations specialize according to the principle of comparative advantage? If so, in which product should each nation specialize?

d. The process of specialization in the production of steel and autos continues in Japan and South Korea until their relative product prices, or *MRTs*, become equal. With specialization, suppose the *MRTs* of the two nations converge at $MRT = 1$. Starting at Japan's autarky point, slide along its production possibilities schedule until the slope of the tangent line equals one. This becomes Japan's production point under partial specialization. How many tons of steel and how many autos will Japan produce at this point? In like manner, determine South Korea's production point under partial specialization. How many tons of steel and how many autos will South Korea produce? For the two countries, do their combined production of steel and autos with partial specialization exceed their output in the absence of specialization? If so, by how much?

e. With the relative product prices in each nation now in equilibrium at 1 ton of steel equal to 1 auto ($MRT = 1$), suppose 500 autos are exchanged at this terms of trade.

(1) Determine the point along the terms-of-trade line at which Japan will locate after trade occurs. What are Japan's consumption gains from trade?

(2) Determine the point along the terms-of-trade line at which South Korea will locate after trade occurs. What are South Korea's consumption gains from trade?

13. Develop an arithmetic example that illustrates how a nation could have an absolute disadvantage in the production of two goods and could still have a comparative advantage in the production of one of them.

14. With a given level of world resources, international trade may bring about an increase in total world output. Explain.

15. How did Smith's views on international trade differ from those of the mercantilists?

16. What is meant by the term *trade triangle*?

17. Identify the basic questions with which modern trade theory is concerned.

Exploring Further   2.1

Comparative Advantage in Money Terms

To illustrate comparative advantage in money terms, refer to the comparative-advantage example of Table 2.3 (p. 35) that assumes that labor is the only input and is homogeneous. Recall that (1) the United States has an absolute advantage in the production of both cloth and wine; and (2) the United States has a comparative advantage in cloth production, while the United Kingdom has a comparative advantage in wine production. This information is restated in Table EF 2.1. As we shall see, even though the United Kingdom is absolutely less efficient in producing both goods, it will export wine (the product of its comparative advantage) when its money wages are so much lower than those of the United States that it is cheaper to make wine in the United Kingdom. Let's see how this works.

Suppose the wage rate is $20 per hour in the United States, as indicated in Table 1. If U.S. workers can produce 40 yards of cloth in an hour, the average cost of producing a yard of cloth is $0.50 ($20/40 yards = $0.50 per yard); similarly, the average cost of producing a bottle of wine in the United States is $0.50. Because Ricardian theory assumes that markets are perfectly competitive, in the long term a product's price equals its average cost of production. The prices of cloth and wine produced in the United States are shown in the table.

Suppose now that the wage rate is £5 per hour in the United Kingdom. Thus, the average cost (price) of producing a yard of cloth in the United Kingdom is £0.50 (£5/10 yards = £0.50 per yard), and the average cost (price) of producing a bottle of wine is £0.25. These prices are also shown in Table EF 2.1.

Is cloth less expensive in the United States or the United Kingdom? In which nation is wine less expensive? When U.S. prices are expressed in dollars and UK prices are expressed in pounds, we cannot answer this question. We must therefore express all prices in terms of one currency—say, the U.S. dollar. To do this, we must know the prevailing exchange rate at which the pound and the dollar trade for each other.

Suppose the dollar/pound exchange rate is $1.60 = £1. In Table EF 2.1, we see that the UK hourly wage rate (£5) is equivalent to $8 at this exchange rate (£5 × $1.60 = $8). The average dollar cost of producing a yard of cloth in the United Kingdom is $0.80 ($8/10 yards = $0.80 per yard), and the average dollar cost of producing a bottle of wine is $0.40 ($8/20 bottles = $0.40 per bottle). Compared to the costs of producing these products in the United States, we see that the United Kingdom has lower costs in wine production but higher costs in cloth production. The United Kingdom thus has a comparative advantage in wine.

TABLE EF 2.1

RICARDO'S COMPARATIVE-ADVANTAGE PRINCIPLE EXPRESSED IN MONEY PRICES

Nation	Labor Input	Hourly Wage Rate	CLOTH (YARDS)		WINE (BOTTLES)	
			Quantity	Price	Quantity	Price
United States	1 hour	$20	40	$0.50	40	$0.50
United Kingdom	1 hour	£5	10	£0.50	20	£0.25
United Kingdom*	1 hour	$8	10	$0.80	20	$0.40

*Dollar prices of cloth and wine, when the prevailing exchange rate is $1.60 = £1. This exchange rate was chosen for this example because at other exchange rates it would not be possible to have balanced trade and balance in the foreign-exchange market.

We conclude that even though the United Kingdom is not as efficient as the United States in the production of wine (or cloth), its lower wage rate in terms of dollars more than compensates for its inefficiency. At this wage rate, the UK average cost in dollars of producing wine is less than the U.S. average cost. With perfectly competitive markets, the UK selling price is lower than the U.S. selling price, and the United Kingdom exports wine to the United States.

Exploring Further   2.2

Indifference Curves and Trade

In this section, we introduce indifference curves to show the role of each country's tastes and preferences in determining the autarky points and how gains from trade are distributed.

The role of tastes and preferences can be illustrated graphically by a consumer's indifference curve. An **indifference curve** depicts the various combinations of two commodities that are equally preferred in the eyes of the consumer; that is, yield the same level of satisfaction (utility). The term indifference curve stems from the idea that the consumer is indifferent about the many possible commodity combinations that provide identical amounts of satisfaction.

Figure EF 2.1 illustrates a consumer's indifference map, which consists of a set of indifference curves. Referring to indifference curve I, a consumer is just as happy consuming, say, six bushels of wheat and one auto at point A as consuming three bushels of wheat and two autos at point B. All combination points along an indifference curve are equally desirable because they yield the same level of satisfaction. Besides this fundamental characteristic, indifference curves have several other features:

- Indifference curves pass through every point in the figure;
- Indifference curves slope downward to the right;
- Indifference curves are bowed in (convex) to the diagram's origin;
- Indifference curves never intersect each other;
- Indifference curves lying farther from the origin (higher curves) represent greater levels of satisfaction.

Having developed an indifference curve for one individual, can we assume that the preferences of all consumers in the entire nation could be added up and summarized by a **community indifference curve**? Strictly speaking, the answer is no,

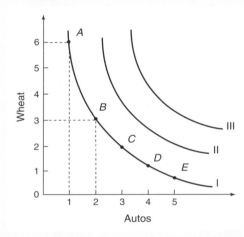

FIGURE EF 2.1

A CONSUMER'S INDIFFERENCE MAP

An indifference map is a graph that illustrates an entire set of indifference curves. Each higher indifference curve represents a greater level of satisfaction for the consumer. A community indifference curve denotes various combinations of two goods that yield equal amounts of satisfaction to the nation as a whole.

because it is impossible to make interpersonal comparisons of satisfaction. For example, person A may prefer a lot of coffee and little sugar, but person B prefers the opposite. The dissimilar nature of individuals' indifference curves results in their being noncomparable. Despite these theoretical problems, a community indifference curve can be used as a pedagogical device that depicts the role of consumer preferences in international trade.

Using indifference curves, let us now develop a trade example to restate the basis-for-trade and the gains-from-trade issues. Figure EF 2.2 depicts the trading position of the United States. The United States in the absence of trade will maximize

INDIFFERENCE CURVES AND TRADE

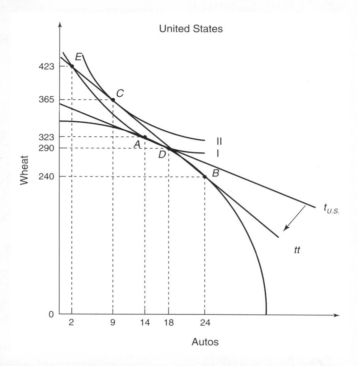

A nation benefits from international trade if it can achieve a higher level of satisfaction (indifference curve) than it can attain in the absence of trade. Maximum gains from trade occur at the point where the international terms-of-trade line is tangent to a community indifference curve.

satisfaction if it can reach the highest attainable indifference curve, given the production constraint of its production possibilities schedule. This will occur when the U.S. production possibilities schedule is just tangent to indifference curve I, at point A. At this point, the U.S. relative price ratio is denoted by line $t_{U.S.}$, which equals the absolute slope of the production possibilities curve at that point.

Suppose that the United States has a comparative advantage vis-à-vis Canada in the production of autos. The United States will find it advantageous

to specialize in auto production until the two countries' relative prices of autos equalize. Suppose this occurs at production point B, where the U.S. price rises to Canada's price, depicted by line tt. Also suppose that tt becomes the international terms-of-trade line. Starting at production point B, the United States will export autos and import wheat, trading along line tt. The immediate problem the United States faces is to determine the level of trade that will maximize its satisfaction.

Suppose that the United States exchanges 6 autos for 50 bushels of wheat at terms of trade tt.

This exchange would shift the United States from production point *B* to post-trade consumption point *D*. But the United States would be no better off with trade than it was in the absence of trade. This is because in both cases the consumption points are located along indifference curve *I*. Trade volume of 6 autos and 50 bushels of wheat thus represents the minimum acceptable volume of trade for the United States. Any smaller volume would force the United States to locate on a lower indifference curve.

Suppose instead that the United States trades 22 autos for 183 bushels of wheat. The United States would move from production point *B* to post-trade consumption point *E*. With trade, the United States would again locate on indifference curve *I*, resulting in no gains from trade. From the U.S. viewpoint, trade volume of 22 autos and 183 bushels of wheat therefore represents the maximum acceptable volume of trade. Any greater volume would find the United States moving to a lower indifference curve.

Trading along terms-of-trade line *tt*, the United States can achieve maximum satisfaction if it exports 15 autos and imports 125 bushels of wheat. The U.S. post-trade consumption location would be at point *C* along indifference curve *II*, the highest attainable level of satisfaction. Comparing point *A* and point *C* reveals that with trade the United States consumes more wheat, but fewer autos, than it does in the absence of trade. Yet point *C* is clearly a preferable consumption location. This is because under indifference-curve analysis, the gains from trade are measured in terms of total satisfaction rather than in terms of the number of goods consumed.

2.3   Exploring Further

Offer Curves and the Equilibrium Terms of Trade

John Stuart Mill's theory of reciprocal demand considered the significance of demand's influence on the terms of trade. But his theory was somewhat vague and generalized. It was Alfred Marshall who formally demonstrated the usefulness of offer curves as a graphic method of illustrating how the interaction of supply and demand determines the equilibrium terms of trade.[1]

Nature of an Offer Curve

An offer curve depicts the various amounts of two products that a country wishes to trade, given different price ratios. For each price ratio, the offer curve shows how much of one product a country is willing to trade for certain amounts of another product. Therefore, an offer curve can be thought of as both a *supply* curve and a *demand* curve. An offer curve is a supply curve in the sense that it shows the amounts of an export product that will be offered for sale at various terms of trade. Reflecting domestic supply factors, such as technology and resource endowments, an offer curve shows that more of an export product will be supplied on the market as its relative price increases. This is especially plausible if it assumes that the country produces under increasing cost conditions.

In Figure EF 2.3, as the U.S. terms of trade improve (the terms-of-trade line rotates upward), the United States finds that a given amount of its autos trades for larger quantities of the import good, wheat. This results in the United States being

FIGURE EF 2.3

OFFER CURVE: DEMAND AND SUPPLY INTERPRETATIONS

[1] Marshall, Alfred, *The Pure Theory of Foreign Trade*, London: London School of Economics and Political Science, 1930.

willing to offer more autos for sale. Similarly, improving terms of trade for Canada results in it being willing to offer additional amounts of its export product (wheat) for sale.

As a demand curve, an offer curve shows the quantities of imports that will be demanded at various terms of trade. Reflecting domestic demand conditions, the offer curve shows that more of the import product will be demanded as its relative price falls. In Figure EF 2.3 [1], we see that as the terms of trade improve for the United States, the relative price of its import good falls; that is, it requires fewer auto exports for the United States to purchase a given quantity of Canadian wheat. The United States thus moves upward along its offer curve, demanding larger amounts of wheat. The reverse holds equally true for Canada.

Offer Curve Construction

The shape and location of a country's offer curve are based on its supply and demand conditions, which are reflected in its production possibilities curve and community indifference curve. These tools can be used to build an offer curve.

Referring to Figure EF 2.4, suppose that its upper part represents U.S. production possibilities under increasing cost conditions. Assume that in the absence of trade the United States achieves the equilibrium point of production and consumption at point R, at which community indifference curve I is tangent to the production possibility curve. At this point, the U.S. price ratio is indicated by $t_{\text{U.S.}}$. With international trade, suppose the United States finds the international price ratio to be given by line tt_S. United States production thus moves to point S, where community indifference curve II is tangent to tt_S. By exchanging AP_S autos for AS wheat, the United States can attain a post-trade equilibrium at point S. Should the international price ratio be at tt_T, the United States could produce at point T, exchanging BP_T autos for BT wheat.

To build the U.S. offer curve, first redraw the price ratios (from the figure's upper part) in the lower part of the figure as positively sloped lines. At international terms of trade tt_S, the United States can offer OA (equal to AP_S) autos in exchange for OC (equal to AS) wheat. This exchange results in point S, one point along the U.S. offer curve. In like manner, other points along the offer curve can be established. The main point to be emphasized in this example is that the construction of an offer curve reflects both the supply and demand conditions of a country.

The Equilibrium Terms of Trade

Offer curve analysis is intended to determine the relative prices at which trade actually takes place—that is, the equilibrium terms of trade. By bringing together the supply characteristics embodied in a country's production possibilities curve and the demand preferences depicted in a community indifference curve, offer curve analysis exhibits the condition of a market equilibrium.

If the existing terms of trade are to be the equilibrium terms of trade, the amount of a product that a country wants to export must match the amount demanded as imports by another country. In Figure EF 2.5, point E represents the market equilibrium of the United States and Canada. At terms of trade tt_0, the quantity of autos the United States is willing to export (OA_0) equals the quantity of autos demanded by Canada (OA_0). In like manner, Canada's wheat exports (OW_0) just match U.S. wheat imports (OW_0). However, what if market equilibrium does not exist? Are there forces that will restore market balance?

Figure EF 2.5 also illustrates a case of market disequilibrium. At the terms of trade tt_1, the number of autos that the United States is willing to supply (OA_1) is less than the number of autos demanded by Canada (OA_2). A shortage of autos thus exists. At terms of trade tt_1, the amount of wheat that Canada is willing to supply (OW_2) exceeds the amount demanded by the United States (OW_1).

FIGURE EF 2.4

CONSTRUCTING AN OFFER CURVE

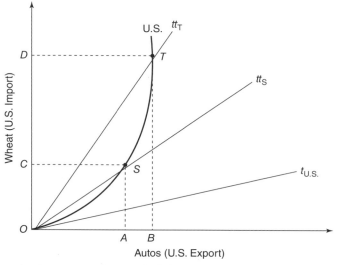

OFFER CURVES AND EQUILIBRIUM TERMS OF TRADE

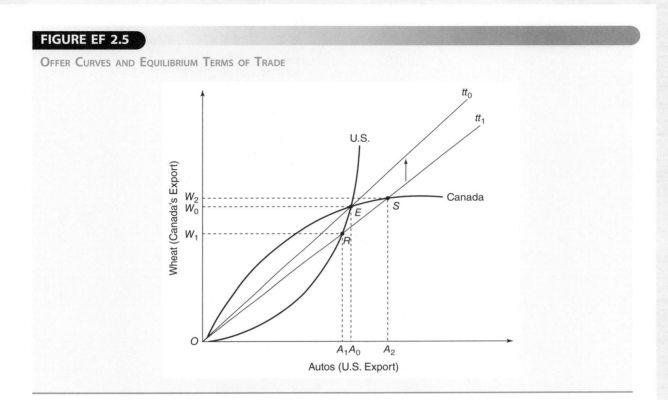

Therefore, there is a surplus of wheat. The relative price of autos will rise and wheat's relative price will fall until all surpluses and shortages are eliminated. At equilibrium point E, the supply matches the demand for both products. Conversely, a shortage of wheat and a surplus of autos results in the relative price of wheat rising and the relative price of autos falling until market equilibrium is restored at point E.

Shifting Offer Curves: Changes in the Equilibrium Terms of Trade

Because an offer curve is derived from a country's production possibilities curve and community indifference curve, changes in the supply and demand conditions underlying these schedules induce a shift in the offer curve's location. This shift in location results in a change in the equilibrium terms of trade and the volume of trade. Let us consider two possibilities.

Referring to Figure EF 2.6, suppose the United States and Canada are initially in equilibrium at point E, trading at terms of trade tt_0. Holding constant the Canadian supply of resources and technology, suppose that Canada's demand shifts away from autos, its import good, toward wheat, its export good. Because Canada now desires autos less intensely, it is willing to trade less wheat than before for a given number of autos. Canada's offer

FIGURE EF 2.6

CHANGES IN THE TERMS OF TRADE: INCREASED DEMAND FOR EXPORT GOOD

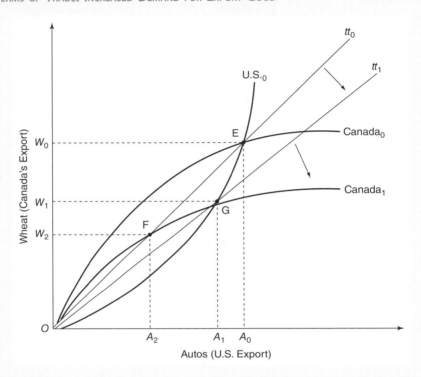

curve thus shifts from $Canada_0$ to $Canada_1$. At the initial terms of trade, tt_0, the market now is in disequilibrium: There exists an excess demand for wheat and an excess supply of autos. The relative price of wheat rises until market equilibrium is restored at point G. Both countries now trade at terms of trade tt_1. This trading situation affects Canada's welfare in two ways. The reduction in the volume of trade reduces its welfare, but the improving terms of trade increases its welfare. The actual effect that these opposing forces have on Canada's welfare depends on their relative

strength. It is left to the reader to verify that if Canada's demand shifts away from wheat to autos, its terms of trade will worsen and its volume of trade will increase.

Referring to Figure EF 2.7, again assume that the United States and Canada are initially in equilibrium at point E, trading at terms of trade tt_0. Holding constant U.S. demand for wheat and autos, suppose that technological advances result in the United States becoming more productive in manufacturing autos, its exportable good. This productivity causes a rightward shift in the U.S. offer

FIGURE EF 2.7

CHANGES IN THE TERMS OF TRADE: INCREASED SUPPLY OF EXPORT PRODUCT

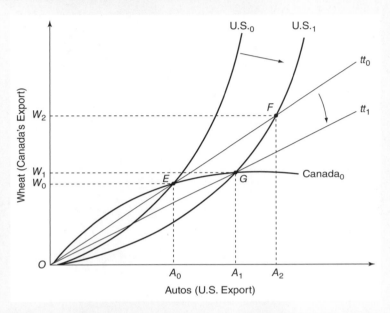

curve, from $U.S._0$ to $U.S._1$. At point F on the initial terms-of-trade line tt_0, the United States is now willing to sell a larger number of autos than Canada is willing to purchase. Market equilibrium is restored at point G, when the fall in the relative price of autos is sufficient to clear the market of the surplus of autos. Therefore, the terms of trade worsen for the United States although its volume of trade increases.

Sources of Comparative Advantage

CHAPTER 3

In Chapter 2, we learned how the principle of comparative advantage applies to the trade patterns of countries. The United States, for example, has a comparative advantage in, and thus exports considerable amounts of chemicals, semiconductors, computers, generating equipment, jet aircraft, agricultural products, and the like. It has comparative disadvantages in, and thus depends on other countries for cocoa, coffee, tea, raw silk, spices, tin, and natural rubber. Imported products also compete with U.S. products in many domestic markets: Japanese automobiles and televisions, Swiss cheese, and Austrian snow skis are some examples. Even the American pastime of baseball relies greatly on imported baseballs and gloves.

What determines a country's comparative advantage? There is no single answer to this question. Sometimes comparative advantage is determined by natural resources or climate, sometimes by the abundance of cheap labor, sometimes by accumulated skills and capital, and sometimes by government assistance granted to a particular industry. Some sources of comparative advantage are long lasting, such as huge oil deposits in Saudi Arabia; others can evolve over time, such as worker skills, education, and technology.

In this chapter, we consider the major sources of comparative advantage: differences in technology, resource endowments, and consumer demand; and also, the existence of government policies, economies of scale in production, and external economies.

Factor Endowments as a Source of Comparative Advantage

When Ricardo formulated the principle of comparative advantage, he did not explain what ultimately determines comparative advantage. He simply took it for granted that relative labor productivity, and thus relative labor costs and relative product prices, differed in the two countries before trade. Moreover, Ricardo's assumption of labor as the only factor of production ruled out an explanation of how trade affects the **distribution of income** among various factors of production within a nation and why certain groups favor free trade, whereas other groups oppose it. As we will see, trade theory suggests that some people will suffer losses from free trade.

In the 1920s and 1930s, Swedish economists Eli Heckscher and Bertil Ohlin formulated a theory addressing two questions left largely unexplained by Ricardo: What determines comparative advantage? And what effect does international trade have on the earnings of various factors of production in trading nations? Because Heckscher and Ohlin maintained that factor (resource) endowments determine a nation's comparative advantage, their theory became known as the **factor-endowment theory**. It is also known as the **Heckscher-Ohlin theory**.[1] Ohlin was awarded the 1977 Nobel prize in economics for his contribution to the theory of international trade.

The Factor-Endowments Theory

The factor-endowment theory asserts that the immediate basis for trade is the difference between pretrade relative product prices of trading nations. These prices depend on the production possibilities curves and tastes and preferences (demand conditions) in the trading countries. Because production possibilities curves, in turn, depend on technology and resource endowments, the ultimate determinants of comparative advantage are technology, resource endowments, and demand. The factor-endowment theory assumes that technology and demand are approximately the same between countries, and thus it emphasizes the role of relative differences in resource endowments as the ultimate determinant of comparative advantage.[2] Note that it is the resource-endowment ratio, rather than the absolute amount of each resource available, that determines comparative advantage.

According to the factor-endowment theory, a nation will export the product that uses a large amount of its relatively abundant resource, and it will import the product which in production uses the relatively scarce resource. Therefore, the factor-endowment theory predicts that India, with its relative abundance of labor, will export shoes and shirts while the United States, with its relative abundance of capital, will export machines and chemicals.

What does it mean to be relatively abundant in a resource? Table 3.1 illustrates hypothetical resource endowments in the United States and China that are used in the production of aircraft and textiles. The U.S. **capital/labor ratio** equals 0.5 (100 machines/200 workers = 0.5) which means that there is 0.5 machines per worker. In China, the capital/labor ratio is 0.02 (20 machines/1,000 workers = 0.02) which means that there is 0.02 machines per worker. Since the U.S. capital/labor ratio

---

[1] Eli Heckscher's explanation of the factor-endowment theory is outlined in his article "The Effects of Foreign Trade on the Distribution of Income," *Economisk Tidskrift* 21 (1919), pp. 497–512. Bertil Ohlin's account is summarized in his *Interregional and International Trade* (Cambridge, MA: Harvard University Press, 1933).

[2] The factor-endowment theory also assumes that the production of goods is conducted under perfect competition, suggesting that individual firms exert no significant control over product price; that each product is produced under identical production conditions in the two countries; that if a producer increases the use of both resources by a given proportion, output will increase by the same proportion; that resources are free to move within a country, so that the price of each resource is the same in the two industries within each country; that resources are not free to move between countries, so that pretrade payments to each resource can differ internationally; and that there are no transportation costs nor barriers to trade.

TABLE 3.1

Producing Aircraft and Textiles: Factor
Endowments in the United States and China

Resource	United States	China
Capital	100 machines	20 machines
Labor	200 workers	1,000 workers

exceeds China's capital/labor ratio, we call the United
States the relatively capital-abundant country and
China the relatively capital-scarce country. Conversely, China is called the relatively labor-abundant
country and the United States the relatively labor-
scarce country.

How does the relative abundance of a resource
determine comparative advantage according to the
factor-endowment theory? When a resource is relatively abundant, its relative cost is less than in coun-
tries where it is relatively scarce. Therefore, before the two countries trade, their
comparative advantages are that capital is relatively cheap in the United States and
labor is relatively cheap in China. So, the United States has a lower relative price in
aircraft, which use more capital and less labor. China's relative price is lower in textiles,
which use more labor and less capital. The effect of resource endowments on comparative advantage can be summarized as follows:

Differences in relative resource endowments	➔	Differences in relative resource prices	➔	Differences in relative product prices	➔	Pattern of comparative advantage

The predictions of the factor-endowment theory can be applied to the data in
Table 3.2 that illustrates capital/labor ratios for selected countries in 1997. To permit
useful international comparisons, capital stocks are shown in 1990 U.S. dollar prices
to reflect the actual purchasing power of the dollar in each country. We see that
the United States had less capital per worker than many other industrial countries,
but more capital per worker than the developing countries. According to the factor-
endowment theory, we can conclude that the United States has a comparative
advantage in capital-intensive products in relation to developing countries, but not
with many industrial countries.

TABLE 3.2

Capital Stock per Worker of Selected Countries in 1997*

Industrial Country	1997	Developing Country	1997
Japan	$77,429	South Korea	$26,635
Germany	61,673	Chile	17,699
Canada	61,274	Mexico	14,030
France	59,602	Turkey	10,780
United States	50,233	Thailand	8,106
Italy	48,943	Philippines	6,095
Spain	38,897	India	3,094
United Kingdom	30,226	Kenya	1,412

*In 1990 international dollar prices

Source: From A. Heston, R. Summers, and B. Aten, Penn World Table (January 2003, Version 6.0), available at **http://pwt.econ.upenn.edu/**.

Visualizing the Factor-Endowment Theory

Figure 3.1 provides a graphical illustration of the factor-endowment theory. It shows the production possibilities curves of the United States, assumed to be the relatively capital-abundant country, and of China, assumed to be the relatively labor-abundant country. The figure also assumes that aircraft are relatively capital intensive in their production process and textiles are relatively labor intensive in their production process.

Because the United States is the relatively capital-abundant country and aircraft are the relatively capital-intensive good, the United States has a greater capability in producing aircraft than China. Thus, the production possibilities curve of the United States is skewed (biased) toward aircraft, as shown in Figure 3.1. Similarly, because China is the relatively labor-abundant country and textiles are a relatively labor-intensive good, China has a greater capability in producing textiles than does the United States. Thus, China's production possibilities curve is skewed toward textiles.

Suppose that in autarky, both countries have the same demand for textiles and aircraft that results in both countries producing and consuming at point A in Figure 3.1(a).[3] At this point, the absolute slope of the line tangent to the U.S. production

FIGURE 3.1

THE FACTOR-ENDOWMENT THEORY

(a) Autarky Equilibrium

(b) Posttrade Equilibrium

A country exports the good whose production is intensive in its relatively abundant factor. It imports the good whose production is intensive in its relatively scarce factor.

---

[3]Note that the factor-endowment theory does not require that tastes and preferences be identical for the United States and China. It only requires that they be approximately the same. This approximation means that community indifference curves have about the same shape and position in all countries, as discussed in Exploring Further 2.2 in Chapter 2. For simplicity, Figure 3.1 assumes exact equality of tastes and preferences.

possibilities curve is smaller (U.S. $MRT = 0.33$) than that of the absolute slope of the line tangent to China's production possibilities curve (China's $MRT = 4.0$). Thus, the United States has a lower relative price for aircraft than China. This finding means that the United States has a comparative advantage in aircraft while China has a comparative advantage in textiles.

Although Figure 3.1(a) helps us visualize the pattern of comparative advantage, it does not identify the ultimate cause of comparative advantage. In our trading example, capital is relatively cheap in the relatively capital-abundant country (the United States) and labor is relatively cheap in the relatively labor-abundant country (China). It is because of this difference in relative resource prices that the United States has a comparative advantage in the relatively capital-intensive good (aircraft) and China has a comparative advantage in the relatively labor-intensive good (textiles). Simply put, the factor endowment theory asserts that the difference in relative resource abundance is the cause of the pretrade differences in the relative product prices between the two countries.

Most of the analysis of the gains from trade in Chapter 2 apply to the factor-endowment model, as seen in Figure 3.1(b). With trade, each country continues to specialize in the production of the product of its comparative advantage until its product price equalizes with that of the other country. Specialization continues until the United States reaches point B' and China reaches point B, the points at which each country's production possibilities curve is tangent to the common relative price line that is assumed to have an absolute slope of 1.0. This relative price line becomes the equilibrium terms of trade. Also, let's assume that with trade both nations prefer a post-trade consumption combination of aircraft and textiles given by point C. To achieve this point, the United States exports 6 aircraft for 6 units of textiles and China exports 6 units of textiles for 6 aircraft. Because point C is beyond the autarky consumption point A, each country realizes gains from trade.

Applying the Factor-Endowment Theory to U.S.-China Trade

The essence of the factor-endowment theory is seen in trade between the United States and China. In the United States, human capital (skills), scientific talent, and engineering talent are relatively abundant, but unskilled labor is relatively scarce. Conversely, China is relatively rich in unskilled labor while relatively scarce in scientific and engineering talent. Thus, the factor-endowment theory predicts that the United States will export to China goods embodying relatively large amounts of skilled labor and technology, such as aircraft, software, pharmaceuticals, and high-tech components of electrical machinery and equipment; China will export to the United States goods for which a relatively large amount of unskilled labor is used, such as apparel, footwear, toys, and the final assembly of electronic machinery and equipment.

Table 3.3 lists the top ten U.S. exports to China and the top ten Chinese exports to the United States in 2007. The pattern of U.S.-China trade appears to fit quite well to the predictions of the factor-endowment theory. Most of the U.S. exports to China were concentrated in higher skilled industries, which include machinery, aircraft, and medical equipment. Conversely, Chinese exports to the United States tended to fall into the lower-skilled industries such as toys, sporting equipment, footwear, and sound equipment. However, note that these trade data provide only a rough overview of U.S.-Chinese trade patterns and do not prove the validity of the factor-endowment theory.

TABLE 3.3

U.S.-CHINA TRADE: TOP TEN PRODUCTS, 2007 (THOUSANDS OF DOLLARS)

U.S. Exports to China		U.S. Imports from China	
Electrical machinery	65,236,121	Sound equipment, TVs	76,719,118
Nuclear reactors, boilers	10,693,159	Machinery	64,025,786
Grain, seed, fruit	8,849,565	Toys, sporting equipment	26,127,241
Aircraft, spacecraft	7,198,055	Apparel	23,965,281
Plastics	3,600,940	Furniture	20,361,512
Optic, photo, medical	3,314,019	Footwear	14,134,828
Iron, steel	2,255,434	Iron and steel products	9,764,720
Wood pulp	2,053,178	Plastics	8,249,394
Aluminum	1,819,115	Leather articles	7,230,980
Organic chemicals	2,101,193	Vehicles	6,384,209

Source: From U.S. Department of Commerce, International Trade Administration, available at **http:www.ita.doc.gov**. Scroll down to TradeStats Express (**http:// tse.export.gov/**) and to *National Trade Data*. See also Foreign Trade Division, U.S. Census Bureau.

Factor-Price Equalization

In Chapter 2, we learned that international trade tends to equalize product prices among trading partners. Can the same be said for resource prices?[4]

To answer this question, consider Figure 3.2. It continues our example of comparative advantage in aircraft and textiles by illustrating the process of **factor-price equalization**. Recall that the Chinese demand for inexpensive American aircraft results in an increased American demand for its abundant resource, capital; the price of capital thus rises in the United States. As China produces fewer aircraft, its demand for capital decreases, and the price of capital falls. The effect of trade is thus to equalize the price of capital in the two nations. Similarly, the American demand for cheap Chinese textiles leads to an increased demand for more labor in China, its abundant resource; the price of labor thus rises in China. With the United States producing fewer textiles, its demand for labor decreases, and the price of labor falls. With trade, the price of labor tends to equalize in the two trading partners. We conclude that by redirecting demand away from the scarce resource and toward the abundant resource in each nation; trade leads to factor-price equalization. In each nation, the cheap resource becomes relatively more expensive, and the expensive resource becomes relatively less expensive, until price equalization occurs.

Indian computer engineers provide an example of factor-price equalization. Without immigration restrictions, the computer engineers could migrate to the United States where wage rates are much higher, thus increasing the relative supply of computer-engineering skills and lessening the upward pressure on computer-engineering wages in the United States. Although such migration in fact has occurred, it has been limited by immigration restrictions. What was the market's response to the restrictions? Computer engineering-skills that could no longer be supplied through migration now arrive through trade in services. Computer-engineering services occur in India and are

---

[4]See Paul A. Samuelson, "International Trade and Equalization of Factor Prices," *Economic Journal*, June 1948, pp. 163–184 and "International Factor-Price Equalization Once Again," *Economic Journal*, June 1949, pp. 181–197.

FIGURE 3.2

THE FACTOR-PRICE EQUALIZATION THEORY

(a) Trade Alters the Mix of Factors (resources) Used in Production

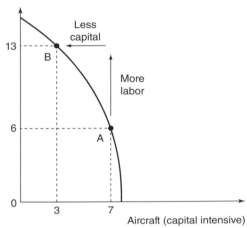

(b) Trade Promotes Factor Prices Moving into Equality across Countries

By forcing product prices into equality, international trade also tends to force factor prices into equality across countries.

transmitted via the Internet to business clients in the United States and other countries. In this manner, trade serves as a substitute for immigration.

However, the forces of globalization have begun to even things out between the United States and India. As more U.S. tech companies poured into India in the first decade of the 2000s, they soaked up the pool of high-end computer engineers who were making about 25 percent of what their counterparts earned in the United

TABLE 3.4

INDEXES OF HOURLY COMPENSATION FOR
MANUFACTURING WORKERS IN 2006 (U.S. = 100)

Norway	173
Germany	142
Sweden	132
Austria	130
Canada	109
Japan	83
Hong Kong	24
Brazil	21
Mexico	11

Source: From U.S. Department of Labor, Bureau of Labor Statistics, available at Web site **http://www.bls.gov**. Scroll to International Labor Comparisons and to Indexes of Hourly Compensation in U.S. Dollars (U.S. = 100).

States. The result was increasing competition for the most skilled Indian computer engineers and a narrowing U.S.-India gap in their compensation. By 2007, India's software-and-service association estimated wage inflation in its industry at 10 to 15 percent a year, while some tech executives said it was closer to 50 percent. In the United States, wage inflation in the software sector was less than three percent. For experienced, top-level Indian engineers, salaries increased to between $60,000 and $100,000 a year, pressing against salaries earned by computer engineers in the United States. Simply put, wage equalization was occurring between India and the United States. Taking into account the time difference with India, some Silicon Valley firms concluded that they were not saving any money by locating there anymore, and thus they began to bring jobs home to American workers.

Although the tendency toward the equalization of resource prices may sound plausible, in the real world we do not see full factor-price equalization. Table 3.4 shows indexes of hourly compensation for nine countries in 2006. Notice that wages differed by a factor of more than 15, from workers in the highest-wage country (Norway) to workers in the lowest-wage country (Mexico). There are several reasons why differences in resource prices exist.

Most income inequality across countries results from uneven ownership of human capital. The factor-endowment model assumes that all labor is identical. However, labor across countries differs in terms of human capital, which includes education, training, skill, and the like. We do not expect a computer engineer in the United States with a Ph.D. and 25 years' experience to be paid the same wage as a college graduate taking his/her first job as a computer engineer in Peru.

Also, the factor-endowment model assumes that all countries use the same technology for producing a particular good. When a new and better technology is developed, it tends to replace older technologies. But this process can take a long time, especially between advanced and developing countries. Therefore, returns paid to resource owners across countries will not equalize when two countries produce some good using different technologies. Machinery workers using superior production technologies in Germany tend to be paid more than workers using inferior production technologies in Algeria.

Moreover, transportation costs and trade barriers can prevent product prices from equalizing. Such market imperfections reduce the volume of trade, limiting the extent to which product prices and thus resource prices can become equal.

Simply put, that resource prices may not fully equalize across nations can be explained in part by the fact that the assumptions underlying the factor-endowment theory are not completely borne out in the real world.

Who Gains and Loses From Trade? The Stolper-Samuelson Theorem

Recall that in Ricardo's theory, a country as a whole benefits from comparative advantage. Also, Ricardo's assumption of labor as the only factor of production rules out an explanation of how trade affects the distribution of income among various factors of production within a nation and why certain groups favor free trade, whereas other groups oppose it. In contrast, the factor-endowment theory provides a more comprehensive way to analyze the gains and losses from trade. It does this by providing predictions of how trade affects the income of groups representing different factors of production, such as workers and owners of capital.

The effects of trade on the distribution of income are summarized in the **Stolper-Samuelson theorem**, an extension of the theory of factor-price equalization.[5] According to this theorem, the export of a product that embodies large amounts of a relatively cheap, abundant resource makes this resource more scarce in the domestic market. Thus, the increased demand for the abundant resource results in an increase in its price and an increase in its income. At the same time, the income of the resource used intensively in the import-competing product (the initially scarce resource) decreases as its demand falls. The increase in the income to each country's abundant resource thus comes at the expense of the scarce resource's income. Simply put, the Stolper-Samuelson theorem states that an increase in the price of a product increases the income earned by resources that are used intensively in its production. Conversely, a decrease in the price of a product reduces the income of the resources that it uses intensively.

Note that the Stolper-Samuelson theorem does not state that all the resources used in the export industries are better off, nor that all the resources used in the import-competing industries are harmed. Rather, the abundant resource that fosters comparative advantage realizes an increase in income, and the scarce resource realizes a decrease in its income, regardless of industry. Simply put, trade theory concludes that some people will suffer losses from free trade, even in the long term.

Although the Stolper-Samuelson theorem provides some insights regarding the income distribution effects of trade, it tells only part of the story. An extension of the Stolper-Samuelson theorem is the **magnification effect**, which suggests that the change in the price of a resource is greater than the change in the price of the good that uses the resource relatively intensively in its production process. Suppose that as the United States starts trading, the price of aircraft increases by six percent and the price of textiles decreases by three percent. According to the magnification effect, the price of capital must increase by more than six percent, and the price of labor must decrease by more than two percent. Thus, if the price of capital increases by eight percent, owners of capital are better off because their ability to consume aircraft and textiles (that is, their real income) is increased. However, workers, because their ability to consume the two goods is decreased (their real income falls), are worse off. Therefore, in the United States, owners of capital gain from free trade, while workers lose.

The Stolper-Samuelson theorem has important policy implications. It suggests that even though free trade may provide overall gains for a country, there are winners and losers. Given this conclusion, it is not surprising that owners of relatively abundant resources tend to favor free trade, while owners of relatively scarce factors tend to favor trade restrictions. For example, the U.S. economy has a relative abundance of skilled labor, so its comparative advantage is in producing skill-intensive

---

[5]Stolper, W. F., and P. A. Samuelson, "Protection and Real Wages." *Review of Economic Studies*, Vol.9, pp. 58–73, 1941.

GLOBALIZATION DRIVES CHANGES FOR U.S. AUTOMAKERS

As we have learned, workers in industries facing intense competition from imports tend to encounter downward pressure on their compensation levels, as seen in the case of the U.S. auto industry.

The history of the U.S. automobile industry can be divided into distinct eras: the emergence of Ford Motor Company as a dominant producer in the early 1900s; the shift of dominance to General Motors in the 1920s; and the rise of foreign competition since the 1970s.

Foreign producers have become effective rivals of the Big Three (GM, Ford, and Chrysler) which used to be insulated from competitive pressures on their costs and product quality. The result has been a steady decrease in the Big Three's share of the U.S. automobile market from more than 70 percent in 1999 to only 52 percent in 2009. For decades, the competitive threat of foreign companies was greatest in the small car segment of the U.S. market. Now, the Big Three also face stiff competition on the lucrative turf of pickup trucks, minivans, and sport-utility vehicles.

Intense foreign competition has shaken up the management and workers of the Big Three and has caused them to rethink their way of doing business. For example, the Big Three are saddled with large pension obligations and health care costs for hundreds of thousands of retirees. Generous benefit packages were negotiated by the United Auto Workers and the Big Three when times were better for these firms and foreign competition was less severe in the U.S. market. In 2008, GM spent about $4.8 billion on health care, an amount that increased the cost of every vehicle that it produced by about $1,500. Also, GM has about 96,000 active U.S. employees plus 497,000 retired workers. Including the dependents of retired workers who are covered by GM, the auto company

provides health care for almost one million people. Although Ford and Chrysler pay less than GM for health care, they are in the same ballpark.

However, for Japanese competitors the picture is much different. Concerning Toyota, analysts estimate its health care costs amount to only about $200 per vehicle. This is because Toyota provides health care coverage for substantially fewer employees in the United States than any of the Big Three: Toyota constructed its first auto assembly plant in the United States in 1986, so hardly any of its workers have reached retirement age. Thus, Toyota's health care cost advantage is about $1,300 per vehicle, compared to the Detroit Three. That is money the Big Three cannot pour into features that make vehicles more competitive—everything from fancy engines to smooth suspensions and tailored interiors.

Relatively high wages represent another cost disadvantage of the Big Three, as seen in Table 3.5. In 2008, the hourly wage of workers at the Big Three averaged $30 (and also $30 in benefits) while it averaged $24 (and also $24 in benefits) for workers at Toyota's and Honda's factories in the United States. Higher wages of the Big Three were not offset by their productivity advantage over their Japanese competitors who are widely viewed as the most efficient producers of automobiles in the world.

By 2008, the Big Three faced the worst decrease in sales since World War II. This decline was exasperated by a worsening economy and a credit crunch that dampened consumers' demand for new vehicles, high legacy costs, increased competition from foreign automakers, and stricter federal fuel-economy standards. Responding to a plea from GM and Chrysler, the administrations of outgoing President George W. Bush and incoming President

goods. The factor-endowment model suggests that the United States will tend to export goods requiring relatively large amounts of skilled labor and import goods requiring relatively large amounts of unskilled labor. International trade in effect increases the supply of unskilled labor to the U.S. economy, lowering the wages of unskilled American workers relative to those of skilled workers. Skilled workers— who are already at the upper end of the income distribution—find their incomes

TABLE 3.5

LABOR-COST GAP PER VEHICLE HURTS COMPETITIVENESS OF BIG THREE AUTOMAKERS

Labor-related costs affecting the higher costs per vehicle of Ford, General Motors, and Chrysler, compared with Toyota, Nissan, and Honda

Labor-Related Cost	Cost Gap Per Vehicle
Retiree health care	$490-705
Active worker health care	$220
Work rule gap*	$250
Vacations, holidays	$120-$160
Total	$1,080-$1,335

*Includes absenteeism rules, break times, seniority rights, job classifications and limits on outsourcing.

Source: Data taken from Jim Harbour and Laurie Harbour-Felax, *Automotive Competitive Challenges: Going Beyond Lean*, 2006, Harbour-Felax Group, Royal Oak, MI. See also, "Desparate to Cut Costs, Ford Gets Union's Help," *Wall Street Journal* March 2, 2007, p. A1.

Barack Obama provided them with a $17.4 billion loan to prevent them from failing and going into bankruptcy; Ford Motor Company did not request financial assistance from the federal government. In return, Obama insisted that GM and Chrysler shrink their labor costs, including retiree health care expenses; slash debt; terminate or sell low-performing brands; and decrease the number of models for sale and the number of dealers selling them. In spite of receiving billions of dollars of government assistance, the financial positions of GM and Chrysler continued to deteriorate and the companies filed for bankruptcy in 2009. As for Ford, its market share increased and the firm returned to profitability at the end of 2009, at the writing of this text.

As competition in the U.S. auto market has become truly international, it is highly unlikely that the Big Three will ever regain the dominance that allowed them to dictate which vehicles Americans bought and at what prices. Pressures will continue for them to downsize and restructure to turn themselves around. Simply put, fat wages and benefits cannot last when global competition is cutthroat.

Source: U.S. Department of Commerce, International Trade Administration, *The Road Ahead for the U.S. Auto Industry*, June 2005, Washington, DC and J. D. Harbour and Associates, *The Harbour Report 2007*, Troy, MI.

increasing as exports expand, while unskilled workers are forced into accepting even lower wages in order to compete with imports. According to the factor-endowment theory, then, international trade can aggravate income inequality, at least in a country such as the United States where skilled labor is relatively abundant. This is a reason why unskilled workers in the United States often support trade restrictions.

Is International Trade a Substitute for Migration?

Immigrants provide important contributions to the U.S. economy. They help the economy grow by increasing the size of the labor force, they assume jobs at the lower of the skill distribution where few native-born Americans are available to work, and they take jobs that contribute to the United States being a leader in technological innovation. In spite of these advantages, critics maintain that immigrants take jobs away from Americans, suppress domestic wages, and consume sizable amounts of public services. They contend that legal barriers are needed to lessen the flow of immigrants into the United States. If the policy goal is to reduce immigration, could international trade be used to achieve this result rather than adopting legal barriers? The factor-endowment model of Heckscher and Ohlin addresses this question.

According to the factor-endowment theory, international trade can provide a substitute for the movement of resources from one country to another in its effects on resource prices. Indeed, the endowments of resources among the countries of the world are not equal. A possible market effect would be movements of capital and labor from countries where they are abundant and inexpensive to countries where they are scarce and more costly, thus decreasing the price differences.

The factor-endowment theory also supports the idea that such international movements in resources are not essential, because the international trade in products can achieve the same result. Countries that have abundant capital can specialize in capital-intensive products and export them to countries where capital is scarce. In a sense, capital is embodied in products and redistributed through international trade. The same conclusion pertains to land, labor, and other resources.

A key effect of an international movement of a resource is to change the relative scarcity or abundance of that resource and therefore to alter its price; that is, to increase the price of the abundant resource by making it more scarce compared to other resources. For example, when Polish workers migrate to France, wage rates tend to increase in Poland because labor becomes somewhat more scarce there; also, wage rates in France tend to decrease (or at least increase more slowly than they would otherwise) because the relative scarcity of labor declines. The same outcome occurs when the French purchase Polish products that are manufactured by relatively labor-intensive methods: Polish export industries demand more workers, and Polish wages tend to increase. In this manner, international trade can serve as a substitute for international movements of resources through its effect on resource prices.[6]

An example of international trade as a substitute for labor migration is the North American Free Trade Agreement of 1995. Signed by Canada, Mexico, and the United States, the agreement eliminated trade restrictions among the three nations. At that time, former President Bill Clinton noted that NAFTA would result in an even more rapid closing of the gap between the wage rates of Mexico and the United States. And as the benefits of economic growth spread in Mexico to working people, they will have more income to buy more American products and there will be less illegal immigration because more Mexicans will be able to support their children by staying home. While NAFTA may have helped lessen the flow of migrants from Mexico to the United States, other factors continued to encourage migration—high

---

[6]Robert Mundell, "International Trade and Factor Mobility," *American Economic Review*, June 1957.

birth rates in Mexico, the collapse of the peso which resulted in recession, and the loss of jobs to other countries, especially China, where average wages are less than half of Mexico's. Although international trade and economic growth can help lessen the flow of Mexicans to the United States, achieving this result could take years, perhaps decades.

However, international trade and labor migration are not necessarily substitutes: They may be complements, especially over the short and near-long terms. As trade expands and an economy attempts to compete with imports, some of its workers may become unemployed. The uprooting of these workers may force some of them to seek employment abroad where job prospects are better. In this manner, increased trade can result in an increase in migration flows. For example, during the first decade of the 2000s, Mexico lost thousands of jobs to China, whose average wages were half of Mexico's and whose exports to other countries were increasing. This loss provided additional incentive for Mexican workers to migrate to the United States to find jobs. The topic of immigration is further discussed in Chapter 9.

Specific Factors: Trade and the Distribution of Income in the Short Run

A key assumption of the factor-endowment model and its Stolper-Samuelson theorem is that resources such as labor and capital can move effortlessly among industries within a country while they are completely immobile among countries. For example, Japanese workers are assumed to be able to shift back and forth between automobile and rice production in Japan, although they cannot move to China to produce these products.

Although such factor mobility among industries may occur in the long term, many factors are immobile in the short term. Physical capital (such as factories and machinery), for example, is generally used for specific purposes; a machine designed for computer production cannot suddenly be used to manufacture jet aircraft. Similarly, workers often acquire certain skills suited to specific occupations and cannot immediately be assigned to other occupations. These types of factors are known in trade theory as **specific factors**. Specific factors are those that cannot move easily from one industry to another. Thus, the **specific-factors theory** analyzes the income-distribution effects of trade in the short term when resources are immobile among industries. This is in contrast to the factor-endowment theory and its Stolper-Samuelson theorem which apply to the long-term mobility of resources in response to differences in returns.

To understand the effects of specific factors and trade, consider steel production in the United States. Suppose that capital is specific to producing steel, labor is mobile between the steel industry and other industries, and capital is not substitutable for labor in producing steel. Also suppose that the United States has a comparative disadvantage in steel. With trade, output decreases in the import-competing steel industry. As the relative price of steel decreases, labor moves out of the steel industry to take employment in export industries having comparative advantage. This movement causes the fixed stock of capital to become less productive for U.S. steel companies. As output per machine declines, the returns to capital invested in the steel industry decrease. At the same time, as output in export industries increases, labor moves to these industries and begins working. Hence, output per machine increases in the export industries, and the return to capital increases. Simply put, the specific-factors theory concludes that resources that are specific to import-competing industries tend to lose as a result of trade, while resources specific to export industries tend to gain as a result of trade. This analysis helps explain why U.S. steel companies since the 1960s have lobbied for import restrictions so as to protect their specific factors that suffer from foreign competition.

The specific-factors theory helps to explain Japan's rice policy. Japan permits only small quantities of rice to be imported, even though rice production in Japan is more costly than in other nations such as the United States. It is widely recognized that Japan's overall welfare would rise if free imports of rice were permitted. However, free trade would harm Japanese farmers. Although rice farmers displaced by imports might find jobs in other sectors of Japan's economy, they would find changing employment to be time consuming and costly. Moreover, as rice prices decrease with free trade, so would the value of Japanese farming land. It is no surprise that Japanese farmers and landowners strongly object to free trade in rice; their unified political opposition has influenced the Japanese government more than the interests of Japanese consumers. *Exploring Further 3.1* provides a more detailed presentation of the specific-factors theory.

Does Trade Make the Poor Even Poorer?

Before leaving the factor-endowment theory, consider this question: Is your income pulled down by workers in Mexico or China? That question has underlined many Americans' fears about their economic future. They worry that the growth of trade with low-wage developing nations could reduce the demand for low-skilled workers in the United States and cause unemployment and wage decreases for U.S. workers.

The wage gap between skilled and unskilled workers has widened in the United States during the past 40 years. Over the same period, imports increased as a percentage of gross domestic product. These facts raise two questions: Is trade harming unskilled workers? If it is, then is this an argument for an increase in trade barriers?

Economists agree that some combination of trade, technology, education, immigration, and union weakness has held down wages for unskilled American workers; but apportioning the blame is tough, partly because income inequality is so pervasive. Economists have attempted to disentangle the relative contributions of trade and other influences on the wage discrepancy between skilled workers and unskilled workers. Their approaches share the analytical framework shown by Figure 3.3. This framework views the wages of skilled workers "relative" to those of unskilled workers as the outcome of the interaction between supply and demand in the labor market.

The vertical axis of Figure 3.3 shows the wage ratio, which equals the wage of skilled workers divided by the wage of unskilled workers. The figure's horizontal axis shows the labor ratio, which equals the quantity of skilled workers available divided by the quantity of unskilled workers. Initially we assume that the supply curve of skilled workers relative to unskilled workers is fixed and is denoted by S_0. The demand curve for skilled workers relative to unskilled workers is denoted by D_0. The equilibrium wage ratio is 2.0, found at the intersection of the supply and demand curves, and suggests that the wages of skilled workers are twice as much as the wages of unskilled workers.

In the figure, a shift in either the supply curve or demand curve of skilled workers available relative to unskilled workers will induce a change in the equilibrium

FIGURE 3.3

INEQUALITY OF WAGES BETWEEN SKILLED AND UNSKILLED WORKERS

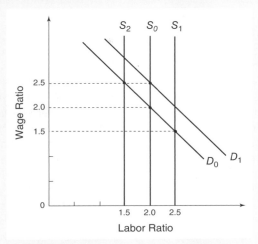

By increasing the demand for skilled relative to unskilled workers, expanding trade or technological improvements result in greater inequality of wages between skilled and unskilled workers. Also, immigration of unskilled workers intensifies wage inequality by decreasing the supply of skilled workers relative to unskilled workers. However, expanding opportunities for college education results in an increase in the supply of skilled relative to unskilled workers, thus reducing wage inequality. In the figure, the wage ratio equals wage of skilled workers/wage of unskilled workers. The labor ratio equals the quantity of skilled workers/quantity of unskilled workers.

wage ratio. Let us consider resources that can affect wage inequality in the United States.

- *International trade and technological change.* Trade liberalization and falling transportation and communication costs result in an increase in the demand curve of skilled workers relative to unskilled workers, say, to D_1 in the figure. Assuming a constant supply curve, the equilibrium wage ratio rises to 2.5, suggesting that the wages of skilled workers are 2½ times as much as the wages of unskilled workers. Similarly, skill-based technological improvements lead to an increase in the demand for skilled workers relative to unskilled workers, thus promoting higher degrees of wage inequality.

- *Immigration.* Immigration of unskilled workers results in a decrease in the supply of skilled workers relative to unskilled workers. Assuming that the demand curve is constant, as the supply curve shifts from S_0 to S_2, the equilibrium wage ratio rises to 2.5, thus intensifying wage inequality.

- *Education and training.* As the availability of education and training increases, so does the ratio of skilled workers to unskilled workers, as seen by the increase in the supply curve from S_0 to S_1. If the demand curve remains constant, then the equilibrium wage ratio will fall from 2.0 to 1.5. Additional opportunities for

DOES A "FLAT WORLD" MAKE RICARDO WRONG?

The possibility that the United States could lose from free trade is at the heart of some recent critiques of globalization. One critique contends that the world has tended to become "flat" as comparative advantages have dwindled or dried up. Proponents of this view note that as countries such as China and India undergo economic development and become more similar to the United States, a level playing field emerges. The flattening of the world is largely due to countries becoming interconnected as the result of the Internet, wireless technology, search engines, and other innovations. Consequently, capitalism has spread like wildfire to China, India, and other countries where factory workers, engineers and software programmers are paid a fraction of what their American counterparts are paid. As China and India develop and become more similar to the United States, the United States could become worse off with trade.

However, not all economists agree with this view. They see several problems with this critique. First, the general view of globalization is that it is a phenomenon marked by increased international economic interdependence. However, the above critique is of a situation in which development in China and India lead to less trade, not more. If China and the United States have differences that allow for gains from trade (for example, differences in technologies and productive capabilities), then removing those differences may decrease the amount of trade and thus decrease the gains from that trade. The worst-case scenario in this situation would be a complete elimination of trade. This is the opposite of the typical concern that globalization involves an overly rapid pace of international economic interdependence.

The second problem with the critique is that it ignores the ways in which modern trade differs from Ricardo's simple model. The advanced nations of the world have substantially similar technology and factors of production, and seemingly similar products such as auto-

mobiles and electronics are produced in many countries, with substantial trade back and forth. This is at odds with the simplest prediction of the Ricardian model under which trade should disappear once each country is able to make similar products at comparable prices. Instead, the world has observed substantially increased trade since the end of World War II. This increase reflects the fact that there are gains to *intra-industry trade* in which broadly similar products are traded in both directions between nations; for example, the United States both imports and exports computer components. Intra-industry trade reflects the advantages garnered by consumers and firms from the increased varieties of similar products made available by trade, as well as the increased competition and higher productivity spurred by trade. Given the historical experience that trade flows have continued to increase between advanced economies even as production technologies have become more similar, one would expect the potential for mutually advantageous trade to remain even if China and India were to develop so rapidly as to have similar technologies and prices as the United States.

Finally, it is argued that the world is not flat at all. While India and China may have very large labor forces, only a small fraction of Indians are prepared to compete with Americans in industries like information technology, while China's authoritarian regime is not compatible with the personal computer. The real problem is that comparative advantage can change very rapidly in a dynamic economy. Boeing might win today, Airbus tomorrow, and then Boeing may be back in play again.

Source: Thomas Friedman, *The World Is Flat,* Farrar, (New York: Straus and Girous, 2005); Jagdish Bhagwati, *In Defense of Globalization*, (New York: Oxford University Press, 2004); Martin Wolf, *Why Globalization Works*, (New Haven, CT: Yale University Press, 2004); and *Economic Report of the President*, 2005, pp. 174–175.

education and training thus serve to reduce the wage inequality between skilled and unskilled workers.

We have seen how trade and immigration can promote wage inequality. However, economists have found that their effects on the wage distribution have been small. In fact, the vast majority of wage inequality is due to domestic sources, especially technology. One often cited study, by William Cline, estimated that during the past three decades technological change has been about four times more powerful in widening wage inequality in the United States than trade, and that trade accounted for only seven percentage points of all the unequalizing forces at work during that period. His conclusions are reinforced by the research of Robert Lawrence that concludes that rising wage inequality during the first decade of the 2000s more closely corresponds to asset-market performance and technological and institutional innovations than to international trade in goods and services. The minor importance of trade implies that any policy that focuses narrowly on trade to deal with wage inequality is likely to be ineffective.[7]

Economists generally agree that trade has been relatively unimportant in widening wage inequality. Also, trade's impact on wage inequality is overwhelmed not just by technology but also by education and training. Indeed, the shifts in labor demand, away from less-educated workers, are the most important factors behind the eroding wages of the less educated. Such shifts appear to be the result of economy-wide technological and organizational changes in how work is performed.

Skill as a Source of Comparative Advantage

Following the development of the factor-endowment theory, little empirical evidence was brought to bear about its validity. All that came forth were intuitive examples such as labor-abundant India exporting textiles or shoes, capital-abundant Germany exporting machinery and automobiles, or land-abundant Australia exporting wheat and meat. However, some economists demanded stronger evidence concerning the validity of the factor-endowment theory.

The first attempt to investigate the factor-endowment theory empirically was undertaken by Wassily Leontief in 1954.[8] It had been widely recognized that in the United States capital was relatively abundant and labor was relatively scarce. According to the factor-endowment theory, the United States will export capital-intensive goods and its import-competing goods will be labor intensive. Leontief tested this proposition by analyzing the capital/labor ratios for some 200 export industries and import-competing industries in the United States, based on trade data for 1947. As shown in Table 3.6, Leontief found that the capital/labor ratio for U.S. export industries was lower (about $14,000 per worker year) than that of its import-competing industries (about $18,000 per worker year). Leontief concluded that exports were *less* capital intensive than import-competing goods. These findings, which contradicted the predictions of the factor-endowment theory, became known as the **Leontief paradox**. To strengthen his conclusion, Leontief repeated his investigation in

---

[7]William Cline, *Trade and Income Distribution*, Institute for International Economics, Washington, DC, 1997, p. 264 and Robert Lawrence, *Blue-Collar Blues: Is Trade to Blame for Rising U.S. Income Inequality?* Institute for International Economics, Washington DC, 2008, pp. 73–74.

[8]Wassily W. Leontief, "Domestic Production and Foreign Trade: The American Capital Position Reexamined," *Proceedings of the American Philosophical Society* 97, September 1953.

FACTOR CONTENT OF U.S. TRADE: CAPITAL AND LABOR REQUIREMENTS PER MILLION DOLLARS OF U.S. EXPORTS AND IMPORT SUBSTITUTES

Empirical Study	Import Substitutes	Exports	Import/Export Ratio
Leontief			
Capital	$3,091,339	$2,550,780	
Labor (person years)	170	182	
Capital/person years	$18,184	$14,015	1.30

Source: Wassily Leontief, "Domestic Production and Foreign Trade: The American Capital Position Re-examined," *Economia Internazionale*, February 1954, pp. 3–32. See also Wassily Leontief, "Factor Proportions and the Structure of American Trade: Further Theoretical and Empirical Analysis," *Review of Economics and Statistics*, November 1956, pp. 386–407.

1956 only to again find that U.S. import-competing goods were more capital intensive than U.S. exports. Simply put, Leontief's discovery was that America's comparative advantage was something other than capital-intensive goods.

The resolution of the Leontief paradox depends on the definition of capital. The exports of the United States are not intensive in capital such as tools and factories. Instead, they are skill intensive, meaning that they are intensive in "human capital." U.S. exporting industries use a significantly higher proportion of highly educated workers to other workers as compared to U.S. import-competing industries. For example, Boeing represents one of America's largest exporting companies. It employs

EDUCATION, SKILL INTENSITY, AND U.S. IMPORT SHARES, 1998

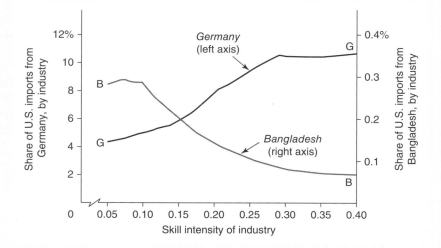

The figure suggests that countries that are abundant in skilled labor capture larger shares of U.S. imports in industries that intensively use those factors. Conversely, countries that are abundant in unskilled labor capture larger shares of U.S. imports in industries that intensively use those factors.

Source: John Romalis, "Factor Proportions and the Structure of Commodity Trade," *American Economic Review*, Vol. 94, No. 1, 2004, pp. 67–97.

large numbers of mechanical and computer engineers having graduate degrees relative to the number of manual workers. Conversely, Americans import lots of shoes and textiles which are often manufactured by workers with little formal education.

In general, countries endowed with highly-educated workers have their exports concentrated in skill-intensive goods, while countries with less-educated workers export goods that require little skilled labor. Figure 3.4 provides an example of this tendency. It compares the goods the United States imports from Germany, where the average adult has in excess of ten years of formal education, with the goods the United States imports from Bangladesh, where the average adult has only 2.5 years of formal education. In each country, industries are ranked according to their skill intensity: increasing skill intensity is shown by a rightward movement along the horizontal axis of the figure. The figure shows that Germany captures large shares of U.S. imports of skill-intensive goods, and much smaller shares for goods that sparingly require skilled labor. This is seen by the schedule representing Germany (GG) to be upward sloping: as a German industry becomes more skill intensive, its share of exports to the United States increases. Conversely, Bangladesh exhibits the opposite trade pattern, with its exports to the United States concentrated in goods that require little skilled labor. Given the downward slope of Bangladesh's schedule (BB); as a Bangladesh industry becomes less skill intensive, its share of exports to the United States increases. The figure concludes that countries capture larger shares of the world trade of goods that more intensively use their abundant factors.

Increasing Returns to Scale and Comparative Advantage

Although comparative-advantage theory has great appeal, it has little ability to explain why regions with similar productivity levels trade to the extent that they do—why Europe and the United States, for example, trade in such a great volume. Nor does it shed light on intra-industry trade: the fact that Germany and Japan will trade automobiles with each other.

In response to these weaknesses, economists developed a new theory of trade in the 1980s.[9] This theory is founded on the concept of **increasing returns to scale**, also known as **economies of scale**. The increasing-returns explanation for trade does not attempt to replace the comparative-advantage explanation; it just supplements it.

According to the increasing-returns trade theory, nations with similar factor endowments, and thus negligible comparative-advantage differences, may nonetheless find it beneficial to trade because they can take advantage of massive economies of scale, a phenomenon prevalent in a number of industries. In the automobile and pharmaceutical industries, for example, the first unit is very expensive to produce, but each subsequent unit costs much less than the one before because the large setup costs can be spread across all units. Companies such as Toyota and Honda reduce costs by specializing in machinery and labor and obtaining quantity discounts in the purchase of inputs.

Increasing-returns trade theory asserts that a nation can develop an industry that has economies of scale, produce that good in great quantity at low average unit costs, and then trade those low-cost goods to other nations. By doing the same

---

[9]Paul Krugman, "New Theories of Trade Among Industrial Countries," *American Economic Review* 73, no. 2, May 1983, pp. 343–47, and Elhanan Helpman, "The Structure of Foreign Trade," *Journal of Economic Perspectives* 13, no. 2, Spring 1999, pp. 121–44.

for other increasing-returns goods, all trading partners can take advantage of economies of scale through specialization and exchange.

Figure 3.5 illustrates the effect of economies of scale on trade. Assume that a U.S. auto firm and a Mexican auto firm are each able to sell 100,000 vehicles in their respective countries. Also assume that identical cost conditions result in the same long-term average cost curve for the two firms, *AC*. Note that scale economies result in decreasing unit costs over the first 275,000 autos produced.

Initially, there is no basis for trade, because each firm realizes a production cost of $10,000 per auto. Suppose that rising income in the United States results in demand for 200,000 autos, while the Mexican auto demand remains constant. The larger demand allows the U.S. firm to produce more output and take advantage of economies of scale. The firm's cost curve slides downward until its cost equals $8,000 per auto. Compared to the Mexican firm, the U.S. firm can produce autos at a lower cost. With free trade, the United States will now export autos to Mexico.

Economies of scale thus provide additional cost incentives for *specialization* in production. Instead of manufacturing only a few units of each and every product that domestic consumers desire to purchase, a country specializes in the manufacture of large amounts of a limited number of goods and trades for the remaining goods. Specialization in a few products allows a manufacturer to benefit from longer production runs, which lead to decreasing average costs.

A key aspect of increasing-returns trade theory is the **home market effect**: Countries will specialize in products that have a large domestic demand. Why? By

FIGURE 3.5

ECONOMIES OF SCALE AS A BASIS FOR TRADE

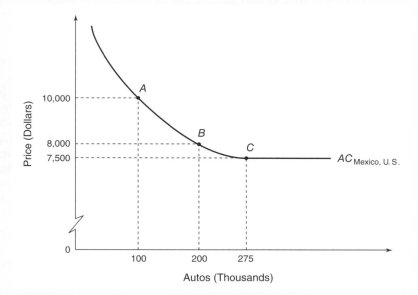

By adding to the size of the domestic market, international trade permits longer production runs by domestic firms, which can lead to greater efficiency and reductions in unit costs.

locating close to its largest market, an industry can minimize the cost of shipping its products to its customers while still taking advantage of economies of scale. That is, auto companies will locate in Germany rather than France if it is clear that Germans are likely to buy more cars. That way the company can produce low-cost cars and not have to pay much to ship them to its largest market.

But the home market effect also has a disturbing implication. If industries tend to locate near their largest markets, what happens to small market areas? Other things equal, they're likely to become de-industrialized as factories and industries move to take advantage of scale economies and low transportation costs. Hence, trade could lead to small countries and rural areas becoming peripheral to the economic core, the backwater suppliers of commodities. As Canadian critics have phrased it, "With free trade, Canadians would become hewers of wood and drawers of water." However, other things are not strictly equal: comparative-advantage effects exist alongside the influence of increasing returns, so the end result of open trade is not a foregone conclusion.

External Economies of Scale and Comparative Advantage

The previous section considered how economies of scale that are internal to a firm affect comparative advantage; that is, the increase in the size of the firm itself is the basis for the decrease in its average cost. Economies of scale can also be external to the individual firm and affect comparative advantage, as explained below.

External economies of scale for a firm relate to the size of an entire industry within a particular geographic area. The average cost of the typical firm decreases as the output of the industry within this area increases. For example, the concentration of an industry's firms in a particular geographic area may attract larger pools of a specialized type of worker needed by the industry. External economies can also occur as new knowledge about production technology spreads among firms in the area, through direct contacts among firms or as workers transfer from firm to firm. Therefore, external economies help explain why New York has a comparative advantage in financial services or California's Silicon Valley has a comparative advantage in semiconductors.

External economies have resulted in Dalton, Georgia becoming the carpet-making capital of the world. The location of the carpet industry in Dalton can be traced back to a wedding gift given in 1895 by a teenage girl, Catherine Whitener, to her brother and his bride. The gift was an unusual tufted bedspread. Copying a quilt pattern, Catherine sewed thick cotton yarns with a running stitch into unbleached muslin, clipped the ends of the yarn so they would fluff out, and washed the spread in hot water to hold the yarns by shrinking the fabric. Interest grew in Catherine's bedspreads, and in 1900, she made the first sale of a spread for $2.50. Demand became so great for the spreads that by the 1930s, local women had haulers take the stamped sheeting and yarns to front porch workers. Often entire families worked to hand tuft the spreads for 10 to 25 cents per spread. Nearly 10,000 local men, women, and children were involved in the industry. When mechanized carpet making was developed after World War II, Dalton became the center of the new industry because specialized tufting skills were required and the city had a ready pool of workers with those skills.

Dalton is now home to more than 170 carpet plants and 100 carpet outlet stores, and more than 30,000 people are employed by these firms. Supporting the carpet industry are local yarn manufacturers, machinery suppliers, dye plants, printing shops, and maintenance firms. The local workforce has acquired specialized skills for operating carpet-making equipment. Because firms that are located outside of Dalton cannot use the suppliers or the skilled workers available to factories in Dalton, they tend to have higher production costs. Although there is no particular reason why Dalton became the carpet-making capital of the world, external economies of scale provided the area with a comparative advantage in carpet making once firms established there.

Overlapping Demands as a Basis for Trade

The home market effect has implications for another theory of trade, the so-called **theory of overlapping demands**. This theory was formulated by Staffan Linder, a Swedish economist, in the 1960s.[10] According to Linder, the factor-endowment theory has considerable explanatory power for trade in primary products (natural resources) and agricultural goods. But it does not explain trade in *manufactured goods* because the main force influencing manufactured-good trade is domestic *demand conditions*. Because much of international trade involves manufactured goods, demand conditions play an important role in explaining overall trade patterns.

Linder states that firms within a country are generally motivated to manufacture goods for which there is a large domestic market. This market determines the set of goods that these firms will have to sell when they begin to export. The foreign markets with greatest export potential will be found in nations with consumer demand similar to those of domestic consumers. A nation's exports are thus an extension of the production for the domestic market.

Going further, Linder contends that consumer demand is conditioned strongly by income levels. Therefore, a country's average or *per capita income* will yield a particular pattern of demand. Nations with high per capita incomes will demand high-quality manufactured goods (luxuries), while nations with low per capita incomes will demand lower-quality goods (necessities).

The Linder hypothesis explains which types of nations will most likely trade with each other. Nations with similar per capita incomes will have overlapping demand structures and will likely consume similar types of manufactured goods. Wealthy (industrial) nations are more likely to trade with other wealthy nations, and poor (developing) nations are more likely to trade with other poor nations.

Linder does not rule out all trade in manufactured goods between wealthy and poor nations. Because of unequal income distribution within nations, there will always be some overlapping of demand structures; some people in poor nations are wealthy, and some people in wealthy nations are poor. However, the potential for trade in manufactured goods is small when the extent of demand overlap is small.

Linder's theory is in rough accord with the facts. A high proportion of international trade in manufactured goods takes place among the relatively high-income (industrial) nations: Japan, Canada, the United States, and the European nations. Moreover, much of this trade involves the exchange of similar products: each nation exports products that are much like the products it imports. However, Linder's theory is not borne out by developing country trade. The bulk of lower-income, developing countries tend to have more trade with high-income countries than with other lower-income countries.

---

[10]Staffan B. Linder, *An Essay on Trade and Transformation* (New York: Wiley, 1961), Chapter 3.

Intra-industry Trade

The trade models considered so far have dealt with **interindustry trade**–the exchange between nations of products of different industries; examples include computers and aircraft traded for textiles and shoes, or finished manufactured items traded for primary materials. Interindustry trade involves the exchange of goods with *different* factor requirements. Nations having large supplies of skilled labor tend to export sophisticated manufactured products, while nations with large supplies of natural resources export resource-intensive goods. Much of interindustry trade is between nations having vastly different resource endowments (such as developing countries and industrial countries) and can be explained by the principle of comparative advantage (the Heckscher-Ohlin model).

Interindustry trade is based on **interindustry specialization**: Each nation specializes in a particular industry (say, steel) in which it enjoys a comparative advantage. As resources shift to the industry with a comparative advantage, certain other industries having comparative disadvantages (say, electronics) contract. Resources thus move geographically to the industry where comparative costs are lowest. As a result of specialization, a nation experiences a growing *dissimilarity* between the products that it exports and the products that it imports.

Although some interindustry specialization occurs, this generally has not been the type of specialization that industrialized nations have undertaken in the post-World War II era. Rather than emphasizing entire industries, industrial countries have adopted a narrower form of specialization. They have practiced **intra-industry specialization**, focusing on the production of particular products or groups of products within a given industry (for example, subcompact autos rather than autos). With intra-industry specialization, the opening up of trade does not generally result in the elimination or wholesale contraction of entire industries within a nation; however, the range of products produced and sold by each nation changes.

Advanced industrial nations have increasingly emphasized **intra-industry trade**—two-way trade in a similar commodity. For example, computers manufactured by IBM are sold abroad, while the United States imports computers produced by Hitachi of Japan. Table 3.7 provides examples of intra-industry trade for the United States. As the table indicates, the United States is involved in two-way trade in many manufactured goods such as airplanes and electrical machinery.

The existence of intra-industry trade appears to be *incompatible* with the models of comparative advantage previously discussed. In the Ricardian and Heckscher-Ohlin models, a country does not simultaneously export and import the same product. However, California is a major importer of French wines as well as a large exporter of its own wines; the Netherlands imports Lowenbrau beer while exporting Heineken. Intra-industry trade involves flows of goods with *similar* factor requirements. Nations that are net exporters of manufactured goods embodying sophisticated technology also purchase such goods

TABLE 3.7

INTRA-INDUSTRY TRADE EXAMPLES: SELECTED U.S. EXPORTS AND IMPORTS, 2007 (IN MILLIONS OF DOLLARS)

Category	Exports	Imports
Airplanes	51,854	13,286
Aluminum	5,806	13,947
Electrical machinery	81,452	113,613
Footwear	578	19,408
Gem diamonds	5,305	18,937
Optical goods	3,210	4,698
Power generating machinery	49,933	50,191
Scientific instruments	42,315	35,604
Vehicles	95,187	210,431

Source: From U.S. Census Bureau, *Statistical Abstract of the U.S.*, 2009, Table 1267.

from other nations. Most of intra-industry trade is conducted among industrial countries, especially those in Western Europe, whose resource endowments are similar. The firms that produce these goods tend to be oligopolies, with a few large firms constituting each industry.

Intra-industry trade includes trade in homogeneous goods as well as in differentiated products. For *homogeneous goods*, the reasons for intra-industry trade are easy to grasp. A nation may export and import the same product because of *transportation costs*. Canada and the United States, for example, share a border whose length is several thousand miles. To minimize transportation costs (and thus total costs), a buyer in Albany, New York, may import cement from a firm in Montreal, Quebec, while a manufacturer in Seattle, Washington, sells cement to a buyer in Vancouver, British Columbia. Such trade can be explained by the fact that it is less expensive to transport cement from Montreal to Albany than to ship cement from Seattle to Albany.

Another reason for intra-industry trade in homogeneous goods is *seasonal*. The seasons in the Southern Hemisphere are opposite those in the Northern Hemisphere. Brazil may export seasonal items (such as agricultural products) to the United States at one time of the year and import them from the United States at another time during the same year. Differentiation in time also affects electricity suppliers. Because of heavy fixed costs in electricity production, utilities attempt to keep plants operating close to full capacity, meaning that it may be less costly to export electricity at off-peak times, when domestic demand is inadequate to ensure full-capacity utilization, and import electricity at peak times.

Although some intra-industry trade occurs in homogeneous products, available evidence suggests that most intra-industry trade occurs in *differentiated products*. Within manufacturing, the levels of intra-industry trade appear to be especially high in machinery, chemicals, and transportation equipment. A significant share of the output of modern economies consists of differentiated products within the same broad product group. Within the automobile industry, a Ford is not identical to a Honda, a Toyota, or a Chevrolet. Two-way trade flows can occur in differentiated products within the same broad product group.

For industrial countries, intra-industry trade in differentiated manufactured goods often occurs when manufacturers in each country produce for the "majority" consumer demand within their country while ignoring "minority" consumer demand. This unmet need is fulfilled by imported products. For example, most Japanese consumers prefer Toyotas to General Motors vehicles; yet some Japanese consumers purchase vehicles from General Motors, while Toyotas are exported to the United States. Intra-industry trade increases the range of choices available to consumers in each country, as well as the degree of competition among manufacturers of the same class of product in each country.

Intra-industry trade in differentiated products can also be explained by overlapping demand segments in trading nations. When U.S. manufacturers look overseas for markets in which to sell, they often find them in countries having market segments that are similar to the market segments in which they sell in the United States, for example, luxury automobiles sold to high-income buyers. Nations with similar income levels can be expected to have similar tastes, and thus sizable overlapping market segments, as envisioned by Linder's theory of overlapping demand; they are expected to engage heavily in intra-industry trade.

Besides marketing factors, economies of scale associated with differentiated products also explain intra-industry trade. A nation may enjoy a cost advantage over its foreign competitor by specializing in a few varieties and styles of a product (for example, subcompact autos with a standard transmission and optional equipment), while its foreign competitor enjoys a cost advantage by specializing in other variants of the same product (subcompact autos with automatic transmission, air conditioning, DVD player, and other optional equipment). Such specialization permits longer production runs, economies of scale, and decreasing unit costs. Each nation exports its particular type of auto to the other nation, resulting in two-way auto trade. In contrast to interindustry trade, which is explained by the principle of comparative advantage, intra-industry trade can be explained by *product differentiation and economies of scale.*

With intra-industry specialization, fewer adjustment problems are likely to occur than with interindustry specialization, because intra-industry specialization requires a shift of resources within an industry instead of between industries. Interindustry specialization results in a transfer of resources from import-competing to export-expanding sectors of the economy. Adjustment difficulties can occur when resources, notably labor, are occupationally and geographically immobile in the short term; massive structural unemployment may result. In contrast, intra-industry specialization often occurs without requiring workers to exit from a particular region or industry (as when workers are shifted from the production of large-size automobiles to subcompacts); the probability of structural unemployment is thus lessened.

Technology as a Source of Comparative Advantage: The Product Cycle Theory

The explanations of international trade presented so far are similar in that they presuppose a *given* and unchanging state of technology, which is the process firms use to turn inputs into goods and services. The basis for trade was ultimately attributed to such factors as differing labor productivities, factor endowments, and national demand structures. However, in a dynamic world, technological changes occur in different nations at different rates of speed. Technological innovations commonly result in new methods of producing existing commodities, in the production of new commodities, or in commodity improvements. These factors can affect comparative advantage and the pattern of trade.

For example, Japanese automobile companies, such as Toyota and Honda, have succeeded by greatly improving the processes for designing and manufacturing automobiles. This improvement allowed Japan to become the world's largest exporter of automobiles, selling large numbers to Americans and people in other countries. Japan's comparative advantage in automobiles has been supported by the superior production techniques developed by that country's manufacturers, which allowed them to produce more vehicles with a given amount of capital and labor than their European or American counterparts. Therefore, Japan's comparative advantage in automobiles is caused by differences in technology, the techniques in production.

Although differences in technology are an important source of comparative advantage at a particular point in time, technological advantage is often transitory. That is, a country may lose its comparative advantage as its technological advantage disappears. Recognition of the importance of such dynamic changes has given rise to another explanation of international trade: the **product life cycle theory**. This theory focuses on the role of technological innovation as a key determinant of the trade patterns in manufactured products.[11]

According to this theory, many manufactured goods such as electronic products and office machinery undergo a predictable *trade cycle*. During this cycle, the home country initially is an exporter, then loses its competitive advantage vis-à-vis its trading partners, and eventually may become an importer of the commodity. The stages that many manufactured goods go through comprise the following:

1. Manufactured good is introduced to home market.
2. Domestic industry shows export strength.
3. Foreign production begins.
4. Domestic industry loses competitive advantage.
5. Import competition begins.

The introduction stage of the trade cycle begins when an innovator establishes a technological breakthrough in the production of a manufactured good. At the start, the relatively small local market for the product and technological uncertainties imply that mass production is not feasible. The manufacturer will most likely operate close to the local market to gain quick feedback on the quality and overall appeal of the product. Production occurs on a small scale using relatively high-skilled workers. The relatively high price of the new product will also offer relatively high returns to the specialized capital stock needed to produce the new product.

During the trade cycle's next stage, the domestic manufacturer begins to export its product to foreign markets having similar tastes and income levels. The local manufacturer finds that, during this stage of growth and expansion, its market becomes large enough to expand production operations and sort out inefficient production techniques. The home-country manufacturer is therefore able to supply increasing amounts to the world markets.

As the product matures and its price falls, the capability for standardized production results in the possibility that more efficient production can occur by using low-wage labor and mass production. At this stage in the product's life, it is most likely that production will move toward economies that have resource endowments relatively plentiful in low-wage labor, such as China or Malaysia. The domestic industry enters its mature stage as innovating businesses establish branches abroad and the outsourcing of jobs occurs.

Although an innovating nation's monopoly position may be prolonged by legal patents, it will most likely break down over time, because in the long term knowledge tends to be a free good. The benefits an innovating nation achieves from its technological gap are short lived, as import competition from foreign producers begins. Once the innovative technology becomes fairly commonplace, foreign producers begin to imitate the production process. The innovating nation gradually loses its comparative advantage, and its export cycle enters a declining phase.

The trade cycle is complete when the production process becomes so standardized that it can be easily used by other nations. The technological breakthrough therefore no longer benefits only the innovating nation. In fact, the innovating nation may itself become a net importer of the product as its monopoly position is eliminated by foreign competition.

---

[11]See Raymond Vernon, "International Investment and International Trade in the Product Life Cycle," *Quarterly Journal of Economics* 80, 1966, pp. 190–207.

The product life cycle theory has implications for innovating countries such as the United States. The gains from trade for the United States are significantly determined by the dynamic balance between its rate of technological innovation and the rate of its technological diffusion to other countries. Unless the United States can generate a pace of innovation to match the pace of diffusion, its share of the gains from trade will decrease. Also, it can be argued that the advance of globalization has accelerated the rate of technological diffusion. What this advance suggests is that preserving or increasing the economy's gains from trade in the face of globalization will require an acceleration in the pace of innovation in goods and service-producing activities.

The product life cycle theory also provides lessons for a firm desiring to maintain its competitiveness: To prevent rivals from catching up, it must continually innovate so as to become more efficient. For example, Toyota Motor Corporation is generally regarded as the industry leader in production efficiency. To maintain this position, the firm has continually overhauled its operations and work practices. In 2008, for example, Toyota was working to decrease the number of components it uses in a typical vehicle by half and develop faster and more flexible plants to assemble these simplified cars. This simplification would allow workers to churn out nearly a dozen different cars on the same production line at a speed of one every 50 seconds, compared to Toyota's current fastest plant that produces a vehicle every 56 seconds. The cut would increase the output per worker and reduce costs by about $1,000 per vehicle. By pushing out the efficiency target, Toyota was attempting to prevent the latter stages of the product cycle from occurring.

Radios, Pocket Calculators, and the International Product Cycle

The experience of U.S. and Japanese radio manufacturers illustrates the product life cycle model. Following World War II, the radio was a well-established product. U.S. manufacturers dominated the international market for radios because vacuum tubes were initially developed in the United States. But as production technologies spread, Japan used cheaper labor and captured a large share of the world radio market. The transistor was then developed by U.S. companies. For a number of years, U.S. radio manufacturers were able to compete with the Japanese, who continued to use outdated technologies. Again, the Japanese imitated the U.S. technologies and were able to sell radios at more competitive prices.

Pocket calculators provide another illustration of a product that has moved through the stages of the international product cycle. This product was invented in 1961 by engineers at Sunlock Comptometer, Inc., and was marketed soon after at a price of approximately $1,000. Sunlock's pocket calculator was more accurate than slide rules (widely used by high school and college students at that time) and more portable than large mechanical calculators and computers that performed many of the same functions.

By 1970, several U.S. and Japanese companies had entered the market with competing pocket calculators; these firms included Texas Instruments, Hewlett-Packard, and Casio (of Japan). The increased competition forced the price down to about $400. As the 1970s progressed, additional companies entered the market. Several began to assemble their pocket calculators in foreign countries, such as Singapore and Taiwan, to take advantage of lower labor costs. These calculators were then shipped to the United States. Steadily improving technologies resulted in product improvements and falling prices; by the mid-1970s, pocket calculators sold routinely for $10 to $20, sometimes even less. It appears that pocket calculators had reached the standardized-product stage of the product cycle by the late 1970s, with product technology available throughout the industry, price competition (and thus costs) of major significance, and product differentiation widely adopted. In a period of less than two decades, the international product cycle for pocket calculators was complete.

Dynamic Comparative Advantage: Industrial Policy

David Ricardo's theory of comparative advantage has influenced international trade theory and policy for almost 200 years. It implies that nations are better off by promoting free trade and allowing competitive markets to determine what should be produced and how.

Ricardian theory emphasizes specialization and reallocation of existing resources found domestically. It is essentially a static theory that does not allow for a dynamic change in industries' comparative advantage or disadvantage over the course of several decades. The theory overlooks the fact that additional resources can be made available to the trading nation because they can be created or imported.

The remarkable postwar economic growth of the East Asian countries appears to be based on a modification of the static concept of comparative advantage. The Japanese were among the first to recognize that comparative advantage in a particular industry can be created through the mobilization of skilled labor, technology, and capital. They also realized that, in addition to the business sector, government can establish policies to promote opportunities for change through time. Such a process is known as **dynamic comparative advantage**. When government is actively involved in creating comparative advantage, the term **industrial policy** applies.

In its simplest form, industrial policy is a strategy to revitalize, improve, and develop an industry. Proponents maintain that government should enact policies that encourage the development of emerging, "sunrise" industries (such as high technology). This strategy requires that resources be directed to industries in which productivity is highest, linkages to the rest of the economy are strong (as with semiconductors), and future competitiveness is important. Presumably, the domestic economy will enjoy a higher average level of productivity and will be more competitive in world markets as a result of such policies.

A variety of government policies can be used to foster the development and revitalization of industries; examples are antitrust immunity, tax incentives, R&D subsidies, loan guarantees, low-interest-rate loans, and trade protection. Creating comparative advantage requires government to identify the "winners" and encourage resources to move into industries with the highest growth prospects.

To better understand the significance of dynamic comparative advantage, we might think of it in terms of the classic example of Ricardo's theory of comparative advantage. His example showed that, in the eighteenth century, Portugal and England would each have gained by specializing respectively in the production of wine and cloth, even though Portugal might produce both cloth and wine more cheaply than England. According to static comparative-advantage theory, both nations would be better off by specializing in the product in which they had an existing comparative advantage.

However, by adhering to this prescription, Portugal would sacrifice long-term growth for short-term gains. If Portugal adopted a dynamic theory of comparative advantage instead, it would specialize in the growth industry of that time (cloth). The Portuguese government (or Portuguese textile manufacturers) would thus initiate policies to foster the development of its cloth industry. This strategy would require Portugal to think in terms of acquiring or creating strength in a "sunrise" sector instead of simply accepting the existing supply of resources and using that endowment as productively as possible.

Countries have used industrial policies to develop or revitalize basic industries, including steel, autos, chemicals, transportation, and other important manufactures. Each of these industrial policies differs in character and approach; common to all is an active role for government in the economy. Usually, industrial policy is a strategy developed collectively by government, business, and labor through some sort of tripartite consultation process.

Advocates of industrial policy typically cite Japan as a nation that has been highly successful in penetrating foreign markets and achieving rapid economic growth. Following World War II, the Japanese were the high-cost producers in many basic industries (such as steel). In this situation, a static notion of comparative advantage would require the Japanese to look to areas of lesser disadvantage that were more labor intensive (such as textiles). Such a strategy would have forced Japan into low-productivity industries that would eventually compete with other East Asian nations having abundant labor and modest living standards.

Instead, the Japanese invested in basic industries (steel, autos, and later electronics, including computers) that required intensive employment of capital and labor. From a short term, static perspective, Japan appeared to pick the wrong industries. But from a long-term perspective, those were the industries in which technological progress was rapid, labor productivity rose quickly, and unit costs decreased with the expansion of output. They were also industries in which one would expect rapid growth in demand as national income increased.

These industries combined the potential to expand rapidly, thus adding new capacity, with the opportunity to use the latest technology and thus promote a strategy of cost reduction founded on increasing productivity. Japan, placed in a position similar to that of Portugal in Ricardo's famous example, refused to specialize in "wine" and chose "cloth" instead. Within three decades, Japan became the world's premier low-cost producer of many of the products for which it initially started in a high-cost position.

However, critics of industrial policy contend that the causal factor in Japanese industrial success is unclear. They admit that some of the Japanese government's targeted industries—such as semiconductors, steel, shipbuilding, and machine tools—are probably more competitive than they would have been in the absence of government assistance. But they assert that Japan also targeted some losers, such as petrochemicals and aluminum, for which the returns on investment were disappointing and capacity had to be reduced. Moreover, several successful Japanese industries did not receive government assistance—motorcycles, bicycles, paper, glass, and cement.

Industrial-policy critics contend that if all trading nations took the route of using a combination of trade restrictions on imports and subsidies on exports, a "beggar-thy-neighbor" process of trade-inhibiting protectionism would result. They also point out that the implementation of industrial policies can result in pork-barrel politics in which politically powerful industries receive government assistance. Also, it is argued that, in a free market, profit-maximizing businesses have the incentive to develop new resources and technologies that change a country's comparative advantage. This incentive raises the question of whether the government does a better job than the private sector in creating comparative advantage.

Government Subsidies Support Boeing and Airbus

An example of industrial policy is the government subsidies that apply to the commercial jetliner industry, as seen in Boeing and Airbus. The world's manufacturers of commercial jetliners operate in an oligopolistic market that has been dominated by Boeing of the United States and the Airbus Company of Europe. During the 1970s, Airbus sold less than five percent of the world's jetliners; today, it accounts for more than half of the world market.

The United States has repeatedly complained that Airbus receives unfair subsidies from European governments. American officials argue that these subsidies place their company at a competitive disadvantage. Airbus allegedly receives loans for the development of new aircraft; these loans are made at below-market interest rates and can amount to 70 to 90 percent of an aircraft's development cost. Rather than repaying the loans according to a prescribed timetable as typically would occur in a competitive market, Airbus can repay them after it delivers an aircraft. Also, Airbus can avoid repaying the loans in full if sales of its aircraft fall short. Although Airbus says that has never occurred, Boeing contends that Airbus has an advantage by lowering its commercial risk, making it easier to obtain financing. The United States maintains that these subsidies allow Airbus to set unrealistically low prices, offer concessions and attractive financing terms to airlines, and write off development costs.

Airbus has defended its subsidies on the grounds that they prevent the United States from holding a worldwide monopoly in commercial jetliners. In the absence of Airbus, European airlines would have to rely exclusively on Boeing as a supplier. Fears of dependence and the loss of autonomy in an area on the cutting edge of technology motivate European governments to subsidize Airbus.

Airbus also argues that Boeing benefits from government assistance. Rather than receiving direct subsidies like Airbus, Boeing receives indirect subsidies. For example, governmental organizations support aeronautics and propulsion research that is shared with Boeing. Support for commercial jetliner innovation also comes from military-sponsored research and military procurement. Research financed by the armed services yields indirect but important technological spillovers to the commercial jetliner industry, most notably in aircraft engines and aircraft design. Also, Boeing subcontracts part of the production of its jetliners to nations such as Japan and China, whose producers receive substantial governmental subsidies. And, the state of Washington provides tax breaks to Boeing, which has substantial production facilities in the state. According to Airbus, these subsidies enhance Boeing's competitiveness.

As a result of the subsidy conflict between Boeing and Airbus, the United States and Europe in 1992 negotiated an agreement to curb subsidies for the two manufacturers. The principal element of the accord was a 33 percent cap on the amount of government subsidies that these manufacturers could receive for product development. In addition, the indirect subsidies were limited to four percent of a firm's commercial-jetliner revenue.

Although the subsidy agreement helped calm trade tensions between the United States and Europe, by the first decade of the 2000s the subsidy dispute was heating up again. The United States criticized the European Union for granting subsidies to Airbus and called for the European Union to renegotiate the 1992 subsidy deal.

What inspired the United States to renew its efforts to force European compliance with its interpretation of the subsidy pact was severe price discounting by Airbus. In 2004, for example, Airbus offered discounts of 40 to 45 percent off list price to win contracts to supply jetliners to airlines. Boeing contended that such discounts could not possibly occur without subsidies. Moreover, Airbus developed a new super-jumbo jetliner, the A380, capable of carrying 555 passengers. The Airbus jetliner would challenge the market supremacy of the Boeing 747 (with about 400 seats), the only other jumbo jet available for sale. To pay for the development costs of the A380, which could reach $15 billion, Airbus will get 40 percent of its funding from parts suppliers, 30 percent from government loans arranged by its partners, and the final chunk from its own resources.

In 2005, Boeing and Airbus filed suits at the World Trade Organization (WTO) which contended that each company was receiving illegal subsidies from the governments of Europe and the United States. In 2009, the WTO made a preliminary finding that Airbus did receive illegal subsidies from European governments. This finding was to be followed by another WTO finding concerning Airbus's contention that Boeing will receive illegal support from the U.S. government, which would likely occur in 2010. At the writing of this text in 2010, it remains to be seen how renewed tensions between Boeing and Airbus will be resolved. Please refer to *Exploring Further* 3.2: "Boeing Airbus Subsidy Dispute".

Government Regulatory Policies and Comparative Advantage

Besides providing subsidies to enhance competitiveness, governments impose regulations on business to pursue goals such as workplace safety, product safety, and a clean environment. In the United States, these regulations are imposed by the Occupational Safety and Health Administration, the Consumer Product Safety Commission, and the Environmental Protection Agency. Although government regulations may improve the well-being of the public, they can result in higher costs for domestic firms. According to the American Iron and Steel Institute, U.S. steel producers today are technologically advanced, low cost, environmentally responsible, and customer focused. Yet they continue to face regulatory burdens from the U.S. government that impair their competitiveness and trade prospects, as seen in Table 3.8.

Strict government regulations applied to the production of goods and services tend to increase costs and erode an industry's competitiveness. This is relevant for both export- and import-competing firms. Even if government regulations are justified on social welfare grounds, the adverse impact on trade competitiveness and the associated job loss have long been a cause for policy concern. Let us examine how governmental regulations on business can affect comparative advantage.

Figure 3.6 illustrates the trade effects of pollution regulations imposed on the production process. Assume a world of two steel producers, South Korea and the United States. The supply and demand schedules of South Korea and those of the United States are indicated by $S_{S.K.0}$ and $D_{S.K.0}$, and by $S_{U.S.0}$ and $D_{U.S.0}$. In the absence of trade, South Korean producers sell 5 tons of steel at $400 per ton, while

TABLE 3.8

U.S. STEELMAKERS COMPLAIN ABOUT REGULATORY BURDENS

Below are some examples of U.S. regulations affecting domestic steel producers:

- **Health Care**. U.S. steel companies spent more than $1.5 billion for health care in 2003 for workers, retirees, and dependents. This adversely affects the competitiveness of U.S. steel companies vis-à-vis foreign competitors, many of whose health care costs are borne by government through general tax revenues.
- **OSHA**. The complexity and cost of compliance with Occupational Safety and Health Administration (OSHA) regulations continue to increase. Many OSHA rules do not have a sound scientific or medical basis and thus are impractical and cost ineffective.
- **Electricity Policy**. Electricity is a major component of steel-manufacturing costs, but it cannot be purchased on a competitive basis as are other commodities.
- **Global Climate Change**. Efforts by the United States to achieve a seven percent decrease in greenhouse gas emissions from 1990 levels by the year 2012, as dictated by the Kyoto Protocol, could result in $5 billion in extra annual energy costs for U.S. steel companies.
- **Clean Air**. Proposed tighter standards for pollutants could place much of the United States—including many steel industry sites—in nonattainment areas. The result would be enormous new costs for steel, with no comparable requirements for U.S. trading partners.

Source: From *Domestic Policies That Impact American Steel's International Competitiveness*, (Washington, DC: American Iron and Steel Institute, 2001), pp. 1–2.

FIGURE 3.6

TRADE EFFECTS OF GOVERNMENTAL REGULATIONS

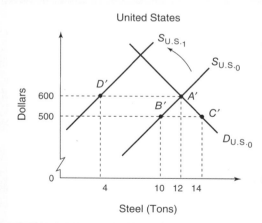

The imposition of government regulations (clean environment, workplace safety, product safety) on U.S. steel companies leads to higher costs and a decrease in market supply. This imposition detracts from the competitiveness of U.S. steel companies and reduces their share of the U.S. steel market.

12 tons of steel are sold in the United States at $600 per ton. South Korea thus enjoys a comparative advantage in steel production.

With free trade, South Korea moves toward greater specialization in steel production, and the United States produces less steel. Under increasing-cost conditions, South Korea's costs and prices rise, while prices and costs fall in the United States. The basis for further growth of trade is eliminated when prices in the two countries are equal at $500 per ton. At this price, South Korea produces 7 tons, consumes 3 tons, and exports 4 tons, and the United States produces 10 tons, consumes 14 tons, and imports 4 tons.

Suppose that the production of steel results in discharges into U.S. waterways, leading the Environmental Protection Agency to impose pollution regulations on domestic steel producers. Meeting these regulations adds to production costs, resulting in the U.S. supply schedule of steel shifting to $S_{U.S.1}$. The environmental regulations thus provide an additional cost advantage for South Korean steel companies. As South Korean companies expand steel production, say, to 9 tons, higher production costs result in a rise in price to $600. At this price, South Korean consumers demand only 1 ton. The excess supply of 8 tons is earmarked for sale to the United States. As for the United States, 12 tons of steel are demanded at the price of $600, as determined by South Korea. Given supply schedule $S_{U.S.1}$, U.S. firms now produce only 4 tons of steel at the $600 price. The excess demand, 8 tons, is met by imports from South Korea. For U.S. steel companies, the costs imposed by pollution regulations lead to further comparative disadvantage and a smaller share of the U.S. market.

Environmental regulation thus results in a policy trade-off for the United States. By adding to the costs of domestic steel companies, environmental regulations make the United States more dependent on foreign-produced steel. However, regulations provide American households with cleaner water and air, and thus a higher quality of life. Also, the competitiveness of other American industries, such as forestry products, may benefit from cleaner air and water. These effects must be considered when forming an optimal environmental regulatory policy. The same principle applies to the regulation of workplace safety by the Occupational Safety and Health Administration and the regulation of product safety by the Consumer Product Safety Commission.

Transportation Costs and Comparative Advantage

Besides embodying production costs, the principle of comparative advantage includes the costs of moving goods from one nation to another. **Transportation costs** refer to the costs of moving goods, including freight charges, packing and handling expenses, and insurance premiums. These costs are an obstacle to trade and impede the realization of gains from trade liberalization. Simply put, differences across countries in transport costs are a source of comparative advantage and affect the volume and composition of trade.

Trade Effects

The trade effects of transportation costs can be illustrated with a conventional supply and demand model based on increasing cost conditions. Figure 3.7(a) illustrates the

FIGURE 3.7

FREE TRADE UNDER INCREASING-COST CONDITIONS

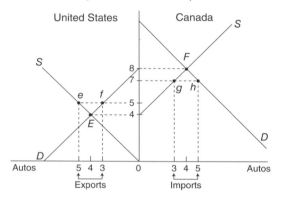

In the absence of transportation costs, free trade results in the equalization of prices of traded goods, as well as resource prices, in the trading nations. With the introduction of transportation costs, the low cost exporting nation produces less, consumes more, and exports less; the high cost importing nation produces more, consumes less, and imports less. The degree of specialization in production between the two nations decreases as do the gains from trade.

supply and demand curves of autos for the United States and Canada. Reflecting the assumption that the United States has the comparative advantage in auto production, the U.S. and Canadian equilibrium locations are at points *E* and *F*, respectively. In the absence of trade, the U.S. auto price, $4,000, is lower than that of Canada, $8,000.

When trade is allowed, the United States will move toward greater specialization in auto production, whereas Canada will produce fewer autos. Under increasing-cost conditions, the U.S. cost and price levels rise, and Canada's price falls. The basis for further growth of trade is eliminated when the two countries' prices are equal, at $6,000. At this price, the United States produces 6 autos, consumes 2 autos, and exports 4 autos; Canada produces 2 autos, consumes 6 autos, and imports 4 autos. Therefore, $6,000 becomes the equilibrium price for both countries because the excess auto supply of the United States just matches the excess auto demand in Canada.

The introduction of transportation costs into the analysis modifies the conclusions of this example. Suppose the per-unit cost of transporting an auto from the United States to Canada is $2,000, as shown in Figure 3.7(*b*). The United States would find it advantageous to produce autos and export them to Canada until its relative price advantage is eliminated. But when transportation costs are included in the analysis, the U.S. export price reflects domestic production costs *plus* the cost of transporting autos to Canada. The basis for trade thus ceases to exist when the U.S. auto price plus the transportation cost rises to equal Canada's auto price.

This equalization occurs when the U.S. auto price rises to $5,000 and Canada's auto price falls to $7,000, the difference between them being the $2,000 per-unit transportation cost. Instead of a single price ruling in both countries, there will be two domestic auto prices, differing by the cost of transportation.

Compared with free trade in the absence of transportation costs, when transportation costs are included, the high-cost importing country will produce more, consume less, and import less. The low-cost exporting country will produce less, consume more, and export less. Transportation costs, therefore, tend to reduce the volume of trade, the degree of specialization in production among the nations concerned, and thus the gains from trade.

The inclusion of transportation costs in the analysis modifies our trade-model conclusions. A product will be traded internationally as long as the pretrade price differential between the trading partners is greater than the cost of transporting the product between them. When trade is in equilibrium, the price of the traded product in the exporting nation is less than the price in the importing country by the amount of the transportation cost.

Transportation costs also have implications for the factor-price-equalization theory presented earlier in this chapter. Recall that this theory suggests that free trade tends to equalize product prices and factor prices so that all workers earn the same wage rate and all units of capital earn the same interest income in both nations. Free trade permits factor-price equalization to occur because factor inputs that cannot move to another country are implicitly being shipped in the form of products. However, looking at the real world, we see U.S. autoworkers earning more than South Korean autoworkers. One possible reason for this differential is transportation costs. By making low-cost South Korean autos more expensive for U.S. consumers, transportation costs reduce the volume of autos shipped from South Korea to the United States. This reduced trade volume stops the process of commodity- and factor-price equalization before it is complete. In other words, the prices of U.S. autos and the wages of U.S. autoworkers do not fall to the levels of those in South Korea. Transportation costs thus provide some relief to high-cost domestic workers who are producing goods subject to import competition.

The cost of shipping a product from one point to another is determined by a number of factors, including distance, weight, size, value, and the volume of trade between the two points in question. Table 3.9 shows the average importance of transportation costs for imports of the United States and other countries. Since the 1960s, the cost of international transportation has decreased significantly relative to the value of U.S. imports. From 1965 to the first decade of the 2000s, transportation costs as a percentage of the value of all U.S. imports decreased from ten percent to less than four percent. This decline in the relative cost of international transportation has made imports more competitive in U.S. markets and contributed to a higher volume of trade for the United States. Falling transportation costs have been due largely to technological improvements, including the development of large dry-bulk containers, large-scale tankers, containerization, and wide-bodied jets. Moreover, technological advances in telecommunications have reduced the economic distances among nations.

Falling Transportation Costs Foster Trade Boom

If merchants everywhere appear to be selling imports, there is a reason. International trade has been growing at a startling pace. What underlies the expansion of international

When Telsa Motors, a leader in electric-powered vehicles, set out to manufacture a luxury model for the American consumer, it had a global perspective. Telsa intended to produce 1,000-pound battery packs in Thailand, ship them to Britain for installation, then bring the mostly assembled vehicles back to the United States. When it started production in 2008, however, Telsa decided to manufacture the batteries and assemble the cars near its headquarters in California, slashing more than 5,000 miles from the transportation cost of each vehicle. This decision was obvious according to the firm's management: their primary objective was to avoid the increasing shipping charges caused by higher energy costs.

The movement of factories to low-cost countries far away from the United States has provided mixed effects for the U.S. economy, forcing workers out of high-paying manufacturing jobs even as it decreased the price of goods for consumers. But after surging over the past decade, that process slowed in 2008 as increasing energy costs caused transportation costs to rise.

In global shipping, recent changes in transportation have resulted in rising sensitivity to increased energy costs. Of primary importance is the shift toward containerization. Container ships can be unloaded more quickly than ships that carry goods in bulk, so they spend much more time traveling at sea than in ports. Speed is another element. During the past twenty years, the speed of the world's fleet of ships has increased, which necessitates greater use of energy. In global shipping, the increase in ship speed during 1990–2008 resulted in a doubling of fuel consumption per unit of freight.

The last three decades have witnessed an unprecedented growth in world trade that was supported by decreases in tariffs and other trade barriers. However, when oil prices surged in 2008, rising transport costs, not tariffs, represented a major challenge to world trade. Economists estimated that transportation costs were the equivalent of a 10–11 percent tariff on goods coming into U.S. ports when the price of a barrel of oil rose to $145 per barrel in 2008. This is compared with the equivalent of only three percent when oil was selling for $20 a barrel in 2000.

Rising shipping costs suggest that trade should be both dampened and diverted as markets look for shorter, and thus, less costly transportation routes. As transportation cost rise, markets tend to substitute goods that are from closer locations rather than from locations half-way around the world carrying hugely inflated shipping costs. For example, Emerson Electric Co., a St. Louis-based manufacturer of appliance motors and other electrical equipment, shifted some of its production from Asia to Mexico and the United States in 2008, in part to offset increasing transportation costs by being closer to customers in North America.

A key question is to what extent would substantial increases in transport costs alter the large wage differential between Chinese labor and North American labor? Although this question remains unanswered, there appears some change in capital-intensive manufacturing whose products carry a high ratio of freight costs to final selling price. Take steel for example. When the price of oil rose to $145 in 2008, rising transport costs had offset China's cost advantage in steel, giving US. steel a competitive advantage in its own market. Simply put, in a world of rapidly rising transportation costs, instead of finding cheap labor half-way around the world, the incentive will be to find the cheapest labor force within reasonable shipping distance to one's market. In that type of world, manufacturing plants in Mexico or Canada, or even the United States, may increasingly look attractive when it comes to supplying the North American market.

However, moving production to the American market would not avoid all the problems associated with increasing transportation costs. As transportation costs increased in the first decade of the 2000s, for example, U.S. manufacturers encountered sizable surcharges on domestic shipments by train and truck. Also, congested domestic transportation systems may have difficulty handling a sudden upswing in demand from manufacturers buying and moving more raw materials and other supplies over U.S. highways and rails. What's more, in certain industries the benefits stemming from offshore production may continue to outweigh increased transportation costs. Electronics firms, for example, are now clustered in Asia and realize a significant advantage of proximity to one another. Simply put, higher transportation costs may slow the outsourcing of goods in the future, instead of triggering a sizable shift back of those items that have previously been outsourced.

Source: Jeff Rubin and Benjamin Tal, "Will Soaring Transport Costs Reverse Globalization?" *StrategEcon*, CIBC World Markets Inc., Toronto, May 27, 2008. See also "Stung by Soaring Transport Costs, Factories Bring Jobs Home Again," *The Wall Street Journal*, June 13, 2008 and "Energy Costs Undercutting Globalization," *The Seattle Times*, August 3, 2008.

TABLE 3.9

THE SIZE OF TRANSPORTATION COSTS FOR SELECTED
COUNTRIES IN 2007

Country	Freight and Insurance Costs as a Percent of Import Value*
Philippines	18.2
Poland	14.9
Russia	9.9
New Zealand	7.1
Brazil	5.0
Australia	4.5
United States	3.3
Germany	2.8

*The freight and insurance factor is calculated by dividing the value of a country's imports, including freight and insurance costs (the cost-insurance-freight value), by the value of its imports excluding freight and insurance costs (the free-on-board value).

Source: From International Monetary Fund, *International Financial Statistics*, August 2007. See also International Monetary Fund, *International Financial Statistics Yearbook*, 1996, pp. 122–125.

commerce? The worldwide decrease in trade barriers, such as tariffs and quotas, is certainly one reason. The economic opening of nations that have traditionally been minor players, such as Mexico and China, is another. But one factor behind the trade boom has largely been unnoticed: the declining costs of getting goods to the market.

Today, transportation costs are a less severe obstacle than they used to be. One reason is that the global economy has become much less transport intensive than it once was. In the early 1900s, for example, manufacturing and agriculture were the two most important industries in most nations. International trade thus emphasized raw materials, such as iron ore and wheat, or processed goods such as steel. These sorts of goods are heavy and bulky, resulting in a relatively high cost of transporting them compared with the value of the goods themselves. As a result, transportation costs had much to do with the volume of trade. Over time, however, world output has shifted into goods whose value is unrelated to their size and weight. Finished manufactured goods, not raw commodities, dominate the flow of trade. Therefore, less transportation is required for every dollar's worth of exports or imports.

Productivity improvements for transporting goods have also resulted in falling transportation costs. In the early 1900s, the physical process of importing or exporting was difficult. Imagine a British textile firm desiring to sell its product in the United States. First, at the firm's loading dock, workers would lift bolts of fabric into the back of a truck. The truck would head to a port and unload its cargo, bolt by bolt, into a dockside warehouse. As a vessel prepared to set sail, dockworkers would remove the bolts from the warehouse and hoist them into the hold, where other dockworkers would stow them in place. When the cargo reached the United States, the process would be reversed. Indeed, this sort of shipment was a complicated task, requiring much effort and expense. With the passage of time came technological improvements such as modern ocean liners, standard containers for shipping goods, computerized loading ports, and freight companies such as United Parcel Service and Federal Express that specialize in using a combination of aircraft and trucks to deliver freight quickly. These and other factors have resulted in falling transportation costs and increased trade among nations.

Terrorist Attack Results in Added Costs and Slowdowns for U.S. Freight System: A New Kind of Trade Barrier?

Once in a great while, an event occurs that is so horrific that it sears its way into the national psyche. Such an event occurred on September 11, 2001, when terrorists launched an assault on the very symbols of American economic and military might—the twin towers of New York's World Trade Center and the Pentagon complex in Washington, D.C.

Immediately following the terrorist attack, Quality Carriers, Inc., the country's biggest liquid-bulk trucker, rehired the $5,000-a-month night-shift security guard it had previously let go at its tanker-truck terminal in Newark, New Jersey. The company also paid two drivers a total of $1,200 to re-park any vehicles loaded with chemicals in plain view and under security lights. To get in at night, the terminal's 52 drivers now must wait for supervisors to open the gate with new electronic gadgets. For Quality Carriers, extra security measures added to the firm's costs. Company officials noted that the carrier would try to pass along most of the added costs to its customers.

Also at risk were the nation's 361 public seaports, which handle more than 95 percent of overseas trade. Following the attack, President George W. Bush instructed the U.S. Coast Guard to take additional measures to guard bridges in U.S. harbors and sites such as the Statue of Liberty. For example, Coast Guard personnel board each inbound cargo ship some 11 miles outside the harbor and inspect the ship's cargo. Once inside the harbor, ships must travel at slow speeds, flanked on each side by a tugboat, to prevent ships from ramming into bridge supports. Shipping companies are charged up to $1,500 for each tugboat escort. Once ships are at their berths, random containers are opened and their contents removed and inspected by government officials. Such tightened security measures add about two hours to each ship's arrival process.

Before the terrorist attack on the World Trade Center and Pentagon, U.S. border enforcement overwhelming focused on limiting the inflow of illegal drugs and immigrants. However, the terrorist attack complicated business as usual along U.S. borders. This is because the cross-border transportation and communications networks used by terrorists are also the arteries of a highly interdependent economy. Analysts note that U.S. prosperity relies on its ready access to global networks of transport, energy, information, finance, and labor. It would be self-defeating for the United States to embrace security measures that isolate it from these networks.

The U.S. border security measures adopted since 2001 have consisted of taking the old drug and immigration enforcement infrastructure and adapting it to counter-terrorism efforts. As understandable as these measures may be, a sustained crack-down at U.S. ports of entry risks a considerable impact on legitimate travel and trade. For example, the United States and Canada conduct more than $1.3 billion worth of two-way trade a day, most of which is transported by truck. Analysts estimate that a truck crosses this border every 2.5 seconds, amounting to 45,000 trucks and 40,000 commercial shipments every day. Immediately following the terrorist attack of 2001 and the subsequent clampdown, the result was a drastic slowing of cross-border traffic. Delays for trucks hauling cargo across the U.S.-Canadian border rose from 1 to 2 minutes to 10 to 15 hours, stranding shipments of perishable goods and parts. Automobile firms, many of which produce parts in Ontario and ship them to U.S. assembly plants on a cost-efficient, just-in-time basis, were especially vulnerable. Ford closed an engine plant in Windsor and a vehicle plant in Michigan because of parts shortages. Extensive traffic jams and long delays also plagued the U.S.-Mexican border, where some 300 million people, 90 million cars, and 4.3 million trucks cross the border annually.

Although border delays are now not as long as immediately following the terrorist attack, heightened security concerns can have an adverse effect on cross-border trade. Simply put, security can become a new kind of trade barrier. The U.S.

response immediately following September 11, 2001, was the equivalent of imposing a trade embargo on itself. While the long-term process of North American interdependence has not been reversed, it has been complicated by the squeeze on the cross-border transportation arteries that provide its lifeblood.[12]

Summary

1. The immediate basis for trade stems from relative product price differences among nations. Because relative prices are determined by supply and demand conditions, such factors as resource endowments, technology, and national income are ultimate determinants of the basis for trade.

2. The factor-endowment theory suggests that differences in relative factor endowments among nations underlie the basis for trade. The theory asserts that a nation will export that product in the production of which a relatively large amount of its abundant and cheap resource is used. Conversely, it will import commodities in the production of which a relatively scarce and expensive resource is used. The theory also states that with trade, the relative differences in resource prices between nations tend to be eliminated.

3. According to the Stolper-Samuelson theorem, increases in income occur for the abundant resource that is used to determine comparative advantage. Conversely, the scarce factor realizes a decrease in income.

4. The specific-factors theory analyzes the income-distribution effects of trade in the short run when resources are immobile among industries. It concludes that resources specific to export industries tend to gain as a result of trade.

5. Contrary to the predictions of the factor-endowment model, the empirical tests of Wassily Leontief demonstrated that for the United States exports are labor intensive and import-competing goods are capital intensive. His findings became known as the Leontief paradox.

6. By widening the size of the domestic market, international trade permits firms to take advantage of longer production runs and increasing efficiencies (such as mass production). Such economies of scale production can be translated into lower product prices, which improve a firm's competitiveness.

7. Staffan Linder offers two explanations for world trade patterns. Trade in primary products and agricultural goods conforms well to the factor-endowment theory. But trade in manufactured goods is best explained by overlapping demand structures among nations. For manufactured goods, the basis for trade is stronger when the structure of demand in the two nations is more similar; that is, when the nations' per capita incomes are similar.

8. Besides interindustry trade, the exchange of goods among nations includes intra-industry trade—two way trade in a similar product. Intra-industry trade occurs in homogeneous goods as well as in differentiated products.

9. One dynamic theory of international trade is the product life cycle theory. This theory views a variety of manufactured goods as going through a trade cycle, during which a nation initially is an exporter, then loses its export markets, and finally becomes an importer of the product. Empirical studies have demonstrated that trade cycles do exist for manufactured goods at some times.

10. Dynamic comparative advantage refers to the creation of comparative advantage through the mobilization of skilled labor, technology, and capital; it can be initiated by either the private or public sector. When government attempts to create comparative advantage, the term *industrial policy* applies. Industrial policy seeks to encourage the development of emerging, sunrise

---

[12]Peter Andreas, "Border Security in the Age of Globalization," *Regional Review*, Federal Reserve Bank of Boston, Third Quarter, 2003, pp. 3–7. See also "After Terror Attacks, U.S. Freight Services Get Slower, Costlier," *The Wall Street Journal*, September 27, 2001, pp. A1 and A7.

industries through such measures as tax incentives and R&D subsidies.

11. Business regulations can affect the competitive position of industries. These regulations often result in cost-increasing compliance measures, such as the installation of pollution-control equipment, which can detract from the competitiveness of domestic industries.

12. International trade includes the flow of services between countries as well as the exchange of manufactured goods. As with trade in manufactured goods, the principle of comparative advantage applies to trade in services.

13. Transportation costs tend to reduce the volume of international trade by increasing the prices of traded goods. A product will be traded only if the cost of transporting it between nations is less than the pretrade difference between their relative commodity prices.

Key Concepts & Terms

- Capital/labor ratio (p. 80)
- Distribution of income (p. 79)
- Dynamic comparative advantage (p. 106)
- Economies of scale (p. 97)
- External economies of scale (p. 99)
- Factor-endowment theory (p. 80)
- Factor-price equalization (p. 84)
- Heckscher-Ohlin theory (p. 80)
- Home market effect (p. 98)
- Increasing returns to scale (p. 97)
- Industrial policy (p. 106)
- Intra-industry specialization (p. 101)
- Intra-industry trade (p. 101)
- Interindustry specialization (p. 101)
- Interindustry trade (p. 101)
- Leontief paradox (p. 95)
- Magnification effect (p. 87)
- Product life cycle theory (p. 103)
- Specific factor (p. 91)
- Specific-factors theory (p. 91)
- Stolper-Samuelson theorem (p. 87)
- Theory of overlapping demands (p. 100)
- Transportation costs (p. 111)

Study Questions

1. Do recent world-trade statistics support or refute the notion of a product life cycle for manufactured goods?

2. Table 3.10 illustrates the supply and demand schedules for calculators in Sweden and Norway. On graph paper, draw the supply and demand schedules of each country.

   a. In the absence of trade, what are the equilibrium price and quantity of calculators produced in Sweden and Norway? Which country has the comparative advantage in calculators?

   b. Assume there are no transportation costs. With trade, what price brings about balance in exports and imports? How many calculators are traded at this price? How many calculators are produced and consumed in each country with trade?

   c. Suppose the cost of transporting each calculator from Sweden to Norway is $5. With trade, what is the impact of the transportation cost on the price of calculators in Sweden and Norway? How many calculators will each country produce, consume, and trade?

TABLE 3.10

Supply and Demand Schedules for Calculators

	SWEDEN			NORWAY	
Price	Quantity supplied	Quantity demanded	Price	Quantity supplied	Quantity demanded
$ 0	0	1200	$ 0	—	1800
5	200	1000	5	—	1600
10	400	800	10	—	1400
15	600	600	15	0	1200
20	800	400	20	200	1000
25	1000	200	25	400	800
30	1200	0	30	600	600
35	1400	—	35	800	400
40	1600	—	40	1000	200
45	1800	—	45	1200	0

d. In general, what can be concluded about the impact of transportation costs on the price of the traded product in each trading nation? The extent of specialization? The volume of trade?

3. How does the Leontief paradox challenge the overall applicability of the factor-endowment model?

4. International trade in services is determined by what factors?

5. According to Staffan Linder, there are two explanations for international trade patterns—one for manufactures and another for primary (agricultural) goods. Explain.

6. How can governmental regulatory policies affect an industry's international competitiveness?

7. The factor-endowment theory demonstrates how trade affects the distribution of income within trading partners. Explain.

8. What is meant by the term *industrial policy*? How do governments attempt to create comparative advantage in sunrise sectors of the economy? What are some problems encountered when attempting to implement industrial policy?

9. How does the factor-endowment theory differ from Ricardian theory in explaining international trade patterns?

10. Distinguish between intra-industry trade and interindustry trade. What are some major determinants of intra-industry trade?

11. Explain how the international movement of products and of factor inputs promotes an equalization of the factor prices among nations.

12. How can economies of scale production affect world trade patterns?

13. What are the effects of transportation costs on international trade patterns?

3.1 Exploring Further

The Specific Factors Theory

Figure EF 3.1 provides a graphic illustration of the specific factors theory. Suppose the United States produces steel and computers using labor and capital. Also, assume that labor is perfectly mobile between the steel and computer industries, but capital is industry-specific: steel capital cannot be used in computer production, and computer capital cannot be used in steel production. Also assume that the total U.S. labor force equals 30 workers.

In each industry, labor is combined with a fixed quantity of the other factor (steel capital or computer capital) to produce the good. Labor is thus subject to diminishing marginal productivity,

FIGURE EF 3.1

RELATIVE PRICES AND THE SPECIFIC FACTORS MODEL

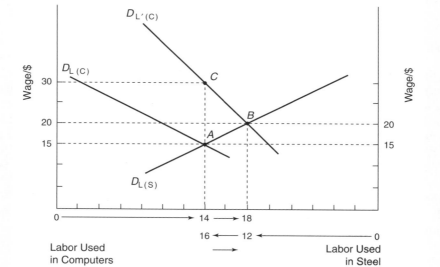

The computer-labor demand schedule increases in proportion to the rise in the price of computers (100 percent); however, the wage rate increases less than proportionately (33 percent). Labor is transferred from steel to computer production. Output of computers thus increases, while output of steel falls.

and the labor demand schedule in each industry is downward sloping.[1] The computer industry's labor demand schedule is denoted by $D_{L(C)}$, while $D_{L(S)}$ denotes the labor demand schedule in the steel industry. Because labor is assumed to be the mobile factor, it will move from the low-wage industry to the high-wage industry until wages are equalized. Let the equilibrium wage rate equal $15 per hour, seen at the intersection point A of the two labor demand schedules. At this wage, 14 workers are hired for computer production (reading from left to right) and 16 are used in steel production (reading from right to left).

Suppose the United States has a comparative advantage in computer production. With free trade and expanded output, the domestic price of computers increases, say, from $2,000 to $4,000 per unit, a 100 percent increase; the demand for labor in computer production increases by the same proportion as the computer price increase and is denoted by demand schedule $D_{L'(C)}$.[2] The result of the demand increase is a shift in equilibrium from point A to point B.

The increased demand for labor in computer production has two effects. First, the equilibrium wage rate rises, from $15 to $20, which is a smaller increase (33 percent) than the computer price increase (100 percent). Second, the increased labor demand in computer production draws workers away from steel production. At the new equilibrium point B, 18 workers are employed in computer production and 12 workers are employed in steel manufacturing; compared to equilibrium point A, 4 workers are shifted from steel to computers. Output of computers thus rises, and output of steel falls.

How does trade affect the *distribution of income* for the three groups: workers, owners of computer capital, and owners of steel capital? Workers find that although their nominal wages are higher than before, their real wages (that is, the purchasing power of the nominal wage) have fallen relative to the price of computers but have risen relative to the price of steel, which is assumed to be unchanged. Given this information, we are uncertain whether workers are better off or worse off. Their welfare will rise, fall, or remain the same depending on whether they purchase computers or steel or a combination of the two goods.

However, owners of computer capital are better off with trade. More computers are being manufactured, and the price received per computer has risen more than the wage cost per unit. The difference between the price and the wage rate is the income of capital owners for each computer sold. Conversely, owners of steel capital are worse off as the rise in computer prices decreases the purchasing power of any given income—that is, real income falls.[3] In general, owners of factors specific to *export* industries tend to *gain* from international trade, while owners of factors specific to *import-competing* industries *suffer*. International trade thus gives rise to potential conflict between different resource suppliers within a society.

---

[1]The value of marginal product (VMP) refers to the price of a product (P) times the marginal product of labor (MP). The VMP schedule is the labor demand schedule. This is because a business hiring under competitive conditions finds it most profitable to hire labor up to the point at which the price of labor (wage rate) equals its VMP. The VMP schedule is downward sloping because of the law of diminishing returns: As extra units of labor are added to capital, beyond some point the marginal product attributable to each additional unit of labor will decrease. Because VMP 1/4 P 3 MP, falling MP means that VMP decreases as more units of labor are hired.

[2]Because VMP 1/4 P 3 MP, a 100-percent rise in computer prices (P) leads to a 100-percent increase in VMP. As a result, the labor demand schedule shifts upward by 100 percent from $D_{L(C)}$ to $D_{L'(C)}$ following the price increase. To visualize this shift, compare point A and point C along the two demand schedules. After the increase in demand, computer firms will be willing to hire a given amount of labor, say 14 workers, at a wage rate of up to $30 instead of $15, a 100-percent increase. In like manner, all points along $D_{L'(C)}$ are located at a wage rate that is 100 percent greater than the corresponding wage rate along $D_{L(C)}$.

[3]Not only do the real incomes of steel-capital owners fall, but so do their nominal incomes. Trade results in a decrease in their VMP due to a decline in their MP, even if the price of steel remains the same.

3.2   Exploring Further

WTO Makes Ruling on Boeing-Airbus Aircraft Subsidy Dispute

During the first decade of the 2000s, Boeing and Airbus engaged in an intense subsidy dispute. In 2005, each company filed a suit at the World Trade Organization (WTO), claiming that its competitor received unfair subsidies from its government to maintain market share and jobs.

In March 2010, the WTO made a condemnation of European export subsidies for Airbus, noting that Airbus received about $20 billion in unfair subsidies to build commercial jetliners. The WTO said that the illegal aid consisted of research grants and loans known as launch aid. The launch aid was found to violate international trade regulations because it was priced below market-rate terms.

The ruling's immediate effect was that it put the European Union in position to file an appeal: It noted that it would do so, but it did not specify a precise timeline. Over the long term, the decision could result in Airbus repaying billions of dollars in past aid or risk allowing the United States to retaliate by increasing tariffs on products imported from Europe. It could also provide Boeing with additional resolve to challenge future government funding for Airbus. However, the WTO has no power to force any of its members to take an action that they are unwilling to take.

Airbus officials emphasized that the WTO's decision did not rule out launch aid in principle, indicating that Airbus has fostered competition that facilitates healthy choice for its customer airlines. They also claimed that the WTO's report did not find that the subsidies caused material injury to Boeing in the form of lost jobs or profits. However, Boeing officials said that the landmark decision was good news for aerospace workers in America who for decades have competed against a heavily subsidized Airbus: The decision should "level the playing field" and provide a vital precedent for other Airbus products or other nations with intentions to enter the commercial jetliner business. Airbus officials said they are looking forward to the WTO's preliminary ruling on more than $20 billion in U.S. government aid to Boeing. That report will come out in June or July of 2010, according to WTO officials.

According to industry experts, the subsidy dispute will likely drag on several more years and that a resolution will only be achieved through transatlantic negotiations. It remains to be seen how this subsidy dispute will be resolved.

Tariffs

According to the free-trade argument, open markets based on comparative advantage and specialization result in the most efficient use of world resources. Not only do free trade and specialization enhance world welfare, but they can also benefit each participating nation. Every nation can overcome the limitations of its own productive capacity to consume a combination of goods that exceeds the best it can produce in isolation.

However, free-trade policies often meet resistance among those companies and workers who face losses in income and jobs because of import competition. Policymakers are thus torn between the appeal of greater global efficiency in the long term made possible by free trade and the needs of the voting public whose main desire is to preserve short term interests such as employment and income. The benefits of free trade may take years to achieve and are spread out over wide segments of society, whereas the costs of free trade are immediate and fall on specific groups such as workers in an import-competing industry.

When forming an international trade policy, a government must decide where to locate along the following spectrum:

Autarky   ← Protectionism   Free Trade
(closed market)   Trade liberalization →   (open market)

As a government protects its producers from foreign competition, it encourages its economy to move closer to a state of isolationism, or autarky. Nations like Cuba and North Korea have traditionally been highly closed economies and therefore are closer to autarky. Conversely, if a government does not regulate the exchange of goods and services between nations, it moves to a free-trade policy. Countries such as Hong Kong (now part of the People's Republic of China) and Singapore are largely free-trade countries. The remaining countries of the world lie somewhere in between these extremes. Rather than considering which of these two extremes a government should pursue, policy discussions generally consider where along this spectrum a country should locate—that is, "how much" trade liberalization or protectionism to pursue.

This chapter considers barriers to trade. In particular, it focuses on the role that tariffs play in the global trading system.

The Tariff Concept

A **tariff** is simply a tax (duty) levied on a product when it crosses national boundaries. The most widespread tariff is the *import tariff,* which is a tax levied on an imported product. A less common tariff is an *export tariff,* which is a tax imposed on an exported product. Export tariffs have often been used by developing nations. For example, cocoa exports have been taxed by Ghana, and oil exports have been taxed by the Organization of Petroleum Exporting Countries (OPEC) in order to raise revenue or promote scarcity in global markets and hence increase the world price.

Did you know that the United States cannot levy export tariffs? When the U.S. Constitution was written, southern cotton-producing states feared that northern textile-manufacturing states would pressure the federal government into levying export tariffs to depress the price of cotton. An export duty would lead to decreased exports and thus a fall in the price of cotton within the United States. As the result of negotiations, the Constitution was worded so as to prevent export taxes: "No tax or duty shall be laid on articles exported from any state."

Tariffs may be imposed for protection or revenue purposes. A **protective tariff** is designed to reduce the amount of imports entering a country, thus insulating import-competing producers from foreign competition. This tariff allows an increase in the output of import-competing producers that would not have been possible without protection. A **revenue tariff** is imposed for the purpose of generating tax revenues and may be placed on either exports or imports.

Over time, tariff revenues have decreased as a source of government revenue for industrial nations, including the United States. In 1900, tariff revenues constituted more than 41 percent of U.S. government receipts; in 2007, the figure stood at one percent. However, many developing nations currently rely on tariffs as a sizable source of government revenue. Table 4.1 shows the percentage of government revenue that several selected nations derive from tariffs.

TABLE 4.1

TARIFF REVENUES AS A PERCENTAGE OF GOVERNMENT REVENUES, 2007: SELECTED COUNTRIES

Developing Countries	Percentage	Industrial Countries	Percentage
The Bahamas	51.2	New Zealand	2.6
Guinea	47.9	Australia	2.5
Ethiopia	33.5	Japan	1.2
Ghana	28.5	Canada	1.2
Sierra Leone	27.6	Switzerland	1.2
Madagascar	26.9	United States	1.1
Dominican Republic	20.9	United Kingdom	1.0
Jordan	11.3	Iceland	1.0

Source: From International Monetary Fund, *Government Finance Statistics, Yearbook,* Washington, DC, 2008.

TABLE 4.2

Selected U.S. Tariffs

Product	Duty Rate
Brooms	32 cents each
Fishing reels	24 cents each
Wrist watches (without jewels)	29 cents each
Ball bearings	2.4% ad valorem
Electrical motors	6.7% ad valorem
Bicycles	5.5% ad valorem
Wool blankets	1.8 cents/kg + 6% ad valorem
Electricity meters	16 cents each + 1.5% ad valorem
Auto transmission shafts	25 cents each + 3.9% ad valorem

Source: From U.S. International Trade Commission, *Tariff Schedules of the United States*, Washington, DC, Government Printing Office, 2008, available at **http://www.usitc.gov/tata/index.htm**.

Some tariffs vary according to the time of entry into the United States, as occurs with agricultural goods such as grapes, grapefruit, and cauliflower. This tariff reflects the harvest season for these products. When these products are out of season in the United States, the tariff is low. Higher tariffs are imposed when U.S. production in these goods increases during harvest season.

Types of Tariffs

Tariffs can be specific, ad valorem, or compound. A **specific tariff** is expressed in terms of a fixed amount of money per physical unit of the imported product. For example, a U.S. importer of a German computer may be required to pay a duty to the U.S. government of $100 per computer, regardless of the computer's price. Therefore, if 100 computers are imported, the tariff revenue of the government equals $10,000 (100 × 100 = 10,000).

An **ad valorem** (of value) **tariff**, much like a sales tax, is expressed as a fixed percentage of the value of the imported product. Suppose that an ad valorem duty of 2.5 percent is levied on imported automobiles. Therefore, if $100,000 worth of autos are imported, the government collects $2,500 in tariff revenue (100,000 × 2.5% = 2,500). This $2,500 is collected whether five $20,000 Toyotas are imported or ten $10,000 Nissans.

A **compound tariff** is a combination of specific and ad valorem tariffs. For example, a U.S. importer of a television might be required to pay a duty of $20 plus five percent of the value of the television. Table 4.2 lists U.S. tariffs on certain items.

What are the relative merits of specific, ad valorem, and compound tariffs?

Specific Tariff

As a fixed monetary duty per unit of the imported product, a specific tariff is relatively easy to apply and administer, particularly for standardized commodities and staple products where the value of the dutiable goods cannot be easily observed. A main disadvantage of a specific tariff is that the degree of protection it affords domestic producers varies *inversely* with changes in import prices. For example, a specific tariff of $1,000 on autos will discourage imports priced at $20,000 per auto to a greater degree than those priced at $25,000. During times of rising import prices, a given specific tariff loses some of its protective effect. The result is to encourage the domestic producer to produce less expensive goods, for which the degree of protection against imports is higher. On the other hand, a specific tariff has the advantage of providing domestic producers more protection during a business recession, when cheaper products are purchased. Specific tariffs thus cushion domestic producers progressively against foreign competitors who cut their prices.

Ad Valorem Tariff

Ad valorem tariffs usually lend themselves more satisfactorily to manufactured goods, because they can be applied to products with a wide range of grade variations. As a percentage applied to a product's value, an ad valorem tariff can distinguish among small differentials in product quality to the extent that they are reflected in product price. Under a system of ad valorem tariffs, a person importing a $20,000 Honda would have to pay a higher duty than a person importing a $19,900 Toyota. Under a system of specific tariffs, the duty would be the same.

Another advantage of an ad valorem tariff is that it tends to maintain a constant degree of protection for domestic producers during periods of changing prices. If the tariff rate is a 20 percent ad valorem and the imported product price is $200, the duty is $40. If the product's price increases, say, to $300, the duty collected rises to $60; if the product price falls to $100, the duty drops to $20. An ad valorem tariff yields revenues proportionate to values, maintaining a constant degree of relative protection at all price levels. An ad valorem tariff is similar to a proportional tax in that the real proportional tax burden or protection does not change as the tax base changes. In recent decades, in response to global inflation and the rising importance of world trade in manufactured products, ad valorem duties have been used more often than specific duties.

The determination of duties under the ad valorem principle at first appears to be simple, but in practice it has suffered from administrative complexities. The main problem has been trying to determine the value of an imported product, a process referred to as **customs valuation**. Import prices are estimated by customs appraisers, who may disagree on product values. Moreover, import prices tend to fluctuate over time, which makes the valuation process rather difficult.

Another customs-valuation problem stems from variations in the methods used to determine a commodity's value. For example, the United States has traditionally used **free-on-board (FOB) valuation**, whereby the tariff is applied to a product's value as it leaves the exporting country. But European countries have traditionally used a **cost-insurance-freight (CIF) valuation**, whereby ad valorem tariffs are levied as a percentage of the imported commodity's total value as it arrives at its final destination. The CIF price thus includes transportation costs, such as insurance and freight.

Compound Tariff

Compound duties are often applied to manufactured products embodying raw materials that are subject to tariffs. In this case, the specific portion of the duty neutralizes the cost disadvantage of domestic manufacturers that results from tariff protection granted to domestic suppliers of raw materials, and the ad valorem portion of the duty grants protection to the finished-goods industry. In the United States, for example, there is a compound duty on woven fabrics (48.5 cents per kilogram plus 38 percent). The specific portion of the duty (48.5 cents) compensates U.S. fabric manufacturers for the tariff protection granted to U.S. cotton producers, while the ad valorem portion of the duty (38 percent) provides protection for their own woven fabrics.

How high are import tariffs around the world? Table 4.3 provides examples of tariffs of selected industrial and developing countries.

TABLE 4.3

EXAMPLES OF TARIFFS FOR SELECTED COUNTRIES (IN PERCENTAGES)

	United States	Canada	Japan	China	European Union
Textiles and clothing	9.6	11.7	7.4	17.5	7.9
Footwear	4.3	5.7	6.4	14.6	4.2
Metals	2.1	1.9	1.3	7.3	1.9
Chemicals	3.4	3.0	2.5	7.5	4.5
Nonelectrical machinery	1.2	1.5	0.0	9.9	1.7
Electrical machinery	1.9	2.4	0.2	10.4	2.5
Petroleum	1.9	3.0	1.7	5.0	3.1
Sugar	13.0	4.3	10.2	33.6	11.4
Dairy products	19.0	7.4	28.0	24.5	7.7
Average	3.9	4.1	3.2	12.4	4.2

Source: From World Trade Organization, *World Trade Report*, 2007, Appendix.

Effective Rate of Protection

In our previous discussion of tariffs, we assumed that a given product is produced entirely in one country. For example, a desktop computer produced by Dell (a U.S. firm) could be the output that results from using only American labor and components. However, this ignores the possibility that Dell imports some inputs used in producing desktops, such as memory chips, hard-disk drives, and microprocessors.

When some inputs used in producing finished desktops are imported, the amount of protection given to Dell depends not only on the tariff rate applied to desktops, but also on whether there are tariffs on inputs used to produce them. The main point is that when Dell imports some of the inputs required to produce desktops, the tariff rate on desktops may not accurately indicate the protection being provided to Dell.

In analyzing tariffs, economists distinguish between the nominal tariff rate and the effective tariff rate. The **nominal tariff rate** is the tariff rate that is published in the country's tariff schedule. It applies to the value of a *finished product* that is imported into a country. The **effective tariff rate** takes into account not only the nominal tariff rate on a finished product, but also any tariff rate applied to *imported inputs* that are used in producing the finished product.[1]

It is apparent that if a finished desktop enters the United States at a zero tariff rate, while imported components used in desktop production are taxed, then Dell is taxed instead of protected. A nominal tariff on a desktop protects the production of Dell, while a tariff on imported components taxes Dell by increasing its costs. The effective tariff rate nets out these two effects.

The effective tariff rate refers to the level of protection being provided to Dell by a nominal tariff on desktops and the tariff on inputs used in desktop production. Specifically, it measures the percentage increase in domestic production activities

---

[1]The effective tariff is a measure that applies to a single nation. In a world of floating exchange rates, if all nominal or effective tariff rates rose, the effect would be offset by a change in the exchange rate.

(value added) per unit of output made possible by tariffs on both the finished desktop and on imported inputs. Simply put, a given tariff on a desktop will have a greater protective effect if it is combined with a low tariff on imported inputs, than if the tariff on components is high.

To illustrate this principle, assume that Dell adds value by assembling computer components that are produced abroad. Suppose the imported components can enter the United States on a duty-free basis (zero tariff). Suppose also that 20 percent of a desktop's final value can be attributed to domestic assembly activities (value added). The remaining 80 percent reflects the value of the imported components. Furthermore, let the cost of the desktop's components be the same for both Dell and its foreign competitor, say, Sony Inc. of Japan. Next, assume that Sony can produce and sell a desktop for $500.

Suppose the United States imposes a nominal tariff of ten percent on desktops, so that the domestic import price rises from $500 to $550 per unit, as seen in Table 4.4. Does this mean that Dell realizes an effective rate of protection equal to ten percent? Certainly not! The imported components enter the country duty-free (at a nominal tariff rate less than that on the finished desktop), so the effective rate of protection is 50 percent. Compared with what would exist under free trade, Dell can incur 50 percent more production activities and still be competitive.

Table 4.4 shows the figures in detail. Under free trade (zero tariff), a Sony desktop could be imported for $500. To meet this price, Dell would have to hold its assembly costs down to $100. But under the protective umbrella of the tariff, Dell can incur up to $150 of assembly costs and still meet the $550 price of imported desktops. The result is that Dell's assembly costs could rise to a level of 50 percent above what would exist under free-trade conditions: ($150 − $100)/$100 = 0.5).

In general, the effective tariff rate is given by the following formula:

$$e = \frac{(n - ab)}{(1 - a)},$$

where

$e =$ The effective rate of protection
$n =$ The nominal tariff rate on the final product
$a =$ The ratio of the value of the imported input to the value of the finished product
$b =$ The nominal tariff rate on the imported input

TABLE 4.4

THE EFFECTIVE RATE OF PROTECTION

Sony's Desktop Computer	Cost	Dell's Desktop Computer	Cost
Component parts	$400	Imported component parts	$400
Assembly activity (value added)	100	Assembly activity (value added)	150
Nominal tariff	50	Domestic price	$550
Import price	$550		

When the values from the desktop example are plugged into this formula, we obtain the following:

$$e = \frac{0.1 - 0.8(0)}{1 - 0.8} = 0.5, \text{ or } 50 \text{ percent}.$$

The nominal tariff rate of ten percent levied on the finished desktop thus allows a 50 percent increase in domestic production activities—five times the nominal rate.

However, a tariff on imported desktop components reduces the level of effective protection for Dell. This reduction means that in the above formula, the higher the value of b, the lower the effective-protection rate for any given nominal tariff on the finished desktop. For example, suppose that imported desktop components are subject to a tariff rate of five percent. The effective rate of protection would equal 30 percent:

$$e = \frac{0.1 - 0.8(0.05)}{1 - 0.8} = 0.3, \text{ or } 30 \text{ percent}.$$

This is less than the 50 percent effective rate of protection that occurs when there is no tariff on imported components.

From these examples we can draw several conclusions. When the tariff on the finished product exceeds the tariff on the imported input, the effective rate of protection exceeds the nominal tariff. However, if the tariff on the finished product is less than the tariff on the imported input, the effective rate of protection is less than the nominal tariff, and may even be negative. Such a situation might occur if the home government desired to protect domestic suppliers of raw materials more than domestic manufacturers.[2] Because national governments generally admit raw materials and other inputs either duty free or at a lower rate than finished goods, effective tariff rates are usually higher than nominal rates. Table 4.5 provides examples of nominal and effective tariff rates for China in 2001.

Tariff Escalation

When analyzing the tariff structures of nations, we often see that processed goods face higher import tariffs than those levied on basic raw materials. For example, logs may be imported tariff-free while processed goods such as plywood, veneers, and furniture face higher import tariffs. The purpose of this tariff strategy is to protect, say, the domestic plywood industry by enabling it to import logs (which are

TABLE 4.5

CHINA'S NOMINAL AND EFFECTIVE TARIFF RATES IN FORESTRY PRODUCTS, 2001

Product	Nominal Rate (%)	Effective Rate (%)
Mouldings	9.4	26.6
Furniture	11.0	21.8
Veneers	4.0	9.4
Plywood	8.4	11.7
Fiberboard	7.5	9.2
Particleboard	9.6	10.6

Source: From Manatu Aorere, *Tariff Escalation in the Forestry Sector*, New Zealand Ministry of Foreign Affairs and Trade, Wellington, New Zealand, August 2002.

---

[2]Besides depending on the tariff rates on finished desktops and components used to produce them, the effective rate of protection depends on the ratio of the value of the imported input to the value of the finished product. The degree of effective protection for Dell increases as the value added by Dell declines (the ratio of the value of the imported input to the value of the final product increases). That is, the higher the value of a in the formula, the greater the effective-protection rate for any given nominal tariff rate on desktops.

FIGURE 4.1

TARIFF ESCALATION ON INDUSTRIAL COUNTRIES' IMPORTS FROM DEVELOPING COUNTRIES

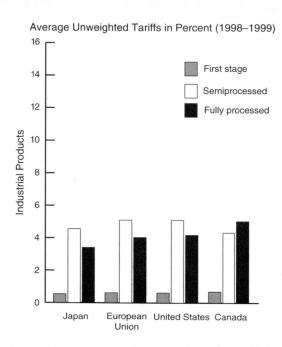

Tariffs often rise significantly with the level of processing (tariff escalation) in many industrial countries. This is especially true for agricultural products. Tariff escalation in industrial countries has the potential of reducing demand for processed imports from developing countries, hampering diversification into higher-value added exports.

Source: Data taken from The World Bank, *Global Economic Prospects and the Developing Countries*, 2002 and World Trade Organization, *Market Access: Unfinished Business*, 2001, available at **http://www.wto.org/**.

used to produce plywood) tariff-free or at low rates while maintaining higher tariffs on imported plywood that competes against domestic plywood.

This policy is referred to as **tariff escalation**: although raw materials are often imported at zero or low tariff rates, the nominal and effective protection increases at each stage of production. As seen in Figure 4.1, tariffs often rise significantly with the level of processing in many industrial countries. This is especially true for agricultural products.

The tariff structures of the industrialized nations may indeed discourage the growth of processing, thus hampering diversification into higher value-added exports for the less-developed nations. The industrialized nations' low tariffs on primary commodities encourage the developing nations to expand operations in these sectors, while the high protective rates levied on manufactured goods pose a significant entry barrier for any developing nation wishing to compete in this area. From the point of view of less-developed nations, it may be in their best interest to discourage disproportionate tariff reductions on raw materials. The effect of these tariff reductions is to magnify the discrepancy between the nominal and effective tariffs of the industrialized nations, worsening the potential competitive position of the less-developed nations in the manufacturing and processing sectors.

Outsourcing and Offshore-Assembly Provision

Outsourcing is a key aspect of the global economy. It may occur when certain aspects of a product's manufacture are performed in more than one country. For example, electronic components made in the United States are shipped to a regionally accessible country with low labor costs, say, Singapore, for assembly into television sets. The assembled sets are then returned to the United States for further processing or packaging and distribution. This foreign assembly type of production sharing has evolved into an important competitive strategy for many U.S. producers of low-cost, labor-intensive products. Market share, in the United States and abroad, can often be preserved as a result of improvements in cost competitiveness by way of foreign assembly, which allows firms to retain higher production and employment levels in the United States than might otherwise be possible.

In addition to the use of foreign assembly plants to reduce labor costs, outsourcing operations may be designed to penetrate foreign markets where high tariffs or other trade barriers restrict the direct export of finished goods. Outsourcing may also take advantage of certain unique foreign production technologies, labor skills, raw materials, or specialized components.

U.S. trade policy includes an **offshore-assembly provision (OAP)** that provides favorable treatment to products assembled abroad from U.S.-manufactured components. Under OAP, when a finished component originating in the United States (such as a semiconductor) is sent overseas and assembled there with one or more other components to become a finished good (such as a television set), the cost of the U.S. component is not included in the dutiable value of the imported assembled article into which it has been incorporated. American import duties thus apply only to the *value added in the foreign assembly process*, provided that U.S.-manufactured components are used by overseas companies in their assembly operations. Manufactured goods entering the United States under OAP have included motor vehicles, office machines, television sets, aluminum cans, and semiconductors.

The U.S. OAP pertains not only to U.S. firms, but also to foreign companies. For example, a U.S. computer company could produce components in the United States, send them to Taiwan for assembly, and ship computers back to the United States under favorable OAP. Alternatively, a Japanese photocopier firm desiring to export to the United States could purchase U.S.-manufactured components, assemble them in Malaysia, and ship photocopiers to the United States under favorable OAP.

Suppose that the United States imports television sets from South Korea at a price of $300 per set. If the tariff rate on such televisions is ten percent, a duty of $30 would be paid on each television entering the United States, and the price to the U.S. consumer would be $330.[3] Now, suppose that U.S. components are used in the television sets assembled by the Koreans and that these components have a value of $200. Under OAP, the ten percent U.S. tariff rate is levied on the value of

---

[3]This assumes that the United States is a "small" country, as discussed later in this chapter.

the imported set *minus* the value of the U.S. components used in manufacturing the set. When the set enters the United States, its dutiable value is thus $300 − $200 = $100, and the duty is 0.1 × $100 = $10. The price to the U.S. consumer after the tariff has been levied is $300 + $10 = $310. With the OAP system, the consumer is better off because the effective tariff rate is only 3.3 percent ($10/$300) instead of the ten percent shown in the tariff schedule.

The OAP provides potential advantages for the United States. By reducing import tariffs on foreign-assembled sets embodying U.S. components, OAP provides incentives for Korean manufacturers, which desire to export to the United States, to purchase components from U.S. sources; this generates sales and jobs in the U.S. component industries. However, television-assembly workers in the United States object to OAP, which they claim exports jobs that rightfully belong to them; it is in their best interest to lobby for the abolition of OAP.

Dodging Import Tariffs: Tariff Avoidance and Tariff Evasion

When a country imposes a tariff on imports, there are economic incentives to dodge it. One way of escaping a tariff is to engage in **tariff avoidance**, the legal utilization of the tariff system to one's own advantage in order to reduce the amount of tariff that is payable by means that are within the law. By contrast, **tariff evasion** occurs when individuals or firms evade tariffs by illegal means, such as smuggling imported goods into a country. Let us consider each of these methods.

Ford Strips Its Wagons to Avoid High Tariff

Several times a month, Ford Motor Company ships its Transit Connect five-passenger wagons from its factory in Turkey to Baltimore, Maryland. Once the passenger wagons arrive in Baltimore, the majority of them are driven to a warehouse, where workers listening to rock music rip out the rear windows, seats, and seat belts. Why?

Ford's behavior is part of its efforts to cope with a lengthy trade conflict. In the 1960s, Europe imposed high tariffs on imported chickens, primarily intended to discourage American sales to West Germany. President Lyndon Johnson retaliated with a 25 percent tariff on imports of foreign-made trucks and commercial vans (motor vehicles for the transport of goods). This tariff exists today and applies to trucks and commercial vans even if they are produced by an American company in a foreign country. However, the U.S. tariff on imports of vehicles in the category of "wagons" and "cars" (motor vehicles for the transport of persons) face a much lower 2.5 percent tariff.

Realizing that a 25 percent tariff would significantly add to the price of its cargo vans sold in the United States, and thus detract from their competitiveness, in 2009 Ford embarked on a program to avoid this tariff. Here's how it works. Ford ships the Transit Connects wagons to the United States, which face a 2.5 percent tariff. Then, once the wagons reach a processing facility in Baltimore, they are transformed into cargo vans. The rear windows are removed and replaced by a sheet of metal, and the rear seats and seat belts are removed and a new floorboard is screwed into place. Although the vehicles start as five-passenger wagons, Ford converts them into two-seat cargo vans. The fabric is shredded, the steel parts are broken down, and everything is sent along with the glass to be recycled. According to U.S. customs officials, this practice complies with the letter of the law.

Transforming wagons into cargo vans costs Ford hundreds of dollars per vehicle, but the process saves the company thousands in terms of tariff duties. For example, on a $25,000 passenger wagon a 2.5 percent tariff would result in a duty of only $625 (25,000 × 0.025 = 625). This compares to a duty of $6,250 that would result from a 25 percent tariff imposed on a cargo van (25,000 × 0.25 = 6,250). The avoidance of the higher tariff on cargo vans would save Ford $5,625 on each vehicle (6,250 − 625 = 5,625), minus the cost of transforming the passenger wagon into a cargo van. Smart, huh?

Ford's transformation process is only one way to avoid tariffs. Other auto makers have avoided U.S. tariffs using different techniques. For example, Toyota Motor Corp., Nissan Motor Co., and Honda Motor Co. took the straightforward route and built plants in the United States, instead of exporting vehicles from Japan to the United States that are subject to import tariffs.[4]

Smuggled Steel Evades U.S. Tariffs

Each year, about 38 million tons of steel with a value of about $12 billion are imported by the United States. About half of this steel is subject to tariffs that range from pennies to hundreds of dollars a ton. The amount of the tariff depends on the type of steel product (of which there are about 1,000) and on the country of origin (of which there are about 100). These tariffs are applied to the selling price of the steel in the United States. American customs inspectors scrutinize the shipments that enter the United States to make sure that tariffs are properly assessed. However, monitoring shipments is difficult given the limited staff of the customs service. Therefore, the risk of being caught for smuggling and the odds of penalties being levied are modest, while the potential for illegal profit is high.

For example, Ivan Dubrinski smuggled 20,000 tons of steel into the United States in the first decade of the 2000s. It was easy. All he did was modify the shipping documents on a product called "reinforcing steel bar" to make it appear that it was part of a shipment of another type of steel called "flat-rolled." This deception saved him about $38,000 in import duties. Multiply this tariff-evasion episode many times over and you have smuggled steel avoiding millions of dollars in duties. The smuggling of steel concerns the U.S. government, which loses tariff revenue, and also the U.S. steel industry, which maintains that it cannot afford to compete with products made cheaper by tariff evasion.

Although larger U.S. importers of steel generally pay correct duties, it is the smaller, often fly-by-night importers that are more likely to try to slip illegal steel into the country. These traders use one of three methods to evade tariffs. One method is to falsely reclassify steel that would be subject to a tariff as a duty-free product. Another is to detach markings which indicate that the steel came from a country subject to tariffs and make it appear to have come from one that is exempt. A third method involves altering the chemical composition of a steel product enough so that it can be labeled duty-free.

Although customs inspectors attempt to scrutinize imports, once the steel gets by them they can do little about it. They cannot confiscate the smuggled steel because it is often already sold and in use. Meanwhile, the people buying the steel

---

[4]Drawn from "To Outfox the Chicken Tax, Ford Strips Its Own Vans," *The Wall Street Journal*, September 23, 2009, p. A-1.

get a nice price break, and the American steel companies that compete against smuggled steel find their sales and profits declining.[5]

Postponing Import Tariffs

Besides allowing for the avoidance of tariffs, U.S. tariff law allows the postponement of tariffs. Let us see how a bonded warehouse and a foreign trade zone can facilitate the postponing of tariffs.

Bonded Warehouse

According to U.S. tariff law, dutiable imports can be brought into the U.S. and temporarily left in a **bonded warehouse**, duty-free. Importers can apply for authorization from the U.S. Customs Service to have a bonded warehouse on their own premises, or they can use the services of a public warehouse that has received such authorization. Owners of storage facilities must be bonded to ensure that they will satisfy all customs duty obligations. This condition means that the bonding company guarantees payment of customs duties in the event that the importing company is unable to do so.

Imported goods can be stored, repacked, or further processed in the bonded warehouse for up to five years. Domestically produced goods are not allowed to enter a bonded warehouse. If warehoused at the initial time of entry, no customs duties are owed. When the time arrives to withdraw the imported goods from the warehouse, duties must be paid on the value of the goods at the time of withdrawal rather than at the time of entry into the bonded warehouse. If the goods are withdrawn for exportation, payment of duty is not required.

While the goods are in the warehouse, the owner may subject them to various processes necessary to prepare them for sale in the market. Such processes might include the repacking and mixing of tea, the bottling of wines, and the roasting of coffee. However, imported components cannot be assembled into final products in a bonded warehouse, nor can the manufacturing of products take place.

A main advantage of a bonded warehouse entry is that no duties are collected until the goods are withdrawn for domestic consumption. The importer has the luxury of controlling the money for the duty until it is paid upon withdrawal of the goods from the bonded warehouse. If the importer cannot find a domestic buyer for its goods, or if the goods cannot be sold at a good price domestically, the importer has the advantage of selling merchandise for exportation that cancels the obligation to pay duties. Also, paying duties when goods first arrive in the country can be expensive, and using a bonded warehouse allows importers time to access funds from the sale of the goods to pay the duties, rather than having to pay duties in advance.

Foreign-Trade Zone

Created in the 1930s, the **foreign-trade zone (FTZ)** program of the United States broadens the concept of a bonded warehouse. A FTZ is an area within the United States where business can operate without the responsibility of paying customs

---

[5]Drawn from "Steel Smugglers Pull Wool over the Eyes of Customs Agents to Enter U.S. Market," *The Wall Street Journal*, November 1, 2001, pp. A1 and A14.

duties on imported products or materials for as long as they remain within this area and do not enter the U.S. marketplace. Customs duties are due only when goods are transferred from the FTZ for U.S. consumption. If the goods never enter the U.S. marketplace, then no duties are paid on those items. For example, if imported components enter a FTZ, are assembled into a final product, and re-exported abroad, no customs duty is paid. Moreover, both foreign and domestic goods can be stored inside a FTZ and there is no time limit on how long goods can be stored.

Many FTZs are situated at U.S. seaports, such as the Port of Seattle, but some are located at inland distribution points. There are currently more than 230 FTZs throughout the United States. Among the businesses that enjoy FTZ status are Exxon, Caterpillar, General Electric, and International Business Machines (IBM). Once merchandise has moved into an FTZ, you can do just about anything to it. You can re-package goods, repair or destroy damaged ones, assemble component parts into finished products, and re-export either the parts or finished products. The manufacturing of goods is also allowed in FTZs. Therefore, importers who use FTZs can conduct a broader range of business activities than can occur in bonded warehouses that permit only the storage of imported goods and limited repackaging and processing activities.

FTZs are divided into general-purpose zones and subzones. General-purpose zones consist of public facilities that are used by more than one firm, and are typically ports or industrial parks used by small- to medium-sized businesses for product assembly, processing, warehousing, and distribution. There are also subzones that involve a single firm's site that is used for more extensive manufacturing or assembly, which cannot be accomplished easily in a general-purpose zone.

The FTZ program encourages U.S.-based business operations by removing certain disincentives associated with manufacturing in the United States. The duty on a product manufactured abroad and imported into the United States is paid at the rate of the finished product rather than that of the individual parts, materials, or components of the product. A U.S.-based company would thus find itself at a disadvantage relative to its foreign competitor if it had to pay a higher rate on parts, materials, or components imported for use in the manufacturing process (this is known as "inverted tariffs"). The FTZ program corrects this imbalance by treating a product manufactured in a FTZ, for purposes of tariff assessment, as if it were produced abroad.

For example, suppose a FTZ user imports a motor, which carries a five percent duty rate, and uses it in the manufacture of a lawn mower, which is free of duty. When the lawn mower leaves the FTZ and enters the U.S. marketplace, the duty rate on the motor drops from the five percent rate to the free lawn mower rate. By participating in the FTZ program, the lawn mower manufacturer has eliminated the duty on this component, and thus decreased the component cost by five percent.

A FTZ can also help a firm eliminate import duties on product waste and scrap. For example, suppose a U.S. chemical company imports raw material, which carries a ten percent duty, to produce a particular chemical that also carries a ten percent duty. Part of the production process involves bringing the imported raw material to very high temperatures. During this process, 20 percent of the raw material is lost as heat. If the chemical company imports $1 million of raw material per year, it will pay $100,000 (1 million $\times$ 0.1 = 100,000) in duty as the raw material enters the United States. However, by participating in the FTZ program, it does not pay duty on the raw material until it leaves the zone and enters the U.S. marketplace. Because 20 percent of the raw material is lost as heat during the manufacturing process, the raw material is now worth only $800,000. Assuming that all of the finished chemical is sold into the United States, the ten percent customs duty totals only $80,000. This is a savings of $20,000. While it may appear that the FTZ program benefits only the U.S. chemical company, it is important to remember that its competitors who make the same product abroad already have the benefit of not having to pay on the waste loss in the production of their chemical.

FTZ's Benefit Motor Vehicle Importers

Toyota Motor Co. is an example of a company that benefits from the U.S. FTZ program. For example, Toyota has vehicle processing centers located within FTZ sites in the United States. Before imported Toyotas are shipped to American dealers, the processing centers clean them, install accessories such as radios and CD players, and so on. A primary benefit of the processing center being located within a FTZ site is customs duty deferral—the postponement of the payment of duties until the vehicle has been processed and shipped to the dealer.

For parts imported into the United States, Toyota also has parts distribution centers that are located within FTZ sites. Due to extended warranties, Toyota must maintain a large inventory of parts within the United States for a lengthy period of time, which makes the FTZ program attractive from the perspective of duty deferral. Also, a large number of parts may become obsolete and have to be destroyed. By obtaining FTZ designation on its parts distribution center, Toyota can avoid the payment of customs duties on those parts that become obsolete and are destroyed.

Another benefit to Toyota of a FTZ is the potential reduction in the dutiable value of the imported vehicle according to the inverted duty principle, as discussed above. Suppose that a CD player that is imported from Japan is installed at a Toyota processing center within a FTZ site. In 2009 the duty on the imported CD player was 4.4 percent and the duty on a final Toyota automobile was 2.5 percent. Thus, Toyota has the ability to reduce the duty on the cost of the CD player by 1.9 percent (4.4 − 2.5 = 1.9) by having the CD player installed at its processing center within the FTZ site.

Tariff Effects: An Overview

Before we make a detailed investigation of tariffs, let us consider an introductory overview of their effects.

Tariffs are taxes on imports. They make the item more expensive for consumers, thus reducing demand. To illustrate, suppose there is a U.S. company and a foreign company supplying computers. The price of the U.S.-made computer is $1,000 and the price of foreign-made computer is $750. The U.S. computer company is not able to stay competitive in this situation.

Suppose that the United States imposes an import tariff of $300 per computer. The tariff increases the price of imported computers above the foreign price by the amount of the tariff, $300. American suppliers of computers, who compete with suppliers of imported computers, can now sell their computers for the foreign price plus the amount of the tariff, $1,050 (750 + 300 = 1,050). As the price of imported computers increases, domestic demand for them decreases. At the same time, the higher price has encouraged American suppliers to expand output, so that imports are reduced. Notice that a tariff need not push the price of the imported computer above the price of its domestic counterpart for the American computer industry to prosper. It should be just high enough to reduce the price differential between the imported computer and the American-made computer.

If no tariff were imposed, as under free trade, Americans would have saved money by buying the cheaper foreign computer. The U.S. computer industry would either have to become more efficient in order to compete with the less expensive imported product or face extinction.

Although the tariff benefits producers in the U.S. computer industry, it imposes costs to the U.S. economy:

- Computer buyers will have to pay more for their protected U.S.-made computers than they would have for the imported computers under free trade.
- Jobs will be lost at retail and shipping companies that import foreign-made computers.
- Jobs will be lost in any domestic industries that suffer from retaliatory tariffs.
- The extra cost of the computers gets passed on to whatever products and services that use these computers in the production process.

These costs will have to be weighed against the number of jobs the tariff would save to get a true picture of the impact of the tariff.

Now that we have an overview of the effects of a tariff, let us consider tariffs in a more detailed manner. We will examine the effects of tariffs for a small importing country and a large importing country. Let us begin by reviewing the concepts of consumer surplus and producer surplus, as discussed in the next section of this text.

Tariff Welfare Effects: Consumer Surplus and Producer Surplus

To analyze the effect of trade policies on national welfare, it is useful to separate the effects on consumers from those on producers. For each group, a measure of welfare is needed; these measures are known as consumer surplus and producer surplus.

Consumer surplus refers to the difference between the amount that buyers would be willing and able to pay for a good and the actual amount they do pay. To illustrate, assume that the price of a Pepsi is $0.50. Being especially thirsty, suppose you would be willing to pay up to $0.75 for a Pepsi. Your consumer surplus on this purchase is $0.25 ($0.75 − $0.50 = $0.25). For all Pepsis bought, consumer surplus is merely the sum of the surplus for each unit.

Consumer surplus can also be depicted graphically. Let us first remember that the height of the market demand curve indicates the maximum price that buyers are willing and able to pay for each successive unit of the good, and, second, in a competitive market, buyers pay a single price (the equilibrium price) for all units purchased. Referring now to Figure 4.2(a), assume the market price of gasoline is $2 per gallon. If buyers purchase four gallons at this price, they spend $8, represented by area *ACED*. For those four gallons, buyers would be willing and able to spend $12, as shown by area *ABCED*. The difference between what buyers actually spend and the amount they are willing and able to spend is consumer surplus; in this case, it equals $4 and is denoted by area *ABC*.

FIGURE 4.2

CONSUMER SURPLUS AND PRODUCER SURPLUS

Consumer surplus is the difference between the maximum amount buyers are willing to pay for a given quantity of a good and the amount actually paid. Graphically, consumer surplus is represented by the area under the demand curve and above the good's market price. Producer surplus is the revenue producers receive over and above the minimum necessary for production. Graphically, producer surplus is represented by the area above the supply curve and below the good's market price.

The size of the consumer surplus is affected by the market price. A decrease in the market price will lead to an increase in the quantity purchased and a larger consumer surplus. Conversely, a higher market price will reduce the amount purchased and shrink the consumer surplus.

Let us now consider the other side of the market: producers. **Producer surplus** is the revenue producers receive over and above the minimum amount required to induce them to supply a good. This minimum amount has to cover the producer's total variable costs. Recall that total variable cost equals the sum of the marginal cost of producing each successive unit of output.

In Figure 4.2(*b*), the producer surplus is represented by the area above the supply curve of gasoline and below the good's market price. Recall that the height of the market supply curve indicates the lowest price at which producers will be willing to supply gasoline; this minimum price increases with the level of output because of rising marginal costs. Suppose that the market price of gasoline is $2 per gallon, and four gallons are supplied. Producers receive revenues totaling $8, represented by area *ACDB*. The minimum revenue they must receive to produce four gallons equals the total variable cost, which equals $4 and is depicted by area *BCD*. Producer surplus is the difference, $4 ($8 − $4 = $4), and is depicted by *area ABC*.

If the market price of gasoline rises, more gasoline will be supplied, and the producer surplus will rise. It is equally true that if the market price of gasoline falls, the producer surplus will fall.

In the following sections, we will use the concepts of consumer surplus and producer surplus to analyze the effects of import tariffs on a nation's welfare.

Tariff Welfare Effects: Small-Nation Model

To measure the effects of a tariff on a nation's welfare, consider the case of a nation whose imports constitute a very small portion of the world market supply. This **small nation** would be a *price taker*, facing a constant world price level for its import commodity. This is not a rare case; many nations are not important enough to influence the terms at which they trade.

In Figure 4.3, a small nation before trade produces autos at market equilibrium point E, as determined by the intersection of its domestic supply and demand schedules. At the equilibrium price of $9,500, the quantity supplied is 50 autos, and the quantity demanded is 50 autos. Now suppose that the economy is opened to foreign

---

FIGURE 4.3

TARIFF TRADE AND WELFARE EFFECTS: SMALL NATION MODEL

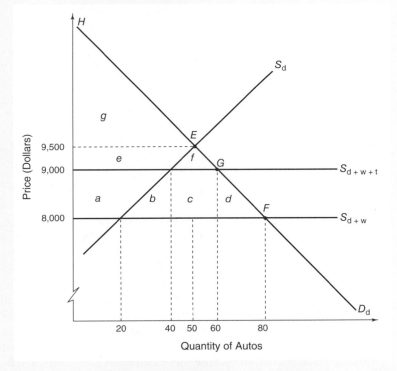

For a small nation, a tariff placed on an imported product is shifted totally to the domestic consumer via a higher product price. Consumer surplus falls as a result of the price increase. The small nation's welfare decreases by an amount equal to the protective effect and consumption effect, the so-called deadweight losses due to a tariff.

TRADE PROTECTIONISM INTENSIFIES AS GLOBAL ECONOMY FALLS INTO RECESSION

TABLE 4.6

CREEPING PROTECTIONISM DURING GLOBAL ECONOMIC DOWNTURN OF 2008–2009: NUMBER OF PROTECTIONIST MEASURES INITIATED*

NUMBER OF NATIONS THAT HAVE IMPOSED PROTECTIONIST MEASURES ON EACH COUNTRY

Targeted Country	Number of Nations Imposing Protectionist Measures
China	55
United States	49
Japan	46
Germany	29
France	29

NUMBER OF PROTECTIONIST MEASURES IMPOSED ON EACH CATEGORY OF PRODUCTS

Product Category	Number of Protectionist Measures
Machinery	44
Foods	22
Financial Services	21
Agricultural Goods	20
Grain and Starch Goods	19

*State aid funds, higher tariffs, immigration restrictions, export subsidies initiated during the period November 2008–September 2009
Source: From *Broken Promises: A G-20 Summit Report*, Global Economic Alert, London, UK, September 17, 2009.

trade and that the world auto price is $8,000. Because the world market will supply an unlimited number of autos at the price of $8,000, the world supply schedule would appear as a horizontal (perfectly elastic) line. Line S_{d+w} shows the supply of autos available to small-nation consumers from domestic and foreign sources combined. This overall supply schedule is the one that would prevail in free trade.

Free-trade equilibrium is located at point F in the figure. Here the number of autos demanded is 80, whereas the number produced domestically is 20. The import of 60 autos fulfills the excess domestic demand. Compared with the situation before trade occurred, free trade results in a fall in the domestic auto price from $9,500 to $8,000. Consumers are better off because they can import more autos at a lower price. However, domestic producers now sell fewer autos at a lower price than they did before trade.

Under free trade, the domestic auto industry is being damaged by foreign competition. Industry sales and revenues are falling, and workers are losing their jobs. Suppose management and labor unite and convince the government to levy a protective tariff on auto imports. Assume the small nation imposes a tariff of $1,000 on auto imports. Because this small nation is not important enough to influence world market

Global economic downturns are often a catalyst for trade protectionism. As economies shrink, nations have incentive to protect their struggling producers by establishing barriers against imported goods (see Table 4.6).

As the global economy fell deeper into recession during 2007–2009, there occurred a decrease in the demand for goods and services and thus a decline in international trade. The credit crunch provided an extra squeeze on trade due to a shortfall of some $100 billion in trade finance, which lubricates 90 percent of world trade. Just as notable as the substantial decrease in trade was its indiscriminate nature. Exports declined by 30 percent or more for countries as diverse as Indonesia, France, South Africa, and the Philippines.

Increasingly, domestic firms and workers worried about the harm that was inflicted on them by their foreign competitors who were seeking customers throughout the globe. China was the country targeted by the most governments for protectionist measures. Although leaders of the Group of 20 large economies unanimously pledged not to resort to protectionism in 2008 and 2009, virtually all of them slipped at least a little bit.

For example, Russia increased tariffs on imported automobiles, India raised tariffs on steel imports, and Argentina established new obstacles to imported auto parts and shoes. In the United States, steel companies prepared complaints against foreign steel being sold in the country at prices below cost of production. Also, American steel companies hoped that increased tariffs would prohibit foreign steel firms from increasing sales in portions of the approximately $100 billion U.S. steel market that were not protected by the "Buy American" legislation of President Barack Obama: The fiscal stimulus program signed by Obama in 2009 shut out foreign companies from U.S. government contracts, which represented about 25 percent of new steel orders in 2009. Moreover, in 2009 the United States imposed tariffs of between 25 percent and 35 percent on imports of tires from China for the next three years. This policy essentially priced out of the market 17 percent of all tires sold in the United States, and forced up the market price for consumers.

During the Great Depression of the 1930s, countries raised import tariffs to protect producers damaged by foreign competition. The United States, for example, increased import tariffs on some 20,000 goods which provoked widespread retaliation from its trading partners. Such tariff increases contributed to the volume of world trade shrinking by a quarter. A lesson from this era is that once trade barriers are increased, they can severely damage global supply chains. It can take years of negotiation to dismantle trade barriers and years before global supply chains can be restored.

conditions, the world supply price of autos remains constant, unaffected by the tariff. This lack of price change means that the small nation's terms of trade remains unchanged. The introduction of the tariff *raises the home price of imports by the full amount of the duty, and the increase falls entirely on the domestic consumer*. The overall supply shifts upward by the amount of the tariff, from S_{d+w} to S_{d+w+t}.

The protective tariff results in a new equilibrium quantity at point G, where the domestic auto price is $9,000. Domestic production increases by 20 units, whereas domestic consumption falls by 20 units. Imports decrease from their pretariff level of 60 units to 20 units. This reduction can be attributed to falling domestic consumption and rising domestic production. The effects of the tariff are to impede imports and protect domestic producers. But what are the tariff's effects on the *nation's welfare*?

Figure 4.3 shows that before the tariff was levied, *consumer surplus* equaled areas $a + b + c + d + e + f + g$. With the tariff, consumer surplus falls to areas $e + f + g$, an overall loss in consumer surplus equal to areas $a + b + c + d$. This change affects the nation's welfare in a number of ways. The welfare effects of a tariff include a revenue effect, a redistribution effect, a protective effect, and a consumption effect.

As might be expected, the tariff provides the government with additional tax revenue and benefits domestic auto producers; at however, the same time, it wastes resources and harms the domestic consumer.

The tariff's **revenue effect** represents the government's collections of duty. Found by multiplying the number of imports (20 units) times the tariff ($1,000), government revenue equals area *c*, or $20,000. This revenue represents the portion of the loss in consumer surplus, in monetary terms, that is transferred to the government. For the nation as a whole, the revenue effect does *not* result in an overall welfare loss; the consumer surplus is merely shifted from the private to the public sector.

The **redistributive effect** is the transfer of the consumer surplus, in monetary terms, to the domestic producers of the import-competing product. This is represented by area *a*, which equals $30,000. Under the tariff, domestic home consumers will buy from domestic firms 40 autos at a price of $9,000, for a total expenditure of $360,000. At the free-trade price of $8,000, the same 40 autos would have yielded $320,000. The imposition of the tariff thus results in home producers' receiving additional revenues totaling areas *a* + *b*, or $40,000 (the difference between $360,000 and $320,000). However, as the tariff encourages domestic production to rise from 20 to 40 units, producers must pay part of the increased revenue as higher costs of producing the increased output, depicted by area *b*, or $10,000. The remaining revenue, $30,000, area *a*, is a net gain in producer income. The redistributive effect, therefore, is a transfer of income from consumers to producers. Like the revenue effect, it does *not* result in an overall loss of welfare for the economy.

Area *b*, totaling $10,000, is referred to as the **protective effect** of the tariff. It illustrates the loss to the domestic economy resulting from wasted resources used to produce additional autos at increasing unit costs. As the tariff-induced domestic output expands, resources that are less adaptable to auto production are eventually used, increasing unit production costs. This increase means that resources are used less efficiently than they would have been with free trade, in which case autos would have been purchased from low-cost foreign producers. A tariff's protective effect thus arises because less efficient domestic production is substituted for more efficient foreign production. Referring to Figure 4.3, as domestic output increases from 20 to 40 units, the domestic cost of producing autos rises, as shown by supply schedule Sd. But the same increase in autos could have been obtained at a unit cost of $8,000 before the tariff was levied. Area *b*, which depicts the protective effect, represents a loss to the economy equal to $10,000. Notice that the calculation of the protection effect simply involves the calculation of the area of triangle *b*. Recall from geometry that the area of a triangle equals (base × height)/2. The height of triangle *b* equals the increase in price due to the tariff ($1,000); the triangle's base (20 autos) equals the increase in domestic auto production due to the tariff. The protection effect is thus (20 × $1,000)/2 = $10,000.

Most of the consumer surplus lost because of the tariff has been accounted for: *c* went to the government as revenue; *a* was transferred to home producers as income; and *b* was lost by the economy because of inefficient domestic production. The **consumption effect,** represented by area *d*, which equals $10,000, is the residual not accounted for elsewhere. It arises from the decrease in consumption resulting from the tariff's artificially increasing the price of autos from $8,000 to $9,000. A loss of welfare occurs because of the increased price and lower consumption. Notice that the calculation of the consumption effect involves the calculation of the area of triangle *d*. The height of the triangle ($1,000) equals the price increase in autos due to the tariff; the base (20 autos) equals the reduction in domestic consumption due to the tariff. The consumption effect is thus $(20 \times \$1,000)/2 = \$10,000$.

Like the protective effect, the consumption effect represents a real cost to society, not a transfer to other sectors of the economy. Together, these two effects equal the **deadweight loss** of the tariff (areas b + d in the figure).

As long as it is assumed that a nation accounts for a negligible portion of international trade, its levying an import tariff necessarily lowers its national welfare. This is because there is no favorable welfare effect resulting from the tariff that would offset the deadweight loss of the consumer surplus. If a nation could impose a tariff that would improve its terms of trade vis-à-vis its trading partners, it would enjoy a larger share of the gains from trade. This larger share would tend to increase its national welfare, offsetting the deadweight loss of the consumer surplus. However, because it is so insignificant relative to the world market, a small nation is unable to influence the terms of trade. Levying an import tariff, therefore, *reduces* a small nation's welfare.

Tariff Welfare Effects: Large-Nation Model

The support for free trade by economists may appear so pronounced that one might conclude that a tariff could never be beneficial. However, this is not necessarily true. A tariff may increase national welfare when it is imposed by an importing nation that is large enough so that changes in the quantity of its imports, by means of tariff policy, influence the world price of the product. This **large-nation** status applies to the United States, which is a large importer of autos, steel, oil, and consumer electronics, and to other economic giants such as Japan and the European Union.

If the United States imposes a tariff on automobile imports, prices increase for American consumers. The result is a decrease in the quantity demanded, which may be significant enough to force Japanese firms to reduce the prices of their exports. Because Japanese firms can produce and export smaller amounts at a lower marginal cost, they are likely to prefer to reduce their price to the United States to limit the decrease in their sales. The tariff's effect is thus shared between U.S. consumers, who pay a higher price than under free trade for each auto imported, and Japanese firms, who realize a lower price than under free trade for each auto exported. The difference between these two prices is the tariff duty. The welfare of the United States rises when it can shift some of the tariff to Japanese firms via export price reductions. The *terms of trade* improve for the United States at the expense of Japan.

Table 4.7 illustrates the extent to which U.S. import tariffs can reduce world prices of imported goods. For example, an 11 percent increase in the U.S. tariff on ball bearing imports would increase the price to the American consumer by an estimated 10.2 percent. This increased price leads to a decrease in the quantity of ball bearings demanded in the United States and an 0.8 percent decrease in the world price.

What are the economic effects of an import tariff for a large country? Referring to Figure 4.4, line Sd represents the domestic supply schedule, and line D_d depicts the home demand schedule. Autarky equilibrium occurs at point E. With free trade, the importing nation faces a total supply schedule of S_{d+w}. This schedule shows the number of autos that both domestic and foreign producers together offer domestic consumers. The total supply schedule is upward sloping rather than horizontal because the foreign supply price is not a fixed constant. The price depends on the quantity purchased by an importing country who is a large buyer of the product.

TABLE 4.7

EFFECTS OF INCREASES IN U.S. TARIFFS ON THE WORLD PRICE OF IMPORTED GOODS

Product	Tariff (or Equivalent)	Increase in U.S. Price	Decrease in World Price
Ball bearings	11.0%	10.2%	0.8%
Chemicals	9.0	6.5	2.5
Jewelry	9.0	5.4	3.6
Orange juice	30.0	21.7	8.3
Glassware	11.0	7.3	3.7
Luggage	16.5	11.0	5.5
Resins	12.0	5.4	6.6
Footwear	20.0	16.1	3.9
Lumber	6.5	4.1	2.4

Source: From G. Hufbauer and K. Elliot, *Measuring the Costs of Protection in the United States* Washington, DC: Institute for International Economics, 1994, pp. 28–29.

FIGURE 4.4

TARIFF TRADE AND WELFARE EFFECTS: LARGE NATION MODEL

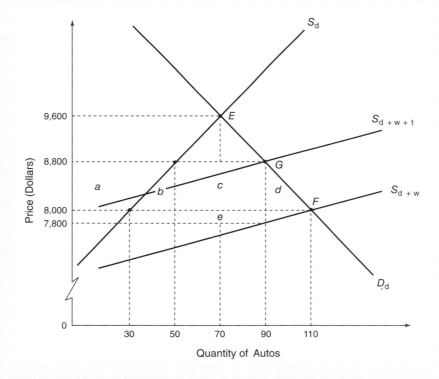

For a large nation, a tariff on an imported product may be partially shifted to the domestic consumer via a higher product price and partially absorbed by the foreign exporter via a lower export price. The extent by which a tariff is absorbed by the foreign exporter constitutes a welfare gain for the home country. This gain offsets some (all) of the deadweight welfare losses due to the tariff's consumption and protective effects.

With free trade, our country achieves market equilibrium at point *F*. The price of autos falls to $8,000, domestic consumption rises to 110 units, and domestic production falls to 30 units. Auto imports totaling 80 units satisfy the excess domestic demand.

Suppose that the importing nation imposes a specific tariff of $1,000 on imported autos. By increasing the selling cost, the tariff results in a shift in the total supply schedule from S_{d+w} to S_{d+w+t}. Market equilibrium shifts from point *F* to point *G*, while the product price rises from $8,000 to $8,800. The tariff-levying nation's consumer surplus falls by an amount equal to areas *a* + *b* + *c* + *d*. Area *a*, totaling $32,000, represents the *redistributive effect*; this amount is transferred from domestic consumers to domestic producers. Areas *d* + *b* depict the tariff's deadweight loss, the deterioration in national welfare because of reduced consumption (*consumption effect* = $8,000) and an inefficient use of resources (*protective effect* = $8,000).

As in the small nation example, a tariff's *revenue effect* equals the import tariff multiplied by the quantity of autos imported. This effect yields areas *c* + *e*, or $40,000. However, notice that the tariff revenue accruing to the government now comes from foreign producers as well as domestic consumers. This result differs from the small nation case in which the supply schedule is horizontal and the tariff's burden falls entirely on domestic consumers.

The tariff of $1,000 is added to the free-trade import price of $8,000. Although the price in the protected market will exceed the foreign supply price by the amount of the duty, it will *not* exceed the free-trade foreign supply price by this amount. Compared with the free-trade foreign supply price, $8,000, the domestic consumers pay only an additional $800 per imported auto. This is the portion of the tariff shifted to the consumer. At the same time, the foreign supply price of autos falls by $200. This means that foreign producers earn smaller revenues, $7,800, for each auto exported. Because foreign production takes place under increasing-cost conditions, the reduction of imports from abroad triggers a decline in foreign production, and unit costs decline. The reduction in the foreign supply price, $200, represents that portion of the tariff borne by the foreign producer. The levying of the tariff raises the domestic price of the import by only part of the duty as foreign producers lower their prices in an attempt to maintain sales in the tariff-levying nation. The importing nation finds that its terms of trade has improved if the price it pays for auto imports decreases while the price it charges for its exports remains the same.

Thus, the *revenue effect* of an import tariff in the large nation includes two components. The first is the amount of tariff revenue shifted from domestic consumers to the tariff-levying government; in Figure 4.4, this amount equals the level of imports (40 units) multiplied by the portion of the import tariff borne by domestic consumers ($800). Area *c* depicts the **domestic revenue effect**, which equals $32,000. The second element is the tariff revenue extracted from foreign producers in the form of a lower supply price. Found by multiplying auto imports (40 units) by the portion of the tariff falling on foreign producers ($200), the **terms-of-trade effect** is shown as area *e*, which equals $8,000. Note that the terms-of-trade effect represents a redistribution of income from the foreign nation to the tariff-levying nation because of the new terms of trade. The tariff's revenue effect thus includes the domestic revenue effect and the terms-of-trade effect.

A nation that is a major importer of a product is in a favorable trade situation. It can use its tariff policy to improve the terms at which it trades, and therefore its national welfare. But remember that the negative welfare effect of a tariff is the dead-weight loss of the consumer surplus that results from the protection and consumption effects. Referring to Figure 4.4, to decide if a tariff-levying nation can improve its national welfare, we must compare the impact of the deadweight loss (areas $b + d$) with the benefits of a more favorable terms of trade (area e). The conclusions regarding the welfare effects of a tariff are as follows:

1. If $e > (b + d)$, national welfare is increased.
2. If $e = (b + d)$, national welfare remains constant.
3. If $e > (b + d)$, national welfare is diminished.

In the preceding example, the domestic economy's welfare would decline by an amount equal to $8,000. This is because the deadweight welfare losses, totaling $16,000, more than offset the $8,000 gain in welfare attributable to the terms-of-trade effect.

The Optimum Tariff and Retaliation

We have seen that a large nation can improve its terms of trade by imposing a tariff on imports. However, a tariff causes the volume of imports to decrease, which lessens the nation's welfare by reducing its consumption of low-cost imports. There is thus a gain due to improved terms of trade and a loss due to reduced import volume.

Referring to Figure 4.4, a nation optimizes its economic welfare by imposing a tariff rate at which the positive difference between the gain of improving terms of trade (area e) and the loss in economic efficiency from the protective effect (area b) and the consumption effect (area d) is at a maximum. The **optimum tariff** refers to such a tariff rate. It makes sense that the lower the foreign elasticity of supply, the more the large country can get its trading partners to accept lower prices for the large country's imports.

A likely candidate for a nation imposing an optimum tariff would be the United States; it is a large importer, compared with world demand, of autos, electronics, and other products. Note, however, that an optimum tariff is only beneficial to the importing nation. Because any benefit accruing to the importing nation through a lower import price implies a loss to the foreign exporting nation, imposing an optimum tariff is a **beggar-thy-neighbor** policy that could invite retaliation. After all, if the United States were to impose an optimal tariff of 25 percent on its imports, why should Japan and the European Union not levy tariffs of 40 or 50 percent on their imports? When all countries impose optimal tariffs, it is likely that everyone's economic welfare will decrease as the volume of trade declines. The possibility of foreign retaliation may be a sufficient deterrent for any nation considering whether to impose higher tariffs.

A classic case of a tariff-induced trade war was the implementation of the Smoot-Hawley Tariff Act by the U.S. government in 1930. This tariff was initially intended to provide relief to U.S. farmers. However, senators and members of Congress from industrial states used the technique of vote trading to obtain increased tariffs on manufactured goods. The result was a policy that increased tariffs on more than a thousand products, with an average nominal duty on protected goods of 53 percent! Viewing the Smoot-Hawley tariff as an attempt to force unemployment on its workers, 12 nations promptly increased their duties against the United

GAINS FROM ELIMINATING IMPORT TARIFFS

TRADE CONFLICTS

TABLE 4.8

ECONOMIC WELFARE GAINS FROM LIBERALIZATION OF SIGNIFICANT IMPORT RESTRAINTS*, 2005 (MILLIONS OF DOLLARS)

Annual change in Economic Welfare	Import-Competing Industry
Textiles and apparel	$1,885 millions
Sugar	811
Dairy	573
Footwear	249
Ethyl alcohol	120
Beef	48
Tuna	24
Glass products	20
Tobacco	19

*Import tariffs, tariff-rate quotas, and import quotas

Source: From U.S. International Trade Commission, *The Economic Effects of Significant U.S. Import Restraints*, Washington, D.C.: Government Printing Office, February 2007.

What would be the effects if the United States unilaterally removed tariffs and other restraints on imported products? On the positive side, tariff elimination lowers the price of the affected imports and may lower the price of the competing U.S. good, resulting in economic gains to the U.S. consumer. Lower import prices also decrease the production costs of firms that buy less costly intermediate inputs, such as steel. On the negative side, the lower price to import-competing producers, as a result of eliminating the tariff, results in profit reductions; workers become

displaced from the domestic industry that loses protection; and the U.S. government loses tax revenue as the result of eliminating the tariff.

In 2007 the U.S. International Trade Commission estimated the annual economic welfare gains from eliminating significant import restraints from their 2005 levels. The result would have been equivalent to a welfare gain of about $3.7 billion to the U.S. economy. The largest welfare gain would come from liberalizing trade in textiles and apparel, as seen in Table 4.8.

States. American farm exports fell to one-third of their former level, and between 1930 and 1933 total U.S. exports fell by almost 60 percent. Although the Great Depression accounted for much of that decline, the adverse psychological impact of the Smoot-Hawley tariff on business activity cannot be ignored. For an analysis on tariff welfare effects using offer curves, go to *Exploring Further 4.1*.

How a Tariff Burdens Exporters

The benefits and costs of protecting domestic producers from foreign competition, as discussed earlier in this chapter, are based on the direct effects of an import tariff. Import-competing producers and workers can benefit from tariffs through increases in output, profits, jobs, and compensation. A tariff imposes costs on domestic consumers in the form of higher prices for protected products and reductions in the consumer surplus. There is also a net welfare loss for the economy because not all of the loss in the consumer surplus is transferred as gains to domestic producers and the government (the protective effect and consumption effects).

A tariff carries additional burdens. In protecting import-competing producers, a tariff leads indirectly to a reduction in domestic exports. The net result of protectionism is to move the economy toward greater self-sufficiency, with lower imports and exports. For domestic workers, the protection of jobs in import-competing producers comes at the expense of jobs in other sectors of the economy, including exports. Although a tariff is intended to help domestic producers, the economy-wide implications of a tariff are adverse for the export sector. The welfare losses due to restrictions in output and employment in the economy's export producers may offset the welfare gains enjoyed by import-competing producers.

Because a tariff is a tax on imports, the burden of a tariff falls initially on importers, who must pay duties to the domestic government. However, importers generally try to shift increased costs to buyers through price increases. The resulting higher prices of imports injure domestic exporters in at least three ways.

First, exporters often purchase imported inputs subject to tariffs that *increase the cost of inputs*. Because exporters tend to sell in competitive markets where they have little ability to dictate the prices they receive, they generally cannot pass on a tariff-induced increase in cost to their buyers. Higher export costs thus lead to higher prices and reduced overseas sales.

Consider the hypothetical case of Caterpillar Inc, a U.S. exporter of tractors. In Figure 4.5, suppose the firm realizes constant long-term costs, suggesting that marginal cost equals average cost at each level of output. Let the production cost of a tractor equal $100,000, denoted by $MC_0 = AC_0$. Caterpillar Inc. maximizes profits by producing 100 tractors, the point at which marginal revenue equals marginal cost, and selling them at a price of $110,000 per unit. The firm's revenue thus totals $11 million (100 × $110,000) while its costs total $10 million (100 × $100,000); as a result, the firm realizes profits of $1 million. Suppose now that the U.S. government levies a tariff on steel imports, while foreign nations allow steel to be imported duty-free. If the production of tractors uses imported steel, and competitively priced domestic steel is not available, the tariff leads to an increase in Caterpillar's costs to, say, $105,000 per tractor, as denoted by $MC_1 = AC_1$. Again the firm maximizes profits by operating where marginal revenue equals marginal cost. However, Caterpillar must charge a higher price, $112,500; the firm's sales thus decrease to 90 tractors and profits decrease to $675,000 [($112,500 − $105,000) × 90 = $675,000]. The import tariff applied to steel represents a tax on Caterpillar that reduces its international competitiveness. Protecting domestic steel producers from import competition can thus lessen the export competitiveness of domestic steel-using producers.

Tariffs also *raise the cost of living* by increasing the price of imports. Workers thus have the incentive to demand correspondingly higher wages, resulting in higher production costs. Tariffs lead to expanding output for import-competing producers that in turn bid for workers, causing wages to rise. As these higher wages pass through the economy, export producers ultimately face higher wages and production costs, which lessen their competitive position in international markets.

In addition, import tariffs have *international repercussions* that lead to reductions in domestic exports. Tariffs cause the quantity of imports to decrease, which

FIGURE 4.5

HOW AN IMPORT TARIFF BURDENS DOMESTIC EXPORTERS

A tariff placed on imported steel increases the costs of a steel-using manufacturer. This increase leads to a higher price charged by the manufacturer and a loss of international competitiveness.

in turn decreases other nations' export revenues and ability to import. The decline in foreign export revenues results in a smaller demand for a nation's exports and leads to falling output and employment in its export industries.

If domestic export producers are damaged by import tariffs, why don't they protest such policies more vigorously? One problem is that tariff-induced increases in costs for export producers are subtle and invisible. Many exporters may not be aware of their existence. Also, the tariff-induced cost increases may be of such magnitude that some potential export producers are incapable of developing and have no tangible basis for political resistance.

U.S. steel-using companies provide an example of exporters opposing tariffs on imported steel. Their officials contend that restrictions on steel imports are harmful to U.S. steel-using industries that employ about 13 million workers compared to less than 200,000 workers employed by American steel producers. In the global economy, U.S. steel users must compete with efficient foreign manufacturers of all types of consumer and industrial installations, machines, and conveyances—everything from automobiles and earth-moving equipment to nuts and bolts. Forcing U.S. manufacturers to pay considerably more for steel inputs than their foreign competitors would deal U.S. manufacturers a triple blow: increase raw material costs, threaten access to steel products not manufactured in the United States, and increase competition from abroad for the products they make. It would simply send our business offshore, devastating U.S. steel-using companies, most of them small businesses.[6]

Steel Tariffs Buy Time for Troubled Industry

In 1950, U.S. steelmakers dominated the world market. Accounting for half of global steel output, they produced almost 20 times as much steel as Japan and more steel than all of Europe combined. However, the market dominance of U.S. steelmakers gradually declined as they became complacent and insensitive to changing market conditions. By 2000, foreign steelmakers had made significant inroads into the American market, turning the United States into a net importer of steel. As sales and profits of U.S. steel mills declined, thousands of American steelworkers lost their jobs.

In response to pressure from U.S. steelmakers, in 2001 President Bush enacted an import tariff program intended to revitalize the industry. During the first year of the program, 30 percent tariffs were imposed on imported steel that competed with the main products of most of the big American mills. Other steel products faced tariffs from 15 to 8 percent, as seen in Table 4.9. These tariffs were followed by reductions in them during the second year of the program. In return for granting steelmakers protection from imports, President Bush insisted that they bring their labor costs down and upgrade equipment.

Critics of the steel tariffs argued that the American steel companies suffered from a lack of competitiveness due to previous poor investment decisions, diversion of funds into non-steel businesses, and a reduction of investment during previous periods of import protection. They also noted that protecting steel would place a heavy burden on American steel-using industries such as automobiles and earth-moving equipment. Although the tariffs would temporarily save roughly 6,000 jobs, the cost of saving these jobs to U.S. consumers and steel-using firms was between $800,000 and $1.1 million per job. Moreover, the steel tariffs would cost as many as 13 jobs in steel-using industries for every one steel manufacturing job protected.[7]

The Bush tariffs did provide some relief to U.S. steelmakers from imports. Also, some cost-cutting occurred among steelmakers during 2002–2003: producers merged and labor contracts were renegotiated, though often at considerable cost to the approximately 150,000 workers still employed the industry. However, the tariffs aroused heavy opposition among a large number of U.S. companies that use steel. In numerous lobbying trips to Washington, chief

TABLE 4.9

PRESIDENT BUSH'S STEEL TRADE REMEDY PROGRAM OF 2002–2003: SELECTED PRODUCTS

Products	TARIFF RATES	
	Year 1	Year 2
Semi-finished slab	30%	24%
Cold-rolled sheet, coated sheet	30%	24%
Hot-rolled bar	30%	24%
Cold-finished bar	30%	24%
Rebar	15%	12%
Welded tubular products	15%	12%
Carbon and alloy flanges	13%	10%
Stainless steel bar	15%	12%

Source: From President of the United States, *Message to Congress* (House Doc. 107–185), March 6, 2002.

---

[6]U.S. Senate Finance Committee, *Testimony of John Jenson*, February 13, 2002.

[7]Robert W. Crandall, *The Futility of Steel Trade Protection*, Criterion Economics, 2002. See also U.S. International Trade Commission, *Steel-Consuming Industries: Competitive Conditions With Respect to Steel Safeguard Measures*, September 2003.

executives of these firms noted that the tariffs drove up their costs and imperiled more jobs across the manufacturing belt than they saved in the steel industry.

By 2007, the U.S. steel industry was strong and profitable. Yet import tariffs still remained on steel, other than the tariffs imposed by Bush during 2002–2003. This time, a new tilt occurred in the balance of political power between steel producers and steel-using industries. Government trade regulators voted to revoke tariffs on high-end steel imports from certain countries. They were especially influenced by the argument of U.S. auto makers that elimination of the tariffs would inject more competition into the steel industry and help reduce the cost of a key raw material for the auto industry at a time when domestic automakers were under financial stress. The case brought together rival U.S. and Japanese automakers—General Motors, Ford, and Chrysler joined forces with Toyota, Honda, and Nissan—to present a united front in their opposition to high steel tariffs.

Tariffs and the Poor

Empirical studies often maintain that the welfare costs of tariffs can be high. Tariffs also affect the distribution of income within a society. A legitimate concern of government officials is whether the welfare costs of tariffs are shared uniformly by all people in a country, or whether some income groups absorb a disproportionate share of the costs.

Several studies have considered the income-distribution effects of import tariffs. They conclude that tariffs tend to be inequitable because they impose the most severe costs on *low-income families*. Tariffs, for example, are often applied to products at the lower end of the price and quality range. Basic products such as shoes and clothing are subject to tariffs, and these items constitute a large share of the budgets of low-income families. Tariffs thus can be likened to sales taxes on the products protected, and, as typically occurs with sales taxes, their effects are *regressive*. Simply put, U.S. tariff policy is tough on the poor: young single mothers purchasing cheap clothes and shoes at Wal-Mart often pay tariff rates five to ten times higher than rich families pay when purchasing at elite stores such as Nordstrom.[8] International trade agreements have eliminated most U.S. tariffs on high-technology products like airplanes, semiconductors, computers, medical equipment, and medicines. The agreements have also reduced rates to generally less than five percent on mid-range manufactured products like autos, TV sets, pianos, felt-tip pens, and many luxury consumer goods. Moreover, tariffs on natural resources such as oil, metal ores, and farm products like chocolate and coffee that are not grown in the United States are generally close to zero. However, inexpensive clothes, luggage, shoes, watches, and silverware have been excluded from most tariff reforms, and thus tariffs remain relatively high. Clothing tariffs, for example, are usually in the 10 to 32 percent range.

Tariffs vary from one consumer good to the next. They are much higher on cheap goods than on luxuries. This disparity occurs because elite firms such as

---

[8]Edward Gresser, "Toughest on the Poor: America's Flawed Tariff System," *Foreign Affairs*, November-December, 2002, pp. 19–23 and Susan Hickok, "The Consumer Cost of U.S. Trade Restraints," Federal Reserve Bank of New York, *Quarterly Review*, Summer 1985, pp. 10–11.

TABLE 4.10

U.S. Tariffs are High on Cheap Goods, Low on Luxuries

Product	Tariff Rate (percent)
Women's Underwear	
Man-made fiber	16.2
Cotton	11.3
Silk	2.4
Men's knitted shirts	
Synthetic fiber	32.5
Cotton	20.0
Silk	1.9
Drinking glasses	
30 cents or less	30.4
$5 or more	5.0
Leaded glass	3.0
Handbags	
Plastic-sided	16.8
Leather, under $20	10.0
Reptile leather	5.3

Source: From U.S. International Trade Commission, *Tariff Schedules of the United States*, Washington, DC: Government Printing Office, 2008, available at **http://www.usitc.gov/taffairs.htm**.

Ralph Lauren, Coach, or Oakley, which sell brand name and image, find small price advantages relatively unimportant. Because they have not lobbied the U.S. government for high tariffs, rates on luxury goods such as silk lingerie, silver-handled cutlery, leaded-glass beer mugs, and snakeskin handbags are very low. But producers of cheap water glasses, stainless steel cutlery, nylon lingerie, and plastic purses benefit by adding a few percentage points to their competitors' prices. So on the cheapest goods, tariffs are even higher than the overall averages for consumer goods suggest, as seen in Table 4.10. Simply put, U.S. tariffs are highest on goods that are the most important to the poor. The U.S. tariff system is not unique in being toughest on the poor. The tariffs of most U.S. trade partners operate in a similar fashion.

Besides bearing down hard on the poor, U.S. tariff policy affects different countries in different ways. It especially burdens countries that specialize in the cheapest goods, noticeably very poor countries in Asia and the Middle East. For example, average tariffs on European exports to the United States—mainly autos, computers, power equipment, and chemicals—today barely exceed one percent. Developing countries such as Malaysia, which specializes in information-technology goods, face tariff rates just as low. So do oil exporters such as Saudi Arabia and Nigeria. However, Asian countries like Cambodia and Bangladesh are hit hardest by U.S. tariffs; their cheap consumer goods often face tariff rates of 15 percent or more, some ten times the world average.

Arguments for Trade Restrictions

The **free-trade argument** is, in principle, persuasive. It states that if each nation produces what it does best and permits trade, in the long term all will enjoy lower prices and higher levels of output, income, and consumption than could be achieved in isolation. In a dynamic world, comparative advantage is constantly changing due to shifts in technologies, input productivities, and wages, as well as demand. A free market compels adjustment to take place. Either the efficiency of an industry must improve, or else resources will flow from low-productivity uses to those with high productivity. Tariffs and other trade barriers are viewed as tools that prevent the economy from undergoing adjustment, resulting in economic stagnation.

Although the free-trade argument tends to dominate in the classroom, virtually all nations have imposed restrictions on the international flow of goods, services, and capital. Often, proponents of protectionism say that free trade is fine in theory, but it does not apply in the real world. Modern trade theory assumes perfectly competitive markets whose characteristics do not reflect real-world market conditions. Moreover, even though protectionists may concede that economic losses occur with tariffs and other restrictions, they often argue that noneconomic benefits such as national security more than offset the economic losses. In seeking protection from imports, domestic industries and labor unions attempt to secure their economic welfare. Over the years, many arguments have been advanced to pressure the president and Congress to enact restrictive measures.

Job Protection

The issue of jobs has been a dominant factor in motivating government officials to levy trade restrictions on imported goods. During periods of economic recession, workers are especially eager to point out that cheap foreign goods undercut domestic production, resulting in a loss of domestic jobs to foreign labor. Alleged job losses to foreign competition historically have been a major force behind the desire of most U.S. labor leaders to reject free-trade policies.

However, this view has a serious omission: It fails to acknowledge the dual nature of international trade. Changes in a nation's imports of goods and services are closely related to changes in its exports. Nations export goods because they desire to import products from other nations. When the United States imports goods from abroad, foreigners gain purchasing power that will eventually be spent on U.S. goods, services, or financial assets. American export industries then enjoy gains in sales and employment, whereas the opposite occurs with U.S. import-competing producers. Rather than promoting overall unemployment, imports tend to generate job opportunities in some industries as part of the process by which they decrease employment in other industries. However, the job gains due to open trade policies tend to be less visible to the public than the readily observable job losses stemming from foreign competition. The more conspicuous losses have led many U.S. business and labor leaders to combine forces in their opposition to free trade.

Trade restraints raise employment in the protected industry (such as steel) by increasing the price (or reducing the supply) of competing import goods. Industries that are primary suppliers of inputs to the protected industry also gain jobs. However, industries that purchase the protected product (such as auto manufacturers) face higher costs. These costs are then passed on to the consumer through higher prices, resulting in decreased sales. Therefore, employment falls in these related industries.

Economists at the Federal Reserve Bank of Dallas have examined the effects on U.S. employment of trade restrictions on textiles and apparel, steel, and automobiles. They conclude that trade protection has little or no positive effect on the level of employment in the long run. Trade restraints tend to provide job gains for only a few industries, while they result in job losses spread across many industries.[9]

A striking fact about efforts to preserve jobs is that each job often ends up costing domestic consumers more than the worker's salary! In 1986, the annual consumer cost of protecting each job preserved in the specialty steel industry in the United States was reported to be $1 million a year; this was far above the salary a production employee in that industry receives. The fact that costs to consumers for each production job saved are so high supports the argument that an alternative approach should be used to help workers, and that workers departing from an

---

[9]Linda Hunter, "U.S. Trade Protection: Effects on the Industrial and Regional Composition of Employment," Federal Reserve Bank of Dallas, *Economic Review*, January 1990, pp. 1–13.

TABLE 4.11

HOURLY COMPENSATION COSTS IN U.S. DOLLARS FOR PRODUCTION WORKERS IN MANUFACTURING, 2007

Country	Hourly Compensation (dollars per hour)
Canada	31.91
United States	30.56
Japan	23.95
South Korea	18.30
Czech Republic	9.67
Taiwan	8.15
Brazil	7.13
Mexico	3.91

Source: From U.S. Department of Labor, Bureau of Labor Statistics, *International Comparisons of Hourly Compensation Costs in Manufacturing, 2007* available at **http://www.bls.gov**.

industry facing foreign competition should be liberally compensated (subsidized) for moving to new industries or taking early retirement.[10]

Protection Against Cheap Foreign Labor

One of the most common arguments used to justify the protectionist umbrella of trade restrictions is that tariffs are needed to defend domestic jobs against cheap foreign labor. As indicated in Table 4.11, production workers in Canada and the United States have been paid much higher wages, in terms of the U.S. dollar, than workers in countries such as Brazil and Mexico. So it could be argued that low wages abroad make it difficult for U.S. producers to compete with producers using cheap foreign labor and that unless U.S. producers are protected from imports, domestic output and employment levels will decrease.

Indeed, it is widely believed that competition from goods produced in low-wage countries is unfair and harmful to American workers. Moreover, it is thought that companies that produce goods in foreign countries to take advantage of cheap labor should not be allowed to dictate the wages paid to American workers. A solution: Impose a tariff or tax on goods brought into the United States equal to the wage differential between foreign and U.S. workers in the same industry. That way, competition would be confined to who makes the best product, not who works for the least amount of money. Therefore, if Calvin Klein wants to manufacture sweatshirts in Pakistan, his firm would be charged a tariff or tax equal to the difference between the earnings of a Pakistani worker and a U.S. apparel worker.

Although this viewpoint may have widespread appeal, it fails to recognize the links among efficiency, wages, and production costs. Even if domestic wages are higher than those abroad, if domestic labor is more productive than foreign labor, domestic labor costs may still be competitive. Total labor costs reflect not only the wage rate but also the output per labor hour. If the productive superiority of domestic labor more than offsets the higher domestic wage rate, the home nation's labor costs will actually be less than they are abroad.

Table 4.12 shows labor productivity (output per worker), wages, and unit labor costs in manufacturing, relative to the United States, for several nations in 2002. We see that wages in these nations were only fractions of U.S. wages; however, labor productivity levels in these nations were also fractions of U.S. labor productivity. Even if wages in a foreign country are lower than in the United States, the country would have higher unit labor costs if its labor productivity is sufficiently lower than U.S. labor productivity. This was the case for Hong Kong, Poland, the United Kingdom, Norway, Hungary, and Denmark where the unit labor cost ratio (unit labor

---

[10]Other examples of the annual cost of import restrictions per job saved to the American consumer include: bolts and nuts, $550,000; motorcycles, $150,000; mushrooms, $117,000; automobiles, $105,000; and footwear, $55,000. See Gary Hufbauer, et. al. *Trade Protection in the United States: 31 Case Studies*, Washington, D.C: Institute for International Economics, 1986.

TABLE 4.12

PRODUCTIVITY, WAGES, AND UNIT LABOR COSTS, RELATIVE TO THE UNITED STATES:
TOTAL MANUFACTURING, 2002 (UNITED STATES = 1.0)

Country	Labor Productivity Relative to United States	Wages Relative to United States*	Unit Labor Cost Relative to United States	
Hong Kong	0.25	0.57	2.28	
Poland	0.08	0.13	1.63	
United Kingdom	0.56	0.82	1.46	
Norway	0.57	0.82	1.44	
Hungary	0.07	0.10	1.43	U.S. More Competitive
Denmark	0.60	0.69	1.15	
Japan	0.89	0.79	0.89	U.S. Less Competitive
Mexico	0.27	0.21	0.78	
India	0.05	0.03	0.60	
South Korea	0.66	0.39	0.59	
China	0.09	0.03	0.33	

*At market exchange rate.

Source: The author wishes to thank Professor Steven Golub of Swarthmore College, who provided data for this table. Also, refer to his publications, *Labor Cost and International Trade*, American Enterprise Institute, Washington, D.C., 1999 and "Comparative and Absolute Advantage in the Asia-Pacific Region," *Pacific Basin Working Paper Series*, Federal Reserve Bank of San Francisco, October 1995. See also J. Ceglowski and S. Golub, "Just How Low are China's Labor Costs?" The *World Economy*, April 2007.

cost ratio = wage ratio/labor productivity ratio) was greater than 1.0. These nations' unit labor costs exceeded those of the United States because the productivity gap of their workers exceeded the wage gap. Simply put, low wages by themselves do not guarantee low production costs.

Another limitation of the cheap-foreign-labor argument is that low-wage nations tend to have a competitive advantage only in the production of goods requiring greater labor and little of the other factor inputs—that is, only when the wage bill is the largest component of the total costs of production. It is true that a high-wage nation may have a relative cost disadvantage compared with its low-wage trading partner in the production of labor-intensive commodities. But this does not mean that foreign producers can undersell the home country across the board in all lines of production, causing the overall domestic standard of living to decline. Foreign nations should use the revenues from their export sales to purchase the products in which the home country has a competitive advantage—products requiring a large share of the factors of production that are abundant domestically.

Recall that the factor-endowment theory suggests that as economies become interdependent through trade, resource payments tend to become equal in different nations, given competitive markets. A nation with expensive labor will tend to import products embodying large amounts of labor. As imports rise and domestic output falls, the resulting decrease in demand for domestic labor will cause domestic wages to fall to the foreign level.

Fairness in Trade: A Level Playing Field

Fairness in trade is another reason given for protectionism. Business firms and workers often argue that foreign governments play by a different set of rules than the home government, giving foreign firms unfair competitive advantages. Domestic producers contend that import restrictions should be enacted to offset these foreign advantages, thus creating a **level playing field** on which all producers can compete on equal terms.

American companies often allege that foreign firms are not subject to the same government regulations regarding pollution control and worker safety; this is especially true in many developing nations (such as Mexico and South Korea), where environmental laws and enforcement have been lax. Moreover, foreign firms may not pay as much in corporate taxes and may not have to comply with employment regulations such as affirmative action, minimum wages, and overtime pay. Also, foreign governments may erect high trade barriers that effectively close their markets to imports, or they may subsidize their producers so as to enhance their competitiveness in world markets.

These fair-trade arguments are often voiced by organized lobbies that are losing sales to foreign competitors. They may sound appealing to the voters because they are couched in terms of fair play and equal treatment. However, there are several arguments against levying restrictions on imports from nations that have high trade restrictions or that place lower regulatory burdens on their producers.

First, trade benefits the domestic economy even if foreign nations impose trade restrictions. Although foreign restrictions that lessen our exports may decrease our welfare, retaliating by levying our own import barriers—which protect inefficient domestic producers—decreases our welfare even more.

Second, the argument does not recognize the potential impact on global trade. If each nation were to increase trade restrictions whenever foreign restrictions were higher than domestic restrictions, a worldwide escalation in restrictions would occur; this would lead to a lower volume of trade, falling levels of production and employment, and a decline in welfare. There may be a case for threatening to levy trade restrictions unless foreign nations reduce their restrictions; but if negotiations fail and domestic restrictions are employed, the result is undesirable. Other countries' trade practices are seldom an adequate justification for domestic trade restrictions.

Maintenance of the Domestic Standard of Living

Advocates of trade barriers often contend that tariffs are useful in maintaining a high level of income and employment for the home nation. It is argued that by reducing the level of imports, tariffs encourage home spending, which stimulates domestic economic activity. As a result, the home nation's level of employment and income will be enhanced.

Although this argument appears appealing on the surface, it merits several qualifications. All nations together cannot levy tariffs to bolster domestic living standards. This is because tariffs result in a redistribution of the gains from trade among nations. To the degree that one nation imposes a tariff that improves its income and employment, it does so at the expense of its trading partner's living standard. Nations adversely affected by trade barriers are likely to impose retaliatory tariffs, resulting in a lower level of welfare for all nations. It is little wonder that tariff restrictions designed to enhance a nation's standard of living at the expense of its trading partner are referred to as *beggar-thy-neighbor* policies.

Equalization of Production Costs

Proponents of a **scientific tariff** seek to eliminate what they consider to be unfair competition from abroad. Owing to such factors as lower wage costs, tax concessions, or government subsidies, foreign sellers may enjoy cost advantages over domestic firms. To offset any such advantage, tariffs equivalent to the cost differential should be imposed. Such provisions were actually part of the U.S. Tariff Acts of 1922 and 1930.

In practice, the scientific tariff suffers from a number of problems. Because costs differ from business to business within a given industry, how can costs actually be compared? Suppose that all U.S. steelmakers were extended protection from all foreign steelmakers. This protection would require the costs of the most efficient foreign producer to be set equal to the highest costs of the least efficient U.S. company. Given today's cost conditions, prices would certainly rise in the United States. This rise would benefit the more efficient U.S. companies, which would enjoy economic profits, but the U.S. consumer would be subsidizing inefficient production. Because the scientific tariff approximates a prohibitive tariff, it completely contradicts the notion of comparative advantage and wipes out the basis for trade and gains from trade.

Infant-Industry Argument

One of the more commonly accepted cases for tariff protection is the **infant-industry argument**. This argument does not deny the validity of the case for free trade. However, it contends that for free trade to be meaningful, trading nations should temporarily shield their newly developing industries from foreign competition. Otherwise, mature foreign businesses, which are at the time more efficient, can drive the young domestic businesses out of the market. Only after the young companies have had time to become efficient producers should the tariff barriers be lifted and free trade take place.

Although there is some truth in the infant-industry argument, it must be qualified in several respects. First, once a protective tariff is imposed, it is very difficult to remove, even after industrial maturity has been achieved. Special-interest groups can often convince policy makers that further protection is justified. Second, it is very difficult to determine which industries will be capable of realizing comparative-advantage potential and thus merit protection. Third, the infant-industry argument generally is not valid for mature, industrialized nations such as the United States, Germany, and Japan. Fourth, there may be other ways of insulating a developing industry from cutthroat competition. Rather than adopt a protective tariff, the government could grant a subsidy to the industry. A subsidy has the advantage of not distorting domestic consumption and relative prices; its drawback is that instead of generating revenue, as an import tariff does, a subsidy spends revenue.

Noneconomic Arguments

Noneconomic considerations also enter into the arguments for protectionism. One such consideration is *national security*. The national-security argument contends that a country may be put in jeopardy in the event of an international crisis or war if it is heavily dependent on foreign suppliers. Even though domestic producers are not as efficient, tariff protection should be granted to ensure their continued existence. A good application of this argument involves the major oil-importing nations, which saw several Arab nations impose oil boycotts on the West to win support for the Arab position against Israel during the 1973 Middle East conflict. However, the problem is stipulating what constitutes an essential industry. If the term is defined broadly, many industries may be able to win import protection, and then the argument loses its meaning.

The national security argument for protectionism also has implications for foreign investments, such as foreign acquisitions of American companies and assets. Although the United States has traditionally welcomed foreign investment, it provides authority to the president to suspend or prohibit any foreign acquisition, merger, or takeover of a U.S. corporation determined to threaten the national security of the United States. Examples of actions generally considered harmful to the security of the United States include the denial of critical technology or key products to the U.S. government or U.S. industry, moving critical technology or key products offshore that are important for national defense or homeland security, and shutting down or sabotaging a critical facility in the United States. Therefore, the U.S. government reviews foreign investment transactions beyond the defense industrial base, including energy and natural resources, technology, telecommunications, transportation, and manufacturing. Such reviews have become more stringent since the September 11, 2001, terrorist attack against the United States.[11]

Another noneconomic argument is based on *cultural* and *sociological* considerations. New England may desire to preserve small-scale fishing; West Virginia may argue for tariffs on hand-blown glassware, on the grounds that these skills enrich the fabric of life; certain products such as narcotics may be considered socially undesirable, and restrictions or prohibitions may be placed on their importation. These arguments constitute legitimate reasons and cannot be ignored. All the economist can do is point out the economic consequences and costs of protection and identify alternative ways of accomplishing the same objective.

In Canada, many nationalists maintain that Canadian culture is too fragile to survive without government protection. The big threat: U.S. cultural imperialism. To keep the Yanks in check, Canada has long maintained some restrictions on sales of U.S. publications and textbooks. By the 1990s, the envelope of Canada's cultural protectionism was expanding. The most blatant example was a 1994 law that levied an 80 percent tax on Canadian ads in Canadian editions of U.S. magazines—in effect, an effort to kill off the U.S. intruders. Without protections for the Canadian media, the cultural nationalists feared that U.S. magazines such as *Sports Illustrated*, *Time*, and *Business Week* could soon deprive Canadians of the ability to read about themselves in *Maclean's* and *Canadian Business*. Although U.S. protests of the tax ultimately led to its abolishment, the Canadian government continued to examine other methods of preserving the culture of its people.

It is important to note that most of the arguments justifying tariffs are based on the assumption that the national welfare, as well as the individual's welfare, will be enhanced. The strategic importance of tariffs for the welfare of import-competing producers is one of the main reasons that reciprocal tariff liberalization has been so gradual. It is no wonder that import-competing producers make such strong

---

[11]Edward Graham and David Marchick, *U.S. National Security and Foreign Direct Investment*, Washington, D.C.: Institute for International Economics, 2006.

PETITION OF THE CANDLE MAKERS   TRADE CONFLICTS

Free-trade advocate Frederic Bastiat presented the French Chamber of Deputies with a devastating satire of protectionists' arguments in 1845. His petition asked that a law be passed requiring people to shut all windows, doors, and so forth so that the candle industry would be protected from the "unfair" competition of the sun. He argued that this would be a great benefit to the candle industry, creating many new jobs and enriching suppliers. Consider the following excerpts from his satire:

We are subjected to the intolerable competition of a foreign rival, who enjoys, it would seem, such superior facilities for the production of light, that he is flooding the domestic market with it at an incredibly low price. From the moment he appears, our sales cease, all consumers turn to him, and a branch of French industry whose ramifications are innumerable is at once reduced to complete stagnation. This rival is no other than the sun.

We ask you to be so good as to pass a law requiring the closing of all windows, dormers, skylights, shutters, curtains, and blinds—in short, all openings, holes, chinks, and fissures through which the light of the sun is wont to enter houses, to the detriment of our industries.

By shutting out as much as possible all access to natural light, you create the necessity for artificial light. Is there in France an industry which will not, through some connection with this important object, be benefited by it? If more tallow be consumed, there will arise a necessity for an increase of cattle and sheep. If more oil be consumed, it will cause an increase in the cultivation of the olive tree. Navigation will profit as thousands of vessels would be employed in the whale fisheries. There is, in short, no market which would not be greatly developed by the granting of our petitions.

Although it is undoubtedly true that the French candle industry would benefit from a lack of sunlight, consumers would obviously not be happy about being forced to pay for light that they could get for free were there no government intervention.

Sources: Frederic Bastiat, *Economic Sophisms*, edited and translated by Arthur Goddard, New York, D. Van Nostrand, 1964.

and politically effective arguments that increased foreign competition will undermine the welfare of the nation as a whole as well as their own. Although a liberalization of tariff barriers may be detrimental to a particular group, we must be careful to differentiate between the individual's welfare and the national welfare. If tariff reductions result in greater welfare gains from trade and if the adversely affected party can be compensated for the loss it has faced, the overall national welfare will increase. However, proving that the gains more than offset the losses in practice is very difficult.

The Political Economy of Protectionism

Recent history indicates that increasing dependence on international trade yields uneven impacts across domestic sectors. The United States has enjoyed comparative advantages in such products as agricultural commodities, industrial machinery, chemicals, and scientific instruments. However, some of its industries have lost their comparative advantage and suffered from international trade—among them are apparel and textiles, motor vehicles, electronic goods, basic iron and steel, and footwear. Formulating international trade policy in this environment is difficult. Free trade can yield substantial benefits for the overall economy through increased productivity and lower prices, but specific groups may benefit if government provides them some relief from import competition. Government officials must consider these opposing interests when setting the course for international trade policy.

Considerable attention has been devoted to what motivates government officials when formulating trade policy. As voters, we do not have the opportunity to go to the polls and vote for a trade bill. Instead, formation of trade policy rests in the hands of elected officials and their appointees. It is generally assumed that elected officials form policies to maximize votes and thus remain in office. The result is a bias in the political system that favors protectionism.

The **protection-biased sector** of the economy generally consists of import-competing producers, labor unions representing workers in that industry, and suppliers to the producers in the industry. Seekers of protectionism are often established firms in an aging industry that have lost their comparative advantage. High costs may be due to lack of modern technology, inefficient management procedures, outmoded work rules, or high payments to domestic workers. The **free-trade-biased sector** generally comprises exporting producers, their workers, and their suppliers. It also consists of consumers, including wholesalers and retail merchants of imported goods.

Government officials understand that they will likely lose the political support of, say, the United Auto Workers (UAW) if they vote against increases in tariffs on auto imports. They also understand that their vote on this trade issue will not be the key factor underlying the political support provided by many other citizens. Their support can be retained by appealing to them on other issues while voting to increase the tariff on auto imports to maintain UAW support.

The United States' protection policy is thus dominated by special-interest groups that represent producers. Consumers generally are not organized, and their losses due to protectionism are widely dispersed, whereas the gains from protection are concentrated among well-organized producers and labor unions in the affected sectors. Those harmed by a protectionist policy absorb individually a small and difficult-to-identify cost. Many consumers, though they will pay a higher price for the protected product, do not associate the higher price with the protectionist policy and thus are unlikely to be concerned about trade policy. However, special-interest groups are highly concerned about protecting their industries against import competition. They provide support for government officials who share their views and lobby against the election of those who do not. Clearly, government officials seeking reelection will be sensitive to the special-interest groups representing producers.

The political bias favoring domestic producers is seen in the tariff escalation effect, discussed earlier in this chapter. Recall that the tariff structures of industrial nations often result in lower import tariffs on intermediate goods and higher tariffs on finished goods. For example, U.S. imports of cotton yarn have traditionally faced low tariffs, while higher tariffs have been applied to cotton fabric imports. The higher tariff on cotton fabrics appears to be the result of the ineffective lobbying efforts of diffused consumers, who lose to organized U.S. fabric producers lobbying for protectionism. But for cotton yarn, the protectionist outcome is less clear. Purchasers of cotton yarn are U.S. manufacturers who want low tariffs on imported inputs. These companies form trade associations and can pressure Congress for low tariffs as effectively as U.S. cotton suppliers, who lobby for high tariffs. Protection applied to imported intermediate goods, such as cotton yarn, is then less likely.

Not only does the interest of the domestic producer tend to outweigh that of the domestic consumer in trade policy deliberations, but import-competing producers also tend to exert stronger influence on legislators than do export producers. A problem faced by export producers is that their gains from international trade are often in addition to their prosperity in the domestic market; producers that are efficient enough to sell overseas are often safe from foreign competition in the domestic market. Most deliberations on trade policy emphasize protecting imports, and the indirect damage done by import barriers to export producers tends to be spread over many export industries. But import-competing producers can gather evidence of immediate damage caused by foreign competition, including falling levels of sales, profits, and employment. Legislators tend to be influenced by the more clearly identified arguments of import-competing producers and see that a greater number of votes are at stake among their constituents than among the constituents of the export producers.

A Supply and Demand View of Protectionism

The political economy of import protection can be analyzed in terms of supply and demand. Protectionism is supplied by the domestic government, while domestic companies and workers are the source of demand. The supply of protection depends on (1) the costs to society, (2) the political importance of import-competing producers, (3) adjustment costs, and (4) public sympathy.

Enlightened government officials realize that although protectionism provides benefits to domestic producers, society as a whole pays the *costs*. These costs include the losses of consumer surplus because of higher prices and the resulting deadweight losses as import volume is reduced, lost economies of scale as opportunities for further trade are foregone, and the loss of incentive for technological development provided by import competition. The higher the costs of protection to society, the less likely it is that government officials will shield an industry from import competition.

The supply of protectionism is also influenced by the *political importance* of the import-competing industry. An industry that enjoys strong representation in the legislature is in a favorable position to win import protection. It is more difficult for politicians to disagree with 1 million autoworkers than with 20,000 copper workers. The national security argument for protection is a variant on the consideration of the political importance of an industry. For example, the U.S. coal and oil industries were successful in obtaining a national-security clause in U.S. trade law permitting protection if imports threaten to impair domestic security.

The supply of protection also tends to increase when domestic producers and workers face large costs of adjusting to rising import competition (for example, unemployment or wage concessions). This protection is seen as a method of delaying the full burden of *adjustment*.

Also, as *public sympathy* for a group of domestic producers or workers increases (for example, if workers are paid low wages and have few alternative work skills), a greater amount of protection against foreign-produced goods tends to be supplied.

On the demand side, factors that underlie the domestic industry's demand for protectionism are (1) comparative disadvantage, (2) import penetration, (3) concentration, and (4) export dependence.

The demand for protection rises as the domestic industry's *comparative disadvantage* intensifies. This is seen in the U.S. steel industry, which has vigorously pursued protection against low-cost Japanese and South Korean steel manufacturers in recent decades.

Higher levels of *import penetration*, which suggests increased competitive pressures for domestic producers, also trigger increased demands for protection. A significant change in the nature of support for protectionism occurred in the late 1960s, when the AFL-CIO abandoned its long-held belief in the desirability of open markets and supported protectionism. This shift in the union's position was due primarily to the rapid rise in import-penetration ratios that occurred during the 1960s in such industries as electrical consumer goods and footwear.

Another factor that may affect the demand for protection is *concentration* of domestic production. The U.S. auto industry, for example, is dominated by the Big Three. Support for import protection can be financed by these firms without fear that a large share of the benefits of protectionism will accrue to nonparticipating firms. Conversely, an industry that comprises many small producers (for example, meat packing) realizes that a substantial share of the gains from protectionism may accrue to producers who do not contribute their fair share to the costs of winning protectionist legislation. The demand for protection thus tends to be stronger the more concentrated the domestic industry.

Finally, the demand for protection may be influenced by the degree of *export dependence*. One would expect that companies whose foreign sales constitute a substantial portion of total sales (for example, Boeing) would not be greatly concerned about import protection. Their main fear is that the imposition of domestic trade barriers might invite retaliation overseas, which would ruin their export markets.

Summary

1. Even though the free-trade argument has strong theoretical justifications, trade restrictions are widespread throughout the world. Trade barriers consist of tariff restrictions and nontariff trade barriers.

2. There are several types of tariffs. A specific tariff represents a fixed amount of money per unit of the imported commodity. An ad valorem tariff is stated as a fixed percentage of the value of an imported commodity. A compound tariff combines a specific tariff with an ad valorem tariff.

3. Concerning ad valorem tariffs, several procedures exist for the valuation of imports. The free-on-board (FOB) measure indicates a commodity's price as it leaves the exporting nation. The cost-insurance-freight (CIF) measure shows the product's value as it arrives at the port of entry.

4. The effective tariff rate tends to differ from the nominal tariff rate when the domestic import-competing industry uses imported resources whose tariffs differ from those on the final commodity. Developing nations have traditionally argued that many advanced nations escalate the tariff structures on industrial commodities to yield an effective rate of protection several times the nominal rate.

5. American trade laws mitigate the effects of import duties by allowing U.S. importers to postpone and prorate over time their duty obligations by means of bonded warehouses and foreign trade zones.

6. The welfare effects of a tariff can be measured by its protective effect, consumption effect, redistributive effect, revenue effect, and terms-of-trade effect.

7. If a nation is small compared with the rest of the world, its welfare necessarily falls by the total amount of the protective effect plus the consumption effect if it levies a tariff on imports.

If the importing nation is large relative to the world, the imposition of an import tariff may improve its international terms of trade by an amount that more than offsets the welfare losses associated with the consumption effect and the protective effect.

8. Because a tariff is a tax on imports, the burden of a tariff falls initially on importers, who must pay duties to the domestic government. However, importers generally try to shift increased costs to buyers through price increases. Domestic exporters, who purchase imported inputs subject to tariffs, thus face higher costs and a reduction in competitiveness.

9. Although tariffs may improve one nation's economic position, any gains generally come at the expense of other nations. Should tariff retaliations occur, the volume of international trade decreases, and world welfare suffers. Tariff liberalization is intended to promote freer markets so that the world can benefit from expanded trade volumes and the international specialization of inputs.

10. Tariffs are sometimes justified on the grounds that they protect domestic employment and wages, help create a level playing field for international trade, equate the cost of imported products with the cost of domestic import-competing products, allow domestic industries to be insulated temporarily from foreign competition until they can grow and develop, or protect industries necessary for national security.

Key Concepts & Terms

- Ad valorem tariff (p. 125)
- Beggar-thy-neighbor policy (p. 146)
- Bonded warehouse (p. 134)
- Compound tariff (p. 125)
- Consumer surplus (p. 137)
- Consumption effect (p. 142)
- Cost-insurance-freight (CIF) valuation (p. 126)
- Customs valuation (p. 126)
- Deadweight loss (p. 143)
- Domestic revenue effect (p. 145)
- Effective tariff rate (p. 127)
- Foreign-trade zone (FTZ) (p. 134)
- Free-on-board (FOB) valuation (p. 126)
- Free-trade argument (p. 152)
- Free-trade-biased sector (p. 160)
- Infant-industry argument (p. 157)
- Large-nation (p. 143)
- Level playing field (p. 156)
- Nominal tariff rate (p. 127)
- Offshore-assembly provision (OAP) (p. 131)
- Optimum tariff (p. 146)
- Outsourcing (p. 131)
- Producer surplus (p. 138)
- Protection-biased sector (p. 160)
- Protective effect (p. 142)
- Protective tariff (p. 124)
- Redistributive effect (p. 142)
- Revenue effect (p. 142)
- Revenue tariff (p. 124)
- Scientific tariff (p. 157)
- Small nation (p. 139)
- Specific tariff (p. 125)
- Tariff (p. 124)
- Tariff avoidance (p. 132)
- Tariff escalation (p. 130)
- Tariff evasion (p. 132)
- Terms-of-trade effect (p. 145)

Study Questions

1. Distinguish between consumer surplus and producer surplus. How do these concepts relate to a country's economic welfare?

2. Less-developed nations sometimes argue that the industrialized nations' tariff structures discourage the less-developed nations from undergoing industrialization. Explain.

3. When a nation imposes a tariff on the importation of a commodity, economic inefficiencies develop that detract from the national welfare. Explain.

4. Describe a specific tariff, an ad valorem tariff, and a compound tariff. What are the advantages and disadvantages of each?

5. Under what conditions does a nominal tariff applied to an import product overstate or understate the actual, or effective, protection afforded by the nominal tariff?

6. What methods do customs appraisers use to determine the values of commodity imports?

7. Assume the nation of Australia is "small" and thus unable to influence world price. Its demand and supply schedules for TV sets are shown in Table 4.13. Using graph paper, plot the demand and supply schedules on the same graph.

TABLE 4.13

DEMAND AND SUPPLY: TV SETS (AUSTRALIA)

Price of TVS	Quantity Demanded	Quantity Supplied
$500	0	50
400	10	40
300	20	30
200	30	20
100	40	10
0	50	0

a. Determine Australia's market equilibrium for TV sets.
   (1) What are the equilibrium price and quantity?
   (2) Calculate the value of Australian consumer surplus and producer surplus.

b. Under free-trade conditions, suppose Australia imports TV sets at a price of $100 each. Determine the free-trade equilibrium, and illustrate graphically.
   (1) How many TV sets will be produced, consumed, and imported?
   (2) Calculate the dollar value of Australian consumer surplus and producer surplus.

c. To protect its producers from foreign competition, suppose the Australian government levies a specific tariff of $100 on imported TV sets.
   (1) Determine and show graphically the effects of the tariff on the price of TV sets in Australia, the quantity of TV sets supplied by Australian producers, the quantity of TV sets demanded by Australian consumers, and the volume of trade.
   (2) Calculate the reduction in Australian consumer surplus due to the tariff-induced increase in the price of TV sets.

   (3) Calculate the value of the tariff's consumption, protective, redistributive, and revenue effects.
   (4) What is the amount of deadweight welfare loss imposed on the Australian economy by the tariff?

8. What is meant by the terms *bonded warehouse* and *foreign-trade zone*? How does each of these help importers mitigate the effects of domestic import duties?

9. Would a tariff imposed on U.S. oil imports promote energy development and conservation for the United States?

10. Suppose that the production of $1 million worth of steel in Canada requires $100,000 worth of taconite. Canada's nominal tariff rates for importing these goods are 20 percent for steel and 10 percent for taconite. Given this information, calculate the effective rate of protection for Canada's steel industry.

11. What factors influence the size of the revenue, protective, consumption, and redistributive effects of a tariff?

12. A nation that imposes tariffs on imported goods may find its welfare improving should the tariff result in a favorable shift in the terms of trade. Explain.

13. Which of the arguments for tariffs do you feel are most relevant in today's world?

14. Although tariffs may improve the welfare of a single nation, the world's welfare may decline. Under what conditions would this be true?

15. What impact does the imposition of a tariff normally have on a nation's terms of trade and volume of trade?

16. Assume that the United States, as a steel-importing nation, is large enough so that changes in the quantity of its imports influence the world price of steel. The U.S. supply and demand schedules for steel are illustrated in Table 4.14, along with the overall amount of steel supplied to U.S. consumers by domestic and foreign producers.
   Using graph paper, plot the supply and demand schedules on the same graph.
   a. With free trade, the equilibrium price of steel is $ _____ per ton. At this price, _____ tons are purchased by U.S. buyers, _____ tons are

supplied by U.S. producers, and _____ tons are imported.

TABLE 4.14

Supply and Demand: Tons of Steel (United States)

Price/Ton	Quantity Supplied (Domestic)	Quantity Supplied (Domestic + Imports)	Quantity Demanded
$100	0	0	15
200	0	4	14
300	1	8	13
400	2	12	12
500	3	16	11
600	4	20	10
700	5	24	9

b. To protect its producers from foreign competition, suppose the U.S. government levies a specific tariff of $250 per ton on steel imports.

(1) Show graphically the effect of the tariff on the overall supply schedule of steel.

(2) With the tariff, the domestic price of steel rises to $_____ per ton. At this price, U.S. buyers purchase _____ tons, U.S. producers supply _____ tons, and _____ tons are imported.

(3) Calculate the reduction in U.S. consumer surplus due to the tariff-induced price of steel, as well as the consumption, protective, redistribution, and domestic revenue effects. The deadweight welfare loss of the tariff equals $_____.

(4) By reducing the volume of imports with the tariff, the United States forces the price of imported steel down to $_____. The U.S. terms of trade thus (improves/worsens), which leads to (an increase/a decrease) in U.S. welfare. Calculate the terms-of-trade effect.

(5) What impact does the tariff have on the overall welfare of the United States?

4.1   Exploring Further

Offer Curves and Tariffs

Chapter 4 uses conventional supply and demand figures to show how an import tariff can affect the welfare of a tariff-levying country. Let us now consider how offer curves provide a more general analysis of this topic.

Figure EF 4.1 represents the trade offer curves of the United States and Canada, assumed to be equally important trading countries (large-country model). The United States exports autos and imports wheat, while Canada exports wheat and imports autos. Market equilibrium is achieved at the point where the two countries' offer curves intersect, shown as point E. The slope of tt_0 then defines the equilibrium terms of trade.

Suppose that the United States levies a 100 percent import tariff on wheat, payable in terms of this import good. The United States now demands twice as many wheat imports per auto exported. Alternately stated, the United States is willing to offer only half as many autos in exchange for each unit of wheat imported. The result is a leftward shift in the U.S. offer curve from U.S.$_0$ to U.S.$_1$. The new tariff-distorted offer curve is drawn so that any point on it lies twice as far above the auto (horizontal) axis as any point directly below on the free-trade offer curve. Market equilibrium now exists at point F. At terms of trade tt_1, U.S. traders exchange $0A_1$ autos for $0W_1$ wheat, turning over W_1W_2 wheat to the government as the tariff duty.

FIGURE EF 4.1

TARIFF WELFARE EFFECTS USING OFFER CURVES

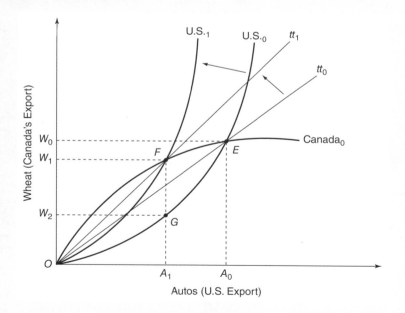

As a result of the tariff, the terms of trade have shifted in favor of the United States. This is because each auto export now buys a greater amount of wheat imports. Before the tariff, the United States would have been willing to trade along offer curve U.S.$_0$ and offer, say, OA_1 autos in exchange for OW_2 wheat. With the import tariff, the United States trades along its tariff-distorted offer curve U.S.$_1$, requiring OW_1 wheat for the same amount of auto exports. The U.S. share of the gains from trade increases at the expense of Canada. On the other hand, the world volume of trade has fallen because of the tariff. Comparing free-trade equilibrium point E with tariff equilibrium point F, the volume of autos traded has declined A_0A_1, while wheat sales have decreased W_0W_1. What impact do these two effects have on each country's welfare?

For Canada, the tariff has resulted in a decline in its level of welfare. Not only has Canada's terms of trade worsened, resulting in a smaller portion of the gains from trade, but its volume of trade has fallen. Both effects are negative from the viewpoint of Canada's welfare. For the United States, its level of welfare will improve if the positive terms-of-trade effect more than offsets the negative trade volume effect. Should the opposite occur, U.S. welfare would decrease. United States welfare would remain constant if the relative strength of the effects were equal. Therefore, the tariff's impact on U.S. welfare depends on which of these two opposing forces has the stronger effect.

Tariff Restrictions: Single-Country View Versus World View

The analysis so far has looked at an import tariff from the viewpoint of a single country. It has been shown how a single country may be able to enhance its national welfare by imposing a tariff on imported products. This will occur if the favorable terms-of-trade effect outweighs the unfavorable trade volume effect. But what may be true for the single country is not true for the world as a whole. All countries together not only are unable to improve their welfare with tariffs, but actually find that tariffs tend to deteriorate world welfare.

By modifying the relative prices at which countries exchange good and services, a tariff results in a redistribution of the gains from trade among countries: A favorable terms of trade yielding a larger share of the gains from trade for one country means the opposite for the other country. The welfare gains for the tariff-levying country therefore come at the expense of its trading partner. Because tariffs are unable to increase the world gains from trade, they provide no positive effect for global welfare. Tariffs do produce a negative welfare effect, the reduction in the volume of world trade. The net result is that for the world as a whole tariffs reduce the level of welfare.

A single country that is dissatisfied with the distribution of the world gains from trade may consider whether it should initiate a tariff on imports. But in an interdependent world, the country realizes that this act would not be welcomed by its trading partners. The possibility of foreign tariff retaliation may be a sufficient deterrent for any country considering whether to impose higher tariffs.

Tariff Retaliation and World Welfare

If one country imposes a tariff on imports and its trading partner does not, the tariff-levying country's welfare may improve. But this improvement would occur at the other country's expense. In order to recoup part of its welfare loss, the trading partner may levy a retaliatory tariff. Should this process recur a number of times, a trade war would result. In the end, both countries would be worse off than they were when free trade existed.

Figure EF 4.2 illustrates the impact of a trade war on the national welfare of the United States and Japan. Starting at free-trade equilibrium point E, suppose that the United States levies a tariff on steel imports. The U.S. offer curve shifts to the left from U.S.$_0$ to U.S.$_1$. Market equilibrium is restored at point F. The U.S. terms of trade would improve from tt_0 to tt_1, implying that the terms at which

FIGURE EF 4.2

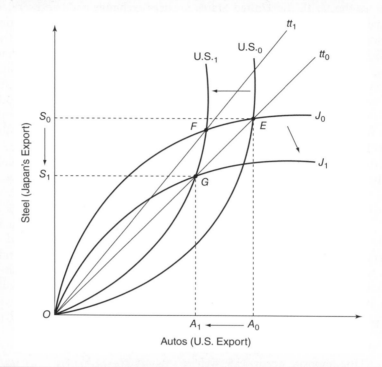

Japan trades have worsened. In order to regain its loss of welfare, suppose Japan retaliates by imposing a tariff on auto imports. The Japanese offer curve shifts from J_0 to J_1, market equilibrium being restored at point G. In this case, the terms at which Japan trades improve and move back to the original level, denoted by line tt_0. This improvement means that Japan's retaliatory tariff has wiped out the initial relative price advantage of the United States. But the total volume of world trade has shrunk. Finding its temporary advantage eliminated, the United States may counteract with a still higher import tariff. This new tariff may lead to a Japanese counter retaliation. Should this process continue, a full-scale trade war would break out.

The effect of the retaliatory tariffs would be a reduction in the welfare of both countries below their free-trade levels. By lowering the volume of trade, tariffs reduce the overall gains from trade resulting from comparative advantage. Both countries tend to lose in their attempt to improve their shares of the gains from trade. The tariff war in effect results in the two countries fighting over larger shares of smaller and smaller gains from trade. Although a tariff-levying country may be able to improve its terms of trade temporarily, the shrinking trade volume would tend to reduce the level of national welfare. Both countries therefore lose as a result of the retaliatory tariffs.

Nontariff Trade Barriers

This chapter considers policies other than tariffs that restrict international trade. Referred to as **nontariff trade barriers (NTBs)**, such measures have been on the rise since the 1960s and have become the most widely discussed topics at recent rounds of international trade negotiations. Although tariffs have come down in recent decades, nontariff trade barriers have multiplied. This is not surprising. After all, the political forces that give rise to high tariffs do not disappear once tariffs are brought down. Instead, they must seek protection through other channels.

Nontariff trade barriers encompass a variety of measures. Some have unimportant trade consequences; for example, labeling and packaging requirements can restrict trade, but generally only marginally. Other NTBs significantly affect trade patterns; examples include import quotas, voluntary export restraints, subsidies, and domestic content requirements. These NTBs are intended to reduce imports and thus benefit domestic producers.

Import Quota

An **import quota** is a physical restriction on the quantity of goods that can be imported during a specific time period; the quota generally limits imports to a level below what would occur under free-trade conditions. For example, a quota might state that no more than 1 million kilograms of cheese or 20 million kilograms of wheat can be imported during some specific time period. Table 5.1 gives examples of import quotas that have been used by the United States.

A common practice to administer an import quota is for the government to require an **import license**. The license specifies the total volume of imports allowed. The license requires the importer to spend time filling out forms and waiting for official permission. Licenses can be sold to importing companies at a competitive price, or simply at a fee. Instead, a government may just give away licenses to preferred importers. However, this allocation method provides incentives for political lobbying and bribery.

TABLE 5.1

EXAMPLES OF U.S. IMPORT QUOTAS*

Imported Article	Quota Quantity (yearly)
Condensed milk (Australia)	91,625 kg*
Condensed milk (Denmark)	605,092 kg
Evaporated milk (Germany)	9,997 kg
Evaporated milk (Netherlands)	548,393 kg
Blue-mold cheese (Argentina)	2,000 kg
Blue-mold cheese (Chile)	80,000 kg
Cheddar cheese (New Zealand)	8,200,000 kg
Italian cheese (Poland)	1,325,000 kg
Italian cheese (Romania)	500,000 kg
Swiss cheese (Switzerland)	1,850,000 kg

*kg = kilograms.

Source: From U.S. International Trade Commission, *Tariff Schedules of the United States*, Washington, DC, Government Printing Office, 2000.

Import quotas on manufactured goods have been outlawed by the World Trade Organization. Advanced countries such as Japan and the United States have used import quotas to protect agricultural producers. However, recent trade negotiations have called for countries to convert their quotas to equivalent tariffs.

One way to administer import limitations is through a **global quota**. This technique permits a specified number of goods to be imported each year, but it does not specify from where the product is shipped or who is permitted to import. When the specified amount has been imported (the quota is filled), additional imports of the product are prevented for the remainder of the year.

In practice, the global quota becomes unwieldy because of the rush of both domestic importers and foreign exporters to get their goods shipped into the country before the quota is filled. Those who import early in the year get their goods; those who import late in the year may not. Moreover, goods shipped from distant locations tend to be discriminated against because of the longer transportation time. Smaller merchants without good trade connections may also be at a disadvantage relative to large merchants. Global quotas are thus plagued by accusations of favoritism against merchants fortunate enough to be the first to capture a large portion of the business.

To avoid the problems of a global quota system, import quotas are usually allocated to specific countries; this type of quota is known as a **selective quota**. For example, a country might impose a global quota of 30 million apples per year, of which 14 million must come from the United States, 10 million from Mexico, and 6 million from Canada. Customs officials in the importing nation monitor the quantity of a particular good that enters the country from each source; once the quota for that source has been filled, no more goods are permitted to be imported.

Selective quotas suffer from many of the same problems as global quotas. Consider the case of Kmart, which ordered more than a million dollars' worth of wool sweaters from China in the 1980s. Before the sweaters arrived in the United States, the Chinese quota was filled for the year; Kmart could not bring them into the country until the following year. By that time, the sweaters were out of style and had to be sold at discounted prices. The firm estimated that it recovered only 60 cents on the dollar for these sweater sales.

Another feature of quotas is that their use may lead to a domestic monopoly of production and higher prices. Because a domestic firm realizes that foreign producers cannot surpass their quotas, it may raise its prices. Tariffs do not necessarily lead to monopoly power, because no limit is established on the amount of goods that can be imported into the nation.

Trade and Welfare Effects

Like a tariff, an import quota affects an economy's welfare. Figure 5.1 represents the case of cheese, involving U.S. trade with the European Union (EU). Suppose the

FIGURE 5.1

IMPORT QUOTA: TRADE AND WELFARE EFFECTS

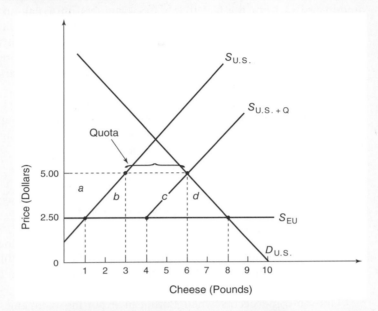

By restricting available supplies of an imported product, a quota leads to higher import prices. This price umbrella allows domestic producers of the import-competing good to raise prices. The result is a decrease in the consumer surplus. Of this amount, the welfare loss to the importing nation consists of the protective effect, the consumption effect, and that portion of the revenue effect that is captured by the foreign exporter.

United States is a "small" country in terms of the world cheese market. Assume that $S_{U.S.}$ and $D_{U.S.}$ denote the supply and demand schedules for cheese in the United States. The S_{EU} denotes the supply schedule of the EU. Under free trade, the price of EU cheese and U.S. cheese equals $2.50 per pound. At this price, U.S. firms produce one pound, U.S. consumers purchase eight pounds, and imports from the EU total seven pounds.

Suppose the United States limits its cheese imports to a fixed quantity of three pounds by imposing an import quota. Above the free-trade price, the total U.S. supply of cheese now equals U.S. production plus the quota. In Figure 5.1, this is illustrated by a shift in the supply curve from $S_{U.S.}$ to $S_{U.S.+Q}$. The reduction in imports from seven to three pounds raises the equilibrium price to $5.00; this leads to an increase in the quantity supplied by U.S. firms from one to three pounds and a decrease in the U.S. quantity demanded from eight to six pounds.

Import quotas can be analyzed in terms of the same welfare effects identified for tariffs in the preceding chapter. Because the quota in our example results in a price increase to $5.00 per pound, the U.S. consumer surplus falls by an amount equal to area $a + b + c + d$ ($17.50). Area a ($5.00) represents the *redistributive effect*, area b ($2.50) represents the *protective effect*, and area d ($2.50) represents the *consumption effect*. The *deadweight loss* of welfare to the economy resulting from the quota is depicted by the protective effect plus the consumption effect.

But what about the quota's *revenue effect*, denoted by area *c* ($7.50)? This amount arises from the fact that U.S. consumers must pay an additional $2.50 for each of the three pounds of cheese imported under the quota, as a result of the quota-induced scarcity of cheese. The revenue effect represents a "windfall profit," also known as a "quota rent." It accrues to whoever has the right to bring imports into the country and to sell these goods in the protected market. Where does this windfall profit go?

To determine the distribution of the quota's revenue effect, it is useful to think of a series of exchanges as seen in the following example. Suppose that European exporting companies sell cheese to grocery stores (importing companies) in the United States, that sell it to U.S. consumers:[1]

European $\rightarrow$ U.S. grocery $\rightarrow$ U.S.
exporting stores consumers
companies (importing companies)

The distribution of the quota's revenue effect will be determined by the prices that prevail in the exchanges between these groups. Who obtains this windfall profit will depend on the competitive relations between the exporting and importing companies concerned.

One outcome occurs when European exporting companies are able to collude and in effect become a monopoly seller. If grocers in the United States behave as competitive buyers, they will bid against one another to buy European cheese. The delivered price of cheese will be driven up from $2.50 to $5.00 per pound. European exporting companies thus capture the windfall profit of the quota. The windfall profit captured by European exporters becomes a welfare loss for the U.S. economy, in addition to the deadweight losses resulting from the protective and consumption effects.

Instead, suppose that U.S. grocers organize as a single importing company (for example, Safeway grocery stores) and become a monopoly buyer. Also assume that European exporting companies operate as competitive sellers. Now, U.S. importing companies can purchase cheese at the prevailing world price of $2.50 per pound and resell it to U.S. consumers at a price of $5.00 per pound. In this case, the quota's revenue effect accrues to the importing companies. Because these companies are American, this accrual does not represent a welfare loss for the U.S. economy.

Alternatively, the U.S. government may collect the quota's revenue effect from the importing companies. Suppose the government sells import licenses to U.S. grocers. By charging for permission to import, the government receives some or all of the quota's windfall profit. If import licenses are auctioned off to the highest bidder in a competitive market, the government will capture all of the windfall profit that would have accrued to importing companies under the quota. Because the quota's revenue effect accrues to the U.S. government, this accrual does not represent a welfare loss for the U.S. economy (assuming that the government returns the revenue to the economy). This point will be discussed further in the next section of this text.

---

[1]This example assumes that European exporting companies purchase cheese from European producers who operate in a competitive market. Because each producer is thus too small to affect the market price, it cannot capture any windfall profit arising under an import quota.

Allocating Quota Licenses

Because an import quota restricts the quantity of imports, usually below the free-trade quantity, not all domestic importers can obtain the same number of imports that they could under free trade. Governments thus allocate the limited supply of imports among domestic importers.

In oil and dairy products, the U.S. government has issued import licenses on the basis of their historical share of the import market. But this method discriminates against importers seeking to import goods for the first time. In other cases, the U.S. government has allocated import quotas on a pro rata basis, whereby U.S. importers receive a fraction of their demand equal to the ratio of the import quota to the total quantity demanded collectively by U.S. importers.

The U.S. government has also considered using another method of allocating licenses among domestic importers: the auctioning of import licenses to the highest bidder in a competitive market. This technique has also been used in Australia and New Zealand.

Consider a hypothetical quota on U.S. imports of textiles. The quota pushes the price of textiles in the United States above the world price, making the United States an unusually profitable market. Windfall profits can be captured by U.S. importers (for example, Sears and Wal-Mart) if they buy textiles at the lower world price and sell them to U.S. buyers at the higher price made possible because of the quota. Given these windfall profits, U.S. importers would likely be willing to pay for the rights to import textiles. By auctioning import licenses to the highest bidder in a competitive market, the government could capture the windfall profits (the revenue effect shown as area c in Figure 5.1). Competition among importers to obtain the licenses would drive up the auction price to a level at which no windfall profits would remain, thus transferring the entire revenue effect to the government. The auctioning of import licenses would turn a quota into something akin to a tariff, which generates tax revenue for the government. In practice, few nations have used auctions to allocate rights to import products under quotas.

Quotas Versus Tariffs

Previous analysis suggests that the revenue effect of import quotas differs from that of import tariffs. These two commercial policies can also differ in the impact they have on the volume of trade. The following example illustrates how, during periods of growing demand, an import quota restricts the volume of imports by a greater amount than does an equivalent import tariff.

Figure 5.2 represents a hypothetical trade situation for the United States in autos. The U.S. supply and demand schedules for autos are given by $S_{U.S._0}$ and $D_{U.S._0}$, and S_{J0} represents the Japanese auto supply schedule. Suppose the U.S. government has the option of levying a tariff or a quota on auto imports to protect U.S. companies from foreign competition.

In Figure 5.2(a), a tariff of $1,000 raises the price of Japanese autos from $6,000 to $7,000; auto imports would fall from seven million units to three million units. In Figure 5.2(b), an import quota of three million units would put the United States in a trade position identical to that which occurs under the tariff: the quota-induced scarcity of autos results in a rise in the price from $6,000 to $7,000. So far, it appears

FIGURE 5.2

TRADE EFFECTS OF TARIFFS VERSUS QUOTAS

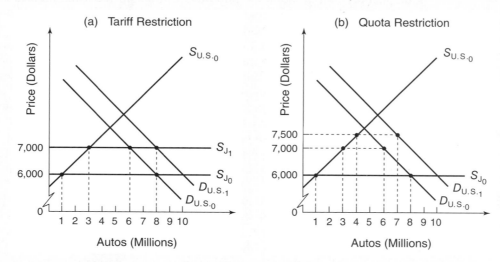

In a growing market, an import tariff is a less restrictive trade barrier than an equivalent import quota. With an import tariff, the adjustment that occurs in response to an increase in domestic demand is an increase in the amount of the product that is imported. With an import quota, an increase in demand induces an increase in product price. The price increase leads to a rise in production and a fall in consumption of the import-competing good, while the level of imports remains constant.

that the tariff and the quota are equivalent with respect to their restrictive impact on the volume of trade.

Now suppose the U.S. demand for autos rises from $D_{U.S._0}$ to $D_{U.S._1}$. Figure 5.2(a) shows that, despite the increased demand, the price of auto imports remains at $7,000. This is because the U.S. price cannot differ from the Japanese price by an amount exceeding the tariff duty. Auto imports rise from three million units to five million units. Under an import tariff, then, domestic adjustment takes the form of an increase in the quantity of autos imported rather than a rise in auto prices.

In Figure 5.2(b), an identical increase in demand induces a rise in domestic auto prices. Under the quota, there is no limit on the extent to which the U.S. price can rise above the Japanese price. Given an increase in domestic auto prices, U.S. companies are able to expand production. The domestic price will rise until the increased production plus the fixed level of imports are commensurate with the domestic demand. Figure 5.2(b) shows that an increase in demand from $D_{U.S._0}$ to $D_{U.S._1}$ forces auto prices up from $7,000 to $7,500. At the new price, domestic production equals four million units and domestic consumption equals seven million units. Imports total three million units, the same amount as under the quota before the increase in domestic demand. Adjustment thus occurs in domestic *prices* rather than in the quantity of autos imported.

During periods of growing demand, then, an import quota is a more restrictive trade barrier than an equivalent import tariff. Under a quota, the government arbitrarily limits the quantity of imports. Under a tariff, the domestic price can rise above the world price only by the amount of the tariff; domestic consumers can still buy unlimited quantities of the import if they are willing and able to pay that amount. Even if the domestic industry's comparative disadvantage grows more severe, the quota prohibits consumers from switching to the imported good. Thus, a quota assures the domestic industry a ceiling on imports regardless of changing market conditions.[2]

Simply put, a quota is a more restrictive barrier to imports than a tariff. A tariff increases the domestic price, but it does not necessarily limit the number of goods that can be imported into a country. Importers who are successful enough to be able to pay the tariff duty still get the product. Moreover, a tariff may be offset by the price reductions of a foreign producer that can cut costs or slash profit margins. Tariffs thus allow for some degree of competition. However, by imposing an absolute limit on the imported good, a quota is more restrictive than a tariff and suppresses competition. Simply put, the degree of protection provided by a tariff is determined by the market mechanism, but a quota forecloses the market mechanism. As a result, member countries of the World Trade Organization have decided to phase out import quotas and replace them with tariffs—a process known as tariffication.

Tariff-Rate Quota: A Two-Tier Tariff

Another restriction used to insulate a domestic industry from foreign competition is the **tariff-rate quota**. The U.S. government has imposed this restriction on imports such as steel, brooms, cattle, fish, sugar, milk, and other agricultural products.

As its name suggests, a tariff-rate quota displays both tariff-like and quota-like characteristics. This device allows a specified number of goods to be imported at one tariff rate (the *within-quota rate*), whereas any imports above this level face a higher tariff rate (the *over-quota rate*). The over-quota tariff rate is often set high enough to prohibit the importation of the product into the domestic market. A tariff-rate quota thus has two components: a quota that defines the maximum volume of imports and charges the within-quota tariff, and an over-quota tariff. Simply put, a tariff-rate quota is a *two-tier tariff*. Tariff-rate quotas are applied for each trade year and if not filled during a particular year, the market access under the quota is lost. Table 5.2 provides examples of tariff-rate quotas applied to U.S. imports.

The tariff-rate quota appears to differ little from the import quota discussed earlier in this chapter. The distinction is that under an import quota it is legally impossible to import more than a specified amount. However, under a tariff-rate quota, imports can exceed this specified amount, but a higher, over-quota tariff is applied on the excess.

In principle, a tariff-rate quota provides more access to imports than an import quota. In practice, many over-quota tariffs are prohibitively high and effectively exclude imports in excess of the quota. It is possible to design a tariff-rate quota so that it reproduces the trade-volume limit of an import quota.

Concerning the administration of tariff-rate quotas, **license on demand allocation** is the most common technique of enforcement for the quotas. Under this system, licenses are required to import at the within-quota tariff. Before the quota period

---

[2]You might test your understanding of the approach used here by working out the details of two other hypothetical situations: (a) a reduction in the domestic supply of autos caused by rising production costs and (b) a reduction in domestic demand due to economic recession.

TABLE 5.2

Examples of U.S. Tariff-Rate Quotas

Product	Within-Quota Tariff Rate	Import-Quota Threshold	Over-Quota Tariff Rate
Peanuts	9.35 cents/kg	30,393 tons	187.9 percent ad valorem
Beef	4.4 cents/kg	634,621 tons	31.1 percent ad valorem
Milk	3.2 cents/L	5.7 million L	88.5 cents/L
Blue cheese	10 cents/kg	2.6 million kg	$2.60/kg
Cotton	4.4 cents/kg	2.1 million kg	36 cents/kg

Source: From U.S. International Trade Commission, *Harmonized Tariff Schedule of the United States*, (Washington, DC, U.S. Government Printing Office, 2006).

begins, potential importers are invited to apply for import licenses. If the demand for licenses is less than the quota, the system operates like a first-come, first-serve system. Usually, if demand exceeds the quota, the import volume requested is reduced proportionally among all applicants. Other techniques for allocating quota licenses are historical market share and auctions.

When the World Trade Organization (WTO) was established in 1995 (see Chapter 6), member countries changed their systems of import protection for those agricultural products helped by government farm programs. The WTO requires members to convert to tariffs all nontariff trade barriers (import quotas, variable levies, discretionary licensing, outright import bans, etc.) applicable to imports from other members. In other words, it put all nontariff barriers on a common standard—tariffs—that any exporter could readily measure and understand. Members are allowed to adopt tariff-rate quotas as a transitional instrument during this conversion period. At the writing of this text, the duration of this conversion period had not been defined. Thus, tariff-rate quotas will likely be around for some time to come.

Tariff-rate quotas have also been used as temporary protection against surging imports of nonagricultural products into the United States. Examples of these products include steel, brooms, stainless steel flatware, and fish. The welfare effects of a tariff-rate quota are discussed in *Exploring Further 5.1*.

Sugar Tariff-Rate Quota Bittersweet for Consumers

The U.S. sugar industry provides an example of the effects of a tariff-rate quota. Traditionally, U.S. sugar growers have received government subsidies in the form of price supports that result in a higher price than the free-market price. This artificially high price can attract lower-priced imported sugar, which will drive down the price. To prevent this outcome, the U.S. government intervenes in the market a second time by implementing tariff-rate quotas.

Tariff-rate quotas for raw cane sugar are allocated on a country-by-country basis among 41 countries in total, while those for refined sugar are allocated in a global first-come, first-serve basis. For sugar entering the U.S. market within the tariff-rate quota, a lower tariff is applied. For sugar imports in excess of the tariff-rate quota, a much higher tariff rate is established that virtually prohibits these imports. In this manner, the tariff-rate quota approximates the trade-volume limit of an import quota that was discussed earlier in this chapter. However, the U.S. government has the option of establishing higher tariff-rate quota amounts whenever it believes that the domestic supply of sugar may be inadequate to meet domestic demand at reasonable prices.

The effect of the tariff-rate quota is to restrict the supply of foreign sugar from entering the United States, thus causing the price of sugar in the domestic market to increase substantially. The U.S. price of sugar has often been twice the world market price because of the tariff-rate quota. In 2006, for example, the difference between the U.S. price (20.94 cents per pound) and the world price (10.42 cents per pound) for raw cane sugar was 101 percent. This difference resulted in American consumers spending an extra $2 billion a year on sugar.

The sugar tariff-rate quota is a classic example of concentrated benefits and dispersed costs. It provides enormous revenues for a very small number of American sugar growers and refiners. However, the costs of providing these benefits are spread across the U.S. economy, specifically to American families as consumers and sugar-using producers such as soft drink companies. Simply put, the U.S. government's trade policy for sugar is "bittersweet" for American consumers.[3]

Export Quotas

Besides implementing import quotas, countries have used **export quotas** to restrain trade. When doing so, they typically negotiate a market sharing pact known as a voluntary export restraint agreement, also known as an orderly marketing agreement. Its main purpose is to moderate the intensity of international competition, allowing less efficient domestic producers to participate in markets that would otherwise have been lost to foreign producers that sell a superior product at a lower price. For example, Japan may impose quotas on its steel exports to Europe, or Taiwan may agree to cutbacks on textile exports to the United States. The export quotas are voluntary in the sense that they are an alternative to more stringent trade restraints that might be imposed by an importing nation. Although voluntary export quotas governed trade in television sets, steel, textiles, autos, and ships during the 1980s, recent international trade agreements have prevented further use of this trade restriction.

Voluntary export quotas tend to have identical economic effects to equivalent import quotas, except for being implemented by the exporting nation. Thus, the revenue effect of an export quota is captured by the foreign exporting company or its government. The welfare effects of an export quota are further examined in *Exploring Further 5.2*.

An analysis of three major U.S. voluntary export restraint agreements of the 1980s (automobiles, steel, and textiles and apparel) concluded that about 67 percent of the costs to American consumers of these restraints was captured by foreign exporters as profit.[4] From the viewpoint of the U.S. economy as a whole, voluntary export restraints tend to be more costly than tariffs. Let us consider a voluntary export restraint agreement from the 1980s.

---

[3] U.S. International Trade Commission, *The Economic Effects of Significant U.S. Import Restraints*, Washington, D.C., 2007, Chapter 2 and Mark Groombridge, *America's Bittersweet Sugar Policy*, Cato Institute, Washington, D.C., December 4, 2001.

[4] David Tarr, *A General Equilibrium Analysis of the Welfare and Employment Effects of U.S. Quotas in Textiles, Autos, and Steel*, Washington, D.C., Federal Trade Commission, 1989.

Japanese Auto Restraints Put Brakes on U.S. Motorists

In 1981, as domestic auto sales fell, protectionist sentiment gained momentum in the U.S. Congress, and legislation was introduced calling for import quotas. This momentum was a major factor in the Reagan administration's desire to negotiate a voluntary restraint pact with the Japanese. Japan's acceptance of this agreement was apparently based on its view that voluntary limits on its auto shipments would derail any protectionist momentum in Congress for more stringent measures.

The restraint program called for self-imposed export quotas on Japanese auto shipments to the United States for three years, beginning in 1981. First-year shipments were to be held to 1.68 million units, 7.7 percent below the 1.82 million units exported in 1980. The quotas were extended annually, with some upward adjustment in the volume numbers, until 1984.

The purpose of the export agreement was to help U.S. automakers by diverting U.S. customers from Japanese to U.S. showrooms. As domestic sales increased, so would jobs for American autoworkers. It was assumed that Japan's export quota would assist the U.S. auto industry as it went through a transition period of reallocating production toward smaller, more fuel-efficient autos and adjusting production to become more cost competitive.

Not all Japanese auto manufacturers were equally affected by the export quota. By requiring Japanese auto companies to form an export cartel against the U.S. consumer, the quota allowed the large, established firms (Toyota, Nissan, and Honda) to increase prices on autos sold in the United States. To derive more revenues from a limited number of autos, Japanese firms shipped autos to the United States with fancier trim, bigger engines, and more amenities such as air conditioners and deluxe stereos as standard equipment. Product enrichment also helped the Japanese broaden their hold on the U.S. market and enhance the image of their autos. As a result, the large Japanese manufacturers earned record profits in the United States. However, the export quota was unpopular with smaller Japanese automakers, such as Suzuki and Isuzu, who felt that the quota allocation favored large producers over small producers.

The biggest loser was the U.S. consumer who had to pay an extra $660 for each Japanese auto purchased and an extra $1,300 for each American-made auto in 1984. From 1981 to 1984, U.S. consumers paid an additional $15.7 billion to purchase autos because of the quota. Although the quota saved some 44,000 jobs for American autoworkers, the consumer cost per job saved was estimated to be more than $100,000.[5]

By 1985, Toyota, Honda, and Nissan had established manufacturing plants in the United States. This result had been sought by the United Auto Workers (UAW) and the U.S. auto companies. Their view was that in taking such action, the Japanese would have to hire American workers and would also face the same competitive manufacturing conditions as U.S. auto companies. However, things did not turn out the way that the American auto interests anticipated. When manufacturing in the U.S. market, the Japanese companies adjusted their production and developed new vehicles specifically designed for this market. Although their exports did decrease, vehicles produced at the Japanese transplant factories more than filled the market gap, so that the U.S. producers' share of the market declined. Moreover, the UAW

---

[5]U.S. International Trade Commission, *A Review of Recent Developments in the U.S. Automobile Industry Including an Assessment of the Japanese Voluntary Restraint Agreements*, Washington, DC, Government Printing Office, 1985.

was unsuccessful in organizing workers at most transplant factories and therefore the Japanese were able to continue to keep labor costs down.

Domestic Content Requirements

Today, many products, such as autos and aircraft, embody worldwide production. Domestic manufacturers of these products purchase resources or perform assembly functions outside the home country, a practice known as outsourcing or production sharing. For example, General Motors obtains engines from its subsidiaries in Mexico, Chrysler purchases ball joints from Japanese producers, and Ford acquires cylinder heads from European companies. Firms have used outsourcing to take advantage of lower production costs overseas, including lower wage rates. Domestic workers often challenge this practice, maintaining that outsourcing means that cheap foreign labor takes away their jobs and imposes downward pressure on the wages of those workers who are able to keep their jobs.

To limit the practice of outsourcing, organized labor has lobbied for the use of **domestic content requirements**. These requirements stipulate the minimum percentage of a product's total value that must be produced domestically if the product is to qualify for zero tariff rates. The effect of content requirements is to pressure both domestic and foreign firms that sell products in the home country to use domestic inputs (workers) in the production of those products. The demand for domestic inputs thus increases, contributing to higher input prices. Manufacturers generally lobby against domestic content requirements, because they prevent manufacturers from obtaining inputs at the lowest cost, thus contributing to higher product prices and the loss of competitiveness.

Worldwide, local content requirements have received the most attention in the automobile industry. Developing countries have often used content requirements to foster domestic automobile production, as shown in Table 5.3.

TABLE 5.3

DOMESTIC CONTENT REQUIREMENTS APPLIED TO AUTOMOBILES IN SELECTED COUNTRIES

Country	Minimum Domestic Content Required (percent) to Qualify for Zero Duty Rates
Argentina	76
Mexico	62
Brazil	60
Uruguay	60
Chinese Taipei	40
Ecuador	35
Venezuela	30
Colombia	30

Source: From U.S. Department of Commerce, International Trade Administration, Office of Automotive Affairs, *Compilation of Foreign Motor Vehicle Import Requirements*, July 2008, at **http://www.ita.doc.gov/**.

Figure 5.3 illustrates possible welfare effects of an Australian content requirement on automobiles. Assume that D_A denotes the Australian demand schedule for Toyota automobiles while S_J depicts the supply price of Toyotas exported to Australia, $24,000. With free trade, Australia imports 500 Toyotas. Japanese resource owners involved in manufacturing this vehicle realize incomes totaling $12 million, denoted by area $c+d$.

Suppose the Australian government imposes a domestic content requirement on autos. This policy causes Toyota to establish a factory in Australia to produce vehicles replacing the Toyotas previously imported by Australia. Assume that the transplant factory combines Japanese management with Australian resources (labor and materials) in vehicle production. Also assume that high Australian resource prices (wages) cause the transplant's supply price to be $33,000, denoted by S_T. Under the content requirement, Australian consumers demand 300 vehicles. Because production has shifted from Japan to Australia, Japanese resource

FIGURE 5.3

WELFARE EFFECTS OF A DOMESTIC CONTENT
REQUIREMENT

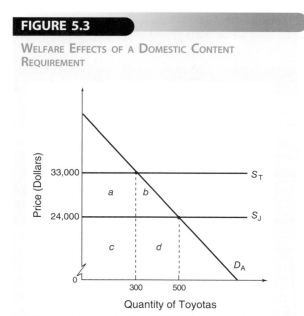

A domestic content requirement leads to rising
production costs and prices to the extent that manufacturers are "forced" to locate production facilities in a
high-cost nation. Although the content requirement
helps preserve domestic jobs, it imposes welfare losses
on domestic consumers.

owners lose $12 million in income. Australian resource
owners gain $9.9 million in income (area $a + c$) minus
the income paid to Japanese managers and the return to
Toyota's capital investment (factory) in Australia.

However, the income gains of Australian resource
owners inflict costs on Australian consumers. Because
the content requirement causes the price of Toyotas to
increase by $9,000, the Australian consumer surplus
decreases by area $a + b$ ($3.6 million). Of this amount,
area b ($900,000) is a deadweight welfare loss for Aus-
tralia. Area a ($2.7 million) is the consumer cost of
employing higher-priced Australian resources instead
of lower-priced Japanese resources; this amount represents a redistribution of welfare from Australian consumers to Australian resource owners. Similar to other
import restrictions, content requirements lead to the
subsidizing by domestic consumers of the domestic
producer.

Subsidies

National governments sometimes grant **subsidies** to
their producers to help improve their market position.
By providing domestic firms a cost advantage, a subsidy allows them to market their products at prices
lower than warranted by their actual cost or profit
considerations. Governmental subsidies assume a variety of forms, including outright cash disbursements, tax
concessions, insurance arrangements, and loans at below-market interest rates.

For purposes of our discussion, two types of subsidies can be distinguished: a
domestic production subsidy, which is granted to producers of import-competing
goods; and an **export subsidy**, which goes to producers of goods that are to be sold
overseas. In both cases, the government adds an amount to the price the purchaser
pays rather than subtracting from it. The net price actually received by the producer
equals the price paid by the purchaser plus the subsidy. The subsidized producer is
thus able to supply a greater quantity at this price. Let us use Figure 5.4 to analyze
the effects of these two types of subsidies.

Domestic Production Subsidy

If a country decides that the public welfare necessitates the maintenance of a semiconductor industry or aircraft industry, would it not be better just to subsidize it directly,
rather than preventing imports of a product? The purpose of a domestic production
subsidy is to encourage the output and thus vitality of import-competing producers.

Figure 5.4(a) illustrates the trade and welfare effects of a production subsidy
granted to import-competing producers. Assume that the initial supply and demand
schedules for steel in the United States are depicted by curves $S_{U.S._0}$ and $D_{U.S._0}$, so
that the market equilibrium price is $430 per ton. Assume also that, because the United

FIGURE 5.4

TRADE AND WELFARE EFFECTS OF SUBSIDIES

(a) Domestic Production Subsidy

(b) Export Subsidy

A government subsidy granted to import-competing producers leads to increased domestic production and reduced imports. The subsidy revenue accruing to the producer is absorbed by producer surplus and high-cost production (protective effect). A subsidy granted to exporters allows them to sell their products abroad at prices below their costs. However, it entails a deadweight welfare loss to the home country in the form of the protective effect and the consumption effect.

States is a small buyer of steel, changes in its purchases do not affect the world price of $400 per ton. Given a free-trade price of $400 per ton, the United States consumes 14 million tons of steel, produces 2 million tons, and imports 12 million tons.

To partially insulate domestic producers from foreign competition, suppose the U.S. government grants them a production subsidy of $25 per ton of steel. The cost advantage made possible by the subsidy results in a shift in the U.S. supply schedule from $S_{U.S._0}$ to $S_{U.S._1}$. Domestic production expands from 2 to 7 million tons, and imports fall from 12 to 7 million tons. These changes represent the subsidy's trade effect.

The subsidy also affects the national welfare of the United States. According to Figure 5.4(a), the subsidy permits U.S. output to rise to 7 million tons. Note that, at this output, the net price to the steelmaker is $425—the sum of the price paid by the consumer ($400) plus the subsidy ($25). To the U.S. government, the total cost of protecting its steelmakers equals the amount of the subsidy ($25) times the amount of output to which it is applied (7 million tons), or $175 million.

Where does this subsidy revenue go? Part of it is redistributed to the more efficient U.S. producers in the form of a *producer surplus*. This amount is denoted by area *a* ($112.5 million) in the figure. There is also a *protective effect*, whereby more costly domestic output is allowed to be sold in the market as a result of the subsidy. This effect is denoted by area *b* ($62.5 million) in the figure. To the United States as a whole, the protective effect represents a deadweight loss of welfare.

HOW "FOREIGN" IS YOUR CAR?

TABLE 5.4

NORTH AMERICAN CONTENT OF AUTOMOBILES SOLD
IN THE UNITED STATES, 2007 (SALES WEIGHTED)

Automaker	North American Content
Chrysler (domestic brands)	78%
Ford (domestic brands)	78
GM (domestic brands)	74
Honda, Acura	59
Nissan/Infiniti	46
Toyota/Lexus	47
Mitsubishi	36
Subaru	26
Isuzu	17
BMW	10
Foreign automaker average	40

Source: From Level Field Institute at **http://www.levelfieldinstitute.org.**

Did you know that U.S. buyers of cars and light trucks can learn how American or foreign their new vehicle is? On cars and trucks weighing 8,500 pounds or less, the law requires content labels telling buyers where the parts of the vehicle were made. Content is measured by the dollar value of components, not the labor cost of assembling vehicles. The percentages of North American (U.S. and Canadian) and foreign parts must be listed as an average for each car line. Manufacturers are free to design the label, which can be included on the price sticker or fuel economy sticker or can be separate. Table 5.4 provides examples of the North American content of vehicles sold in the United States for the 2007 model year.

To encourage production by its import-competing producers, a government might levy tariffs or quotas on imports. But tariffs and quotas involve larger sacrifices in national welfare than occur under an equivalent subsidy. Unlike subsidies, tariffs and quotas distort choices for domestic consumers (resulting in a decrease in the domestic demand for imports), in addition to permitting less efficient home production to occur. The result is the familiar consumption effect of protection, whereby a deadweight loss of the consumer surplus is borne by the home nation. This welfare loss is absent in the subsidy case. Thus, a subsidy tends to yield the same result for domestic producers as does an equivalent tariff or quota, but at a *lower* cost in terms of the nation's welfare.

However, subsidies are not free goods, for they must be financed by someone. The direct cost of the subsidy is a burden that must be financed out of tax revenues paid by the public. Moreover, when a subsidy is given to an industry, it is often in return for accepting government conditions on key matters (such as wage and salary levels). Therefore, a subsidy may not be as superior to other types of commercial policies as this analysis suggests.

Export Subsidy

Rather than granting a production subsidy to import-competing producers, a government could pay a subsidy on exports only. The most common product groups where export subsidies are applied are agricultural and dairy products.

Figure 5.4(b) shows the effects of an export subsidy. Assume that the supply and demand curves of the United States for wheat are shown by curves $S_{U.S.}$ and $D_{U.S.}$, so that the autarky equilibrium price is $4 per bushel. Assume also that because the United States is a relatively small producer of wheat, changes in its output do not affect the world price. At the world price of, say, $5 per bushel, the United States produces eight million bushels, purchases four million bushels, and thus exports four million bushels.

Suppose that the U.S. government makes a payment of $1 on each bushel of wheat exported in order to encourage export sales. The subsidy allows U.S. exporting firms to receive revenue of $6 per bushel which is equal to the world price ($5) plus the subsidy ($1). Although the subsidy is not available on domestic sales, these firms are willing to sell to domestic consumers only at the higher price of $6 per bushel. This is because the firms would not sell wheat in the United States for a price less than $6 per bushel; they could always earn that amount on sales to the rest of the world. As the price rises from $5 to $6 per bushel, the quantity purchased in the United States falls from four million bushels to two million bushels, the quantity supplied rises from eight million bushels to ten million bushels, and the quantity of exports increases from four million bushels to eight million bushels.

The welfare effects of the export subsidy on the U.S. economy can be analyzed in terms of the consumer and producer surpluses. The export subsidy results in a decrease in the consumer surplus of area $a + b$ in the figure ($3 million) and an increase in the producer surplus of area $a + b + c$ ($9 million). The taxpayer cost of the export subsidy equals the per-unit subsidy ($1) times the quantity of wheat exported (8 million bushels), resulting in area $b + c + d$ ($8 million). Thus, U.S. wheat producers gain at the expense of the U.S. consumer and taxpayer.

Also, the export subsidy entails a deadweight loss of welfare to the U.S. economy. This consists of area d ($1 million), which is a deadweight loss due to the increasing domestic cost of producing additional wheat and area b ($1 million), which is due to lost consumer surplus because the price has increased.

In this example, we assumed that the exporting country is a relatively small country. However, in the real world, the exporting country may be a relatively large producer in the world market, and thus will realize a decrease in its terms of trade when it imposes a subsidy on exports. Why would this occur? In order to export more product, its firms would have to reduce the price. A decrease in the price of the exported good would worsen the exporting country's terms of trade.

The Export Enhancement Program provides an example of the use of export subsidies by the United States. Established in 1985, this program attempts to offset the adverse effects on U.S. agricultural exports due to unfair trade practices or subsidies by competing exporters, particularly the EU. This program allows U.S. exporters to sell their products in targeted markets at prices below their costs by providing cash bonuses. It has played a major role in the export of many agricultural products; such as wheat, barley, poultry, and dairy products.

Dumping

The case for protecting import-competing producers from foreign competition is bolstered by the antidumping argument. **Dumping** is recognized as a form of international price discrimination. It occurs when foreign buyers are charged lower prices than domestic buyers for an identical product, after allowing for transportation costs and tariff duties. Selling in foreign markets at a price below the cost of production is also considered dumping.

Forms of Dumping

Commercial dumping is generally viewed as sporadic, predatory, or persistent in nature. Each type is practiced under different circumstances.

Sporadic dumping (distress dumping) occurs when a firm disposes of excess inventories on foreign markets by selling abroad at lower prices than at home. This form of dumping may be the result of misfortune or poor planning by foreign producers. Unforeseen changes in supply and demand conditions can result in excess inventories and thus in dumping. Although sporadic dumping may be beneficial to importing consumers, it can be quite disruptive to import-competing producers, who face falling sales and short-term losses. Temporary tariff duties can be levied to protect home producers, but because sporadic dumping has minor effects on international trade, governments are reluctant to grant tariff protection under these circumstances.

Predatory dumping occurs when a producer temporarily reduces the prices charged abroad to drive foreign competitors out of business. When the producer succeeds in acquiring a monopoly position, prices are then raised commensurate with its market power. The new price level must be sufficiently high to offset any losses that occurred during the period of cutthroat pricing. The firm would presumably be confident in its ability to prevent the entry of potential competitors long enough for it to enjoy economic profits. To be successful, predatory dumping has to be practiced on a massive basis to provide consumers with a sufficient opportunity for bargain shopping. Home governments are generally concerned about predatory pricing for monopolizing purposes and may retaliate with antidumping duties that eliminate the price differential. Although predatory dumping is a theoretical possibility, economists have not found empirical evidence that supports its existence. With the prospect of a long and costly period of predation and the likelihood of a limited ability to deter subsequent entry by new rivals, the chances of actually earning full monopoly profits seems remote.

Persistent dumping, as its name suggests, goes on indefinitely. In an effort to maximize economic profits, a producer may consistently sell abroad at lower prices than at home. The rationale underlying persistent dumping is explained in the next section.

International Price Discrimination

Consider the case of a domestic seller that enjoys market power as a result of barriers that restrict competition at home. Suppose this firm sells in foreign markets that are highly competitive. This scenario means that the domestic consumer response to a change in price is less than that abroad; the home demand is less elastic than the foreign demand. A profit-maximizing firm would benefit from international price discrimination, charging a *higher* price at home, where competition is weak and demand is less elastic, and a *lower* price for the same product in foreign markets to meet competition. The practice of identifying separate groups of buyers of a product and charging different prices to these groups results in increased revenues and profits for the firm as compared to what would occur in the absence of price discrimination.

Figure 5.5 illustrates the demand and cost conditions of South Korean Steel Inc. (SKS), who sells steel to buyers in South Korea (less elastic market) and in Canada (more elastic market); the total steel market consists of these two submarkets. Let D_{SK} be the South Korean steel demand and D_C be the Canadian demand, with the corresponding marginal revenue schedules represented by MR_{SK} and MR_C, respectively. The D_{SK+C} denotes the market demand schedule, found by adding horizontally the demand schedules of the two submarkets; similarly, MR_{SK+C} depicts the market marginal revenue schedule. The marginal cost and average total cost schedules of SKS are denoted respectively by MC and ATC.

South Korea Steel maximizes total profits by producing and selling 45 tons of steel at which marginal revenue equals marginal cost. At this output level, $ATC =$ \$300 per ton, and total cost equals \$13,500 (\$300 × 45 tons). The firm faces the problem of how to distribute the total output of 45 tons, and thus set price, in the

FIGURE 5.5

INTERNATIONAL PRICE DISCRIMINATION

A price-discriminating firm maximizes profits by equating marginal revenue, in each submarket, with marginal cost. The firm will charge a higher price in the less-elastic-demand (less competitive) market and a lower price in the more-elastic-demand (more competitive) market. Successful dumping leads to additional revenue and profits for the firm compared to what would be realized in the absence of dumping.

two submarkets in which it sells. Should the firm sell steel to South Korean and Canadian buyers at a uniform (single) price, or should the firm practice discriminating pricing?

As a *nondiscriminating* seller, SKS sells 45 tons of steel to South Korean and Canadian buyers at the single price of $500 per ton, the maximum price permitted by demand schedule D_{SK+C} at the $MR = MC$ output level. To see how many tons of steel are sold in each submarket, construct a horizontal line in Figure 5.5 at the price of $500. The optimal output in each submarket occurs where the horizontal line intersects the demand schedules of the two nations. Thus, SKS sells 35 tons of steel to South Korean buyers at a price of $500 per ton and receives revenues totaling $17,500. The firm sells 10 tons of steel to Canadian buyers at a price of $500 per ton and realizes a revenue of $5,000. Sales revenues in both submarkets combined equal $22,500. With a total cost of $13,500, SKS realizes a profit of $9,000.

Although SKS realizes a profit as a nondiscriminating seller, its profit is not optimal. By engaging in price discrimination, the firm can increase its total revenue without increasing its cost, and thus increase its profit. The firm accomplishes this by charging *higher* prices to South Korean buyers, who have less elastic demand schedules, and *lower* prices to Canadian buyers, who have more elastic demand schedules.

As a price-discriminating seller, SKS again faces the problem of how to distribute the total output of 45 tons of steel, and thus set price, in the two submarkets in which it sells. To accomplish this, the firm follows the familiar $MR = MC$ principle, whereby the marginal revenue of each submarket equals the marginal cost at the profit-maximizing output. This principle can be shown in Figure 5.5 by first constructing a horizontal line from $200, the point where $MC = MR_{SK+C}$. The optimal output and price in each submarket is then found where this horizontal line intersects the MR schedules of the submarkets. Thus, SKS sells 25 tons of steel to South Korean buyers at a price of $700 per ton and receives revenues totaling $17,500. The firm sells 20 tons of steel to Canadian buyers at a price of $400 per ton and collects revenues of $8,000. The combined revenues of the two submarkets equal $25,500, a sum $3,000 greater than in the absence of price discrimination. With a total cost of $13,500, the firm realizes a profit of $12,000, compared to $9,000 under a single pricing policy. As a price-discriminating seller, SKS thus enjoys a higher revenue and profit.

Notice that the firm took advantage of its ability to price-discriminate, charging different prices in the two submarkets: $700 per ton to South Korean steel buyers and $400 per ton to Canadian buyers. For international price discrimination to be successful, certain conditions must hold. First, to ensure that at any price the demand schedules in the two submarkets have different demand elasticities, the submarkets' demand conditions must differ. Domestic buyers, for example, may have income levels or tastes and preferences that differ from those of the buyers abroad. Second, the firm must be able to separate the two submarkets, preventing any significant resale of commodities from the lower-priced to the higher-priced market. This is because any resale by consumers will tend to neutralize the effect of differential prices and will narrow the discriminatory price structure to the point at which it approaches a single price to all consumers. Because of high transportation costs and governmental trade restrictions, markets are often easier to separate internationally than nationally.

Antidumping Regulations

Despite the benefits that dumping may offer to importing consumers, governments have often levied penalty duties against commodities they believe are being dumped into their markets from abroad. U.S. antidumping law is designed to prevent price discrimination and below-cost sales that injure U.S. industries. Under U.S. law, an **antidumping duty** is levied when the U.S. Department of Commerce determines a class or kind of foreign merchandise is being sold at *less than fair value* (LTFV) and the U.S. International Trade Commission (ITC) determines that LTFV imports are causing or threatening material injury (such as unemployment and lost sales and profits) to a U.S. industry. Such antidumping duties are imposed in addition to the normal tariff in order to neutralize the effects of price discrimination or below-cost sales.

The **margin of dumping** is calculated as the amount by which the foreign market value exceeds the U.S. price. Foreign market value is defined in one of two ways. According to the **priced-based definition**, dumping occurs whenever a foreign company sells a product in the U.S. market at a price below that for which the same product sells in the home market. When a home-nation price of the good is not available (for example, if the good is produced only for export and is not sold domestically), an effort is made to determine the price of the good in a third market.

In cases where the price-based definition cannot be applied, a **cost-based definition** of foreign market value is permitted. Under this approach, the Commerce Department "constructs" a foreign market value equal to the sum of (1) the cost of manufacturing the merchandise, (2) general expenses, (3) profit on home-market sales, and (4) the cost of packaging the merchandise for shipment to the United States. The amount for general expenses must equal at least ten percent of the cost of manufacturing, and the amount for profit must equal at least eight percent of the manufacturing cost plus general expenses.

Antidumping cases begin with a complaint filed concurrently with the Commerce Department and the International Trade Commission. The complaint comes from within an import-competing industry (for example, from a firm or labor union) and consists of evidence of the existence of dumping and data that demonstrate material injury or threat of injury.

The Commerce Department first makes a preliminary determination as to whether or not dumping has occurred, including an estimate of the size of the dumping margin. If the preliminary investigation finds evidence of dumping, U.S. importers must immediately pay a special tariff (equal to the estimated dumping margin) on all imports of the product in question. The Commerce Department then makes its final determination as to whether or not dumping has taken place, as well as the size of the dumping margin. If the Commerce Department rules that dumping did not occur, special tariffs previously collected are rebated to U.S. importers. Otherwise, the International Trade Commission determines whether or not material injury has occurred as the result of the dumping.

If the International Trade Commission rules that import-competing firms were not injured by the dumping, the special tariffs are rebated to U.S. importers. But if both the International Trade Commission and the Commerce Department rule in favor of the dumping petition, a permanent tariff is imposed that equals the size of the dumping margin calculated by the Commerce Department in its final investigation.

In recent years, the average antidumping duty imposed by the United States has been about 45 percent, with some duties exceeding 100 percent. The impact of these duties on trade has been substantial, with targeted imports typically falling 50 to 70 percent over the first three years of protection. Let us consider some cases involving dumping.

Smith Corona Finds Antidumping Victories Are Hollow

Although antidumping duties are intended to protect domestic producers from unfairly priced imports, they can be an inconclusive weapon. Consider the case of Smith Corona, Inc., which won several antidumping cases from the 1970s to the 1990s but had little to show for it.

Trouble erupted for Smith Corona in the 1970s when it encountered ferocious competition from Brother Industries Ltd. of Japan, which flooded the U.S. market with its portable typewriters. Responding to Smith Corona's dumping complaint, in 1980 the U.S. government imposed antidumping duties of 49 percent on Brother portables. However, Smith Corona's antidumping victory proved to be hollow, because Brother realized that the antidumping ruling applied only to typewriters without a memory or calculating function. Through the tactic of *product evolution*, Brother evaded the duties by upgrading its typewriter to include a tiny computer memory. It took until 1990 for Smith Corona to get this loophole plugged by the federal court of appeals in Washington, DC. By that time, Brother had found a more permanent method of circumventing antidumping duties: It began assembling portable typewriters in the United States from components manufactured in Malaysia and Japan. These typewriters were no longer "imported," and thus the 1980s duties did not apply.

Then competition shifted to another product, the personal word processor. By 1990, Smith Corona complained that Brother and other Japanese manufacturers were dumping word processors in the United States. This complaint led the U.S. government to impose import duties of almost 60 percent on Japanese word processors in 1991. But that victory was also hollow, because it applied only to word processors manufactured in Japan; the Japanese firms assembled their word processors in the United States.

Undeterred, Smith Corona filed another complaint, invoking a provision in U.S. trade law that was designed to deter foreign firms from evading antidumping duties by importing components and assembling them in the United States. But the provision assumed that imported components would come from domestic (Japanese) factories, so it did not cover components produced in third countries. Recognizing this loophole, Brother demonstrated that its imported components came from third countries, and therefore its word processors were not subject to antidumping duties. All in all, obtaining relief from foreign dumped goods was a difficult process for Smith Corona!

Canadians Press Washington Apple Producers for Level Playing Field

Not only have foreign producers dumped products in the United States, but U.S. firms have sometimes dumped goods abroad.

In 1989, the Canadian government ruled that U.S. Delicious apples, primarily those grown in Washington, had been dumped on the Canadian market, causing injury to 4,500 commercial apple growers. As a result of the ruling, a 42-pound

SWIMMING UPSTREAM: THE CASE OF VIETNAMESE CATFISH

TRADE CONFLICTS

In 2003, the U.S. government was strongly criticized for assaulting catfish imports from Vietnam. According to Senator John McCain and other critics, this policy was an example of how wealthy countries preach the gospel of free trade when it comes to finding markets for their manufactured goods, but become highly protectionist when their farmers face competition. Let us consider this trade dispute.

After pursuing pro-capitalistic reforms, Vietnam became one of globalization's success stories in the 1990s. The nation transformed itself from being a rice importer to the world's second largest rice exporter and also an exporter of coffee. Vietnam's rural poverty rate declined from 70 to 30 percent. The normalization of communication between the governments of Vietnam and the United States resulted in American trade missions intended on increasing free enterprise in Vietnam.

On one of these trade missions, delegates saw much promise in Vietnamese catfish, with the country's Mekong Delta and cheap labor providing a competitive advantage. Within several years, some half-million Vietnamese were earning income from the catfish trade. Vietnam captured 20 percent of the frozen catfish-fillet market in the United States, forcing down prices. To the alarm of catfish farmers in Mississippi, the hub of the U.S. catfish industry, even local restaurants were serving Vietnamese catfish.

Before long, Vietnamese farmers faced a nasty trade war waged by Mississippi's catfish farmers involving product labeling and antidumping tariffs. Although these farmers are usually not large agribusinesses, they were strong enough to persuade the U.S. government to close the catfish market to the very Vietnamese farmers whose enterprise it had originally encouraged. The government declared that out of 2,000 types of catfish, only the American-born family could be called "catfish." So the Vietnamese could market their fish in America only by using Vietnamese words such as "tra" and "basa." Mississippi catfish farmers issued warnings of a "slippery catfish wannabe," saying such fish were "probably not even sporting real whiskers" and "floating around in Third World rivers nibbling on who knows what." This disinformation campaign resulted in decreased sales of Vietnamese catfish in the United States.

Not satisfied with its labeling success, the Mississippi catfish farmers initiated an antidumping case against Vietnamese catfish. In this case, the U.S. Department of Commerce did not have strong evidence that the imported fish were being sold in America more cheaply than in Vietnam, or below their cost of production. But rather than leaving Mississippi catfish farmers to the forces of international competition, the department declared Vietnam a "nonmarket" economy. This designation implied that Vietnamese farmers must not be covering all the costs they would in a market economy such as the United States, and thus were dumping catfish into the American market. Thus, tariffs ranging from 37 to 64 percent were imposed by the department on Vietnamese catfish. The U.S. International Trade Commission made the tariffs permanent by stating that the American catfish industry was injured by unfair competition due to dumping by Vietnam. According to critics, this nonmarket designation should not have been used because the U.S. government was encouraging Vietnam to become a market economy.

Source: "Harvesting Poverty: The Great Catfish War," *The New York Times*, July 22, 2003, p. 18 and The World Bank, *Global Economic Prospects*, 2004, Washington, D.C., p. 85.

box of Washington apples could not be sold in Canada for less than $11.87 (in USD), the "normal value" (analogous to the U.S. concept of "fair value") established by the Canadian government for regular-storage apples. Canadian importers purchasing U.S. apples at below-normal value had to pay an antidumping duty to the Canadian government so that the total purchase price equaled the established value. The antidumping order was for the five years from 1989 to 1994.

TABLE 5.5

NORMAL VALUE AND THE MARGIN OF DUMPING: DELICIOUS APPLES, REGULAR STORAGE, 1987–1988*

U.S. FOB per Packed Box (42 pounds)	Normal Value (in dollars)
Growing and harvesting costs	5.50
Packing, marketing, and storing costs	5.49
Total costs	10.99
Profit (8% margin)	0.88
Total normal value	11.87

Margin of Dumping	Percentage
Range	0–63.44
Weighted-average margin	32.53

*The weighted-average dumping margin for controlled-atmosphere-storage apples was 23.86 percent.

Source: From *Statement of Reasons: Final Determination of Dumping Respecting Delicious Apples Originating in or Exported from the United States of America*, Revenue Canada, Customs and Excise Division, December 1988.

The Canadian apple growers' complaint alleged that extensive tree planting in the United States during the late 1970s and early 1980s resulted in excess apple production. In 1987 and 1988, Washington growers experienced a record harvest and inventories that exceeded storage capacities. The growers dramatically cut prices in order to market their crop, leading to a collapse of the North American price of Delicious apples.

When Washington apple growers failed to provide timely information, the Canadian government estimated the normal value of a box of U.S. apples using the best information available. As seen in Table 5.5, the normal value for a box of apples in the crop-year 1987–1988 was $11.87 (in USD). During this period, the U.S. export price to Canada was about $9 (in USD) a box. Based on a comparison of the export price and the normal value of apples, the weighted-average dumping margin was determined to be 32.53 percent.

The Canadian government determined that the influx of low-priced Washington apples into the Canadian market displaced Canadian apples and resulted in losses to Canadian apple growers of $1 to $6.40 (in Canadian $) per box during the 1987–1988 growing season. The Canadian government ruled that the dumped apples injured Canadian growers, and thus imposed antidumping duties on Washington apples.

Is Antidumping Law Unfair?

Supporters of antidumping laws maintain that they are needed to create a "level playing field" for domestic producers that face unfair import competition. Antidumping laws ensure a level playing field by offsetting artificial sources of competitive advantage. By making up the difference between the dumped price and fair market value, an antidumping duty puts the domestic producer back on an equal footing. However, critics note that although protected industries may gain from antidumping duties, consumers of the protected good and the wider economy typically lose more, as discussed in Chapter 4. Hence, it is not surprising that antidumping law is subject to criticism, as discussed below.

Should Average Variable Cost Be the Yardstick for Defining Dumping?

Under current rules, dumping can occur when a foreign producer sells goods in the United States at less than fair value. Fair value is equated with average total cost plus an eight percent allowance for profit. However, many economists argue that fair value should be based on *average variable cost* rather than average total cost, especially when the domestic economy realizes a temporary downturn in demand.

Consider the case of a radio producer under the following assumptions: (1) The producer's physical capacity is 150 units of output over the given time period, and

TABLE 5.6

DUMPING AND EXCESS CAPACITY

	No Dumping	Dumping
Home sales	100 units @ $300	100 units @ $300
Export sales	0 units @ $300	50 units @ $250
Sales revenue	$30,000	$42,500
Less variable costs of $200 per unit	−20,000	−30,000
	$10,000	$12,500
Less total fixed costs of $10,000	−10,000	−10,000
Profit	$ 0	$ 2,500

(2) The domestic market's demand for radios is price-inelastic, whereas foreign demand is price-elastic. Refer to Table 5.6. Suppose the producer charges a uniform price (no dumping) of $300 per unit to both domestic and foreign consumers. With domestic demand inelastic, domestic sales total 100 units. But with elastic demand conditions abroad, suppose the producer cannot market any radios at the prevailing price. Sales revenues would equal $30,000, with variable costs plus fixed costs totaling $30,000. Without dumping, the firm would find itself with an excess capacity of 50 radios. Moreover, the firm would just break even on its domestic market operations.

Suppose this producer decides to dump radios abroad at lower prices than at home. As long as all variable costs are covered, any price that contributes to fixed costs will permit larger profits (smaller losses) than those realized with idle plant capacity at hand. According to Table 5.6, by charging $300 to home consumers, the firm can sell 100 units. Suppose that by charging a price of $250 per unit, the firm is able to sell an additional 50 units abroad. The total sales revenue of $42,500 would not only cover variable costs plus fixed costs, but would permit a profit of $2,500.

With dumping, the firm is able to increase profits even though it is selling abroad at a price less than the average total cost (average total cost = $40,000/150 = $267). Firms facing excess production capacity may thus have the incentive to stimulate sales by cutting prices charged to foreigners—perhaps to levels that just cover average variable cost. Of course, domestic prices must be sufficiently high to keep the firm operating profitably over the relevant time period.

Put simply, many economists argue that antidumping law, which uses average total cost as a yardstick to determine fair value, is unfair. They note that economic theory suggests that under competitive conditions, firms price their goods at average variable costs, which are below average total costs. Therefore, the antidumping laws punish firms that are simply behaving in a manner typical of competitive markets. Moreover, the law is unfair because U.S. firms selling at home are not subject to the same rules. Indeed, it is quite possible for a foreign firm that is selling at a loss both at home and in the United States to be found guilty of dumping, when U.S. firms are also taking losses and selling in the domestic market at exactly the same price.

Should Antidumping Law Reflect Currency Fluctuations?

Another criticism of antidumping law is that it does not account for currency fluctuations. Consider the price-based definition of dumping: selling at lower prices in a foreign market. Because foreign producers often must set their prices for foreign customers in terms of a foreign currency, fluctuations in exchange rates can cause them to "dump" according to the legal definition. For example, suppose the Japanese yen appreciates against the U.S. dollar, which means that it takes fewer yen to buy a dollar. But if Japanese steel exporters are meeting competition in the United States and setting their prices in dollars, the appreciation of the yen will cause the price of their exports in terms of the yen to decrease, making it appear that they are dumping in the United States. Under the U.S. antidumping law, American firms are not required to meet the standard imposed on foreign firms selling in the United States. Does the antidumping law redress unfairness—or create it?

Are Antidumping Duties Overused?

Until the 1990s, antidumping actions were a protectionist device used almost exclusively by a few rich countries: the United States, Canada, Australia, and Europe. Since then, there has been an explosion of antidumping cases brought by many developing nations such as Mexico, India, and Turkey. Rising use by other nations has meant that the United States itself has become an ever more frequent target of antidumping measures.

The widening use of antidumping duties is not surprising given the sizable degree of trade liberalization that has occurred across the world economy. However, the proliferation of antidumping duties is generally viewed by economists as a disturbing trend, a form of backdoor protectionism that runs counter to the post-World War II trend of reducing barriers to trade. Although antidumping actions are legal under the rules of the World Trade Organization, there is concern of a vicious cycle where antidumping duties by one country invite retaliatory duties by other countries.

For U.S. producers, it has become much easier to obtain relief from import competition in the form of antidumping duties. One reason is that the scope for initiating an antidumping action has been widened from preventing predatory pricing to any form of international price discrimination. More aggressive standards for assessing the role of imports in harming domestic industries have also contributed to greater use of antidumping duties.

Critics of U.S. antidumping policy maintain that the U.S. Department of Commerce almost always finds that dumping has occurred, although positive findings of material injury by the U.S. International Trade Commission are less frequent. Critics also note that in many cases where imports were determined to be dumped under existing rules, they would not have been questioned as posing an anticompetitive threat under the same countries' antitrust laws. In other words, the behavior of the importers, if undertaken by a domestic firm, would not have been questioned as anticompetitive or otherwise generally harmful.

Other Nontariff Trade Barriers

Other NTBs consist of governmental codes of conduct applied to imports. Even though such provisions are often well disguised, they remain important sources of commercial policy. Let's consider three such barriers: government procurement policies, social regulations, and sea transport and freight regulations.

Government Procurement Policies

Because government agencies are large buyers of goods and services, they are attractive customers for foreign suppliers. If governments purchased goods and services only from the lowest-cost suppliers, the pattern of trade would not differ significantly from that which occurs in a competitive market. However, most governments favor domestic suppliers over foreign ones in the procurement of materials and products. This is evidenced by the fact that the ratio of imports to total purchases in the public sector is much smaller than in the private sector.

Governments often extend preferences to domestic suppliers in the form of **buy-national policies**. The U.S. government, through explicit laws, openly discriminates against foreign suppliers in its purchasing decisions. Although most other governments do not have formally legislated preferences for domestic suppliers, they often discriminate against foreign suppliers through hidden administrative rules and practices. Such governments utilize closed bidding systems that restrict the number of companies allowed to bid on sales, or they may publicize government contracts in such a way as to make it difficult for foreign suppliers to make a bid.

To stimulate domestic employment during the Great Depression, in 1933 the U.S. government passed the Buy American Act. This act requires federal agencies to purchase materials and products from U.S. suppliers if their prices are not "unreasonably" higher than those of foreign competitors. A product, to qualify as domestic, must have at least a 50 percent domestic component content and must be manufactured in the United States. As it stands today, U.S. suppliers of civilian agencies are given a six percent preference margin. This margin means that a U.S. supplier receives the government contract as long as the U.S. low bid is no more than six percent higher than the competing foreign bid. This preference margin rises to 12 percent if the low domestic bidder is situated in a labor-surplus area, and to 50 percent if the purchase is made by the Department of Defense. These preferences are waived when it is determined that the U.S.-produced good is not available in sufficient quantities or is not of satisfactory quality.

By discriminating against low-cost foreign suppliers in favor of domestic suppliers, buy-national policies are a barrier to free trade. Domestic suppliers are given the leeway to use less efficient production methods and to pay resource prices higher than those permitted under free trade. This leeway yields a higher cost for government projects and deadweight welfare losses for the nation in the form of the protective and consumption effects.

The Buy American restrictions of the U.S. government have been liberalized with the adoption of the Tokyo Round of Multilateral Trade Negotiations in 1979. However, the pact does not apply to the purchase of materials and products by state and local government agencies. More than 30 states currently have Buy American laws, ranging from explicit prohibitions on purchases of foreign products to loose policy guidelines favoring U.S. products.

For example, during 2001–2004 the California Transit Authority rebuilt portions of the earthquake-damaged San Francisco–Oakland Bay Bridge. However, the project cost about $4 billion, three times more than the agency originally expected. One reason was California's Buy American rules, which required that foreign steel could be used on the bridge only if its cost was at least 25 percent less than domestic steel. In this case, the difference was only 23 percent, so the state had to purchase domestic steel. That difference added $400 million to the price tag. Although this requirement

U.S. FISCAL STIMULUS AND BUY AMERICAN LEGISLATION

As the U.S. government moved toward enacting its $787 billion fiscal stimulus legislation during the recession of 2007–2009, debate emerged over whether government-funded projects should use only U.S.-made materials. According to proponents of Buy American legislation, not one dollar of stimulus expenditures should be spent on foreign goods; instead, taxpayers' dollars should be used to buy U.S.-made goods and thus support the jobs of Americans.

The initial fiscal stimulus bill sponsored by the House of Representatives stipulated that none of the funds made available by the bill could be used for infrastructure projects unless all of the iron and steel used in a project are produced in the United States. The Senate version went even further, mandating that all manufactured goods used in construction projects come from U.S. producers. This legislation was strongly favored by U.S. labor unions and companies such as U.S. Steel Corp.

Although President Barack Obama supported Buy American legislation during his presidential campaign in 2008, his enthusiasm weakened by 2009. The initial foreign reaction to possible Buy American legislation was outrage. The European Union, for example, warned that passage of the legislation would result in the United States violating past trade agreements and intensifying the possibility of a trade war that could plunge the world into depression. Also, U.S. exporting companies such as Caterpillar argued that foreign retaliation would greatly reduce their sales abroad: Caterpillar noted that in 2009, 60 percent of its revenue was from foreign sales.

In response to these concerns, Obama came out against Buy American provisions that signaled blatant protectionism. He wound up signing a fiscal stimulus bill that included a watered-down version of the Buy American provisions contained in the House and Senate stimulus bills. For example, federal agencies can waive Buy American preferences if they inflate the cost of a construction project by more than 25 percent or are deemed to be against the public interest. Also, Buy American preferences are waived if they violate past trade agreements such as the North American Free Trade Agreement (NAFTA) reached by the United States, Canada, and Mexico. This waiver means that NAFTA protects the ability of firms in Canada and Mexico to bid on U.S. government contracts even though their products do not embody steel made in America. However, city and state (municipal) governments in the United States are not obligated to honor the trade agreements of the federal government: They have been able to enact Buy American preferences that exclude firms in Canada, Mexico, and other countries from bidding on municipal construction contracts for schools, water treatment plants, and the like.

At the writing of this book, many nations expressed unhappiness with Buy American legislation. For example, China and other developing countries, which do not have free trade agreements with the United States, complained that Buy American legislation is being used to shut out their products from the additional spending that the U.S. government was making to counter its recession. Moreover, Canadian producers resent being prevented from bidding on municipal contracts in the United States and thus pressured their municipal governments to exclude U.S. bidders from their contracts. Indeed, officials in Washington were scrambling to avoid an all out trade war.

benefited domestic steel producers, it was difficult to see how it helped California taxpayers.[6]

Social Regulations

Since the 1950s, nations have assumed an ever-increasing role in regulating the quality of life for society. **Social regulation** attempts to correct a variety of undesirable

---

[6]"Steep Cost Overruns, Delays Plague Efforts to Rebuild Bay Bridge," *Los Angeles Times*, May 29, 2004.

side effects in an economy that relate to health, safety, and the environment—effects that markets, left to themselves, often ignore. Social regulation applies to a particular issue, say environmental quality, and affects the behavior of firms in many industries such as automobiles, steel, and chemicals.

CAFÉ Standards

Although social regulations may advance health, safety, and environmental goals, they can also serve as barriers to international trade. Consider the case of fuel economy standards imposed by the U.S. government on automobile manufacturers.

Originally enacted in 1975, **corporate average fuel economy standards (CAFÉ)** represent the foundation of U.S. energy conservation policy. Applying to all passenger vehicles sold in the United States, the standards are based on the average fuel efficiency of all vehicles sold by all manufacturers. Since 1990, the CAFÉ requirement for passenger cars has been 27.5 miles per gallon. Manufacturers whose average fuel economy falls below this standard are subject to fines.

During the 1980s, CAFÉ requirements were used not only to promote fuel conservation but also to protect the jobs of U.S. autoworkers. The easiest way for U.S. car manufacturers to improve the average fuel efficiency of their fleets would have been to import smaller, more fuel-efficient vehicles from their subsidiaries in Asia and Europe. However, this would have decreased employment in an already depressed industry. The U.S. government thus enacted *separate but identical* standards for domestic and imported passenger cars. Therefore, General Motors, Ford, and Chrysler, which manufactured vehicles in the United States and also sold imported cars, would be required to fulfill CAFÉ targets for *both* categories of vehicles. Thus, U.S. firms could not fulfill CAFÉ standards by averaging the fuel economy of their imports with their less fuel-efficient, domestically produced vehicles. By calculating domestic and imported fleets separately, the U.S. government attempted to force domestic firms not only to manufacture more efficient vehicles but also to produce them in the United States! In short, government regulations sometimes place effective import barriers on foreign commodities, whether they are intended to do so or not, which aggravates foreign competitors.

Europe Has a Cow Over Hormone-Treated U.S. Beef

The EU's ban on hormone-treated meat is another case where social regulations can lead to a beef. Growth-promoting hormones are used widely by livestock producers to speed up growth rates and produce leaner livestock more in line with consumer preferences for diets with reduced fat and cholesterol. However, critics of hormones maintain that they can cause cancer for consumers of meat.

In 1989, the EU enacted its ban on the production and importation of beef derived from animals treated with growth-promoting hormones. The EU justified the ban as necessary to protect the health and safety of consumers.

The ban was immediately challenged by U.S. producers, who used the hormones in about 90 percent of their beef production. According to the United States, there was no scientific basis for the ban that restricted beef imports on the basis of health concerns. Instead, the ban was merely an attempt to protect the relatively high-cost European beef industry from foreign competition. American producers noted that when the ban was imposed, European producers had accumulated large, costly-to-store beef surpluses that resulted in enormous political pressure to limit imports of beef. The EU's emphasis on health concerns was thus a smokescreen for protecting an industry with comparative disadvantage, according to the United States.

The trade dispute eventually went to the WTO (see Chapter 6), which ruled that the EU's ban on hormone-treated beef was illegal and resulted in lost annual U.S. exports of beef to the EU in the amount of $117 million. Nonetheless, the EU, citing consumer preference, refused to lift its ban. Therefore, the WTO authorized the United States to impose tariffs high enough to prohibit $117 million of European exports to the United States. The United States exercised its right and slapped 100 percent tariffs on a list of European products that included tomatoes, Roquefort cheese, prepared mustard, goose liver, citrus fruit, pasta, hams, and other products. The U.S. hit list focused on products from Denmark, France, Germany, and Italy— the biggest supporters of the EU's ban on hormone-treated beef.

By effectively doubling the prices of the targeted products, the 100 percent tariffs pressured the Europeans to liberalize their imports of American beef products. In 2009, the EU and the United States took a first step in resolving their trade dispute by negotiating a four-year deal. During this period, the EU will quadruple import quotas for hormone-free U.S. beef, but it will not import hormone-treated American beef. In return, the United States will not impose sanctions on additional EU products, although it will maintain existing sanctions. By the end of the fourth-year, the two sides will seek to conclude a longer-term agreement regarding trade in beef whereupon the U.S. sanctions against the EU will be eliminated. It remains to be seen if this first step results in a permanent trade deal in beef.

Sea Transport and Freight Regulations

During the 1990s, U.S. shipping companies serving Japanese ports complained of a highly restrictive system of port services. They contended that Japan's association of stevedore companies (companies that unload cargo from ships) used a system of prior consultations to control competition, allocate harbor work among themselves, and frustrate the implementation of any cost-cutting by shipping companies.

In particular, shipping companies contended that they were forced to negotiate with the Japanese stevedore-company association on everything from arrival times to choice of stevedores and warehouses. Because port services were controlled by the stevedore-company association, foreign carriers could not negotiate with individual stevedore companies about prices and schedules. Moreover, U.S. carriers maintained that the Japanese government approved these restrictive practices by refusing to license new entrants into the port service business and by supporting the requirement that foreign carriers negotiate with Japan's stevedore-company association.

A midnight trip to Tokyo Bay illustrates the frustration of U.S. shipping companies. The lights are dimmed and the wharf is quiet, even though the Sealand Commerce has just docked. At 1:00 a.m., lights turn on, cranes swing alive, and trucks appear to unload the ship's containers, which carry paper plates, computers, and pet food from the United States. However, at 4:00 a.m. the lights shut off and the work ceases. Longshoremen won't return until 8:30 a.m. and will take three more hours off later in the day. They have unloaded only 169 of 488 containers that they must handle before the ship sails for Oakland. At this rate, the job will take until past noon; but at least it isn't Sunday, when docks close altogether.

When the Sealand Commerce reaches Oakland, however, U.S. dockworkers will unload and load 24 hours a day, taking 30 percent less time for about half the price. To enter Tokyo Bay, the ship had to clear every detail of its visit with Japan's stevedore-company association; to enter the U.S. port, it will merely notify port authorities and the Coast Guard. According to U.S. exporters, this unequal treatment on waterfronts is a trade barrier because it makes U.S. exports more expensive in Japan.

In 1997, the United States and Japan found themselves on the brink of a trade war after the U.S. government decided to direct its Coast Guard and customs service to bar Japanese-flagged ships from unloading at U.S. ports. The U.S. government demanded that foreign shipping companies be allowed to negotiate directly with Japanese stevedore companies to unload their ships, thus giving carriers a way around the restrictive practices of Japan's stevedore-company association. After consultation between the two governments, an agreement was reached to liberalize port services in Japan. As a result, the United States rescinded its ban against Japanese ships.

Summary

1. With the decline in import tariffs in the past two decades, nontariff trade barriers have gained in importance as a measure of protection. Nontariff trade barriers include such practices as (a) import quotas, (b) orderly marketing agreements, (c) domestic content requirements, (d) subsidies, (e) antidumping regulations, (f) discriminatory government procurement practices, (g) social regulations, and (h) sea transport and freight restrictions.

2. An import quota is a government-imposed limit on the quantity of a product that can be imported. Quotas are imposed on a global (worldwide) basis or a selective (individual country) basis. Although quotas have many of the same economic effects as tariffs, they tend to be more restrictive. A quota's revenue effect generally accrues to domestic importers or foreign exporters, depending on the degree of market power they possess. If government desired to capture the revenue effect, it could auction import quota licenses to the highest bidder in a competitive market.

3. A tariff-rate quota is a two-tier tariff placed on an imported product. It permits a limited number of goods to be imported at a lower tariff rate, whereas any imports beyond this limit face a higher tariff. Of the revenue generated by a tariff-rate quota, some accrues to the domestic government as tariff revenue and the remainder is captured by producers as windfall profits.

4. Because an export quota is administered by the government of the exporting nation (supply-side restriction), its revenue effect tends to be captured by sellers from the exporting nation. For the importing nation, the quota's revenue effect is a welfare loss in addition to the protective and consumption effects.

5. Domestic content requirements try to limit the practice of foreign sourcing and encourage the development of domestic industry. They typically stipulate the minimum percentage of a product's value that must be produced in the home country for that product to be sold there tariff-free. Domestic content protection tends to impose welfare losses on the domestic economy in the form of higher production costs and higher-priced goods.

6. Government subsidies are sometimes granted as a form of protection to domestic exporters and import-competing producers. They may take the form of direct cash bounties, tax concessions, credit extended at low interest rates, or special insurance arrangements. Direct production subsidies for import-competing producers tend to involve a smaller loss in economic welfare than do equivalent tariffs and quotas. The imposition of export subsidies results in a terms-of-trade effect and an export-revenue effect.

7. International dumping occurs when a firm sells its product abroad at a price that is less than average total cost or less than that charged to domestic buyers of the same product. Dumping can be sporadic, predatory, or persistent in nature. Idle productive capacity may be the

reason behind dumping. Governments often impose stiff penalties against foreign commodities that are believed to be dumped in the home economy.

8. Government rules and regulations in areas such as safety and technical standards and marketing requirements can have a significant impact on world trade patterns.

Key Concepts & Terms

- Antidumping duty (p. 187)
- Buy-national policies (p. 193)
- Corporate average fuel economy standards (CAFÉ) (p. 195)
- Cost-based definition of dumping (p. 187)
- Domestic content requirements (p. 179)
- Domestic production subsidy (p. 180)
- Dumping (p. 184)
- Export quotas (p. 177)
- Export subsidy (p. 180)
- Global quota (p. 170)
- Import license (p. 169)
- Import quota (p. 169)
- License on demand allocation (p. 175)
- Margin of dumping (p. 187)
- Nontariff trade barriers (NTBs) (p. 169)
- Persistent dumping (p. 184)
- Predatory dumping (p. 184)
- Price-based definition of dumping (p. 187)
- Selective quota (p. 170)
- Social regulation (p. 194)
- Sporadic dumping (p. 184)
- Subsidies (p. 180)
- Tariff-rate quota (p. 175)

Study Questions

1. A subsidy may provide import-competing producers the same degree of protection as tariffs or quotas but at a lower cost in terms of national welfare. Explain.

2. Rather than generating tax revenue as do tariffs, subsidies require tax revenue. Therefore, they are not an effective protective device for the home economy. Do you agree?

3. In 1980, the U.S. auto industry proposed that import quotas be imposed on foreign-produced cars sold in the United States. What would be the likely benefits and costs of such a policy?

4. Why did the U.S. government in 1982 provide import quotas as an aid to domestic sugar producers?

5. Which tends to result in a greater welfare loss for the home economy: (a) an import quota levied by the home government or (b) a voluntary export quota imposed by the foreign government?

6. What would be the likely effects of export restraints imposed by Japan on its auto shipments to the United States?

7. Why might U.S. steel-using firms lobby against the imposition of quotas on foreign steel sold in the United States?

8. Concerning international dumping, distinguish between the price- and cost-based definitions of foreign market value.

9. Table 5.7 illustrates the demand and supply schedules for television sets in Venezuela, a "small" nation that is unable to affect world prices. On graph paper, sketch Venezuela's demand and supply schedules of television sets.

TABLE 5.7

VENEZUELA SUPPLY OF AND DEMAND FOR TELEVISION SETS

Price per TV set	Quantity Demanded	Quantity Supplied
$100	900	0
200	700	200
300	500	400
400	300	600
500	100	800

a. Suppose Venezuela imports TV sets at a price of $150 each. Under free trade, how many sets does Venezuela produce, consume, and import? Determine Venezuela's consumer surplus and producer surplus.

b. Assume that Venezuela imposes a quota that limits imports to 300 TV sets. Determine the quota-induced price increase and the resulting decrease in consumer surplus. Calculate the quota's redistributive, consumption, protective, and revenue effects. Assuming that Venezuelan import companies organize as buyers and bargain favorably with competitive foreign exporters, what is the overall welfare loss to Venezuela as a result of the quota? Suppose that foreign exporters organize as a monopoly seller. What is the overall welfare loss to Venezuela as a result of the quota?

c. Suppose that, instead of a quota, Venezuela grants its import-competing producers a subsidy of $100 per TV set. In your diagram, draw the subsidy-adjusted supply schedule for Venezuelan producers. Does the subsidy result in a rise in the price of TV sets above the free-trade level? Determine Venezuela's production, consumption, and imports of TV sets under the subsidy. What is the total cost of the subsidy to the Venezuelan government? Of this amount, how much is transferred to Venezuelan producers in the form of a producer surplus, and how much is absorbed by higher production costs due to inefficient domestic production? Determine the overall welfare loss to Venezuela under the subsidy.

10. In the past two decades, nontariff trade barriers have gained in importance as protectionist devices. What are the major nontariff trade barriers?

11. How does the revenue effect of an import quota differ from that of a tariff?

12. What are the major forms of subsidies that governments grant to domestic producers?

13. What is meant by voluntary export restraints, and how do they differ from other protective barriers?

14. Should U.S. antidumping laws be stated in terms of average total costs or average variable costs?

15. Which is a more restrictive trade barrier: an import tariff or an equivalent import quota?

16. Differentiate among sporadic, persistent, and predatory dumping.

17. Table 5.8 illustrates the demand and supply schedules for computers in Ecuador, a "small" nation that is unable to affect world prices. On graph paper, sketch Ecuador's demand and supply schedules of computers.

TABLE 5.8

COMPUTER SUPPLY AND DEMAND: ECUADOR

Price of Computer	Quantity Demanded	Quantity Supplied
$ 0	100	—
200	90	0
400	80	10
600	70	20
800	60	30
1000	50	40
1200	40	50
1400	30	60
1600	20	70
1800	10	80
2000	0	90

a. Assume that Hong Kong and Taiwan can supply computers to Ecuador at a per-unit price of $300 and $500, respectively. With free trade, how many computers does Ecuador import? From which nation does it import?

b. Suppose Ecuador and Hong Kong negotiate a voluntary export agreement in which Hong Kong imposes on its exporters a quota that limits shipments to Ecuador to 40 computers. Assume Taiwan does not take advantage of the situation by exporting computers to Ecuador. Determine the quota-induced price increase and the reduction in the consumer surplus for Ecuador. Determine the quota's redistributive, protective, consumption, and revenue effects. Because the export quota is administered by Hong Kong, its exporters will capture the quota's revenue effect. Determine the overall welfare loss to Ecuador as a result of the quota.

FIGURE 5.6

INTERNATIONAL DUMPING SCHEDULES

(a)   United Kingdom

(b)   Canada

(c)   Total Market

---

c. Again assume that Hong Kong imposes an export quota on its producers that restricts shipments to Ecuador to 40 computers, but now suppose that Taiwan, a nonrestrained exporter, ships an additional 20 computers to Ecuador. Ecuador thus imports 60 computers. Determine the overall welfare loss to Ecuador as a result of the quota.

d. In general, when increases in nonrestrained supply offset part of the cutback in shipments that occur under an export quota, will the overall welfare loss for the importing country be greater or smaller than that which occurs in the absence of nonrestrained supply? Determine the amount in the example of Ecuador.

18. Figure 5.6 illustrates the practice of international dumping by British Toys, Inc. (BTI). Figure 5.6 (a) shows the domestic demand and marginal revenue schedules faced by BTI in the United Kingdom (UK), and Figure 5.6(b) shows the demand and marginal revenue schedules faced by BTI in Canada. Figure 5.6(c) shows the combined demand and marginal revenue schedules

for the two markets, as well as BTI's average total cost and marginal cost schedules.

a. In the absence of international dumping, BTI would charge a uniform price to U.K. and Canadian customers (ignoring transportation costs). Determine the firm's profit-maximizing output and price, as well as total profit. How much profit accrues to BTI on its U.K. sales and on its Canadian sales?

b. Suppose now that BTI engages in international dumping. Determine the price that BTI charges its U.K. buyers and the profits that accrue on U.K. sales. Also determine the price that BTI charges its Canadian buyers and the profits that accrue on Canadian sales. Does the practice of international dumping yield higher profits than the uniform pricing strategy? If so, by how much?

19. Why is a tariff-rate quota viewed as a compromise between the interests of the domestic consumer and those of the domestic producer? How does the revenue effect of a tariff-rate quota differ from that of an import tariff?

Exploring Further   5.1

Tariff-Rate Quota Welfare Effects

The welfare effects of tariff-rate quotas have been briefly discussed in this chapter. Let us further examine these welfare effects.

Figure EF 5.1 illustrates the welfare effects of a hypothetical tariff-rate quota on sugar. Assume that the U.S. demand and supply schedules for sugar are given by $D_{U.S.}$ and $S_{U.S.}$, and the equilibrium (autarky) price of sugar is $540 per ton. Assuming free trade, suppose the United States faces a constant world price of sugar equal to $400 per ton. At the free-trade price, U.S. production

equals 5 tons, U.S. consumption equals 40 tons, and imports equal 35 tons.

To protect its producers from foreign competition, suppose the United States enacts a tariff-rate import quota of 5 tons. Imports within this limit face a 10 percent tariff, but a 20 percent tariff applies to imports in excess of the limit.

Because the United States initially imports an amount exceeding the limit as defined by the tariff-rate quota, both the within-quota rate and the over-quota rate apply. This two-tier tariff causes

---

FIGURE EF 5.1

TARIFF-RATE QUOTA WELFARE EFFECTS

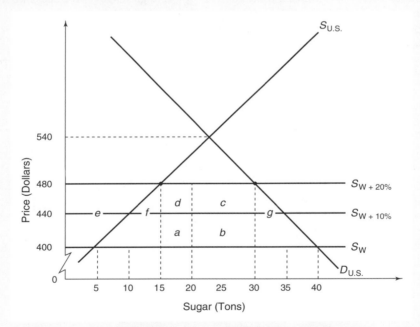

The imposition of a tariff-rate quota leads to higher product prices and a decrease in consumer surplus for domestic buyers. Of the tariff-rate quota's revenue effect, a portion accrues to the domestic government, while the remainder accrues to domestic importers or foreign exporters as windfall profits.

the price of sugar sold in the United States to rise from $400 to $480 per ton. Domestic production increases to 15 tons, domestic consumption falls to 30 tons, and imports fall to 15 tons. Increased sales allow the profits of U.S. sugar producers to rise by an amount equal to area e ($800). The deadweight losses to the U.S. economy, in terms of production and consumption inefficiencies, equal areas f ($400) and g ($400), respectively.

An interesting feature of the tariff-rate quota is the revenue it generates. Some of it accrues to the domestic government as tariff revenue, but the remainder is captured by businesses as windfall profits—a gain to businesses resulting from sudden or unexpected government policy.

In this example, after enactment of the tariff quota, imports total 15 tons of sugar. The U.S. government collects area a ($200), found by multiplying the within-quota duty of $40 times 5 tons. Area $b + c$ ($800), found by multiplying the remaining 10 tons of imported sugar times the over-quota duty of $80, also accrues to the government.

Area d ($200) in the figure represents windfall profits. Under the tariff-rate quota, the domestic price of the first 5 tons of sugar imported is $440, reflecting the foreign supply price of $400 plus the import duty of $40. Suppose U.S. import companies can obtain foreign sugar at $440 per ton. By reselling the 5 tons to U.S. consumers at $480 per ton, the price of over-quota sugar, U.S. importers would capture area d as windfall profits. But this opportunity will not last long, because foreign sugar suppliers will want to capture the windfall gain. To the extent that they can restrict sugar exports to the United States, foreign producers could force up the price of sugar and expropriate profits from U.S. importing companies. Foreign producers conceivably could capture the entire area d by raising their supply price to $480 per ton. The portion of the windfall profit captured by foreign sugar producers represents a welfare loss to the U.S. economy.

Exploring Further 5.2

Export Quota Welfare Effects

Typical orderly marketing agreements have involved limitations on export sales administered by one or more exporting nations or industries. What are the welfare effects of export quotas?

Figure EF 5.2 illustrates these effects in the case of trade in autos between the United States, Japan, and Germany. Assume that $S_{U.S.}$ and $D_{U.S.}$ depict the supply and demand schedules of autos for the United States. The S_J denotes the supply schedule of Japan, assumed to be the world's

low-cost producer, and S_G denotes the supply schedule of Germany.

Referring to Figure EF 5.2(a), the price of autos to the U.S. consumer is $20,000 under free trade. At that price, U.S. firms produce one auto, and U.S. consumers purchase seven autos, with imports from Japan totaling six autos. Note that German autos are too costly to be exported to the United States at the free-trade price.

WELFARE EFFECTS OF AN EXPORT QUOTA

By reducing the available supplies of a product, an export quota (levied by the foreign nation) leads to higher prices in the importing nation. The price increase induces a decrease in consumer surplus. Of this amount, the welfare loss to the importing nation equals the protective effect, the consumption effect, and the portion of the revenue effect that is captured by the foreign exporter. To the extent that nonrestrained countries augment shipments to the importing nation, the welfare loss of an export quota decreases.

Suppose that Japan, responding to protectionist sentiment in the United States, decides to restrain auto shipments to the United States rather than face possible mandatory restrictions on its exports. Assume that the Japanese government imposes an export quota on its auto firms of two units, down from the free-trade level of six units. Above the free-trade price, the total U.S. supply of autos now equals U.S. production plus the export quota; the auto supply curve thus shifts from $S_{U.S.}$ to $S_{U.S.+Q}$ in Figure EF 5.2(a). The reduction in imports from six autos to two autos raises the equilibrium price to \$30,000. This price leads to an increase in the quantity supplied by U.S. firms from one auto to three autos and a decrease in the U.S. quantity demanded from seven autos to five autos.

The export quota's price increase causes consumer surplus to fall by area $a + b + c + d + e + f + g + h + i + j + k + l$, an amount totaling \$60,000. Area $a+h$ (\$20,000) represents the transfer to U.S. auto companies as *profits*. The export quota results in a deadweight welfare loss for the U.S. economy equal to the *protective effect*, denoted by area $b + c + i$ (\$10,000), and the *consumption effect*, denoted by area $f + g + l$ (\$10,000). The export quota's *revenue effect* equals area $d + e + j + k$ (\$20,000), found by multiplying the quota-induced increase in the Japanese price times the volume of autos shipped to the United States.

Remember that under an import quota, the disposition of the revenue effect is indeterminate: It will be shared between foreign exporters and domestic importers, depending on the relative concentration of bargaining power. But under an export quota, it is the foreign exporter who is able to capture the larger share of the quota revenue. In our example of the auto export quota, the Japanese exporters, in compliance with their government, self-regulate shipments to the United States. This supply-side restriction, resulting from Japanese firms behaving like a monopoly, leads to a scarcity of autos in the United States. Japanese automakers then are able to raise the price of their exports, capturing the quota revenue.

For this reason, it is not surprising that exporters might prefer to negotiate a voluntary restraint pact in lieu of facing other protectionist measures levied by the importing country. As for the export quota's impact on the U.S. economy, the expropriation of revenue by the Japanese represents a welfare loss in addition to the deadweight losses of production and consumption.

Another characteristic of a voluntary export agreement is that it typically applies only to the most important exporting nation(s). This is in contrast to a tariff or import quota, which generally applies to imports from all sources. When voluntary limits are imposed on the chief exporter, the exports of the **nonrestrained suppliers** may be stimulated. Nonrestrained suppliers may seek to increase profits by making up part of the cutback in the restrained nation's shipments. They may also want to achieve the maximum level of shipments against which to base any export quotas that might be imposed on them in the future. For example, Japan was singled out by the United States for restrictions in textiles during the 1950s and in color television sets during the 1970s. Other nations quickly increased shipments to the United States to fill in the gaps created by the Japanese restraints. Hong Kong textiles replaced most Japanese textiles, and TV sets from Taiwan and Korea supplanted Japanese sets.

Referring to Figure EF 5.2(b), let us start again at the free-trade price of \$20,000, with U.S. imports from Japan totaling six autos. Assume that Japan agrees to reduce its shipments to two units. However, suppose Germany, a nonrestrained supplier, exports two autos to the United States in response to the Japanese cutback. Above the free-trade price, the total U.S. supply of autos now equals U.S. production plus the Japanese export quota plus the nonrestrained exports coming from Germany. In Figure EF 5.2(b), this is illustrated by a shift in the supply curve from $S_{U.S.}$ to $S_{U.S.+Q+N}$. The reduction in imports from six autos to four autos raises the equilibrium price to \$25,000. The resulting deadweight losses of production and consumption inefficiencies equal area $b + g$ ($5,000), less than the deadweight losses under Japan's export quota in the absence of nonrestrained supply. Assuming that Japan administers the export restraint program, Japanese companies would be able to raise the price of their auto exports from $20,000 to $25,000 and earn profits equal to area $c + d$ ($10,000). Area $e + f$ ($10,000) represents a **trade-diversion effect**, which reflects inefficiency losses due to the shifting of two units from Japan, the world's low-cost producer, to Germany, a higher-cost source. Such trade diversion results in a loss of welfare to the world because resources are not being used in their most productive manner. The overall welfare of the United States thus decreases by area $b + c + d + e + f + g$ under the export-quota policy.

When increases in the nonrestrained supply offset part of the cutback in shipments that occurs under an export quota, the overall inefficiency loss for the importing nation (deadweight losses plus revenue expropriated by foreign producers) is *less* than that which would have occurred in the absence of nonrestrained exports. In the preceding example, this reduction amounts to area $i + j + k + l$ ($15,000).

Trade Regulations and Industrial Policies

CHAPTER 6

Previous chapters have examined the benefits and costs of tariff and nontariff trade barriers. This chapter discusses the major trade policies of the United States. It also considers the role of the World Trade Organization in the global trading system, the industrial policies implemented by nations to enhance the competitiveness of their producers, and the nature and effects of international economic sanctions used to pursue foreign policy objectives.

U.S. Tariff Policies Before 1930

As Table 6.1 makes clear, U.S. tariff history has been marked by fluctuations. The dominant motive behind the early tariff laws of the United States was to provide the government with an important source of tax revenue. This *revenue* objective was the main reason Congress passed the first tariff law in 1789 and followed it up with 12 more tariff laws by 1812. But as the U.S. economy diversified and developed alternative sources of tax revenue, justification for the revenue argument was weakened. The tariffs collected by the federal government today are about one percent of total federal revenues, a negligible amount.

As the revenue argument weakened, the *protective* argument for tariffs developed strength. In 1791, Alexander Hamilton presented to Congress his famous "Report on Manufacturers," which proposed that the young industries of the United States be granted import protection until they could grow and prosper—the *infant-industry* argument. Although Hamilton's writings did not initially have a legislative impact, by the 1820s protectionist sentiments in the United States were well established. During the 1920s, the average level of tariffs on U.S. imports was three to four times the eight percent levels of 1789.

The surging protectionist movement reached its high point in 1828 with the passage of the so-called Tariff of Abominations. This measure increased duties to an average level of 45 percent, the highest in the years prior to the Civil War, and

TABLE 6.1

U.S. TARIFF HISTORY: AVERAGE TARIFF RATES

Tariff Laws and Dates	Average Tariff Rate* (%)
McKinley Law, 1890	48.4
Wilson Law, 1894	41.3
Dingley Law, 1897	46.5
Payne-Aldrich Law, 1909	40.8
Underwood Law, 1913	27.0
Fordney-McCumber Law, 1922	38.5
Smoot-Hawley Law, 1930	53.0
1930–1949	33.9
1950–1969	11.9
1970–1989	6.4
1990–1999	5.2
2008	3.5

*Simple average.

Source: From U.S. Department of Commerce, *Statistical Abstract of the United States*, various issues and World Trade Organization, *World Tariff Profiles*, 2008.

provoked the South, which wanted low duties for its imported manufactured goods. The South's opposition to this tariff led to the passage of the Compromise Tariff of 1833, which provided for a downsizing of the tariff protection afforded U.S. manufacturers. During the 1840s and 1850s, the U.S. government found that it faced an excess of tax receipts over expenditures. Therefore, the government passed the Walker tariffs, which cut duties to an average level of 23 percent in order to eliminate the budget surplus. Further tariff cuts took place in 1857, bringing the average tariff levels to their lowest point since 1816, at around 16 percent.

During the Civil War era, tariffs were again raised with the passage of the Morill Tariffs of 1861, 1862, and 1864. These measures were primarily intended as a means of paying for the Civil War. By 1870, protection climbed back to the heights of the 1840s; however, this time the tariff levels would not be reduced. During the latter part of the 1800s, U.S. policy makers were impressed by the arguments of American labor and business leaders who complained that *cheap foreign labor* was causing goods to flow into the United States. The enactment of the McKinley and Dingley Tariffs largely rested upon this argument. By 1897, tariffs on protected imports averaged 46 percent.

Although the Payne-Aldrich Tariff of 1909 marked the turning point against rising protectionism, it was the enactment of the Underwood Tariff of 1913 that reduced duties to 27 percent on average. Trade liberalization might have remained on a more permanent basis had it not been for the outbreak of World War I. Protectionist pressures built up during the war years and maintained momentum after the war's conclusion. During the early 1920s, the *scientific tariff* concept was influential and in 1922 the Fordney-McCumber Tariff contained, among other provisions, one that allowed the president to increase tariff levels if foreign production costs were below those of the United States. Average tariff rates climbed to 38 percent under the Fordney-McCumber law.[1]

Smoot-Hawley Act

The high point of U.S. protectionism occurred with the passage of the **Smoot-Hawley Act** in 1930, under which U.S. average tariffs were raised to 53 percent on protected imports. As the Smoot-Hawley bill moved through the U.S. Congress, formal protests

---

[1]Throughout the 1800s, the United States levied high tariffs on imported goods, the infant-industry argument being an important motive. The second half of the 1800s was also a period of rapid economic growth for the country. According to protectionists, these tariffs provided the foundation for a growing economy. However, free traders note that such conclusions are unwarranted because this era was also a time of massive immigration to the United States, which fostered economic growth. See T. Norman Van Cott and Cecil Bohanon, "Tariffs, Immigration, and Economic Insulation," *The Independent Review*, Spring 2005, pp. 529–542.

FIGURE 6.1

SMOOT-HAWLEY PROTECTIONISM AND WORLD TRADE, 1929–1933 (MILLIONS OF DOLLARS)

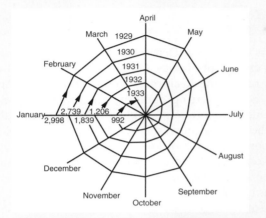

The figure shows the pattern of world trade from 1929 to 1933. Following the Smoot-Hawley Tariff Act of 1930, which raised U.S. tariffs to an average level of 53 percent, other nations retaliated by increasing their own import restrictions, and the volume of world trade decreased as the global economy fell into the Great Depression.

Source: Data taken from League of Nations, *Monthly Bulletin of Statistics*, February, 1934. See also Charles Kindleberger, *The World in Depression* (Berkeley, CA: University of California Press, 1973), p. 170.

from foreign nations flooded Washington, eventually adding up to a document of some 200 pages. Nevertheless, both the House of Representatives and the Senate approved the bill. Although about a thousand U.S. economists beseeched President Herbert Hoover to veto the legislation, he did not do so, and the tariff was signed into law on June 17, 1930. Simply put, the Smoot-Hawley Act tried to divert national demand away from imports and toward domestically produced goods.

The legislation provoked retaliation by 25 trading partners of the United States. Spain implemented the Wais Tariff in reaction to U.S. tariffs on cork, oranges, and grapes. Switzerland boycotted U.S. exports to protest new tariffs on watches and shoes. Canada increased its tariffs threefold in reaction to U.S. tariffs on timber, logs, and many food products. Italy retaliated against tariffs on olive oil and hats with tariffs on U.S. automobiles. Mexico, Cuba, Australia, and New Zealand also participated in the tariff wars. Other beggar-thy-neighbor policies, such as foreign-exchange controls and currency depreciations, were also implemented. The effort by several nations to run a trade surplus by reducing imports led to a breakdown of the international trading system. Within two years after the Smoot-Hawley Act, U.S. exports decreased by nearly two-thirds. Figure 6.1 shows the decline of world trade as the global economy fell into the Great Depression.

How did President Hoover fall into such a protectionist trap? The president felt compelled to honor the 1928 Republican platform calling for tariffs to aid the weakened farm economy. The stock market crash of 1929 and the imminent Great Depression further led to a crisis atmosphere. Republicans had been sympathetic to protectionism for decades. Now they viewed import tariffs as a method of fulfilling demands that government should initiate positive steps to combat domestic unemployment.

President Hoover felt bound to tradition and to the platform of the Republican Party. Henry Ford spent an evening with Hoover requesting a presidential veto of what he referred to as "economic stupidity." Other auto executives sided with Ford. However, tariff legislation had never before been vetoed by a president, and Hoover was not about to set a precedent. Hoover remarked that "with returning normal conditions, our foreign trade will continue to expand."

By 1932, U.S. trade with other nations had collapsed. Presidential challenger Franklin Roosevelt denounced the trade legislation as ruinous. Hoover responded that Roosevelt would have U.S. workers compete with peasant labor overseas. Following Hoover's defeat in the presidential election of 1932, the Democrats dismantled the Smoot-Hawley legislation. But they used caution, relying on reciprocal trade agreements instead of across-the-board tariff concessions by the United States. Sam Rayburn, the speaker of the House of Representatives, insisted that any party member who wanted to be a member of the House Ways and Means Committee had to support trade reciprocity instead of protectionism. The Smoot-Hawley approach was discredited, and the United States pursued trade liberalization via reciprocal trade agreements.

Reciprocal Trade Agreements Act

The combined impact on U.S. exports of the Great Depression and the foreign retaliatory tariffs imposed in reaction to the Smoot-Hawley Act resulted in a reversal of U.S. trade policy. In 1934, Congress passed the **Reciprocal Trade Agreements Act**, which changed U.S. trade policies by transferring authority from the Congress, which generally favored domestic import-competing producers, to the president, who tended to consider the national interest when forming trade policy. This change tipped the balance of power in favor of lower tariffs and set the stage for a wave of trade liberalization. Specifically aimed at tariff reduction, the act contained two features: negotiating authority and generalized reductions.

Under this law, the president was given the unprecedented authority to negotiate bilateral tariff-reduction agreements with foreign governments (for example, between the United States and Sweden). Without congressional approval, the president could lower tariffs by up to 50 percent of the existing level. Enactment of any tariff reductions was dependent on the willingness of other nations to reciprocally lower their tariffs on U.S. goods. From 1934 to 1947, the United States entered into 32 bilateral tariff agreements, and over this period the average level of tariffs on protected products fell to about half of the 1934 levels.

The Reciprocal Trade Agreements Act also provided for generalized tariff reductions through the **most favored nation (MFN)** clause. This clause is an agreement between two nations to apply tariffs to each other at rates as low as those applied to any other nation having MFN status. For example, if the United States extends MFN treatment to Brazil and then grants a low tariff on imports of machinery from France, the United States is obligated to provide the identical low-tariff treatment on imports of machinery from Brazil. Brazil thus receives the same treatment as the initially most-favored nation, France. The advantage to Brazil of MFN status is that it can investigate all of the tariff policies of the United States concerning imported machinery to see if treatment to some nation is more favorable than theirs; if any more favorable terms are found, Brazil can call for equal treatment. Simply put, the MFN clause resulted in tariff reductions being made on a nondiscriminatory basis: If a country reduced a tariff to one country, it would reduce them to all. In 1998, the U.S. government replaced the term most favored nation with **normal trade relations**.

Although the Reciprocal Trade Agreements Act tipped the political balance of power in favor of lower tariffs, its piecemeal, bilateral approach limited the trade liberalization efforts of the United States. The United States recognized that a more comprehensive approach was needed to liberalize trade on a multilateral basis.

General Agreement on Tariffs and Trade

Partly in response to trade disruptions during the Great Depression, the United States and some of its allies sought to impose order on trade flows after World War II. The first major postwar step toward liberalization of trade on a multilateral basis was the **General Agreement on Tariffs and Trade** (GATT), signed in 1947. GATT was crafted as an agreement among contracting parties, the member nations, to decrease trade barriers and to place all nations on an equal footing in trading relations. GATT was never intended to become an organization; instead, it was a set of agreements among countries around the world to reduce trade barriers and establish broad rules for commercial policy.

In 1995, GATT was transformed into the **World Trade Organization (WTO)**. The WTO embodies the main provisions of GATT, but its role was expanded to include a mechanism intended to improve GATT's process for resolving trade disputes among member nations. Let us first discuss the major principles of the original GATT system.

Trade Without Discrimination

According to GATT, a member country should not discriminate between its trading partners. The two pillars of the nondiscrimination principle were the MFN principle (normal trade relations) and the national treatment principle.

According to the MFN principle, if a member of GATT granted another member a lower tariff rate for one of its products, it had to do the same for all other GATT members. The MFN thus meant "favor one, favor all." Members of GATT were obligated to apply the MFN principle only to other GATT members, but they were free to apply it to nonmember countries as well. However, MFN status did not always mean equal treatment. Prior to GATT, bilateral trade agreements set up exclusive clubs among a country's MFN partners. Under GATT, the MFN club was no longer exclusive; the MFN principle ensured that each country treated all other GATT members equally.

According to GATT, there were two exceptions to the MFN clause: industrial nations could grant preferential tariffs to imports from developing nations that were not granted to imports from other industrial nations, and nations belonging to a regional trading arrangement (for example, the North American Free Trade Agreement) could eliminate tariffs applied to imports of goods coming from other members while maintaining tariffs on imports from nonmembers.

Granting MFN status or imposing differential tariffs has been used as an instrument of foreign policy. For example, a nation may punish unfriendly nations with high import tariffs on their goods and reward friendly nations with low tariffs. The United States has granted MFN status to most of the nations with which it trades. As of 2010, the United States did not grant MFN status to Cuba and North Korea. Tariffs on imports from these countries are often three or four (or more) times as high as those on comparable imports from nations receiving MFN status, as seen in Table 6.2. Also, the United States provided temporary MFN status to several countries such as Russia and Vietnam.

The second aspect of trade without discrimination involved *national treatment*; that is, treating foreigners and locals equally. Under the national treatment principle, GATT members had to treat other members' industries no less favorably than they do their own domestic industries. Therefore, domestic regulations and internal taxes could not be biased against foreign products, once foreign goods have entered the domestic market. However, tariffs could apply to foreign products when they entered a country as imports.

TABLE 6.2

U.S. Tariffs on Imports from Nations Granted, and not Granted, Normal Trade Relation Status: Selected Examples

	TARIFF (PERCENT)	
Product	**With Normal Trade Relation Status**	**Without Normal Trade Relation Status**
Hams	1.2 cents/kg	7.2 cents/kg
Sour cream	3.2 cents/liter	15 cents/liter
Butter	12.3 cents/liter	30.9 cents/liter
Fish	3% ad valorem	25% ad valorem
Saws	4% ad valorem	30% ad valorem
Cauliflower	10% ad valorem	50% ad valorem
Coffee	10% ad valorem	20% ad valorem
Woven fabrics	15.7% ad valorem	81% ad valorem
Babies' shirts	20.2% ad valorem	90% ad valorem
Gold necklaces	5% ad valorem	80% ad valorem

Source: From U.S. International Trade Commission, *Harmonized Tariff Schedule of the United States*, Washington, D.C., Government Printing Office, various issues.

The Canadian periodicals industry illustrates the use of discriminatory taxes for the purpose of imposing a higher burden on a foreign product than on a domestic product. For example, a long-standing policy of the Canadian government has been to protect its magazine industry as a medium of Canadian ideas and interests, and a tool for the promotion of Canadian culture. In the 1990s, the Canadian government levied a steep tax on U.S. magazines, such as *Sports Illustrated*, that were sold to Canadians. The intent of the tax was to make it unprofitable for U.S. firms to publish special edition periodicals aimed at the Canadian market, thereby protecting the advertising revenues of Canadian publications. These taxes were found to violate the national treatment rules established in GATT because they discriminated against foreign magazines.

Promoting Freer Trade

Another goal of GATT was to promote freer trade through its role in the settlement of trade disputes. Historically, trade disputes consisted of matters strictly between the disputants; no third party was available to which they might appeal for a favorable remedy. As a result, conflicts often remained unresolved for years. When they were settled, the stronger country generally won at the expense of the weaker country. GATT improved the dispute-resolution process by formulating complaint procedures and providing a conciliation panel to which a victimized country could express its grievance. However, GATT's dispute-settlement process did not include the authority to enforce the conciliation panel's recommendations—a weakness that inspired the formation of the World Trade Organization.

GATT also obligated its members to use tariffs rather than quotas to protect their domestic industry. GATT's presumption was that quotas were inherently more trade distorting than tariffs because they allowed the user to discriminate between suppliers, were not predictable and transparent to the exporter, and imposed a maximum ceiling on imports. Here, too, exceptions were made to GATT's prohibition of quotas. Member nations could use quotas to safeguard their balance of payments, promote economic development, and allow the operation of domestic agricultural-support programs. Voluntary export-restraint agreements, which used quotas, also fell outside the quota restrictions of GATT because the agreements were voluntary.

Predictability: Through Binding and Transparency

Sometimes, promising not to increase a trade barrier can be as important as reducing one, because the promise provides businesses a clearer view of their future opportunities. Under GATT, when countries agreed to open their markets for goods or services, they would "bind" their commitments. These bindings amounted to ceilings on import tariff rates for developed countries, the bound rates have generally been the rates actually charged. Most developing countries have bound the rates somewhat higher than the actual rates charged, so the bound rates serve as a ceiling. A country could change its bindings, but only after negotiating with its trading partners, which meant compensating them for a loss of trade. The result of this was a much higher degree of market security for traders and investors.

Also, the GATT system tried to improve predictability and stability by making countries' trade rules as clear and public (transparent) as possible. Countries were required to disclose their trade policies and practices publically within the country or by notifying the GATT secretariat.

Multilateral Trade Negotiations

Prior to GATT, trade agreements involved bilateral negotiation between, say, the United States and a single foreign country. With the advent of GATT, trade negotiations were conducted on a multilateral basis which involved all GATT members participating in the negotiations. With the passage of time, GATT evolved to include almost all the main trading nations, although some were nonmembers. Therefore, "multilateral" was used to describe the GATT system instead of "global" or "world." To promote freer trade, GATT sponsored a series of negotiations, or rounds, to reduce tariffs and nontariff trade barriers, as summarized in Table 6.3.

The first round of GATT negotiations, completed in 1947, achieved tariff reductions averaging 21 percent. However, tariff reductions were much smaller in the GATT rounds of the late 1940s and 1950s. During this period, protectionist pressures intensified in the United States as the war-damaged industries of Japan and Europe were reconstructed: the negotiation process was slow and tedious, and nations often were unwilling to consider tariff cuts on many goods.

During the period 1964–1967, GATT members participated in the so-called **Kennedy Round** of trade negotiations, named after U.S. President

TABLE 6.3

GATT Negotiating Rounds

Negotiating Round and Coverage	Dates	Number of Participants	Tariff Cut Achieved (percent)
Addressed tariffs			
Geneva	1947	23	21
Annecy	1949	13	2
Torquay	1951	38	3
Geneva	1956	26	4
Dillon Round	1960–1961	26	2
Kennedy Round	1964–1967	62	35
Addressed tariff and nontariff barriers			
Tokyo Round	1973–79	99	33
Uruguay Round	1986–93	125	34
Doha Round	2002–	149	—

John F. Kennedy, who issued an initiative calling for the negotiations. A multilateral meeting of GATT participants occurred at which the form of negotiations shifted from a product-by-product format to an across-the-board format. Tariffs were negotiated on broad categories of goods, and a given rate reduction applied to the entire group—a more streamlined approach. The Kennedy Round cut tariffs on manufactured goods by an average of 35 percent, to an average ad valorem level of 10.3 percent.

The GATT rounds from the 1940s to the 1960s focused almost entirely on tariff reduction. As average tariff rates in industrial nations decreased during the postwar period, the importance of nontariff barriers increased. In response to these changes, negotiators shifted emphasis to the issue of nontariff distortions in international trade.

At the **Tokyo Round** of 1973–1979, signatory nations agreed to tariff cuts that took the across-the-board form initiated in the Kennedy Round. The average tariff on manufactured goods of the nine major industrial countries was cut from 7.0 percent to 4.7 percent, a 39 percent decrease. Tariff reductions on finished products were deeper than those on raw materials, thus tending to decrease the extent of tariff escalation. After the Tokyo Round, tariffs were so low that they were not a significant barrier to trade in industrial countries. A second accomplishment of the Tokyo Round was the agreement to remove or lessen many nontariff barriers. Codes of conduct were established in six areas: customs valuation, import licensing, government procurement, technical barriers to trade (such as product standards), antidumping procedures, and countervailing duties.

In spite of the trade liberalization efforts of the Tokyo Round, during the 1980s, world leaders felt that the GATT system was weakening. Members of GATT had increasingly used bilateral arrangements, such as voluntary export restraints, and other trade-distorting actions, such as subsidies, that stemmed from protectionist domestic policies. World leaders also felt that GATT needed to encompass additional areas, such as trade in intellectual property, services, and agriculture. They also wanted GATT to give increasing attention to the developing countries, which had felt bypassed by previous GATT rounds of trade negotiations.

These concerns led to the **Uruguay Round** from 1986–1993. As seen in Table 6.4, the Uruguay Round achieved across-the-board tariff cuts for industrial countries averaging 40 percent. Tariffs were eliminated entirely in several sectors, including steel, medical equipment, construction equipment, pharmaceuticals, and paper. Also, many nations agreed for the first time to bind, or cap, a significant portion of their tariffs, giving up the possibility of future rate increases above the bound levels. Progress was also made by the Uruguay Round in decreasing or eliminating nontariff barriers. The government-procurement code opened a wider range of markets for signatory nations. The Uruguay Round made extensive efforts to eliminate quotas on agricultural products and required nations to rely instead on tariffs. In the apparel and textile sector,

TABLE 6.4

URUGUAY ROUND TARIFF REDUCTIONS ON INDUSTRIAL PRODUCTS BY SELECTED COUNTRIES

Country	AVERAGE TARIFF RATE (PERCENT)	
	Pre-Uruguay Round	Post-Uruguay Round
Industrial countries		
Australia	20.1	12.2
Canada	9.0	4.8
European Union	5.7	3.6
Japan	3.9	1.7
United States	5.4	3.5
Developing countries		
Argentina	38.2	30.9
Brazil	40.7	27.0
Chile	34.9	24.9
Colombia	44.3	35.3
India	71.4	32.4

Source: From "Uruguay Round Outcome Strengthens Framework for Trade Relations," *IMF Survey*, November 14, 1994, p. 355.

various bilateral quotas were phased out by 2005. The safeguards agreement prohibited the use of voluntary export restraints.

World Trade Organization

On January 1, 1995, the day on which the Uruguay Round took effect, GATT was transformed into the World Trade Organization. This transformation turned GATT from a trade accord into a membership organization, responsible for governing the conduct of trade relations among its members. The GATT obligations remain at the core of the WTO. However, the WTO agreement requires that its members adhere not only to GATT rules, but also to the broad range of trade pacts that have been negotiated under GATT auspices in recent decades. This undertaking ends the free ride of many GATT members (especially developing countries) that benefited from, but refused to join in, new agreements negotiated in GATT since the 1970s. Today, the WTO consists of 153 nations, accounting for over 97 percent of world trade.

How different is the WTO from the old GATT? The WTO is a full-fledged international organization, headquartered in Geneva, Switzerland; the old GATT was basically a provisional treaty serviced by an ad hoc secretariat. The WTO has a far wider scope than the old GATT, bringing into the multilateral trading system, for the first time, trade in services, intellectual property, and investment. The WTO also administers a unified package of agreements to which all members are committed; in contrast, the GATT framework included many side agreements (for example, anti-dumping measures and subsidies) whose membership was limited to a few nations. Moreover, the WTO reverses policies of protection in certain "sensitive" areas (for example, agriculture and textiles) that were more or less tolerated in the old GATT. The WTO is not a government; individual nations remain free to set their own appropriate levels of environment, labor, health, and safety protections.

Through various councils and committees, the WTO administers the many agreements contained in the Uruguay Round, plus agreements on government procurement and civil aircraft. It oversees the implementation of the tariff cuts and reduction of nontariff measures agreed to in the negotiations. It is also a watchdog of international trade, regularly examining the trade regimes of individual members. In its various bodies, members flag proposed or draft measures by others that can cause trade conflicts. Members are also required to update various trade measures and statistics, which are maintained by the WTO in a large database.

Under the WTO, when members open their markets through the removal of barriers to trade, they "bind" their commitments. Therefore, when they reduce their tariffs through negotiations, they commit to bind the tariff reduction at a fixed level negotiated with their trading partners beyond which tariffs may not be increased. The binding of tariffs in the WTO provides a stable and predictable basis for trade, a fundamental principle underlying the operation of the institution. However, a provision is made for the renegotiation of bound tariffs. This provision means that a country can increase a tariff if it receives the approval of other countries, which generally requires providing compensation by decreasing other tariffs. Currently, virtually all tariff rates in developed countries are bound, as are about 75 percent of the rates in developing countries.

Settling Trade Disputes

A major objective of the WTO is to strengthen the GATT mechanism for settling trade disputes. The old GATT dispute mechanism suffered from long delays, the ability of accused parties to block decisions of GATT panels that went against them, and inadequate enforcement. The dispute-settlement mechanism of the WTO addresses each of these weaknesses. It guarantees the formation of a dispute panel once a case is brought and sets time limits for each stage of the process. The decision of the panel may be taken to a newly created appellate body, but the accused party can no longer block the final decision. The dispute-settlement issue was especially important to the United States because this nation was the most frequent user of the GATT dispute mechanism.

The first case settled by the WTO involved a dispute between the United States and several other countries. In 1994, the U.S. government adopted a regulation imposing certain conditions on the quality of the gasoline sold in the United States. The aim of this resolution, established by the Environmental Protection Agency (EPA) under the Clean Air Act, was to improve air quality by reducing pollution caused by gasoline emissions. The regulation set different pollution standards for domestic and imported gasolines. It was challenged before the WTO by Venezuela and later by Brazil.

According to Venezuelan officials, there was a violation of the WTO's principle of national treatment, which suggests that once imported gasoline is on the U.S. market it cannot receive treatment less favorable than domestically produced gasoline. Venezuela argued that its gasoline was being submitted to controls and standards much more rigorous than those imposed on gasoline produced in the United States.

The United States argued that this discrimination was justified under WTO rules. The United States maintained that clean air is an exhaustible resource and that it was justified under WTO rules to preserve it. It also claimed that its pollution regulations were necessary to protect human health, which is also allowed by the WTO. The major condition is that these provisions should not be protectionism in disguise.

Venezuela refuted that argument. Venezuela was in no way questioning the right of the United States to impose high environmental standards. However, it said that if the United States wanted clean gasoline then it should have submitted both the domestic and imported gasolines to the same high standards.

The new regulations put in place by the United States had an important impact for Venezuela and for its gasoline producers. Venezuela maintained that producing the gasoline according to the EPA's double standard was much more expensive than if Venezuela had followed the same specifications as American producers. Moreover, the U.S. market was critically important for Venezuela because two-thirds of Venezuela's gasoline exports were sold to the United States.

When Venezuela realized that the discriminatory aspects of the American gasoline regime would not be modified by the United States, it brought the case to the WTO. Brazil also complained about the discriminatory aspect of U.S. regulation. The two complaints were heard by a WTO panel, which ruled in 1996 that the United States unjustly discriminated against imported gasoline. When the United States appealed this ruling, a WTO appellate board confirmed the findings of the panel. The United States agreed to cease its discriminatory actions against imported gasoline by revising its environmental laws. Venezuela and Brazil were satisfied by the action of the United States.

Does the WTO Reduce National Sovereignty?

Do WTO rules or dispute settlements reduce the sovereignty of the United States or other countries? The United States benefits from WTO dispute settlement by having a set of rules to which it can hold other countries accountable for their trade actions. At the same time, the U.S. government was careful to structure the WTO dispute-settlement rules to preserve the rights of Americans. Nevertheless, critics on both the left and right, such as Ralph Nader and Patrick Buchanan, contend that by participating in the WTO the United States has seriously undermined its sovereignty.

However, proponents note that the findings of a WTO dispute-settlement panel cannot force the United States to change its laws. Only the United States determines exactly how it will respond to the recommendations of a WTO panel, if at all. If a U.S. measure is found to be in violation of a WTO provision, the United States may on its own decide to change the law; compensate a foreign country by lowering its trade barriers of an equivalent amount in another sector; or do nothing and possibly undergo retaliation by the affected country in the form of increased barriers to U.S. exports of an equivalent amount. But America retains full sovereignty in its decision of whether or not to implement a panel recommendation. Simply put, WTO agreements do not preclude the United States from establishing and maintaining its own laws or limit the ability of the United States to set its environmental, labor, health, and safety standards at the level it considers appropriate. However, the WTO does not allow a nation to use trade restrictions to enforce its own environmental, labor, health, and safety standards when they have selective and discriminatory effects against foreign producers.

Most trade-dispute rulings of the WTO are resolved amicably, without resorting to retaliatory trade barriers. However, retaliation is sometimes used. For example, in 1999 the United States won its hormone-treated beef and banana cases in which the WTO ruled that the EU unfairly restricted imports of these products. The WTO thus authorized the U.S. government to raise tariffs on European exports to the United States. After a prolonged struggle, the banana dispute was resolved, but the EU has steadfastly refused to revise its policy on hormone-treated beef. The chance that the EU will accept U.S. hormone-treated beef appears dim.

Economists generally agree that the real issue raised by the WTO is not whether it decreases national sovereignty, but whether the specific obligations that it imposes on a nation are greater or less than the benefits the nation receives from applying the same requirements to others (along with itself). According to this standard, the benefits of the United States of joining the WTO greatly exceed the costs. By granting the United States the status of normal trade relations with all 153 members, the agreement improves U.S. access to foreign markets. Moreover, it reduces the ability of other nations to impose restrictions to limit access to their markets. If the United States withdrew from the WTO, it would lose the ability to use the WTO mechanism to induce other nations to decrease their own trade barriers, and would thus harm U.S. exporting firms and their workers. Simply put, economists generally contend that the WTO puts some constraints on the decision making of the private and public sectors. But the costs of these constraints are outweighed by the economic benefits that citizens derive from freer trade.

Should Retaliatory Tariffs Be Used for WTO Enforcement?

Critics contend that the WTO's dispute-settlement system based on tariff retaliation places smaller countries, without much market power, at a disadvantage. Suppose that Ecuador, a small country, receives WTO authorization to retaliate against unfair trade practices of the United States, a large country. With competitive conditions, if Ecuador applies a higher tariff to imports from the United States, its national welfare will decrease, as explained in Chapter 4. Therefore, Ecuador may be reluctant to impose a retaliatory tariff even though it has the approval of the WTO.

However, for countries large enough to affect prices in world markets, the issue is less clear. This is because a retaliatory tariff may improve a large country's terms of trade, thus enhancing its national welfare. If the United States raises a tariff barrier, it reduces the demand for the product on world markets. The decreased demand makes imports less expensive for the United States, so that to pay for these imports, the United States can export less. The terms of trade (ratio of export prices to import prices) thus improves for the United States. This improvement offsets at least some of the welfare reductions that take place through less efficiency due to increasing the tariff.

Simply put, although a small country could decide to impose retaliatory tariffs to teach a larger trading partner a lesson, it will find such behavior relatively more costly to initiate than its larger trading partner because it cannot obtain favorable movements in its terms of trade. Therefore, the limited market power of small countries makes them less likely to induce compliance to WTO rulings through retaliation. However, the problems smaller nations face in retaliating are the opposite of the special benefits they gain in obtaining WTO tariff concessions without being required to make reciprocal concessions.

Some maintain that the WTO's current dispute-settlement system should be modified. For example, free traders object to retaliatory tariffs on the grounds that the WTO's purpose is to reduce trade barriers. Instead, they propose that offending countries should be assessed monetary fines. A system of fines has the advantage of avoiding additional trade protection and not placing smaller countries at a disadvantage. However, this system encounters the problem of deciding how to place a monetary value on violations. Also, fines might be difficult to collect because the offending country's government would have to initiate specific budgetary authorization. Moreover, the notion of accepting an obligation to allow foreigners to levy monetary fines on a nation such as the United States would likely be criticized as taxation without representation, and the WTO would be attacked as undermining national sovereignty.

American export subsidies provide an example of retaliatory tariffs authorized by the WTO. From 1984 to 2004, the U.S. tax code provided a tax benefit that enabled American exporters to exempt between 15 to 30 percent of their export income from U.S. taxes. In 1998, the EU lodged a complaint with the WTO, arguing that the U.S. tax benefit was an export subsidy in violation of WTO agreements. This complaint led to the WTO's ruling in 2003 that the tax benefit was illegal and that the EU could immediately impose $4 billion in punitive duties on U.S. exports to Europe. Although the EU gave the U.S. government time to eliminate its export subsidy program, inertia resulted in continuation of the program. Therefore, Europe began implementing retaliatory tariffs in 2004. A five percent penalty tariff was levied on U.S. exports such as jewelry, refrigerators, toys, and paper. The penalty climbed by one percentage point for each month that U.S. lawmakers failed to bring

U.S. tax laws in line with the WTO ruling. This tariff marked the first time that the United States came under WTO penalties for failure to adhere to its rulings. Although some in Congress resisted surrendering to the WTO on anything, the pressure provided by the tariffs convinced Congress to repeal the export subsidies.

Does the WTO Harm the Environment?

In recent years, the debate has intensified on the links between trade and the environment, and the role that the WTO should play in promoting environment-friendly trade. A central concern of those who have raised the profile of this issue in the WTO is that there are circumstances where trade and the pursuit of trade liberalization may have harmful environmental effects. Indeed, these concerns were voiced when thousands of environmentalists descended on the World Trade Organization summit in Seattle in 1999. They protested the WTO's influence on everything from marine destruction to global warming. Let us consider the opposing views on the links between trade and the environment.[2]

Harming the Environment

Two main arguments are made as to how trade liberalization may harm the environment. First, trade liberalization leads to a "race to the bottom" in environmental standards. If some countries have low environmental standards, industry is likely to shift production of environmentally intensive or highly polluting products to such pollution havens. Trade liberalization can make the shift of smokestack industries across borders to pollution havens even more attractive. If these industries then create pollution with globally adverse effects, trade liberalization can, indirectly, promote environmental degradation. Worse, trade-induced competitive pressure may force countries to lower their environmental standards, thus encouraging trade in products creating global pollution.

Why would developing nations adopt less stringent environmental policies than industrial nations? Poorer nations may place a higher priority on the benefits of production (more jobs and income) relative to the benefits of environmental quality than wealthy nations. Moreover, developing nations may have greater environmental capacities to reduce pollutants by natural processes (such as Latin America's rainforest capacity to reduce carbon dioxide in the air) than do industrial nations that suffer from the effects of past pollution. Developing nations can thus tolerate higher levels of emissions without increasing pollution levels. Also, the introduction of a polluting industry into a sparsely populated developing nation will likely have less impact on the capacity of the environment to reduce pollution by natural processes than it would have in a densely populated industrial nation.

A second concern of environmentalists about the role of trade relates to social preferences. Some practices may simply be unacceptable for certain people or societies, so they oppose trade in products that encourage such practices. These practices can include killing dolphins in the process of catching tuna and using leghold traps for catching animals for their furs. During the 1990s, relations between environmentalists and the WTO clashed when the WTO ruled against a U.S. ban on the imports of shrimp from countries using nets that trap turtles, after complaints by India, Malaysia, Pakistan, and Thailand. Also, the United States was found guilty of

---

[2]World Trade Organization, *Annual Report*, Geneva, Switzerland, 1998, pp. 54–55 and "Greens Target WTO's Plan for Lumber," *The Wall Street Journal*, November 24, 1999, pp. A2 and A4.

violating world trade law when it banned imports of Mexican tuna caught in ways that drown dolphins. Indeed, critics maintained that the free-trade policies of the WTO contradicted the goal of environmental quality.

To most economists, any measure that liberalizes trade enhances productivity and growth, puts downward pressure on inflation by increasing competition, and creates jobs. In Japan, tariffs are so high on imported finished-wood products that U.S. firms don't have much of a market there. High local prices limit domestic demand in Japan. But if tariffs were abolished, demand for lumber products from the United States could surge, creating additional logging jobs in the United States and additional import-related jobs in Japan.

But environmentalists view the tariff elimination differently. Their main concern is that a nontariff market, which would result in lower prices, would stimulate so much demand that logging would intensify in the world's remaining ancient forests, which they say serve as habitat for complex ecosystems that would otherwise not survive intact in forests that have been cut into fragments. Such old forests still exist across much of Alaska, Canada, and Russia's Siberian region. Environmentalists note that in Pennsylvania, New York, and other states in the Northeast, the forests have been so chopped up that many large predators have been driven from the land, leaving virtually no check on the deer population. Therefore, deer are in a state of overpopulation.

However, trade liberalization proponents play down the adverse impacts, arguing that reduced tariffs would boost world economies by decreasing the cost of housing, paper, and other products made from wood, while actually helping forest conditions. For example, timber officials in the United States say they could go into a country like Indonesia and persuade local firms to adopt more conservation-minded techniques.

Improving the Environment

On the other hand, it is argued that trade liberalization may improve the quality of the environment rather than promote degradation. First, trade stimulates economic growth, and growing prosperity is one of the key factors in societies' demand for a cleaner environment. As people get richer, they want a cleaner environment—and they acquire the means to pay for it. Granted, trade can increase the cost of the wrong environmental policies. If farmers freely pollute rivers, for instance, higher agricultural exports will increase pollution. But the solution to this is not to shut off exports: it is to impose tougher environmental laws that make polluters pay.

Second, trade and growth can encourage the development and dissemination of environment friendly production techniques as the demand for cleaner products grows and trade increases the size of markets. International companies may also contribute to a cleaner environment by using the most modern and environmentally clean technology in all their operations. This is less costly than using differentiated technology based on the location of production and helps companies to maintain a good reputation.

Although there is no dispute that in theory intensified competition could give rise to pollution havens, the empirical evidence suggests that it has not happened on a significant scale. The main reason is that the costs imposed by environmental regulation are small relative to other cost considerations, so this factor is unlikely to be at the basis of relocation decisions. The U.S. Census Bureau finds that even the most polluting industries spend no more than two percent of their revenues on abating pollution. Other factors such as labor costs, transportation costs, and the adequacy of infrastructure are much more important. For all the talk of a race to the bottom, there is no evidence of a competitive lowering of environmental standards.

BURNING RUBBER: OBAMA'S TIRE TARIFF IGNITES CHINESE OFFICIALS

TRADE CONFLICTS

President Barack Obama's import tariffs on tires provide an example of U.S. safeguard (escape clause) policy. As a condition for China's entering the World Trade Organization in 2001, it agreed that other nations could clamp down on surges of imports from China without having to prove unfair trade practices. This special safeguard lasts until 2013. The surge became real when China increased its shipments of tires for automobiles and light trucks to the United States by 215 percent during 2004–2008. Four American tire plants were closed and about 4,500 tire production jobs were lost during that period, according to the United Steelworkers (USW) union.

In response to a complaint by the USW, Obama imposed a tariff in 2009, in addition to the existing tariff, for a three-year period, on imports of tires from China. The tariff was applied to low-price tires, roughly $50 to $60 apiece, which constitute the bulk of the tires China exports to the United States. The amount of the additional tariff was set at 35 percent in the first year, 30 percent in the second year, and 25 percent in the third year. The move would cut off about 17 percent of all tires sold in the United States. Obama justified his tariff policy by stating that he was simply enforcing the rule the Chinese had accepted. However, critics maintained that Obama was pandering to blue-collar workers and union leaders who were needed to support his legislative agenda regarding health care and other issues.

The tariff signaled Obama's desire to keep his word, announced during his presidential campaign, about protecting American jobs, many of which have moved to China and left employment holes in American manufacturing industries. The USW hailed the decision by declaring that it was the right thing to do for beleaguered American tire workers. However, officials of China's government stated that Obama's decision sent the wrong signal to the world: not only was it a grave act of trade protectionism, but it violated rules of the World Trade Organization and contradicted open-market commit-

ments that the U.S. government made at the G20 financial summit in 2009.

According to the Obama administration, the tariffs would significantly reduce tire imports from China and boost U.S. industry sales and prices, resulting in increased profitability. This profitability would result in the preservation of jobs and the creation of new ones, as well as encourage investment. Also, the tariff would have little or no impact on the U.S. production of automobiles and light trucks because tires account for a very small share of the total cost of those products. Moreover, tires account for a relatively small share of the annual cost of owning and operating an automobile or light truck.

However, critics contended that the story was more complicated. They noted that the USW petition for the tariff increase was not supported by American tire companies because they had already abandoned making low-cost tires in the United States: Tire company officials declared that it was not profitable to produce inexpensive tires in domestic plants in view of competition from foreign companies. Most American tire companies, such as Goodyear Tire and Rubber Co. and Cooper Tire and Rubber Co., manufacture low-cost tires in China that they sell in the United States. Any other American tire manufacturer that wanted to get involved in the low-end business would have to revamp factory lines to produce such tires, a costly and complicated practice that would require considerable time. Critics also noted that if Chinese tire exports to the United States were blocked by the tariff, low-wage manufacturers in other countries would replace them. However, it would take many months for producers in places like Brazil and Indonesia to pick up the slack. In the meantime, shortages of low-end tires would likely appear in the U.S. market, resulting in prices increasing by an estimated 20 to 30 percent. Therefore, it was not clear that the Obama tariffs would actually lead to more jobs for the American tire worker or be good for the nation as a whole, according to the critics.

From Doha To Hong Kong: Failed Trade Negotiations

Although the WTO attempts to foster trade liberalization, such an achievement can be difficult. Let's see why.

In 1999, members of the WTO kicked off a new round of trade negotiations in Seattle, Washington for the 2000s. The participants established an agenda that included trade in agriculture, intellectual property rights, labor and environmental matters, and help for less-developed nations. Believing that they had been taken to the cleaners in previous trade negotiations, developing nations were determined not to allow that to occur again. Disagreements among developing nations and industrial nations were a major factor that resulted in a breakdown of the meetings. The meeting became known as "The Battle in Seattle" because of the rioting and disruption that took place in the streets during the meeting.

Although trade liberalization proponents were discouraged by the collapse of the Seattle meeting, they continued to press for another round of trade talks. The result was the Doha Round, which was launched in Doha, Qatar. The rhetoric of the Doha Round was elaborate: it would decrease trade-distorting subsidies on farm goods; it would slash manufacturing tariffs by developing countries; it would cut tariffs on textiles and apparel products that poor countries especially cared about; it would free up trade in services; and it would negotiate global rules in four new areas—in competition, investment, government procurement, and trade facilitation.

This round was formally called the "Doha development agenda" because the majority of the WTO's members rank as medium- to low-income, developing countries. These nations have the highest trade barriers and the most difficulty meeting the existing obligations of the WTO. The developing countries would benefit significantly from the liberalization of remaining trade barriers in the United States, Japan, and Europe, as well as reform of their own trade restrictions.

In spite of its ambitious aims, the Doha Round showed little progress. From the start, countries disowned major portions of the agenda. The EU, for example, denied it had ever promised to get rid of export subsidies. Led by India, many poor countries denied that they had ever signed up for talks on new rules regarding intellectual property and competition policy. Other poor countries spent more time complaining about their grievances over earlier trade rounds than they did in negotiating the new one. Several rich countries showed little interest in compromise. Japan, for example, appeared content simply to reject any cuts in rice tariffs. This kind of posturing resulted in self-imposed deadlines being missed and all tough political decisions, with regard to opening economies to trade, being put off.

Trade ministers had hoped to finalize the Doha Round at their December 2005 meetings in Hong Kong. But all that could be signed was a substantially weakened deal that included a pledge to eliminate farm subsidies by 2013 and modest cuts in tariffs. All of this fell far short of the original objectives for this Doha Round of trade negotiations. Skeptics noted that if the Doha talks could not advance soon, it was probably time to reconsider the size of these huge multilateral rounds and perhaps resort to bilateral trade agreements among a relatively small number of countries as the next best alternative.

Throughout the past 50 years, members of the WTO (GATT) have been able to negotiate the easy issues, and many of the difficult ones. However, at the time of the Doha Round only the difficult issues remained, such as subsidies to farmers with substantial political power. It is possible that these remaining issues may be too difficult to negotiate. Even if the Doha Round does not succeed, the trade liberalization provisions of previous rounds remain in place and global trade is remarkably open by historical standards.

Trade Promotion Authority (Fast-Track Authority)

If international trade agreements were subject to congressional amendments, achieving such pacts would be arduous, if not hopeless. The provisions that had been negotiated by the president would soon be modified by a deluge of congressional amendments, which would quickly meet the disapproval of the trading partner, or partners, that had accepted the original terms.

To prevent this scenario, the mechanism of **trade promotion authority** (also known as **fast-track authority**) was devised in 1974. Under this provision, the president must formally notify Congress of his/her intent to enter trade negotiations with another country. This notification starts a clock in which Congress has 60 legislative days to permit or deny "fast-track" authority. If fast-track authority is approved, the president has a limited time period in which to complete the trade negotiations; extensions of this time period are permissible with congressional approval. Once the negotiations are completed, their outcome is subject only to a straight up-or-down vote (without amendment) in both houses of Congress within 90 legislative days of submission. In return, the president agrees to consult actively with Congress and the private sector throughout the negotiation of the trade agreement.

Fast-track authority was instrumental in negotiating and implementing major trade agreements such as the Uruguay Round Agreements Act of 1994 and the North American Free Trade Agreement of 1993. Most analysts contend that the implementation of future trade agreements will require fast-track authority for the president. Efforts to renew fast-track authority have faced stiff opposition, largely due to congressional concerns about delegating too much discretionary authority to the president and disagreements over the goals of U.S. trade negotiations. In particular, labor unions and environmentalists have sought to ensure that trade agreements will address their concerns. They believe that high labor and environmental standards in the United States put American producers at a competitive disadvantage and that increased trade with countries with lax standards may lead to pressure to lower U.S. standards. If other countries are to trade with the United States, shouldn't they have similar labor and environmental standards?

Supporters of fast-track authority have generally argued that, although labor and environmental standards are important, they do not belong in a trade agreement. Instead, these issues should be negotiated through secondary agreements that accompany a trade agreement. However, labor leaders and environmentalists contend that past secondary agreements have lacked enforcement provisions and thus have done little to improve the quality of life abroad.

Safeguards (The Escape Clause): Emergency Protection From Imports

In addition to the WTO's addressing of unfair trade practices, the United States itself has adopted a series of **trade remedy laws** designed to produce a fair trading environment for all parties engaging in international trade. These laws include the escape clause, countervailing duties, antidumping duties, and unfair trading

TABLE 6.5

TRADE REMEDY LAW PROVISIONS

Statute	Focus	Criteria for Action	Response
Fair trade (escape clause)	Increasing imports	Increasing imports are substantial cause of injury	Duties, quotas, tariff-rate quotas, orderly marketing arrangements, adjustment assistance
Subsidized imports (countervailing duty)	Manufacturing production, or export subsidies	Material injury or threat of material injury	Duties
Dumped imports (antidumping duty)	Imports sold below cost of production or below foreign market price	Material injury or threat of material injury	Duties
Unfair trade (Section 301)	Foreign practices violating a trade agreement or injurious to U.S. trade	Unjustifiable, unreasonable, or discriminatory practices, burdensome to U.S. commerce	All appropriate and feasible action

practices. Table 6.5 summarizes the provisions of the U.S. trade remedy laws, which are discussed in the following sections.

The **escape clause** provides temporary **safeguards** (relief) to U.S. firms and workers who are substantially injured from surges in imports that are fairly traded. To offset surging imports, the escape clause allows the president to terminate or make modifications in trade concessions granted to foreign nations and to levy trade restrictions. The most common form of relief is tariff increases, followed by tariff-rate quotas and trade adjustment assistance. Import relief can be enacted for an initial period of four years and extended for another four years. The temporary nature of safeguards is to give the domestic industry time to adjust to import competition. It is common for safeguards to decline during the period in which they are imposed so as to gradually wean the domestic industry from protectionism.

An escape clause is initiated by a petition from an American industry to the USITC, which investigates and recommends a response to the president. To receive relief, the industry must demonstrate that it has been substantially injured by foreign competition. The industry must also prepare a statement that shows how safeguards will help it adjust to import competition. An affirmative decision by the USITC is reported to the president, who determines what remedy is in the national interest.

Most recipients of safeguard relief come from manufacturing, such as footwear, steel, fishing tackle and rods, and clothespins. Agricultural products are the second largest category, including asparagus, mushrooms, shrimp, honey, and cut flowers. Table 6.6 provides examples of safeguard relief granted to U.S. industries.

Although safeguard relief was invoked often during the 1970s, in recent decades it has been rarely used. This is partly because safeguard relief has proven to be a very difficult way to win protection against imports because presidential action is required for it to be granted, and presidents have often been reluctant to grant such relief. Instead, safeguard relief has been overshadowed by antidumping duties, whose implementation does not require presidential action and whose injury standards are not as stringent.

TABLE 6.6

SAFEGUARD RELIEF GRANTED UNDER THE ESCAPE CLAUSE: SELECTED EXAMPLES

Product	Type of Relief
Porcelain-on-steel cooking ware	Additional duties imposed for four years of 20 cents, 20 cents, 15 cents, and 10 cents per pound in the first, second, third, and fourth years, respectively
Prepared or preserved mushrooms	Additional duties imposed for three years of 20%, 15%, and 10% ad valorem in the first, second, and third years, respectively
High-carbon ferrochromium	Temporary duty increase
Color TV receivers	Orderly marketing agreements with Taiwan and Korea
Footwear	Orderly marketing agreements with Taiwan and Korea

Source: From *Annual Report of the President of the United States on the Trade Agreements Program*, Washington, DC, Government Printing Office, various issues.

One argument for safeguard provisions is that they are a political necessity for the formation of agreements to liberalize trade. Without the assurance of a safety net to protect domestic producers from surging imports, trade liberalization agreements would be impossible to achieve. Another argument for safeguards is a more practical political argument. Governments appease domestic producers that maintain strong lobbying power, even at the detriment of foreign producers of like products, simply because the domestic producers are voting constituents. It is argued that a better solution to the pressure on domestic producers is to impose these temporary measures from time to time to reduce strain on the industry rather than to take any permanent action that might dismantle liberal trade policies in general. The problem with this justification is that there are usually other possible ways to reduce this pressure that do not involve restrictions on imports to the disadvantage of foreign producers, such as government aid and tax relief.

U.S. Safeguards Limit Surging Imports of Textiles from China

Surging textile exports from China to the United States provide an example of how safeguards can be used to stabilize a market. Producers of textiles and apparel have benefitted from some of the most substantial and long-lasting trade protection granted by the U.S. government in recent times. In 1974, the United States and Europe negotiated a system of rules to restrict competition from developing exporting countries employing low-cost labor. Known as the **Multifiber Arrangement** (MFA), quotas were negotiated each year on a country-by-country basis, assigning the quantities of specific textile and apparel items which could be exported from developing countries to the industrial countries. Although the MFA was initially intended to be a short-term measure primarily to give industrialized countries time to adjust to the rigors of global competition, due to extensions it lasted until 2005.

The MFA helped create textile and apparel industries in some countries where such sectors would likely not have emerged on their own, simply because these countries were granted rights to export. Impoverished countries such as Bangladesh, Cambodia, and Costa Rica grew to rely on garment exports as a means of providing jobs and income for their people. Without the MFA, many developing countries that benefitted from the quotas might have lost out in a more competitive environment.

When the MFA came to an end in 2005, importers were allowed to buy textile products in any volume from any country. This affected the geographic distribution of industrial production in favor of China, the world's lowest-cost and largest supplier of textile products. China was poised to become the main beneficiary of trade liberalization under the removal of the quota.

The superior competitive position of China resulted in its textile and apparel exports surging to the markets of Europe and the United States in 2005. To soften the shock wave, the Chinese government took voluntary measures including strengthening self-discipline among its textile exporters, curbing investment in the sector, and encouraging big textile companies to invest abroad. The government also added an export tax to reduce the competitiveness of 148 textile and apparel products in foreign markets. Nevertheless, Chinese exports continued to flow rapidly to the markets of the United States and Europe.

Alarmed that Chinese garments might overwhelm domestic producers, the U.S. government imposed safeguard quotas that restricted the rise in imports to 7.5 percent on Chinese trousers, shirts, and underwear. In November 2005, the safeguard quotas were replaced by a textile agreement with China that imposed annual limits on 34 categories of clothing running through 2008. Economists estimated that the restrictions would drive up clothing prices between $3 billion and $6 billion annually, an amount that would translate into $10 to $20 higher bills for the average U.S. family.

Countervailing Duties: Protection Against Foreign Export Subsidies

As consumers, we tend to appreciate the low prices of foreign subsidized steel. But foreign export subsidies are resented by import-competing producers, who must charge higher prices because they do not receive such subsidies. From their point of view, the export subsidies give foreign producers an unfair competitive advantage.

As viewed by the World Trade Organization, export subsidies constitute unfair competition. Importing countries can retaliate by levying a **countervailing duty**. The size of the duty is limited to the amount of the foreign export subsidy. Its purpose is to increase the price of the imported good to its fair market value.

Upon receipt of a petition from a U.S. industry or firm, the U.S. Department of Commerce will conduct a preliminary investigation as to whether or not an export subsidy was given to a foreign producer. If the preliminary investigation finds a reasonable indication of an export subsidy, U.S. importers must immediately pay a special tariff (equal to the estimated subsidy margin) on all imports of the product in question. The Commerce Department then conducts a final investigation to determine whether an export subsidy was in fact granted, as well as the amount of the subsidy. If it determines that there was no export subsidy, the special tariff is rebated to the U.S. importers. Otherwise, the case is investigated by the U.S. International Trade Commission, which determines if the import-competing industry suffered material injury as a result of the subsidy.[3] If both the Commerce Department and the International Trade Commission rule in favor of the subsidy petition, a permanent countervailing duty

---

[3]For those nations that are signatories to the WTO Subsidy Code, the International Trade Commission must determine that their export subsidies have injured U.S. producers before countervailing duties are imposed. The export subsidies of nonsignatory nations are subject to countervailing duties immediately following the Commerce Department's determination of their occurrence; the International Trade Commission does not have to make an injury determination.

is imposed that equals the size of the subsidy margin calculated by the Commerce Department in its final investigation. Once the foreign nation stops subsidizing exports of that product, the countervailing duty is removed.

Lumber Duties Hammer Home Buyers

Let us consider a countervailing duty involving the U.S. lumber industry. Since the 1980s, the United States and Canada have quarreled over softwood lumber. The stakes are enormous: Canadian firms export billions of dollars' worth of lumber annually to U.S. customers.

The lumber dispute has followed a repetitive pattern. U.S. lumber producers accuse their Canadian rivals of receiving government subsidies. In particular, they allege that the Canadians pay unfairly low tree-cutting fees to harvest timber from lands owned by the Canadian government. In the United States, lumber producers pay higher fees for the right to cut trees in government forests. Moreover, Canadian regulations permit provincial governments to reduce their tree-cutting fees when lumber prices decline so as to keep Canadian sawmills profitable. To U.S. producers, this amounts to an unfair subsidy granted to their Canadian competitors.

For example, in 1996, the Coalition for Fair Lumber Imports, a group of U.S. sawmill companies, won a countervailing-duty petition with the U.S. government charging that domestic lumber companies were hurt by subsidized exports from Canada. The complaint led to the imposition of a tariff-rate quota to protect U.S. producers. According to the trade restraint, up to 14.7 billion board feet of Canadian lumber exports from Canada to the United States could enter duty free. The next 0.65 billion board feet of exports was subject to a tariff of $50 per thousand board feet. The Canadian government also agreed to raise the tree-cutting fees it charged provincial producers. The result was that Canadian lumber exports to the United States fell about 14 percent.

The U.S. lumber industry maintained that this tariff-rate quota created a level playing field in which American and Canadian producers could fairly compete. However, critics argued that the trade restriction failed to take into account the interests of American lumber users in the lumber-dealing, homebuilding, and home-furnishing industries. It also overlooked the interests of American buyers of new homes and home furnishings according to the critics. They noted that the trade restrictions increased the price of lumber from between 20 to 35 percent; thus, the cost of the average new home increased from between $800 to $1,300.[4]

U.S. and Canadian lumber producers have continued to wrestle over the issue of lumber subsidies since the 1990s. It remains to be seen how this issue will be resolved.

Antidumping Duties: Protection Against Foreign Dumping

In recent years, relatively few American firms have chosen to go through the cumbersome process of obtaining relief though countervailing duties. Instead, they have found another way to obtain protection against imports: They have found it much

---

[4]Brink Lindsey, Mark Groombridge, and Prakash Loungani, *Nailing the Homeowner: The Economic Impact of Trade Protection of the Softwood Lumber Industry*, CATO Institute, July 6, 2000, pp. 5–8.

easier to accuse foreign firms of dumping in the U.S. market, and convince the U.S. government to impose antidumping duties on these goods. From the perspective of American firms trying to obtain protection from imports, antidumping is where the action is.

The objective of U.S. antidumping policy is to offset two unfair trading practices by foreign nations: export sales in the United States at prices below the average total cost of production, and price discrimination in which foreign firms sell in the United States at a price less than that charged in the exporter's home market. Both practices can inflict economic hardship on U.S. import-competing producers; by reducing the price of the foreign export in the U.S. market, they encourage U.S. consumers to buy a smaller quantity of the domestically produced good.

Antidumping investigations are initiated upon a written request by the import-competing industry that includes evidence of (1) dumping; (2) material injury, such as lost sales, profits, or jobs; and (3) a link between the dumped imports and the alleged injury. Antidumping investigations commonly involve requests that foreign exporters and domestic importers fill out detailed questionnaires. Parties that elect not to complete questionnaires can be put at a disadvantage with respect to case decisions; findings are made on the best information available, which may simply be information supplied by the domestic industry in support of the dumping allegation. The number of antidumping cases dwarfs those of other trade remedies. The Commerce Department determines if dumping did occur and the International Trade Commission determines if the domestic industry was harmed because of dumping.

If these agencies determine that dumping is occurring and is causing material injury to the domestic industry, then the U.S. response is to impose an antidumping duty (tariff) on dumped imports equal to the margin of dumping. The effect of the duty is to offset the extent to which the dumped goods' prices fall below average total cost, or below the price at which they are sold in the exporter's home market. Antidumping duties are generally large, often in the neighborhood of 60 percent. According to the International Trade Commission, imports subject to antidumping duties of over 50 percent tend to increase by 33 percent in price and decrease by 73 percent in volume as compared to the year prior to the petition for antidumping duties.[5]

An antidumping case can be terminated prior to conclusion of the investigation if the exporter of the product to the United States agrees to cease dumping, to stop exporting the product to the United States, to increase the price to eliminate the dumping, or to negotiate some other agreement that will decrease the quantity of imports. Indeed, the mere threat of an antidumping investigation may induce foreign companies to increase their export prices and thus to stop any dumping they were practicing.

Are antidumping laws good for a nation? Economists tend to be dubious of antidumping duties because they increase the price of imported goods and thus decrease consumer welfare. According to economic analysis, low prices are a problem in need of remedy only if they tend to result in higher prices in the long term. Economists generally consider antidumping duties appropriate only when they combat predatory pricing, designed to monopolize a market by knocking competitors out of business.

---

[5]U.S. International Trade Commission, *The Economic Effects of Antidumping and Countervailing Duty Orders and Suspension Agreements*, Washington, DC: International Trade Commission, June 1995.

The consensus among economists is that antidumping laws have virtually nothing to do with addressing predatory pricing, so their existence is without economic justification.

Supporters of antidumping laws admit that they are not intended to combat predatory pricing, or to enhance consumer welfare in the economists' definition of the term. However, they justify antidumping laws, not on the criterion of efficiency, but on the criterion of fairness. Even though dumping may benefit consumers in the short term, they contend that it is unfair for domestic producers to have to compete with unfairly traded goods.

Remedies Against Dumped and Subsidized Imports

Recall that the direct effect of dumping and subsidizing imports is to lower import prices, an effect that provides benefits and costs for the importing country. There are benefits to consumers if imports are finished goods and to consuming industries that use imports as intermediate inputs into their own production (*downstream* industry). Conversely, there are costs to the import-competing industry, its workers, and other domestic industries selling intermediate inputs to production of the import-competing industry (*upstream* industry). Dumping at prices below fair market value and subsidizing exports are considered unfair trade practices under international trade law; they can be neutralized by the imposition of antidumping or countervailing duties on dumped or subsidized imports.

Figure 6.2 illustrates the effects of unfair trade practices on Canada, a nation too small to influence the foreign price of steel; for simplicity, the figure assumes that Canada's steel, iron ore, and auto companies operate in competitive markets. In Figure 6.2(a), S_C and D_C represent the Canadian supply and demand for steel. Suppose that South Korea, which has a comparative advantage in steel, supplies steel to Canada at the fair-trade price of $600 per ton. At this price, Canadian production equals 200 tons, Canadian consumption equals 300 tons, and imports equal 100 tons.

Now suppose that as a result of South Korean dumping and subsidizing practices, Canada imports steel at a price of $500 per ton; the margin of dumping and subsidization would thus equal $100 ($600 − $500 = $100). The unfair trade practice reduces Canadian production from 200 tons to 100 tons, increases Canadian consumption from 300 tons to 400 tons, and increases Canadian imports from 100 tons to 300 tons. Falling prices and quantities, in turn, lead to falling investment and employment in the Canadian steel industry. Although the producer surplus of Canadian steelmakers decreases by area *a* due to unfair trade, Canadian buyers find their consumer surplus rising by area *a* + *b* + *c* + *d*. The Canadian steel market as a whole benefits from unfair trade because the gains to its consumers exceed the losses to its producers by area *b* + *c* + *d*!

Unfair trade also affects Canada's upstream and downstream industries. If the Canadian iron-ore industry (upstream) supplies mainly to Canadian steelmakers, the demand for Canadian iron ore will decrease as their customers' output falls due to competition from cheaper imported steel. As illustrated in Figure 6.2(b), without unfair trade, the quantity of iron ore demanded by Canadian steelmakers is Q_0 tons at a price of P_0 per ton. Because of unfair trade in the steel industry, the demand for iron ore decreases from D_C to $D_{C'}$; production thus falls as do revenues and employment in this industry. In autos (downstream), production will increase as

FIGURE 6.2

EFFECTS OF DUMPED AND SUBSIDIZED IMPORTS AND THEIR REMEDIES

Dumped or subsidized imports provide benefits to consumers if imports are finished goods and to consuming producers that use the imports as intermediate inputs into their own production; they inflict costs on import-competing domestic producers, their workers, and other domestic producers selling intermediate inputs to import-competing producers. An antidumping or countervailing duty inflicts costs on consumers if imports are finished goods and on consuming producers that use the imports as intermediate inputs into their own production; benefits are provided to import-competing domestic producers, their workers, and other domestic producers selling intermediate inputs to the protected industry.

manufacturing costs decrease because of the availability of cheaper imported steel. As illustrated in Figure 6.2(c), Canadian auto production increases from Q_0 units to Q_1 units, as the supply curve shifts downward from S_C to $S_{C'}$, with accompanying positive effects on revenues and employment; the decrease in production costs also improves the Canadian auto industry's competitiveness in international markets.

Suppose that unfair trade in steel results in the imposition by the Canadian government of an antidumping duty or countervailing duty on imported steel equal to the margin of dumping or subsidization ($100). The effect of an exact offsetting duty in the steel industry is a regaining of the initial prices and quantities in Canada's steel, iron-ore, and auto industries, as seen in Figure 6.2. The duty raises the import price of unfairly traded steel in Canada, leading to increased steel production by Canadian steelmakers; this results in increased demand, and therefore higher prices, for Canadian iron ore, but also implies increased production costs, higher prices, and lower sales for Canadian automakers. With the import duty, the decrease in the consumer surplus more than offsets the increase in the producer surplus in the Canadian steel market.

The U.S. International Trade Commission estimated the economic effects of antidumping duties and countervailing duties for U.S. petitioning industries and their upstream suppliers and downstream consumers for the year 1991. The study concluded that these duties typically benefited successful petitioning industries by raising prices and improving output and employment. However, the costs to the rest of the economy were far greater. The study estimated that the U.S. economy would have experienced a net welfare gain of $1.59 billion in the year 1991 had U.S. antidumping duties and countervailing duties *not* been in effect. In other words, these duties imposed costs on consumers, downstream industries, and the economy as a whole at least $1.59 billion greater than the benefits enjoyed by the successful petitioning industries and their employees.[6] However, remember that the purpose of antidumping and countervailing duty laws is not to protect consumers, but rather to discourage unfairly traded imports that cause harm to competing domestic industries and workers.

U.S. Steel Companies Lose an Unfair Trade Case and Still Win

For years, the U.S. steel industry has dominated at the complaint department of the U.S. International Trade Commission. During the 1980s and 1990s, it accounted for almost half of the nation's unfair-trade complaints, even though steel constituted less than five percent of U.S. imports. Year after year, the steel industry swamped the USITC with petitions alleging that foreign steel was being subsidized or dumped into the U.S. market. However, the steel industry was not very successful in its petitions against cheap imports. During the 1990s, for example, it lost more than half its cases.

To the steel industry, however, winning isn't everything. Filing and arguing its cases is part of the competitive strategy of the Big Steel consortium—U.S. Steel, Bethlehem, AK Steel, LTV Corp., Inland Steel Industries Inc., and National Steel. The consortium knows that it can use the trade laws to influence the supply of steel in the marketplace and thus limit foreign competition. Whenever the market gets weak, for whatever reason, the consortium files an unfair-trade case.

Here's how the strategy works. The market gets soft, and the consortium files trade cases alleging foreign subsidization or dumping, and then imports from the target companies decrease. The case proceeds for a year or so, allowing domestic steelmakers to increase market share and raise prices. Even if the USITC rules against the case, the market has time to recover.

Once a case is filed, it takes months to proceed through a four-stage legal process, and time benefits domestic steelmakers. American steelmakers usually win the first round in which the industry has to show the USITC a "reasonable indication" of harm from imports. Armed with that finding, the U.S. Department of Commerce can set preliminary duties on the imports. Importers must post a financial bond to cover those duties. Then, the Commerce Department determines the final duties, based on the extent of foreign subsidization or dumping, and the case goes back to the USITC for a final determination of injury. If the U.S. companies lose, the duty is never collected, and the bond is lifted. However, if they win, the importer may be liable for the full amount.

During this process, U.S. importers have the right to continue importing. They might continue to import if they feel strongly that the U.S. steelmakers will lose the case. However, the USITC is a political body, with some of its presidentially appointed commissioners being free traders and others tending to be more protectionist. Because

---

[6]U.S. International Trade Commission, *The Economic Effects of Antidumping and Countervailing Duty Orders and Suspension Agreements*, Washington, DC: International Trade Commission, June 1995.

U.S. importers realize that they run a big risk if they are wrong, the response is usually to stop importing when a case is filed.

In 1997, Trinidad was hit with a complaint on steel wire rod, which is used to make wire. Wire-rod producers in Trinidad cut their U.S. shipments by 40 percent after the preliminary ruling, even though Trinidad's steelmakers eventually won the case.

Put simply, just by filing unfair trade cases, the U.S. steel industry may win. Whatever it spends on legal fees, it may recoup many times over in extra revenue. That's the great thing about filing: even if you lose, you still win.

Section 301: Protection Against Unfair Trading Practices

Section 301 of the Trade Act of 1974 gives the U.S. trade representative (USTR) the authority, subject to the approval of the president, and the means to respond to unfair trading practices by foreign nations. Included among these unfair practices are foreign-trade restrictions that hinder U.S. exports and foreign subsidies that hinder U.S. exports to third-country markets. The USTR responds when he or she determines that such practices result in "unreasonable" or "discriminatory" burdens on U.S. exporters. The legislation was primarily a congressional response to dissatisfaction with GATT's ineffectiveness in resolving trade disputes. Table 6.7 provides examples of Section 301 cases.

Section 301 investigations are usually initiated on the basis of petitions by adversely affected U.S. companies and labor unions; they can also be initiated by the president. If, after investigation, it is determined that a foreign nation is engaging in unfair trading practices, the USTR is empowered to (1) impose tariffs or other import restrictions on products and services and (2) deny the foreign country the benefits of trade-agreement concessions.

Although the ultimate sanction available to the United States is retaliatory import restrictions, the purpose of Section 301 is to obtain the successful resolution of conflicts. In a large majority of cases, Section 301 has been used to convince foreign nations to modify or eliminate what the United States has considered to be unfair trading practices; only in a small minority of cases has the United States retaliated against foreign producers by means of tariffs or quotas. However, foreign nations have often likened Section 301 to a "crowbar" approach to resolving trade disputes, which invites retaliatory trade restrictions. At least two reasons have been

TABLE 6.7

SECTION 301 INVESTIGATIONS OF UNFAIR TRADING PRACTICES: SELECTED EXAMPLES

U.S. Petitioner	Product	Unfair Trading Practice
Heilman Brewing Co.	Beer	Canadian import restrictions
Amtech Co.	Electronics	Norwegian government procurement code
Great Western Sugar Co.	Sugar	European Union subsidies
National Soybean Producers Assoc.	Soybeans	Brazilian subsidies
Association of American Vintners	Wine	South Korean import restrictions

Source: From U.S. International Trade Commission, *Operation of the Trade Agreements Program*, Washington, DC, Government Printing Office, various issues.

advanced for the limitations of this approach to opening foreign markets to U.S. exports: (1) Nationalism unites the people of a foreign nation against U.S. threats of trade restrictions; and (2) The foreign nation reorients its economy toward trading partners other than the United States.

An example of a Section 301 case is the banana dispute between the United States and Europe. In 1993, the EU implemented a single EU-wide regime on banana imports. The regime gave preferential entry to bananas from the EU's former colonies, including parts of the Caribbean, Africa, and Asia. It also restricted entry from other countries, including several in Latin America where U.S. companies predominate. According to the United States, the EU's banana regime resulted in unfair treatment for American companies. United States trade officials maintained that Chiquita Brands International and Dole Food Co., which handle and distribute bananas from Latin American nations, lost half of their business because of the EU's banana regime. As a result, the United States and several Latin American countries brought this issue to the World Trade Organization and successfully argued their case. The WTO ruled that the EU's banana regime discriminated against U.S. and Latin American distribution companies and banana exports from Latin American countries. After a prolonged struggle, Europe modified its behavior and the tariff was lifted.

Protection of Intellectual Property Rights

In the 1800s, Charles Dickens criticized U.S. publishers for printing unauthorized versions of his works without paying him one penny. But U.S. copyright protection did not apply to foreign (British) authors, so Dickens's popular fiction could be pirated without punishment. In recent years, it is U.S. companies whose profit expectations have been frustrated. Publishers in South Korea run off copies of bootlegged U.S. textbooks without providing royalty payments. American research laboratories find themselves in legal tangles with Japanese electronics manufacturers concerning patent infringement.

Certain industries and products are well-known targets of pirates, counterfeiters, and other infringers of **intellectual property rights (IPRs)**. Counterfeiting has been common in industries such as automobile parts, jewelry, sporting goods, and watches. Piracy of audio and videotapes, computer software, and printed materials has been widespread throughout the world. Industries in which product life cycles are shorter than the time necessary to obtain and enforce a patent are also subject to thievery; examples are photographic equipment and telecommunications. Table 6.8 provides examples of IPR violations in China.

Intellectual property is an invention, idea, product, or process that has been registered with the government and that awards the inventor (or author) exclusive rights to use the invention for a given time period. Governments use several techniques to protect intellectual property. *Copyrights* are awarded to protect works of original authorship (for example, music compositions and textbooks); most nations issue copyright protection for the remainder of the author's life plus 50 years. *Trademarks* are awarded to manufacturers and provide exclusive rights to a distinguishing name or symbol (for example, Coca-Cola). *Patents* secure to an inventor for a term, usually 15 years or more, the exclusive right to make, use, or sell the invention.

TABLE 6.8

EXAMPLES OF INTELLECTUAL PROPERTY RIGHT VIOLATIONS IN CHINA

Affected Firm	Violation in China
Epson	Copying machines and ink cartridges are counterfeited.
Microsoft	Counterfeiting of Windows and Windows NT, with packaging virtually indistinguishable from the real product and sold in authorized outlets.
Yamaha	Five of every six JYM150-A motorcycles and ZY125 scooters bearing Yamaha's name are fake in China. Some state-owned factories manufacture copies four months following the introduction of a new model.
Gillette	Up to one-fourth of its Parker pens, Duracell batteries, and Gillette razors sold in China are pirated.
Anheuser-Busch	Some 640 million bottles of fake Budweiser beer are sold annually in China.
Bestfoods	Bogus versions of Knorr bouillon and Skippy Peanut Butter lead to tens of millions of dollars in forgone sales each year.

Source: From U.S. Trade Representative, *National Trade Estimate Report on Foreign Trade Barriers*, various issues, available at **http://www.ustr.gov**.

In spite of efforts to protect IPRs, competing firms sometimes infringe on the rights of others by making a cheaper imitation of the original product. In 1986, the courts ruled that Kodak had infringed on Polaroid's patents for instant cameras and awarded Polaroid more than $900 million in damages. Another infringement would occur if a company manufactured an instant camera similar to Polaroid's and labeled and marketed it as a Polaroid camera; this is an example of a counterfeit product.

The lack of effective international procedures for protecting IPRs becomes a problem when the expense of copying an innovation (including the cost of penalties if caught) is less than the cost of purchasing or leasing the technology. Suppose that Warner-Lambert Drug Co. develops a product that cures the common cold, called "Cold-Free," and that the firm plans to export it to Taiwan. If Cold-Free is not protected by a patent in Taiwan, either because Taiwan does not recognize IPRs or Warner-Lambert has not filed for protection, cheaper copies of Cold-Free could legally be developed and marketed. Also, if Warner-Lambert's trademark is not protected, counterfeit cold remedies that are indistinguishable from Cold-Free could be legally sold in Taiwan. These copies would result in reduced sales and profits for Warner-Lambert. Moreover, if "Cold-Free" is a trademark that consumers strongly associate with Warner-Lambert, a counterfeit product of noticeably inferior quality could adversely affect Warner-Lambert's reputation and thus detract from the sales of both Cold-Free and other Warner-Lambert products.

Although most nations have regulations protecting IPRs, many problems have been associated with trade in products affected by IPRs. One problem is differing IPR regulations across nations. For example, the United States uses a first-to-invent rule when determining patent eligibility, whereas most other nations employ a first-to-file rule. Another problem is lack of enforcement of international IPR agreements. These problems stem largely from differing incentives to protect intellectual property, especially between nations that are innovating, technological exporters and those that are noninnovating, technological importers. Developing nations, lacking in research and development and patent innovation, sometimes pirate foreign technology and use it to produce goods at costs lower than could be achieved in the innovating nation. Poorer developing nations often find it difficult to pay the higher prices that would prevail if innovated products (such as medical supplies) were provided patent protection. Therefore, they have little incentive to provide patent protection to the products they need.

As long as the cost of pirating technology, including the probability and costs of being caught, is less than the profits captured by the firm doing the pirating, technology pirating tends to continue. However, pirating reduces the rate of profitability earned by firms in the innovating nations, which in turn deters them from investing in research and development. Over time, this lack of investment leads to fewer products and welfare losses for the people of both nations.

The United States has faced many obstacles in trying to protect its intellectual property. Dozens of nations lack adequate legal structures to protect the patents of foreign firms. Others have consciously excluded certain products (such as chemicals) from protection to support their industries. Even in developed nations, where legal safeguards exist, the fast pace of technological innovation often outruns the protection provided by the legal system.

Trade Adjustment Assistance

According to the free-trade argument, in a dynamic economy in which trade proceeds according to the comparative-advantage principle, resources flow from uses with lower productivity to those with higher productivity. Consumers gain by having a wider variety of goods to choose from at lower prices. It is also true that as countries adopt freer trade policies, both winners and losers emerge. Some firms and industries will become more efficient and grow as they expand into overseas markets, whereas others will contract, merge, or perhaps even fail when faced with increased competition. While this adjustment process may be healthy for a dynamic economy, it can be a harsh reality for firms and workers in import-competing industries.

One way to balance the gains of freer trade that are realized broadly throughout the economy, with the costs that tend to be more concentrated, is to address the needs of firms and workers that have been adversely affected. Many industrial nations have done this by enacting programs for giving **trade adjustment assistance** to those who incur hardships because of trade liberalization. The underlying rationale comes from the notion that if society in general enjoys welfare gains from the increased efficiency stemming from trade liberalization, some sort of compensation should be provided for those who are injured by import competition. As long as freer trade generates significant gains to the nation, the winners can compensate the losers and still enjoy some of the gains from freer trade.

The U.S. trade adjustment assistance program assists domestic workers displaced by foreign trade and increased imports. The program provides benefits such as extended income support beyond normal unemployment insurance benefits, services such as job training, and allowances for job search and relocation. To businesses and communities, the program offers technical aid in moving into new lines of production, market research assistance, and low-interest loans. The major beneficiaries of the program have been workers and firms in the apparel and textile industry, followed by the oil and gas, electronics, and metal and machinery industries. Traditionally, trade-displaced workers are older and less educated than typical workers, and have worked only in one industry. They take longer to find another job and, when they find one, are more likely to see their wages decrease.

According to the trade adjustment assistance program, unemployed workers typically receive 26 weeks of unemployment compensation payments. If they use up this benefit and are declared eligible for trade adjustment assistance by the Department of Labor, they can then receive trade adjustment assistance benefits for an extra 52 weeks, resulting in a total support of 78 weeks. In recent years, about two-thirds of all workers filing for trade adjustment assistance have been declared eligible by the Department of Labor.

Although the trade adjustment assistance program is considered a significant innovation in trade policy, critics maintain that it has suffered from inadequate funding. They note that the United States spends only about $1 billion a year on helping trade-displaced workers, while the economy as a whole gains some $1 trillion a year from freer trade. Also, trade adjustment assistance cannot resolve all the workers' challenges, especially those faced by low-skilled workers. For example, many workers applying for training assistance do not have a high school education, have been out of the educational system for 20 years or more, or have limited English skills. Therefore, training programs are unlikely to complete the match between these workers and the kinds of jobs available in a high-skilled economy. Moreover, the trade adjustment program covers manufacturing workers, but not service workers whose jobs have been outsourced to foreign workers. Critics also maintain that trade adjustment assistance has sometimes been used to financially sustain a losing concern rather than help it become more competitive by switching to superior technologies and developing new products. Also, critics note that the program provides a motive for trade-displaced workers to remain unemployed for a longer period of time than other displaced workers. Should people who lose their jobs because of competition from imports receive special support over and above those who lose their jobs because of changes in consumers' tastes, domestic competition, or as a result of new technologies?

Will Wage and Health Insurance Make Free Trade More Acceptable to Workers?

Although the trade adjustment assistance program assists domestic workers displaced by foreign trade and increased imports, many workers feel threatened by international trade. Workers' fears about globalization and union pressure on government officials hinder efforts to liberalize trade. That's why economists have increasingly advocated that the trade adjustment assistance program be expanded to include wage and health insurance.

The concept of wage and health insurance is simple. Trade, although a benefit to the economy overall, harms workers who produce things or provide services susceptible to import competition. Trade-related job losses are concentrated in manufacturing industries where import competition is strong, including the automobile, steel, textile, apparel, computing, and electronics industries. Compensating the losers makes more sense than trying to protect them by denying the benefits of trade to all.

When trade or technology puts someone out of work, a worker often takes a new job that pays less. On average, a worker in a manufacturing industry hit by import competition who loses one job and gets another earns 13 percent less, according to the estimates of Professor Lori Kletzer of the University of California at Santa Cruz.[7] About a third earn as much or more, and they don't need help. But about a quarter take jobs that pay 30 percent less, or worse. Because the rest of us benefit—by getting cheaper goods, more efficient services, and a more productive economy—we can afford to make up some of the difference.

Rather than protecting workers by restricting imports, which results in losses for the overall economy, why not provide wage and health insurance? Proponents of wage insurance contend that it encourages workers to find a new job quickly, in contrast to unemployment insurance, which creates an incentive to delay looking for work. They also contend that wage insurance yields benefits for both younger workers and older workers. It makes it easier for younger workers to acquire the training and new skills that will make them more employable over the course of their working lives. Wage insurance can enable older workers to reach retirement without having to sharply lower their standard of living or dip into retirement savings after a job loss. Simply put, proponents of wage insurance contend that, by reducing worker anxiety, wage insurance will reduce worker opposition to trade liberalization and globalization more broadly.

To win authority for fast-track power to negotiate future trade agreements with Latin America, in 2002 President George Bush bowed to congressional pressure and expanded the trade adjustment assistance program. First, he initiated a program of wage insurance for trade-displaced workers. To receive income maintenance benefits, eligible workers must be over 50 years old, earn less than $50,000 a year, and be employed fulltime at the firm from which they were separated. The government pays half the difference between the old and new wage for two years, up to a maximum of $10,000. To receive this income subsidy, workers must prove they do not have skills that are easily transferrable to other jobs, and some cannot do that.

Moreover, President Bush implemented the Health Coverage Tax Credit program. This program provides a federal income tax credit that pays 65 percent of qualified health plan premiums for eligible trade-displaced workers. Congress established the tax credit with the goal of making health coverage more accessible and affordable for those who might otherwise not be able to afford it. For workers to receive the benefits of this program, the Labor Department must certify that they have lost their jobs to imports from certain countries or to a shift in production there. However, during the first five years of the program, just 11 percent of those potentially eligible for the subsidy took it. This is because many laid-off workers were unable to come up with 35 percent of the health insurance premium, which can run about $250 per month. Critics note that those who get health coverage on the job typically pay only 15 to 25 percent of the total cost of their insurance. Thus, they maintain that the Health Coverage Tax Credit program needs to be liberalized to make health insurance more accessible for trade-displaced workers.

---

[7]Lori Kletzer and Robert Litan, *A Prescription to Relieve Worker Anxiety*, International Economics Policy Briefs, Institute for International Economics, Washington, DC, February 2001. See also Trade Deficit Review Commission, *The U.S. Trade Deficit*, Washington, DC, 2000.

It remains to be seen whether these new income maintenance programs will reduce workers' distrust of liberal trade agreements.

Industrial Policies of the United States

Besides enacting regulations intended to produce a fair trading environment for all parties engaging in international business, the United States has implemented *industrial policies* to enhance the competitiveness of domestic producers. As discussed in Chapter 3, such policies involve government channeling of resources into specific, targeted industries that it views as important for future economic growth. Among the methods used to channel resources are tax incentives, loan guarantees, and low-interest loans.

Today, almost all nations implement some industrial policies. Although industrial policies are generally associated with the formal, explicit efforts of governments (as in Japan and France) to enhance the development of specific industries (such as steel or electronics), other traditionally free-enterprise nations (such as Germany and the United States) also have less formal, implicit industrial policies.

What has been the U.S. approach to industrial policy? The U.S. government has attempted to provide a favorable climate for business, given the social, environmental, and safety constraints imposed by modern society. Rather than formulating a coordinated industrial policy to affect particular industries, the U.S. government has generally emphasized macroeconomic policies (such as fiscal and monetary policies) aimed at such objectives as economic stability, growth, and the broad allocation of the gross domestic product.

However, there is no doubt that the U.S. government uses a number of measures to shape the structure of the economy that would be called "industrial policies" in other nations. The most notable of these measures is agricultural policy. In agriculture, a farmer who initiates a major innovation can be imitated by many other farmers, who capture the benefits without sharing the risks. To rectify this problem, the U.S. government is involved in research in agricultural techniques and in the dissemination of this information to farmers through its agricultural extension service, as well as the fostering of large-scale projects such as irrigation facilities. The U.S. government has also provided support for the shipping, shipbuilding, and energy industries, primarily on the grounds of national security.

United States defense spending is often cited as an industrial policy. As the world's largest market for military goods, it is no wonder that the United States dominates their production. American spending on military goods supports domestic manufacturers and permits them to achieve large economies of scale. United States defense spending has provided spillover benefits to civilian industries, especially commercial aircraft, computers, and electronics. Military research and development provides U.S. companies with expertise that they can apply elsewhere.

In manufacturing, the U.S. government has provided assistance to financially troubled industries. In automobiles, for example, the government provided a $1.5 billion loan guarantee in 1979 and 1980 to bail out Chrysler Corporation. It also negotiated voluntary export restrictions with the Japanese on autos in the 1980s to ease the burden of import competition. The steel and textile industries have been major recipients of trade protection as well.

Export Promotion and Financing

Another element of U.S. industrial policy is export promotion. The U.S. government furnishes exporters with marketing information and technical assistance, in addition to trade missions that help expose new exporters to foreign customers. The government also promotes exports by sponsoring exhibits of U.S. goods at international trade fairs and establishing overseas trade centers that enable U.S. businesses to exhibit and sell machinery and equipment.

The United States also encourages exports by allowing its manufacturers to form export trade associations to facilitate the marketing of U.S. products abroad. Moreover, U.S. manufacturers and financial institutions are permitted to combine their resources into joint export trading companies to export their own products or to act as an export service for other producers. Sears, Rockwell, General Electric, Control Data, and General Motors are examples of firms that have formed export trading companies.

Moreover, the United States provides export subsidies to its producers in the form of low-cost credit. The maintenance of competitive credit terms for U.S. exporters is a function of the U.S. Export-Import Bank and the Commodity Credit Corporation. The **Export-Import Bank (Eximbank)** is an independent agency of the U.S. government established to encourage the exports of U.S. businesses. The Eximbank provides the following:

- Guarantees of working capital loans for U.S. exporters to cover pre-export costs
- Export credit insurance that protects U.S. exporters or their lenders against commercial or political risks of nonpayment by foreign buyers
- Guarantees of commercial loans to creditworthy foreign buyers of U.S. goods and services
- Direct loans to these foreign buyers when private financing is unavailable
- Special programs to promote U.S. exports of environmentally beneficial goods and services
- Asset-based financing for large commercial aircraft and other appropriate exports
- Project financing to support U.S. exports to international infrastructure projects

In offering competitive interest rates in financing exports, Eximbank has sometimes been criticized because part of its funds are borrowed from the U.S. Treasury. Critics question whether U.S. tax revenues should subsidize exports to foreign countries at interest rates lower than could be obtained from private institutions. To this extent, it is true that tax funds distort trade and redistribute income toward exporters.

Table 6.9 provides examples of direct loans and loan guarantees made by Eximbank. Major beneficiaries of Eximbank credit have included aircraft, telecommunications, power-generating equipment, and energy developments. Firms such as Boeing, McDonnell Douglas, and Westinghouse have enjoyed substantial benefits from these programs.

Officially supported lending for U.S. exports is also provided by the **Commodity Credit Corporation (CCC)**, a government-owned corporation administered by the U.S. Department of Agriculture. The CCC makes available export credit financing for eligible agricultural commodities. The interest rates charged by the CCC are usually slightly below the prevailing rates charged by private financial institutions.

TABLE 6.9

EXAMPLES OF LOANS PROVIDED BY EXIMBANK OF THE UNITED STATES (IN MILLIONS OF DOLLARS)

Foreign Borrower/U.S. Exporter	Purpose	Loan or Loan Guarantee
Banco Santander Noroeste of Brazil/General Electric	Locomotives	87.7
Government of Bulgaria/Westinghouse	Instruments	81.8
Air China/Boeing	Aircraft	69.8
Government of Croatia/Bechtel International	Highway construction	228.7
Government of Ghana/Wanan International	Electrical equipment	21.1
Government of Indonesia/IBM	Computer hardware	20.2
Japan Airlines/Boeing	Aircraft	212.3
Fevisa Industrial of Mexico/Pennsylvania Crusher Inc.	Glass manufacturing equipment	17.7
Delta Communications of Mexico/Motorola	Communications equipment	11.5

Source: From Export-Import Bank of the United States, *Annual Report*, various issues, **http://www.exim.gov**.

Industrial Policies of Japan

Although the United States has generally not used explicit industrial policies to support specific industries, such policies have been used elsewhere. Consider the case of Japan.

Japan has become a technological leader in the post-World War II era. During the 1950s, Japan's exports consisted primarily of textiles and other low-tech products. By the 1960s and 1970s, its exports emphasized capital-intensive products such as autos, steel, and ships. By the 1980s and 1990s, Japan had become a major world competitor in high-tech goods, such as optical fibers and semiconductors.

Advocates of industrial policy assert that government assistance for emerging industries has helped transform the Japanese economy from low-tech to heavy industry to high-tech. They claim that protection from imports, R&D subsidies, and the like fostered the development of Japanese industry. Clearly, the Japanese government provided assistance to shipbuilding and steel during the 1950s, to autos and machine tools during the 1960s, and to high-tech industries beginning in the early 1970s. Japanese industrial policy has had two distinct phases: From the 1950s to the early 1970s, the Japanese government assumed strong control over the nation's resources and the direction of the economy's growth. Since the mid-1970s, the government's industrial policy has been more modest and subtle.

To implement its industrial policies in manufacturing, the Japanese government has created the **Ministry of Economy, Trade and Industry (METI)**. This ministry attempts to facilitate the shifting of resources into high-tech industries by targeting specific industries for support. With the assistance of consultants from leading corporations, trade unions, banks, and universities, METI forms a consensus on the best policies to pursue. The next step of industrial policy is to increase domestic R&D, investment, and production. Targeted industries have received support in the form of trade protection, allocations of foreign exchange, R&D subsidies, loans at below-market interest rates, loans that must be repaid only if a firm becomes profitable, favorable tax treatment, and joint government-industry research projects intended to develop promising technologies.

Without government support, it is improbable that Japanese semiconductor, telecommunications equipment, fiber optics, and machine-tool industries would be as competitive as they are. Not all Japanese industrial policies have been successful, however, as seen in the cases of computers, aluminum, and petrochemicals. Even industries in which Japan is competitive in world markets, such as shipbuilding and steel, have witnessed prolonged periods of excess capacity. Moreover, some of Japan's biggest success stories (TVs, stereos, and VCRs) were not the industries most heavily targeted by the Japanese government.

The extent to which industrial policy has contributed to Japan's economic growth since World War II is unclear. Japan has benefited from a high domestic savings rate, an educated and motivated labor force, good labor-management relations, a shift of labor from low-productivity sectors (such as agriculture) to high-productivity manufacturing, entrepreneurs willing to assume risks, and the like. These factors have enhanced Japan's transformation from a low-tech nation to a high-tech nation. It is debatable how rapidly this transformation would have occurred in the absence of an industrial policy. Although Japan has the most visible industrial policy of the industrialized nations, the importance of that policy to Japan's success should not be exaggerated.[8]

Strategic Trade Policy

Beginning in the 1980s, a new argument for industrial policy gained prominence. The theory behind **strategic trade policy** is that government can assist domestic companies in capturing economic profits from foreign competitors.[9] Such assistance entails government support for certain "strategic" industries (such as high-technology) that are important to future domestic economic growth and that provide widespread benefits (externalities) to society.

The essential notion underlying strategic trade policy is *imperfect competition*. Many industries participating in trade, the argument goes, are dominated by a small number of large companies—large enough for each company to significantly influence market price. Such market power gives these companies the potential to attain long-term economic profits. According to the strategic trade policy argument, government policy can alter the terms of competition to favor domestic companies over foreign companies and shift economic profits in imperfectly competitive markets from foreign to domestic companies.

A standard example is the aircraft industry. With the high fixed costs of introducing a new aircraft and a significant learning curve in production that leads to decreasing unit production costs, this industry can support only a small number of manufacturers. It is also an industry that typically is closely associated with national prestige.

Assume that two competing manufacturers, Boeing (representing the United States) and Airbus (a consortium owned jointly by four European governments), are considering whether to construct a new aircraft. If *either* firm manufactures the

---

[8]R. Beason and D. Weinstein, "Growth, Economies of Scale, and Targeting in Japan: 1955–1990," Review of economics and Statistics, May 1996.

[9]The argument for strategic trade policy was first presented in J. Brander and B. Spencer, "International R&D Rivalry and Industrial Strategy," *Review of Economic Studies* 50 (1983), pp. 707–722. See also P. Krugman, ed., *Strategic Trade Policy and the New International Economics* (Cambridge, MA: MIT Press, 1986) and P. Krugman, "Is Free Trade Passe?" *Economic Perspectives*, Fall 1987, pp. 131–144.

FIGURE 6.3

EFFECTS OF A EUROPEAN SUBSIDY GRANTED TO AIRBUS

Hypothetical Payoff Matrix: Millions of Dollars

Without Subsidy

		Airbus	
		Produces	Does Not Produce
Boeing	Produces	Airbus −5 Boeing −5	Airbus 0 Boeing 100
Boeing	Does Not Produce	Airbus 100 Boeing 0	Airbus 0 Boeing 0

With European Subsidy

		Airbus	
		Produces	Does Not Produce
Boeing	Produces	Airbus 5 Boeing −5	Airbus 0 Boeing 100
Boeing	Does Not Produce	Airbus 110 Boeing 0	Airbus 0 Boeing 0

According to the theory of strategic trade policy, government subsidies can assist domestic firms in capturing economic profits from foreign competitors.

Source: Paul Krugman, "Is Free Trade Passe?" *Economic Perspectives*, Fall 1987, pp. 131–144.

aircraft by itself, it will attain *profits* of $100 million. If *both* firms manufacture the aircraft, they will each suffer a *loss* of $5 million.

Now assume the European governments decide to subsidize Airbus production in the amount of $10 million. Even if both companies manufacture the new aircraft, Airbus is now certain of making a $5 million profit. But the point is this: Boeing will *cancel* its new aircraft project. The European subsidy thus ensures not only that Airbus will manufacture the new aircraft but also that Boeing will suffer a loss if it joins in. The result is that Airbus achieves a profit of $110 million and can easily repay its subsidy to the European governments. If we assume that the two manufacturers produce entirely for export, the subsidy of $10 million results in a transfer of $100 million in profits from the United States to Europe. Figure 6.3 summarizes these results. The welfare effects of strategic trade policy are discussed in *Exploring Further 6.1*.

Consider another example. Suppose the electronics industry has just two companies, one in Japan and one in the United States. In this industry, learning-by doing reduces unit production costs indefinitely with the expansion of output. Suppose the Japanese government considers its electronics industry to be "strategic" and imposes trade barriers that close its domestic market to the U.S. competitor; assume the United States keeps its electronics market open. The Japanese manufacturer can expand its output and thus reduce its unit cost. Over a period of time, this competitive advantage permits it to drive the U.S. manufacturer out of business. The profits that the U.S. company had extracted from U.S. buyers are transferred to the Japanese.

Advocates of strategic trade policy recognize that the classical argument for free trade considered externalities at length. The difference, they maintain, is that the classical theory was based on *perfect competition* and thus does not appreciate the most likely source of the externality, whereas modern theories based on imperfect competition does. The externality in question is the ability of companies to capture the fruits of expensive innovation. Classical theory based on perfect competition neglected this factor because large fixed costs are involved in innovation and research and development, and such costs ensure that the number of competitors in an industry will be small.

The strategic-trade policy concept has been criticized on several grounds. From a political perspective, special-interest groups may dictate who will receive government support. Also, if a worldwide cycle of activist trade-policy retaliation and counter retaliation were to occur, all nations would be worse off. Moreover, governments lack the information to intervene intelligently in the marketplace. In the Boeing-Airbus example, the activist government must know how much profit would be achieved as a result of proceeding with the new aircraft, both with and without foreign competition. Minor miscalculations could result in an intervention that makes the home economy worse off, instead of better off. Finally, the mere existence of imperfect competition does not guarantee that there is a strategic opportunity to be pursued, even by an omniscient government. There must also be a continuing source of economic profits, with no potential competition to erase them. But *continuing* economic profits are probably less common than governments think.

The case of the European subsidization of aircraft during the 1970s provides an example of the benefits and costs encountered when applying the strategic-trade policy concept. During the 1970s, Airbus received a government subsidy of $1.5 billion. The subsidy was intended to help Airbus offset the 20 percent cost disadvantage it faced on the production of its A300 aircraft compared to that of its main competitor, the Boeing 767. Did the subsidy help the European nations involved in the Airbus consortium? Evidence suggests that it did not. Airbus itself lost money on its A300 plane and continued to face cost disadvantages relative to Boeing. European airlines and passengers did benefit because the subsidy kept Airbus prices lower; however, the amount of Airbus's losses roughly matched this gain. Because the costs of the subsidy had to be financed by higher taxes, Europe was probably worse off with the subsidy. The United States also lost, because Boeing's profits were smaller and were not fully offset by lower prices accruing to U.S. aircraft users; but the European subsidy did not drive Boeing out of the market. The only obvious gainers were other nations, whose airlines and passengers enjoyed benefits from lower Airbus prices at no cost to themselves.[10]

Economic Sanctions

Instead of promoting trade, governments may *restrict* trade for domestic and foreign-policy objectives. **Economic sanctions** are government-mandated limitations placed on customary trade or financial relations among nations. They have been used to protect the domestic economy, reduce nuclear proliferation, set compensation for property expropriated by foreign governments, combat international terrorism, preserve national security, and protect human rights. The nation initiating the economic sanctions, the *imposing nation*, hopes to impair the economic capabilities of the *target nation* to such an extent that the target nation will succumb to its objectives.

The imposing nation can levy several types of economic sanctions. *Trade sanctions* involve boycotts on imposing-nation exports. The United States has used its

---

[10]R. Baldwin and P. Krugman, "Industrial Policy and International Competition in Wide-Bodied Jet Aircraft," in R. Baldwin, ed., *Trade Policy Issues and Empirical Analysis* (Chicago: University of Chicago Press, 1988), pp. 45–77.

TABLE 6.10

SELECTED ECONOMIC SANCTIONS OF THE UNITED STATES

Year	Target Country	Objectives
2007	Iran	Discourage nuclear proliferation
1998	Pakistan and India	Discourage nuclear proliferation
1993	Haiti	Improve human rights
1992	Serbia	Terminate civil war in Bosnia-Herzegovina
1990	Iraq	Terminate Iraq's military takeover of Kuwait
1985	South Africa	Improve human rights
1981	Soviet Union	Terminate martial law in Poland
1979	Iran	Release U.S. hostages; settle expropriation claims
1961	Cuba	Improve national security

role as a major producer of grain, military hardware, and high-technology goods as a lever to win overseas compliance with its foreign-policy objectives. Trade sanctions may also include quotas on imposing-nation imports from the target nation. *Financial sanctions* can entail limitations on official lending or aid. During the late 1970s, the U.S. policy of freezing the financial assets of Iran was seen as a factor in the freeing of the U.S. hostages. Table 6.10 provides examples of economic sanctions levied by the United States for foreign-policy objectives.

Figure 6.4 can be used to illustrate the goal of economic sanctions levied against a target country, say, Iraq. The figure shows the hypothetical production possibilities curve of Iraq for machines and oil. Prior to the imposition of sanctions, suppose that Iraq is able to operate at maximum efficiency as shown by point A along production possibilities curve PPC_0. Under the sanctions program, a refusal of the imposing nations to purchase Iraqi oil leads to idle wells, refineries, and workers in Iraq. Unused production capacity thus forces Iraq to move inside PPC_0. If imposing nations also impose export sanctions on productive inputs, and thus curtail equipment sales to Iraq, the output potential of Iraq would decrease. This is shown by an inward shift of Iraq's production possibilities curve to PPC_1. Economic inefficiencies and reduced production possibilities, caused by economic sanctions, are intended to inflict hardship on the people and government of Iraq. Over time, sanctions may cause a reduced growth rate for Iraq. Even if short-term welfare losses from sanctions are not large, they can appear in inefficiencies in the usage of labor and capital, deteriorating domestic expectations, and reductions in savings, investment, and employment. Sanctions do reduce Iraq's output potential.

FIGURE 6.4

EFFECTS OF ECONOMIC SANCTIONS

Economic sanctions placed against a target country have the effect of forcing it to operate inside its production possibilities curve. Economic sanctions can also result in an inward shift in the target nation's production possibilities curve.

Factors Influencing the Success of Sanctions

The historical record of economic sanctions provides some insight into the factors that govern their effectiveness. Among the most important determinants of the success of economic sanctions are (1) the number of nations imposing sanctions, (2) the degree to which the target nation has economic and political ties to the imposing nation(s), (3) the extent of political opposition in the target nation, and (4) cultural factors in the target nation.

Although unilateral sanctions may have some success in achieving intended results, it helps if sanctions are imposed by a large number of nations. Multilateral sanctions generally result in greater economic pressure on the target nation than do unilateral measures. Multilateral measures also increase the probability of success by demonstrating that more than one nation disagrees with the target nation's behavior, which enhances the political legitimacy of the effort. International ostracism can have a significant psychological impact on the people of a target nation. However, failure to generate strong multilateral cooperation can result in sanctions' becoming counterproductive; disputes among the imposing nations over sanctions can be interpreted by the target nation as a sign of disarray and weakness.

Sanctions tend to be more effective if the target nation had substantial economic and political relations with the imposing nation(s) before the sanctions are imposed. Then the potential costs to the target nation are very high if it does not comply with the wishes of the imposing nation(s). For example, Western sanctions against South Africa during the 1980s helped convince the government to reform its apartheid system, in part because South Africa conducted four-fifths of its trade with six Western industrial nations and obtained almost all of its capital from the West.

Strength of political opposition within the target nation also affects the success of sanctions. When the target government faces substantial domestic opposition, economic sanctions can lead powerful business interests (such as companies with international ties) to pressure the government to conform to the imposing nation's wishes. Selected, moderate sanctions, with the threat of more severe measures to follow, inflict some economic hardship on domestic residents, while providing an incentive for them to lobby for compliance to forestall more severe sanctions; thus, the political advantage of levying graduated sanctions may outweigh the disadvantage of giving the target nation time to adjust its economy. If harsh, comprehensive sanctions are imposed immediately, domestic business interests have little incentive to pressure the target government to modify its policy; the economic damage has already been done.

When the people of the target nation have strong cultural ties to the imposing nation(s), they are likely to identify with the imposing nation's objectives, which enhances the effectiveness of sanctions. For example, South African whites have generally thought of themselves as part of the Western community. When economic sanctions were imposed on South Africa in the 1980s because of its apartheid practices, many liberal whites felt isolated and morally ostracized by the Western world; this encouraged them to lobby the South African government for political reforms.

Economic Sanctions and Weapons of Mass Destruction: North Korea and Iran

For decades, the United States and the United Nations have imposed economic sanctions against countries that have been implicated in the use of terrorism and the development of chemical, biological, and nuclear weapons. Are economic sanctions useful in discouraging this behavior? Let us consider the cases of Iran and North Korea.

Since 1950 when North Korea invaded South Korea, the United States and the United Nations have imposed numerous sanctions against North Korea. The use of sanctions has been justified on the grounds that North Korea is a threat to global security through its sponsorship of terrorism and its proliferation of weapons of mass destruction such as nuclear bombs and missiles.

Among the sanctions that have been used against North Korea are bans on trade and the entry of North Korean ships and people into other countries. Also, the United States has applied financial sanctions to banks that conduct business with North Korea. Once a bank is targeted, it is effectively terminated from the U.S. financial system. It cannot clear U.S. dollars and it cannot have transactions with other U.S. banks and financial institutions.

In 2005, for example, the United States blacklisted a bank in Macao, called Banco Delta Asia, which provided illicit financial services to the government of North Korea: It helped the North Koreans feed counterfeit U.S. $100 bills into circulation, laundered money from drug deals, and financed cigarette smuggling. Because this bank was a main conduit for North Korea to the international financial system, the sanctions had a chilling effect on North Korean trade and finance. Nevertheless, the sanctions were unable to halt North Korea from testing a nuclear weapon.

One reason why sanctions have not been able to pressure North Korea into changing its behavior is because North Korea's trade and financial relations with the rest of the world are limited. These limited relations restrict the scope of sanctions and their leverage on North Korea. Another problem is that China and South Korea, the main economic lifelines of North Korea, have refrained from implementing substantial sanctions against their neighbor for fear of possible turmoil in the region. To date, it appears that the government of North Korea considers nuclear weapons as vital to its political survival. It will be difficult for sanctions to fulfill their goal of stopping North Korea from developing nuclear weapons.

The case of Iran also demonstrates the limitations of sanctions as a deterrent to the development of nuclear weapons. Since 1987, the United States has implemented numerous sanctions against Iran, such as trade and financial sanctions. These sanctions were intensified in 2006 when Iran openly pursued the development of a nuclear reactor. Iran insisted that it was merely fostering nuclear energy, but other countries have been suspicious that this technology can be shifted to the development of nuclear bombs.

Proponents of sanctions have maintained that Iran's economy is vulnerable to outside economic pressure. It relies on foreign capital and investment to develop its untapped oil fields and fledgling nuclear energy sector. However, Iran's sizeable role in oil production makes it difficult for oil-dependent countries such as the United States to impose severe sanctions against Iran. Also, as U.S. trade with Iran has decreased in the past two decades, Iran's trade with the rest of the world has increased, thus reducing the leverage that the United States has against Iran.

For decades, U.S. sanctions have attempted to discourage Iran and North Korea from destabilizing global security. However, skeptics feel that the overall impact of sanctions, and the extent to which they can advance the objectives of the United States, are questionable in this situation. They maintain that sanctions will not work

DO AUTOMAKER SUBSIDIES WEAKEN THE WTO?

GLOBALIZATION

During 2008–2009, the turmoil in financial markets and the economic downturn brought substantial financial stress to the automobile industry. The economic reach of the auto industry in the United States is broad, affecting autoworkers, auto suppliers, stock and bondholders, dealers, and certain states. The Big Three (Ford, General Motors, and Chrysler) appealed to the U.S. government for financial assistance, noting that if they collapsed, there would be a costly domino effect through the U.S. economy and abroad in terms of falling income and rising unemployment. Simply put, these firms maintained that they were "too big to fail."

The U.S. government considered several methods of assisting the Big Three including outright loans for GM and Chrysler, a "cash for clunkers" program to encourage the purchase of newer vehicles, a tax credit for new purchases, and the bailout of auto-parts firms.

In December 2008, the U.S. government allocated $36 billion for the purpose of making bridge loans to Chrysler and GM. The initial loans consisted of $4 billion to Chrysler and $13.4 billion to GM, and they required both automakers to submit restructuring plans in 2009 if they were to receive additional assistance.

Turbulence in the auto industry was not unique to the United States. As auto sales decreased throughout the world, other countries implemented their own assistance programs. For example, France provided up to $7.7 billion to its failing automakers in the form of loans, and it also established a cash for clunkers scheme. In the United Kingdom, ailing auto companies received $3.2 billion in governmental loan guarantees.

Do these loans and loan-guarantees constitute illegal subsidies according to the rules of the WTO? According to WTO rules, for government assistance to be illegal it must meet several criteria. First, a financial contribution must be made by a government to a particular firm, not to a wide spectrum of firms. Also, it must provide the firm an advantage that would not occur under normal market conditions. Next, the subsidy must cause serious injury, or threat of serious injury, to imports from foreign firms.

Analysts generally maintained that the auto bailouts in the United States and other countries largely adhered to the WTO definition of illegal subsidies. Then why were these subsidies not contested? A key reason is that because virtually all of the major auto-exporting countries enacted some level of assistance to help their ailing auto producers, it would be hard for one country to file a case against another country without inviting retaliation. Therefore, it was unlikely that WTO cases would arise on auto-subsidy programs. Nevertheless, skeptics worried that if a major industry, such as autos, is not subject to the rules of the WTO, the ability of the WTO to maintain open markets based on comparative advantage could be greatly weakened.

Source: Claire Brunel and Gary Clyde Hufbauer, *Money for the Auto Industry: Consistent with WTO Rules?* Policy Brief No. PB09–4, Peterson Institute for International Economics, Washington, D.C., February 2009.

as a stand-alone tool of foreign policy regarding Iran and North Korea. If that is true, policymakers may have to negotiate and offer positive incentives as a method of encouraging cooperation from these countries, short of military conflict, to achieve political objectives.

Summary

1. United States trade policies have reflected the motivation of many groups, including government officials, labor leaders, and business management.

2. United States tariff history has been marked by ups and downs. Many of the traditional arguments for tariffs (revenue, jobs) have been incorporated into U.S. tariff legislation.

3. The Smoot-Hawley Act of 1930 raised U.S. tariffs to an all-time high, with disastrous results. Passage of the Reciprocal Trade Act of 1934 resulted in generalized tariff reductions by the United States, as well as the enactment of most favored nation provisions.

4. The purposes of the General Agreement on Tariffs and Trade were to decrease trade barriers and place all nations on an equal footing in trading relations. In 1995, GATT was transformed into the World Trade Organization, which embodies the main provisions of GATT and provides a mechanism intended to improve the process of resolving trade disputes among member nations. The Tokyo Round and Uruguay Round of multilateral trade negotiations went beyond tariff reductions to liberalize various nontariff trade barriers.

5. Trade remedy laws can help protect domestic firms from stiff foreign competition. These laws include the escape clause, provisions for antidumping and countervailing duties, and Section 301 of the 1974 Trade Act, which addresses unfair trading practices of foreign nations.

6. The escape clause provides temporary protection to U.S. producers who desire relief from foreign imports that are fairly traded.

7. Countervailing duties are intended to offset any unfair competitive advantage that foreign producers might gain over domestic producers because of foreign subsidies.

8. Economic theory suggests that if a nation is a net importer of a product subsidized or dumped by foreigners, the nation as a whole gains from the foreign subsidy or dumping. This is because the gains to domestic consumers of the subsidized or dumped good more than offset the losses to domestic producers of the import-competing goods.

9. U.S. antidumping duties are intended to neutralize two unfair trading practices: export sales in the United States at prices below average total cost, and international price discrimination in which foreign firms sell in the United States at a price lower than that charged in the exporter's home market.

10. Section 301 of the Trade Act of 1974 allows the U.S. government to levy trade restrictions against nations that are practicing unfair competition, if trade disagreements cannot be successfully resolved.

11. Intellectual property includes copyrights, trademarks, and patents. Foreign counterfeiting of intellectual property has been a significant problem for many industrial nations.

12. Because foreign competition may displace import-competing producers and workers, the United States and other nations have initiated programs of trade adjustment assistance involving government aid to adversely affected businesses, workers, and communities.

13. The United States has been reluctant to formulate an explicit industrial policy in which government picks winners and losers among products and firms. Instead, the U.S. government has generally taken a less activist approach in providing assistance to domestic producers (such as the Export-Import Bank and export trade associations).

14. According to the strategic trade policy concept, government can assist firms in capturing economic profits from foreign competitors. The strategic trade policy concept applies to firms in imperfectly competitive markets.

15. Economic sanctions consist of trade and financial restraints imposed on foreign nations. They have been used to preserve national security, protect human rights, and combat international terrorism.

Key Concepts & Terms

- Commodity Credit Corporation (CCC) (p. 239)
- Countervailing duty (p. 226)
- Economic sanctions (p. 243)
- Escape clause (p. 224)
- Export-Import Bank (p. 239)
- Fast-track authority (p. 223)

- General Agreement on Tariffs and Trade (GATT) (p. 211)
- Intellectual property rights (IPRs) (p. 233)
- Kennedy Round (p. 213)
- Ministry of Economy, Trade and Industry (METI) (p. 240)
- Most favored nation (MFN) clause (p. 210)

- Multifiber Arrangement (MFA) (p. 225)
- Normal trade relations (p. 210)
- Reciprocal Trade Agreements Act (p. 210)
- Safeguards (p. 224)
- Section 301 (p. 232)
- Smoot-Hawley Act (p. 208)
- Strategic trade policy (p. 241)

- Tokyo Round (p. 214)
- Trade adjustment assistance (p. 235)
- Trade promotion authority (p. 223)
- Trade remedy laws (p. 223)
- Uruguay Round (p. 214)
- World Trade Organization (WTO) (p. 211)

Study Questions

1. Assume that the nation of Spain is "small" and unable to influence the Brazilian (world) price of steel. Spain's supply and demand schedules are illustrated in Table 6.11. Assume that Brazil's price is $400 per ton of steel. Using graph paper, plot the demand and supply schedules of Spain and Brazil on the same graph.

TABLE 6.11

STEEL SUPPLY AND DEMAND FOR SPAIN

Price	Quantity Supplied	Quantity Demanded
$ 0	0	12
200	2	10
400	4	8
600	6	6
800	8	4
1000	10	2
1200	12	0

a. With free trade, how many tons of steel will be produced, purchased, and imported by Spain? Calculate the dollar value of Spanish producer and consumer surpluses.

b. Suppose the Brazilian government grants its steel firms a production subsidy of $200 per ton. Plot Brazil's subsidy-adjusted supply schedule on your graph.

(1) What is the new market price of steel? At this price, how much steel will Spain produce, purchase, and import?

(2) The subsidy helps/hurts Spanish firms because their producer surplus rises/falls by $\_\_\_\_$; Spanish steel users realize a rise/fall in the consumer surplus of $\_\_\_\_$. The Spanish economy as a whole benefits/ suffers from the subsidy by an amount totaling $\_\_\_\_$.

2. What is the purpose of strategic trade policy?

3. What is the purpose of economic sanctions? What problems do they pose for the nation initiating the sanctions? When are sanctions most successful in achieving their goals?

4. If the United States is a net importer of a product that is being subsidized or dumped by Japan, not only do U.S. consumers gain, but they also gain more than U.S. producers lose from the Japanese subsidies or dumping. Explain why this is true.

5. Describe the industrial policies adopted by the U.S. government. How have these policies differed from those adopted by Japan?

6. Under the Tokyo Round of trade negotiations, what were the major policies adopted concerning nontariff trade barriers? What about the Uruguay Round?

7. What is intellectual property? Why has intellectual property become a major issue in recent rounds of international trade negotiations?

8. How does the trade adjustment assistance program attempt to help domestic firms and workers who are displaced as a result of import competition?

9. What are trade remedy laws? How do they attempt to protect U.S. firms from unfairly (fairly) traded goods?

10. What is meant by the most-favored nation clause, and how does it relate to the tariff policies of the United States?

11. GATT and its successor, the World Trade Organization, have established a set of rules for the commercial conduct of trading nations. Explain.

12. To what extent have the traditional arguments that justify protectionist barriers actually been incorporated into U.S. trade legislation?

13. At what stage in U.S. trade history did protectionism reach its high point?

Exploring Further   6.1

Welfare Effects of Strategic Trade Policy

The welfare effects of governmental subsidies in the commercial jetliner industry can be analyzed in terms of the theory of strategic trade policy. Analysts generally agree that commercial jetliners fit the requirements for strategic trade policy. The jetliner industry is highly concentrated, with Boeing and Airbus competing in what is essentially a duopoly market. Also, the commercial jetliner industry provides spillover benefits to a number of sectors of the economy.

To analyze the strategic trade implication of subsidies, we can consider an example in which Boeing and Airbus vie for monopoly profits in the Japanese market for commercial jetliners. Figure EF 6.1 illustrates several possible outcomes. These outcomes depend on which producer first

FIGURE EF 6.1

WELFARE EFFECTS OF STRATEGIC TRADE POLICY

Japan's Commercial Jetliner Market

A subsidy granted by the governments of Europe to Airbus improves its competitiveness in the Japanese market; a sufficiently large European subsidy will convince Boeing to retreat from the Japanese market, assuming that no retaliatory subsidies are granted by the U.S. government. Although Airbus realizes increased export profits, European taxpayers pick up the tab for the subsidy. If these export profits exceed the subsidy's cost to European taxpayers, Europe achieves net gains. Airline companies in Japan realize consumer surplus gains resulting from lower-priced jetliners due to the subsidy.

penetrates the Japanese market, how much government assistance is granted to producers, and the reaction of the producer's rival.

Suppose that Boeing is the first to develop and market commercial jetliners and thus becomes a monopoly seller in Japan. In our example, Boeing faces a constant marginal production cost of $130 million per jet, denoted by schedule MC_0. For production with constant marginal cost, average variable cost and marginal cost are identical. Marginal cost always lies below average total cost for such processes. The average total cost schedule is downward sloping because of declining average fixed cost.

As a monopoly, Boeing maximizes profit by selling that output at which marginal revenue equals marginal cost; 5 jets are sold at a price of $150 million. Boeing realizes a profit of $20 million per jet and a total profit of $100 million (minus the fixed costs of becoming established in Japan). Japanese airlines, who purchase jetliners, also realize a consumer surplus of $50 million (the area under

the demand schedule down to the price of $150 million) from the availability of the jets. World welfare thus rises by these two amounts, which total $150 million. Table EF 6.1 summarizes these effects.

Suppose that Airbus is formed to produce commercial jetliners and that its marginal costs are identical to those of Boeing, $130 million per jet. To enhance international competitiveness, assume the governments of Europe grant a subsidy of $30 million on each jet produced by Airbus. The marginal costs of Airbus now equal $100 million ($130 million less the $30 million subsidy), as shown by MC_1. With the help of government, Airbus is in a position to export to Japan. If the subsidy policy convinces Boeing that it can no longer compete with Airbus, Boeing will exit the Japanese market and Airbus will become the monopoly seller of jetliners. The subsidy thus facilitates Airbus's success in the Japanese market.

TABLE EF 6.1

WELFARE EFFECTS OF STRATEGIC TRADE POLICY: COMMERCIAL JETLINERS

Situation	GAINS (LOSSES): MILLIONS OF DOLLARS			
	Boeing/Airbus Profit* −	Subsidy Cost to U.S./European Taxpayers +	Consumer surplus of Japanese Airlines =	World Welfare*
a. Boeing is the first to penetrate the Japanese market, and thus becomes a monopoly seller.	100	0	50	150
b. European governments grant a subsidy to Airbus, which now monopolizes the Japanese market.	400	−300	150	250
c. U.S. and European governments grant offsetting subsidies to their producers; both nations compete in the Japanese market.	0	−750	875	125

*Minus fixed costs.

With the subsidy, Airbus maximizes profits by selling 10 jets, where marginal revenue equals marginal cost, at a price of $140 million per jet. Airbus realizes a profit of $40 million per jet and a total profit of $400 million on the 10 jets (minus fixed costs). European taxpayers lose the $300 million granted to Airbus as a subsidy ($30 million × 10 jets). However, Europe realizes overall gains equal to the amount by which its export profits (less fixed costs) exceed the taxpayer cost of the subsidy, or $100 million ($400 million − $300 million = $100 million). At the price of $140 million, Japanese airlines attain consumer surplus of $150 million from the availability of jetliners. The welfare gains to the world would total $250 million ($100 million + $150 million = $250 million).

This example assumes that if Europe provides a subsidy to Airbus, it will drive Boeing out of the Japanese market, thus capturing its profits. Suppose, however, that the United States retaliates and subsidizes Boeing. In this case, the welfare of the United States and Europe tends to decrease, while Japanese welfare increases.

To illustrate, assume that Boeing and Airbus initially have identical marginal production costs of $130 million and that the United States and Europe provide a per-unit subsidy of $30 million to their producers; the subsidy-adjusted marginal costs for Boeing and Airbus are now $100 million. With government support, neither firm will back down and exit the Japanese market. With competition and intense price cutting, Boeing and Airbus will reduce their prices to $100 million, at which price 25 jets are sold and no profits are realized by either firm. Because Boeing and Airbus compete with each other, each must accept a price no higher than marginal cost. Both firms lose the fixed costs of becoming established in Japan. Over time, one or both firms may go bankrupt. The total cost of the subsidy to the U.S. and European governments is $750 million ($30 million × 25 jets). The United States and Europe are clearly worse off than in the case of no subsidies. Their taxpayers bear the burdens of the subsidy, but their firms do not realize the profits that come with increased market share. On the other hand, Japanese airlines realize consumer surplus of $875 million. To the extent that the gains to the Japanese airlines exceed the losses of Europe and the United States, the subsidy enhances world welfare.

Trade Policies for the Developing Nations

It is a commonly accepted practice to array all nations according to real income and then to draw a dividing line between the advanced and developing ones. Included in the category of **advanced nations** are those of North America and Western Europe, plus Australia, New Zealand, and Japan. Most nations of the world are classified as developing, or less-developed, nations. The **developing nations** are most of those in Africa, Asia, Latin America, and the Middle East. Table 7.1 provides economic and social indicators for selected nations. In general, advanced nations are characterized by relatively high levels of gross domestic product per capita, longer life expectancies, and higher levels of adult literacy.

Although international trade can provide benefits to domestic producers and consumers, some economists maintain that the current international trading system hinders economic development in the developing nations. They believe that conventional international trade theory based on the principle of comparative advantage is irrelevant for these nations. This chapter examines the reasons some economists provide to explain their misgivings about the international trading system. It also considers policies aimed at improving the economic conditions of the developing nations.

Developing-Nation Trade Characteristics

If we examine the characteristics of developing-nation trade, we find that developing nations are highly dependent on advanced nations. A majority of developing-nation exports go to the advanced nations, and most developing-nation imports originate in advanced nations. Trade among developing nations is relatively minor, although it has increased in recent years.

Another characteristic is the composition of developing-nations' exports, with its emphasis on **primary products** (agricultural goods, raw materials, and fuels). Of the manufactured goods that are exported by developing nations, many (such as

TABLE 7.1

BASIC ECONOMIC AND SOCIAL INDICATORS FOR
SELECTED NATIONS, 2007

	Gross National Product per Capita[*]	Life Expectancy (years)	Adult Literacy (percent)
United States	$45,840	78	Over 95%
Switzerland	44,410	82	Over 95
Japan	34,750	83	Over 95
Mexico	13,910	75	90
Chile	12,330	78	Over 95
Algeria	7,640	72	70
Indonesia	3,570	71	88
Guinea	1,120	56	65
Burundi	330	49	26

*At purchasing power parity.

Source: From The World Bank Group, *Data and Statistics: Country At a Glance Tables,* **http://www.worldbank.org/data/**. See also the World Bank, *World Development Report, 2009.*

textiles) are labor intensive and include only modest amounts of technology in their production. Table 7.2 presents the structure of output for selected advanced and developing nations.

In the past three decades, the dominance of primary products in developing-nation trade has greatly diminished. Many developing nations have been able to increase their exports of manufactured goods and services relative to primary products: these nations include China, India, Mexico, South Korea, Hong Kong, Bangladesh, Sri Lanka, Turkey, Morocco, Indonesia, Vietnam, and so on. Nations that have integrated into the world's industrial markets have realized significant poverty reduction.

How have developing nations been able to move into exports of manufactured products? Investments in both people and factories have played a role. The average educational levels and capital stock per worker have risen sharply throughout the developing world. Also, improvements in transport and communications, in conjunction with developing-nation reforms, allow the production chain to be broken up into components, with developing nations playing a key role in global production sharing. Also, the liberalization of trade barriers in developing nations after the mid-1980s increased their competitiveness. This increase was especially true for manufactured goods and processed primary products. Simply put, developing nations are

TABLE 7.2

STRUCTURE OF OUTPUT FOR SELECTED ADVANCED NATIONS AND DEVELOPING NATIONS, 2007

	VALUE ADDED AS A PERCENT OF GDP		
Economy	Agriculture, Forestry, and Fishing	Industry	Services
Advanced Nations			
United States	1	22	71
Japan	2	30	68
Canada	2	33	65
France	2	21	77
Italy	2	27	71
Developing Nations			
Albania	21	20	59
Chad	23	44	32
Pakistan	21	26	53
Tanzania	45	18	37
Mali	37	24	39

Source: From The World Bank Group, *Data and Statistics: Country at a Glance Tables.* See also The World Bank Group, *Data and Statistics: Country Profiles,* available at **http://www.worldbank.org/data**.

gaining ground in higher-technology exports. Nevertheless, they have been frustrated about their modest success in exporting these goods to advanced nations.

However, many developing nations, with a total population of around 2 billion people, still have not integrated strongly into the global industrial economy; these nations are in Africa and the former Soviet Union. Their exports usually consist of a narrow range of primary products. These nations have often been handicapped by poor infrastructure, inadequate education, rampant corruption, and high trade barriers. Also, transport costs to advanced-nation markets are often higher than the tariffs on their goods, so that transport costs are even more of a barrier to integration than the trade policies of rich nations. For these developing nations, incomes have been falling and poverty has been rising in the past 20 years. It is important for them to diversify exports by breaking into global markets for manufactured goods and services where possible.

Tensions Between Developing and Advanced Nations

In spite of the trade frustrations of developing nations, most scholars and policy-makers today agree that the best strategy for a poor nation to develop is to take advantage of international trade. In the past two decades, many developing nations saw the wisdom of this strategy and opened their markets to international trade and foreign investment. Ironically, in spite of scholars' support for this change, the advanced world has sometimes increased its own barriers to imports from these developing nations. Why is this so?

Think of the world economy as a ladder. On the bottom rungs are developing nations that produce mainly textiles and other low-tech goods. Toward the top are the United States, Japan, and the other advanced nations that manufacture sophisticated software, electronics, and pharmaceuticals. Up and down the middle rungs are all the other nations, producing everything from memory chips, to autos, to steel. From this perspective, economic development is simple: Everyone attempts to climb to the next rung. This process works well if the topmost nations can create new industries and products, thus adding another rung to the ladder: older industries can move overseas while new jobs are generated at home. But if innovation stalls at the highest rung, then Americans must compete with lower-wage workers in developing nations.

A predicament faced by developing nations is that in order to make progress, they must displace producers of the least advanced goods that are still being produced in the advanced nations. For example, if Zambia is going to produce textiles and apparel, it will compete against American and European producers of these goods. As producers in advanced nations suffer from import competition, they tend to seek trade protection in order to avoid it. However, this protection denies critical market access to developing nations, thwarting their attempts to grow. Thus, there is a bias against their catching up to the advanced nations.

Those who are protected in advanced nations from competition with developing nations tend to include those who are already near the bottom of the advanced nations' income distributions. Many of these people work in labor-intensive industries and have limited skills and low wages. Income redistribution programs ought to aid, not hinder, these people. To some extent, advanced nations face a trade-off between helping their own poor and helping the world's poor. But critics note that the world as a whole needs to treat all poor as its own and that international institutions ought to ensure fairness to all who are in poverty. For example, the World Trade Organization (WTO) is responsible for preventing advanced nations' trade policies from tilting too far in favor of their own people and against the rest of the world's. This is why recent WTO meetings have been filled with tensions between poor and rich nations.

However, providing developing nations with greater access to the markets of advanced nations will not solve all the developing nations' problems. They face structural weaknesses in their economies, which are compounded by nonexistent or inadequate institutions and policies in the fields of law and order, sustainable macroeconomic management, and public services.

Trade Problems of the Developing Nations

The theory of comparative advantage maintains that all nations can enjoy the benefits of free trade if they specialize in production of those goods in which they have a comparative advantage and exchange some of them for goods produced by other nations. Policy makers in the United States and many other advanced nations maintain that the market-oriented structure of the international trading system furnishes a setting in which the benefits of comparative advantage can be realized. They claim that the existing international trading system has provided widespread benefits and that the trading interests of all nations are best served by pragmatic, incremental changes in the existing system. Advanced nations also maintain that to achieve trading success, they must administer their own domestic and international economic policies.

On the basis of their trading experience with advanced nations, some developing nations have become dubious of the *distribution* of trade benefits between themselves and advanced nations. They have argued that the protectionist trading policies of advanced nations hinder the industrialization of many developing nations. Accordingly, developing nations have sought a new international trading order with improved access to the markets of advanced nations. Among the problems that have plagued developing nations have been unstable export markets, worsening terms of trade, and limited access to the markets of advanced nations.

TABLE 7.3

DEVELOPING NATION DEPENDENCE ON PRIMARY PRODUCTS, 2007

Nation	Major Export Product	Major Export Product as a Percentage of Total Exports
Saudi Arabia	Oil	91%
Venezuela	Oil	90
Burundi	Coffee	89
Nigeria	Oil	88
Zambia	Copper	56
Malawi	Tobacco	50
Ethiopia	Coffee	36
Benin	Cotton	35

Source: From The World Bank Group, *Data and Statistics: Country At a Glance Tables*, available at **http://www.worldbank.org/data**.

Unstable Export Markets

One characteristic of many developing nations is that their exports are concentrated in only one or a few primary products. This situation is shown in Table 7.3, which illustrates the dependence of selected developing nations on a single primary product. A poor harvest or a decrease in market demand for that product can significantly reduce export revenues and seriously disrupt domestic income and employment levels.

FALLING COMMODITY PRICES THREATEN GROWTH OF EXPORTING NATIONS

TRADE CONFLICTS

During the first decade of the 2000s, increasing commodity prices and favorable growing conditions benefited producers and governments in many developing nations. Higher prices resulted in rising profits and increasing tax revenues that were used by governments to pay off some of their debts and spend more on social programs. In Latin America, stronger commodity markets contributed to economic growth, which averaged 5 percent per year during 2003–2008 as compared to 3.5 percent per year during the previous three decades.

However, that upward cycle took a sharp hit when many advanced economies plunged into recession in 2008 and 2009. As these economies shrank, so did their demand for commodities. Lower demand resulted in a dramatic tumbling in the prices of copper, tin, iron ore, soybeans, oil, and the like. As export revenues declined, commodity-producing nations such as Peru and Bolivia had to put on the shelf natural-resource investments such as iron ore extraction.

Brazil paid a steep price for relying on primary products, such as soybeans and iron ore, for 40 percent of its exports. For example, the price of soybeans decreased from $600 per ton to $365 per ton during 2008–2009. As Brazil's export prices declined, so did its once sizable trade surplus. Brazil's corporations, such as mining giant Cia Vale do Rio Doce, had to cut back production and lay off workers. Also, the region's big gas and oil producers, including Bolivia, Ecuador, and Venezuela, were hit hard by the global economic downturn.

Simply put, the economies of many developing nations are tied to primary products and a majority of their exports go to advanced nations. When advanced nations encounter economic downturns, they can be quickly transmitted to their developing-nation trading partners as seen in the global economic downturn of 2008–2009.

Source: "Latin America Gets Squeezed by Dive in Commodity Prices," *The Wall Street Journal*, February 11, 2009, p. A-1.

Economists maintain that a key factor underlying the instability of primary-product prices and producer revenues is the low price elasticity of the demand and supply schedules for products such as tin, copper, and coffee.[1] Recall that the price elasticity of demand (supply) refers to the percentage change in quantity demanded (supplied) resulting from a one percent change in price. To the extent that demand and supply schedules are relatively *inelastic*, suggesting that the percentage change in price exceeds the percentage change in quantity, a small shift in either schedule can induce a large change in price and revenues.

Figure 7.1 illustrates the supply and demand schedules for coffee, pertaining to the market as a whole. Assume that these schedules are highly inelastic. The market is in equilibrium at point A, where the market supply schedule S_0 intersects the market demand schedule D_0. The revenues of coffee producers total $22.5 million, found by multiplying the equilibrium price ($4.50) times the quantity of pounds sold (5 million).

---

[1] For most commodities, price elasticities of demand and supply are estimated to be in the range of 0.2–0.5, suggesting that a one percent change in price results in only a 0.2 percent change in quantity. A classic empirical study of this topic comes from Jerre Behman, "International Commodity Agreements: An Evaluation of the UNCTAD Integrated Commodity Program," in William Cline, ed., *Policy Alternatives for a New International Economic Order* (New York: Praeger, 1979), pp. 118–121.

FIGURE 7.1

EXPORT PRICE INSTABILITY FOR A DEVELOPING NATION

(a) Elasticity of Supply Effect

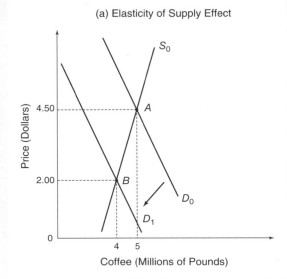

(b) Elasticity of Demand Effect

When the supply of a commodity is highly price-inelastic, decreases (or increases) in demand will generate wide variations in price. When the demand for a commodity is highly price-inelastic, increases (or decreases) in supply will generate wide variations in price.

Referring to Figure 7.1(a), suppose that decreasing foreign incomes cause the market demand curve for coffee to decrease to D_1. With the supply of coffee being inelastic, the decrease in demand causes a substantial decline in market price, from $4.50 to $2.00 per pound. The revenues of coffee producers thus fall to $8 million. Part of this decrease represents a fall in producer profit. We conclude that coffee prices and earnings can be highly volatile when market supply is inelastic.

Not only do changes in demand induce wide fluctuations in price when supply is inelastic, but changes in supply induce wide fluctuations in price when demand is inelastic. The latter situation is illustrated in Figure 7.1(b). Suppose that favorable growing conditions cause a rightward shift in the market supply curve of coffee to S_1. The result is a substantial drop in price from $4.50 to $2 per pound, and producer revenues fall to $14 million ($2 × 7 million = $14 million). We see that prices and revenues can be very volatile when demand conditions are inelastic.

Worsening Terms of Trade

How the gains from international trade are distributed among trading partners has been controversial, especially among developing nations whose exports are concentrated in primary products. These nations generally maintain that the benefits of international trade accrue disproportionately to the advanced nations.

Developing nations complain that their commodity terms of trade has deteriorated in the past century or so, suggesting that the prices of their exports relative to their imports have fallen. Worsening terms of trade has been used to justify the refusal of many developing nations to participate in trade-liberalization negotiations. It also has underlain developing nations' demands for preferential treatment in trade relations with advanced nations.

Observers maintain that the monopoly power of manufacturers in the advanced nations results in higher prices. Gains in productivity accrue to manufacturers in the form of higher earnings rather than price reductions. Observers further contend that the export prices of primary products of developing nations are determined in competitive markets. These prices fluctuate downward as well as upward. Gains in productivity are shared with foreign consumers in the form of lower prices. Developing nations maintain that market forces cause the prices they pay for imports to rise faster than the prices commanded by their exports, resulting in a deterioration in their commodity terms of trade. Moreover, as income rises people tend to spend more on manufactured goods than primary goods, thus contributing to a worsening in the developing nations' terms of trade.

The developing nations' assertion of worsening commodity terms of trade was supported by a United Nations (UN) study in 1949.[2] The study concluded that from the period 1876–1880 to 1946–1947, the prices of primary products compared with those of manufactured goods fell by 32 percent. However, because of inadequacies in data and the problems of constructing price indexes, the UN study was hardly conclusive. Other studies led to opposite conclusions about terms-of-trade movements.

In 2004, economists at the United Nations found that between 1961 and 2001, the average prices of agricultural commodities sold by developing nations fell by almost 70 percent relative to the price of manufactured goods purchased from developed nations. Such terms of trade declines were especially harmful for the very poorest nations of Sub-Saharan Africa. Also, the World Bank estimated that between 1970 and 1997 declining terms of trade cost non-oil-exporting nations in Africa the equivalent of 119 percent of their combined annual gross domestic product in lost revenues. In theory, a decline in the terms of trade could be counteracted by increases in the quantity produced and exported so as to maintain or increase the value of export earnings. In practice, export quantities did not grow sufficiently in the nations of Africa to cover the loss.[3]

Regarding other developing nations—such as China, India, and Russia—and other developing world oil exporters, the declining terms of trade argument appears to hold less well in recent years. Many of these nations have been able to realize economies of scale in the production of certain other primary products, such as corn or cotton, and have diversified their economies away from exclusive reliance on oil exports.

It is difficult to conclude whether the developing nations as a whole have experienced a deterioration or an improvement in their terms of trade. Conclusions about terms-of-trade movements become clouded by the choice of the base year

---

[2]United Nations Commission for Latin America, *The Economic Development of Latin America and Its Principal Problems*, 1950.

[3]Food and Agriculture Organization (FAO) of the United Nations, *The State of Agricultural Commodity Markets*, Rome, Italy, 2004, pp. 8–12. See also Kevin Watkins and Penny Fowler, *Rigged Rules and Double Standards: Trade, Globalization and the Fight Against Poverty*, (Oxford, England: Oxfam Publishing, 2002), Chapter 6.

used in comparisons, by the problem of making allowances for changes in technology and productivity as well as for new products and product qualities, and by the methods used to value exports and imports and to weight the commodities used in the index.

Limited Market Access

In the past two decades, developing nations as a whole have improved their penetration of world markets. However, global protectionism has been a hindrance to their market access. This is especially true for agriculture and labor-intensive manufactured products such as clothing and textiles, as seen in Figure 7.2. These products are important to the world's poor because they represent more than half of low-income nations' exports and about 70 percent of least-developed nations' export revenues.

Tariffs imposed by the advanced nations on imports from developing nations tend to be higher than those they levy on other advanced nations. The differences in tariff averages reflect in part the presence of major trading blocks such as the European Union (EU) and the North American Free Trade Agreement (NAFTA), which have abolished tariffs for advanced-nation trade partners. Also, because developing nations did not actively participate in multilateral trade liberalization agreements prior to the 1990s, their products tended to be omitted from the sharp reductions in tariffs made in those rounds. Simply put, average tariff rates in advanced nations are low, but they maintain barriers in exactly the areas where developing nations have comparative advantage: agriculture and labor-intensive manufactured goods.

Developing nations also are plagued by tariff escalation, as discussed in Chapter 4. In advanced nations, tariffs escalate steeply, especially on agricultural products. Tariff escalation has the potential of decreasing demand for processed imports from developing nations, thus restricting their diversification into higher value-added exports. Though less prevalent, tariff escalation also affects imports of industrial products, especially at the semiprocessed stage. Examples of such products, in which many developing nations have a comparative advantage, include textiles and clothing, leather and leather products, wood, paper, furniture, metals, and rubber products.

Moreover, protectionist barriers have caused developing-nation producers of textiles and clothing to forego sizable export earnings. For decades, advanced nations imposed quotas on imports of these products. Although the Uruguay Round Agreement on Textiles and Clothing resulted in the abolishment of the quotas in 2005, market access in textiles and clothing will remain restricted because tariff barriers are high.

However, antidumping and countervailing duties have become popular substitutes for traditional trade barriers, which are gradually being reduced in the course of regional and multilateral trade liberalization. Developing nations have argued that advanced nations such as the United States have limited access to their markets through aggressive use of antidumping and countervailing duties. Such policies have resulted in significant reductions in export volumes and market shares, according to the developing nations.

Indeed, poor nations have leaned on the United States and Europe to reduce trade barriers. However, rich nations note that poor nations need to reduce their own tariffs, which are often higher than those of their rich counterparts. The average tariff rate of developing nations is more than 20 percent compared with less than

FIGURE 7.2

TRADE BARRIERS LIMIT EXPORT OPPORTUNITIES OF DEVELOPING NATIONS

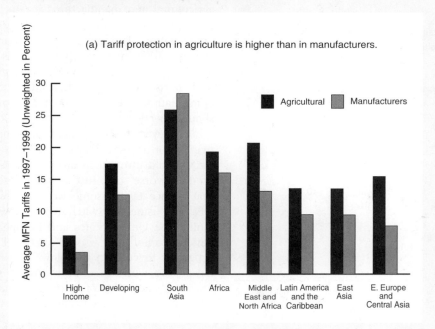

(a) Tariff protection in agriculture is higher than in manufacturers.

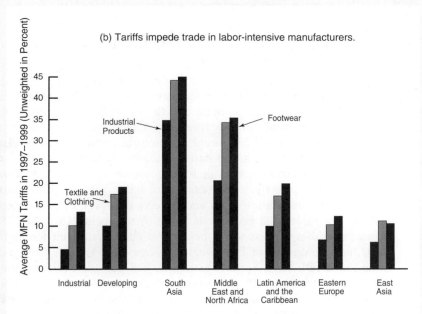

(b) Tariffs impede trade in labor-intensive manufacturers.

They Face High Tariff Walls, Especially in Agricultural Commodities and Labor-Intensive Manufacturers.

Source: From World Trade Organization, *World Trade Report 2004*, Appendix I and The World Bank, *Global Economic Prospects and Developing Countries*, 2002.

TABLE 7.4

TARIFFS OF SELECTED DEVELOPING NATIONS AND ADVANCED NATIONS

Poor nations typically impose higher tariffs than rich nations. Simple average bound tariff rates for selected nations for all goods in 2008.

Developing Nations	Average Tariff Rate (percent)
Kenya	95.7
Ghana	92.5
Barbados	78.1
Angola	59.2
Mexico	36.1
China	10.0
Advanced Nations	
Canada	6.5
European Communities	5.4
Japan	5.1
United States	3.5

Source: From the World Trade Organization, *World Tariff Profiles*, 2008.

6 percent of advanced nations, as seen in Table 7.4. Tariff escalation is also widely practiced by developing nations; their average tariff for fully processed agricultural and manufactured products is higher than on unprocessed products. Although trade among developing nations is a much smaller share of total trade, average tariffs in manufactured goods are about three times higher for trade among developing nations than for exports to advanced nations. Critics note that developing nations are part of their own problem and they should liberalize trade.

However, this argument does not sit well with many poor nations. They contend that quickly reducing tariffs could throw their already fragile economies into an even worse state. Just as is the case in rich nations that reduce tariffs, some workers will inevitably lose jobs as businesses switch to the lowest-cost centers. Unlike the United States and European nations, poor nations do not have a social safety net and reeducation programs to cushion the blow. The message that the developing world receives is that it should do some market liberalization of its own. Nevertheless, it is paradoxical for advanced nations to want developing nations to lift their trade barriers, yet advanced nations like the United States and Canada benefited from significant trade barriers during their developing stages.

Agricultural Export Subsidies of Advanced Nations

Global protectionism in agriculture is another problem for developing nations. In addition to using tariffs to protect their farmers from import-competing products, advanced nations support their farmers with sizable subsidies. Subsidies are often rationalized on the noneconomic benefits of agriculture, such as food security and maintenance of rural communities. By encouraging the production of agricultural commodities, subsidies discourage agricultural imports, thus displacing developing-nation shipments to advanced-nation markets. Also, the unwanted surpluses of agricultural commodities that result from government support are often dumped onto world markets with the aid of export subsidies. This dumping depresses prices for many agricultural commodities and reduces the revenues of developing nations.

For example, rice farmers in West Africa complain that U.S. and European export subsidies depress world prices and make it difficult for them to compete. In 2007, an average ton of U.S. rough rice cost $240 to sow, tend and harvest. By the time that rice left a U.S. port for export, U.S. subsidies reduced the price to foreign buyers to $205. However, the production cost in West Africa was $230 a ton. Thus, West African farmers could not compete in their own market. As rice farmers have gone bankrupt in West Africa, they have often attempted to journey illegally to Europe to find jobs. Thousands have died as they crossed the Mediterranean at more dangerous spots to avoid detection by European patrols.

The complaints of West Africa's cotton farmers have mirrored those of its rice farmers. They note that U.S. exports of cotton have been aided by sizable subsidies.

West African farmers feel that life is unfair when they must compete against American farmers as well as the U.S. government.

American food-aid policies tend to intensify this controversy. It is true that U.S. food donated to the developing world has saved millions of lives made destitute by the failure of their farms. But growers in developing nations complain that the U.S. government purchases surplus grain from American farmers and sends it halfway around the world, instead of first purchasing what foreigners grow. By law, the United States is bound to send homegrown food for assistance, instead of spending cash on foreign produce, in all but the most exceptional cases. This policy supports American farmers, processors, and shippers, as well as the world's hungry. The complaints of West African farmers do not get much sympathy in the United States, where farmers oppose the U.S. government's spending of taxpayer money to purchase foreign crops.

However, many developing nations are net importers of agricultural products and therefore benefit from these subsidies. Because these subsidies decrease the prices of the products that they purchase on global markets, many developing nations would suffer by their elimination.

Stabilizing Primary-Product Prices

Although developing nations have shown some improvement in exports of manufactured goods, agriculture and natural resource products remain a main source of employment. As we have learned, the export prices and revenues for these products can be quite volatile.

In an attempt to stabilize export prices and revenues of primary products, developing nations have attempted to form **international commodity agreements (ICAs)**. These agreements are between leading producing and consuming nations of commodities such as coffee, rubber and cocoa about matters such as stabilizing prices, assuring adequate supplies to consumers, and promoting the economic development of producers. To promote stability in commodity markets, ICAs have relied on production and export controls, buffer stocks, and multilateral contracts. We should note that these measures have generally had only limited (if any) success in improving the economic conditions of developing nations, and that other methods of helping these nations are needed.

Production and Export Controls

If an ICA accounts for a large share of total world output (or exports) of a commodity, its members may agree on **production and export controls** to stabilize export revenues. Production and export controls affect the price of commodities by influencing the world supply of the commodity. The total quantity of production or exports allowed under a commodity agreement is based on the *target price* that is agreed to by member nations. If it is thought that the price of, say, tin will decrease below the target price in the future, producing nations will be assigned a lower production level or export quota. By making tin more scarce, its price will remain at the target level. Conversely, if it is anticipated that the price of tin will increase above the target price in the future, producing nations will be allowed to increase their levels of production and exports.

An obstacle in attempting to impose limits on production and exports is the distribution of the limits among producing nations. For example, if a decline in the total quantity of coffee exports is needed to offset a falling price, how would that decline be allocated among individual producers? Small producers may be hesitant to decrease their levels of output when prices are declining. Another problem is the appearance of new producers of coffee that may be drawn into the market by artificially high prices. Producing nations just embarking on the production or export of coffee would likely be reluctant to reduce their levels of production or exports at that time. Moreover, producers have the incentive to cheat on output restrictions, and enforcement is difficult.

Buffer Stocks

Another technique for limiting commodity price swings is the **buffer stock**, in which a producers' association (or international agency) is prepared to buy and sell a commodity in large amounts. The buffer stock consists of supplies of a commodity financed and held by the producers' association. The buffer stock manager *buys* from the market when supplies are abundant and prices are falling below acceptable levels, and *sells* from the buffer stock when supplies are tight and prices are high.

Figure 7.3 illustrates the hypothetical price-stabilization efforts of the International Tin Agreement. Assume that the association sets a price range, with a floor of $3.27 per pound and a ceiling of $4.02 per pound to guide the stabilization operations of the buffer-stock manager. Starting at equilibrium point A in Figure 7.3(a), suppose the buffer-stock manager sees the demand for tin rising from D_0 to D_1. To defend the ceiling price of $4.02, the manager must be prepared to sell 20,000 pounds of tin to offset the excess demand for tin at the ceiling price. Conversely, starting at equilibrium point E in Figure 7.3(b), suppose the supply of tin rises from S_0 to S_1. To defend the floor price of $3.27, the buffer-stock manager must purchase the 20,000-pound excess supply that exists at that price.

Proponents of buffer stocks contend that the scheme offers the primary producing nations several advantages. A well-run buffer stock can promote economic efficiency because primary producers can plan investment and expansion if they know that prices will not gyrate. It is also argued that soaring commodity prices invariably ratchet industrial prices upward, whereas commodity price decreases exert no comparable downward pressure. By stabilizing commodity prices, buffer stocks can moderate the price inflation of the industrialized nations. Buffer stocks in this context are viewed as a means of providing primary producers more stability than is allowed by the free market.

Setting up and administering a buffer-stock program is not without costs and problems. The basic difficulty in stabilizing prices with buffer stocks is agreeing on a target price that reflects long-term market trends. If the target price is set too low, the buffer stocks will become depleted as the stock manager sells the commodity on the open market in an attempt to hold market prices in line with the target price. If the target price is set too high, the stock manager must purchase large quantities of the commodity in an effort to support market prices. The costs of holding the stocks tend to be high, for they include transportation expenses, insurance, and labor costs. In their choice of price targets, buffer-stock officials have often made poor decisions. Rather than conduct massive stabilization operations, buffer-stock officials will periodically revise target prices should they fall out of line with long-term price trends.

FIGURE 7.3

BUFFER STOCK: PRICE CEILING AND PRICE SUPPORT

(a) Offsetting a Price Increase

(b) Offsetting a Price Decrease

During periods of rising tin demand, the buffer-stock manager sells tin to prevent the price from rising above the ceiling level. However, prolonged defense of the ceiling price may result in depletion of the tin stockpile, which undermines the effectiveness of this price-stabilization tool and leads to an upward revision of the ceiling price. During periods of abundant tin supplies, the manager purchases tin to prevent the price from falling below the floor level. Again, prolonged defense of the price floor may exhaust the funds to purchase excess supplies of tin at the floor price and may lead to a downward revision of the floor price.

Multilateral Contracts

Multilateral contracts are another method of stabilizing commodity prices. Such contracts generally stipulate a *minimum price* at which importers will purchase guaranteed quantities from the producing nations and a *maximum price* at which producing nations will sell guaranteed amounts to the importers. Such purchases and sales are designed to hold prices within a target range. Trading under a multilateral contract has often occurred among several exporting and importing nations, as in the case of the International Sugar Agreement and the International Wheat Agreement.

One possible advantage of the multilateral contract as a price-stabilization device is that, in comparison with buffer stocks or export controls, it results in less distortion of the market mechanism and the allocation of resources. This result is because the typical multilateral contract does not involve output restraints and thus does not check the development of more efficient low-cost producers. If target prices are not set near the long-term equilibrium price; however, discrepancies will occur between supply and demand. Excess demand would indicate a ceiling too low, whereas excess supply would suggest a floor too high. Multilateral contracts also tend to furnish only limited market stability, given the relative ease of withdrawal and entry by participating members.

Does the Fair-Trade Movement Help Poor Coffee Farmers?

We have seen that low commodity prices are troublesome for producers in developing nations. Can consumers of commodities be of assistance to producers? Consider the case of coffee produced in Nicaragua.

Nicaraguan coffee farmer Santiago Rivera has traveled far beyond his mountain home to publicize what is known as the "fair trade" coffee movement. Have you heard of fair-trade coffee? You soon may. Started in Europe in the early 1990s, the objective of the fair-trade coffee movement is to increase the income of poor farmers in developing nations by implementing a system where the farmers can sell their beans directly to roasters and retailers, bypassing the traditional practice of selling to middlemen in their own nations.

This arrangement permits farmers, who farm mainly in the mountainous regions of Latin America and other tropical regions where high-flavor, high-priced beans sold to gourmet stores are grown, to earn as much as $1.26 per pound for their beans, compared with the $0.40 per pound they were getting from middlemen.

Under the fair-trade system, farmers organize in cooperatives of as many as 2,500 members, which set prices and arrange for export directly to brokerage firms and other distributors. Middlemen—known as "coyotes" in Nicaragua—previously handled this role. So far, 500,000 of the developing world's 4 million coffee farmers have joined the fair-trade movement. However, the movement has led to incidents of violence in some places in Latin America, mostly involving middlemen who are being bypassed.

The fair-trade coffee movement is the latest example of how social activists are using free-market economics to foster social change. Organizers of the movement say they have signed up eight gourmet roasters and about 120 stores, including big chains like Safeway, Inc. Fair-trade coffee carries a logo identifying it as such.

Fair trade achieved great success in Europe, where fair-trade coffee sells in 35,000 stores and has sales of $250 million a year. In some nations like the Netherlands and Switzerland, fair-trade coffee accounts for as much as five percent of total coffee sales. Based on those achievements, organizers in Europe are expanding their fair-trade efforts to include other commodity items, including sugar, tea, chocolate, and bananas. But fair-trade activists admit that selling Americans on the idea of buying coffee with a social theme will be more challenging than it was in Europe. Americans, they note, tend to be less aware of social problems in the developing world than Europeans. The fair-trade movement has yet to get the support of major U.S. coffee houses such as Maxwell and Folgers. Nevertheless, organizers are trying to nudge Seattle's two coffee giants, Starbuck's Coffee Co. and the Seattle Coffee Co., into agreeing to purchase some of the fair-trade coffee. However, critics question the extent to which "fair-traded" coffee actually helps. They note that the biggest winners are not the farmers, but rather the retailers that sometimes charge huge markups on fair-traded coffee while promoting themselves as corporate citizens. They can get away with it because consumers generally are given little or no information about how much of a product's price goes to farmers.

The OPEC Oil Cartel

Although many developing nations have not seen significant improvements in their economies in recent decades, some have realized notable gains: once such group is those developing nations endowed with oil reserves. Instead of just forming agreements to stabilize prices and revenues, oil exporting nations have formed cartels intended to increase price and thus realize "monopoly" profits. The most successful cartel in recent history is the Organization of Petroleum Exporting Nations.

The **Organization of Petroleum Exporting Nations (OPEC)** is a group of nations that sells petroleum on the world market. The OPEC nations attempt to support prices higher than would exist under more competitive conditions to maximize member-nation profits. After operating in obscurity throughout the 1960s, OPEC was able to capture control of petroleum pricing in 1973 and 1974, when the price of oil rose from approximately $3 to $12 per barrel. Triggered by the Iranian revolution in 1979, oil prices doubled from early 1979 to early 1980. By 1981, the price of oil averaged almost $36 per barrel. The market power of OPEC stemmed from a strong and inelastic demand for oil combined with its control of about half of world oil production and two-thirds of world oil reserves. Largely because of world recession and falling demand, oil prices fell to $11 per barrel in 1986, only to rebound thereafter. By 2007, the price of oil was about $98 per barrel as demand soared and supply was tight.

Prior to OPEC, oil-producing nations behaved like individual competitive sellers. Each nation by itself was so unimportant relative to the overall market that changes in its export levels did not significantly affect international prices over a sustained period of time. By agreeing to restrict competition among themselves via production quotas, the oil-exporting nations found that they could exercise considerable control over world oil prices, as seen in the price hikes of the 1970s.

Maximizing Cartel Profits

A **cartel** attempts to support prices higher than they would be under more competitive conditions, thus increasing the profits of its members. Let us consider some of the difficulties encountered by a cartel in its quest for increased profits.

Assume that there are ten suppliers of oil, of equal size, in the world oil market and that oil is a standardized product. As a result of previous price wars, each supplier charges a price equal to minimum average cost. Each supplier is afraid to raise its price because it fears that the others will not do so and all of its sales will be lost.

Rather than engage in cutthroat price competition, suppose these suppliers decide to collude and form a cartel. How will a cartel go about maximizing the collective profits of its members? The answer is, by behaving like a profit-maximizing monopolist: restrict output and drive up price.

Figure 7.4 illustrates the demand and cost conditions of the ten oil suppliers as a group [Figure 7.4(a)] and the group's average supplier [Figure 7.4(b)]. Before the cartel is organized, the market price of oil under competition is $20 per barrel. Because each supplier is able to achieve a price that just covers its minimum average cost, economic profit equals zero. Each supplier in the market produces 150 barrels per day. Total industry output equals 1,500 barrels per day ($150 \times 10 = 1500$).

FIGURE 7.4

MAXIMIZING OPEC PROFITS

As a cartel, OPEC can increase the price of oil from $20 to $30 per barrel by assigning production quotas to its members. The quotas decrease output from 1,500 to 1,000 barrels per day and permit producers that were pricing oil at average cost to realize a profit. Each producer has the incentive to increase output beyond its assigned quota, to the point at which the OPEC price equals marginal cost. But if all producers increase output in this manner, there will be a surplus of oil at the cartel price, forcing the price of oil back to $20 per barrel.

Suppose the oil suppliers form a cartel in which the main objective is to maximize the collective profits of its members. To accomplish this objective, the cartel must first establish the profit-maximizing level of output; this output is where marginal revenue equals marginal cost. The cartel then divides up the cartel output among its members by setting up production quotas for each supplier.

In Figure 7.4(a), the cartel will maximize group profits by restricting output from 1,500 barrels per day to 1,000 barrels per day. This means that each member of the cartel must decrease its output from 150 barrels to 100 barrels per day, as shown in Figure 7.4(b). This production quota results in a rise in the market price of a barrel of oil from $20 to $30. Each member realizes a profit of $8 per barrel ($30 − $22 = $8) and a total profit of $800 on the 100 barrels of oil produced (area a).

The next step is to ensure that no cartel member sells more than its quota. This is a difficult task, because each supplier has the incentive to sell more than its assigned quota at the cartel price. But if all cartel members sell more than their quotas, the cartel price will fall toward the competitive level, and profits will vanish. Cartels thus attempt to establish penalties for sellers that cheat on their assigned quotas.

In Figure 7.4(b), each cartel member realizes economic profits of $800 by selling at the assigned quota of 100 barrels per day. However, an *individual* supplier knows that it can increase its profits if it sells more than this amount at the cartel price. Each individual supplier has the incentive to increase output to the level at which the cartel price, $30, equals the supplier's marginal cost; this occurs at 180 barrels per day. At this output level, the supplier would realize economic profits of $1,440, represented by area $a + b$. By cheating on its agreed-upon production quota, the supplier is able to realize an increase in profits of $640 ($1,440 − $800 = $640), denoted by area b. Note that this increase in profits occurs if the price of oil does not decrease as the supplier expands output; that is, if the supplier's extra output is a negligible portion of the industry supply.

A single supplier may be able to get away with producing more than its quota without significantly decreasing the market price of oil. But if each member of the cartel increases its output to 180 barrels per day to earn more profits, total output will be 1,800 barrels (180 × 10 = 1,800). To maintain the price at $30, however, industry output must be held to only 1,000 barrels per day. The excess output of 800 barrels puts downward pressure on price, which causes economic profits to decline. If economic profits fall back to zero (the competitive level), the cartel will likely break up.

Besides the problem of cheating, several other obstacles arise in forming a cartel:

Number of Sellers

Generally speaking, the larger the number of sellers, the more difficult it is to form a cartel. Coordination of price and output policies among three sellers that dominate the market is more easily achieved than when there are ten sellers each having ten percent of the market.

Cost and Demand Differences

When cartel members' costs and product demands differ, it is more difficult to agree on price. Such differences result in a different profit-maximizing price for each member, so there is no single price that can be agreed upon by all members.

Potential Competition

The potential increased profits under a cartel may attract new competitors. Their entry into the market triggers an increase in product supply, which leads to falling prices and profits. A successful cartel thus depends on its ability to block the market entry of new competitors.

Economic Downturn

Economic downturn is generally problematic for cartels. As market sales dwindle in a weakening economy, profits fall. Cartel members may conclude that they can escape serious decreases in profits by reducing prices, in expectation of gaining sales at the expense of other cartel members.

Substitute Goods

The price-making ability of a cartel is weakened when buyers can substitute other goods (coal and natural gas) for the good that it produces (oil).

OPEC as a Cartel

OPEC has generally disavowed the term *cartel*. However, its organization is composed of a secretariat, a conference of ministers, a board of governors, and an economic commission. OPEC has repeatedly attempted to formulate plans for systematic production control among its members as a way of firming up oil prices. However, OPEC hardly controls prices. The group currently controls less than 40 percent of

ARE INTERNATIONAL LABOR STANDARDS NEEDED TO PREVENT SOCIAL DUMPING?

In recent years, labor unions and human rights activists in advanced nations have feared that advanced-nation wages and benefits are being forced down by unfair competition from nations with much lower labor costs: so-called "social dumping." They also maintain that market access to advanced nations should be conditional, and based on raising labor standards in developing nations to prevent a "race to the bottom" in wages and benefits. Trade sanctions imposed in response to violations of labor standards are sometimes referred to as a "social clause."

Two main arguments can be made for the international harmonization of labor standards. The economic argument suggests that low wages and labor standards in developing nations threaten the living standards of workers in developed nations. The moral argument asserts that low wages and labor standards violate the human rights of workers in developing nations. Human rights activists believe that raising labor standards in developing nations will benefit workers in these nations and that some labor practices are morally intolerable, such as the exploitation of working children and discrimination based on gender.

Proponents of the international harmonization of labor standards will not usually admit openly to any protectionist intent. However, developing nations remain deeply suspicious that disguised protectionism motivates many of the calls for compliance with the labor standards of advanced nations, especially if the latter are to be enforced with trade sanctions. Some unions and human rights groups in the United States continue to insist that

conditions on wages and benefits should be attached to agreements on labor standards.

That fairness should be observed in international competition seems indisputable. What constitutes fairness is not so obvious. Does the abundance of cheap labor in China render it an unfair competitor in the production of goods requiring relatively large amounts of unskilled labor? If so, do the plentiful coconut trees in the Philippines render it an unfair competitor in the production of coconut oil?

Another question concerns the implementation of international labor standards. Most advanced-nation labor standards are not feasible for many developing nations. Concerning child labor, for example, it is indeed disturbing that young children in developing nations toil under harsh conditions for low pay. But the earnings of these children may be important to their families' survival—and their own. Moreover, setting strict standards in a developing nation's regulated sector may consign children to even more degrading, less remunerative work in the unregulated sector. To be sure, exploitative child labor and forced labor may suppress wage rates, but such practices also prevent those victimized from shifting readily into activities that best match their skills and goals, and thus reduce their productivity.

Source: Stephen Golub, "Are International Labor Standards Needed to Prevent Social Dumping?" *Finance and Development*, December 1997, pp. 20–23.

world supply, an insufficient amount to establish an effective cartel. Moreover, OPEC's production agreements have not always lived up to expectations because too many member nations have violated the agreements by producing more than their assigned quotas. Since 1983, when production quotas were first assigned to members, OPEC's actual production levels have almost always been greater than its target levels, meaning that nations have been selling more oil than their authorized amounts of oil. Simply put, OPEC does not have any club with which to enforce its edicts.

The exception is Saudi Arabia, owner of the world's largest reserves and lowest production costs. The Saudis spend immense capital to maintain more production capacity than they use, allowing them to influence, or threaten to influence, prices over the short term.

To offset the market power of OPEC, the United States and other importing nations might initiate policies to increase the supply and/or decrease demand. However, achieving these measures involves difficult choices for Americans, such as the following:

- *Raising the fuel economy standards mandated by the federal government.* Analysts estimate that if the gas mileage of new cars had increased by only one mile per gallon each year since 1987, and the mileage of light trucks by a half-mile per gallon, the United States would be saving 1.3 million barrels of oil each day. However, increasing fuel economy standards would meet resistance from auto producers, who would see their production costs increasing because of this policy.
- *Increasing the federal excise tax on gasoline.* Although the resulting hike in the price of gasoline would provide an incentive for consumers to conserve, this would conflict with the preference of Americans for low-priced gasoline. Moreover, rising gasoline prices would especially harm low-income consumers with the least ability to pay.
- *Allowing oil companies to drill on federal land designated as wilderness in Alaska, where there is a good chance that oil might be found.* Perhaps, but what happens when the wilderness is destroyed, never to return? Who pays for that?
- *Diversifying imports.* Although it could be expensive, the United States might forge closer ties with oil producers outside the Middle East to diminish dependence on this unstable region. However, this would require the United States to work even more closely with unsavory regimes in nations like Angola, Indonesia, and Vietnam. Also, OPEC oil is very cheap to extract from the ground. While it costs deepwater drillers like ExxonMobil or Conoco $6 to $8 to produce a barrel in the Gulf of Mexico or the North Sea, the Saudis and Kuwaitis spend a fraction of that—$1 a barrel or less. This cost advantage enhances OPEC's market power.
- *Developing alternate sources of energy such as biofuels and wind power.* Perhaps. But these tend to require governmental subsidies financed by taxpayers.

Aiding the Developing Nations

We have learned that the oil-exporting nations are a special group of developing nations that have realized substantial wealth in recent decades. However, most developing nations are not in this favorable situation. Dissatisfied with their economic performance and convinced that many of their problems are due to the shortcomings of the existing international trading system; developing nations have pressed collective demands on the advanced nations for institutions and policies that improve the climate for economic development. Among the institutions and policies that have been created to support developing nations are the World Bank, the International Monetary Fund, and the generalized system of preferences.

The World Bank

During the 1940s, two international institutions were established to ease the transition from a wartime to a peacetime environment and to help prevent a recurrence of the turbulent economic conditions of the Great Depression era. The World Bank and the International Monetary Fund were established at the United Nations

Monetary and Financial Conference held at Bretton Woods, New Hampshire, in July 1944. The developing nations view these institutions as sources of funds to promote economic development and financial stability.

The **World Bank** is an international organization that provides loans to developing nations aimed toward poverty reduction and economic development. It lends money to member governments and their agencies and to private firms in the member nations. The World Bank is not a "bank" in the common sense. It is one of the UN's specialized agencies, made up of 185 member nations. These nations are jointly responsible for how the institution is financed and how its money is spent.

The "World Bank Group" is the name that has come to be used for five closely associated institutions. The International Bank for Reconstruction and Development and the International Development Association provide low-cost loans and grants to developing nations. The International Finance Corporation provides equity, long-term loans, loan guarantees, and advisory services to developing nations that would otherwise have limited access to capital. The Multilateral Investment Guarantee Agency encourages foreign investment in developing nations by providing guarantees to foreign investors against losses caused by war, civil disturbance, and the like. In addition, the International Center for Settlement of Investment Disputes encourages foreign investment by providing international facilities for conciliation and arbitration of investment disputes, thus helping foster an atmosphere of mutual confidence between developing nations and foreign investors.

The World Bank provides both loans and grants to developing members that cannot obtain money from other sources at reasonable terms. These funds are for specific development projects such as hospitals, schools, highways, and dams. The World Bank is involved in projects as diverse as raising AIDS awareness in Guinea, supporting the education of girls in Bangladesh, improving health-care delivery in Mexico, and helping India rebuild after a devastating earthquake. The World Bank provides low-interest rate loans, and in some cases interest-free loans, to developing nations that have little or no capacity to borrow on market terms.

In recent years, the World Bank has financed debt-refinancing activities of some of the heavily indebted developing nations. The bank encourages private investment in member nations. In 2008, the World Bank lent more than $24 billion to developing nations, as seen in Table 7.5. The World Bank receives its funds from contributions of wealthy developed nations.

Some 10,000 development professionals from nearly every nation in the world work in the World Bank's Washington, DC, headquarters or in its 109 nation offices. They provide many technical assistance services for members.

When attempting to help developing nations fight malaria and build dams and schools, the World Bank must also deal with the problem of fraud and corruption: Corrupt government officials and contractors sometimes divert development dollars into their pockets rather than allowing them to benefit the masses of

TABLE 7.5

WORLD BANK LENDING BY SECTOR, 2008 (MILLIONS OF DOLLARS)

Developing-Nation Sector

Agriculture, Fishing, and Forestry	$ 1,361
Education	1,927
Energy and Mining	4,180
Finance	1,541
Health and Social Services	1,608
Industry and Trade	1,544
Information and Communication	57
Law and Justice	5,296
Transportation	4,830
Water, Sanitation, and Flood Protection	2,360
	$24,704

Source: From the World Bank, "World Bank Lending by Theme and Sector," *Annual Report 2008*, available at Internet site **http://www.worldbank.org/**.

the poor. Because money is fungible, it is difficult for the World Bank to trace the disbursed funds so as to identify the source of corruption. Thus, poor nations lose huge amounts of funds from the World Bank because of the misuse of money, yet their taxpayers still have to repay the World Bank. According to critics, between 5 and 25 percent of the funds the World Bank has lent since 1946 have been misused. This misuse has resulted in millions of poverty-stricken people losing opportunities to improve their health, education, and economic condition. Moreover, for two decades, the World Bank has poured money into poor nations clearly unable to repay. It remains to be seen if the World Bank can adopt safeguards that would ensure that the funds entrusted to it are used productively for their intended purpose.

Moreover, as globalization transforms the world economy, the World Bank's role is diminishing. There are new competitors that channel funds to developing nations. Sovereign wealth funds from Singapore to Abu Dhabi are searching for profit in remote places. Also, nations such as China, Brazil, India and Russia are funding infrastructure and industry for even the poorest nations, to lock in access to raw materials and export markets.

International Monetary Fund

Another source of aid to developing nations (as well as advanced nations) is the **International Monetary Fund (IMF)** which is headquartered in Washington, DC. Consisting of 185 nations, the IMF can be thought of as a bank for the central banks of member nations. Over a given time period, some nations will face balance-of-payments surpluses, and others will face deficits. A nation with a deficit initially draws on its stock of foreign currencies, such as the dollar, that are accepted in payment by other nations. However, the deficit nation will sometimes have insufficient amounts of currency. That is when other nations, via the IMF, can provide assistance. By making available currencies to the IMF, the surplus nations channel funds to nations with temporary deficits. Over the long term, deficits must be corrected, and the IMF attempts to ensure that this adjustment will be as prompt and orderly as possible.

IMF funds come from two major sources: quotas and loans. Quotas (or subscriptions), which are pooled funds of member nations, generate most IMF funds. The size of a member's quota depends on its economic and financial importance in the world; nations with larger economic importance have larger quotas. The quotas are increased periodically as a means of boosting the IMF's resources. The IMF also obtains funds through loans from member nations. The IMF has lines of credit with major industrial nations as well as with Saudi Arabia.

All IMF loans are subject to some degree of *conditionality*. This attachment means that to obtain a loan, a deficit nation must agree to implement economic and financial policies as stipulated by the IMF. These policies are intended to correct the member's balance-of-payments deficit and promote noninflationary economic growth. However, the conditionality attachment to IMF lending has often met strong resistance from deficit nations. The IMF has sometimes demanded that deficit nations undergo austerity programs including severe reductions in public spending, private consumption, and imports in order to live within their means.

Critics of the IMF note that its bailouts may contribute to the so-called *moral-hazard* problem, whereby nations realize the benefits of their decisions when things go well but are protected when things go poorly. If nations do not suffer the costs of bad decisions, won't they be encouraged to make other bad decisions in the future?

A second area of concern is the contractionary effect of the IMF's restrictive monetary and fiscal policy conditions. Won't such conditions cause business and bank failures, induce a deeper recession, and limit government spending to help the poor? Many analysts feel the answer is yes.

Generalized System of Preferences

Given inadequate access to markets of advanced nations, developing nations have pressed them to reduce their tariff walls. To help developing nations strengthen their international competitiveness and expand their industrial base, many industrialized nations have extended nonreciprocal tariff preferences to exports of developing nations. Under this **generalized system of preferences (GSP)**, major industrial nations temporarily reduce tariffs on designated manufactured imports from developing nations below the levels applied to imports from other industrial nations. However, the GSP is not a uniform system because it consists of many individual schemes that differ in the types of products covered and the extent of tariff reduction. Simply put, the GSP attempts to promote economic development in developing nations through increased trade, rather than foreign aid.

Trade preferences granted by advanced nations are voluntary. They are not WTO obligations. Donor nations determine eligibility criteria, product coverage, the size of preference margins, and the duration of the preference. In practice, advanced-nation governments rarely grant deep preferences in sectors where developing nations have a large export potential. Thus, developing nations often obtain only limited preferences in sectors where they have a comparative advantage. The main reason for limited preferences is that in some sectors there is strong domestic opposition to liberalization in advanced nations.

Since its origin in 1976, the U.S. GSP program has extended duty-free treatment to about 3,000 items. Criteria for eligibility include not aiding international terrorists and complying with international environmental, labor, and intellectual property laws. The U.S. program grants complete tariff-free and quota-free access to eligible products from eligible nations. Beneficiaries of the U.S. program include some 130 developing nations and their dependent territories. Like the GSP programs of other advanced nations, the U.S. program excludes certain import-sensitive products from preferential tariff treatment. Textiles and apparel, footwear, and some agricultural products are not eligible for the GSP. Also, a nation's GSP eligibility for a given product may be removed if annual exports of that product reach $100 million or if there is significant damage to a domestic industry. From time to time, as GSP participants have grown wealthier, they have been "graduated" out of the program. Among the alumni are Hong Kong, Singapore, Malaysia, Taiwan, and Singapore.

Although the GSP program provides preferential access to advanced nations' markets, several factors erode its effectiveness in reducing trade barriers faced by developing nations. First, preferences mainly apply to products that already face relatively low tariffs. Second, tariff preferences can also be eroded by nontariff measures, such as antidumping duties and safeguards. Moreover, products and nations have been removed from GSP eligibility because of lobbying by domestic interest groups in importing nations. Also, preferences do little to assist the majority of the world's poor. Most of those living on less than $1 per day live in nations like India and Pakistan, which receive limited preferences in products in which they have a comparative advantage. As a result, developing nations have been frustrated about limited access to the markets of the advanced nations.

Does Aid Promote Growth of Developing Nations?

Does aid promote growth indeveloping nations? Debates about the effectiveness of aid go back decades. Critics maintain that aid has fostered government bureaucracies, prolonged bad governments, favored the wealthy in poor nations, or just been squandered. They note widespread poverty in South Asia and Africa despite four decades of aid, and point out that nations which have received sizable aid have had miserable records—such as Haiti, the Democratic Republic of the Congo, Somalia, and Papua, New Guinea. In their view, aid programs should be substantially altered, drastically cut, or eliminated altogether.

Proponents counter that these contentions, while partially true, are overstated. They indicate that, although aid has sometimes been ineffective, it has enhanced poverty reduction and growth in some nations and prevented worse performance in others. Many of the shortcomings of aid have more to do with donors than beneficiaries, especially since much aid is dolled out to political allies instead of promoting development. They cite a number of successful nations that have received significant aid such as South Korea, Indonesia, Botswana, Mozambique, and Tanzania. In the 40 years since aid became widespread, they note that poverty indicators have declined in many nations, and health and education indicators have increased faster than during any other 40-year period in human history.

Researchers at the Center for Global Development in Washington D.C. have attempted to resolve this debate by distinguishing between types of aid granted to developing nations. Aid for the development of infrastructure—such as transportation systems, communications, energy generation, and banking services—is considered to have relatively strong effects on economic growth, and thus is designated as *growth-oriented aid*. However, aid for disaster and humanitarian relief, food supply, water sanitation, and the like tend to have less immediate effects on economic growth. Each $1 in growth-oriented aid over a four year period was found to yield $1.64 in increased income in the average recipient nation, amounting to an annual rate of return of about 13 percent. The researchers concluded that there is a positive, causal relation between growth-oriented aid and growth on average, although not in every nation. Simply put, aid flows aimed at growth have produced results.[4]

How to Bring Developing Nations in From the Cold

Nobel Prize-winning economist Joseph Stiglitz has been an outspoken critic of the World Bank and the International Monetary Fund since resigning from his position as chief economist at the World Bank in 1999. These organizations generally view trade liberalization and market economies as sources of economic growth. However, Stiglitz contends that developing nations that have opened themselves to trade, deregulated their financial markets, and abruptly privatized national enterprise have too often experienced more economic and social disruption than growth. Therefore,

---

[4]Steven Radelet, Michael Clemens, and Rikhil Bhavnani, "Aid and Growth," *Finance and Development*, September 2005, pp. 16–20.

pressing these nations to liberalize their economies may result in failure. Let us consider excerpts from a speech that Stiglitz gave on this topic.[5]

"I am delighted that Mr. Michael Moore, the Director General of the World Trade Organization, has called on members to provide more help to developing countries. I want to reinforce Mr. Moore's call. I will argue that basic notions of equity and a sense of fair play require that the next round of trade negotiations be more balanced—that is, more reflective of the interests and concerns of the developing world—than has been the case in earlier rounds.

The stakes are high. There is a growing gap between the developed and the less developed countries. The international community is doing too little to narrow this gap. Even as the ability of developing countries to use aid effectively has increased, the level of development assistance has diminished, with aid per capita to the developing world falling by nearly a third in the 1990s. Too often, the cuts in aid budgets have been accompanied by the slogan of "Trade, not aid," together with exhortations for the developing world to participate fully in the global marketplace. Developing countries have been lectured about how government subsidies and protectionism distort prices and impede growth. But all too often there is a hollow ring to these exhortations. As developing countries do take steps to open their economies and expand their exports, in too many sectors they find themselves confronting significant trade barriers—leaving them, in effect, with neither aid nor trade. They quickly run up against dumping duties, when no economist would say they are really engaged in dumping, or they face protected or restricted markets in their areas of natural comparative advantage, like agriculture or textiles.

In these circumstances, it is not surprising that critics of liberalization within the developing world quickly raise cries of hypocrisy. Developing countries often face great pressure to liberalize quickly. When they raise concerns about job loss, they receive the doctrinaire reply that markets create jobs, and that the resources released from the protected sector can be redeployed productively elsewhere. But all too often, the jobs do not appear quickly enough for those who have been displaced; and all too often, the displaced workers have no resources to buffer themselves, nor is there a public safety net to catch them as they fall.

What are developing countries to make of the rhetoric in favor of rapid liberalization, when rich countries—countries with full employment and strong safety nets—argue that they need to impose protective measures to help those adversely affected by trade? Or when rich countries play down the political pressures within developing countries—insisting that they must "face up to the hard choices"—but at the same time excuse their own trade barriers and agricultural subsidies by citing "political pressures"?

Let me be clear: there is no doubt in my mind that trade liberalization will be of benefit to the developing countries, and to the world more generally. But trade liberalization must be balanced, and it must reflect the concerns of the developing world. It must be balanced in agenda, process, and outcomes. It must take in not only those sectors in which developed countries have a comparative advantage, like financial services, but also those in which developing countries have a special interest, like agriculture and construction services. Trade liberalization must take into account

---

[5]Excerpts from Joseph Stiglitz, "Two Principles for the Next Round, Or, How to Bring Developing Nations in from the Cold," The World Bank, Washington, DC, September 21, 1999. See also Joseph Stiglitz, *Globalization and Its Discontents*, (New York: W. W. Norton, 2002).

the marked disadvantage that developing countries have in participating meaningfully in negotiations.

Moreover, we must recognize the differences in circumstances between developed and developing countries. We know that developing countries face greater volatility, that opening to trade in fact contributes to that volatility, that developing countries have weak or non-existent safety nets, and that high unemployment is a persistent problem in many if not most developing countries. Simply put, the developed and less developed countries play on a playing field that is not level.

Standard economic analysis argues that trade liberalization, even unilateral opening of markets, benefits a country. In this view, job loss in one sector will be offset by job creation in another, and the new jobs will be higher-productivity than the old. It is this movement from low- to high-productivity jobs that represents the gain from the national perspective, and explains why, in principle, everyone can be made better off as a result of trade liberalization. This economic logic requires markets to be working well, however, and in many countries, underdevelopment is an inherent reflection of poorly functioning markets. Thus, new jobs are not created, or not created automatically. Moving workers from a low-productivity sector to unemployment does not increase output. A variety of factors contribute to the failure of jobs to be created, from government regulations, to rigidities in labor markets, to lack of access of capital.

Concerning future rounds of trade negotiations, adherence to the principles of fairness and comprehensiveness could hold open the promise of a more liberal and more equitable trading regime. While participants in previous rounds have often paid lip service to these principles, they have been honored mostly in the breach. Future adherence to these principles is absolutely essential for the success of the next round, and in particular if the developing countries are to become full partners in the process of trade liberalization."

Economic Growth Strategies: Import Substitution Versus Export-Led Growth

Besides seeking economic assistance from advanced nations, developing nations have pursued two competing strategies for industrialization: an inward-looking strategy (import substitution) in which industries are established largely to supply the domestic market, and foreign trade is assigned negligible importance; and an outward-looking strategy (export-led growth) of encouraging the development of industries in which the nation enjoys comparative advantage, with heavy reliance on foreign nations as purchasers of the increased production of exportable goods.

Import Substitution

During the 1950s and 1960s, the industrialization strategy of **import substitution** became popular in developing nations such as Argentina, Brazil, and Mexico; some nations still use it today. Import substitution involves extensive use of trade barriers to protect domestic industries from import competition. The strategy is inward-oriented in that trade and industrial incentives favor production for the domestic market over the export market. For example, if fertilizer imports occur, import substitution calls for establishment of a domestic fertilizer industry to produce replacements for fertilizer imports. In the extreme, import-substitution policies could lead to complete self-sufficiency.

The rationale for import substitution arises from the developing nations' perspective on trade. Many developing nations feel that they cannot export manufactured goods because they cannot compete with established firms of the advanced nations, especially in view of the high trade barriers maintained by these nations. Given the need for economic growth and development, developing nations have no choice but to manufacture for themselves some of the goods they now import. The use of tariffs and quotas restricts imports, and the domestic market is reserved for domestic manufacturers. This rationale is often combined with the infant-industry argument: protecting start-up industries will allow them to grow to a size where they can compete with the industries of advanced nations.

In one respect, import substitution appears logical: If a good is demanded and imported, why not produce it domestically? The economist's answer is that it may be more costly to produce it domestically and cheaper to import it; comparative advantage should decide which goods are imported and which are exported.

Encouraging economic development via import substitution has several advantages as follows:

- The risks of establishing a home industry to replace imports are low because the home market for the manufactured good already exists.
- It is easier for a developing nation to protect its manufacturers against foreign competitors than to force advanced nations to reduce their trade restrictions on products exported by developing nations.
- To avoid the import tariff walls of the developing nation, foreigners have an incentive to locate manufacturing plants in the nation, thus providing jobs for local workers.

In contrast to these advantages, there are several disadvantages as follows:

- Because trade restrictions shelter domestic industries from international competition, they have no incentive to increase their efficiency.
- Given the small size of the domestic market in many developing nations, manufacturers cannot take advantage of economies of scale and thus have high unit costs.
- Because the resources employed in the protected industry would otherwise have been employed elsewhere, protection of import-competing producers automatically discriminates against all other producers, including potential exporting ones.
- Once investment is sunk in activities that were profitable only because of tariffs and quotas, any attempt to remove those restrictions is generally strongly resisted.
- Import substitution also breeds corruption. The more protected the economy, the greater the gains to be had from illicit activity such as smuggling.

Import-Substitution Laws Backfire on Brazil

Although import-substitution laws have often been used by developing nations in their industrialization efforts, they sometimes backfire. Let us consider the example of Brazil.

In 1991, Enrico Misasi was the president of the Brazilian unit of Italian computer-maker Olivetti Inc., but he did not have an Olivetti computer. The computer on his desk was instead manufactured by two Brazilian firms; it cost three times more than an Olivetti, and its quality was inferior. Rather than manufacturing computers in Brazil, Olivetti, Inc. was permitted to manufacture only typewriters and calculators.

This anomaly was the result of import-substitution policies practiced by Brazil until 1991. From the 1970s until 1991, importing a foreign personal computer—or a microchip, a fax, or dozens of other electronic goods—was prohibited. Not only were electronic imports prohibited, but foreign firms willing to invest in Brazilian manufacturing plants were also banned. Joint ventures were deterred by a law that kept foreign partners from owning more than 30 percent of a local business. These restrictions were intended to foster a homegrown electronics industry. Instead, even the law's proponents came to admit that the Brazilian electronics industry was uncompetitive and technologically outdated.

The costs of the import ban were clearly apparent by the early 1990s. Almost no Brazilian automobiles were equipped with electronic fuel injection or antiskid brake systems, both widespread throughout the world. Products such as Apple's Macintosh computer were not permitted to be sold in Brazil. Brazil chose to allow Texas Instruments to shut down its Brazilian semiconductor plant, resulting in a loss of 250 jobs, rather than permit Texas Instruments to invest $133 million to modernize its product line. By adhering to its import-substitution policy, Brazil wound up a largely computer-unfriendly nation: By 1991, only 12 percent of small- and medium-sized Brazilian companies were at least partially computerized, and only 0.5 percent of Brazil's classrooms were equipped with computers. Many Brazilian companies postponed modernization because computers available overseas were not manufactured in Brazil and could not be imported. Some Brazilian companies resorted to smuggling computers and other electrical equipment; those companies that adhered to the rules wound up with outdated and overpriced equipment.

Realizing that the import-substitution policy had backfired on its computer industry, in 1991 the Brazilian government scrapped a cornerstone of its nationalistic approach by lifting the electronics import ban—though continuing to protect domestic industry with high import duties. The government also permitted foreign joint-venture partners to raise their ownership shares from 30 to 49 percent and to transfer technology into the Brazilian economy.

Export-Led Growth

Another development strategy is **export-led growth**, or **export-oriented policy**. This strategy is outward oriented because it links the domestic economy to the world economy. Instead of pursuing growth through the protection of domestic industries suffering comparative disadvantage, the strategy involves promoting growth through the export of manufactured goods. Trade controls are either nonexistent or very low, in the sense that any disincentives to export resulting from import barriers are counterbalanced by export subsidies. Industrialization is viewed as a natural outcome of development instead of being an objective pursued at the expense of the economy's efficiency. By the 1970s, many developing nations were abandoning their import-substitution strategies and shifting their emphasis to export-led growth.

Export-oriented policies have three advantages: They encourage industries in which developing nations are likely to have a comparative advantage, such as labor-intensive manufactured goods. By providing a larger market in which to sell, they allow domestic manufacturers greater scope for exploiting economies of scale. By

FIGURE 7.5

OPENNESS AND ECONOMIC GROWTH

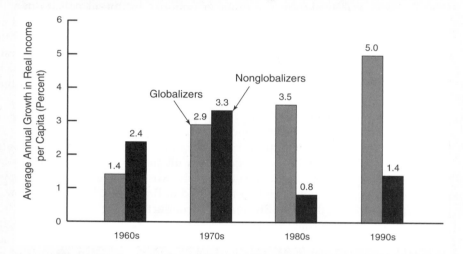

During the 1980s and 1990s, developing nations that were more open to the international economy grew faster than those remaining more closed.

Source: Data taken from David Dollar and Aart Kraay, *Trade, Growth, and Poverty*, World Bank Development Research Group, 2001.

maintaining low restrictions on imported goods, they impose a competitive discipline on domestic firms that forces them to increase efficiency.

Figure 7.5 illustrates the relation between openness to international trade and economic growth for developing nations. A sample of 72 nations is split into "globalizers" and "nonglobalizers." The globalizers are defined as the 24 nations that achieved the largest increases in their ratio of trade to gross domestic product from 1975 to 1995. During the 1960s and 1970s, the nonglobalizers experienced somewhat faster growth of real income per capita on average than the globalizers. However, during the 1980s, globalizers experienced much higher growth rates; real income per capita grew an average of 3.5 percent a year in these nations, compared with 0.8 percent for the nonglobalizers. The divergence was even greater during the 1990s, with 5.0 percent annual growth for the globalizers versus 1.4 percent for the rest. To put these differences into perspective, had the average globalizer and the average nonglobalizer each begun with an income per capita of $1,000 in 1980, by 2000 the globalizer's income per capita would have grown to $2,300, and the nonglobalizer's only to $1,240.

These findings support the concept that the economic performance of nations implementing export-led growth policies has been superior to that of nations using import-substitution policies. Export-led growth policies introduce international competition to domestic markets, which encourages efficient firms and discourages inefficient ones. By creating a more competitive environment, they also promote higher productivity and hence faster economic growth. Conversely, import-substitution policies relying on trade protection switch demand to products produced domestically. Exporting is then discouraged by both the increased cost of imported inputs and the increased cost of domestic inputs relative to the price received by exporters.

Is Economic Growth Good for the Poor?

Although the evidence strongly suggests that trade is good for growth, is growth good for poor workers in developing nations? Critics argue that growth tends to be bad for the poor if the growth in question has been promoted by trade or foreign investment. Investment inflows, they say, make economies less stable, exposing workers to the risk of financial crisis and to the attentions of advanced-nation banks. Moreover, they contend that growth driven by trade provides Western multinational corporations a dominant role in third-world development. That is bad, because Western multinationals are not interested in development at all, only in making larger profits by ensuring that the poor stay poor. The proof of this, say critics, lies in the evidence that economic inequality increases even as developing nations and advanced nations increase their national income, and in the multinationals' use of sweatshops when producing goods. So if workers' welfare is your primary concern, the fact that trade promotes growth, even if true, misses the point.

However, there is strong evidence that growth aids the poor. Developing nations that have achieved continuing growth, as in East Asia, have made significant progress in decreasing poverty. The nations where widespread poverty persists, or is worsening, are those where growth is weakest, notably in Africa. Although economic policy can affect the extent of poverty, in the long term, growth is much more important.

There is intense debate over the extent to which the poor benefit from economic growth. Critics argue that the potential benefits of economic growth for the poor are undermined or even offset entirely by sharp increases in inequality that accompany growth. On the other hand, proponents contend that liberal economic policies such as open markets and monetary and fiscal stability raise the incomes of the poor and everyone else in society proportionately. Researchers at the World Bank have investigated this topic. They confirm that, in a sample of 92 industrial and developing nations across the world, the incomes of the poor have risen one for one with overall growth.[6] This income growth implies that growth generally does benefit the poor as much as everyone else, so that growth-enhancing policies should be at the center of successful poverty reduction strategies.

Suppose it were true that income inequality is increasing between the advanced and developing nations. Would this be a terrible indictment of globalization? Perhaps not. It would be disturbing if inequality throughout the world were increasing because incomes of the poorest were decreasing in absolute terms, instead of in relative terms. However, this is rare. Even in Africa, which is behaving poorly in relative terms, incomes have been increasing and broader indicators of development have been improving. Perhaps it is too little, but something is better than nothing.

Can All Developing Nations Achieve Export-Led Growth?

Although exporting can promote growth for developing economies, it depends on the willingness and ability of advanced nations to go on absorbing large amounts of goods from developing nations. Pessimists argue that this process involves a fallacy of composition. If all developing nations tried to export simultaneously, the price of their exports would be driven down on world markets. Moreover, advanced

---

[6]David Dollar and Aart Kraay, *Growth Is Good for the Poor*, The World Bank, Washington, DC, 2001, p. 45.

nations may become apprehensive of foreign competition, especially during eras of high unemployment, and thus impose tariffs to reduce competition from imports. Will liberalizing trade be self-defeating if too many developing nations try to export simultaneously?

Although developing nations as a group are enormous in terms of geography and population, in economic terms they are small. Taken together, the exports of all the world's poor and middle-income nations equal only five percent of world output. This is an amount approximately equivalent to the national output of the United Kingdom. Even if growth in the global demand for imports were somehow capped, a concerted export drive by those parts of the developing world not already engaged in the effort would put no great strain on the global trading system.

Pessimists also tend to underestimate the scope for intra-industry specialization in trade, which gives developing nations a further set of new trade opportunities. The same goes for new trade among developing nations, as opposed to trade with the advanced nations. Often, as developing nations grow, they move away from labor-intensive manufactures to more sophisticated kinds of production. This movement makes room in the markets they previously served for goods from nations that are not yet so advanced. For example, in the 1970s, Japan withdrew from labor-intensive manufacturing, making way for exports from South Korea, Taiwan, and Singapore. In the 1980s and 1990s, South Korea, Taiwan, and Singapore did the same, as China began moving into those markets. As developing nations grow through exporting, their own demand for imports rises.

East Asian Economies

In spite of the sluggish economic performance of many developing nations, some have realized strong and sustained economic growth, as seen in Table 7.6. One group of successful developing nations has come from East Asia, such as Hong Kong, South Korea, Singapore, and Taiwan. What accounts for their success?

The East Asian nations are highly diverse in natural resources, populations, cultures, and economic policies. However, they have in common several characteristics underlying their economic success: (1) high rates of investment and (2) high and increasing endowments of human capital due to universal primary and secondary education.

To foster competitiveness, East Asian governments have invested in their people and provided a favorable competitive climate for private enterprise. They have also kept their economies open to international trade. The East Asian economies have actively sought foreign technology, such as licenses, capital-good imports, and foreign training.

The East Asian economies have generally discouraged the organization of trade unions—whether by deliberate suppression (South Korea and Taiwan), by government paternalism (Singapore), or by a laissez-faire policy (Hong Kong). The outcome has

TABLE 7.6

EAST ASIAN ECONOMIES' GROWTH RATES, 2006–2008

Nation	Average Annual Growth Rate
China	11.5%
Indonesia	6.0
Singapore	5.8
Malaysia	5.7
Philippines	5.7
Hong Kong, China	5.4
Thailand	4.6
South Korea	4.2

Source: Central Intelligence Agency, *World Fact Book*, 2009, available at **www.cia.gov**.

been the prevention of minimum-wage legislation and the maintenance of free and competitive labor markets.

In the post-World War II era, trade policies in the East Asian economies (except Hong Kong) began with a period of import substitution. To develop their consumer-good industries, these nations levied high tariffs and quantitative restrictions on imported goods. They also subsidized some manufacturing industries such as textiles. Although these policies initially led to increased domestic production, as time passed they inflicted costs on the East Asian economies. Because import-substitution policies encouraged the importing of capital and intermediate goods and discouraged the exporting of manufactured goods, they led to large trade deficits for the East Asian economies. To obtain the foreign exchange necessary to finance these deficits, the East Asian economies shifted to a strategy of outward orientation and export promotion.

Export-push strategies were enacted in the East Asian economies by the late 1950s and 1960s. Singapore and Hong Kong set up trade regimes that were close to free trade. Japan, South Korea, and Taiwan initiated policies to promote exports while protecting domestic producers from import competition. Indonesia, Malaysia, and Thailand adopted a variety of policies to encourage exports while gradually reducing import restrictions. These measures contributed to an increase in the East Asian economies' share of world exports, with manufactured exports accounting for most of this growth.

The stunning success of the East Asian economies has created problems, however. The industrialize-at-all-costs emphasis has left many of the East Asian economies with major pollution problems. Whopping trade surpluses have triggered a growing wave of protectionist sentiment overseas, especially in the United States, which sees the East Asian economies depending heavily on the U.S. market for future export growth.

Flying-Geese Pattern of Growth

It is widely recognized that East Asian economies have followed a **flying-geese pattern of economic growth** in which nations gradually move up in technological development by following in the pattern of nations ahead of them in the development process. For example, Taiwan and Malaysia take over leadership in apparel and textiles from Japan as Japan moves into the higher-technology sectors of automotive, electronic, and other capital goods. A decade or so later, Taiwan and Malaysia are able to upgrade to automotive and electronics products, while the apparel and textile industries move to Thailand, Vietnam, and Indonesia.

To some degree, the flying-geese pattern is a result of market forces: Labor-abundant nations will become globally competitive in labor-intensive industries, such as footwear, and will graduate to more capital- or skill-intensive industries as savings and education deepen the availability of capital and skilled workers. However, as the East Asian economies have demonstrated, more than just markets are necessary for flying-geese development. Even basic labor-intensive products, such as electronics assembly, are increasingly determined by multinational enterprises and technologies created in advanced nations.

For East Asian economies, a strong export platform has underlain their flying-geese pattern of development. East Asian governments have utilized several versions of an export platform, such as bonded warehouses, free-trade zones, joint ventures, and strategic alliances with multinational enterprises. Governments supported these mechanisms with economic policies that aided the incentives for labor-intensive exports.[7]

China's Transformation to Capitalism

China is another East Asian nation that has had remarkable economic success in recent years. Let us see why.

In the early 1970s, the People's Republic of China was an insignificant participant in the world market for goods. The value of its exports and imports was less than $15 billion, and it was only the 30th largest exporting nation. China was also a negligible participant in world financial markets. By 2005, China had grown to be the world's second largest economy, with a national output over half that of the United States and 60 percent larger than Japan's. What caused this transformation?

Modern China began in 1949, when a revolutionary communist movement captured control of the nation. Soon after the communist takeover, China instituted a Soviet model of central planning and import substitution with emphasis on rapid economic growth, particularly industrial growth. The state took over urban manufacturing, collectivized agriculture, eliminated household farming, and established compulsory production quotas. By discouraging the ability of markets to function, China's government stifled economic growth and left many of its people poor.

In the late 1950s, China departed from the Soviet model and shifted from large-scale, capital-intensive industry to small-scale, labor-intensive industry scattered across the countryside. Little attention was paid to linking individual reward to individual effort. Instead, a commitment to the success of the collective plans was relied on as the motivation for workers. This system proved to be an economic failure. Although manufacturing output rose following the reforms, product quality was low and production costs were high. Because China's agricultural output was insufficient to feed its people, China became a large importer of grains, vegetable oils, and cotton. As a result of this economic deterioration, plant managers, scientists, engineers, and scholars, who favored material incentives and reform, were denounced and sent to work in the fields.

By the 1970s, China could see its once-poor neighbors—Japan, Singapore, Taiwan, and South Korea—enjoying extraordinary growth and prosperity. This led to China's "marketizing" its economy through small, step-by-step changes to minimize economic disruption and political opposition. In agriculture and industry, reforms were made to increase the role of the producing unit, to increase individual incentives, and to reduce the role of state planners. Most goods were sold for market-determined—not state-controlled—prices. Greater competition was allowed both between new firms and between new firms and state firms; by 2000, nonstate firms manufactured about 75 percent of China's industrial output. Moreover, China opened its economy to foreign investment and joint ventures. The Chinese government's monopoly over foreign trade was also disbanded; in its place, economic zones were established in which firms could keep foreign exchange earnings and hire and fire workers. Simply put, China has broken with the path of import substitution,

---

[7]Terutomo Ozawa, *Institutions, Industrial Upgrading, and Economic Performance in Japan: The Flying-Geese Theory of Catch-Up Growth*, Cheltenham, U.K., Edward Elgar, 2005.

where import barriers are established for the development of domestic industry. China is now remarkably open to international trade, and imports play a very large role in the Chinese economy.

By the first decade of the 2000s, China had made all of the easy economic adjustments in its transition toward capitalism: letting farmers sell their own produce and opening its doors to foreign investors and salespeople. Other reforms still needed addressing: (1) a massive restructuring of state-owned industries, which were losing money; (2) a cleanup of bankrupt state banks; (3) the creation of a social security system in a society that once guaranteed a job for life; and (4) establishment of a monetary system with a central bank free of Communist Party or government control. If China were to shut down money-losing enterprises, millions of workers would be laid off with no benefits; their addition to the 100 million-plus workers already adrift in China could be volatile. In addition, banks that lent the state companies cash would require cash infusions if bankruptcies increased in the state sector. Such loans could render a central bank monetary policy ineffective and could fuel inflation.

Although China has dismantled much of its centrally planned economy and has permitted free enterprise to replace it, political freedoms have lagged behind. Recall the Chinese government's use of military force to end a pro-democracy demonstration in Beijing's Tiananmen Square in 1989, which led to loss of life and demonstrated the Communist Party's determination to maintain its political power. Under Communist Party rule, there is no freedom of speech, making independent voices all but inaudible. China's evolution toward capitalism has thus consisted of expanded use of market forces under a communist political system. Today, China describes itself as a *socialist market economy*.

Concerning international trade, China has followed a pattern consistent with the principle of comparative advantage as explained by the factor endowment theory of Eli Heckscher and Berlin Ohlin, as discussed in Chapter 3. China's exports have emphasized the intensive use of labor, its abundant factor of production. Therefore, China has become a center of low-wage manufacturing and exports sporting goods, toys, electronics, footwear, garments, textiles, and other goods. On the import side, China is a growing market for machinery, transportation equipment, and other capital goods that require higher levels of technologies than China can produce domestically. Most of China's economic expansion since 1978 has been driven by rapid growth in exports and investment spending.

After 15 years of negotiations, China became a member of the WTO in 2001. China made its membership a priority because it would represent international recognition of its growing economic power, reduce the threat of restrictions on its exports, and induce the United States to grant China permanent normal trade relations. However, U.S. trade officials insisted that China's membership had to be based on meaningful terms that would require China to significantly reduce trade and investment barriers. When China acceded to the WTO, it agreed to do the following: reduce its average tariff for industrial goods to 8.9 percent and to 15 percent for agricultural goods; limit subsidies for agricultural production to 8.5 percent of the value of farm output and not maintain export subsidies on agricultural exports; grant full trade and distribution rights to foreign enterprises in China; to fully open the banking system to foreign financial institutions; and to protect the intellectual property of foreigners according to internationally agreed-upon standards.

The economic success of China is a testament that its economy has become open to international trade and investment. However, the biggest challenge for

China is to harmonize its society amid growing disparities in growth, income, and living conditions. The question is whether the existing political system can address the environment and other domestic issues. China has no choice but to turn to market principles for help. It is linked to the rest of the world through markets, but internally there is no momentum for market-driven social integration. This is why many observers feel that the solution to China's problem will ultimately involve political reform pushing for a multiparty system.

China's Export Boom Comes at a Cost: How to Make Factories Play Fair

Although China has become a major exporter of manufactured goods, it has come at a cost. As retailers such as Wal-Mart and The Home Depot place pressure on Chinese suppliers to produce cheap goods at the lowest possible prices, concerns about product safety, the quality of the environment, and labor protections are brushed aside.

In 2007, for example, Chinese firms were challenged by consumer advocates on the grounds that they were producing unsafe toys, cribs, electronic products, and the like. Mattel, the world's largest toymaker, issued three separate recalls for toys manufactured in China that contained hazardous lead paint and dangerous magnets; Disney recalled thousands of Baby Einstein blocks; smaller companies recalled everything from children's jewelry, key chains, and notebooks to water bottles and flashlights. The biggest disappointment to children was the double recall of Thomas the Tank Engine toys when it was discovered that they contained unsafe levels of lead in the paint, which can cause brain damage to children. Moreover, the Floating Eyeballs toy was recalled after it was found to be filled with kerosene. Critics maintained that these examples are part of a larger pattern. The U.S. economy has gone global and has outsourced more and more production to nations like China. At the same time, the U.S. government has cut back import regulation and inspection. As a result, American consumers are exposed to increasing numbers of products that are neither produced in the United States nor subject to American safety standards.

Protecting labor is another problem for China. As U.S. retailers such as Eddie Bauer and Target continually demand lower prices from their Chinese suppliers, allowing American consumers to enjoy inexpensive clothes and sneakers, that price pressure creates a powerful incentive for Chinese firms to cheat on labor standards that American companies promote as a badge of responsible capitalism. These standards generally incorporate the official minimum wage of China, which is set by local or provincial governments and ranges from $45 to $101 a month. U.S. companies also typically say they adhere to the government-mandated workweek of 40 to 44 hours, beyond which higher overtime pay is required. However, the pressure to cut costs has resulted in many Chinese factories ignoring these standards. By falsifying payrolls and time sheets, they have been able to underpay their workers and force them to work excessive hours at factories that often have health and safety problems. Conceding that the current system of auditing Chinese suppliers is failing to stop labor abuses, U.S. retailers are searching for ways to improve China's labor protections. It remains to be seen if these efforts will be successful.

Promoting a safe environment is another problem for China. In the last two decades since U.S. firms began turning to Chinese factories to churn out cheap T-shirts and jeans, China's air, land, and water have paid a heavy price. Environmental activists and the Chinese government note the role that U.S. multinational

DOES FOREIGN DIRECT INVESTMENT HINDER OR HELP ECONOMIC DEVELOPMENT?

TRADE CONFLICTS

Foreign investment brings higher wages, and is a major source of technology transfer and managerial skills in host developing nations. This contributes to rising prosperity in the developing nations concerned, as well as enhancing demand for higher value-added exports from advanced economies.

—*OECD Policy Brief*, No. 6, 1998

As investors search the globe for the highest return, they are often drawn to places endowed with bountiful natural resources but handicapped by weak or ineffective environmental laws. Many people and communities are harmed as the environment that sustains them is damaged or destroyed—villagers are displaced by large construction projects, for example, and indigenous peoples watch their homelands disappear as timber companies level old-growth forests. Foreign investment-fed growth also promotes western-style consumerism, boosting car ownership, paper use, and Big Mac consumption rates toward the untenable levels found in the United States-with grave potential consequences for the health of the natural world, the stability of the earth's climate, and the security of food supplies.

—Hilary French, "Capital Flows and the Environment," *Foreign Policy in Focus*, August 1998

One of the requirements for economic development in a low-income economy is an increase in the nation's stock of capital. A developing nation may increase the amount of capital in the domestic economy by encouraging foreign direct investment. Foreign direct investment occurs when foreign firms either locate production plants in the domestic economy or acquire a substantial ownership position in a domestic firm. This topic will be discussed further in Chapter 9. Many developing economies have attempted to restrict foreign direct investment because of nationalist sentiment and concerns about foreign economic and political influence. One reason for this sentiment is that many developing nations have operated as colonies of more developed economies. This colonial experience has often resulted in a legacy of concern that foreign direct investment may serve as a modern form of economic colonialism in which foreign companies might exploit the resources of the host nation.

However, in recent years restrictions on foreign direct investment in many developing economies have been substantially reduced as a result of international treaties, external pressure from the IMF or World Bank, or unilateral actions by governments that have come to believe that foreign direct investment will encourage economic growth in the host nation. This has resulted in a rather dramatic expansion in the level of foreign direct investment in some developing economies.

Foreign direct investment may encourage economic growth in the short term by increasing aggregate demand in the host economy. In the long run, the increase in the stock of capital raises the productivity of labor, leads to higher incomes, and further increases aggregate demand. However, another long-term impact comes through the transfer of technological knowledge from advanced to developing economies. Many economists argue that this transfer of technology may be the primary benefit of foreign direct investment.

It is also often argued that it is necessary to restrict foreign direct investment in a given industry for national security purposes. This reasoning serves as a justification for prohibitions on investment in defense industries and in other industries that are deemed essential for national security. Most governments, for example, would be concerned if their weapons were produced by companies owned by firms in nations that might serve as future enemies.

Environmentalists are concerned that the growth of foreign direct investment in developing economies may lead to a deterioration in the global environment since investment is expanding more rapidly in nations that have relatively lax environmental standards. The absence of restrictive environmental standards, it is argued, is one of the reasons for the relatively high rate of return on capital investment in less-developed economies. Technology transfer from the developed economies; however, may also result in the adoption of more efficient and environmentally sound production techniques than would have been adopted in the absence of foreign investment.

Source: John Kane, *Does Foreign Direct Investment Hinder or Help Economic Development?* South-Western Policy Debate, 2004.

companies play in China's growing pollution problems by demanding ever-lower prices for Chinese products. One way China's factories have historically kept costs down is by dumping wastewater directly into rivers. Treating contaminated water costs more than 13 cents a metric ton, so large factories can save hundreds of thousands of dollars a year by sending waste water directly into rivers in violation of China's water-pollution laws. The result is that prices in the United States are artificially low because Americans are not paying the costs of pollution. American companies that use Chinese products are subject to much criticism for not taking a hard enough line against polluting suppliers in China.

India: Breaking Out of the Third World

India is another example of an economy that has rapidly improved its economic performance following the adoption of freer trade policies. The economy of India is diverse, encompassing agriculture, handicrafts, manufacturing, and a multitude of services. Although two-thirds of the Indian workforce still earns their livelihood directly or indirectly through agriculture, services are a growing sector of India's economy. The advent of the digital age and the large number of young and educated Indians fluent in English are transforming India as an important destination for global outsourcing of customer services and technical support.

India and China have traveled different paths of development. China has followed the traditional development route of nations like Japan and South Korea, becoming a center for low-wage manufacturing of goods. Realizing that it could not go head to head with China in manufacturing, India concluded that it had a better chance in exporting services. Consistent with the Heckscher-Ohlin theory, India's abundant factor has been the relatively well-educated, English-speaking labor that provides a low-cost gateway to global services such as data processing operations, call centers, and the like. Although economic growth rates give China's goods-dominated strategy the superior track record so far, India's approach may pay off better over the long term. A look at per-capita incomes around the world indicates that the wealth of nations eventually depends more in services than industry.

After gaining independence from Britain in 1947, India began practicing socialism and adopted an import-substitution model to run its economy. Both of these resulted from India's fear of imperialism of any kind following its independence. Therefore, India's government initiated protectionist trade barriers and bans on foreign investment to restrict competition, strict regulations over private business and financial markets, a large public sector, and central planning. This resulted in India becoming isolated from the mainstream world from the 1950s to 1980s. During this period, India's economy achieved only a modest rate of growth and poverty was widespread. Increasingly, people in India recognized that public sector policy had failed India.

By 1991, policy makers in India realized that their system of state controls and import substitution was strangling the economy, and that reforms were needed. The result was a clear switch toward an outward-oriented, market-based economy. The requirement that government must approve industrial investment expenditures was terminated, quotas on imports were abolished, export subsidies were eliminated, and import tariffs were slashed from an average of 87 percent in 1990 to 33 percent in 1994. Also, Indian companies were allowed to borrow on international markets and the rupee was devalued. These reforms helped transform India from an agrarian, underdeveloped, and closed economy into a more open and progressive one that encourages foreign investment and draws more wealth from industry and services. The result has been a dramatic increase in economic growth and falling poverty rates.

India's outsourcing business illustrates how foreign investment and trade have benefited the nation. The lifting of restrictions on foreign investment resulted in firms such as General Electric and British Airways moving information technology (IT) and other back-office operations to India in the 1990s. The success of these companies showed the world that India was a viable destination for outsourcing, and additional companies set up operations in the nation. These multinationals trained thousands of Indian workers, many of whom transferred their skills to other emerging Indian firms. Simply put, Indian workers benefited from the thousands of jobs that were created and the rising incomes that resulted from foreign investment.

India's auto industry is another example of the benefits of trade and investment liberalization. Before the 1980s, prohibitions on foreign investment and high import tariffs shielded India's state-owned automakers from global competition. These firms used obsolete technology to produce just two models and sold them at high prices. By the 1990s, tariffs were slashed on auto imports and bans on foreign investment were largely phased out. The result was an increase in autos imported into India and also the entry of foreign automakers that established assembly plants in the nation. As competition increased, labor productivity increased more than threefold for Indian auto workers who benefited from higher wages. Also, auto prices declined, unleashing a surge in consumer demand, a rise in auto sales, and the creation of thousands of autoworker jobs. Today, India's auto industry produces 13 times more cars than it did in the early 1980s, and India exports vehicles to other nations. None of this would have been possible had India's automakers remained isolated from the world.

However, the dynamic growth of India's outsourcing and automobile industries stands in contrast to most of its economy, where restrictions on trade and foreign investment stifle competition and foster the survival of inefficient firms. Food retailing illustrates how Indian industry gets along when foreign investment is prohibited. As of 2007, labor productivity in this industry was only five percent of the U.S. level. Much of this discrepancy is because almost all of India's food retailers are street markets and mom-and-pop counter stores rather than modern supermarkets. Moreover, productivity averages just 20 percent of the U.S. level in Indian supermarkets as a result of their small scale and inefficient merchandising and marketing methods. In other developing nations, such as China and Mexico, global retailers such as Wal-Mart have intensified competition that has increased productivity. However, these retailers have been prohibited from investing in India.

In spite of India's economic gains, the nation cannot afford to rest on its laurels; more than 250 million Indians still live below the official poverty line. Sustaining robust economic growth will require the nation to focus on improving its infrastructure such as roads, electric power generation, rail freight, and ports. India's recent infrastructure investments have not kept pace with economic developments. In contrast, China has invested heavily to build a world-class infrastructure that can attract foreign investment and promote economic growth.

India is expected to become the world's most populous nation by 2030. This rate of population growth provides India the major advantage of an almost limitless labor supply and consumer demand. Nevertheless, it also illustrates the necessity of investing in education and health care and creating adequate opportunities for employment.

Most economists contend that India needs to systematically deregulate sectors such as retailing, the news media, and banking, which have remained crippled by archaic policies. It also needs to eliminate preferences for small-scale, inefficient producers and repeal legislation blocking layoffs in medium- and large-sized firms. With deregulation and the opening of markets, vital foreign investments of capital and skills could flow more readily into India, making its industry more effective and the economy more robust. To ensure that India's economic growth reaches the whole nation, the government needs to reform its agriculture industry in order to generate jobs in rural areas.

India has made great progress, but further efforts will be needed to sustain its economic growth. With a rapidly rising population, India faces the challenge of creating millions of jobs to keep its people out of poverty. It remains to be seen whether India's government, private sector, and society at large will demonstrate the political will needed to work together and make this occur.

Summary

1. Developing nations tend to be characterized by relatively low levels of gross domestic product per capita, shorter life expectancies, and lower levels of adult literacy. Many developing nations believe that the current international trading system, based on the principle of comparative advantage, is irrelevant for them.

2. Among the alleged problems facing the developing nations are (a) unstable export markets, (b) worsening terms of trade, and (c) limited market access.

3. Among the institutions and policies that have been created to support developing nations are the World Bank, the International Monetary Fund, and a generalized system of preferences.

4. International commodity agreements have been formed to stabilize the prices and revenues of producers of primary products. The methods used to attain this stability are buffer stocks, export controls, and multilateral contracts. In practice, these methods have yielded modest success.

5. The OPEC oil cartel was established in 1960 in reaction to the control that the major international oil companies exercised over the posted price of oil. OPEC has used production quotas to support prices and earnings above what could be achieved in more competitive conditions.

6. Besides seeking financial assistance from advanced nations, developing nations have promoted internal industrialization through policies of import substitution and export promotion. Nations emphasizing export promotion have tended to realize higher rates of economic growth than nations emphasizing import-substitution policies.

7. The East Asian economies have realized remarkable economic growth in recent decades. The foundation of such growth has included high rates of investment, the increasing endowments of an educated workforce, and the use of export-promotion policies.

8. By the 1990s, China had become a high-performing Asian economy. Although China has dismantled much of its centrally planned economy and permitted free enterprise to replace it, political freedoms have not increased. Today, China describes itself as a socialist market economy. Being heavily endowed with labor, China specializes in many labor-intensive products. In 2001, China became a member of the WTO.

9. India is another example of an economy that has rapidly improved its economic performance following the adoption of freer trade policies. After becoming independent from Britain in 1947,

India began practicing socialism and adopted an import-substitution policy to run its economy. By 1991, the policymakers of India realized that their system of state controls and import substitution was not working. Therefore, India adopted a more open economy that encourages foreign investment, and economic growth accelerated.

Key Concepts & Terms

- Advanced nations (p. 255)
- Buffer stock (p. 266)
- Cartel (p. 269)
- Developing nations (p. 255)
- Export-led growth (p. 281)
- Export-oriented policy (p. 281)
- Flying-geese Pattern of economic growth (p. 285)
- Generalized system of preferences (GSP) (p. 276)
- Import substitution (p. 279)
- International commodity agreements (ICAs) (p. 265)
- International Monetary Fund (IMF) (p. 275)
- Multilateral contracts (p. 267)
- Organization of Petroleum Exporting Nations (OPEC) (p. 269)
- Primary products (p. 255)
- Production and export controls (p. 265)
- World Bank (p. 274)

Study Questions

1. Why is cheating a typical problem for cartels?
2. What led India in the 1990s to abandon its system of import substitution, and what growth strategy did India adopt?
3. The average person probably had never heard of the Organization of Petroleum Exporting Countries until 1973 or 1974, when oil prices skyrocketed. In fact, OPEC was founded in 1960. Why did OPEC not achieve worldwide prominence until the 1970s? What factors contributed to OPEC's problems in the 1980s?
4. How has China achieved the status of a high-performing Asian economy? Why has China's normal-trade-relation status been a source of controversy in the United States? What are the likely effects of China's entry into the WTO?
5. Why are the developing nations concerned with commodity-price stabilization?
6. How are import-substitution and export-promotion policies used to aid in the industrialization of developing nations?
7. What are some examples of international commodity agreements? Why have many of them broken down over time?
8. Describe the strategy that East Asia used from the 1970s to the 1990s to achieve high rates of economic growth. Can the Asian miracle continue in the new millennium?
9. Stabilizing commodity prices has been a major objective of many primary-product nations. What are the major methods used to achieve price stabilization?
10. The generalized system of preferences is intended to help developing nations gain access to world markets. Explain.
11. What are the major reasons for the skepticism of many developing nations regarding the comparative-advantage principle and free trade?

Regional Trading Arrangements

Since World War II, advanced nations have significantly lowered their trade restrictions. This trade liberalization has stemmed from two approaches. The first is a reciprocal reduction of trade barriers on a nondiscriminatory basis. Under the General Agreement on Tariffs and Trade (GATT) and its successor, the World Trade Organization (WTO), member nations acknowledge that tariff reductions agreed on by any two nations would be extended to all other members. Such an international approach encourages a gradual relaxation of tariffs throughout the world.

A second approach to trade liberalization occurs when a small group of nations, typically on a regional basis, form a **regional trading arrangement**. Under this system, member nations agree to impose lower barriers to trade within the group than to trade with nonmember nations. Each member nation continues to determine its domestic policies, but the trade policy of each includes preferential treatment for group members. Regional trading arrangements (free-trade areas and customs unions) have been an exception to the principle of nondiscrimination embodied in the World Trade Organization. This chapter investigates the operation and effects of regional trading arrangements.

Regional Integration Versus Multilateralism

Recall that a major purpose of the WTO is to promote trade liberalization through worldwide agreements. However, getting a large number of countries to agree on reforms can be extremely difficult. By the first decade of the 2000s, the WTO was stumbling in its attempt to achieve a global trade agreement, and countries increasingly looked to more narrow, regional agreements as an alternative. Are regional trading arrangements building blocks or stumbling blocks to a multilateral trading system?

Trade liberalization under a regional trading arrangement is very different from the multilateral liberalization embodied in the WTO. Under regional trading arrangements, nations reduce trade barriers only for a small group of partner nations, thus discriminating against the rest of the world. Under the WTO, trade liberalization by any one nation is extended to all WTO members, 153 nations, on a nondiscriminatory basis.

Although regional trading blocs can complement the multilateral trading system, by their very nature they are discriminatory; and are a departure from the principle of normal trading relations, a cornerstone of the WTO system. Some analysts note that regional trading blocs that decrease the discretion of member nations to pursue trade liberalization with outsiders are likely to become stumbling blocs to multilateralism. For example, if Malaysia has already succeeded in finding a market in the United States, it would have only a limited interest in a free-trade pact with the United States. But its less successful rival, Argentina, would be eager to sign a regional free-trade agreement and thus capture Malaysia's share of the U.S. market: not by making a better or cheaper product, but by obtaining special treatment under U.S. trade law. Once Argentina obtains its special privilege, what incentive would it have to go to WTO meetings and sign a multilateral free-trade agreement that would eliminate those special privileges?

Two other factors suggest that the members of a regional trading arrangement may not be greatly interested in worldwide liberalization. First, trade-bloc members may not realize additional economies of scale from global trade liberalization, which often provides only modest openings to foreign markets. Regional trade blocs, which often provide more extensive trade liberalization, may allow domestic firms sufficient production runs to exhaust scale economies. Second, trade-bloc members may want to invest their time and energy in establishing strong regional linkages rather than investing them in global negotiations.

On the other hand, when structured according to principles of openness and inclusiveness, regional blocs can be building blocs rather than stumbling blocks to global free trade and investment. Regional blocs can foster global market openings in several ways. First, regional agreements may achieve deeper economic interdependence among members than do multilateral accords, because of the greater commonality of interests and the simpler negotiating processes. Second, a self-reinforcing process is set in place by the establishment of a regional free-trade area: as the market encompassed by a free-trade area enlarges, it becomes increasingly attractive for nonmembers to join to receive the same trade preferences as member nations. Third, regional liberalization encourages the partial adjustment of workers out of import-competing industries in which the nation's comparative disadvantage is strong and into exporting industries in which its comparative advantage is strong. As adjustment proceeds, the portion of the labor force that benefits from liberalized trade rises, and the portion that loses falls; this process promotes political support for trade liberalization in a self-reinforcing process. For all of these reasons, when regional agreements are formed according to principles of openness, they may overlap and expand, thus promoting global free trade from the bottom up.

Let us next consider the various types of regional trading blocs and their economic effects.

Types of Regional Trading Arrangements

Since the mid-1950s, the term **economic integration** has become part of the vocabulary of economists. Economic integration is a process of eliminating restrictions on international trade, payments, and factor mobility. Economic integration thus results in the uniting of two or more national economies in a regional trading arrangement. Before proceeding, let us distinguish the types of regional trading arrangements.

A **free-trade area** is an association of trading nations in which members agree to remove all tariff and nontariff barriers among themselves. However, each member maintains its own set of trade restrictions against outsiders. An example of this stage of integration is the **North American Free Trade Agreement (NAFTA)** which consists of Canada, Mexico, and the United States. The United States also has free-trade agreements with Israel and Chile. Another free-trade agreement occurred in 1999 when the European Union and Mexico reached a deal that ended all tariffs on their bilateral trade in industrial goods in 2007.

Like a free-trade association, a **customs union** is an agreement among two or more trading partners to remove all tariff and nontariff trade barriers between themselves. In addition, however, each member nation imposes identical trade restrictions against nonparticipants. The effect of the common external trade policy is to permit free trade within the customs union, whereas all trade restrictions imposed against outsiders are equalized. A well-known example is **Benelux** (Belgium, the Netherlands, and Luxembourg), which was formed in 1948.

A **common market** is a group of trading nations that permits (1) the free movement of goods and services among member nations, (2) the initiation of common external trade restrictions against nonmembers, and (3) the free movement of factors of production across national borders within the economic bloc. The common market thus represents a more complete stage of integration than a free-trade area or a customs union. The **European Union** (EU)[1] achieved the status of a common market in 1992.

Beyond these stages, economic integration could evolve to the stage of **economic union**, in which national, social, taxation, and fiscal policies are harmonized and administered by a supranational institution. Belgium and Luxembourg formed an economic union during the 1920s. The task of creating an economic union is much more ambitious than achieving the other forms of integration. This is because a free-trade area, customs union, or common market results primarily from the abolition of existing trade barriers, but an economic union requires an agreement to transfer economic sovereignty to a supranational authority. The ultimate degree of economic union would be the unification of national monetary policies and the acceptance of a common currency administered by a supranational monetary authority. The economic union would thus include the dimension of a **monetary union**.

The United States serves as an example of a monetary union. Fifty states are linked together in a complete monetary union with a common currency, implying completely fixed exchange rates among the 50 states. Also, the Federal Reserve serves as the single central bank for the nation; it issues currency and conducts the nation's monetary policy. Trade is free among the states, and both labor and capital move freely in pursuit of maximum returns. The federal government conducts the nation's

---

[1]Founded in 1957, the European Community was a collective name for three organizations: the European Economic Community, the European Coal and Steel Community, and the European Atomic Energy Commission. In 1994, the European Community was replaced by the European Union following ratification of the Maastricht Treaty by the 12 member countries of the European Community. For simplicity, the name European Union is used throughout this chapter in discussing events that occurred before and after 1994.

MISSING BENEFITS: THE UNITED STATES FALLS BEHIND ON TRADE LIBERALIZATION

TABLE 8.1

EXAMPLES OF TRADE DEALS INVOLVING COUNTRIES OTHER THAN THE UNITED STATES

South Korea-European Union, 2009
- Applies to $96 billion in annual trade
- Eliminates virtually all tariffs
- Decreases Korean regulatory barriers on imports of automobiles

Canada-Colombia, 2008
- Applies to $1.2 billion in annual trade
- Phases out most Colombian agricultural tariffs
- Addresses Colombian food-safety standards that restrict trade

Japan-Association of Southeast Asian Nations, 2008
- Applies to $211.4 billion in annual trade
- Eliminates Japanese tariffs on 93 percent of import value
- Eliminates six countries' tariffs on 90 percent of Japanese imports

Source: World Trade Organization, *Regional Trade Agreements Information System* available at **http://rtais.wto.org/?lang=1/**.

Does the United States leave itself behind by not negotiating bilateral or regional trade agreements with other countries? There were about 266 bilateral or regional trade pacts in existence in 2009, according to the World Trade Organization. Overall, the United States had trade deals with only 17 countries, such as Mexico and Canada under NAFTA. In contrast, the European Union, Japan, and China have rapidly formed trade alliances ranging from customs unions to large free-trade pacts with a total of 40 countries. Table 8.1 provides examples of recent trade deals involving countries other than the United States.

The expansion of bilateral and regional trade deals stem in part from countries losing faith in the ongoing Doha Round of multilateral trade talks that has dragged on for almost a decade, as discussed in Chapter 6. Others view bilateral and regional deals as a method of liberalizing beyond what the Doha Round would achieve, including areas such as intellectual property protection. These deals can also foster alliances or promote political influence, which is one reason China enthusiastically negotiates trade pacts with its neighbors.

However, when the United States sits on the sidelines, its companies can find themselves on the wrong side of trade pacts negotiated among other countries.

For example, the 2008 treaty between Canada and Colombia gets rid of Colombia's tariffs, which average 12 percent, on nonagricultural goods from Canada, while these tariffs still apply to U.S. exports. Also, Canadian farmers will benefit over time from tariff-free access to Colombia for most of their agricultural exports while farmers in Kansas or Nebraska will face tariffs ranging from 5 to 80 percent.

Many economists maintain that bilateral trade deals are a suboptimal method of fostering global growth. It would be far better for governments to decrease their own trade barriers by signing a multilateral deal like the Doha Round. A complicated system of bilateral and regional deals can plague businesses with the costs of adhering to multiple sets of rules. This spaghetti bowl approach also results in inefficiencies to the degree that businesses make trade and investment decisions based more on where they can get trade preferences than on the highest return on investment.

Source: World Trade Organization, *Regional Trade Agreements*, October 2009 and "America Leaves Itself Behind," *The Wall Street Journal*, November 11, 2009, p. A-20.

fiscal policy and deals in matters concerning retirement and health programs, national defense, international affairs, and the like. Other programs, such as police protection and education, are conducted by state and local governments so that states can keep their identity within the union.

Impetus for Regionalism

Regional trading arrangements are pursued for a variety of reasons. A motivation of virtually every regional trading arrangement has been the prospect of enhanced economic growth. An expanded regional market can allow economies of large-scale production, foster specialization and learning-by-doing, and attract foreign investment. Regional initiatives can also foster a variety of noneconomic objectives, such as managing immigration flows and promoting regional security. Moreover, regionalism may enhance and solidify domestic economic reforms. East European nations, for example, have viewed their regional initiatives with the European Union as a means of locking in their domestic policy shifts toward privatization and market-oriented reform.

Smaller nations may seek safe-haven trading arrangements with larger nations when future access to the larger nations' markets appears uncertain. This kind of access was an apparent motivation for the formation of NAFTA. In North America, Mexico was motivated to join NAFTA partially by fear of changes in U.S. trade policy toward a more managed or strategic trade orientation. Canada's pursuit of a free-trade agreement was significantly motivated by a desire to discipline the use of countervailing and antidumping duties by the United States.

As new regional trading arrangements are formed, or existing ones are expanded or deepened, the opportunity cost of remaining outside an arrangement increases. Nonmember exporters could realize costly decreases in market share if their sales are diverted to companies of the member nations. This prospect may be sufficient to tip the political balance in favor of becoming a member of a regional trading arrangement, as exporting interests of a nonmember nation outweigh its import-competing interests. The negotiations between the United States and Mexico to form a free-trade area appear to have strongly influenced Canada's decision to join NAFTA, and thus not be left behind in the movement toward free trade in North America.

Effects of a Regional Trading Arrangement

What are the possible welfare implications of *regional trading arrangements*? We can delineate the theoretical benefits and costs of such devices from two perspectives. First are the **static effects of economic integration** on productive efficiency and consumer welfare. Second are the **dynamic effects of economic integration**, which relate to member nations' long-term rates of growth. Because a small change in the growth rate can lead to a substantial cumulative effect on national output, the dynamic effects of trade-policy changes can yield substantially larger magnitudes than those based on static models. Combined, these static and dynamic effects determine the overall welfare gains or losses associated with the formation of a regional trading arrangement.

Static Effects

The static welfare effects of lowering tariff barriers among members of a trade bloc are illustrated in the following example. Assume a world composed of three countries: Luxembourg, Germany, and the United States. Suppose that Luxembourg and Germany decide to form a customs union, and the United States is a nonmember. The decision to form a customs union requires that Luxembourg and Germany abolish all tariff restrictions between themselves while maintaining a common tariff policy against the United States.

Referring to Figure 8.1, assume the supply and demand schedules of Luxembourg to be S_L and D_L. Assume also that Luxembourg is very small relative to Germany and to the United States. This assumption means that Luxembourg cannot influence foreign prices, so that foreign supply schedules of grain are perfectly elastic. Let Germany's supply price be $3.25 per bushel and that of the United States, $3 per bushel. Note that the United States is assumed to be the more efficient supplier.

FIGURE 8.1

STATIC WELFARE EFFECTS OF A CUSTOMS UNION

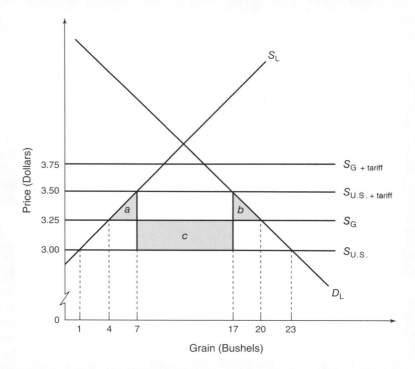

The formation of a customs union leads to a welfare-increasing trade creation effect and a welfare-decreasing trade diversion effect. The overall effect of the customs union on the welfare of its members, as well as on the world as a whole, depends on the relative strength of these two opposing forces.

Before the formation of the customs union, Luxembourg finds that under conditions of free trade, it purchases all of its import requirements from the United States. Germany does not participate in the market because its supply price exceeds that of the United States. In free-trade equilibrium, Luxembourg's consumption equals 23 bushels, production equals 1 bushel, and imports equal 22 bushels. If Luxembourg levies a tariff equal to $0.50 cents on each bushel imported from the United States (or Germany), then imports will fall from 22 bushels to 10 bushels.

Suppose that, as part of a trade liberalization agreement, Luxembourg and Germany form a customs union. Luxembourg's import tariff against Germany is dropped, but it is still maintained on imports from the nonmember United States. By removing the tariff, Germany becomes the low-price supplier. Luxembourg now purchases all of its imports, totaling 16 bushels, from Germany at $3.25 per bushel, while importing nothing from the United States.

The movement toward freer trade under a customs union affects world welfare in two opposing ways: a welfare-increasing **trade-creation effect** and a welfare-reducing **trade-diversion effect**. The overall consequence of a customs union on the welfare of its members, as well as on the world as a whole, depends on the relative strengths of these two opposing forces.

Trade creation occurs when some domestic production of one customs-union member is replaced by another member's lower-cost imports. The welfare of the member countries is increased by trade creation because it leads to increased production specialization according to the principle of comparative advantage. The trade-creation effect consists of a *consumption effect* and a *production effect*.

Before the formation of the customs union and under its own tariff umbrella, Luxembourg imports from the United States at a price of $3.50 per bushel. Luxembourg's entry into the customs union results in it dropping all tariffs against Germany. Facing a lower import price of $3.25, Luxembourg increases its consumption of grain by three bushels. The welfare gain associated with this increase in consumption equals triangle *b* in Figure 8.1.

The formation of the customs union also yields a production effect that results in a more efficient use of world resources. Eliminating the tariff barrier against Germany means that Luxembourg's producers must now compete against lower-cost, more efficient German producers. Inefficient domestic producers drop out of the market, resulting in a decline in home output of three bushels. The reduction in the cost of obtaining this output equals triangle *a* in the figure. This triangle represents the favorable production effect. The overall trade-creation effect is given by the sum of triangles *a* + *b*.

Although a customs union may add to world welfare by way of trade creation, its trade-diversion effect generally implies a welfare loss. Trade diversion occurs when imports from a low-cost supplier outside the union are replaced by purchases from a higher-cost supplier within the union. This diversion suggests that world production is reorganized less efficiently. In Figure 8.1, although the total volume of trade increases under the customs union, part of this trade (ten bushels) has been diverted from a low-cost supplier, the United States, to a high-cost supplier, Germany. The increase in the cost of obtaining these ten bushels of imported grain equals area *c*. This is the welfare loss to Luxembourg, as well as to the world as a whole. Our static analysis concludes that the formation of a customs union will increase the welfare of its members, as well as the rest of the world, if the positive trade-creation effect more than offsets the negative trade-diversion effect. Referring to the figure, this occurs if *a* + *b* is greater than *c*.

This analysis illustrates that the success of a customs union depends on the factors contributing to trade creation and diversion. Several factors that bear on the relative size of these effects can be identified. One factor is the kinds of nations that tend to benefit from a customs union. Nations whose pre-union economies are quite competitive are likely to benefit from trade creation because the formation of the union offers greater opportunity for specialization in production. Also, the larger the size and the greater the number of nations in the union, the greater the gains are likely to be, because there is a greater possibility that the world's low-cost producers will be union members. In the extreme case in which the union consists of the entire world, there can exist only trade creation, not trade diversion. In addition, the scope for trade diversion is smaller when the customs union's common external tariff is lower rather than higher. Because a lower tariff allows greater trade to take place with nonmember nations, there will be less replacement of cheaper imports from nonmember nations by relatively high-cost imports from partner nations.

Did the United Kingdom (UK) Gain from Entering the European Union?

An example of trade creation and trade diversion occurred when the UK entered the European Union in 1973. Upon entry, the UK turned away cheaper agricultural produce from its former colony, Australia. Instead, it increased farm output and purchased produce from its more expensive European neighbors. How did this come about?

In joining the EU, the UK had to comply with its agriculture policy, which set common barriers against agricultural producers outside the EU. Tariffs and quotas increased the price of non-EU produce to UK consumers. Therefore, Australia's preferential access to the UK market ended. It was shut out as the UK fell in line with other more costly European producers.

United Kingdom consumers paid a high price for the change. Before joining the EU, UK food bills were the cheapest in Europe. However, when the UK joined the EU, more expensive produce from Europe pushed its food prices up 25 percent on average. Simply put, the UK lost because trade was diverted from low- to high-cost producers.

Trade in manufactured goods from Europe increased significantly as the UK entered the EU and thus abolished barriers placed on imports of these goods from European nations. This trade allowed lower-priced imports from European trading partners to replace higher-priced UK output, thus increasing national welfare.

Evaluating whether entering the EU was good or bad for the UK became an empirical question. Did the welfare-expanding effect of trade creation in manufactured goods more than offset the welfare-contracting effect of trade diversion in agricultural products? Empirical studies generally maintain that trade creation was the stronger effect, and that the UK's overall welfare improved by joining the EU.

Dynamic Effects

Not all welfare consequences of a regional trading arrangement are static in nature. There may also be dynamic gains that influence member-nation growth rates over the long term. These dynamic gains stem from the creation of larger markets by the movement to freer trade under customs unions. The benefits associated with a customs union's dynamic gains may more than offset any unfavorable static effects. Dynamic gains include *economies of scale, greater competition*, and a *stimulus of investment.*

Perhaps the most noticeable result of a customs union is market enlargement. Being able to penetrate freely into domestic markets of other member nations, producers can take advantage of economies of scale that would not have occurred in smaller markets limited by trade restrictions. Larger markets may permit efficiencies attributable to greater specialization of workers and machinery, the use of the most efficient equipment, and the more complete use of by-products. Evidence suggests that significant economies of scale have been achieved by the EU in such products as steel, automobiles, footwear, and copper refining.

The European refrigerator industry provides an example of the dynamic effects of integration. Prior to the formation of the EU, each of the major European nations that produced refrigerators (Germany, Italy, and France) supported a small number of manufacturers that produced primarily for the domestic market. These manufacturers had production runs of fewer than 100,000 units per year, a level too low to permit the adoption of automated equipment. Short production runs translated into a high per-unit cost. The EU's formation resulted in the opening of European markets and paved the way for the adoption of large-scale production methods, including automated press lines and spot welding. By the late 1960s, the typical Italian refrigerator plant manufactured 850,000 refrigerators annually. This volume was more than sufficient to meet the minimum efficient scale of operation, estimated to be 800,000 units per year. The late 1960s also saw German and French manufacturers averaging 570,000 units and 290,000 units per year, respectively.[2]

Broader markets may also promote greater competition among producers within a customs union. It is often felt that trade restrictions promote monopoly power, whereby a small number of companies dominate a domestic market. Such companies may prefer to lead a quiet life, forming agreements not to compete on the basis of price. But with the movement to more open markets under a customs union, the potential for successful collusion is lessened as the number of competitors expands. With freer trade, domestic producers must compete or face the possibility of financial bankruptcy. To survive in expanded and more competitive markets, producers must cut waste, keep prices down, improve quality, and raise productivity. Competitive pressure can also be an effective check against the use of monopoly power and in general a benefit to the nation's consumers.

In addition, trade can accelerate the pace of technical advance and boost the level of productivity. By increasing the expected rate of return to successful innovation and spreading research and development costs more wisely, trade can propel a higher pace of investment spending in the latest technologies. Greater international trade can also enhance the exchange of technical knowledge among countries as human and physical capital move more freely. These inducements tend to increase an economy's rate of growth, causing, not just a one-time boost to economic welfare, but a persistent increase in income that grows steadily larger as time passes.

---

[2]Nicholas Owen, *Economies of Scale, Competitiveness, and Trade Patterns Within the European Community* (New York: Oxford University Press, 1983), pp. 119–139.

The European Union

In the years immediately after World War II, Western European countries suffered balance-of-payments deficits in response to reconstruction efforts. To shield their firms and workers from external competitive pressures, they initiated an elaborate network of tariff and exchange restrictions, quantitative controls, and state trading. However, in the 1950s these trade barriers were generally viewed as counterproductive. Therefore, Western Europe began to dismantle its trade barriers in response to successful tariff negotiations under the auspices of GATT.

It was against this background of trade liberalization that the European Union, then known as the European Community, was created by the Treaty of Rome in 1957. The EU initially consisted of six nations: Belgium, France, Italy, Luxembourg, the Netherlands, and West Germany. By 1973, the United Kingdom, Ireland, and Denmark had joined the trade bloc. Greece joined the trade bloc in 1981, followed by Spain and Portugal in 1987. In 1995, Austria, Finland, and Sweden were admitted into the EU. In 2004, ten other Central and Eastern European countries joined the EU: Cyprus, the Czech Republic, Estonia, Hungary, Latvia, Lithuania, Malta, Poland, Slovakia, and Slovenia. In 2007, Bulgaria and Romania joined the EU, bringing the membership up to 27 countries. The EU views this enlargement process as an opportunity to promote stability in Europe and further the integration of the continent by peaceful means.

European Union expansion has produced both winners and losers. Most studies agree that Germany, Italy, Austria, Sweden, and Finland, who have close trade and investment ties with Central and Eastern European nations, are gainers. France, Spain, Portugal, Greece, and Ireland are likely to be losers, given the sizable funding they receive from EU programs—especially France's agricultural funds—as the money is stretched over more countries. Clearly, the Central and Eastern European nations stand to gain the most as their economies become integrated with other European economies.

Pursuing Economic Integration

According to the Treaty of Rome, the EU agreed in principle to follow the path of economic integration and eventually become an economic union. In pursuing this goal, EU members first dismantled tariffs and established a free-trade area in 1968. This liberalization of trade was accompanied by a fivefold increase in the value of industrial trade—higher than world trade, in general. The success of the free-trade area inspired the EU to continue its process of economic integration. In 1970, the EU became a full-fledged customs union when it adopted a common external tariff system for its members.

Several studies have been conducted on the overall impact of the EU on its members' welfare during the 1960s and 1970s. In terms of static welfare benefits, one study concluded that trade creation was pronounced in machinery, transportation equipment, chemicals, and fuels, whereas trade diversion was apparent in agricultural commodities and raw materials.[3] A broad conclusion was drawn that trade creation in the manufactured-goods sector during the 1960s and 1970s was significant: 10 to 30 percent of total EU imports of manufactured goods. Moreover, trade

---

[3]Mordechai E. Kreinin, *Trade Relations of the EEC: An Empirical Approach* (New York: Praeger, 1974), Chapter 3.

creation exceeded trade diversion by a wide margin, estimated at 2 to 15 percent. In addition, analysts also noted that the EU realized dynamic benefits from integration in the form of additional competition and investment and also economies of scale. For instance, it has been determined that many firms in small nations, such as the Netherlands and Belgium, realized economies of scale by producing both for the domestic market and for export. However, after becoming members of the EU, sizable additional economies of scale were gained by individual firms, reducing the range of products manufactured and increasing the output of the remaining products.[4]

After forming a customs union, the EU made little progress toward becoming a common market until 1985. The hostile economic climate (recession and inflation) of the 1970s led EU members to shield their citizens from external forces rather than dismantle trade and investment restrictions. By the 1980s, however, EU members were increasingly frustrated with barriers that hindered transactions within the bloc. European officials also feared that the EU's competitiveness was lagging behind that of Japan and the United States.

In 1985, the EU announced a detailed program for becoming a common market. This program resulted in the elimination of remaining nontariff trade barriers to intra-EU transactions by 1992. Examples of these barriers included border controls and customs red tape, divergent standards and technical regulations, conflicting business laws, and protectionist procurement policies of governments. The elimination of these barriers resulted in the formation of a European common market and turned the trade bloc into the second largest economy in the world, almost as large as the U.S. economy.

While the EU was becoming a common market, its heads of government agreed to pursue much deeper levels of integration. Their goal was to begin a process of replacing their central banks with a European Central Bank and replacing their national currencies with a single European currency. The **Maastricht Treaty**, signed in 1991, set 2002 as the date at which this process would be complete. In 2002, a full-fledged **European Monetary Union (EMU)** emerged with a single currency, known as the **euro**.

When the Maastricht Treaty was signed, economic conditions in the various EU members differed substantially. The treaty specified that to be considered ready for monetary union, a country's economic performance would have to be similar to the performance of other members. Countries cannot, of course, pursue different rates of money growth, have different rates of economic growth, and different rates of inflation while having currencies that don't move up or down relative to each other. So the first thing the Europeans had to do was align their economic and monetary policies.

This effort, called convergence, has led to a high degree of uniformity in terms of price inflation, money supply growth, and other key economic factors. The specific **convergence criteria** as mandated by the Maastricht Treaty are as follows:

- **Price stability**. Inflation in each prospective member is supposed to be no more than 1.5 percent above the average of the inflation rates in the three countries with the lowest inflation rates

---

[4]Richard Harmsen and Michael Leidy, "Regional Trading Arrangements," in International Monetary Fund, World Economic and Financial Surveys, *International Trade Policies: The Uruguay Round and Beyond, Volume II*, 1994, p. 99.

- **Low long-term interest rates**. Long-term interest rates are to be no more than 2 percent above the average interest rate in those countries
- **Stable exchange rates**. The exchange rate is supposed to have been kept within the target bands of the monetary union with no devaluations for at least two years prior to joining the monetary union
- **Sound public finances**. One fiscal criterion is that the budget deficit in a prospective member should be at most 3 percent of GDP; the other is that the outstanding amount of government debt should be no more than 60 percent of a year's GDP.

The euro is the official currency of 16 of the 27 member states of the European Union. These states, known collectively as the eurozone, are Austria, Belgium, Cyprus, Finland, France, Germany, Greece, Ireland, Italy, Luxembourg, Malta, the Netherlands, Portugal, Slovakia, Slovenia, and Spain. The euro is also used in another five European countries and is consequently used daily by some 327 million Europeans. Over 175 million people worldwide use currencies that are pegged to the euro, including more than 150 million people in Africa. The euro is the second largest reserve currency and the second most traded currency in the world after the U.S. dollar.

As additional countries join the European Union they are also obligated to join the EMU and adopt the euro as their national currency. Membership in the EMU is not automatic because the accession countries must first satisfy the convergence criteria as mandated by the Maastricht Treaty. However, the candidates see the convergence criteria as a small price to pay for the exchange-rate stability and the low interest rates that come with full entry into the monetary union.

An important motivation for the EMU is the momentum it provides for political union, a long-standing goal of many European policymakers. France and Germany initiated the EMU. Monetary union was viewed as an important way to anchor Germany securely in Europe. Moreover, the EMU provided France with a larger role in determining monetary policy for Europe, which they would achieve with a common central bank. Prior to the EMU, Europe's monetary policy was mainly determined by the German Bundesbank.

French and Dutch Voters Sidetrack Integration

As the EU expanded its membership, it recognized the need to improve its governing institutions and decision-making processes so it could operate effectively and prevent gridlock. A new constitutional treaty was finalized in 2004 that contained changes to the EU's original governing constitution.

Besides containing measures that enable an enlarged EU to function more effectively, the new constitution also contained measures to boost the EU's visibility on the world stage. Major innovations include abolishing the EU's rotating presidency and appointing a single individual to serve as president of the European Council for up to five years, creating a new foreign minister, increasing the powers of the European Parliament, and simplifying EU voting procedures. Almost all of the changes in the constitution represented compromises between member countries who favor greater EU integration and those who prefer to keep the EU on an intergovernmental footing in which member countries can better guard their national sovereignty.

In order to take effect, the constitutional treaty must be ratified by all 25 member countries.

Although 12 countries completed ratification, the constitution's future became questionable following its rejection by French and Dutch voters in separate referenda in 2005. What did these voters react against? Voters in both countries were concerned that the treaty would promote liberal economic trends that could undermine their social protections, such as high minimum wage laws and welfare payments. Also, voters viewed a negative vote as a way to express dissatisfaction with their unpopular national governments, the EU bureaucracy, and Turkey's prospective EU membership. In France, some feared that the constitution, by paving the way for additional EU enlargement, would reduce French influence within the EU. Dutch voters complained that the EU's big countries were already too strong and that certain aspects of the constitution would expand their power even more.

Although EU officials emphasized that the EU could continue to operate and increase membership without the constitution, the rejection shook their confidence. The United Kingdom quickly responded that it would postpone its efforts to ratify the constitution, with no target date being set. Experts predict that the EU may face a period of stagnation, at least in the short term, as members struggle with internal reforms and the EU's future identity.

Agricultural Policy

Besides providing for free trade in industrial goods among its members, the EU has abolished restrictions on agricultural products traded internally. A **common agricultural policy** has replaced the agricultural-stabilization policies of individual member nations, which differed widely before the formation of the EU. A substantial element of the common agricultural policy has been the support of prices received by farmers for their produce. Schemes involving deficiency payments, output controls, and direct income payments have been used for this purpose. In addition, the common agricultural policy has supported EU farm prices through a system of **variable levies**, which applies tariffs to agricultural imports entering the EU. Exports of any surplus quantities of EU produce have been assured through the adoption of **export subsidies**.

One problem confronting the EU's price-support programs is that agricultural efficiencies differ among EU members. Consider the case of grains. German farmers, being high-cost producers, have sought high support prices to maintain their existence. The more efficient French farmers do not need as high a level of support prices as the Germans do to keep them in operation; nevertheless, French farmers have found it in their interest to lobby for high price supports. In recent years, high price supports have been applied to products such as beef, grains, and butter. The common agricultural policy has thus encouraged inefficient farm production by EU farmers and has restricted food imports from more efficient nonmember producers. Such trade diversion has been a welfare-decreasing effect on the EU.

Variable Levies

Figure 8.2 illustrates the operation of a system of variable levies. Assume that S_{EU_0} and D_{EU_0} represent the EU's supply and demand schedules for wheat and that the world price of wheat equals $3.50 per bushel. Also assume that the EU wishes to

FIGURE 8.2

VARIABLE LEVIES

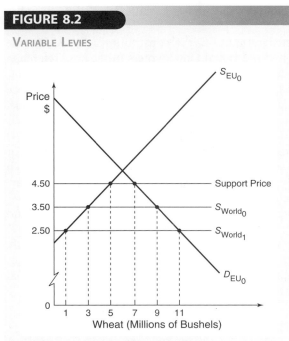

The common agricultural policy of the EU has used variable levies to protect EU farmers from low-cost foreign competition. During periods of falling world prices, the sliding-scale nature of the variable levy results in automatic increases in the EU's import tariff.

guarantee its high-cost farmers a price of $4.50 per bushel. This price cannot be sustained as long as imported wheat is allowed to enter the EU at the free-market price of $3.50 per bushel. Suppose the EU, to validate the support price, initiates a variable levy. Given an import levy of $1 per bushel, EU farmers are permitted to produce 5 million bushels of wheat, as opposed to the 3 million bushels that would be produced under free trade. At the same time, EU imports total 2 million bushels instead of 6 million bushels.

Suppose now that, owing to increased productivity overseas, the world price of wheat falls to $2.50 per bushel. Under a variable levy system, the levy is determined daily and equals the difference between the lowest price on the world market and the support price. The sliding-scale nature of the variable levy results in the EU's increasing its import tariff to $2 per bushel. The support price of wheat is sustained at $4.50, and EU production and imports remain unchanged. Thus, EU farmers are insulated from the consequences of variations in foreign supply. Should EU wheat production decrease, the import levy can be reduced to encourage imports. Then EU consumers are protected against rising wheat prices.

The variable import levy tends to be more restrictive than a fixed tariff. It discourages foreign producers from absorbing part of the tariff and cutting prices to maintain export sales. Cutting prices only triggers higher variable levies. For the same reason, variable levies discourage foreign producers from subsidizing their exports in order to penetrate domestic markets.

The completion of the Uruguay Round of trade negotiations in 1994 brought rules to bear on the use of variable levies. It required that all nontariff barriers, including variable levies, be converted to equivalent tariffs. However, the method of conversion used by the EU essentially maintained the variable levy system, except for one difference. The actual tariff applied on agricultural imports can vary, like the previous variable levy, depending on world prices. Now there is an upper limit applied to how high the tariff can rise.

Export Subsidies

The EU has also used a system of export subsidies to ensure that any surplus agricultural output will be sold overseas. The high price supports of the common agricultural policy have given EU farmers the incentive to increase production, often in surplus quantities. But the world price of agricultural commodities has generally been below the EU price. The EU pays its producers export subsidies so they can sell surplus produce abroad at the low price but still receive the higher, international support price. By encouraging exports, the government will reduce the domestic supply and eliminate the need for the government to purchase the excess.

TABLE 8.2

GOVERNMENT SUPPORT FOR AGRICULTURE, 2007

Producer-Subsidy Equivalents*	Country as a Percent of Farm Prices
Iceland	61
South Korea	60
Norway	53
Switzerland	50
Japan	46
European Union	26
Canada	18
Mexico	14
United States	10
Australia	5
New Zealand	1

*The producer-subsidy equivalent represents the total assistance to farmers in the form of market price support, direct payments, and transfers that indirectly benefit farmers.

Source: From Organization of Economic Cooperation and Development (OECD), *Agricultural Policies in OECD Countries: Monitoring and Evaluation*, 2008. See also World Trade Organization, *Annual Report*, various issues.

The EU's policy of assuring a high level of income for its farmers has been costly. High support prices for products including milk, butter, cheese, and meat have led to high internal production and low consumption. The result has often been huge surpluses that must be purchased by the EU to defend the support price. To reduce these costs, the EU has sold surplus produce in world markets at prices well below the cost of acquisition. These subsidized sales have met with resistance from farmers in other countries. This is especially true for farmers in poor, developing countries who argue that they are handicapped when they face imports whose prices are depressed because of export subsidies or when they face greater competition in their export markets for the same reason.

Virtually every industrial country subsidizes its agricultural products. As seen in Table 8.2, government programs accounted for 26 percent of the value of agricultural products in the EU in 2007. This amount is even higher in certain countries such as Switzerland and Japan, but it is much lower in others, including the United States, Australia, and New Zealand. Countries with relatively low agricultural subsidies have criticized the high-subsidy countries as being too protectionist.

For a discussion of government procurement policy and the European Union, go to *Exploring Further 8.1.*

Is the European Union Really a Common Market?

For decades, members of the EU have tried to build a common market with uniform policies on product regulation, trade, and movement of factors of production. But are the policies of these countries really that common?

Consider the case of Kellogg Co., the American producer of breakfast cereals. For years, Kellogg has petitioned members of the EU to let it market identical vitamin-fortified cereals throughout Europe. But the firm's requests have run into numerous roadblocks. Government regulators in Denmark do not want vitamins added, dreading that cereal consumers who already take multivitamins might surpass recommended daily doses, which could jeopardize health. The Netherlands' regulators don't think that either folic acid or vitamin D is beneficial, so they don't want them included. However, Finland prefers more vitamin D than other nations to help Finns compensate for a lack of sun. So Kellogg has to produce four different varieties of cornflakes and other cereals at its plants in the United Kingdom.

The original concept of the EU was a common market based on uniform regulations. By producing for a single market throughout Europe, firms could attain production runs large enough to realize substantial economies of scale. Instead, persistent national differences have burdened firms with extra costs that stifle plant expansion and job creation.

This lack of consistency extends well beyond the domain of breakfast cereals. Caterpillar Inc. sells tractors throughout Europe. But in Germany, its vehicles must include a louder backup horn and lights that are installed in different locations.

The yield signs and license-plate holders on the backs of tractors and other earth-moving vehicles must differ, sometimes by just centimeters, from nation to nation. Officials at Caterpillar contend that there is no sound justification for such regulatory discrepancies. They only make it hard to mass produce in an efficient manner.

In 2005, the EU attempted to increase market integration in its service sector, which accounts for about 67 percent of its economic activity. But the effort to permit such businesses as medical firms and law practices to expand more easily across borders was stopped by Germany and France which contended that service companies from other nations would put their own providers out of business.

Persistent regulatory differences between markets have also adversely affected business expansion plans throughout Europe. For example, Ikea Group, the Swedish furniture retailer, must pay for studies to prove that its entry into markets will not displace local businesses. According to Ikea, each study costs approximately $25,000, and it takes about a year before a decision is made. Moreover, only 33 to 50 percent of Ikea's petitions result in approval.

Although members of the EU have advanced to higher levels of economic unification in the past 50 years, regulatory differences remain that have created barriers to trade and investment that stifle economic growth. These barriers have resulted in numerous legal battles between producers and national regulators, as well as between the European Commission and individual governments. Simply put, Europe's common market remains uncommon.[5]

Economic Costs and Benefits of a Common Currency: The European Monetary Union

As we have learned, the formation of the EMU in 1999 resulted in the creation of a single currency (the euro) and a European Central Bank. Switching to a new currency is extremely difficult. Just imagine the task if each of the 50 U.S. states had its own currency and its own central bank, and then had to agree with the other 49 states on a single currency and a single financial system. That's exactly what the Europeans have done.

The European Central Bank is located in Frankfurt, Germany, and is responsible for the monetary policy and exchange-rate policies of the EMU. The European Central Bank alone controls the supply of euros, sets the short-term euro interest rate, and maintains permanently fixed exchange rates for the member countries. With a common central bank, the central bank of each participating nation performs operations similar to those of the 12 regional Federal Reserve Banks in the United States.

For Americans, the benefits of a common currency are easy to understand. Americans know they can walk into a McDonald's or Burger King anywhere in the United States and purchase hamburgers with dollar bills in their purses and wallets. The same was not true in European countries prior to the formation of the EMU. Because each was a distinct nation with its own currency, a French person could not buy something at a German store without first exchanging his French francs for German marks. This exchange would be like someone from St. Louis having to

---

[5]"Corn Flakes Clash Shows the Glitches in European Union," *The Wall Street Journal*, November 1, 2005, p. A1.

exchange her Missouri currency for Illinois currency each time she visits Chicago. To make matters worse, because marks and francs floated against each other within a range, the number of marks the French traveler receives today would probably differ from the number he would have received yesterday or tomorrow. On top of exchange-rate uncertainty, the traveler also had to pay a fee to exchange the currency, making a trip across the border a costly proposition indeed. Although the costs to individuals can be limited because of the small quantities of money involved, firms can incur much larger costs. By replacing the various European currencies with a single currency, the euro, the EMU can avoid such costs. Simply put, the euro will lower the costs of goods and services, facilitate a comparison of prices within the EU, and thus promote more uniform prices.

Optimum Currency Area

Much analysis of the benefits and costs of a common currency is based on the theory of optimum currency areas.[6] An **optimum currency area** is a region in which it is economically preferable to have a single official currency rather than multiple official currencies. For example, the United States can be considered an optimal currency area. It is inconceivable that the current volume of commerce among the 50 states would occur as efficiently in a monetary environment of 50 different currencies. Table 8.3 highlights some of the advantages and disadvantages of forming a common currency area.

According to the theory of optimum currency areas, there are gains to be had from sharing a currency across countries' boundaries. These gains include more uniform prices, lower transaction costs, greater certainty for investors, and enhanced competition. Also, a single monetary policy, run by an independent central bank, should promote price stability.

However, a single policy can also entail costs, especially if interest-rate changes affect different economies in different ways. Also, the broader benefits of a single currency must be compared against the loss of two policy instruments: an independent

TABLE 8.3

Advantages and Disadvantages of Adopting a Common Currency

Advantages	Disadvantages
The risks associated with exchange fluctuations are eliminated within a common currency area.	Absence of individual domestic monetary policy to counter macroeconomic shocks.
Costs of currency conversion are lessened.	Inability of an individual country to use inflation to reduce public debt in real terms.
The economies are insulated from monetary disturbances and speculation.	The transition from individual currencies to a single currency could lead to speculative attacks.
Political pressures for trade protection are reduced.	

[6]The theory of "optimum currency areas" was first analyzed by Robert Mundell, who won the 1999 Nobel Prize in Economics. See Robert Mundell, "A Theory of Optimum Currency Areas," *American Economic Review*, Vol. 51, September 1961, pp. 717–725.

monetary policy and the option of changing the exchange rate. Losing these is particularly acute if a country or region is likely to suffer from economic disturbances (recession) that affect it differently from the rest of the single-currency area, because it will no longer be able to respond by adopting a more expansionary monetary policy or adjusting its currency.

Optimum currency theory then considers various reactions to economic shocks, noting three. The first is the mobility of labor: workers in the affected country must be able and willing to move freely to other countries. The second is the flexibility of prices and wages: the country must be able to adjust these in response to a disturbance. The third is some automatic mechanism for transferring fiscal resources to the affected country.

The theory of optimal currency areas concludes that for a currency area to have the best chance of success, countries involved should have similar business cycles and economic structures. Also, the single monetary policy should affect all the participating countries in the same manner. Moreover, there should be no legal, cultural, or linguistic barriers to labor mobility across borders; there should be wage flexibility; and there should be some system of stabilizing transfers.

Europe as a Suboptimal Currency Area

Although Europe may not be an ideal currency area, forming a monetary union has some advantages. A monetary union may improve economic efficiency through lowering the transaction costs of exchanging one currency for another. Tourists are familiar with the time and expense of changing one currency into another while traveling in Europe. Eliminating the transaction costs benefits both consumers and businesses. A single currency also facilitates the genuine comparison of prices within Europe. Another advantage is the elimination of exchange-rate risk; businesses will more readily trade and invest in other European countries if they did not have to consider what the future exchange rate wil be. The EMU also stimulates competition and facilitates the broadening and deepening of European financial markets.

The overall magnitudes of these gains appear to be relatively small. The European Commission estimates that savings in transaction costs are about 0.4 percent of the EU's gross domestic product.[7] Even though small, the efficiency gains are greater the more a country trades with other countries in the monetary union. For example, the Netherlands, whose trade with Germany has typically exceeded 20 percent of its total trade, benefits considerably by a monetary union with Germany. In contrast, only about two percent of the total trade of the Netherlands has typically been with Spain, making the benefits of monetary union with Spain much smaller.

A main disadvantage of the EMU is that each participating European country loses the use of monetary policy and the exchange rate as a tool in adjusting to economic disturbances. If one country experiences a recession, it can no longer relax monetary policy or allow its currency to depreciate to stimulate its economy. The use of fiscal policy, too, may be limited by the need to keep budget deficits in control under the EMU. Economic revival depends on wage flexibility and perhaps the ability and willingness of labor to move to new locations. Because wage rigidity in Europe is

---

[7]Commission of the European Communities, Directorate-General for Economic and Financial Affairs, "One Market, One Money: An Evaluation of the Potential Benefits and Costs of Forming an Economic and Monetary Union," *European Economy*, No. 44, October 1990, p. 11.

considerable and labor mobility is low, recovering from a recession can be difficult, leading to political pressure to ease the single monetary policy, or increased government debt for the country in recession.

Are the members of the EU an optimum currency area? In other words, do the microeconomic gains of greater efficiency outweigh the macroeconomic costs of the loss of the exchange rate as an adjustment tool? Some economists have suggested that the costs exceed the gains for the countries as a whole, and thus monetary union is not a good idea for all countries. However, for a smaller set of countries, the gains may exceed the costs, and monetary union makes sense. Trade among the smaller set of countries is much higher than trade with all countries, so that the efficiency gains are higher.

Challenges for the EMU

The economic effect of the EMU on Europe and the United States will depend mostly on the policy decisions that are made in Europe in the years ahead. The actual move to a single currency, by itself, will likely have only a relatively small effect.

Perhaps the most important monetary policy challenge for the EMU is the ability of the European Central Bank to focus on price stability over the long term. Some are concerned that, over time, monetary policy may become too expansionary given the large number of countries voting on monetary policy and the fact that strong anti-inflationary actions are not well ingrained in countries like Portugal, Spain, and Italy.

The operation of monetary policy may also present some challenges. If there are wide differences in economic growth rates among the EMU countries, it may be difficult to decide on appropriate short-term interest rates. Tightening monetary policy to reduce inflationary pressures may be appropriate for some countries, while loosening monetary policy to stimulate activity may be appropriate for other countries. Therefore, determining monetary policy for the eurozone as a whole, which the European Central Bank is required to do, may be difficult at times.

Although fiscal policy remains the province of national governments, avoidance of excessive budget deficits is important for the success of the EMU. Because large budget deficits can lead to high interest rates and lower economic activity, budgetary restraint is desirable. Most countries have considerable difficulty in reducing budget deficits and debts to meet the convergence criteria of the EMU. Cutting government expenditures, especially on well-established social programs, was (and is) politically difficult. In the face of aging populations in most countries, pressures on budgets may grow even stronger.

Also, the need for structural reform in European countries presents a challenge for EMU countries. Labor-market flexibility is probably the most important structural issue. Real (inflationary adjusted) wage flexibility in Europe is estimated to be half that of the United States. Moreover, labor mobility is quite low in Europe, not only between countries, but also within them. Incentives to work and to acquire new skills are inadequate. Regulations that limit employers' ability to dismiss workers make them unwilling to hire and train new workers. Also, high taxes and generous unemployment benefits provided by European governments contribute to sluggish economies.

Analysts note that structural reforms are necessary for several reasons. First, they would lower the EU's persistently high structural unemployment rate. Second, firms would provide needed flexibility in adjusting to recessions, especially those

THE EURO, TEN YEARS LATER: HOW HAS IT PERFORMED?

During the euro's first decade, it quickly established itself as a global currency without becoming a major rival of the U.S. dollar. Since the launching of the eurozone in 1999, membership has increased from 11 to16 countries, with others showing interest in joining.

The most obvious benefit of the euro is that it removed the cost of exchanging currency for its members. It also eliminated exchange rate risks that companies and individuals bear when investing or trading outside of their currency zones. The reduction in cross-border transaction costs made possible by the euro also has allowed banks to provide a wider array of services that can compete across the eurozone. Moreover, the economic ties that the euro has fostered have helped unite countries throughout Europe, thus reducing political tensions.

However, worries about imbalances have emerged within the euro zone. Germany's substantial trade surplus is offset by big deficits elsewhere, especially in Mediterranean countries that German policymakers had attempted to prevent from joining the eurozone. Consider Spain, for example. By 2008 the country suffered from a painful collapse in its housing market which caused its construction industry to nose dive and helped drive the national unemployment rate to 18 percent. Moreover, Spain realized a sharp deterioration in its balance of trade, with its

domestic firms finding it hard to compete with imports at home and to sell their goods abroad. By being locked into a single currency (the euro), Spain could no longer improve its lost competitiveness by decreasing (devaluing) its exchange rate as it might have done before joining the eurozone.

Another challenge of the eurozone is that its one-size-fits-all monetary policy has not met the needs of all of its members. Although the European Central Bank helped keep the lid on the eurozone's inflation rate at about two percent a year in its first decade, capping inflation in fast growing countries, such as Greece and Spain, required a far tighter monetary policy than in the cooler northern countries like Germany. Interest rates that seemed proper for the eurozone as a whole were too high for sluggish Germany and too low for Spain, Ireland, and Greece which were more prone to inflation. Increasingly, the question has been asked whether such a disparate group of countries can continue to share a common monetary policy.

Although staying in the eurozone has been difficult for some of its members, leaving would be very costly. For example, if Spain dropped out of the eurozone, established a new currency, and reduced its exchange rate, a bank run would likely occur. People would rush to deposit

that effect one or a few countries in the eurozone. If prices and wages were flexible downward, for example, a decline in demand would be followed by lower prices, tending to raise demand. Increased labor mobility would be particularly useful in adjusting to recessions.

Does the Eurozone Need a Bailout Fund?

In 2010 the European Monetary Union faced its toughest challenge since the euro began in 2002. The trouble began when the newly elected Socialist government of Greece revealed that its budget deficit was more than three times as large as previously estimated. The European Union maintained that Greece's financial figures were fudged for years. With debt piling up, investors feared that Greece could not pay its debts. To shore up its financial position, the government of Greece proposed deep budget cuts, a freeze on public sector wages, pension reforms, increased taxes, and efforts to rein in rampant tax evasion. However, the markets remained skeptical about the government's ability to deliver, partly because the austerity programs might crumble as social and their euros with foreign banks to avoid forced conversion into the new, weaker currency. Also, investors would shun the debt of Spain and would demand huge premiums on any loans made to Spain to cover the increased risk of default. Moreover, changing all contracts in euros—such as bank deposits, mortgages, and wage deals—to the new currency would be a nightmare. Although the decision to reduce the currency's exchange value might help make exporters more competitive, it would increase the cost of imports and therefore make domestic consumers poorer. Also, workers would strongly oppose being paid in a weaker currency. In addition, an exit from the euro would not address weak productivity growth and inflexible wages, which are prime causes of low competitiveness.

The 2007–2009 financial crisis was a major test of the eurozone's resiliency, although its implications are unclear. According to critics, the eurozone is a fair weather institution, effective when economies are expanding but poorly equipped to addresses a sinking economy. They note how the lack of a common fiscal policy limited the ability of countries of the eurozone to initiate fiscal stimulus in response to the economic downturn. Conversely, proponents argue that being in the eurozone helped member countries survive the worst financial crisis since the 1930s. They maintain that the instability in the financial markets

during the crisis made the stability of fixed exchange rates appear attractive and that monetary policy was not as powerful a stabilizing tool as had been hoped. Thus, trading an independent monetary policy for the stability of a fixed exchange rate, as occurs in the eurozone, seemed less of a sacrifice. Moreover, proponents argue that without the framework of the eurozone, coordinating a European response to the financial crisis would have been much more difficult. In spite of its shortcomings, the euro did not crack during the financial crisis and eurozone countries did not default on their loans.

Although politicians tend to be disappointed by the euro's failure, so far, to inspire deeper political integration, the euro has succeeded in being accepted throughout much of the world. It has risen to become the world's second most important reserve currency, only behind the U.S. dollar. Moreover, the eurozone is more likely to increase than decrease its membership over the next decade: Most countries of the European Union that remain outside of the eurozone, other than Sweden and Britain, are interested in joining. Apparently, the euro must be doing something right.

Source: "Holding Together: A Special Report on the Euro Area," *The Economist*, June 13, 2009, pp. 51–64.

political discontent increased. Other eurozone countries that faced similar financial difficulties included Spain, Portugal, Ireland, and Italy. Indeed, there were concerns about the long-term viability of the eurozone and its currency, the euro.

While members of the eurozone share a currency and a central bank, they have no institution that can rescue countries in financial difficulty or enforce rules to limit budget deficits and government debt. That is, once a country has become a member of the European Monetary Union, it cannot be forced to adhere to the deficit limit of three percent of GDP and the total debt limit of 60 percent of GDP that applies to prospective member countries. What is needed is greater coordination of eurozone government budgets, which most economists see as essential to avoiding economic crises and guaranteeing the long-term survival of the common currency. Simply put, additional fiscal cooperation in the eurozone is necessary for its stability.

Although most economists thought that a break up of the eurozone was only a remote possibility, they recognized that European governments need to come up with a better mechanism to deal with a financial crisis. A possible interim solution might be the establishment of a European Monetary Fund (EMF). This bailout fund could be financed out of assessed contributions from member country governments. The payments would be larger for governments that miss the deficit limits of the eurozone, an incentive aimed at discouraging excessive debt and deficits. During a financial crisis, a country could call on funds up to the amount it had paid in, providing its fiscal policies were approved by other eurozone members. Help beyond that amount would require an economic adjustment program supervised by eurozone members.

However, critics note that the International Monetary Fund already exists to assist countries facing economic crises. Yet there are two major reasons why eurozone governments might desire their own fund. First, it would put the eurozone in charge of its own destiny. Second, the eurozone members would have greater powers to punish fiscal abusers, for example, by terminating regional aid. In contrast, the IMF can do very little if the country in question does not fulfill its promises, except withhold additional funding.

Skeptics are also concerned that an EMF would undermine the effectiveness of fiscal rules which set limits on government deficits: The bailing out of profligate eurozone members could create "moral hazard;" that is, incentives for governments to act irresponsibly because they would be assured of a financial rescue. However, an EMF might actually toughen the environment for countries violating the rules because an irresponsible country could be punished by other eurozone members. At the writing of this text, the debate on a bailout fund and fiscal-policy cooperation in the eurozone had only just begun, and it could be years before such reforms are made.

For an analysis of the long-term prospects for the euro given the current global economic climate, go to *Exploring Further 8.3.*

North American Free Trade Agreement

The success of Europe in forming the European Union inspired the United States to launch several regional free-trade agreements. During the 1980s, for example, the United States entered into discussions for a free-trade agreement with Canada, which became effective in 1989. This paved the way for Mexico, Canada, and the United States to form the North American Free Trade Agreement, which went into effect in 1994.

NAFTA's visionaries in the United States made a revolutionary gamble. Mexico's authoritarian political system, repressed economy, and resulting poverty were creating problems that could not be contained at the border in perpetuity. Mexican instability would eventually spill over the Rio Grande. The choice was easy: either help Mexico develop as part of an integrated North America, or watch the economic gap widen and the risks for the United States increase.

The establishment of NAFTA was expected to provide each member nation better access to the others' markets, technology, labor, and expertise. In many respects, there were remarkable fits between the nations: The United States would benefit from Mexico's pool of cheap and increasingly skilled labor, while Mexico would benefit from U.S. investment and expertise. However, negotiating the free-trade agreement was difficult because it required meshing two large advanced industrial economies (United States and Canada) with that of a sizable developing nation (Mexico). The huge living-standard gap between Mexico, with its lower wage scale, and the United States and Canada was a politically sensitive issue. One of the main concerns about

TABLE 8.4

WINNERS AND LOSERS IN THE UNITED STATES UNDER FREE TRADE WITH MEXICO

U.S. Winners	U.S. Losers
Higher-skill, higher-tech businesses and their workers benefit from free trade.	Labor-intensive, lower-wage, import—competing businesses lose from reduced tariffs on competing imports.
Labor-intensive businesses that relocate to Mexico benefit by reducing production costs.	Workers in import-competing businesses lose if their businesses close or relocate.
Domestic businesses that use imports as components in the production process save on production costs.	
Consumers in the United States benefit from less expensive products due to increased competition with free trade.	

NAFTA was whether Canada and the United States as developed countries had much to gain from trade liberalization with Mexico. Table 8.4 highlights some of the likely gains and losses of integrating the Mexican and U.S. economies.

NAFTA's Benefits and Costs for Mexico and Canada

NAFTA's benefits to Mexico have been proportionately much greater than for the United States and Canada, because these economies are many times larger than its own. Eliminating trade barriers has led to increases in the production of goods and services for which Mexico has a comparative advantage. Mexico's gains have come at the expense of other low-wage countries, such as Korea and Taiwan. Generally, Mexico has produced more goods that benefit from a low-wage, low-skilled workforce, such as tomatoes, avocados, fruits, vegetables, processed foods, sugar, tuna, and glass; labor-intensive manufactured exports, such as appliances and economy automobiles, have also increased. Rising investment spending in Mexico has helped increase wage incomes and employment, national output, and foreign-exchange earnings; it also has facilitated the transfer of technology.

Although agriculture represents only four to five percent of Mexico's GDP, it supports about a quarter of the country's population. Most Mexican agricultural workers are subsistence farmers who plant grains and oilseeds in small plots that have supported them for generations. Mexican producers of rice, beef, pork, and poultry claim they have been devastated by U.S. competition in the Mexican market resulting from NAFTA. They claim they cannot compete against U.S. imports, where easy credit, better transportation, better technology, and major subsidies give U.S. farmers an unfair advantage.

For Canada, initial concerns about NAFTA had less to do with the flight of low-skilled manufacturing jobs, because trade with Mexico was much smaller than it was for the United States. Instead, the main concern was that closer integration with the U.S. economy would threaten Canada's European-style social welfare model, either by causing certain practices and policies (such as universal health care or a generous minimum wage) to be considered as uncompetitive, or else by imposing downward pressure on the country's base of personal and corporate taxes, thus starving government programs of resources. However, Canada's social-welfare model currently stands intact, and in sharp contrast to the United States. As long as most Canadians are willing to pay the higher taxes necessary to finance generous governmental services, NAFTA poses no threat to the Canadian way of life.

Canada's benefits from NAFTA have been mostly in the form of safeguards: maintenance of its status in international trade, no loss of its current free-trade preferences in the U.S. market, and equal access to Mexico's market. Canada also desired to become part of any process that would eventually broaden market access to Central and South America. Although Canada hoped to benefit from trade with Mexico over time, most researchers have estimated that there have been relatively small gains thus far because of the small amount of existing Canada-Mexico trade.

Economies of scale represent another benefit of NAFTA. A member of NAFTA can overcome the smallness of its domestic markets and realize economies of scale in production by exporting to other members. NAFTA has allowed U.S. manufacturing giants from General Motors to General Electric to use economies of scale for their production lines. Prior to NAFTA, GM's assembly plants in Mexico assembled small volumes of many products, which resulted in high costs and somewhat inferior quality. Now its plants in Mexico specialize in a few high-volume products, resulting in lower costs and higher quality. This result benefits both U.S. and Mexican consumers. For an analysis of the effects of economies of scale in manufacturing, go to *Exploring Further 8.2.*

Although it has succeeded in stimulating increased trade and foreign investment, NAFTA alone has not been enough to modernize Mexico or guarantee prosperity. This result has been a disappointment to many Mexicans. However, trade and investment can do only so much. Since the beginnings of NAFTA, the government of Mexico has struggled to deal with the problems of corruption, poor education, red tape, crumbling infrastructure, lack of credit, and a tiny tax base. These factors greatly influence a country's economic development. For Mexico to become an economically advanced nation, it needs a better educational system, cheaper electricity, better roads, and investment incentives for generating growth—things that NAFTA cannot provide. What NAFTA can provide is additional wealth so that the Mexican government can allocate the gains to things that are necessary. If a government doesn't allocate new wealth correctly, the advantages of free trade quickly erode.

NAFTA's Benefits and Costs for the United States

NAFTA proponents maintain that the agreement has benefited the U.S. economy overall by expanding trade opportunities, reducing prices, increasing competition, and enhancing the ability of U.S. firms to attain economies of large-scale production. The United States has produced more goods that benefit from large amounts of physical capital and a highly-skilled workforce, including chemicals, plastics, cement, sophisticated electronics and communications gear, machine tools, and household appliances. American insurance companies have also benefited from fewer restrictions on foreign insurers operating in Mexico. American companies, particularly larger ones, have realized better access to cheaper labor and parts. Moreover, the United States has benefited from a more reliable source of petroleum, less illegal Mexican immigration, and enhanced Mexican political stability as a result of the nation's increasing wealth. In spite of these benefits, the overall economic gains for the United States are estimated to be modest, because the U.S. economy is 25 times the size of the Mexican economy and many U.S.-Mexican trade barriers were dismantled prior to the implementation of NAFTA.

But even ardent proponents of NAFTA acknowledge that it has inflicted pain on some segments of the U.S. economy. On the business side, the losers have been industries such as citrus growing and sugar that rely on trade barriers to limit imports of low-priced Mexican goods. Other losers are unskilled workers, such as those in the apparel industry, whose jobs are most vulnerable to competition from low-paid workers abroad.

American labor unions have been especially concerned that Mexico's low wage scale encourages U.S. companies to locate in Mexico, resulting in job losses in the United States. Cities such as Muskegon, Michigan, which has thousands of workers cranking out such basic auto parts as piston rings, are especially vulnerable to low-wage Mexican competition. Indeed, the hourly manufacturing compensation for Mexican workers has been a small fraction of that paid to U.S. and Canadian workers.

According to NAFTA critics, there would be a "giant sucking sound" from U.S. companies moving to Mexico to capitalize on Mexico's cheap labor. However, after more than a decade, U.S. companies have not relocated to Mexico in the large numbers forecasted. International trade theory tells us why. As seen in Table 8.5, the productivity of the average American worker (gross domestic product per worker) was $94,120 in 2007 while the productivity of the average Mexican worker was $23,409. The U.S. worker was thus about four times as productive as the Mexican worker. Therefore, employers could pay U.S. workers four times as much as Mexican workers without any difference in cost per unit of output. Also, companies operating in the United States benefit from a more stable legal and political system than exists in Mexico. Simply put, the lower wages of Mexican workers have not motivated large numbers of U.S. companies to move to Mexico.

Another concern is Mexico's environmental regulations, criticized as being less stringent than those of the United States. American labor and environmental activists fear that polluting Mexican plants might cause plants in the United States, which are cleaner but more expensive to operate, to close down. Environmentalists also fear that increased Mexican growth will bring increased air and water pollution. However,

TABLE 8.5

GROSS DOMESTIC PRODUCT, EMPLOYMENT AND LABOR PRODUCTIVITY, 2007

Country	Gross Domestic Product (billions)	Employment (millions)*	Labor Productivity**
United States	$13,751	146.1	$94,120
United Kingdom	2,772	30.2	91,788
Germany	3,317	39.8	83,342
Canada	1,330	16.5	80,606
Australia	821	10.2	80,490
Japan	4,384	63.8	68,714
Mexico	1,023	43.7	23,409
China	3,206	764.0	4,196

*Employment = (1 − unemployment rate) × labor force
**Labor productivity = GDP/number of persons employed. Due to rounding, numbers are not precise.

Source: World Bank Group, Data and Statistics, **http://www.worldbank.org/data**. See also Central Intelligence Agency, *World Fact Book* and International Monetary Fund, *International Financial Statistics*.

NAFTA advocates counter that a more prosperous Mexico might be more willing and able to enforce its environmental regulations; more economic openness is also associated with production closer to state-of-the-art technology, which tends to be cleaner.

Proponents of NAFTA view it as an opportunity to create an enlarged productive base for the entire region through a new allocation of productive factors that would permit each nation to contribute to a larger pie. However, an increase in U.S. and Canadian trade with Mexico resulting from the reduction of trade barriers under NAFTA would partly displace U.S. and Canadian trade with other nations, including those in Central and South America, the Caribbean, and Asia. Some of this displacement would be expected to result in a loss of welfare associated with trade diversion—the shift from a lower-cost supplier to a higher-cost supplier. But because the displacement was expected to be small, it was projected to have a minor negative effect on the U.S. and Canadian economies.

In order to make the NAFTA treaty more agreeable to a skeptical U.S. Congress, President Bill Clinton negotiated side agreements with Mexico and Canada. Concerning the environment, an agency was established in Canada to investigate environmental abuses in any of the three countries. Fines or trade sanctions can be levied on countries that fail to enforce their own environmental laws. As for labor, an agency was established in the United States to investigate labor abuses if two of the three countries agree. Fines or trade sanctions can be imposed if countries fail to enforce minimum-wage standards, child-labor laws, or worker-safety rules.

On balance and to date, the effects of NAFTA on the U.S. economy have been relatively small. These effects have included increases in overall U.S. income and increases in U.S. trade with Mexico, but little impact on overall levels of unemployment, although with some displacement of workers from sector to sector. For particular industries or products with a greater exposure to intra-NAFTA trade, effects have generally been greater, including displacement effects on individual workers.

What are the effects of NAFTA concerning trade creation and trade diversion? As seen in Table 8.6, over the period 1994–1998, the flow of U.S. imports from Canada was estimated to have increased by $1.074 trillion because of NAFTA, with $690 billion of that trade expansion representing trade creation and $384 billion representing trade diversion—imports that previously came into the United States from other lower-cost countries but now come from Canada, the higher-cost producer. Overall,

TABLE 8.6

TRADE EFFECTS OF NAFTA: TRADE CREATION AND TRADE DIVERSION (THOUSANDS OF DOLLARS)

Trade Flow	Trade Expansion	Trade Creation	Trade Diversion
U.S. imports from Canada	$1,074,186	$689,997	$384,189
U.S. imports from Mexico	334,912	284,774	50,138
Canadian imports from the United States	63,656	38,444	25,212
Canadian imports from Mexico	167,264	3,321	163,943
Mexican imports from the United States	77,687	50,036	27,651
Mexican imports from Canada	28,001	902	27,099

Source: From David Karemera and Kalu Ohah, "An Industrial Analysis of Trade Creation and Trade Diversion of NAFTA," *Journal of Economic Integration*, September 1998, pp. 419–420. See also Gary Clyde Hufbauer and Jeffrey Schott, *NAFTA Revisited: Achievements and Challenges*, Washington, DC, Institute for International Economics, 2005.

the table suggests that NAFTA resulted in greater trade creation than trade diversion for the United States, thus improving its welfare. This is consistent with a majority of studies which have found NAFTA to be trade creating rather than trade diverting.[8]

It is in politics, not economics, that NAFTA has had its biggest impact. The trade agreement has come to symbolize a close embrace between the United States and Mexico. Given the history of hostility between the two countries, this embrace is remarkable. Its cause was the realization by U.S. officials that their chance of curbing the flow of illegal immigrants would be far greater were their southern neighbors wealthy instead of poor. Put simply, the United States bought itself an ally with NAFTA.

NAFTA and Trade Diversion: Textiles and Apparel

Textiles and apparel provide an example of trade diversion resulting from NAFTA. Although the NAFTA-created trade diversion initially aided Mexico's textile industry, the benefits were not permanent. When U.S. barriers on imports of Mexican textiles were eliminated under NAFTA, Mexican producers could compete in the U.S. market, even though other nonmember countries could produce textiles more cheaply. By the late 1990s, Mexico increased market share so rapidly against China that it briefly became the dominant textile supplier to the United States. But, China had developed a highly competitive textile export industry, helping it become the world's low-cost producer. Also, barriers to China's textile exports were reduced when it joined the World Trade Organization in 2001. As the playing field leveled, China increased U.S. sales at Mexico's expense. Simply put, the early trade diversion resulting from NAFTA revitalized Mexico's textile industry, but the gains could not be sustained. As subsequent trade agreements eroded Mexico's preferred position, NAFTA no longer provided Mexican textiles producers much benefit. It is hard to predict what will happen to Mexico's textile and apparel companies now that China and other countries have increasing access to the U.S. market.[9]

Mexico Retaliates After the United States Closes Its Highways to Mexican Cargo Trucks

Achieving a global market isn't as easy as it looks. Consider the conflict between free traders, who desire the efficiency of a deregulated trucking system, and social activists who are concerned about highway safety. Or is it outright protectionism that is the real motive?

For decades, the safety of the trucking system has been of concern to Americans and Canadians. The United States and Canada have laws on their books limiting the number of consecutive hours a trucker can be on the road; truck drivers are tested for drug or alcohol use; and trucks are inspected for safety requirements. In contrast, Mexico has no roadside inspection program or drug testing for drivers. It does not require logbooks or have weighing stations for trucks. It doesn't have a requirement for the labeling of hazardous or toxic cargo, or a system to verify drivers' licenses.

---

[8]See Daniel Lederman, William Maloney, and Luis Serven, *Lessons from NAFTA for Latin America and the Caribbean Countries: A Summary of Research Findings*, The World Bank, Washington, DC, December 2003 and Sidney Weintraub, ed., *NAFTA's Impact on North America: The First Decade*, Center for Strategic and International Studies, Washington, DC, 2004.

[9]William Gruben, "NAFTA, Trade Diversion and Mexico's Textiles and Apparel Boom and Bust," *Southwest Economy*, Federal Reserve Bank of Dallas, September-October 2006, pp. 11–15.

According to NAFTA, the United States, Mexico, and Canada agreed to open their roads to each other's rigs. However, in 1995 President Bill Clinton imposed restrictions on Mexican trucks, confining them to stateside areas within 20 miles of the Mexican border. Mexican goods traveling farther than this arbitrary zone had to be loaded onto American trucks, a practice that pleased the U.S. Teamsters (truckers) union. Moreover, in 2002, the U.S. government introduced 22 additional safety requirements that Mexican trucks would have to meet, a measure that was discriminatory as these requirements were not applied to U.S. and Canadian carriers operating in the United States.

In response to these measures, a NAFTA arbitration panel ruled that the United States was in violation of its treaty obligations. The result was an agreement in 2007 that established a pilot program that allowed a limited number of Mexican carriers into the United States under rigid safety regulations. After 18 months, the program proved that Mexican carriers were as safe as their U.S. and Canadian counterparts and that transportation cost savings provided benefits for American consumers. That was bad news for the Teamsters union.

In violation of NAFTA, the U.S. government terminated the pilot program in 2009, thus closing the southern border of the United States to Mexican trucking. Mexico retaliated by releasing a list of 89 U.S. products that would face new tariffs of 10 to 45 percent. Among the states hit hardest by Mexico's tariffs were California, Oregon, and Washington, which exported a variety of agricultural products to Mexico. With the cost of imported American products higher, Mexicans substituted these products with goods from Latin America, Europe, and Canada. Clearly, American agricultural producers paid a dear price for the protectionism granted the Teamsters union. At the writing of this text, it remains to be seen if the trucking dispute will be resolved.

Is NAFTA an Optimum Currency Area?

The increasing convergence of the NAFTA countries has stimulated a debate on the issues of adopting a common currency and forming an American monetary union among Canada, Mexico, and the United States. Of central relevance to the economic suitability of such a monetary union is the concept of the optimum currency area, as discussed in this chapter.

According to the theory of optimum currency areas, the greater the linkages between countries, the more suitable it is for them to adopt a single official currency. One such linkage is the degree of economic integration among the three NAFTA members. As expected, trade within NAFTA is quite substantial. Canada and Mexico rank as the first and second, respectively, largest trading partners of the United States in terms of trade turnover (imports plus exports). Likewise, the United States is the largest trading partner of Canada and Mexico.

Another linkage is the similarity of economic structures among the three NAFTA members. Canada's advanced industrial economy resembles that of the United States. In the past decade, Canada's average real income per capita, inflation rate, and interest rate were very close to those of the United States. However, Mexico is a growing economy that is aspiring to maintain economic and financial stability with a much lower average real income per capita and significantly higher inflation and interest rates compared with those of Canada and the United States. Moreover, the value of the peso relative to the U.S. dollar has been quite volatile, although the peso has been more stable against the Canadian dollar. Other problems endured by Mexico

FROM NAFTA TO CAFTA

TRADE CONFLICTS

In addition to complicated multilateral trade negotiations involving the World Trade Organization, the United States has sought simpler agreements with a smaller number of countries. In particular, the United States has pursued trade liberalization with its neighbors in South and Central America. This came to fruition in 2003 when the United States and Chile signed a bilateral free-trade agreement, and in 2005 when the United States and five nations of Central America signed the Central American Free Trade Agreement (CAFTA). Let us take a brief look at these trade liberalization measures.

Market access was a major reason behind the U.S.-Chile free-trade agreement. When the agreement went into effect in 2004, 87 percent of U.S.-Chilean bilateral trade in consumer and industrial products became duty-free immediately, with the rest receiving reduced tariff treatment over time. Some 75 percent of U.S. farm exports will enter Chile duty-free by 2008, and duties on all goods will be fully phased out by 2016. The agreement also phases out export subsidies on agricultural products and increases market access for a broad range of services including banking and insurance. Proponents of the U.S.-Chile free-trade agreement maintained that it offered both economic and political benefits, with Chile seen as a crucial foothold in South America, a region historically linked closely with Europe and Asia.

Besides market access, political considerations motivated the United States to form a free trade agreement with Central America. In the 1980s, Central America was characterized by civil war, chaos, dictators, and communist insurgencies. By the first decade of the 2000s, the region consisted of fragile democracies that embraced freedom and economic reform. CAFTA was viewed as a way for the United States to support freedom, democracy, and economic reform in its own neighborhood.

CAFTA breaks down most trade barriers between the United States and the five nations of Central America— Costa Rica, El Salvador, Guatemala, Honduras, and Nicaragua plus the Caribbean country of the Dominican Republic. Most products from this region were entering the United States duty-free prior to the agreement; thus, the United States gave up little in liberalizing trade with Central America. CAFTA makes sure that about 80 percent of U.S. exports become duty-free in Central America. According to the American Farm Bureau Federation, CAFTA will likely increase U.S. farm exports by some $1.5 billion a year. American manufacturers will also benefit, especially in sectors like information technology products, agricultural and construction equipment, paper products, and medical and scientific equipment.

To be sure, CAFTA is not perfect. It is really a "freer trade" rather than a free-trade agreement. Certain special interests were successful in creating exceptions to the principle of free trade. Nevertheless, President George Bush maintained that by strengthening economic ties with Central America, progress would be made toward its political and social reform.

are high levels of external debt, balance of payments deficits, and weak financial markets.

Some analysts are skeptical of whether Mexico's adoption of the U.S. dollar as its official currency would be beneficial. If Mexico adopted the dollar, its central bank would be unable to use monetary policy to impact production and employment in the face of economic shocks, which might further weaken its economy. However, adopting the dollar would offer Mexico several advantages, including the achievement of long-term credibility in Mexican financial markets, long-term monetary stability and reduced interest rates, and increased discipline and confidence as a result of reducing inflation to U.S. levels. Put simply, most observers feel that the case for Mexican participation in a North American optimum currency area is questionable on economic grounds. However, the Mexican government has shown interest in dollarizing its economy in an attempt to develop stronger political ties to the United States.

Canadians have generally expressed dissatisfaction concerning adoption of the U.S. dollar as their official currency. In particular, Canadians are concerned about the loss of national sovereignty that such a policy would entail. They also note that there is no added benefit of credibility to monetary and fiscal discipline, since Canada, like the United States, is already committed to achieving low inflation, low interest rates, and a low level of debt relative to gross domestic product. The case for Canadian participation in any North American currency area is less strong on political grounds than economically. At the writing of this text, the likelihood of a North American currency area in the near term appeared to be dim.

Free Trade Area of the Americas

"Never in America has there been a matter requiring more good judgment or more vigilance, or demanding a clearer and more thorough examination." So said Jose Marti, Cuba's independence hero of the first effort by the United States to unite the two halves of the Americas in 1889. By the first decade of the 2000s, the region's governments were still stumbling on toward that goal, but hardly in step.

Attempting to widen the scope of North American economic interdependence, in 1994 the United States convened the Summit of the Americas, which was attended by 34 nations in North and South America; this included all of the nations in the hemisphere except Cuba. The cornerstone of the conference was a call for the creation of a **Free Trade Area of the Americas (FTAA)**. The idea dates back to the 1820s, when Henry Clay, speaker of the House and secretary of state, sought to strengthen U.S. ties with the new Latin republics.

If established, an FTAA would represent the largest trading bloc in the world. It would create a market of more than 850 million consumers with a combined income of more than $14 trillion. It also would level the playing field for U.S. exporters who, at the turn of the century, faced trade barriers more than three times higher than exporters to the United States. The United States tangibly demonstrated its commitment to this objective by entering into free-trade agreements with Chile in 2003 and five Central American countries in 2005, thus providing momentum for negotiations with other nations in Latin America.

Over the past two decades, Latin America has embraced progressively more open trade policies, intraregionally and with the world, as part of its overall economic platform. The larger economies of Latin America, once known for their collective indebtedness, are considered to be among the more promising emerging markets for trade and investment opportunities now in the 2000s. Three economic-policy shifts in Latin America paved the way for this new perspective: reduced roles for government in managing the economies, with greater reliance placed on markets, private ownership, and deregulation; use of conventional and generally restrictive macroeconomic policies to promote economic growth and stability; and the failure of the import-substitution model of development of the 1960s and 1970s. Table 8.7 identifies the major regional trade agreements that exist throughout the Americas.

TABLE 8.7

MAJOR WESTERN HEMISPHERE REGIONAL TRADE AGREEMENTS

Agreement	Members	Year Effective
Free Trade Area of the Americas	34 countries	Negotiating
Central American Free Trade Agreement (CAFTA)	Costs Rica, El Salvador, Guatemala, Honduras Nicaragua, Dominican Republic, United States	2005
North American Free Trade Agreement (NAFTA)	Canada, Mexico, United States	1994
Southern Cone Common Market (MERCOSUR)	Argentina, Brazil, Paraguay, Uruguay	1991
Caribbean Community and Common Market	Antigua, Bahamas, Barbados, Barbuda, Belize, Dominica, Grenada, Guyana, Haiti, Jamaica, Montserrat, St. Kitts, Nevis, St. Lucia, St. Vincent, Surinam, Trinidad, and Tobago	1973
Andean Community	Bolivia, Colombia, Ecuador, Peru, Venezuela	1969
Central American Common Market	Costa Rica, El Salvador, Guatemala, Honduras, Nicaragua	1961

However, there are obstacles that need to be addressed in order for the FTAA to become a reality. One challenge involves the FTAA's allowance for other trade agreements in the hemisphere. Countries in the hemisphere are members of 21 free-trade agreements as well as four customs unions that span the region. Although these agreements can become a "spaghetti bowl" of conflicting arrangements, an FTAA presents an opportunity to simplify these arrangements under a single agreement. Another concern is that smaller partners in the hemisphere should be given special assistance. Skeptics note that an FTAA should not merely reflect the interests of the hemisphere's two largest economies, the United States and Brazil.

Yet another challenge revolves around agricultural issues. Agriculture makes up, on average, seven percent of Latin America's GDP and a significantly larger share of its exports.

In FTAA negotiations, the United States has refused to lower subsidies and tariffs that protect U.S. farmers, arguing that those protections should be negotiated in global trade agreements, not regional ones, because the European Union is the biggest subsidizer of agriculture. But Brazil contends that its farmers cannot compete in U.S. markets, so it demands that subsidies and tariffs be on the bargaining table. However, U.S. farmers fear that a flood of cheap agricultural products from Brazil and other Latin American nations would occur if trade barriers were removed, which would wipe them out. Other difficult negotiating issues for the FTAA involve honoring intellectual property rights and the opening of government contracts to foreign bidders.

These differences have kept the region's governments from uniting the two halves of the Americas. To keep the region on the road to forming an FTAA, in 2003 the governments put together a less ambitious compromise. Out went the wide-ranging accord they had spent years negotiating. Instead, they sought a flexible, 34-country agreement, comprising only a few common standards and some tariff cuts. In spite of this strategy, the FTAA languished in 2005 when its members were unable to reach an agreement on free trade. Instead, a moratorium was placed on future talks until things change on the global scene.

The FTAA is perhaps the most ambitious economic initiative in the Western Hemisphere's history and one that would have a tremendous effect on the lives of its inhabitants. Many roadblocks and detours will likely have to be faced before it is completed.

Asia-Pacific Economic Cooperation

Since 1989, the United States has been a member of the **Asia-Pacific Economic Cooperation (APEC)**, which also includes Australia, Brunei, Canada, Chile, China, Indonesia, Japan, Malaysia, Mexico, New Zealand, Papua New Guinea, the Philippines, Singapore, South Korea, Taiwan, and Thailand. In 1993, leaders of the APEC countries put forth their vision of an Asia-Pacific economic community in which barriers to trade and investment in the region would be eliminated by the year 2020. All countries would begin to liberalize at a common date, but the pace of implementation would take into account the differing levels of economic development among APEC economies: the industrialized countries would achieve free trade and investment no later than 2010, and the developing economies no later than 2020. It remains to be seen whether the APEC goal of economic integration will have to be pushed back.

Transition Economies

Trade preferences have also been extended to commercial and financial practices involving nations making the transition from a centrally planned economy to a market economy; such economies are known as **transition economies**. Prior to the economic reforms in Eastern European nations in the 1990s, these nations were classified as nonmarket economies; the Western nations, including the United States,

TABLE 8.8

GDP Per Capita* for the Transition Economies, 2007 (in dollars)

FORMER REPUBLICS OF THE SOVIET UNION		CENTRAL AND EASTERN EUROPEAN COUNTRIES	
Estonia	$18,330	Slovenia	$26,230
Lithuania	16,830	Czech Republic	22,690
Latvia	15,790	Hungary	17,470
Russia	14,330	Slovakia	19,220
Belarus	10,750	Croatia	15,540
Kazakstan	9,600	Poland	15,500
Ukraine	6,810	Romania	12,350
Azerbaijan	6,570	Boznia-Herzegovina	8,020
Armenia	5,680	Albania	7,240
Moldova	2,800		
Uzbekistan	2,430		
Kyrgyz Republic	1,980		
Tajikistan	1,710		

*At purchasing power parity.

Source: The World Bank Group, **http://www.worldbank.org/**. Select "Data," "By Topic," and "Purchasing Power Parity."

TABLE 8.9

ECONOMIES IN TRANSITION: 2009 INDEX OF
ECONOMIC FREEDOM*

Economy	Overall Score	
Hong Kong	90.0	
Singapore	87.1	Mostly free
United States	80.7	
Lithuania	70.0	
South Korea	68.1	
Jordan	65.4	
France	63.3	Moderately free
Poland	60.3	
Brazil	56.7	
China	53.2	
Angola	47.0	
Zimbabwe	22.7	Mostly unfree
North Korea	2.0	

*Based on 10 broad economic factors in 161 economies across 10 specific
freedoms: business freedom, trade freedom, monetary freedom, freedom
from government, fiscal freedom, property rights, investment freedom,
financial freedom, freedom from corruption, and labor freedom.

Source: From The Heritage Foundation, *2009 Index of Economic Freedom
Rankings*, available at **http://www.heritage.org/index**.

were classified as market economies. Table 8.8 shows
the gross domestic product per capita for the transition
economies as of 2007. Let us consider the major features
of these economic systems.

In a **market economy**, the commercial decisions
of independent buyers and sellers acting in their
own interest govern both domestic and international
trade. Market-determined prices value alternatives and
allocate scarce resources. This allocation means that
prices play rationing and signaling roles that make
the availability of goods consistent with buyer preferences and purchasing power.

In a **nonmarket economy** (one that is centrally
planned), there is less regard for market considerations. State planning and control govern foreign and
sometimes domestic trade. The central plan often controls the prices and output of goods bought and sold,
with small recognition given to considerations of cost
and efficiency. The state fixes prices to ration arbitrary
quantities among buyers, and these prices are largely
insulated from foreign-trade influences. Given these
different pricing mechanisms, trade between market
economies and centrally planned economies can be difficult. Because market-determined prices underlie the
basis for trade according to the theory of comparative
advantage, the theory has little to say about how non-
market economies carry out their international trade policies. Table 8.9 shows the 2009
Index of Economic Freedom for selected economies.

The Transition Toward a Market-Oriented Economy

After a half century of state control, the countries under Soviet hegemony were
backward and isolated, in need of major transformation. In 1989, many of these
countries redefined themselves by moving toward democracy and economic reform.
Countries such as Hungary and the Czech Republic discarded their centrally controlled state economies and moved toward systems in which private ownership of
property predominated and most resources were allocated through markets. Freed
from communism, these countries sought a path to prosperity that lay in emulating
the West's open, free market economic model.[10]

The fundamental motivation for change in the 27 countries once under Soviet
control was the failure of their economies to generate a high standard of living for
their people. The economic policies pursued in these countries failed because they
were unable to provide adequate incentives for producers to efficiently supply the
goods and services that consumers wanted to purchase. Widespread use of price
controls, reliance on inefficient public enterprises, extensive barriers to competition
with the rest of the world, and government regulation of production and investment

---

[10]This section is drawn from Julia Carter, "After the Fall: Globalizing the Remnants of the Communist
Bloc," *Economic Letter*, Federal Reserve Bank of Dallas, February 2007, pp.1–5.

all obstructed the normal operation of markets. The lack of enforceable property rights severely restricted incentives for entrepreneurs.

For the communistic countries, central plans decided production levels. As a result, there was no reason to expect that the output produced would meet the wants or needs of the people. Shortages and surpluses occurred frequently, but managers had little motivation to modify their output as long as quotas were realized. Government investment choices led to the underproduction of consumer goods and widespread rationing. Incentives to innovate were almost completely absent, except in the defense sector; but the countries were unable to transfer their high levels of defense technology into improvements for consumers. Inefficient state-owned enterprises were common, and public funds were channeled into favored industries irrespective of the economic consequences. Over time, the weaknesses of the political and economic systems of the communistic countries and the contrasting success of the market-oriented systems became obvious. This dichotomy created pressure that led to the collapse of some of the Soviet bloc's governments.

However, the reforming countries of Eastern Europe have not marched in unison. The Czech Republic, Lithuania, Estonia, Georgia, Hungary, Slovenia, and Bulgaria have substantially moved toward capitalism and have made significant progress in becoming global players. These countries have brought themselves close to the world standard in monetary discipline, openness to trade, and limited roles of government in the economy. They have decreased red tape for business, deregulated their financial sector, increased flexibility of labor markets, welcomed foreign investment, protected intellectual property rights, and fought social corruption.

Although some former Soviet republics have made significant economic and political reforms, others continue to struggle with the vestiges of their communist pasts. Countries that have not reformed as much include Russia, Poland, Ukraine, Belarus, and Turkmenistan. Their ways of doing business have not changed much since Soviet times. Government interference and ownership are widely practiced. Lack of property rights and social corruption are particularly apparent.

By several economic measures, the countries pursuing economic and political freedom have done much better. Since 1989, the freer countries have realized per-capita incomes that are one and a half times the per capita incomes of the unfree or repressed nations. The freer countries have also realized higher levels of economic growth, as seen in Figure 8.3. Moreover, they have done better at containing inflation, and thus preserving their currencies' value.

Why haven't all of the former Soviet bloc countries made more progress in moving toward globalization and capitalism? Countries are more likely to embrace these concepts if they expect to benefit with jobs, growth, and higher living standards. History shows that global capitalism delivers, but not always in the short run. Communism left a legacy of shoddy production techniques, underemployment and higher costs, so the former Soviet bloc countries faced hurdles in entering the global marketplace.

For example, although workers of the former Soviet bloc countries tend to be better educated than workers in China and India, they are also more costly, even taking into account their higher productivity. For every dollar a U.S. employee earns, a worker gets 73 cents in Poland and 58 cents in Hungary. But China's and India's unit labor costs are much lower, at about 20 percent of U.S. costs. Moreover, workers of the former Soviet bloc countries do not match workers of Western Europe or the United States in years of schooling or instructional quality. Thus, the

FIGURE 8.3

FOR THE FORMER SOVIET BLOC COUNTRIES, FREER ECONOMIES GROW FASTER

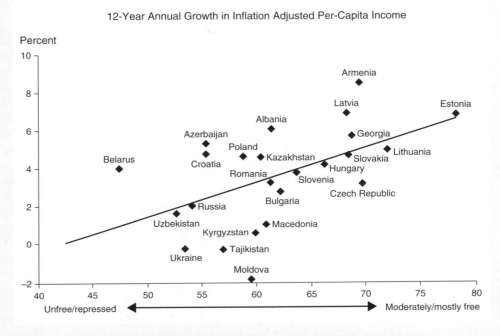

From 1993 to 2005, economic growth was strongest for the freer countries of the former Soviet bloc.

Source: Data taken from Julia Carter, "After the Fall: Globalizing the Remnants of the Communist Bloc," Economic Letter, Federal Reserve Bank of Dallas, February 2007, p. 5.

former communist countries occupy a difficult middle position—not cheap enough to compete with China and India, and not developed enough to compete with the United States and Western Europe. Furthermore, the infrastructures of the former Soviet bloc countries (roads, schools, hospitals) are badly in need of improvement, while social corruption hinders meaningful reforms. Thus, the former Soviet bloc countries have often delayed or slowed globalization and economic reform while addressing the backlog of development needs.

Undoing the repressive legacy of communism has proved to be a daunting task. Two decades after the fall of the Soviet Union, an economic divide has formed along Russia's frontier. On countries to the east, except the Baltic republics, economies have not broken free of government shackles. Countries to the west, further along in progress toward globalization and economic freedom, have oriented themselves to Europe, with many joining the European Union. The vast economic space that was once the Soviet empire is likely to bear the marks of this split for decades to come.

Russia and the World Trade Organization

Although Russia has been slow to move towards globalization and capitalism, since 1995 it has been negotiating terms for accession to the World Trade Organization.

Progress toward accession has been uneven over the years, with negotiations to date consisting of detailed examinations of Russia's trade policies and its legal and administrative framework for trade.

Russia's WTO accession negotiations have been slow for several reasons. Still in transition from a nonmarket to a market economy since the breakup of the Soviet Union, Russia faces the ongoing challenges of restructuring its economy, privatizing government-owned industries, and implementing market-oriented economic reforms. Reaching political consensus on reforms—particularly on reforms that would open the Russian economy to more efficient foreign competitors—has often proved difficult and time-consuming. A 1998 economic crisis, precipitated by a loss of the financial markets' confidence in Russia, was a significant setback that forced Russian policy-makers to prioritize domestic economic-crisis management as their top priority. Also, rising world oil prices beginning in 2000 (oil is Russia's major export) generated a windfall budget surplus and slowed the impetus in Russia for domestic economic reforms and integration into the global economy.

The goal of WTO membership has been the cornerstone of Russian economic policies to integrate Russia into the global economy following decades of Soviet self-imposed isolation. Although the WTO does not require that its members enact specific legislation, its members have requested that Russia develop new laws and regulations in line with international standards, improve enforcement of regulations already compliant with WTO rules, and agree to terms that will open Russian markets to foreign competition before Russia's accession application is approved. Issues that must be addressed include Russian agricultural subsidies, the Russian customs system, foreign investment regulations, market access for Russia's service sectors, Russian technical barriers to trade, and Russia's need to improve its administration and enforcement of intellectual property rights.

Accession to the WTO generally enjoys broad political support in Russia. Russian officials estimate that Russian trade gains could total as much as $18 billion over five years following WTO accession as a result of reduced tariff and nontariff trade barriers with Russia's trading partners. However, critics fear that an open-trade regime could have an adverse impact on many Russian industries that are not globally competitive, such as autos, steel, and agriculture.

Summary

1. Trade liberalization has assumed two main forms. One involves the reciprocal reduction of trade barriers on a nondiscriminatory basis, as seen in the operation of the World Trade Organization. The other approach involves the establishment by a group of nations of regional trading arrangements among themselves. The European Union and the North American Free Trade Agreement are examples of regional trading arrangements.

2. The term *economic interdependence* refers to the process of eliminating restrictions on international trade, payments, and factor input mobility. The stages of economic interdependence are (a) free-trade area, (b) customs union, (c) common market, (d) economic union, and (e) monetary union.

3. The welfare implications of economic interdependence can be analyzed from two perspectives. First are the static welfare effects, resulting from trade creation and trade diversion. Second are the dynamic welfare effects that stem from greater competition, economies of scale, and the stimulus to investment spending that economic interdependence makes possible.

4. From a static perspective, the formation of a customs union yields net welfare gains if the consumption and production benefits of trade

creation more than offset the loss in world efficiency owing to trade diversion.

5. Several factors influence the extent of trade creation and trade diversion: (a) the degree of competitiveness that member-nation economies have prior to formation of the customs union, (b) the number and size of its members, and (c) the size of its external tariff against nonmembers.

6. The European Union was originally founded in 1957 by the Treaty of Rome. Today it consists of 27 members. By 1992, the EU had essentially reached the common-market stage of interdependence. Empirical evidence suggests that the EU has realized welfare benefits in trade creation that have outweighed the losses from trade diversion. One of the stumbling blocks confronting the EU has been its common agricultural policy, which has required large government subsidies to support European farmers. The Maastricht Treaty of 1991 called for the formation of a monetary union for eligible EU members, which was initiated in 1999.

7. The formation of the European Monetary Union in 1999 resulted in the creation of a single currency (the euro) and a European Central Bank. With a common central bank, the central bank of each participating nation performs operations similar to those of the 12 regional Federal Reserve Banks in the United States.

8. Much of the analysis of the benefits and costs of Europe's common currency is based on the theory of optimum currency areas. According to this theory, the gains to be had from sharing a currency across countries' boundaries include more uniform prices, lower transactions costs, greater certainty for investors, and enhanced competition. These gains must be compared against the loss of an independent monetary policy and the option of changing the exchange rate.

9. In 1989, the United States and Canada successfully negotiated a free-trade agreement under which free trade between the two nations would be phased in over a 10-year period. This agreement was followed by negotiation of the North American Free Trade Agreement by the United States, Mexico, and Canada.

10. By the 1990s, nations of Eastern Europe and the former Soviet Union were making the transition from centrally planned economies to market economies. These transitions reflected the failure of central planning systems to provide either political freedom or a decent standard of living.

11. It is widely agreed that the transition of the economies of Eastern Europe and the former Soviet Union into healthy market economies will require major restructuring: (a) establishing sound fiscal and monetary policies; (b) removing price controls; (c) opening economies to competitive market forces; (d) establishing private property rights and a legal system to protect those rights; and (e) reducing government's involvement in the economy.

Key Concepts & Terms

- Asia-Pacific Economic Cooperation (APEC) (p. 326)
- Benelux (p. 297)
- Common agricultural policy (p. 307)
- Common market (p. 297)
- Convergence criteria (p. 305)
- Customs union (p. 297)
- Dynamic effects of economic integration (p. 299)
- Economic integration (p. 296)
- Economic union (p. 297)

- Euro (p. 305)
- European Monetary Union (EMU) (p. 305)
- European Union (p. 297)
- Export subsidies (p. 307)
- Free-trade area (p. 297)
- Free Trade Area of the Americas (FTAA) (p. 324)
- Maastricht Treaty (p. 305)
- Market economy (p. 327)
- Monetary union (p. 297)
- Nonmarket economy (p. 327)

- North American Free Trade Agreement (NAFTA) (p. 297)
- Optimum currency area (p. 311)
- Regional trading arrangement (p. 295)
- Static effects of economic integration (p. 299)
- Trade-creation effect (p. 301)
- Trade-diversion effect (p. 301)
- Transition economies (p. 326)
- Variable levies (p. 307)

Study Questions

1. How do the static welfare effects of trade creation and trade diversion relate to a nation's decision to form a customs union? Of what importance to this decision are the dynamic welfare effects?
2. Why has the so-called common agricultural policy been a controversial issue for the European Union?
3. What is meant by the term *economic integration*? What are the various stages that economic integration can take?
4. What are the welfare effects of trade creation and trade diversion for the European Union, as determined by empirical studies?
5. How can trade liberalization exist on a nondiscriminatory basis versus a discriminatory basis? What are some actual examples of each?
6. Table 8.10 depicts the supply and demand schedules of gloves for Portugal, a small nation that is unable to affect the world price. On graph paper, draw the supply and demand schedules for gloves in Portugal.
   a. Assume that Germany and France can supply gloves to Portugal at a price of $2 and $3, respectively. With free trade, which nation exports gloves to Portugal? How many gloves does Portugal produce, consume, and import?
   b. Suppose Portugal levies a 100-percent nondiscriminatory tariff on its glove imports. Which nation exports gloves to Portugal? How many gloves will Portugal produce, consume, and import?

TABLE 8.10

SUPPLY AND DEMAND FOR GLOVES: PORTUGAL

Price ($)	Quantity Supplied	Quantity Demanded
0	0	18
1	2	16
2	4	14
3	6	12
4	8	10
5	10	8
6	12	6
7	14	4
8	16	2
9	18	0

   c. Suppose Portugal forms a customs union with France. Determine the trade-creation effect and the trade-diversion effect of the customs union. What is the customs union's overall effect on the welfare of Portugal?
   d. Suppose instead that Portugal forms a customs union with Germany. Is this a trade-diverting or trade-creating customs union? By how much does the customs union increase or decrease the welfare of Portugal?

Exploring Further   8.1

Government Procurement Policy and the European Union

Another sensitive issue confronting the EU has been government procurement policies. Governments are major purchasers of goods and services, ranging from off-the-shelf items such as paper and pencils to major projects such as nuclear power facilities and defense systems. Government procurement has been used by EU nations to support national and regional firms and industries for several reasons: (1) national security (for example, aerospace); (2) compensation for local communities near environmentally damaging public industries (such as nuclear fuels); (3) support for emerging high-tech industries (for example, lasers); and (4) politics (as in assistance to highly visible industries, such as automobiles).

Although there may be sound justifications for purchasing locally, by the 1980s it was widely recognized that EU public procurement policies served as formidable barriers to foreign competitors; individual EU nations permitted only a minor fraction, often about two percent, of government contracts to be awarded to foreign suppliers. By downplaying intra–EU competition, governments paid more than they should for the products they needed and, in so doing, supported suboptimal producers within the community.

When the EU became a common market in 1992, it removed discrimination in government procurement by permitting all EU competitors to bid for public contracts. The criteria for awarding

FIGURE EF 8.1

OPENING UP OF GOVERNMENT PROCUREMENT

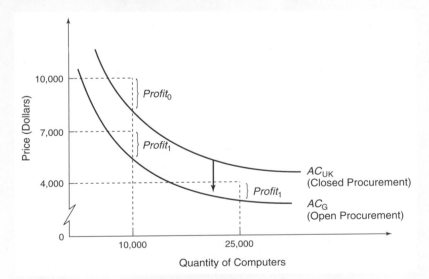

Procurement liberalization allows the UK government to import computers from Germany, the low-cost EU producer. Cost savings result from the trade effect, the competition effect, and the restructuring (economies-of-scale) effect.

public contracts are specified as either the lowest price or the most economically advantageous tender that includes such factors as product quality, delivery dates, and the reliability of supplies.

It was believed that savings from a more competitive government procurement policy would come from three sources: EU governments would be able to purchase from the cheapest foreign suppliers (static trade effect). Increased competition would occur as domestic suppliers decreased prices to compete with foreign competitors that had previously been shut out of the home market (competition effect). Industries would be restructured over the long term, permitting the surviving companies to achieve economies of scale (restructuring effect).

These three sources of savings are illustrated in Figure EF 8.1, which represents public procurement of computers. Suppose a liberalized procurement policy permits the UK government to buy computers from the cheapest EU supplier, assumed to be Germany. The result is a reduction in average costs from $AC_{U.K.}$ to AC_G. At the same time, increased competition results in falling prices and decreased profit margins. At an output of 10,000 computers, unit prices are reduced from $10,000 to $7,000, and profit margins from $Profit_0$ to $Profit_1$. What's more, exploitation of economies of scale gives rise to further decreases in unit costs and prices, as output expands from 10,000 to 25,000 computers along cost schedule AC_G.

Exploring Further   8.2

Economies of Scale and NAFTA

Another benefit of NAFTA for its members is economies-of-scale production. To illustrate, Figure EF 8.2 represents the Canadian auto market, in which Canada is assumed to be a net exporter to the United States. Assume that prior to the elimination of U.S. trade restrictions, the U.S. demand for Canadian autos is $D_{U.S.0}$. Also assume that the Canadian auto demand is D_C. The overall demand schedule is thus denoted by $D_C + D_{U.S.0}$. Economies of scale are denoted in the downward-sloping cost schedule AC. For simplicity, assume that

Canadian manufacturers price their automobiles at average cost. In the absence of a free-trade agreement, the total number of autos demanded is 100 units, and the price received by Canadian manufacturers is $10,000 per unit.

Under bilateral free trade with the United States, Canadian auto companies encounter a danger and an opportunity. The danger is that competing U.S. manufacturers may undercut Canadian companies that maintain prices at $10,000. But bilateral free trade also provides the Canadian

FIGURE EF 8.2

ECONOMIES OF SCALE AND NAFTA: BENEFITS TO CANADA OF THE ELIMINATION OF U.S. TRADE RESTRICTIONS

With bilateral free trade, competing U.S. automakers may undercut Canadian manufacturers who maintain prices at $10,000. But longer production runs for Canadian manufacturers, made possible by the opening of the U.S. auto market, can result in cost reductions with economies of scale.

companies an opportunity. The elimination of U.S. trade restrictions results in a shift in the export demand schedule faced by Canadian manufacturers from $D_{U.S.0}$ to $D_{U.S.1}$; therefore, the overall demand schedule is now $D_C + D_{U.S.1}$. The total number of autos supplied by Canadian manufacturers increases to 120 units, and the resulting cost reductions permit the price charged by Canadian manufacturers to decrease to $8,000. Economies-of-scale production thus permit Canadian firms to adopt more competitive price policies.

For Canadian consumers, the $2,000 price reduction results in an increase in consumer surplus equal to area a, located under demand schedule D_C. Note that the gain to the Canadian consumer does *not* come at the expense of the Canadian manufacturer! The Canadian manufacturer can afford to sell autos at a lower price without any decrease in unit profits because economies of scale lead to reductions in unit costs. Economies-of-scale production therefore can provide benefits for *both* the producer *and* the consumer.

Exploring Further   8.3

Will the Euro Fail?

When the euro was introduced in 1999, the skeptics did not give it much chance of reaching its tenth anniversary. They argued that the euro was doomed because of the wide differential in economic performance and discipline amongst the member countries. At one end there were the highly disciplined economies such as Germany. At the other end there were the poorly disciplined countries such as Greece, Portugal, Spain, and Italy. It was Nobel laureate economist Milton Friedman who famously predicted that the euro would not last past its first major economic crisis.

The skeptics note that there is a fundamental weakness in the way the European currency union is structured. In the United States, arguably the largest currency union in the world, fiscal transfers between member states allow for the federal government to adjust for discrepancies in economic performances. However, there is no such mechanism within the euro area, which explains why the member countries are subjected to a number of rules, such as limiting government budget deficits and debt. Although these rules require members to achieve a high level of economic discipline, in practice, there has often been little or no such discipline.

For a decade, a stable euro and low interest rates hid the profligate spending and structural weaknesses of Greece, Portugal, Spain, and Italy. By 2010, it was widely recognized that the euro area needed to turn its sights to its fundamental problem: this aging continent spends too much and grows too little. It was at this time that the European Commission warned that imbalances between stronger and weaker euro states risk the very existence of the euro itself.

Indeed, Germany has been working hard to impose its monetary and fiscal discipline on the rest of Europe. For example, Germany has a new constitutional amendment that prohibits government budget deficits starting in 2016. Also, the German government has vetoed European Union bailouts of weaker economies, forcing countries like Hungry and Latvia to seek economic assistance from the International Monetary Fund which imposes tough economic conditions when granting loans to troubled economies. Moreover, the German-based European Central Bank has a strict inflation-fighting mandate and is prohibited from using monetary policy to stimulate the economy. In spite of these pressures, countries such as Greece, Portugal, Italy, and Spain have not exercised economic discipline in recent years.

An economic crisis emerged in 2010 when tremors spread through financial markets as the credit ratings of debt-ridden Greece, Portugal, and Spain were downgraded sharply. Questions were raised about whether these countries might default (refuse to repay their debts) and thus have to exit the euro area. Would such a default signify the end of the euro?

A default would certainly end the ideal of the euro area as an organization whose members are all equal and all work toward the common goal of maintaining a stable, common currency. Membership in such an organization protects against financial problems, because members are supposed to behave well and assist each other in case of unwarranted speculative attacks. Although the members are not liable for each other's government debt, there is an implicit political commitment to provide emergency assistance.

If Greece left the euro area and began printing new drachmas (the former currency of Greece), they would immediately fall in value against the euro. A highly devalued drachma would make Greek olives and wines inexpensive for foreigners, but this benefit for Greek competitiveness would be more than offset by rampant inflation, bank runs, and the burden of having to pay back old euro-denominated debts with a highly devalued currency. However, even if the government of Greece decided to leave the euro area, it would likely not cause a break up. The euro would hardly be less stable without Greece, which represents only two percent of euro-area GDP. Rather, a euro centered on Germany, France and a few of the more advanced economies of Europe would make the union stronger rather than weaker. Simply put, the euro area would break up not when smaller, weaker members leave, but when large, strong ones like Germany no longer see benefits from the arrangement.

Although analysts do not generally anticipate the dissolution of the euro area, widespread economic difficulties have cast a dark cloud over its prospects for expansion. During the past decade, European leaders looked forward to having former Communist nations join the euro area. However, since the global economic downturn of 2008–2009, most of the promising candidates have battled their own recessions and swelling budget deficits, draining public support for euro-area membership. It remains to be seen how the euro area will perform in the future.

International Factor Movements and Multinational Enterprises

Our attention so far has been on the international flow of goods and services. However, some of the most dramatic changes in the world economy have been due to the international flow of factors of production, comprising labor and capital. In the 1800s, European capital and labor (along with African and Asian labor) flowed to the United States and fostered its economic development. In the 1960s, the United States sent large amounts of investment capital to Canada and Western Europe; in the 1980s and 1990s, investment flowed from Japan to the United States. Today, workers from southern Europe find employment in northern European factories, while Mexican workers migrate to the United States. The tearing down of the Berlin Wall in 1990 triggered a massive exodus of workers from East Germany to West Germany.

The economic forces underlying the international movement in factors of production are virtually identical to those underlying the international flow of goods and services. Productive factors move, when they are permitted to, from nations where they are abundant (low productivity) to nations where they are scarce (high productivity). Productive factors flow in response to differences in returns (such as wages and yields on capital) as long as these are large enough to more than outweigh the cost of moving from one country to another.

This chapter considers the role of international capital flows (investment) as a substitute for trade in capital-intensive products. Special attention is given to the multinational enterprise that carries on the international reallocation of capital. The chapter also analyzes the international mobility of labor as a substitute for trade in labor-intensive products.

The Multinational Enterprise

Although the term *enterprise* can be precisely defined, there is no universal agreement on the exact definition of a **multinational enterprise (MNE)**. But a close look at some representative MNEs suggests that these businesses have a number of

TABLE 9.1

THE WORLD'S LARGEST CORPORATIONS, 2008

Firm	Headquarters	Revenues ($ billions)
Wal-Mart Stores	United States	378.8
Exxon Mobil	United States	372.8
Royal Dutch Shell	Netherlands	355.8
BP	United Kingdom	291.4
Toyota Motor	Japan	230.2
Chevron	United States	210.8
ING Group	Netherlands	201.5
Total	France	187.3
General Motors	United States	182.3
ConocoPhillips	United States	178.6

Source: From "The 2009 Global 500," *Fortune*, available at http://www.fortune.com.

identifiable features. Operating in many host countries, MNEs often conduct research and development (R&D) activities in addition to manufacturing, mining, extraction, and business-service operations. The MNE cuts across national borders and is often directed from a company planning center that is distant from the host country. Both stock ownership and company management are usually multinational in character. A typical MNE has a high ratio of foreign sales to total sales, often 25 percent or more. Regardless of the lack of agreement as to what constitutes an MNE, there is no doubt that the multinational phenomenon is massive in size. Table 9.1 provides a glimpse of some of the world's largest corporations.

Multinationals may diversify their operations along vertical, horizontal, and conglomerate lines within the host and source countries. **Vertical diversification** often occurs when the parent MNE decides to establish foreign subsidiaries to produce intermediate goods or inputs that go into the production of a finished good. For industries such as oil refining and steel, such *backward* diversification may include the extraction and processing of raw materials. Most manufacturers tend to extend operations backward only to the production of component parts. The major international oil companies represent a classic case of backward vertical diversification on a worldwide basis. Oil-production subsidiaries are located in areas such as the Middle East, whereas the refining and marketing operations occur in the industrial nations of the West. Multinationals may also practice *forward diversification* in the direction of the final consumer market. Automobile manufacturers, for example, may establish foreign subsidiaries to market the finished goods of the parent company. In practice, most vertical foreign diversification is backward. Multinationals often wish to diversify their operations vertically to benefit from economies of scale and international specialization.

Horizontal diversification occurs when a parent company producing a commodity in the source country sets up a subsidiary to produce an identical product in the host country. These subsidiaries are independent units in productive capacity and are established to produce and market the parent company's product in overseas markets. Coca-Cola and Pepsi-Cola, for example, are bottled not only in the United States but also throughout much of the world. Multinationals sometimes locate production facilities overseas to avoid stiff foreign tariff barriers, which would place their products at a competitive disadvantage. Parent companies also like to locate close to their customers because differences in national preferences may require special designs for their products.

Besides making horizontal and vertical foreign investments, MNEs may diversify into nonrelated markets, in what is known as **conglomerate diversification**. For example, in the 1980s, U.S. oil companies stepped up their nonenergy acquisitions in response to anticipated declines in future investment opportunities for oil and gas. ExxonMobil acquired a foreign copper-mining subsidiary in Chile, and Tenneco bought a French company producing automotive exhaust systems.

To carry out their worldwide operations, MNEs rely on **foreign direct investment**—acquisition of a controlling interest in an overseas company or facility. Foreign direct investment typically occurs when (1) the parent company obtains sufficient common stock in a foreign company to assume voting control (the U.S. Department of Commerce defines a company as directly foreign owned when a "foreign person" holds a ten percent interest in the company); (2) the parent company acquires or constructs new plants and equipment overseas; (3) the parent company shifts funds abroad to finance an expansion of its foreign subsidiary; or (4) earnings of the parent company's foreign subsidiary are reinvested in plant expansion.

Table 9.2 summarizes the position of the United States with respect to foreign direct investment in 2007. Data are provided concerning U.S. direct investment abroad and foreign direct investment in the United States. In recent years, the majority of U.S. foreign direct investment has flowed to Europe, Latin America, and Canada, especially in the manufacturing sector. Most foreign direct investment in the United States has come from Europe, Canada, and Asia—areas that have invested heavily in U.S. manufacturing, petroleum, and wholesale trade facilities.

Motives for Foreign Direct Investment

The case for opening markets to foreign direct investment is as compelling as it is for trade. More open economies enjoy higher rates of private investment, which is a major determinant of economic growth and job creation. Foreign direct investment is actively courted by countries, not least because it generates spillovers such as improved management and better technology. As is true with firms that trade, firms and sectors where foreign direct investment is intense tend to have higher average labor productivity and pay higher wages. Outward investment allows firms to remain

TABLE 9.2

DIRECT INVESTMENT POSITION OF THE UNITED STATES ON AN HISTORICAL COST BASIS, 2007[*]

Country	U.S. DIRECT INVESTMENT ABROAD		FOREIGN DIRECT INVESTMENT IN U.S	
	Amount (billions of dollars)	Percentage	Amount (billions of dollars)	Percentage
Canada	257.1	9.2	213.2	10.2
Europe	1,551.2	55.6	1,483.0	70.9
Latin America	472.0	16.9	62.9	3.0
Africa	27.8	1.0	1.1	0.0
Middle East	29.4	1.0	12.9	0.6
Asia and Pacific	453.9	16.3	319.8	15.3
	2,791.4	100.0	2,092.9	100.0

*Historical-cost valuation is based on the time the investment occurred, with no adjustment for price changes.

Source: From U.S. Department of Commerce, *U.S. Direct Investment Position Abroad and Foreign Direct Investment Position in the United States on a Historical-Cost Basis*, available at http://www.bea.doc.gov/. See also U.S. Department of Commerce, *Survey of Current Business*, Washington, DC (Government Printing Office).

competitive and thus supports employment at home. Investment abroad stimulates exports of machinery and other capital goods.

New MNEs do not pop up haphazardly in foreign nations; they develop as a result of conscious planning by corporate managers. Both economic theory and empirical studies support the idea that foreign direct investment is conducted in anticipation of *future profits*. It is generally assumed that investment flows from regions of low anticipated profit to those of high anticipated profit, after allowing for risk. Although expected profits may ultimately explain the process of foreign direct investment, corporate management may emphasize a variety of other factors when asked about their investment motives. These factors include market-demand conditions, trade restrictions, investment regulations, labor costs, and transportation costs. All these factors have a bearing on cost and revenue conditions and hence on the level of profit.

Demand Factors

The quest for profits encourages MNEs to search for new markets and sources of demand. Some MNEs set up overseas subsidiaries to tap foreign markets that cannot be maintained adequately by export products. This set up sometimes occurs in response to dissatisfaction over distribution techniques abroad. Consequently, a business may set up a foreign marketing division and, later, manufacturing facilities. This incentive may be particularly strong with the realization that local taste and design differences exist. A close familiarity with local conditions is of utmost importance to a successful marketing program.

The location of foreign manufacturing facilities may be influenced by the fact that some parent companies find their productive capacity already sufficient to meet domestic demands. If they wish to enjoy growth rates that exceed the expansion of domestic demand, they must either export or establish foreign production operations. General Motors (GM), for example, has felt that the markets of such countries as the United Kingdom, France, and Brazil are strong enough to permit the survival of GM manufacturing subsidiaries. But Boeing has centralized its manufacturing operations in the United States and exports abroad because an efficient production plant for jet planes is a large investment relative to the size of most foreign markets.

Market competition may also influence a firm's decision to set up foreign facilities. Corporate strategies may be defensive in nature if they are directed at preserving market shares from actual or potential competition. The most certain method of preventing foreign competition from becoming a strong force is to acquire foreign businesses. For the United States, the 1960s and early 1970s witnessed a tremendous surge in the acquisition of foreign businesses. Approximately half of the foreign subsidiaries operated by U.S. MNEs were originally acquired through the purchase of already existing concerns during this era. Once again, GM exemplifies this practice, purchasing and setting up auto producers around the globe. General Motors has been successful in gaining control of many larger foreign-model firms, including Monarch (GM Canada) and Opel (GM Germany). It did not acquire smaller-model firms such as Toyota, Datsun, and Volkswagen, all of which have become significant competitors for General Motors.

DO U.S. MULTINATIONALS EXPLOIT FOREIGN WORKERS?

TRADE CONFLICTS

TABLE 9.3

AVERAGE ANNUAL WAGE PAID BY FOREIGN AFFILIATES OF U.S. MULTINATIONALS AND
AVERAGE ANNUAL DOMESTIC MANUFACTURING WAGE BY HOST-COUNTRY[*]

	All Countries	High-Income	Middle-Income	Low-Income
Average wage paid by affiliates/ thousands of Dollars	15.1	32.4	9.5	3.4
Average domestic manufacturing wage/thousands of dollars	9.9	22.6	5.4	1.7
Ratio	1.5	1.4	1.8	2.0

*Calculations exclude wages of the multinationals' expatriate employees

Source: From Edward Graham, *Fighting the Wrong Enemy* (Washington, DC: Institute for International Economics, 2000).

Do U.S. multinational businesses exploit workers in developing countries? According to critics, maximizing profits is the only thing that matters to multinationals: They search the globe for the cheapest labor when deciding where to locate factories. The only gain from this behavior, critics argue, accrues to the owners of the businesses who have shifted operations from low-wage factories in industrialized countries to poverty-wage factories in developing countries. Simply put, workers in developing countries are underpaid, according to critics.

Indeed, multinationals are in business for profits. But this does not seem to be troublesome for many workers in developing countries who compete to work for them. People who go to work for a foreign-owned business do so because they prefer it to the alternative, whatever that may be. In their own view, the new jobs make them better off.

Assume that the critics are right, and that these workers are being exploited. One remedy would be to admonish multinationals for operating in developing countries at all. If multinationals stopped hiring workers in developing countries, the workers would, in their own estimation, become worse off. Another course is to entice multinationals to pay workers in developing countries wages that are as high as the wages paid to workers in industrial countries. However, this would discourage direct investment in developing countries. Why? Workers in developing countries are paid less than workers in industrial countries because they are generally less productive: They often work with less advanced machinery, and the surrounding infrastructure is inadequate, which

reduces productivity. These workers are attractive to multinationals, in spite of their lower productivity, because they are cheap. If you were to wipe out that offsetting advantage, you would make them unemployable. Put simply, bucking under pressure to extend U.S. or European pay scales to developing countries could mean shutting down local factories—hurting people, not helping them.

Productivity aside, should "responsible" multinationals pay their developing-country employees more than other local workers? To hire workers, they may not have to provide a premium over local wages if they can offer other advantages, such as a modern factory in which to work rather than a sweatshop. By participating in the local labor market and adding to the total demand for labor, the multinationals would most likely be increasing wages for all workers, not just those they employ.

However, evidence suggests that multinationals do pay a wage premium, which apparently reflects their desire to recruit relatively skilled workers. Table 9.3 shows that in 1994, the wages paid by multinationals to poor-country workers were about double the local manufacturing wage; wages paid by multinationals to workers in middle-income countries were about 1.8 times the local manufacturing wage. In short, do U.S. multinationals underpay workers in developing countries? By U.S. standards, they do. But U.S. standards are irrelevant in developing countries: Very few workers are paid at U.S. levels in these countries. The key point is that, by local standards, these workers typically fare quite well.

Cost Factors

Multinationals often seek to increase profit levels through reductions in production costs. Such cost-reducing foreign direct investments may take a number of forms. The pursuit of essential raw materials may underlie a company's intent to go multinational. This is particularly true of the extractive industries and certain agricultural commodities. United Fruit, for example, has established banana-producing facilities in Honduras to take advantage of the natural trade advantages afforded by the weather and growing conditions. Similar types of natural trade advantages explain why Anaconda has set up mining operations in Bolivia and why Shell produces and refines oil in Indonesia. Natural supply advantages such as resource endowments or climatic conditions may indeed influence a company's decision to invest abroad.

Production costs include factors other than material inputs, notably labor. *Labor costs* tend to differ among national economies. Multinationals may be able to hold costs down by locating part or all of their productive facilities abroad. Many U.S. electronics firms, for instance, have had their products produced or at least assembled abroad to take advantage of cheap foreign labor. (The mere fact that the United States may pay higher wages than those prevailing abroad does not necessarily indicate higher costs. High wages may result from U.S. workers being more productive than their foreign counterparts. Only when high U.S. wages are not offset by superior U.S. labor productivity will foreign labor become relatively more attractive.)

Multinational location can also be affected by transportation costs, especially in industries where transportation costs are a high fraction of product value. When the cost of transporting raw materials used by an MNE is significantly higher than the cost of shipping its finished products to markets, the MNE will generally locate production facilities closer to its raw material sources than to its markets; lumber, basic chemicals, aluminum, and steel are among the products that fit this description. Conversely, when the cost of transporting finished products is significantly higher than the cost of transporting the raw materials that are used in their manufacture, MNEs locate production facilities close to their markets. Beverage manufacturers, such as Coca-Cola and Pepsi-Cola, transport syrup concentrate to plants all over the world, which add water to the syrup, bottle it, and sell it to consumers. When transportation costs are a minor fraction of product value, MNEs tend to locate where the availability and cost of labor and other inputs provide them the lowest manufacturing cost. Multinationals producing electronic components, garments, and shoes offer examples of such locational mobility.

Government policies may also lead to foreign direct investment. Some nations seeking to lure foreign manufacturers to set up employment-generating facilities in their countries may grant subsidies, such as preferential tax treatment or free factory buildings, to MNEs. More commonly, direct investment may be a way of circumventing import tariff barriers. The very high tariffs that Brazil levies on auto imports means that foreign auto producers wishing to sell in the Brazilian market must locate production facilities in that country. Another example is the response of U.S. business to the formation of the EU, which imposed common external tariffs against outsiders while reducing trade barriers among member nations. American companies were induced to circumvent these barriers by setting up subsidiaries in the member nations. Another example is Japanese businesses that located additional auto-assembly plants in the United States in the 1980s and 1990s to defuse mounting protectionist pressures.

Supplying Products to Foreign Buyers: Whether to Produce Domestically or Abroad

Once a firm knows that foreign demand for its goods exists, it must ascertain the lowest-cost method of supplying these goods abroad. Suppose Anheuser-Busch (A-B) of the United States wants to sell its Budweiser beer in Canada. Anheuser considers these following ways: (1) build a brewery in Wisconsin to produce Bud for sale to U.S. consumers in the Upper Midwest and also to Canadian consumers (direct exporting); (2) build a brewery in Canada to produce Bud and sell it to Canadian consumers (foreign direct investment); or (3) license the rights to a Canadian brewery to produce and market Bud in Canada. The method A-B chooses depends on the extent of economies of scale, transportation and distribution costs, and international trade barriers. These considerations are discussed in the following sections.

Direct Exporting versus Foreign Direct Investment/Licensing

Let us consider A-B's strategy of supplying Bud to Canadians via direct exporting as opposed to foreign direct investment or a licensing agreement. We will first analyze the influence of economies of scale on this strategy. One would expect economies of scale to encourage A-B to export Bud to Canada when the quantity of beer demanded in Canada is relatively small, and to encourage Canadian production, via either a licensing agreement or foreign direct investment, when a relatively large quantity of beer is demanded in Canada.

To illustrate this principle, assume that average production cost curves are identical for A-B's potential brewery in Wisconsin, A-B's potential brewery in Canada, and a Canadian brewery that could be licensed to produce Bud. These cost curves are denoted by AC in Figure 9.1. As these breweries increase output, the average costs of producing a case of beer decrease up to a point, after which average costs no longer decrease, but stabilize.

Suppose A-B estimates that U.S. consumers will demand 200 cases of Bud per year, as seen in Figure 9.1. Producing this quantity at A-B's Wisconsin brewery allows the realization of sizable economies of scale, which result in a production cost of $8 per case. Also assume that Canadians are estimated to demand a relatively small quantity of Bud, say 100 cases. Because the Wisconsin brewery already produces 200 cases for U.S. consumption, increasing output to meet the extra demand in Canada permits the brewery to slide down its average cost curve until it produces 300 cases at a cost of $6 per case.

The alternative to producing Bud in Wisconsin and exporting it to Canada is to produce it in Canada. However, because Canadian consumers are estimated to demand only 100 cases of Bud, the size of the market is too small to allow economies of scale to be fully realized. That is, A-B's potential brewery in Canada or the licensed Canadian brewer would produce Bud at a cost of $11 per case. Therefore, the production cost saving for A-B of brewing Bud in Wisconsin and exporting it to Canada is $5 per case ($11 − $6 = $5). If the cost of transporting and distributing Bud to Canadians is less than this amount, A-B would maximize profits by exporting Bud to Canada.

However, if the quantity of Bud demanded in Canada exceeds 300 cases, it might be more profitable for A-B to use a licensing agreement or foreign direct investment.

FIGURE 9.1

THE CHOICE BETWEEN DIRECT EXPORTING AND FOREIGN DIRECT INVESTMENT/LICENSING

When the Canadian market's size is large enough to permit efficient production in Canada, a U.S. firm increases profits by establishing a Canadian production subsidiary or licensing the rights to a Canadian firm to produce and market its product in Canada. The U.S. firm increases profits by exporting its product to Canada when the Canadian market is too small to permit efficient production.

To illustrate this possibility, refer to Figure 9.1. Suppose that Canadians are estimated to demand 400 cases of Bud per year whereas the quantity of Bud demanded by U.S. consumers remains at 200 cases. With economies of scale exhausted at 300 cases, the larger Canadian demand does not permit A-B to produce Bud at a cost lower than $6 per case. By producing 400 cases, the licensed Canadian brewery or the Canadian subsidiary brewery of A-B could match the efficiency of A-B's Wisconsin brewery, and each would realize a production cost of $6 per case. Given equal production costs, A-B minimizes total cost by avoiding the additional cost of transporting and distributing beer to Canadians. Thus, A-B increases profits by either licensing its beer technology to a Canadian brewer or investing in a brewing subsidiary in Canada.

Similar to transportation costs, trade restrictions can neutralize production-cost advantages. If Canada has high import tariffs, the production-cost advantage of A-B's Wisconsin brewery may be offset, so that foreign direct investment or licensing is the only feasible way of penetrating the Canadian market.

Foreign Direct Investment versus Licensing

Once a firm chooses foreign production as a method of supplying goods abroad, it must decide whether it is more efficient to establish a foreign production subsidiary or license the technology to a foreign firm to produce its goods. In the United Kingdom, there are Kentucky Fried Chicken establishments that are owned and run by local residents. The parent U.S. organization merely provides its name and operating procedures in return for royalty fees paid by the local establishments. Although licensing is widely used in practice, it presupposes that local firms are capable of adapting their operations to the production process or technology of the parent organization.

FIGURE 9.2

<small>THE CHOICE BETWEEN FOREIGN DIRECT INVESTMENT AND LICENSING</small>

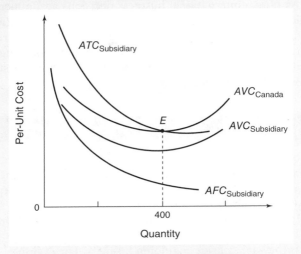

The decision to establish foreign operations through direct investment or licensing depends on (1) the extent to which capital is used in the production process, (2) the size of the foreign market, and (3) the amount of fixed cost a business must bear when establishing an overseas facility.

Figure 9.2 portrays the hypothetical cost conditions confronting A-B as it contemplates whether to license Bud production technology to a Canadian brewery or invest in a Canadian brewing subsidiary. Curve $AVC_{Subsidiary}$ represents the average variable cost (such as labor and materials) of A-B's brewing subsidiary, and AVC_{Canada} represents the average variable cost of a Canadian brewery. The establishment of a foreign brewing subsidiary also entails fixed costs denoted by curve $AFC_{Subsidiary}$. These include expenses of coordinating the subsidiary with the parent organization and the sunk costs of assessing the market potential of the foreign country. The total unit costs that A-B faces when establishing a foreign subsidiary are given by $ATC_{Subsidiary}$.

Comparing $ATC_{Subsidiary}$ with AVC_{Canada}, for a relatively small market of less than 400 cases of beer, the Canadian brewery has an absolute cost advantage. Licensing Bud production technology to a Canadian brewery in this case is more profitable for A-B. But if the Canadian market for Bud exceeds 400 cases, A-B's brewing subsidiary has an absolute cost advantage; A-B increases profits by supplying beer to Canadians via foreign direct investment.

Several factors influence the output level at which A-B's brewing subsidiary begins to realize an absolute cost advantage vis-à-vis the Canadian brewery (400 cases in Figure 9.2). To the extent that production is capital-intensive and A-B's brewing subsidiary can acquire capital at a lower cost than that paid by the Canadian brewery, the variable cost advantage of the subsidiary is greater. This advantage neutralizes the influence of a fixed-cost disadvantage for the subsidiary at a lower level of output. The amount of the brewing subsidiary's fixed costs also has a bearing on this minimum output level. Smaller fixed costs lower the subsidiary's average total costs, again resulting in a smaller output at which the subsidiary first begins to have an absolute cost advantage.

As noted, international business decisions are influenced by such factors as production costs, fixed costs of locating overseas, the relative importance of labor and capital in the production process, and the size of the foreign market. Another factor is the element of risk and uncertainty. When determining where to locate production operations, management is concerned with possibilities such as currency fluctuations and subsidiary expropriations.

Country Risk Analysis

Although investing or lending abroad can be rewarding, these activities come with accompanying risks. For example, the Russian government might expropriate the assets of foreign investors or make foreign loan repayments illegal. Thus, MNES and banks carry out a **country risk analysis** to help them decide whether to do business abroad.

Individuals holding positions of responsibility with internationally oriented firms and banks engage in country risk analysis by evaluating the risk for each country in which they are considering doing business. For example, officers at Chase Manhattan Bank may establish limits on the amount of loans that they are willing to make to clients in Turkey according to the risk of terrorism, as well as market factors. Moreover, if Toyota fears runaway inflation and escalating labor costs in Mexico, it may refrain from establishing an auto assembly plant there.

Assessing the cost and benefits of doing business abroad entails analyses of political, financial, and economic risk. *Political risk* analysis is intended to assess the political stability of a country and includes criteria such as government stability, corruption, domestic conflict, religious tensions, and ethnic tensions. *Financial risk* analysis investigates a country's ability to finance its debt obligations and includes factors such as foreign debt as a percentage of GDP, loan default, and exchange rate stability. And, *economic risk* analysis determines a country's current economic strengths and weaknesses by looking at its rate of growth in GDP, per capita GDP, inflation rate, and the like. Analysts then calculate a composite country risk rating based on these three categories of risk. This composite rating provides an overall assessment of the risk of doing business in some country.

Country risk analysis is intended for a particular user. For example, a company engaged in international tourism will be concerned about country risk as it applies to its attractiveness as a vacation destination. In this case, the composite risk rating of, say Venezuela, may not be of much use. It is possible that Venezuela might be considered high risk in its composite rating, but not present a substantial risk to travelers because its composite risk is decreased by such factors as low financial or economic risk, a miserable investment climate, or other factors that do not threaten tourists. However, Israel might be judged as moderately risky overall due to a stable government and sound economic policies, but still present significant political risk to tourists due to religious and ethnic tensions. In these cases, a better understanding of risk can be ascertained by taking into account particular components of risk, such as law and order or internal conflict, rather than the composite risk rating.

When conducting country risk analysis, MNEs and banks may obtain help from organizations that analyze risk. For example, Political Risk Services publishes a

TABLE 9.4

Selected Country Risks Ranked by Composite Ratings, July 2008

Country	Composite Risk Rating (100 point maximum)	
Norway	91.8	Very Low Risk
Luxembourg	89.3	
Brunei	88.5	↑
Switzerland	88.5	
Germany	86.0	
Hong Kong	85.0	
United States	76.5	
Egypt	65.8	
Iraq	53.0	↓
Somalia	39.3	Very High Risk

Source: From Political Risk Services, *International Country Risk Guide*, 2008, available at https://www.prsgroup.com/FreeSamplePage.aspx/.

monthly report called the *International Country Risk Guide*.[1] The guide provides individual ratings on more than 130 advanced and developing countries for political, financial, and economic risk, plus a composite rating. In calculating the composite risk rating, the political risk factors are given a weighting of 50 percent, while the financial and economic risk factors each contribute 25 percent. Examples of composite ratings are provided in Table 9.4. In assessing a country's composite risk, a higher score indicates a lower risk, and a lower score indicates a higher risk. Such information can be helpful to a firm as a predictive tool for international investments and financial transactions.

After a firm determines a country's risk rating, it must decide whether that risk is tolerable. If the risk is estimated to be too high, then the firm does not need to pursue the feasibility of the proposed project any further. If the risk rating of a country is in the acceptable range, any project related to that country deserves further consideration. In terms of the *International Country Risk Guide's* ratings of country risk, the following categories are used to identify levels of risk: (1) low risk, 80–100 points; (2) moderate risk, 50–79 points; (3) high risk, 0–49 points. However, these broad categories must be tempered to fit the needs of particular MNEs and banks.

International Trade Theory and Multinational Enterprise

Perhaps the main explanation of the development of MNEs lies in the strategies of corporate management. The reasons for engaging in international business can be outlined in terms of the comparative-advantage principle. Corporate managers see advantages they can exploit in the forms of access to factor inputs, new technologies and products, and managerial know-how. Organizations establish overseas subsidiaries largely because profit prospects are best enhanced by foreign production.

From a trade-theory perspective, the multinational-enterprise analysis is fundamentally in agreement with the predictions of the comparative-advantage principle. Both approaches contend that a given commodity will be produced in a low-cost country. The major difference between the multinational-enterprise analysis and the conventional trade model is that the former stresses the international movement of factor inputs, whereas the latter is based on the movement of merchandise among nations.

International trade theory suggests that the aggregate welfare of both the source and host countries is enhanced when MNEs make foreign direct investments for their own benefit. The presumption is that if businesses can earn a higher return on overseas investments than on those at home, resources are transferred from lower to higher productive uses, and on balance the world allocation of resources

---

[1]There are other services that measure country risk, some of the more popular ones being *Euromoney*, Economist Intelligence Unit, Bank of America World Information Services, Business Environment Risk Intelligence, Institutional Investor, Standard and Poor's Rating Group, and Moody's Investor Services.

will improve. Thus, analysis of MNEs is essentially the same as conventional trade theory, which rests on the movement of products among nations.

Despite the basic agreement between conventional trade theory and the multinational-enterprise analysis, there are some notable differences. The conventional model presupposes that goods are exchanged between independent organizations on international markets at competitively determined prices. But MNEs are generally vertically diversified companies whose subsidiaries manufacture intermediate goods as well as finished goods. In an MNE, sales become *intrafirm* when goods are transferred from subsidiary to subsidiary. Although such sales are part of international trade, their value may be determined by factors other than a competitive pricing system.

Japanese Transplants in the U.S. Automobile Industry

Since the 1980s, the growth of Japanese direct investment in the U.S. auto industry has been widely publicized. Japanese automakers have invested billions of dollars in U.S.-based assembly facilities, known as **transplants**, as seen in Table 9.5. Establishing transplants in the United States provides a number of benefits to Japanese automakers, including opportunities to:

- Silence critics who insist that autos sold in the United States must be built there.
- Avoid the potential import barriers of the United States.
- Gain access to an expanding market at a time when the Japanese market is nearing saturation.
- Provide a hedge against fluctuations in the yen–dollar exchange rate.

For example, Toyota has pledged to produce in North America at least two-thirds of the vehicles it sells in the region. It regards manufacturing more vehicles in the United States as a type of political insurance. By sprinkling manufacturing jobs across many states, Toyota has built a network of state and federal government officials friendly to the company.

The growth of Japanese investment in the U.S. auto industry has led to both praise and concern over the future of U.S.-owned auto-manufacturing and parts-supplier industries. Proponents of foreign direct investment maintain that it fosters improvement in the overall competitive position of the domestic auto-assembly and parts industries. They also argue that foreign investment generates jobs and provides consumers with a wider product choice at lower prices than would otherwise be available. However, the United Auto Workers (UAW) union maintains that this foreign investment results in job losses in the auto-assembly and parts-supplier industries.

TABLE 9.5

JAPANESE AUTO PLANTS IN THE UNITED STATES

Plant Name/Parent Company	Location
Honda of America, Inc. (Honda)	Marysville, Ohio East Liberty, Ohio
Nissan Motor Manufacturing Corp. (Nissan)	Smyrna, Tennessee
New United Motor Manufacturing, Inc. (Toyota/General Motors)	Fremont, California
Toyota Motor Manufacturing, USA, Inc. (Toyota)	Georgetown, Kentucky
Mazda Motor Manufacturing, USA, Inc. (Mazda)	Flat Rock, Michigan
Ford Motor Co. (Nissan/Ford)	Avon Lake, Ohio

One factor that influences the number of workers hired is a company's *job classifications*, which stipulate the scope of work each employee performs. As the number of job classifications increases, the scope of work decreases, along with the flexibility of using available employees; this decrease can lead to falling worker productivity and rising production costs.

Japanese-affiliated auto companies have traditionally used significantly fewer job classifications than traditional U.S. auto companies. Japanese transplants use work teams, and each team member is trained to do all the operations performed by the team. A typical Japanese-affiliated assembly plant has three to four job classifications: one team leader, one production technician, and one or two maintenance technicians. Often, jobs are rotated among team members. In contrast, traditional U.S. auto plants have enacted more than 90 different job classifications, and employees generally perform only those operations specifically permitted for their classification. These trends have contributed to the superior labor productivity of Japanese transplants compared to the U.S. Big Three (GM, Ford, and Chrysler). Although powerful forces within the U.S. Big Three have resisted change, international competition has forced U.S. automakers to slowly dismantle U.S. management and production methods and remake them along Japanese lines.

For policy makers, the broader issue is whether the Japanese transplants have lived up to expectations. When the Japanese initiated investment in U.S. auto-manufacturing facilities in the 1980s, many Americans viewed them as models for a revitalized U.S. auto industry and new customers for U.S. auto-parts suppliers. Transplants were seen as a way of providing jobs for U.S. autoworkers whose jobs were dwindling as imports increased. When the transplant factories were announced, Americans anticipated that transplant production would be based primarily on American parts, material, and labor; transplant production would displace imports in the U.S. market while transferring new management techniques and technology to the United States.

Certainly, the transplant factories boosted the economies in the regions where they located. There is also no doubt that the transplants helped to transfer Japanese quality control, just-in-time delivery, and other production techniques to the United States. However, the original expectations of the transplants were only partially fulfilled. Skeptics contended that Japanese manufacturing operations were twice as likely to import parts for assembly in the United States as the average foreign company, and four times as likely to import parts as the average U.S. company. Extensive use of imported parts by Japanese transplants contributed to a U.S. automotive trade deficit with Japan and resulted in fewer jobs for U.S. autoworkers.

International Joint Ventures

Another area of multinational enterprise involvement is **international joint ventures**. A joint venture is a business organization established by two or more companies that combines their skills and assets. It may have a limited objective (research or production) and be short lived. It may also be multinational in character, involving cooperation among several domestic and foreign companies. Joint ventures differ from mergers in that they involve the creation of a *new* business firm, rather than the union of two existing companies. Table 9.6 provides examples of recent joint ventures between U.S. and foreign companies.

TABLE 9.6

JOINT VENTURES BETWEEN U.S. AND FOREIGN COMPANIES

Joint Venture	Partner	Foreign Partner	Products
CAMMI	General Motors	Suzuki (Japan)	Subcompact cars
AutoAlliance	Ford	Mazda (Japan)	Subcompact cars
New United Motor Manufacturing	General Motors	Toyota (Japan)	Subcompact cars
National Steel	National Intergroup	Nippon Kokan	Steel
Siecor	Corning Glass Works	Siemens (Germany)	Optical cable
Himont	Hercules	Montedison (Italy)	Polypropylene resin
International Aero Engines	United Technologies	Rolls-Royce (UK)	Aircraft engines
Tokyo Disneyland	Walt Disney Productions	Oriental Land Company	Entertainment

There are three types of international joint ventures. The first is a joint venture formed by two businesses that conduct business in a third country. For example, a U.S. oil firm and a UK oil firm may form a joint venture for oil exploration in the Middle East. Next is the formation of a joint venture with local private interests. Honeywell Information Systems of Japan was formed by Honeywell, Inc., of the United States and Mitsubishi Office Machinery Company of Japan to sell information system equipment to the Japanese. The third type of joint venture includes participation by local government. Bechtel of the United States, Messerschmitt-Boelkow-Blom of West Germany, and National Iranian Oil (representing the government of Iran) formed the Iran Oil Investment Company for oil extraction in Iran.

Several reasons have been advanced to justify the creation of joint ventures. Some functions, such as R&D, can involve costs too large for any one company to absorb by itself. Many of the world's largest copper deposits have been owned and mined jointly by the largest copper companies on the grounds that joint financing is required to raise enough capital. The exploitation of oil deposits is often done by a consortium of several oil companies. Exploratory drilling projects typically involve several companies united in a joint venture, and several refining companies traditionally own long-distance crude oil pipelines. Oil refineries in foreign countries may be co-owned by several large U.S. and foreign oil companies.

Another factor that encourages the formation of international joint ventures is the restrictions some governments place on the foreign ownership of local businesses. Governments in developing nations often close their borders to foreign companies unless they are willing to take on local partners. Mexico, India, and Peru require that their own national companies represent a major interest in any foreign company conducting business within their borders. The foreign investor is forced to either accept local equity participation or forgo operation in the country. Such government policies are defended on the grounds that joint ventures result in the transfer of managerial techniques and know-how to the developing nation. Joint ventures may also prevent the possibility of excessive political influence on the part of foreign investors. Also, joint ventures help minimize dividend transfers abroad and thus strengthen the developing nation's balance of payments.

International joint ventures are also viewed as a means of forestalling protectionism against imports. Apparently motivated by the fear that rising protectionism might restrict their access to U.S. markets, Japanese manufacturers (Toyota Motor Enterprise) increasingly formed joint ventures with U.S. enterprises in the 1980s. Such ventures typically resulted in U.S. workers assembling Japanese components, with the finished goods sold to U.S. consumers. Not only did this process permit Japanese production to enter the U.S. market, but it also blurred the distinction between U.S. and Japanese production. Just who is us? And who is them? The rationale for protecting domestic output and jobs from foreign competition is thus lessened.

However, there are disadvantages to forming an international joint venture. A joint venture is a cumbersome organization compared with a single organization. Control is divided, creating the problem of "two masters." Success or failure depends on how well companies can work together despite having different objectives, corporate cultures, and ways of doing things. The action of corporate chemistry is difficult to predict, but it is critical, because joint-venture agreements usually provide both partners an ongoing role in management. When joint-venture ownership is divided equally, as often occurs, deadlocks in decision making can take place. If balance is to be preserved between different economic interests, negotiation must establish a hierarchical command. Even when negotiated balance is achieved, it can be upset by changing corporate goals or personnel.

Welfare Effects

International joint ventures can yield both welfare-increasing and welfare-decreasing effects for the domestic economy. Joint ventures lead to *welfare gains* when (1) the newly established business adds to pre-existing productive capacity and fosters additional competition, (2) the newly established business is able to enter new markets that neither parent could have entered individually, or (3) the business yields cost reductions that would have been unavailable if each parent performed the same function separately. However, the formation of a joint venture may also result in *welfare losses*. For instance, it may give rise to increased market power, suggesting greater ability to influence market output and price. This is especially likely to occur when the joint venture is formed in markets in which the parents conduct business. Under such circumstances, the parents, through their representatives in the joint venture, agree on prices and output in the very market that they themselves operate. Such coordination of activities limits competition, reinforces upward pressure on prices, and lowers the level of domestic welfare.

Let's consider an example that contrasts two situations: two competing companies sell autos in the domestic market and form a joint venture that operates as a single seller (a monopoly) in the domestic market. We would expect to see a higher price and smaller quantity when the joint venture behaves as a monopoly. This result will always occur as long as the marginal cost curve for the joint venture is identical to the horizontal sum of the marginal cost curves of the individual competitors. The result of this *market-power effect* is a deadweight welfare loss for the domestic economy—a reduction in consumer surplus that is not offset by a corresponding gain to producers. If, however, the formation of the joint venture entails *productivity gains* that neither parent can realize prior to its formation, domestic welfare may increase. This is because a smaller amount of the domestic economy's resources is now required to produce any given output. Whether domestic welfare rises or falls because of the joint venture depends on the magnitudes of these two opposing forces.

FIGURE 9.3

THE WELFARE EFFECTS OF AN INTERNATIONAL JOINT VENTURE

An international joint venture can yield a welfare-decreasing market-power effect and a welfare-increasing cost-reduction effect. The source of the cost-reduction effect may be lower resource prices or improvements in technology and productivity. The joint venture leads to improvements in national welfare if its cost-reduction effect is due to improvements in technology and productivity and if it more than offsets the market-power effect.

Figure 9.3 illustrates the welfare effects of two parent companies' forming a joint venture in the market in which they operate. Assume that Sony Auto Company of Japan and American Auto Company of the United States are the only two firms producing autos for sale in the U.S. market. Suppose each company realizes constant long-term costs, suggesting that the average total cost equals marginal cost at each level of output. Let the cost schedules of each company prior to the formation of the joint venture be $MC_0 = ATC_0$, which equals \$10,000. Thus, $MC_0 = ATC_0$ becomes the long-term market supply schedule for autos.

Assume that the Sony Auto Company and the American Auto Company initially operate as competitors, charging a price equal to marginal cost. In Figure 9.3, market equilibrium exists at point A, where 100 autos are sold at a price of \$10,000 per unit. Consumer surplus totals area $a + b + c$. Producer surplus does not exist, given the horizontal supply schedule of autos (recall that producer surplus equals the sum of the differences between the market price and each of the minimum prices indicated on the supply schedule for quantities between zero and the market output).

Now suppose that the two competitors announce the formation of a joint venture known as JV Company, which manufactures autos for sale in the United

States. The autos sold by JV replace the autos sold by the two parents in the United States.

Suppose the formation of JV Company entails new production efficiencies that result in cost reductions. Let JV's new cost schedule, $MC_1 = ATC_1$, be located at $7,000. As a monopoly, JV maximizes profit by equating marginal revenue with marginal cost. Market equilibrium exists at point B, where 90 autos are sold at a price of $12,000 per unit. The price increase leads to a reduction in consumer surplus equal to area $a + b$. Of this amount, area a is transferred to JV as producer surplus. Area b represents the loss of consumer surplus that is *not* transferred to JV and that becomes a deadweight welfare loss for the U.S. economy (the consumption effect).

Against this deadweight welfare loss lies the efficiency effect of JV Company: a decrease in unit costs from $10,000 to $7,000 per auto. JV can produce its profit-maximizing output, 90 autos, at a cost reduction equal to area d as compared with the costs that would exist if the parent companies produced the same output. Area d thus represents additional producer surplus, which is a welfare gain for the U.S. economy. Our analysis concludes that, for the United States, the formation of JV Company is desirable if area d exceeds area b.

It has been assumed that JV Company achieves cost reductions that are unavailable to either parent as a stand-alone company. Whether the cost reductions benefit the overall U.S. economy depends on their source. If they result from *productivity* improvements (for example, new work rules leading to higher output per worker), a welfare gain exists for the economy, because fewer resources are required to produce a given number of autos and the excess can be shifted to other industries. However, the cost reductions stemming from JV Company's formation may be *monetary* in nature. Being a newly formed company, JV may be able to negotiate wage concessions from domestic workers that could not be achieved by the American Auto Company. Such a cost reduction represents a transfer of dollars from domestic workers to JV profits and does not constitute an overall welfare gain for the economy.

Multinational Enterprises as a Source of Conflict

Advocates of MNEs often point out the benefits these enterprises can provide for the nations they affect, including both the source country where the parent organization is located and the host country where subsidiary firms are established. Benefits allegedly exist in the forms of additional levels of investment and capital, creation of new jobs, and the development of technologies and production processes. But critics contend that MNEs often create trade restraints, cause conflict with national economic and political objectives, and have adverse effects on a nation's balance of payments. These arguments perhaps explain why some nations frown on direct investment, while others welcome it. This section examines some of the more controversial issues involving multinationals. The frame of reference is the U.S. MNE, although the same issues apply no matter where the parent organization is based.

Employment

One of the most hotly debated issues surrounding the MNE is its effects on employment in both the host and source countries. Multinationals often contend that their foreign direct investment yields favorable benefits to the labor force of the recipient nation. Setting up a new multinational automobile manufacturing plant in Canada creates more jobs for Canadian workers. But the MNE's effect on jobs varies from business to business. One source of controversy arises when the direct investment spending of foreign-based MNEs is used to purchase already existing local businesses rather than to establish new ones. In this case, the investment spending may not result in additional production capacity and may not have noticeable effects on employment in the host country. Another problem arises when MNEs bring in foreign managers and other top executives to run the subsidiary in the host country. In U.S. oil companies located in Saudi Arabia, the Saudis are increasingly demanding that their own people be employed in high-level positions.

As for the source country, the issues of runaway jobs and cheap foreign labor are of vital concern to home workers. Because labor unions are confined to individual countries, the multinational nature of these businesses permits them to escape much of the collective-bargaining influence of domestic unions. It is also pointed out that MNEs can seek out those countries where labor has minimal market power.

The ultimate impact that MNEs have on employment in the host and source countries seems to depend in part on the time scale. In the short term, the source country will likely experience an employment decline when production is shifted overseas. But other industries in the source country may find foreign sales rising over time. This is because foreign labor consumes as well as produces and tends to purchase more as employment and income increase as a result of increased investment. Perhaps the main source of controversy stems from the fact that the MNEs are involved in rapid changes in technology and in the transmission of productive enterprises to host countries. Although such efforts may promote global welfare in the long term, the potential short-term adjustment problems facing source-country labor cannot be ignored.

Technology Transfer

Besides promoting runaway jobs, multinationals can foster the transfer of technology (knowledge and skills applied to how goods are produced) to other nations. Such a process is known as **technology transfer**.

Technology has been likened to a contagious disease: it spreads further and more quickly if there are more personal contacts. Foreign trade is viewed as a channel through which people in different nations make contacts and through which people in one nation get to know about the products of other nations. Foreign direct investment is an even more effective method of technology transfer. When foreign firms with technological advantages establish local production subsidiaries, the personal contacts between these subsidiaries and local firms are more frequent and closer than when firms are located abroad.

International trade and foreign direct investment also facilitate technology transfer via the so-called *demonstration effect*: as a firm shows how its products operate, this sends important information to other firms that such products exist and are usable. Technology transfer is also aided by the *competition effect*: When a foreign firm manufactures a superior product that is popular among consumers, other firms are threatened. To survive, they must innovate and improve the quality of their products.

Although technology transfer may increase the productivity and competitiveness of recipient nations, donor nations may react against it because it is detrimental to their economic base. Donor nations contend that the establishment of production operations abroad by multinational enterprises decreases their export potential and leads to job losses for their workers. By sharing technical knowledge with foreign nations, a donor nation may eventually lose its international competitiveness, thus causing a decrease in its rate of economic growth.

Consider the case of the U.S. technology transfer to China in the mid-1990s. After decades of mutual hostility, the United States hoped that, by the 1990s, China would open itself to the outside world and engage in free trade so that foreign nations could trade with China according to the principle of comparative advantage. Instead, China used its leverage as a large buyer of foreign products to pressure multinational enterprises to localize production and transfer technology to China to help it become competitive. With multinational enterprises willing to outbid each other to woo Chinese bureaucrats, China was in a favorable position to reap the benefits of technology transfer.

For example, Microsoft Corporation, under the threat of having its software banned, co-developed a Chinese version of Windows 95 with a local partner and agreed to aid efforts to develop a Chinese software industry. Another example was General Motors. To beat out Ford for the right to become a partner in manufacturing sedans in Shanghai, GM agreed to bring in dozens of joint ventures for auto parts and to design most of the car in China. It also agreed to establish five research institutes to teach Chinese engineers to turn technological theory in fields such as power trains and fuel-injection systems into commercial applications.

American multinationals argued that transferring technology to China was largely risk-free because a competitive challenge from China was decades away. However, the acceleration of technology transfer in the mid-1990s became increasingly unpopular with U.S. labor unions, which feared that their members were losing jobs to lower-paid Chinese workers. United States government officials also feared that the technology transfer was helping create a competitor of extreme proportions. Let us consider the case of General Electric's technology transfer to China.

General Electric's Trade-Off for Entry into the Chinese Market: Short-Term Sales for Long-Term Competition

For decades, General Electric (GE) had an effective strategy for being competitive in the Chinese market for power-generating equipment: sell the best equipment at the lowest price. However, by the first decade of the 2000s, the formula was altered. Besides offering high quality gas-fired turbines at a competitive price, GE had to agree to share with the Chinese sophisticated technology for producing the turbines. To be considered for turbine contracts worth several billion dollars, GE, Mitsubishi, Siemens, and other competitors were obligated to form joint ventures with state-owned Chinese power companies. General Electric was also required to transfer to its new partners the technology and advanced manufacturing specifications for its gas-fired turbine, which GE had spent more than $500 million to develop. Officials from GE noted that the Chinese wanted to have complete access to its technology, while GE wanted to protect the technology in which it made a large financial investment.

The vast size of China's electricity market convinced GE executives that this market was worth pursuing in spite of the technology demands. The U.S. market for gas-fired turbines was weak because of past spending sprees to increase capacity by power companies and utilities. On the other hand, China was expected to spend more than $10 billion a year constructing electricity plants in the near future. General Electric officials thus faced the trade-off of short-term sales in China for long-term competition from Chinese manufacturers. In the end, GE won an order for 13 of its gas-fired turbines, and as part of the agreement also had to share technology with its Chinese partners.

Before the gas-fired turbine venture with GE, Chinese manufacturers had mastered only the technology required for making much less efficient steam-powered turbines. That technology was obtained in part through previous joint ventures with firms such as Westinghouse Electric Co. However, the Chinese demanded the technology behind the more efficient gas-fired turbines.

General Electric officials noted that Chinese competition was not imminent in highly advanced products like gas-fired turbines. In the past, even after acquiring expertise from foreign corporations, Chinese firms lacked the skill necessary to fully exploit the technology and become competitive in world markets. Moreover, by the time Chinese companies mastered the technology they initially obtained from GE, GE had developed more advanced technologies. Nonetheless, Chinese officials looked ahead to new rounds of power-generating equipment bidding by GE and its competitors, when Chinese officials hoped to obtain even more lucrative technology-sharing deals.[2]

National Sovereignty

Another controversial issue involving the conduct of MNEs is their effect on the economic and political policies of the host and source governments. Many nations fear that the presence of MNEs in a given country results in a loss of its national sovereignty. For example, MNEs may resist government attempts to redistribute national income through taxation. By using accounting techniques that shift profits overseas, an MNE may be able to evade the taxes of a host country. An MNE could accomplish this evasion by raising prices on goods from its subsidiaries in nations with modest tax rates to reduce profits on its operations in a high-tax nation where most of its business actually takes place.

The political influence of MNEs is also questioned by many, as illustrated by the case of Chile. For years, U.S. businesses had pursued direct investments in Chile, largely in copper mining. When Salvador Allende was in the process of winning the presidency, he was opposed by U.S. businesses fearing that their Chilean operations would be expropriated by the host government. International Telephone and Telegraph tried to prevent the election of Allende and attempted to promote civil disturbances that would lead to his fall from power. Another case of MNEs' meddling in host-country affairs is that of United Brands (now Chiquita), who engaged in food-product sales. In 1974, the company paid a $1.25 million bribe to the president of Honduras in return for an export-tax reduction applied to bananas. When the payoff was revealed, the president was removed from office.

There are other areas of controversy. Suppose a Canadian subsidiary of a U.S.-based MNE conducts trade with a country subject to U.S. trade embargoes. Should U.S. policymakers outlaw such activities? The Canadian subsidiary may be pressured by the parent organization to comply with U.S. foreign policy. During

---

[2]"China's Price for Market Entry: Give Us Your Technology, Too," *The Wall Street Journal*, February 26, 2004, pp. A-1 and A-6.

international crises, MNEs may move funds rapidly from one financial center to another to avoid losses (make profits) from changes in exchange rates. This conduct makes it difficult for national governments to stabilize their economies.

In a world where national economies are interdependent and factors of production are mobile, the possible loss of national sovereignty is often viewed as a necessary cost whenever direct investment results in foreign control of production facilities. Whether the welfare gains accruing from the international division of labor and specialization outweigh the potential diminution of national independence involves value judgments by policymakers and interested citizens.

Balance of Payments

The United States offers a good example of how an MNE can affect a nation's balance of payments. In brief, the *balance of payments* is an account of the value of goods and services, capital movements (including foreign direct investment), and other items that flow into or out of a country. Items that make a positive contribution to a nation's payments position include exports of goods and services and capital inflows (foreign investment entering the home country); whereas the opposite flows weaken the payments position. At first glance, we might conclude that when U.S. MNEs make foreign direct investments, these payments represent an outflow of capital from the United States and hence a negative factor on the U.S. payments position. Although this view may be true in the short term, it ignores the positive effects on trade flows and earnings that direct investment provides in the long term.

When a U.S. MNE sets up a subsidiary overseas, it generally purchases U.S. capital equipment and materials needed to run the subsidiary. Once in operation, the subsidiary tends to purchase additional capital equipment and other material inputs from the United States. Both of these factors stimulate U.S. exports, strengthening its balance-of-payments position.

Another long-term impact that U.S. foreign direct investment has on its balance of payments is the return inflow of income generated by overseas operations. Such income includes earnings of overseas affiliates, interest and dividends, and fees and royalties. These items generate inflows of revenues for the economy and strengthen the balance-of-payments position.

Transfer Pricing

Controversy also confronts MNEs in their use of **transfer pricing**, the pricing of goods within an MNE. For example, goods from the company's production division may be sold to its foreign marketing division, or inputs obtained by a parent company can come from a foreign subsidiary. The transfer price may be a purely arbitrary figure which means that it may be unrelated to costs incurred or to operations carried out. The choice of the transfer prices affects the division of the total profit among the parts of the company and thus influences its overall tax burden.

For example, suppose that Dell Inc. produces computers in the United States and buys microchips from its own subsidiary in Malaysia. Also suppose that corporate taxes are 34 percent in the United States and 20 percent in Malaysia. Suppose that Dell tells its subsidiary to sell microchips to Dell at a grossly inflated price (the

DOES THE U.S. TAX CODE SEND AMERICAN JOBS OFFSHORE?

One of the most controversial issues involving MNEs for U.S. policymakers is the taxation of income stemming from foreign direct investment. Labor unions and other groups often contend that U.S. tax laws provide a disincentive to invest at home that results from tax concessions offered by the U.S. government on foreign direct investment. Such tax concessions result in the shipping of American jobs overseas, according to unions. These concessions include *foreign tax credits* and *tax deferrals*.

According to U.S. tax law, an MNE headquartered in the United States is permitted credits against its U.S. income-tax liabilities in an amount equal to the income taxes it pays to foreign governments. Assuming that a Canadian subsidiary earns $100,000 taxable income and that Canada's income-tax rate is 25 percent, the company would pay the Canadian government $25,000. But if that income were applied to the parent organization in the United States, the tax owed to the U.S. government would be $35,000, given an income-tax rate of 35 percent. Under the tax credit system, the parent organization would pay the U.S. government only $10,000 ($35,000 − $25,000 = $10,000). The rationale of the foreign tax credit is that MNEs headquartered in the United States should not be subject to double taxation.

United States-based MNEs also enjoy a tax-deferral advantage. Under U.S. tax laws, the parent organization has the option of deferring U.S. taxes paid on the income of its foreign subsidiary as long as that income is retained overseas rather than repatriated to the United States. This system amounts to an interest-free loan extended by the U.S. government to the parent for as long as the income is maintained abroad. Retained earnings of an overseas subsidiary can be reinvested abroad without being subject to U.S. taxes. Therefore, the tax deferral puts a U.S.-based MNE, which has a subsidiary in, say, China, on the same footing as a local company operating in China or on the same footing as, say, a French-based MNE that operates a subsidiary in China. When the income is repatriated to the United States, it is no longer being used by that subsidiary, so there is no longer any need for that tax leveling. Thus, the MNE gets taxed by the United States but with a foreign tax credit for the foreign tax which has previously been paid.

In 2009, President Barack Obama proposed to close tax loopholes on U.S.-based MNEs and crack down on overseas tax havens. His goal was to help create jobs in the United States, make the tax code fairer, and raise additional revenue for the federal government. Obama's proposal was opposed vigorously by U.S. corporate officials who noted that such a measure would place them at a competitive disadvantage in the global marketplace unless it was accompanied by a reduction in the corporate tax rate. At the writing of this text, it remains to be seen if Obama's proposal will be enacted.

transfer price). Dell thus has a large business expense to deduct when determining its taxable income on its other profitable operations in the United States. To the extent that transfer pricing allows Dell to reduce its taxable income in the United States, the firm avoids being taxed at the rate of 34 percent. Moreover, the increased income of Dell's Malaysian subsidiary, which occurs because of the inflated transfer price, is taxed at the lower rate of 20 percent. Simply put, Dell can reduce its overall tax burden by reporting most of its income in Malaysia, the low tax country, even though the income is earned in the United States, the high-tax country. But note that the tax paid to the U.S. government decreases while the tax paid to the Malaysian government increases. In other words, one government's loss is the other government's gain. So one government can be expected to want to legislate against unfair transfer pricing practices, while the other government can be expected to resist such legislation.

Both foreign governments and the U.S. government are interested in the part that transfer prices play in the realization of corporate profits. Abuses in pricing across national borders are illegal if they can be proved. According to U.S. Internal Revenue Service (IRS) regulations, enterprises dealing with their own subsidiaries are required to set prices "at arms length," just as they would for unrelated customers that are not part of the same corporate structure. This process means that prices must relate to actual costs incurred and to operations actually carried out. However, proving that the prices that one subsidiary charges another are far from market prices is very difficult.

International Labor Mobility: Migration

Historically, the United States has been a favorite target for international **migration**. Because of its vast inflow of migrants, the United States has been described as the melting pot of the world. Table 9.7 indicates the volume of immigration to the United States from the 1820s to 2008. Western Europe was a major source of immigrants during this era, with Germany, Italy, and the United Kingdom among the largest contributors. In recent years, large numbers of Mexicans have migrated to the United States, as well as people from Asia. Migrants have been motivated by better economic opportunities and by noneconomic factors such as politics, war, and religion.

Although international labor movements can enhance the world economy's efficiency, they are often restricted by government controls. The United States, like most countries, limits immigration. Following waves of immigration at the turn of the century, the Immigration Act of 1924 was enacted. Besides restricting the overall flow of immigrants to the United States, the act implemented a quota that limited the number of immigrants from each foreign country. Because the quotas were based on the number of U.S. citizens who had previously emigrated from those countries, the allocation system favored emigrants from northern Europe relative to southern Europe. In the late 1960s, the quota formula was modified, which led to increasing numbers of Asian immigrants to the United States.

TABLE 9.7

U.S. IMMIGRATION, 1820–2008

Period	Number (thousands)
1820–1840	743
1841–1860	4,311
1861–1880	5,127
1881–1900	8,934
1901–1920	14,531
1921–1940	4,636
1941–1960	3,551
1961–1980	7,815
1981–2000	16,433
2001–2008	8,328

Source: From U.S. Department of Homeland Security, Office of Immigration Statistics, *Yearbook of Immigration Statistics*, 2008 available at http://www.uscis.gov/graphics/shared/statistics/yearbook/. See also U.S. Department of Commerce, Bureau of the Census, *Statistical Abstracts of the United States*, Washington, DC: Government Printing Office, available at www.census.gov/.

The Effects of Migration

Figure 9.4 illustrates the economics of labor migration. Suppose the world consists of two countries, the United States and Mexico, which are initially in isolation. The horizontal axes denote the total quantity of labor in the United States and Mexico, and the vertical

FIGURE 9.4

THE EFFECTS OF LABOR MIGRATION FROM MEXICO TO THE UNITED STATES

Prior to migration, the wage rate in the United States exceeds that of Mexico. Responding to the wage differential, Mexican workers immigrate to the United States; this leads to a reduction in the Mexican labor supply and an increase in the U.S. labor supply. Wage rates continue to rise in Mexico and fall in the United States until they eventually are equalized. The labor migration hurts native U.S. workers but helps U.S. owners of capital; the opposite occurs in Mexico. Because migrant workers flow from uses of lower productivity to higher productivity, world output expands.

axes depict the wages paid to labor. For each country, the demand schedule for labor is designated by the value of the marginal product (VMP) of labor.[3] Also assume a fixed labor supply of seven workers in the United States, denoted by $S_{U.S.0}$, and seven workers in Mexico, denoted by S_{M0}.

The equilibrium wage in each country is determined at the point of intersection of the supply and demand schedules for labor. In Figure 9.4(a), the U.S. equilibrium wage is $9, and total labor income is $63; this amount is represented by the area $a + b$. The remaining area under the labor demand schedule is area c, which equals $24.50; this value represents the share of the nation's income accruing to owners

---

[3]The value of the marginal product of labor (VMP) refers to the amount of money producers receive from selling the quantity that was produced by the last worker hired; in other words, VMP = product price × the marginal product of labor. The VMP curve is the labor demand schedule. This curve follows from an application of the rule that a business hiring under competitive conditions finds it most profitable to hire labor up to the point at which the price of labor (wage rate) equals its VMP. The location of the VMP curve depends on the marginal productivity of labor and the price of the product that it produces. Under pure competition, price is constant. Therefore, it is because of diminishing marginal productivity that the labor demand schedule is downward-sloping.

of capital.[4] In Figure 9.4(*b*), the equilibrium wage for Mexico is $3; labor income totals $21, represented by area $f + g$; capital owners enjoy incomes equaling area $h + i + j$, or $24.50.

Suppose labor can move freely between Mexico and the United States and assume that migration is costless and occurs solely in response to wage differentials. Because U.S. wage rates are relatively high, there is an incentive for Mexican workers to migrate to the United States and compete in the U.S. labor market; this process will continue until the wage differential is eliminated. Suppose three workers migrate from Mexico to the United States. In the United States, the new labor supply schedule becomes $S_{U.S.1}$; the excess supply of labor at the $9 wage rate causes the wage rate to fall to $6. In Mexico, the labor emigration results in a new labor supply schedule at S_{M1}; the excess demand for labor at wage rate $3 causes the wage rate to rise to $6. The effect of **labor mobility** is thus to equalize wage rates in the two countries.[5] Our next job is to assess how labor migration in response to wage differentials affects the world economy's efficiency. Does world output expand or contract with open migration? For the United States, migration increases the labor supply from $S_{U.S.0}$ to $S_{U.S.1}$. This increase leads to an expansion of output; the value of the additional output is denoted by area $d + e$ ($22.50). For Mexico, the decrease in labor supply from S_{M0} to S_{M1} results in a contraction in output; the value of the lost output is represented by area $g + i$ ($13.50). The result is a net gain of $9 in world output as a result of labor migration. This is because the *VMP* of labor in the United States exceeds that of Mexico throughout the relevant range. Workers are attracted to the United States by the higher wages paid. These higher wages signal to Mexican labor the higher value of worker productivity, thus attracting workers to those areas where they will be most efficient. As workers are used more productively, world output expands.

Migration also affects the *distribution of income*. As we will see, the gains in world income resulting from labor mobility are not distributed equally among all nations and factors of production. The United States as a whole benefits from immigration; its overall income gain is the sum of the losses by native U.S. workers, gains by Mexican immigrants now living in the United States, and gains by U.S. owners of capital. Mexico experiences overall income losses as a result of its labor emigration; however, workers remaining in Mexico gain relative to Mexican owners of capital. As previously suggested, the Mexican immigrants gain from their relocation to the United States.

For the United States, the gain in income as a result of immigration is denoted by area $d + e$ ($22.50) in Figure 9.4(*a*). Of this amount, Mexican immigrants capture area d ($18), while area e ($4.50) is the extra income accruing to U.S. owners of

---

[4]How do we know that area c represents the income accruing to U.S. owners of capital? My analysis assumes two productive factors, labor and capital. The total income (value of output) that results from using a given quantity of labor with a fixed amount of capital equals the area under the *VMP* curve of labor for that particular quantity of labor. Labor's share of that area is calculated by multiplying the wage rate times the quantity of labor hired. The remaining area under the *VMP* curve is the income accruing to the owners of capital.

[5]Wage-rate equalization assumes unrestricted labor mobility in which workers are concerned only about their incomes. It also assumes that migration is costless for labor. In reality, there are economic and psychological costs of migrating to another country. Such costs may result in only a small number of persons finding the wage gains in the immigrating country high enough to compensate them for their migration costs. Thus, complete wage equalization may not occur.

capital thanks to the availability of additional labor to use with the capital. However, immigration forces wage rates down from $9 to $6. The earnings of the native U.S. workers fall by area b ($21); this amount is transferred to U.S. owners of capital.

As for Mexico, its labor emigration results in a decrease in income equal to $g + i$ ($13.50); this decrease represents a transfer from Mexico to the United States. The remaining workers in Mexico gain area h ($12) as a result of higher wages. However, Mexican capital owners lose because less labor is available for use with their capital.

Although immigration may lower wage rates for some native U.S. workers, it should also be noted that these lower wage rates benefit U.S. producers. Lower wage rates also result in lower equilibrium product prices, thereby benefiting consumers. From society's perspective, the gains from immigration to producers and consumers should be weighed against the losses to low-wage workers.

We can conclude that the effect of labor mobility is to increase overall world income and to redistribute income from labor to capital in the United States and from capital to labor in Mexico. Migration has an impact on the distribution of income similar to an increase in exports of labor-intensive goods from Mexico to the United States.

Immigration as an Issue

The preceding example makes it clear why domestic labor groups in capital-abundant nations often prefer restrictions on immigration; open immigration tends to reduce their wages. When migrant workers are unskilled, as is typically the case, the negative effect on wages mainly affects unskilled domestic workers. Conversely, domestic manufacturers will tend to favor unrestricted immigration as a source of cheap labor.

Another controversy about immigrants is whether they are a drain on government resources. Nations that provide generous welfare payments to the economically disadvantaged may fear they will induce an influx of nonproductive people who will not produce as did the immigrants of Figure 9.4, but will enjoy welfare benefits at the expense of domestic residents and working immigrants. However, fiscal relief may not be far away. The children of immigrants will soon enter the labor force and begin paying taxes, thus supporting not only their children's education, but also their parents' retirement. In a matter of two generations, most immigrant families tend to assimilate to the point that their fiscal burdens are indistinguishable from those of other natives. When it's all added up, most long-term calculations show that immigrants make a net positive contribution to public coffers.

Developing nations have sometimes feared open immigration policies because they can result in a **brain drain**—emigration of highly educated and skilled people from developing nations to industrial nations, thus limiting the growth potential of the developing nations. The brain drain has been encouraged by national immigration laws, as in the United States and other industrial nations, which permit the immigration of skilled persons while restricting that of unskilled workers.

In the previous labor-migration example, we implicitly assumed that the Mexican workers' migration decision was more or less permanent. In practice, most labor migration is temporary, especially in the European Union. That is, a country such as France will allow the immigration of foreign workers on a temporary basis when needed; these workers are known as **guest workers**. During periods of business recession, France will refuse to issue work permits when foreign workers are no longer needed. Such a practice tends to insulate the French economy from labor shortages during business expansions and labor surpluses during business recessions. However, the labor-adjustment problem is shifted to the labor-emigrating countries.

Illegal migration is also a problem. In the United States, this type of migration has become a political hot potato, with millions of illegal immigrants finding employment in the so-called underground economy, often below minimum wage. Some 3 to 15 million illegal immigrants are estimated to be in the United States, many of them from Mexico. For the United States, and especially the southwestern states, immigration of Mexican workers has provided a cheap supply of agricultural and low-skilled workers. For Mexico, it has been a major source of foreign exchange and a safety cushion against domestic unemployment. Illegal immigration also affects the distribution of income for U.S. natives because it tends to reduce the income of low-skilled U.S. workers.

On the other hand, immigrants not only diversify an economy, but they may also contribute to economic growth. It is because immigrants are often different from natives that the economy as a whole profits. In many instances, immigrants both cause prices to fall, which benefits all consumers, and enable the economy to domestically produce a wider variety of goods than natives could alone. If immigrants weren't different from natives, they would only augment the population and the scale of the economy, but not have an effect on the overall growth rate of per capita income. According to the National Research Council, the overall effect of immigration on the U.S. gross domestic product is between $1 billion and $10 billion a year.[6] Although these amounts may seem negligible in an $8 trillion economy (about one-eighth of one percent at most), they are still a gain—and not the drain many believe immigration to be.

As we learned from Figure 9.4, immigrants increase the supply of labor in the economy. This results in a lower market wage for all workers *if all workers are the same*. But all workers are not the same. Some natives will compete with immigrants for positions because they possess similar skills; others will work alongside immigrants, complementing the immigrants' skills with their own. This skill distinction means that not all native workers will receive a lower wage. Those who compete with (are substitutes for) immigrants will receive a lower wage than they would without immigration, while those who complement immigrants will receive a higher wage. Most analyses of various countries have found that a ten percent increase in the immigrant share of the population reduces native wages by one percent at most. This finding suggests that most immigrants are not substituting for native labor—skilled or unskilled—but are, instead, complementing it.[7]

Advocates of increased immigration note that children do not begin working the minute they are born. Producing an adult worker requires substantial expenditures in the form of food, clothing, shelter, education, and other child-rearing costs. These investments in human capital formation are quite substantial. Immigrant workers, unlike newborn children, are able to begin engaging in productive activities upon their arrival in the country. The cost of much of their human capital formation

---

[6]See National Research Council Panel on the Demographic and Economic Impacts of Immigration. *The New Americans: Economic, Demographic, and Fiscal Effects of Immigration* (Washington D.C.: National Academy Press, 1997).

[7]Friedberg, R. M. and J. Hunt, "The Impact of Immigrants on Host Country Wages, Employment and Growth," *Journal of Economic Perspectives*, Spring 1995, pp. 23–44.

DOES U.S. IMMIGRATION POLICY HARM DOMESTIC WORKERS?

The net gains from current immigration are small, so it is unlikely that these gains can play a crucial role in the policy debate. Economic research teaches a very valuable lesson: the economic impact of immigration is essentially distributional. Current immigration redistributes wealth from unskilled workers, whose wages are lowered by immigrants, to skilled workers and owners of companies that buy immigrants' services, and from taxpayers who bear the burden of paying for the social services used by immigrants to consumers who use the goods and services produced by immigrants.

George Borjas, "The New Economics of Immigration," *The Atlantic Online*, November 1996.

Highly skilled immigrants, who also create jobs for Americans, are not the only ones contributing to our economic boom. Even the less-skilled immigrants con-tribute to our economy and our lives by working in jobs most Americans do not want, such as cleaning offices, cooking in restaurants, and ringing up purchases in the grocery store. They, in turn, contribute by buying homes, clothes, and groceries. The wonderful cultural diversity brought to the United States by immigrants has become secondary to their willingness to work hard and become part of today's America.

Bronwyn Lance, "The Economic Impact of Immigrants," May 2000, available at http://www.worldandihomeschool.com/.

Most U.S. residents today are the descendants of immi-grants who arrived in the United States during the past 150 years. Concerns about the effect of immigration on domestic workers, however, have resulted in the passage of several laws designed to restrict immigration. Unions, in

particular, have argued for a more restrictive immigration policy on the grounds that immigration lowers the wage and employment levels for domestic residents.

No substantial restrictions were placed on immigration into the United States until the passage of the Quota Law of 1921. This law set quotas on the number of immigrants based on the country of origin. The Quota Law primarily restricted immigration from eastern and southern Europe. The Immigration and Nationality Act Amendments of 1965 eliminated the country-specific quota system and instead established a limit on the maximum number of immigrants allowed into the United States. Under this act, preferential treatment is given to those who immigrate for the purpose of family reunification. Those possessing exceptional skills are also given priority. However, no limit is placed on the number of political refugees allowed to immigrate into the United States. Not all immigrants, of course, enter the country through legal channels. Individuals often enter on student or tourist visas and begin working in violation of their visa status. Other individuals enter the country illegally without a valid U.S. visa. The Immigration Reform and Control Act of 1986 addresses the issue of illegal immigra-tion by imposing substantial fines on employers that hire illegal immigrants.

The Illegal Immigration Reform and Immigrant Responsibility Act of 1996 provided several new restric-tions to immigration. Host families can only accept immi-grants if the host family receives an income that is at least 125 percent of the poverty level. This act also requires that the Immigration and Naturalization Service maintain stric-ter records of entry and exit by nonresident aliens.

was borne by the country from which they emigrated. Because most immigrants arrive at a stage in their life in which they are relatively productive, higher immigration rates generally result in an increase in the proportion of the population that is working. As the proportion of the population that is working rises, per capita income also rises.

Concern over the future of social security is also used to support relaxed immi-gration restrictions. Declining birthrates in the United States, combined with rising life spans, result in a steady increase in the ratio of retired to working individuals over the next few decades. An increase in the number of younger immigrants could help to alleviate this problem.

TABLE 9.8

Labor Markets Work: Percentage Wage Change Due to 1980–2000 Immigration Influx (in percent)

Labor Category	PERCENTAGE WAGE CHANGE	
	Short Run	Long Run
All workers	−3.3%	0.1%
High school dropouts	−8.2	−4.8
High school graduates	−2.2	1.1
Some college	−2.6	0.8
College graduates	−3.8	−0.5

Source: George Borjas and Lawrence Katz, *The Evolution of the Mexican-Born Workforce in the United States.* National Bureau of Economic Research, Cambridge, MA, 2005.

Do Immigrants Really Hurt American Workers' Wages?

One study of the wage effect of immigration deserves attention. Researchers at the National Bureau of Economic Research have examined whether immigrants entering the U.S. labor market depress the wages of competing U.S. workers. They investigated the wage effect of immigration (mainly of Mexican origin) into the United States during 1980–2000. They found that in the short term, immigration lowered the average wage of competing U.S. workers by three percent. For competing workers that dropped out of high school, the average wage fell by eight percent. The results of the researchers' findings are summarized in Table 9.8.

However, they also noted that over the long term, wages depend on the supply of capital as well as labor. Alone, an influx of immigrants increases the supply of workers and thus decreases wages. But cheaper labor increases the potential return of employers to building new factories. In so doing, they create extra demand for workers. Once capital has fully adjusted, the final effect on overall wages should be a wash, as long as the immigrants have not changed the productivity of the workforce as a whole. It turns out that the researchers found that the wage of the average competing worker was not affected by immigration in the long term, but the wage of high school dropouts still decreased by approximately five percent. These findings confirmed the idea that in the long term, immigration had only a small negative effect on the pay of America's least skilled workers. If Congress wants to reduce wage inequality, building border walls is a very questionable way of going about it.

Summary

1. Today the world economy is characterized by the international movement of factor inputs. The multinational enterprise plays a central part in this process.

2. There is no single agreed upon definition of what constitutes an MNE. Some of the most identifiable characteristics of multinationals are the following: (a) Stock ownership and management are multinational in character; (b) company headquarters may be far removed from the country where a particular activity occurs; and (c) foreign sales represent a high proportion of total sales.

3. Multinationals have diversified their operations along vertical, horizontal, and conglomerate lines.

4. Among the major factors that influence decisions to undertake foreign direct investment are (a) market demand, (b) trade restrictions, (c) investment regulations, and (d) labor productivity and costs.

5. In planning to set up overseas operations, a business must decide whether to construct (or purchase) plants abroad or extend licenses to foreign businesses to produce its goods.

6. The theory of multinational enterprise essentially agrees with the predictions of the comparative-advantage principle. However, conventional trade theory assumes that commodities are traded between independent, competitive businesses, whereas MNEs are often vertically diversified businesses, with substantial intrafirm sales. Thus, MNEs may use transfer pricing to maximize overall company profits rather than the profits of any single subsidiary.

7. In recent years, companies have increasingly linked up with former rivals in a vast array of joint ventures. International joint ventures can yield welfare-increasing effects as well as market-power effects.

8. Some of the more controversial issues involving MNEs are (a) employment, (b) technology transfer, (c) national sovereignty, (d) balance of payments, and (e) taxation.

9. International labor migration occurs for economic and noneconomic reasons. Migration increases output and decreases wages in the country of immigration, as it decreases output and increases wages in the country of emigration. For the world as a whole, migration leads to net increases in output.

Key Concepts & Terms

- Brain drain (p. 364)
- Conglomerate diversification (p. 340)
- Country risk analysis (p. 348)
- Foreign direct investment (p. 341)
- Guest workers (p. 364)
- Horizontal diversification (p. 340)
- International joint ventures (p. 351)
- Labor mobility (p. 363)
- Migration (p. 361)
- Multinational enterprise (MNE) (p. 339)
- Technology transfer (p. 356)
- Transfer pricing (p. 359)
- Transplants (p. 350)
- Vertical diversification (p. 340)

Study Questions

1. What is meant by the term *multinational enterprise*?

2. What are the major issues involving multinational enterprises as a source of conflict for source and host countries?

3. What are the most important motives behind an enterprise's decision to undertake foreign direct investment?

4. Under what conditions would a business wish to enter foreign markets by extending licenses or franchises to local businesses to produce its goods?

5. Why is it that the rate of return on U.S. direct investments in the developing nations often exceeds the rate of return on its investments in industrial nations?

6. Is the theory of multinational enterprise essentially consistent or inconsistent with the traditional model of comparative advantage?

7. What are the major foreign industries in which U.S. businesses have chosen to place direct investments? What are the major industries in the United States in which foreigners place direct investments?

8. What are some examples of welfare gains and welfare losses that can result from the formation of international joint ventures among competing businesses?

9. Multinational enterprises may diversify their operations along vertical, horizontal, and conglomerate lines within the host and source countries. Distinguish among these diversification approaches.

10. Table 9.9 illustrates the revenue conditions facing ABC, Inc., and XYZ, Inc., which operate as competitors in the U.S. calculator market. Each firm realizes constant long-term costs ($MC = AC$) of $4 per unit. On graph paper, plot the enterprise demand, marginal revenue, and $MC = AC$ schedules. On the basis of this information, answer the following questions.

TABLE 9.9

PRICE AND MARGINAL REVENUE:
CALCULATORS

Quantity	Price ($)	Marginal Revenue ($)
0	9	—
1	8	8
2	7	6
3	6	4
4	5	2
5	4	0
6	3	−2
7	2	−4

a. With ABC and XYZ behaving as competitors, the equilibrium price is $ _____ and output is _____. At the equilibrium price, U.S. households attain $ _____ of consumer surplus, while company profits total $ _____.

b. Suppose the two organizations jointly form a new one, JV, Inc., whose calculators replace the output sold by the parent companies in the U.S. market. Assuming that JV operates as a monopoly and that its costs ($MC = AC$) equal $4 per unit, the company's output would be _____ at a price of $_____, and total profit would be $ _____. Compared to the market equilibrium position achieved by ABC and XYZ as competitors, JV as a monopoly leads to a deadweight loss of consumer surplus equal to $_____.

c. Assume now that the formation of JV yields technological advances that result in a per-unit cost of only $2; sketch the new $MC = AC$ schedule in the figure. Realizing that JV results in a deadweight loss of consumer surplus, as described in part b, the net effect of the formation of JV on U.S. welfare is a gain/loss of $ _____. If JV's cost reduction was due to the wage concessions of JV's U.S. employees, the net welfare gain/loss for the United States would equal $ _____. If JV's cost reductions resulted from changes in work rules leading to higher worker productivity, the net welfare gain/loss for the United States would equal $ _____.

11. What effects does labor migration have on the country of immigration? The country of emigration? The world as a whole?

12. Table 9.10 illustrates the hypothetical demand and supply schedules of labor in the United States. Assume that labor and capital are the only two factors of production. On graph paper, plot these schedules.

TABLE 9.10

DEMAND AND SUPPLY OF LABOR

Wage ($)	Quantity Demanded	Quantity Supplied$_0$	Quantity Supplied$_1$
8	0	2	4
6	2	2	4
4	4	2	4
2	6	2	4
0	8	2	4

a. Without immigration, suppose the labor force in the United States is denoted by schedule S_0. The equilibrium wage rate is $_____; payments to native U.S. workers total $ _____, while payments to U.S. capital owners equal $ _____.

b. Suppose immigration from Hong Kong results in an overall increase in the U.S. labor force to S_1. Wages would rise/fall to $ _____, payments to native U.S. workers would total $ _____, and payments to Hong Kong immigrants would total $ _____. U.S. owners of capital would receive payments of $_____.

c. Which U.S. factor of production would gain from expanded immigration? Which U.S. factor of production would likely resist policies permitting Hong Kong workers to freely migrate to the United States?

PART 2
International Monetary Relations

The Balance of Payments

When trade occurs between the United States and other nations, many types of financial transactions are recorded in a summary called the balance of payments. In this chapter, I examine the monetary aspects of international trade by considering the nature and significance of a nation's balance of payments.

The **balance of payments** is a record of the economic transactions between the residents of one country and the rest of the world. Nations keep record of their balance of payments over the course of a one-year period; the United States and some other nations also keep such a record on a quarterly basis.

An *international transaction* is an exchange of goods, services, or assets between residents of one country and those of another. But what is meant by the term *resident*? Residents include businesses, individuals, and government agencies that make the country in question their legal domicile. Although a corporation is considered to be a resident of the country in which it is incorporated, its overseas branch or subsidiary is not. Military personnel, government diplomats, tourists, and workers who emigrate temporarily are considered residents of the country in which they hold citizenship.

Double-Entry Accounting

The arrangement of international transactions into a balance-of-payments account requires that each transaction be entered as a credit or a debit. A **credit transaction** is one that results in a *receipt* of a payment from foreigners. A **debit transaction** is one that leads to a *payment* to foreigners. This distinction is clarified when we assume that transactions take place between U.S. residents and foreigners and that all payments are financed in dollars.

From the U.S. perspective, the following transactions are credits (+), leading to the receipt of dollars from foreigners:

- Merchandise exports
- Transportation and travel receipts

- Income received from investments abroad
- Gifts received from foreign residents
- Aid received from foreign governments
- Investments in the United States by overseas residents

Conversely, the following transactions are debits (−) from the U.S. viewpoint because they involve payments to foreigners:

- Merchandise imports
- Transportation and travel expenditures
- Income paid on the investments of foreigners
- Gifts to foreign residents
- Aid given by the U.S. government
- Overseas investment by U.S. residents

Although we speak in terms of credit and debit transactions, every international transaction involves an exchange of assets and so has both a credit and a debit side. Each credit entry is balanced by a debit entry, and vice versa, so that the recording of any international transaction leads to two offsetting entries. In other words, the balance-of-payments accounts utilize a **double-entry accounting** system. The following two examples illustrate the double-entry technique.

Example 1

IBM sells $25 million worth of computers to a German importer. Payment is made by a bill of exchange, which increases the balances of New York banks at their Bonn correspondents' bank. Because the export involves a transfer of U.S. assets abroad for which payment is to be received, it is entered in the U.S. balance of payments as a credit transaction. IBM's receipt of the payment held in the German bank is classified as a short-term financial movement because the financial claims of the United States against the German bank have increased. The entries on the U.S. balance of payments would appear as follows:

	Credits (+)	Debits (−)
Merchandise exports	$25 million	
Short-term financial movement		$25 million

Example 2

A U.S. resident who owns bonds issued by a Japanese company receives interest payments of $10,000. With payment, the balances owned by New York banks at their Tokyo affiliate are increased. The impact of this transaction on the U.S. balance of payments would be as follows:

	Credits (+)	Debits (−)
Service exports	$10,000	
Short-term financial movement		$10,000

These examples illustrate how every international transaction has two equal sides, a credit and a debit. If we add up all the credits as pluses and all the debits as minuses, the net result is zero; that is, the total credits must always equal the total debits. This

INTERNATIONAL PAYMENTS PROCESS

GLOBALIZATION

FIGURE 10.1

INTERNATIONAL PAYMENTS PROCESS

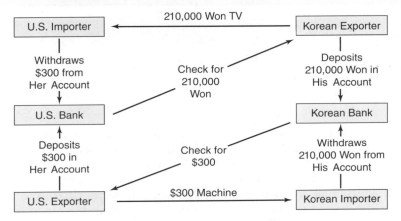

Dollars spent by U.S. importers end up
as dollars received by U.S. exporters.

Won spent by Korean importers end up
as won received by Korean exporters.

When residents in different countries contemplate selling or buying products, they must consider how payments will occur, as seen in Figure 10.1. Assume that you, as a resident of the United States, buy a TV directly from a producer in South Korea. How, when, and where will the South Korean producer obtain his won so that he can spend the money in South Korea?

Initially, you would write a check for $300, which your U.S. bank would convert to 210,000 won (assuming an exchange rate of 700 won per dollar). When the South Korean producer receives your payment in won, he deposits the funds in his bank. The bank in South Korea thus holds a check from a U.S. bank that promises to pay a stipulated amount of won.

Assume that at the same time you paid for your TV, a buyer in South Korea paid a U.S. producer $300 for machinery. The flowchart illustrates the path of both transactions.

When trade is in balance, money of different countries does not actually change hands across the oceans. In this example, the value of South Korea's exports to the United States equals the value of South Korea's imports from the United States; the won that South Korean importers use to purchase dollars to pay for U.S. goods are equal to the won that South Korean exporters receive in payment for the products they ship to the United States. The dollars that would flow, in effect, from U.S. importers to U.S. exporters exhibit a similar equality.

In theory, importers in a country pay the exporters in that same country in the national currency. In reality, however, importers and exporters in a given country do not deal directly with one another; to facilitate payments, banks carry out these transactions.

result means that the *total* balance-of-payments account must always be in balance. There is no such thing as an overall balance-of-payments surplus or deficit.

Even though the entire balance of payments must numerically balance by definition, it does *not* necessarily follow that any single subaccount or subaccounts of the statement must balance. For instance, total merchandise exports may or may not be in balance with total merchandise imports. When reference is made to a balance-of-payments surplus or deficit, it is particular subaccounts of the balance of payments that are referred to, not the overall value. A *surplus* occurs when the balance on a subaccount (subaccounts) is positive; a *deficit* occurs when the balance is negative.

Balance-of-Payments Structure

Let us now consider the structure of the balance of payments by examining its various subaccounts.

Current Account

The **current account** of the balance of payments refers to the monetary value of international flows associated with transactions in goods, services, income flows, and unilateral transfers. Each of these flows will be described in turn.

Merchandise trade includes all of the goods the United States exports or imports: agricultural products, machinery, autos, petroleum, electronics, textiles, and the like. The dollar value of merchandise exports is recorded as a plus (credit) and the dollar value of merchandise imports is recorded as a minus (debit). Combining the exports and imports of goods gives the **merchandise trade balance**. When this balance is negative, the result is a merchandise trade deficit; a positive balance implies a merchandise trade surplus.

Exports and imports of *services* include a variety of items. When U.S. ships carry foreign products or foreign tourists spend money at U.S. restaurants and motels, valuable services are being provided by U.S. residents, who must be compensated. Such services are considered exports and are recorded as credit items on the goods and services account. Conversely, when foreign ships carry U.S. products or when U.S. tourists spend money at hotels and restaurants abroad, then foreign residents are providing services that require compensation. Because U.S. residents are, in effect, importing these services, the services are recorded as debit items. Insurance and banking services are explained in the same way. Services also include items such as transfers of goods under military programs, construction services, legal services, technical services, and the like.

To get a broader understanding of the international transactions of a country, we must add services to the merchandise trade account. This total gives the **goods and services balance**. When this balance is positive, the result is a surplus of goods and services transactions; a negative balance implies a deficit. Just what does a surplus or deficit balance appearing on the U.S. goods and services account mean? If the goods and services account shows a surplus, the United States has transferred more resources (goods and services) to foreigners than it has received from them over the period of one year. Besides measuring the value of the *net transfer of resources,* the goods and services balance also furnishes information about the status of a nation's gross domestic product (GDP). This is because the balance on the goods and services account is defined essentially the same way as the *net export of goods and services,* which is part of a nation's GDP.

Recall from your macroeconomics course that GDP is equal to the value of the goods and services produced in an economy over a period of time. In an economy with trade, GDP is equal to the sum of four different types of spending in the economy: consumption, gross investment, government spending, and net exports of goods and services. In effect, net exports represent the value of goods and services that are produced domestically but not included in domestic consumption.

For a nation's GDP, then, the balance on the goods and services account can be interpreted as follows. A positive balance on the account shows an excess of exports over imports, and this difference must be added to the GDP. When the account is in deficit, the excess of imports over exports must be subtracted from the GDP. If a nation's exports of goods and services equal its imports, the account will have a net imbalance of zero and will not affect the status of the GDP. Therefore, depending on the relative value of exports and imports, the balance on the goods and services account contributes to the level of a nation's national product.

Broadening our balance-of-payments summary further, we must include *income receipts and payments*. This item consists of the net earnings (dividends and interest) on U.S. investments abroad—that is, earnings on U.S. investments abroad less payments on foreign assets in the United States. It also includes compensation to employees.

Also, the balance-of-payments summary is expanded to include **unilateral transfers**. These items include transfers of goods and services (gifts in kind) or financial assets (money gifts) between the United States and the rest of the world. *Private transfer payments* refer to gifts made by individuals and nongovernmental institutions to foreigners. These might include a remittance from an immigrant living in the United States to relatives back home, a birthday present sent to a friend overseas, or a contribution by a U.S. resident to a relief fund for underdeveloped nations. *Governmental transfers* refer to gifts or grants made by one government to foreign residents or foreign governments. The U.S. government makes transfers in the form of money and capital goods to developing nations, military aid to foreign governments, and remittances such as retirement pensions to foreign workers who have moved back home. In some cases, U.S. governmental transfers represent payments associated with foreign assistance programs that can be used by foreign governments to finance trade with the United States. It should be noted that many U.S. transfer (foreign aid) programs are tied to the purchase of U.S. exports (such as military equipment or farm exports) and thus represent a subsidy to U.S. exporters. When investment income and unilateral transfers are combined with the balance on goods and services, we arrive at the current account balance. This is the broadest measure of a nation's balance of payments regularly quoted in the newspapers and in national television and radio news reports.

Capital and Financial Account

Capital and financial transactions in the balance of payments include all international purchases or sales of assets. The term *assets* is broadly defined to include items such as titles to real estate, corporate stocks and bonds, government securities, and ordinary commercial bank deposits. The **capital and financial account** includes both private-sector and official (central bank) transactions.[1]

---

[1]Since 1999, U.S. international transactions have been classified into three groups—the current account, the capital account, and the financial account. The transactions were formerly classified into the current account and capital account. See "Upcoming Changes in the Classification of Current and Capital Transactions in the U.S. International Accounts," *Survey of Current Business*, February 1999.

Capital transactions consist of capital transfers and the acquisition and disposal of certain nonfinancial assets. The major types of capital transfers are debt forgiveness and migrants' goods and financial assets accompanying them as they leave or enter the country. The acquisition and disposal of certain nonfinancial assets include the sales and purchases of rights to natural resources, patents, copyrights, trademarks, franchises, and leases. Though conceptually important, capital transactions are generally very small in U.S. accounts and thus will not be emphasized in this chapter.

The vast majority of transactions appearing in the capital and financial account come from financial transactions. The following are examples of private-sector financial transactions:

Direct Investment: Direct investment occurs when residents of one country acquire a controlling interest (stock ownership of ten percent or more) in a business enterprise in another country.

Securities: Securities are private-sector purchases of short- and long-term debt securities, such as Treasury bills, Treasury notes, Treasury bonds, and securities of private enterprises.

Bank Claims and Liabilities: Bank claims consist of loans, overseas deposits, acceptances, foreign commercial paper, claims on affiliated banks abroad, and foreign government obligations. Bank liabilities include demand deposits and NOW (negotiable order of withdrawal) accounts, passbook savings deposits, certificates of deposit, and liabilities to affiliated banks abroad.

Capital and financial transactions are recorded in the balance-of-payments statement by applying a plus sign (credit) to capital and financial inflows and a minus sign (debit) to capital and financial outflows. For the United States, a *financial inflow* might occur under the following circumstances: (1) U.S. liabilities to foreigners rise (for example, a French resident purchases securities of IBM); (2) U.S. claims on foreigners decrease (Citibank receives repayment for a loan it made to a Mexican enterprise); (3) foreign-held assets in the United States rise (Toyota builds an auto-assembly plant in the United States); or (4) U.S. assets overseas decrease (Coca-Cola sells one of its Japanese bottling plants to a Japanese buyer). A *financial outflow* would imply the opposite.

The following rule may be helpful in appreciating the fundamental difference between credit and debit transactions that make up the capital and financial account. Any transaction that leads to the home country's receiving payments from foreigners can be regarded as a credit item. A capital (financial) inflow can be likened to the *export* of goods and services. Conversely, any transaction that leads to foreigners receiving payments, it is considered a debit item for home countries. A capital (financial) outflow is similar in effect to the *import* of goods and services.

Besides including private-sector transactions, the capital and financial account includes **official settlements transactions** of the home country's central bank. Official settlements transactions refer to the movement of financial assets among official holders (for example, the U.S. Federal Reserve and the Bank of England). These financial assets fall into two categories: official reserve assets (U.S. government assets abroad) and liabilities to foreign official agencies (foreign official assets in the United States).

Official holdings of reserves are used for two purposes. First, they afford a country sufficient international liquidity to finance short-term trade deficits and weather

TABLE 10.1

U.S. RESERVE ASSETS, 2008*

Type	Amount (billions of dollars)
Gold stock**	$11.0
Special drawing rights	9.0
Reserve positions in the International Monetary Fund	7.3
Convertible foreign currencies	46.0
Total	$73.3

*November
**Gold is valued at $42.22/fine troy ounce.

Source: From *Statistical Supplement to the Federal Reserve Bulletin*, December 2008, available at Internet site **http://www.federalreserve.gov**.

TABLE 10.2

SELECTED U.S. LIABILITIES TO FOREIGN OFFICIAL INSTITUTIONS, 2008*

	Amount (billions of dollars)
BY TYPE	
Liabilities reported by U.S. banks**	$ 303.3
U.S. Treasury bills and certificates	360.6
U.S. Treasury bonds and notes	1,542.6
Other U.S. securities	1,245.8
Total	$3,452.3
BY AREA	
Europe	$ 592.3
Canada	12.9
Latin America/Caribbean	279.3
Asia	2,486.4
Other	81.4
Total	$3,452.3

*December
**Includes demand deposits, time deposits, bank acceptances, commercial paper, negotiable time certificates of deposit, and borrowings under repurchase agreements.

Source: From *Statistical Supplement to the Federal Reserve Bulletin*, December 2008, available at Internet site **http://www.federalreserve.gov**.

periodic currency crises. This liquidity function is usually only important to developing countries that do not have a readily convertible currency or ready access to international capital markets on favorable terms. Second, central banks sometimes buy or sell official reserve assets in private-sector markets to stabilize their currencies' exchange rates. For countries with fixed exchange rates, changes in reserves can be large as reserves are bought or sold through foreign exchange intervention. Because the United States has a managed floating exchange rate, which usually requires negligible foreign exchange intervention, changes in its official reserve assets tend to be small. This topic is further discussed in Chapter 15.

Table 10.1 summarizes the **official reserve assets** position of the United States as of 2008. One such asset is the stock of gold reserves held by the U.S. government. Next are convertible currencies, such as the Japanese yen, that are readily acceptable as payment for international transactions and can be easily exchanged for one another. Another reserve asset is the special drawing right (SDR), described in Chapter 17. Last is the reserve position that the United States maintains in the International Monetary Fund, also described in Chapter 17.

Official settlements transactions also include liabilities to foreign official holders. These liabilities refer to foreign official holdings with U.S. commercial banks and official holdings of U.S. Treasury securities. Foreign governments often wish to hold such assets because of the interest earnings they provide. Table 10.2 illustrates the U.S. liabilities to foreign official holders as of 2008.

Statistical Discrepancy: Errors and Omissions

The data-collection process that underlies the published balance-of-payments figures is far from perfect. The cost of collecting balance-of-payments statistics is high, and a perfectly accurate collection system would be prohibitive in cost. Government statisticians thus base their figures partly on information collected and partly on estimates. Probably the most reliable information consists of merchandise trade data, which are collected mainly from customs records. Capital and financial account information is derived from reports by financial institutions indicating changes in their liabilities and claims to foreigners; these data are not matched with specific current account transactions. Because statisticians do not have a system whereby they can simultaneously record the credit and debit side of each transaction, such information for any particular transaction tends to come from different sources. Large numbers of transactions fail to get recorded.

When statisticians sum the credits and debits, it is not surprising when the two totals do not match. Because total debits must equal total credits in principle, statisticians insert a *residual* to make them equal. This corrected entry is known as **statistical discrepancy**, or errors and omissions. In the balance-of-payments statement, statistical discrepancy is treated as part of the capital and financial account because short-term financial transactions are generally the most frequent source of error.

U.S. Balance of Payments

The method the U.S. Department of Commerce uses in presenting balance-of-payments statistics is shown in Table 10.3. This format groups specific transactions together along functional lines to provide analysts with information about the impact of international transactions on the domestic economy. The *partial balances* published on a regular basis include the merchandise trade balance, the balance on goods and services, the current account balance, and information about capital and financial transactions.

The *merchandise trade balance*, commonly referred to as the **trade balance** by the news media, is derived by computing the net exports (imports) in the merchandise accounts. Owing to its narrow focus on traded goods, the merchandise trade balance offers limited policy insight. The popularity of the merchandise trade

TABLE 10.3

U.S. Balance of Payments, 2008 (billions of dollars)

Current Account		Capital and Financial Account	
Merchandise trade balance	−$820.8	Capital account transactions, net	−$2.7
Exports	1,291.4	Financial account transactions, net	546.6
Imports	−2,112.2	Statistical discrepancy	129.3
Services balance	139.7	Balance on capital and financial account	673.2
Travel and transportation, net	160.9		
Military transactions, net	−21.4		
Royalties and license fees, net	61.7		
Other services, net	−61.5		
Goods and services balance	−681.1		
Income balance	127.6		
Investment income, net	134.8		
Compensation of employees, net	−7.2		
Unilateral transfers balance	−119.7		
U.S. Government grants	−34.6		
U.S. Government pensions	−7.9		
Private remittances	−77.2		
Current account balance	−673.2		

Source: From U.S. Department of Commerce, *Survey of Current Business*, June 2009. See also Bureau of Economic Analysis, *U.S. International Transactions Accounts Data* at Internet site **http://www.bea.gov/**.

balance is due largely to its availability on a monthly basis. Merchandise trade data can rapidly be gathered and reported, whereas measuring trade in services requires time-consuming questionnaires.

As seen in Table 10.3, the United States had a merchandise trade deficit of $820.8 billion in 2008, resulting from the difference between U.S. merchandise exports ($1,291.4 billion) and U.S. merchandise imports ($2,112.2 billion). The United States was thus a net importer of merchandise. Table 10.4 shows that the United States has consistently faced merchandise trade deficits in recent decades. This situation contrasts with the 1950s and 1960s, when merchandise trade surpluses were common for the United States.

Trade deficits generally are not popular with domestic residents and policy-makers because they tend to exert adverse consequences on the home nation's terms of trade and employment levels, as well as on the stability of the international money markets. For the United States, economists' concerns over persistent trade deficits have often focused on their possible effects on the terms at which the United States trades with other nations. With a trade deficit, the value of the dollar may fall in international currency markets as dollar outpayments exceed dollar inpayments. Foreign currencies would become more expensive in terms of dollars, so that imports would become more costly to U.S. residents. A trade deficit that induces a decrease in the dollar's international value imposes a real cost on U.S. residents in the form of higher import costs.

Another often-publicized consequence of a trade deficit is its adverse impact on employment levels in certain domestic industries, such as steel or autos. A worsening trade balance may injure domestic labor, not only by the number of jobs lost to foreign workers who produce our imports but also by the employment losses due to deteriorating export sales. It is no wonder that home-nation unions often raise the most vocal arguments about the evils of trade deficits for the domestic economy. Keep in mind, however, that a nation's trade deficit, which leads to decreased employment in some industries, is offset by capital and financial account inflows that generate employment in other industries. Rather than determining total domestic employment, a trade deficit influences the distribution of employment among domestic industries.

TABLE 10.4

U.S. BALANCE OF PAYMENTS, 1980–2008 (IN BILLIONS OF DOLLARS)

Year	Merchandise Trade Balance	Services Balance	Goods and Services Balance	Income Balance	Unilateral Transfers Balance	Current Account Balance
1980	−$25.5	$6.1	−$19.4	$30.1	−$8.3	$2.4
1984	−112.5	3.3	−109.2	30.0	−20.6	−99.8
1988	−127.0	12.2	−114.8	11.6	−25.0	−128.2
1992	−96.1	55.7	−40.4	4.5	−32.0	−67.9
1996	−191.3	87.0	−104.3	17.2	−42.1	−129.2
2000	−452.2	76.5	−375.7	−14.9	−54.1	−444.7
2004	−665.4	47.8	−617.6	30.4	−80.9	−668.1
2008	−820.8	139.7	−681.1	127.6	−119.7	−673.2

Source: From U.S. Department of Commerce, *Survey of Current Business*, various issues.

TRADE CONFLICTS

THE PARADOX OF CAPITAL FLOWS FROM DEVELOPING TO INDUSTRIAL COUNTRIES

The first decade of the 2000s saw the shift of developing countries as a group from net capital importers to net capital exporters. Therefore, capital has been flowing "uphill" from poor developing countries to rich industrial countries, especially the United States. What explains this pattern of capital flows?

The sources of the net capital flow out of the developing economies have been concentrated in China, Japan, Russia, and the members of the Organization of Petroleum Exporting Countries. Economists refer to this situation as capital flowing "uphill" because it appears to contradict economic logic. There are two elements of that logic. First, in developing economies, labor is generally much more available than capital; and thus, capital should be more productive in these economies and should flow there from relatively labor-scarce industrial countries. Second, the relatively rapid income growth expected by developing economies as they catch up to industrial countries should provide them with incentives to borrow against their expected higher future incomes. In spite of this logic, the opposite has occurred during the first decade of the 2000s: capital has flowed from developing countries to rich industrial countries, especially the United States.

One explanation for the uphill flow of capital emphasizes divergent patterns of growth and investment. According to one such view, the increase in U.S. productivity growth boosted perceived rates of return on U.S. assets and thus attracted capital. Also, decreases in investment spending outside the United States resulted in a surplus of saving over investment abroad that was channeled toward the U.S. economy. However, neither a global saving glut nor a U.S. advantage in productivity growth would be expected to persist indefinitely. Thus, net capital flows might reverse direction and head back toward the developing economies at some point.

A second explanation for this paradox focuses on what might be more persistent, structural differences between developing and industrial economies. The financial systems in many developing nations are relatively weak and are not effective at directing saving toward appropriate investment projects. Thus, excess saving flows to countries with better financial systems. Compared with developing economies, industrial countries such as the United States are believed to produce financial assets that are safer, less volatile, and more liquid—although the U.S. financial crisis of 2008–2009 may have raised questions

Discussion of U.S. competitiveness in merchandise trade often gives the impression that the United States has consistently performed poorly relative to other industrial nations. However, the merchandise trade deficit is a narrow concept, because goods are only part of what the world trades. A better indication of the nation's international payments position is the *goods and services balance*. Table 10.3 shows that in 2008, the United States generated a surplus of $139.7 billion on service transactions. Combining this surplus with the merchandise trade deficit of $820.8 billion yields a deficit on the goods and services balance of $681.1 billion. This deficit means that the United States transferred fewer resources (goods and services) to other nations than it received from them during 2008.

In recent decades, the United States has generated a surplus in its services account, as seen in Table 10.4. The United States has been competitive in services categories such as transportation, construction, engineering, brokers' commissions, and certain health care services. The United States also has traditionally registered large net receipts from transactions involving proprietary rights—fees, royalties, and other receipts derived mostly from long-established relations between U.S.-based parent companies and their affiliates abroad.

about that reputation. These are advantages that also draw capital out of developing economies. This explanation also suggests that the uphill flow of capital will be reversed to the extent that the financial systems of developing countries improve. However, such a process is likely to take time.

Also, the current account deficits in the industrial countries—especially the United States—can be traced to increases in both public and private consumption that show up as declines in national savings rates. To an economist, saving money is desirable because it finances productive investments in factories and new equipment, which promote economic growth. But with American households currently saving less than one percent of their income and with politicians unwilling to eliminate the federal budget deficit, the United States has had to rely on the savings of foreigners. These explanations are often advanced when discussing recent global capital flows. While elements of them could account for some aspects of recent trends in global capital flows, none are complete explanations for this complex phenomenon.

The recent net flow of capital toward the industrial world is not in the long-term interest of the developing economies, according to many economists. To increase incomes and reduce poverty, the developing economies must boost their productivity; and that, in turn, will require complementing their large and growing labor forces with increasing amounts of capital. The net flow of capital back toward the developing economies can be best achieved by improving the environment for business investment, strengthening domestic financial systems, and encouraging the development of more attractive financial instruments. At the same time, industrial countries will have to address the implications of their consumption and saving patterns and especially government entitlement programs (Medicare, Social Security, and Medicaid) in view of an aging population.

Sources: Randall Krosner, *International Capital Flows and the Emerging-Market Economies*, Board of Governors of the Federal System, Washington D.C., May 15, 2007. See also Jane Sneddon Little, editor, *Global Imbalances and the Evolving World Economy*, Federal Reserve Bank of Boston, Boston MA, 2008 and the United Nations Council on Trade and Development (UNCTAD), *Trade and Development Report*, Geneva, Switzerland, 2008.

Adjusting the balance on goods and services for income receipts and payments and net unilateral transfers gives the balance of the current account. As Table 10.3 shows, the United States had a *current account* deficit of $673.2 billion in 2008. This deficit means that an excess of imports over exports—of goods, services, income flows, and unilateral transfers—resulted in decreasing net foreign investment for the United States. However, we should *not* become unduly preoccupied with the current account balance, for it ignores capital and financial account transactions. If foreigners purchase more U.S. assets in the United States (such as land, buildings, and bonds), then the United States can afford to import more goods and services from abroad. To look at one aspect of a nation's international payment position without considering the others is misleading.

Taken as a whole, U.S. international transactions always balance. This balance means that any force leading to an increase or decrease in one balance-of-payments account sets in motion a process leading to exactly offsetting changes in the balances of other accounts. As seen in Table 10.3, the United States had a current account deficit in 2008 of $673.2 billion. Offsetting this deficit was a combined surplus of $673.2 billion in the remaining capital and financial accounts, as follows: (1) capital account transactions, net, −$2.7 billion outflow; (2) financial account transactions, net, $546.6 billion inflow; and (3) statistical discrepancy, $129.3 billion inflow.

What Does a Current Account Deficit (Surplus) Mean?

Concerning the balance of payments, the current account and the capital and financial account are not unrelated; they are essentially reflections of one another. Because the balance of payments is a double-entry accounting system, total debits will always equal total credits. It follows that if the current account registers a *deficit* (debits outweigh credits), the capital and financial account must register a *surplus*, or net capital/financial *inflow* (credits outweigh debits). Conversely, if the current account registers a *surplus*, the capital and financial account must register a *deficit*, or net capital/financial *outflow*.

To better understand this concept, assume that in a particular year your spending is greater than your income. How will you finance your "deficit"? The answer is by borrowing or by selling some of your assets. You might liquidate some real assets (for example, sell your personal computer) or perhaps some financial assets (sell a U.S. government security that you own). In like manner, when a nation experiences a current account deficit, its expenditures for foreign goods and services are greater than the income received from the international sales of its own goods and services, after making allowances for investment income flows and gifts to and from foreigners. The nation must somehow finance its current account deficit. But how? The answer lies in selling assets and borrowing. In other words, a nation's current account deficit (debits outweigh credits) is offset by a net financial inflow (credits outweigh debits) in its capital and financial account.

However, one should not treat international capital flows as though they are passively responding to what is happening in the current account. The current account deficit, some say, is "financed" by U.S. borrowing abroad. However, international investors buy U.S. assets not for the purpose of financing the U.S. current account deficit but because they believe these are sound investments, promising a good combination of safety and return. Also, many of these investments have nothing whatsoever to do with borrowing as commonly understood, but instead involve purchases of land, businesses, and common stock in the United States.

Net Foreign Investment and the Current Account Balance

The current account balance is synonymous with **net foreign investment** in national income accounting. A *current account surplus* means an excess of exports over imports of goods, services, investment income, and unilateral transfers. This surplus permits a net receipt of financial claims for home-nation residents. These funds can be used by the home nation to build up its financial assets or to reduce its liabilities to the rest of the world, improving its net foreign investment position (its net worth vis-à-vis the rest of the world). The home nation experiences capital outflows and thus becomes a net *supplier* of funds (lender) to the rest of the world. Conversely, a *current account deficit* implies an excess of imports over exports of goods, services, investment income, and unilateral transfers. This deficit leads to an increase in net foreign claims upon the home nation. The home nation experiences foreign capital inflows and thus becomes a net *demander* of funds from abroad, the demand being met through borrowing from other nations or liquidating foreign assets. The result is a worsening of the home nation's net foreign investment position.

The current account balance thus represents the bottom line on a nation's income statement. If it is positive, then the nation is spending less than its total income and accumulating asset claims on the rest of the world. If it is negative, then domestic expenditure exceeds income and the nation borrows from the rest of the world.

The net borrowing of an economy can be expressed as the sum of the net borrowing by each of its sectors: government and the private sector, including business and households. Net borrowing by government equals its budget deficit: the excess of outlays (G) over taxes (T). Private-sector net borrowing equals the excess of private investment (I) over private saving (S). The net borrowing of the nation is given by the following identity:

$$
\underset{\substack{\text{Government} \\ \text{Deficit}}}{(\text{G} \; - \; \text{T})} \; + \; \underset{\substack{\text{Private} \\ \text{Investment}}}{(\text{I}} \; - \; \underset{\substack{\text{Private} \\ \text{Saving}}}{\text{S})} \; = \; \underset{\substack{\text{Current} \\ \text{Account} \\ \text{Deficit} \\ \text{(net borrowing)}}}{\text{Current}}
$$

An important aspect of this identity is that the current account deficit is a macroeconomic phenomenon: It reflects imbalances between government outlays and taxes as well as imbalances between private investment and saving. Any effective policy to decrease the current account deficit must ultimately reduce these discrepancies. Reducing the current account deficit requires either decreases in the government's budget deficit or increases in private saving relative to investment, or both. However, these options are difficult to achieve. Decreasing budget deficits may require unpopular tax hikes or government program cutbacks. Efforts to reduce investment spending would be opposed because investment is a key determinant of the nation's productivity and standard of living. Also, incentives to stimulate saving, such as tax breaks, may be opposed on the grounds that they favor the rich rather than the poor.

Decreasing a current account deficit is not entirely in the hands of the home nation. For the world as a whole, the sum of all nations' current account balances must equal zero. Thus, a reduction in one nation's current account deficit must go hand in hand with a decrease in the current account surplus of the rest of the world. A complementary policy in foreign nations, especially those with large current account surpluses, can help in a successful transition.

Impact of Capital Flows on the Current Account

In the preceding section, we described a country's capital and financial flows as responsive to developments in the current account. However, the process can, and often does, work the other way around, with capital and financial flows initiating changes in the current account. For example, if foreigners want to purchase U.S. financial instruments exceeding the amount of foreign financial obligations that Americans want to hold, they must pay for the excess with shipments of foreign goods and services. Therefore, a financial inflow to the United States is associated with a U.S. current account deficit.

Let us elaborate on how a U.S. current account deficit can be caused by a net financial inflow to the United States. Suppose domestic saving falls short of desired domestic investment. Therefore, U.S. interest rates rise relative to interest rates abroad, which attracts an inflow of foreign saving to help support U.S. investment. The United States thus becomes a net importer of foreign saving, using the borrowed purchasing power to acquire foreign goods and services, and resulting in a like-sized net inflow of goods and services—a current account deficit. But how does a financial inflow cause a current account deficit for the United States? When foreigners start purchasing more of our assets than we are purchasing of theirs, the dollar becomes more costly in the foreign-exchange market (see Chapter 11). This causes U.S. goods to become more expensive to foreigners, resulting in declining exports; also, foreign goods become cheaper to Americans, resulting in increasing imports. The result is a rise in the current account deficit, or a decline in the current account surplus.

Economists believe that, in the 1980s, a massive financial inflow caused a current account deficit for the United States. The financial inflow was the result of an increase in the U.S. interest rate relative to interest rates abroad. The higher interest rate, in turn, was mainly due to the combined effects of the U.S. federal government's growing budget deficit and a decline in the private saving rate.

Simply put, instead of thinking that capital flows are financing the current account deficit, it may well be that the current account deficit is driven by capital flows: capital inflows keep the dollar stronger than it otherwise would be, tending to boost imports and suppress exports, thus leading to a current account deficit.

Is a Current Account Deficit a Problem?

Contrary to commonly held views, a current account deficit has little to do with foreign trade practices or any inherent inability of a country to sell its goods on the world market. Instead, it is because of underlying macroeconomic conditions at home requiring more imports to meet current domestic demand for goods and services than can be paid for by export sales. In effect, the domestic economy spends more than it produces, and this excess of demand is met by a net inflow of foreign goods and services leading to the current account deficit. This tendency is minimized during periods of recession but expands significantly with the rising income associated with economic recovery and expansion. Simply put, current account deficits are not efficiently reversed by trade policies that attempt to alter the levels of imports or exports such as tariffs, quotas, or subsidies.

When a nation realizes a current account deficit, it experiences foreign capital inflows and thus becomes a net borrower of funds from the rest of the world. Is this a problem? Not necessarily. Foreign capital inflows augment domestic sources of capital, which, in turn, keep domestic interest rates lower than they would be without foreign capital. The benefit of a current account deficit is the ability to push current spending beyond current production. However, the cost is the debt service that must be paid on the associated borrowing from the rest of the world.

Is it good or bad for a country to incur debt? The answer obviously depends on what the country does with the money. What matters for future incomes and living standards is whether the deficit is being used to finance more consumption or more investment. If used exclusively to finance an increase in domestic investment, the burden could be slight. We know that investment spending increases the nation's stock of capital and expands the economy's capacity to produce goods and services. The value of this extra output may be sufficient to both pay foreign creditors and also augment domestic spending. In this case, because future consumption need not fall below what it otherwise would have been, there would be no true economic burden. If, on the other hand, foreign borrowing is used to finance or increase domestic consumption (private or public), there is no boost given to future productivity. Therefore, to meet debt service expense, future consumption must be reduced below what it otherwise would have been. Such a reduction represents the burden of borrowing. This is not necessarily bad; it all depends on how one values current versus future consumption.

During the 1980s, when the United States realized current account deficits, the rate of domestic saving decreased relative to the rate of investment. In fact, the decline of the overall saving rate was mainly the result of a decrease of its public saving component, caused by large and persistent federal budget deficits in this period—budget deficits are in effect negative savings that subtract from the pool of savings. This negative savings indicated that the United States used foreign borrowing to increase current consumption, not productivity-enhancing public investment. The U.S. current account deficits of the 1980s were thus greeted with concern by many economists.

However, in the 1990s, U.S. current account deficits were driven by increases in domestic investment. This investment boom contributed to expanding employment and output. It could not, however, have been financed by national saving alone. Foreign lending provided the additional capital needed to finance the boom. In the absence of foreign lending, U.S. interest rates would have been higher, and investment would inevitably have been constrained by the supply of domestic saving. Therefore, the accumulation of capital and the growth of output and employment would all have been smaller had the United States not been able to run a current account deficit in the 1990s. Rather than choking off growth and employment, the large current account deficit allowed faster long-term growth in the U.S. economy, which improved economic welfare.

Business Cycles, Economic Growth, and the Current Account

How is the current account related to a country's business cycle and long-term economic growth? Concerning the business cycle, *rapid* growth of production and employment is commonly associated with large or growing trade and current account *deficits*, whereas *slow* output and employment growth is associated with large or growing *surpluses*.

During a recession, both saving and investment tend to fall. Saving falls as households try to maintain their consumption patterns in the face of a temporary fall in income; investment declines because capacity utilization declines and profits fall. However, because investment is highly sensitive to the need for extra capacity, it tends to drop more sharply than saving during recessions. The current account balance thus tends to rise. Consistent with this rise, but viewed from a different angle, the trade balance typically improves during a recession, because imports tend to fall with overall consumption and investment demand. The opposite occurs during periods of boom, when sharp increases in investment demand typically outweigh increases in saving, producing a decline in the current account. Of course, factors other than income influence saving and investment, so that the tendency of a country's current account deficit to decline in recessions is not ironclad.

The relation just described between the current account and economic performance typically holds not only on a short-term or cyclical basis, but also on a

ECONOMIC DOWNTURN OF 2007–2009: EFFECT ON FOREIGN INVESTMENT IN THE UNITED STATES

The large capital inflows into the United States in recent decades have provided many benefits for Americans, as discussed in this chapter. However, during the global economic downturn of 2007–2009, there was concern whether these benefits would continue. There were two aspects to this concern.

First, there was the question of whether the supply of credit that net-saver countries provide to the rest of the world would decrease. This credit has flowed from countries with large current-account surpluses, including China, Japan, and the Middle East countries. To the extent that a slowdown in global economic activity decreases the demand for Asian exports and Middle-East petroleum products, the net savings available from these countries might decline if their savings rates do not increase sharply. Also, foreign countries' savings would likely decrease if their governments decided to engage in higher spending to boost their flagging economies, thus decreasing the amount of government saving. This spending would reduce the gap between national saving and domestic investment and reduce the supply of credit to the rest of the world, therefore increasing world interest rates. Some of these factors appeared to be occurring by 2009. For example, China's exports to other countries decreased and China enacted a substantial fiscal stimulus program to pump prime its weakening economy.

A second question was whether the cost of foreign savings to the United States would increase. This cost depended on the U.S. demand for foreign savings and the relative desirability of U.S. assets for foreign investors. As the U.S. government increased expenditures to bolster its economy, the demand for foreign savings increased in 2009. Yet the cost of foreign savings did not noticeably rise for the United States. This was mainly due to an increase in the relative desirability of low-risk U.S. Treasury securities for global investors as compared to higher-risk securities offered by other countries. The net inflow of foreign savings into U.S. Treasury securities allowed the U.S. government to borrow at a relatively low cost, and this low cost helped cushion the impact of the crisis on the U.S. economy.

As the global economy improves, and investors' desire for risk returns, the demand for Treasury securities will likely decline. Whether the cost of foreign savings will increase for the United States will depend on the relative attractiveness of U.S. investments compared to opportunities abroad. At the writing of this text, it remains to be seen how these events will play out.

Source: *Economic Report of the President*, U.S. Government Printing Office, Washington D.C., 2009, pp. 141–142.

long-term basis. Often, countries enjoying *rapid* economic growth possess long-term current account *deficits*, whereas those with *weaker* economic growth have long-term current account *surpluses*. This relation likely derives from the fact that rapid economic growth and strong investment often go hand in hand. Where the driving force is the discovery of new natural resources, technological progress, or the implementation of economic reform, periods of rapid economic growth are likely to be periods in which new investment is unusually profitable. However, investment must be financed with saving, and if a country's national saving is not sufficient to finance all new profitable investment projects, the country will rely on foreign saving to finance the difference. It thus experiences a net financial inflow and a corresponding current account deficit. As long as the new investments are profitable, they will generate the extra earnings needed to repay the claims contracted to undertake them. Thus, when current account deficits reflect strong, profitable investment programs, they work to raise the rate of output and employment growth, not to destroy jobs and production.

Norway provides an example of one of these productive opportunities. In the 1960s, rich petroleum deposits were discovered in the North Sea. Norway was one of the major beneficiaries of this discovery. Getting to these valuable oil and gas deposits required large and repeated investments in off-shore oil platforms, transport pipelines, ships, and helicopters. Norway also had to develop a knowledge of exploration and extraction to precisely locate and exploit these resources. Acquiring these items required sizable imports that created trade deficits for Norway. At the time of these discoveries, Norway lacked the equipment and expertise to take advantage of the opportunity. Although the oil revenue would eventually pay for these investments, they had to be paid for in advance. Norway thus financed the investments by borrowing from the rest of the world. Foreign investors were happy to make these loans because Norway's capital was viewed to be more productive and thus earned a higher return than could be earned abroad. Once the oil came online, Norway began running persistent trade surpluses, which were used to repay its original borrowing and to save for a day when the petroleum reserves are exhausted. Simply put, Norway's initial trade deficit was a sign of strong and continued economic growth, and thus good things to come.

How the United States Has Borrowed at Very Low Cost

Over the past three decades, the U.S. current account has moved from a small surplus to a deficit in 2006 of more than $800 billion. This deficit is financed by either borrowing from or selling assets to foreigners. As the current-account deficit has increased for the United States, the country has become a large net debtor. The legacy of cumulative U.S. current-account deficits resulted in the net accumulation of U.S. liabilities through 2006 of almost $2.7 trillion, which was equivalent to 22 percent of U.S. GDP.

When a country increases its borrowing from abroad, the cost of servicing its debt is expected to increase. This is because the country must make larger payments of interest and principal to foreign lenders. However, during the past two decades, there has been a paradox in U.S. international transactions: U.S. residents have consistently earned more income from their foreign investments than foreigners earn from their larger U.S. investments. In most years the surplus has been between $20 and $30 billion. Therefore, the United States has been able to be a large debtor nation without bearing negative debt service cost. This paradox suggests that the U.S. current account deficits might be less burdensome than often portrayed.

What accounts for this paradox? One explanation concerns asymmetric investment returns. The United States has tended to consistently earn higher returns on its foreign investments than foreigners earn on their U.S. investments. This overall rate of return advantage has generally been one to two percentage points. A main reason for this advantage is that U.S. companies take greater risks when they invest in foreign nations, such as economic and political instability. Investments that involve higher risk will not be undertaken unless they offer the potential for higher rewards. Conversely, because the United States is generally considered as a safe haven for investment, foreign investors are more likely to buy U.S. assets that offer low return and low risk.

This paradox provides an explanation of why the massive foreign borrowing by the United States has been relatively painless in the past two decades. However, future borrowing prospects may not be as favorable. Skeptics fear that if global interest rates rise, the United States will have to pay higher rates to attract foreign investment, thus increasing U.S. interest payments to foreigners. These payments could swing the U.S. investment-income balance from surplus to deficit and cause U.S. debt service costs to become burdensome. As this costs grows, the U.S. current-account deficit and its consequences could increasingly become matters of concern for economic policy makers.[2]

Do Current Account Deficits Cost Americans Jobs?

The sizable U.S. current account deficits that have occurred in recent years have prompted concerns that American jobs are in jeopardy. Increasing competition in the domestic market from low-cost Asian imports could put pressure on U.S. firms to lay off workers. Exporters such as Ford, whose sales decline as a strong dollar raises the price of its autos in foreign markets, could also move to restrict employment. Also, jobs in export-oriented firms such as Boeing were hurt by the 1997–1998 recession in Asia, which weakened the demand for U.S. goods. Weak foreign economies in the first decade of the 2000s also contributed to falling demand for American products. Adding to concerns about the employment effects of the current account deficit is the fear that increasing numbers of U.S. firms will shut down domestic operations and shift production to other countries, largely to take advantage of lower labor costs.

Nevertheless, although export and import trends raise concerns about U.S. job losses, employment statistics do not bear out the relation between a rising current account deficit and lower employment. According to economists at the Federal Reserve Bank of New York, the U.S. current account deficit is not a threat to total employment for the economy as a whole.[3] A high current account deficit may indeed hurt employment in particular firms and industries as workers are displaced by increased imports or by the relocation of production abroad. At the economy-wide level, however, the current account deficit is matched by an equal inflow of foreign funds, which finances employment-sustaining investment spending that would not otherwise occur. When viewed as the net inflow of foreign investment, the current account deficit produces jobs for the economy: both from the direct effects of higher employment in investment-oriented industries and from the indirect effects of higher investment spending on economy-wide employment. Simply put, with a current account deficit some import sensitive industries (such as textiles) will have their output and employment decline, but some credit sensitive industries (such as housing) will have their output and employment increase. Also, the Federal Reserve, using monetary policy, can set the overall level of spending in the economy to a level consistent with full employment. Viewing the current account deficit as a net inflow of foreign investment thus helps to dispel misconceptions about the adverse consequences of economic globalization on the domestic job market.

---

[2]Juann Hung and Angelo Mascaro, *Why Does U.S. Investment Abroad Earn Higher Returns Than Foreign Investment in the United States?* Congressional Budget Office: Washington, D.C., 2005, Craig Elwell, *U.S. External Debt: How Has the United States Borrowed Without Cost? Congressional Research Service*, Washington, D.C., 2006, and William Cline, *The United States as a Debtor Nation*, Washington, D.C., Institute for International Economics, 2005.

[3]Matthew Higgins and Thomas Klitgaard, "Viewing the Current Account Deficit as a Capital Inflow," *Current Issues and Economics and Finance*, Federal Reserve Bank of New York, December 1999, pp. 1–6 and Craig Elwell, *Deindustrialization of the U.S. Economy*, Congressional Research Service, 2004.

Although standard economic analysis indicates that current account deficits do not cause a net loss of output or jobs in the overall economy, they tend to change the composition of output and employment. For example, evidence suggests that over the past two decades, persistent current account deficits have likely caused a reduction in the size of the U.S. manufacturing sector, while output and employment in the economy's service sector have increased.

Can the United States Continue to Run Current Account Deficits Indefinitely?

The United States has benefitted from a surplus of saving over investment in many areas of the world, which has provided a supply of funds. This surplus of saving has been available to the United States because foreigners have remained willing to loan that saving to the United States in the form of acquiring U.S. assets, such as Treasury securities, which have accommodated the current account deficits. During the 1990s and the first decade of the 2000s, for example, the United States experienced a decline in its rate of saving and an increase in the rate of domestic investment. The large increase in the U.S. current account deficit would not have been possible without the accommodating inflows of foreign capital coming from nations with high saving rates, such as Japan, China, and Middle-Eastern nations, as seen in Table 10.5.

For example, China has been the fastest growing supplier of capital to the United States during 2001–2010. This is partly because of China's exchange-rate policy of keeping the value of its yuan low (cheap) so as to export goods to the United States and thus create jobs for its workers (see Chapter 15). In order to offset a rise in the value of the yuan against the dollar, the central bank of China has purchased dollars with yuan. Rather than hold dollars, which earn no interest, China's central bank has converted much of its dollar holdings into U.S. securities that do pay interest. This situation has put the United States in a unique position to benefit from the willingness of China to finance its current-account deficit. Simply put, the United States can "print money" that the Chinese hold in order to finance its excess spending. The buildup of China's dollar reserves helps to support the U.S. stock and bond markets and permits the U.S. government to incur expenditure increases and tax reductions without increases in domestic U.S. interest rates that would otherwise take place. However, some analysts are concerned that at some point Chinese investors may view the increasing level of U.S. foreign debt as unsustainable or more risky and thus suddenly shift their capital elsewhere. They also express concern that the United States will become more politically reliant on China who might use its large holdings of U.S. securities as leverage against policies it opposes.

Can the United States run current account deficits indefinitely and thus rely on inflows of foreign capital? Since the current account deficit arises mainly because foreigners desire to purchase American assets, there is

TABLE 10.5

FOREIGN HOLDERS OF U.S. SECURITIES AS OF 2007

Country	Billions of Dollars	Percent of World Total
Japan	$1,197	12.2%
China	922	9.4
United Kingdom	921	9.4
Cayman Islands	740	7.6
Luxembourg	703	7.2
Canada	475	4.9
Belgium	396	4.0
Other	4,418	45.3
World Total	$9,772	100.0%

Source: U.S. Treasury Department, *Report on Foreign Portfolio Holdings of U.S. Securities as of June 30, 2007*, April 2008, p. 8.

no economic reason why it cannot continue indefinitely. As long as the investment opportunities are large enough to provide foreign investors with competitive rates of return, they will be happy to continue supplying funds to the United States. Simply put, there is no reason why the process cannot continue indefinitely: no automatic forces will cause either a current account deficit or a current account surplus to reverse.

United States history illustrates this point. From 1820 to 1875, the United States ran current account deficits almost continuously. At this time, the United States was a relatively poor (by European standards) but rapidly growing country. Foreign investment helped foster that growth. This situation changed after World War I. The United States was richer, and investment opportunities were more limited. Thus, current account surpluses were present almost continuously between 1920 and 1970. During the last 25 years, the situation has again reversed. The current account deficits of the United States are underlaid by its system of secure property rights, a stable political and monetary environment, and a rapidly growing labor force (compared with Japan and Europe), which make the United States an attractive place to invest. Moreover, the U.S. saving rate is low compared to its major trading partners. The U.S. current account deficit reflects this combination of factors, and it is likely to continue as long as they are present.

At the turn of the century, the United States' current account deficit was high and rising. By 2006, the U.S. current account deficit was about six percent of GDP, the highest in the country's history. Even in the late 1800s, after the Civil War, the U.S. deficit was generally below three percent of GDP. During the budget deficits of President Ronald Reagan in the 1980s, the current account deficit peaked at 3.4 percent of GDP. Because of relatively good prospects for growth in the United States compared to the rest of the world, international capital was flowing to the United States in search of the safety and acceptable returns offered there. However, capital was not flowing to emerging markets as in the 1990s. Europe faced high unemployment and sluggish growth, and Japan faced economic contraction and continuing financial problems. Not surprisingly in this setting, capital flowed into the United States because of the relatively superior past performance and expectations for future growth in the U.S. economy. Simply put, the U.S. current account deficit reflected a surplus of good investment opportunities in the United States and a deficit of growth prospects elsewhere in the world. However, many economists feel that economies become overextended and hit trouble when their current-account deficits reach four to five percent of GDP.

Some economists think that because of spreading globalization, the pool of savings offered to the United States by world financial markets is deeper and more liquid than ever. This pool allows foreign investors to continue furnishing the U.S. with the money it needs without demanding higher interest rates in return. Presumably, a current account deficit of six percent or more of GDP would not have been readily fundable several decades ago. The ability to move that much of world saving to the United States in response to relative rates of return would have been hindered by a far lower degree of international financial interdependence. However, in recent years, the increasing integration of financial markets has created an expanding class of foreigners who are willing and able to invest in the United States.

The consequence of a current account deficit is a growing foreign ownership of the capital stock of the United States and a rising fraction of U.S. income that must be diverted overseas in the form of interest and dividends to foreigners. A serious problem could emerge if foreigners lose confidence in the ability of the United States to generate the resources necessary to repay the funds borrowed from abroad. As a result, suppose that foreigners decide to reduce the fraction of their saving that they send to the United States. The initial effect could be both a sudden and large decline in the value of the dollar as the supply of dollars increases on the foreign-exchange market and a sudden and large increase in U.S. interest rates as an important source of saving was withdrawn from financial markets. Large increases in interest rates could cause problems for the U.S. economy as they reduce the market value of debt securities, cause prices on the stock market to decline, and raise questions about the solvency of various debtors. Simply put, whether the United States can sustain its current account deficit over the foreseeable future depends on whether foreigners are willing to increase their investments in U.S. assets. The current account deficit puts the economic fortunes of the United States partially in the hands of foreign investors.

However, the economy's ability to cope with big current account deficits depends on continued improvements in efficiency and technology. If the economy becomes more productive, then its real wealth may grow fast enough to cover its debt. Optimists note that robust increases in U.S. productivity in recent years have made its current account deficits affordable. But if productivity growth stalls, the economy's ability to cope with current account deficits will deteriorate.

Although the appropriate level of the U.S. current account deficit is difficult to assess, at least two principles are relevant should it prove necessary to reduce the deficit. First, the United States has an interest in policies that stimulate foreign growth, because it is better to reduce the current account deficit through faster growth abroad than through slower growth at home. A recession at home would obviously be a highly undesirable means of reducing the deficit.

Second, any reductions in the deficit are better achieved through increased national saving than through reduced domestic investment. If there are attractive investment opportunities in the United States, we are better off borrowing from abroad to finance these opportunities than forgoing them. On the other hand, incomes in this country would be even higher in the future if these investments were financed through higher national saving. Increases in national saving allow interest rates to remain lower than they would otherwise be. Lower interest rates lead to higher domestic investment, which, in turn, boosts demand for equipment and construction. For any given level of investment, increased saving also results in higher net exports, which would again increase employment in these sectors.

However, shrinking the U.S. current account deficit can be difficult. The economies of foreign nations may not be strong enough to absorb additional American exports, and Americans may be reluctant to curb their appetite for foreign goods. Also, the U.S. government has shown a bias toward deficit spending. Turning around a deficit is associated with a sizable fall in the exchange rate and a decrease in output in the adjusting country, topics that will be discussed in subsequent chapters.

Balance of International Indebtedness

A main feature of the U.S. balance of payments is that it measures the economic transactions of the United States over a period of one year or one quarter. But at any particular moment, a nation will have a fixed stock of assets and liabilities against the rest of the world. The statement that summarizes this situation is known as the **balance of international indebtedness**. It is a record of the international position of the United States at a particular time (year-end data).

The U.S. balance of international indebtedness indicates the accumulated value of U.S.-owned assets abroad as opposed to foreign-owned assets in the United States. These assets include such financial assets as corporate stocks and bonds, government securities, and direct investment in businesses and real estate. The value of these assets can change as a result of purchases and sales of new or existing assets, changes in the value of assets that arise through appreciation/depreciation or inflation, and so on. The United States is considered a **net creditor** to the rest of the world when the accumulated value of U.S.-owned assets abroad exceeds the value of foreign-owned assets in the United States. When the reverse occurs, the United States assumes a **net debtor** position. Table 10.6. shows the international investment position of the United States for various years.

Of what use is the balance of international indebtedness? Perhaps of greatest significance is that it breaks down international investment holdings into several categories so that policy implications can be drawn from each separate category about the *liquidity status* of the nation. For the short-term investment position, the strategic factor is the amount of short-term liabilities (bank deposits and government securities) held by foreigners. This is because these holdings potentially can be withdrawn at very short notice, resulting in a disruption of domestic financial markets. The balance of official monetary holdings is also significant. Assume that this balance is negative from the U.S. viewpoint. Should foreign monetary authorities decide to liquidate their holdings of U.S. government securities and have them converted into official reserve assets, the financial strength of the dollar would be reduced. As for a nation's long-term investment position, it is of less importance for the U.S. liquidity position because long-term investments generally respond to basic economic trends and are not subject to erratic withdrawals.

TABLE 10.6

INTERNATIONAL INVESTMENT POSITION OF THE U.S. AT YEAR-END (IN BILLIONS OF DOLLARS)

Type of Investment*	1995	2000	2007
U.S.-owned assets abroad			
U.S. government assets	$ 257	$ 214	$ 2,656
U.S. private assets	3,149	5,954	14,984
Total	$3,406	$6,168	$17,640
Foreign-owned assets in the United States			
Foreign official assets	$ 672	$ 922	$ 3,337
Foreign private assets	3,234	7,088	16,745
Total	$3,906	$8,010	$20,082
Net international investment position	−500	−1,842	−2,442
Relative share: U.S. Net international investment position/U.S. gross domestic product	6%	15%	18%

*At current cost.

Source: From U.S. Department of Commerce, Bureau of Economic Analysis, *The International Investment Position of the United States at Year End*, available at **http://www.bea.gov**. See also U.S. Department of Commerce, *Survey of Current Business*, various June and July issues.

United States as a Debtor Nation

In the early stages of its industrial development, the United States was a net international debtor. Relying heavily on foreign funds, the United States built up its industries by mortgaging part of its wealth to foreigners. After World War I, the United States became a net international creditor. The U.S. international investment position evolved steadily from a net-creditor position of $6 billion in 1919 to a position of $337 billion in 1983. However, by 1987 the United States had become a net international debtor, in the amount of $23 billion, for the first time since World War I; since then, the United States has continued to be a net international debtor, as seen in Table 10.6.

How did this turnabout occur so rapidly? The reason was that foreign investors placed more funds in the United States than U.S. residents invested abroad. The United States was considered attractive to investors from other countries because of its rapid economic recovery from the recession of the early 1980s, its political stability, and its relatively high interest rates. American investments overseas fell because of the sluggish loan demand in Europe, the desire by commercial banks to reduce their overseas exposure as a reaction to the debt-repayment problems of Latin American countries, and the decreases in credit demand by oil-importing developing nations as the result of declining oil prices. Of the foreign investment funds in the United States, less than one-fourth went to direct ownership of U.S. real estate and business. Most of the funds were in financial assets such as bank deposits, stocks, and bonds.

For the typical U.S. resident, the transition from net creditor to net debtor went unnoticed. However, the net-debtor status of the United States raised an issue of propriety. To many observers, it seemed inappropriate for the United States, one of the richest nations in the world, to be borrowing on a massive scale from the rest of the world.

Summary

1. The balance of payments is a record of a nation's economic transactions with all other nations for a given year. A credit transaction is one that results in a receipt of payments from foreigners, whereas a debit transaction leads to a payment abroad. Owing to double-entry bookkeeping, a nation's balance of payments will always balance.

2. From a functional viewpoint, the balance of payments identifies economic transactions as (a) current account transactions and (b) capital and financial account transactions.

3. The balance on goods and services is important to policymakers because it indicates the net transfer of real resources overseas. It also measures the extent to which a nation's exports and imports are part of its gross national product.

4. The capital and financial account of the balance of payments shows the international movement of loans, investments, and the like. Capital and financial inflows (outflows) are analogous to exports (imports) of goods and services because they result in the receipt (payment) of funds from (to) other nations.

5. Official reserves consist of a nation's financial assets: (a) monetary gold holdings, (b) convertible currencies, (c) special drawing rights, and (d) drawing positions on the International Monetary Fund.

6. The current method employed by the Department of Commerce in presenting the U.S. international payments position makes use of a functional format emphasizing the following *partial* balances: (a) merchandise trade balance,

(b) balance on goods and services, and (c) current account balance.

7. Because the balance of payments is a double-entry accounting system, total debits will always equal total credits. It follows that if the current account registers a deficit (surplus), the capital and financial account must register a surplus (deficit), or net capital/financial inflow (outflow). If a country realizes a deficit (surplus) in its current account, it becomes a net demander (supplier) of funds from (to) the rest of the world.

8. Concerning the business cycle, rapid growth of production and employment is commonly associated with large or growing trade and current account deficits, whereas slow output and employment growth is associated with large or growing current account surpluses.

9. The international investment position of the United States at a particular time is measured by the balance of international indebtedness. Unlike the balance of payments, which is a flow concept (over a period of time), the balance of international indebtedness is a stock concept (at a single point in time).

Key Concepts & Terms

- Balance of international indebtedness (p. 394)
- Balance of payments (p. 373)
- Capital and financial account (p. 377)
- Credit transaction (p. 373)
- Current account (p. 376)
- Debit transaction (p. 373)
- Double-entry accounting (p. 374)
- Goods and services balance (p. 376)
- Merchandise trade balance (p. 376)
- Net creditor (p. 394)
- Net debtor (p. 394)
- Net foreign investment (p. 384)
- Official reserve assets (p. 379)
- Official settlements transactions (p. 378)
- Statistical Discrepancy (p. 380)
- Trade Balance (p. 380)
- Unilateral Transfers (p. 377)

Study Questions

1. What does the balance of international indebtedness measure? How does this statement differ from the balance of payments?
2. Why does the balance-of-payments statement "balance"?
3. What financial assets are categorized as official reserve assets for the United States?
4. What economic transactions give rise to the receipt of dollars from foreigners? What transactions give rise to payments to foreigners?
5. Why has the goods and services balance sometimes shown a surplus while the merchandise trade balance shows a deficit?
6. What is meant by the balance of payments?
7. What is the meaning of a surplus (deficit) on the (a) merchandise trade balance, (b) goods and services balance, and (c) current account balance?
8. From a functional viewpoint, a nation's balance of payments can be grouped into several categories. What are these categories?
9. Given the hypothetical items shown in Table 10.7, determine the international investment position of the United States. Is the United States a net-creditor nation or a net-debtor nation?

TABLE 10.7

INTERNATIONAL INVESTMENT POSITION OF THE UNITED STATE (IN BILLIONS OF DOLLARS)

Foreign official assets in the United States	$25
Other foreign assets in the United States	225
U.S. government assets abroad	150
U.S. private assets abroad	75

10. Table 10.8 summarizes hypothetical transactions, in billions of U.S. dollars, that took place during a given year.

TABLE 10.8

INTERNATIONAL TRANSACTIONS OF THE UNITED STATES
(BILLIONS OF DOLLARS)

Travel and transportation receipts, net	$25
Merchandise imports	450
Unilateral transfers, net	−20
Allocation of SDRs	15
Receipts on U.S. investments abroad	20
Statistical discrepancy	40
Compensation of employees	−5
Changes in U.S. assets abroad, net	−150
Merchandise exports	375
Other services, net	35
Payments on foreign investments in the United States	−10

a. Calculate the U.S. merchandise trade, services, goods and services, income, unilateral transfers, and current account balances.

b. Which of these balances pertains to the net foreign investment position of the United States? How would you describe that position?

11. Indicate whether each of the following items represents a debit or a credit on the U.S. balance of payments:
   a. A U.S. importer purchases a shipload of French wine.
   b. A Japanese automobile firm builds an assembly plant in Kentucky.
   c. A British manufacturer exports machinery to Taiwan on a U.S. vessel.
   d. A U.S. college student spends a year studying in Switzerland.
   e. American charities donate food to people in drought-plagued Africa.
   f. Japanese investors collect interest income on their holdings of U.S. government securities.
   g. A German resident sends money to her relatives in the United States.
   h. Lloyds of London sells an insurance policy to a U.S. business firm.
   i. A Swiss resident receives dividends on her IBM stock.

Foreign Exchange

CHAPTER 11

Among the factors that make international economics a distinct subject is the existence of different national monetary units of account. In the United States, prices and money are measured in terms of the dollar. The peso represents Mexico's unit of account, whereas the franc and yen signify the units of account of Switzerland and Japan, respectively.

A typical international transaction requires two distinct purchases. First, the foreign currency is bought; second, the foreign currency is used to facilitate the international transaction. For example, before French importers can purchase commodities from, say, U.S. exporters, they must first purchase dollars to meet their international obligation. Some institutional arrangements are required that provide an efficient mechanism whereby monetary claims can be settled with a minimum of inconvenience to both parties. Such a mechanism exists in the form of the foreign-exchange market.[1]

In this chapter, we will examine the nature and operation of this market.

Foreign-Exchange Market

The **foreign-exchange market** refers to the organizational setting within which individuals, businesses, governments, and banks buy and sell foreign currencies and other debt instruments.[2] Only a small fraction of daily transactions in foreign exchange actually involve the trading of currency. Most foreign-exchange transactions involve the transfer of electronic balances between commercial banks or foreign exchange

---

[1]This chapter considers the foreign-exchange market in the absence of government restrictions. In practice, foreign-exchange markets for many currencies are controlled by governments; therefore, the range of foreign-exchange activities discussed in this chapter are not all possible.

[2]This section draws from Sam Cross, *The Foreign Exchange Market in the United States*, Federal Reserve Bank of New York, 1998.

dealers. Major U.S. banks, such as JP Morgan Chase or Bank of America, maintain inventories of foreign exchange in the form of foreign-denominated deposits held in their branches or correspondent banks in foreign cities. Americans can obtain this foreign exchange from hometown banks that, in turn, purchase it from Bank of America.

The foreign-exchange market is by far the largest and most liquid market in the world. The estimated worldwide amount of foreign-exchange transactions is about $3 trillion a day. Individual trades of $200 to $500 million are not uncommon. Quoted prices change as often as 20 times a minute. It has been estimated that the world's most active exchange rates can change up to 18,000 times during a single day.

The foreign-exchange market is dominated by four currencies: the U.S. dollar, the euro, the Japanese yen, and the British pound. Not all currencies are traded on the foreign-exchange market. Currencies that are not traded are avoided for reasons ranging from political instability to economic uncertainty. Sometimes a country's currency is not exchanged for the simple reason that the country produces very few products of interest to other countries.

Unlike stock or commodity exchanges, the foreign-exchange market is not an organized structure. It has no centralized meeting place and no formal requirements for participation. Nor is the foreign-exchange market limited to any one country. For any currency, such as the U.S. dollar, the foreign-exchange market consists of all locations where dollars are exchanged for other national currencies. Three of the largest foreign-exchange markets in the world are located in London, New York, and Tokyo; they handle the majority of all foreign-exchange transactions. A dozen or so other market centers also exist around the world, such as Paris and Zurich. Because foreign-exchange dealers are in constant telephone and computer contact, the market is very competitive; in effect, it functions no differently than if it were a centralized market.

The foreign-exchange market opens on Monday morning in Hong Kong, which is still Sunday evening in New York. As the day progresses, markets open in Tokyo, Frankfurt, London, New York, Chicago, San Francisco, and elsewhere. As the West Coast markets of the United States close, Hong Kong is only one hour away from opening for Tuesday business. Indeed, the foreign-exchange market is a round-the-clock operation.

A typical foreign-exchange market functions at three levels: in transactions between commercial banks and their commercial customers, who are the ultimate demanders and suppliers of foreign exchange; in the domestic interbank market conducted through brokers; and in active trading in foreign exchange with banks overseas.

Exporters, importers, investors, and tourists buy and sell foreign exchange from and to commercial banks rather than each other. As an example, consider the import of German autos by a U.S. dealer. The dealer is billed for each car it imports at the rate of 50,000 euros per car. The U.S. dealer cannot write a check for this amount because it does not have a checking account denominated in euros. Instead, the dealer goes to the foreign-exchange department of, say, Bank of America to arrange payment. If the exchange rate is 1.1 euros = $1, the auto dealer writes a check to Bank of America for $45,454.55 (50,000/1.1 = 45,454.55) per car. Bank of America will then pay the German manufacturer 50,000 euros per car in Germany. Bank of America is able to do this because it has a checking deposit in euros at its branch in Bonn.

The major banks that trade foreign exchange generally do not deal directly with one another but instead use the services of *foreign-exchange brokers*. The purpose of a broker is to permit the trading banks to maintain desired foreign-exchange balances. If at a particular moment a bank does not have the proper foreign-exchange balances, it can turn to a broker to buy additional foreign currency or sell the surplus. Brokers thus provide a wholesale, interbank market in which trading banks can buy and sell foreign exchange. Brokers are paid a commission for their services by the selling bank.

The third tier of the foreign-exchange market consists of the transactions between the trading banks and their overseas branches or foreign correspondents. Although several dozen U.S. banks trade in foreign exchange, it is the major New York banks that usually carry out transactions with foreign banks. The other, inland trading banks meet their foreign-exchange needs by maintaining correspondent relations with the New York banks. Trading with foreign banks permits the matching of supply and demand of foreign exchange in the New York market. These international transactions are carried out primarily by telephone and computers.

Commercial and financial transactions in the foreign-exchange market represent large nominal amounts, they are small in comparison to the amounts based on speculation. By far, most of currency trading is based on speculation in which traders purchase and sell for short-term gains based on minute-to-minute, hour-to-hour, and day-to-day price fluctuations. Estimates are that speculation accounts for about 90 percent of the daily trading activity in the foreign-exchange market.

Until the 1980s, most foreign-exchange trading was done over the phone. However, most foreign-exchange trading is now executed electronically. Trading occurs through computer terminals at thousands of locations worldwide. When making a currency trade, a trader will key an order into his or her computer terminal, indicating the amount of a currency, the price, and an instruction to buy or sell. If the order can be filled from other orders outstanding, and it is the best price available in the system from other traders, the deal will be made. If a new order cannot be matched with outstanding orders, the new order will be entered into the system and traders in the system from other banks will have access to it. Another trader may accept the order by pressing a "buy" or "sell" button and a transmit button. Proponents of electronic trading note that there are benefits from the certainty and clarity of trade execution. This is unlike trading via telephone, where conflicts between traders sometimes occur about the supposedly agreed upon currency prices.

Prior to 2000, companies that needed hard currency on a daily basis to meet foreign payrolls or to convert sales in foreign currencies into U.S. dollars traditionally dealt with traders at major banks such as JP Morgan Chase. This required corporate customers to work the phones, talking to traders at several banks at once to get the right quotation. However, there was little head-to-head competition among the banks, and corporate clients were looking for alternatives. All of this changed when start-up Currenex, Inc. built an online marketplace where banks could compete to offer foreign-currency exchange service to companies. The concept was embraced by major banks as well as corporate clients such as The Home Depot. Being online makes the currency-trading process more transparent. Corporate clients can see multiple quotes instantly and shop for the best deal.

Types of Foreign-Exchange Transactions

When conducting purchases and sales of foreign currencies, banks promise to pay a stipulated amount of currency to another bank or customer at an agreed upon date. Banks typically engage in three types of foreign-exchange transactions: spot, forward, and swap.

A **spot transaction** is where you can make an outright purchase or sale of a currency *now*, as in "on the spot." A spot deal will settle (in other words, the physical exchange of currencies takes place) two working days after the deal is struck. The two-day period is known as *immediate delivery*. By convention, the settlement date is the second business day after the date on which the transaction is agreed to by the two traders. The two-day period provides ample time for the two parties to confirm the agreement and arrange the clearing and necessary debiting and crediting of bank accounts in various international locations.

Here's how a spot transaction works:

- A trader calls another trader and asks for the price of a currency, say, the euro. This call expresses only a potential interest in a deal, without the caller indicating whether he or she wants to buy or sell.
- The second trader provides the first trader with prices for both buying and selling.
- When the traders agree to do business, one will send euros and the other will send, say, dollars. By convention, the payment is actually made two days later.

Spot dealing has the advantage of being the simplest way to meet your foreign currency requirements, but it also carries with it the greatest risk of exchange rate fluctuations, as there is no certainty of the rate until the transaction is made. Exchange rate fluctuations can effectively increase or decrease prices and can be a financial planning ordeal for companies and individuals.

In many cases, a business or financial institution knows it will be receiving or paying an amount of foreign currency on a specific date in the future. For example, in August a U.S. importer may arrange for a special Christmas season shipment of Japanese radios to arrive in October. The agreement with the Japanese manufacturer may call for payment in yen on October 20. To guard against the possibility of the yen's becoming more expensive in terms of the dollar, the importer might contract with a bank to buy yen at a stipulated price, but not actually receive them until October 20 when they are needed. When the contract matures, the U.S. importer pays for the yen with a known amount of dollars. This is known as a **forward transaction**. Simply put, a forward transaction will protect you against unfavorable movements in the exchange rate, but will not allow gains to be made should the exchange rate move in your favor in the period between entering the contract and final settlement of the currency.

Forward transactions differ from spot transactions in that their maturity date is more than two business days in the future. A forward-exchange contract's maturity date can be a few months or even years in the future. The exchange rate is fixed when the contract is initially made. No money necessarily changes hands until the transaction actually takes place, although dealers may require some customers to provide collateral in advance. Notice that in a forward transaction, the buyer and seller are locked into a contract at a fixed price that cannot be affected by any changes in market exchange rates. This tool allows the market participants to plan more safely, since they know in advance what their foreign exchange will cost. It also allows them to avoid an immediate outlay of cash.

Trading foreign currencies among banks and companies also involves swap transactions. A **currency swap** is the conversion of one currency to another currency at one point in time, with an agreement to reconvert it back to the original currency

TABLE 11.1

DISTRIBUTION OF FOREIGN-EXCHANGE TRANSACTIONS BY U.S. BANKS

AVERAGE DAILY VOLUME (BILLIONS OF DOLLARS)

Foreign-Exchange Instrument	Amount	Percent
Spot transactions	$319	45%
Foreign-exchange swaps	221	31
Forward transactions	109	15
Foreign-exchange options	66	9
Total	$715	100%

Source: From Federal Reserve Bank of New York, 2007, *Triennial Central Bank Survey of Foreign Exchange and Derivatives Market*, available at **http://www.newyorkfed.org/**. See also Bank for International Settlements, *Triennial Central Bank Survey of Foreign Exchange and Derivatives Market*.

at a specified time in the future. The rates of both exchanges are agreed to in advance. Here's how a swap transaction works:

- Suppose a U.S. company needs 15 million Swiss francs for a three-month investment in Switzerland.
- It may agree to a rate of 1.5 francs to a dollar and swap $10 million with a company willing to swap 15 million francs for three months.
- After three months, the U.S. company returns the 15 million francs to the other company and gets back $10 million, with adjustments made for interest rate differentials.

The key aspect is that the two traders arrange the swap as a single transaction in which they agree to pay and receive stipulated amounts of currencies at specified rates. Swaps provide an efficient mechanism through which traders can meet their foreign-exchange needs over a period of time. Traders are able to use a currency for a period in exchange for another currency that is not needed during that time.

Table 11.1 illustrates the distribution of foreign-exchange transactions by U.S. banking institutions, by transaction type. As of 2007, spot transactions accounted for the largest share of foreign-exchange transactions. Also, the U.S. dollar was the most important currency traded in foreign-exchange markets, being involved in more than 90 percent of all transactions. The euro was the second most actively traded currency. Other leading currencies were the Japanese yen, Canadian dollar, and Swiss franc.

Interbank Trading

In the foreign-exchange market, currencies are actively traded around the clock and throughout the world. Banks are linked by telecommunications equipment that permits instantaneous communication. A relatively small number of money center banks carry out most of the foreign-exchange transactions in the United States. Virtually all the big New York banks have active currency-trading operations, as do their counterparts in London, Tokyo, Hong Kong, Frankfurt, and other financial centers. Large banks in cities such as Los Angeles, Chicago, San Francisco, and Detroit also have active currency-trading operations. For most U.S. banks, currency transactions are not a large part of their business; these banks have ties to correspondent banks in New York and elsewhere to conduct currency transactions.

All these banks are prepared to purchase or sell foreign currencies to facilitate speculation for their own accounts, and to provide trading services for their customers such as corporations, government agencies, and wealthy private individuals. Bank purchases from and sales to their customers are classified as *retail transactions* when the amount involved is less than 1 million currency units. *Wholesale transactions*, involving more than 1 million currency units, generally occur between banks or with large corporate customers.

An international community of about 400 banks constitute the daily currency exchanges for buyers and sellers worldwide. A bank's foreign-exchange dealers are in constant contact with other dealers to buy and sell currencies. In most large banks, dealers specialize in one or more foreign currencies. The chief dealer establishes the overall trading policy and direction of trading, trying to service the foreign-exchange needs of the bank's customers and make a profit for the bank. Currency trading is conducted on a 24-hour basis, and exchange rates may fluctuate at any moment. Bank dealers must be light sleepers, ready to react to a nighttime phone call that indicates exchange rates are moving sharply in foreign markets. Banks often allow senior dealers to conduct exchange trading at home in response to such developments.

With the latest electronic equipment, currency exchanges are negotiated on computer terminals; a push of a button confirms a trade. Dealers use electronic trading boards, such as Reuters Dealing and EBS, that permit them to instantly register transactions and verify their bank's positions. Besides trading currencies during daytime hours, major banks have established night-trading desks to capitalize on foreign-exchange fluctuations during the evening and to accommodate corporate requests for currency trades. In the **interbank market**, currencies are traded in amounts involving at least 1 million units of a specific foreign currency. Table 11.2 lists leading banks that trade in the foreign-exchange market.

How do banks such as Bank of America earn profits in foreign-exchange transactions in the interbank market? They quote both a bid and an offer rate to other banks. The **bid rate** refers to the price that the bank is willing to pay for a unit of foreign currency; the **offer rate** is the price at which the bank is willing to sell a unit of foreign currency. The difference between the bid and the offer rate is the **spread** that varies by the size of the transaction and the liquidity of the currencies being traded. At any given time, a bank's bid quote for a foreign currency will be less than its offer quote. The spread is intended to cover the bank's costs of implementing the exchange of currencies. The large trading banks are prepared to "make a market" in a currency by providing bid and offer rates on request. The use of bid and offer rates allows banks to make profits on foreign-exchange transactions in the spot and forward markets.

Foreign-exchange dealers who simultaneously purchase and sell foreign currency earn the spread as profit. For example, Citibank might quote bid and offer rates for the Swiss franc at $0.5851/0.5854. The bid rate is $0.5851 per franc. At this price, Citibank would be prepared to buy 1 million francs for $585,100. The offer rate is $0.5854 per franc. Citibank would be willing to sell 1 million francs for $585,400. If Citibank is able to simultaneously buy and sell 1 million francs, it will earn $300 on the transaction. This profit equals the spread ($0.0003) multiplied by the amount of the transaction (1 million francs).

Besides earning profits from a currency's bid/offer spread, foreign-exchange dealers attempt to profit by anticipating correctly the future direction of currency movements. Suppose a Citibank dealer expects the

TABLE 11.2

TOP TEN BANKS BY SHARE OF FOREIGN-EXCHANGE MARKET, 2009

Bank	Share of Foreign-Exchange Market
Deutsche Bank	20.96%
UBS	14.48
Barclays Capital	10.45
RBS	8.19
Citi	7.32
J.P. Morgan Chase	5.43
HSBC	4.09
Goldman Sachs	3.35
Credit Suisse	3.05
BNP Paribas	2.26

Source: From "Foreign Exchange Survey," *Euromoney*, May 2009, available at **http://www.euromoney.com**.

Japanese yen to *appreciate* (strengthen) against the U.S. dollar. The dealer will likely *raise* both bid and offer rates, attempting to persuade other dealers to sell yen to Citibank and dissuade other dealers from purchasing yen from Citibank. The bank dealer thus purchases more yen than are sold. If the yen appreciates against the dollar as predicted, the Citibank dealer can sell the yen at a higher rate and earn a profit. Conversely, should the Citibank dealer anticipate that the yen is about to *depreciate* (weaken) against the dollar, the dealer will *lower* the bid and offer rates. Such action encourages sales and discourages purchases; the dealer thus sells more yen than are bought. If the yen depreciates as expected, the dealer can purchase yen back at a lower price to make a profit.

If exchange rates move in the desired direction, foreign-exchange traders earn profits. However, losses accrue if exchange rates move in the opposite, unexpected direction. To limit possible losses on exchange-market transactions, banks impose financial restrictions on their dealers' trading volume. Dealers are subject to *position limits* that stipulate the amount of buying and selling that can be conducted in a given currency. Although banks maintain formal restrictions, they have sometimes absorbed substantial losses from unauthorized trading activity beyond position limits. Because foreign-exchange departments are considered by bank management to be profit centers, dealers feel pressure to generate an acceptable rate of return on the bank's funds invested in this operation.

When a bank sells foreign currency to its business and household customers, it charges a "retail" exchange rate. This rate is based on the interbank (wholesale) rate that the bank pays when it buys foreign currency plus a markup that compensates the bank for the services it provides. This markup depends on the size of the currency transaction, the market volatility, and the currency pairs.

Reading Foreign-Exchange Quotations

Most daily newspapers publish foreign-exchange rates for major currencies. The **exchange rate** is the price of one currency in terms of another—for example, the number of dollars required to purchase 1 British pound (£). In shorthand notation, ER = $/£, where ER is the exchange rate. For example, if ER = 2, then purchasing £1 will require $2 (2/1 = 2). It is also possible to define the exchange rate as the number of units of foreign currency required to purchase one unit of domestic currency, or ER′ = £/$. In our example, ER′ = 0.5 (½ = 0.5), which implies that it requires £0.5 to buy $1. Of course, ER′ is the reciprocal of ER (ER′ = 1/ER).

Table 11.3 shows the exchange rates listed for May 13, 2009. In columns 2 and 3 of the table, the selling prices of foreign currencies are listed in dollars (In USD). Note that for all exchange rates, only one exchange rate is reported: This is the midrange between the bid and offer prices. The columns state how many dollars are required to purchase one unit of a given foreign currency. For example, the quote for the Argentinean peso for Wednesday (May 13) was 0.2686. This rate means that $0.2686 was required to purchase 1 peso. Columns 4 and 5 (Per USD) show the foreign-exchange rates from the opposite perspective, telling how many units of a foreign currency are required to buy a U.S. dollar. Again referring to Wednesday, it would take 3.7230 Argentinean pesos to purchase 1 U.S. dollar.

The term *exchange rate* in the table's heading refers to the price at which a New York bank will sell foreign exchange, in amounts of $1 million or more, to

TABLE 11.3

FOREIGN-EXCHANGE QUOTATIONS

Exchange Rates

May 13, 2009

The foreign-exchange rates below apply to trading among banks in amounts of $1 million and more, as quoted at 4:00 P.M. Eastern time by Reuters and other sources. Retail transactions provide fewer units of foreign currency per dollar.

Country/currency	In U.S. $		Per U.S. $	
	Wed.	Tues.	Wed.	Tues.
Americas				
Argentina peso	.2686	.2688	3.7230	3.7202
Brazil real	.4740	.4833	2.1097	2.0691
Canada dollar	.8506	.8605	1.1756	1.1621
1-month forward	.8507	.8607	1.1755	1.1618
3-months forward	.8511	.8611	1.1750	1.1613
6-months forward	.8517	.8619	1.1741	1.1602
Chile peso	.001750	.001756	571.43	569.48
Colombia peso	.0004426	.0004476	2259.38	2234.14
Ecuador U.S. dollar	1	1	1	1
Mexico peso	.0751	.0756	13.3156	13.2240
Peru new sol	.3289	.3333	3.040	3.000
Uruguay peso	.04220	.04180	23.70	23.92
Venezuela bolivar	.465701	.465701	2.1473	2.1473
Asia-Pacific				
Australian dollar	.7517	.7647	1.3303	1.3077
China yuan	.1466	.1466	6.8225	6.8215
Hong Kong dollar	.1290	.1290	7.7502	7.7502
India rupee	.02015	.02029	49.628	49.285
Indonesia rupiah	.0000967	.0000967	10341	10341
Japan yen	.010495	.010377	95.28	96.37
1-month forward	.010499	.010381	95.25	96.33
3-months forward	.010506	.010389	95.18	96.26
6-months forward	.010519	.010403	95.07	96.13
Malaysia ringgit	.2836	.2847	3.5261	3.5125
New Zealand dollar	.5907	.6061	1.6929	1.6499
Pakistan rupee	.01237	.01243	80.841	80.451
Philippines peso	.0212	.0212	47.125	47.081
Singapore dollar	.6824	.6841	1.4654	1.4618

Country/currency	In U.S. $		Per U.S. $	
	Wed.	Tues.	Wed.	Tues.
South Korea won	.0008065	.0008071	1239.93	1239.00
Taiwan dollar	.03040	.03044	32.895	32.852
Thailand baht	.02896	.02894	34.530	34.554
Vietman dong	.00005627	.00005625	17773	17777
Europe				
Czech Rep. koruna	.05034	.05091	19.865	19.463
Denmark krone	.1824	.1831	5.4825	5.4615
Euro area euro	1.3583	1.3640	.7362	.7331
Hungary forint	.004753	.004869	210.39	205.38
Norway krone	.1531	.1550	6.5317	6.4516
Poland zloty	.3049	.3102	3.2798	3.2237
Russia ruble	.03120	.03116	32.051	32.092
Sweden krona	.1264	.1282	7.9114	7.8003
Switzerland franc	.9029	.9044	1.1075	1.1057
1-month forward	.9032	.9047	1.1072	1.1053
3-months forward	.9041	.9057	1.1061	1.1041
6-months forward	.9054	.9071	1.1045	1.1024
Turkey lira	.6332	.6374	1.5793	1.5689
UK pound	1.5139	1.5269	.6605	.6549
1-month forward	1.5137	1.5267	.6606	.6550
3-months forward	1.5134	1.5265	.6608	.6551
6-months forward	1.5131	1.5261	.6609	.6553
Middle East/Africa				
Bahrain dinar	2.6525	2.6525	.3770	.3770
Egypt pound	.1780	.1780	5.6173	5.6173
Israel shekel	.2415	.2442	4.1408	4.0950
Jordan dinar	1.4139	1.4114	.7073	.7085
Kuwait dinar	3.4486	3.4521	.2900	.2897
Lebanon pound	.0006656	.0006634	1502.40	1507.39
Saudi Arabia riyal	.2667	.2667	3.7495	3.7495
South Africa rand	.1174	.1185	8.5179	8.4388
UAE dirham	.2723	.2722	3.6724	3.6738
SDR	1.5205	1.5181	.6577	.6587

Source: From Reuters, *Currency Calculator*, at **http://www.reuters.com**. See also Federal Reserve Bank of New York, *Foreign Exchange Rates*, at **http://www.newyorkfed.org/markets/fxrates/ten.AM.cfm/**.

another bank. The table's heading also states at what time during the day the quotation was made (4:00 P.M. Eastern time) because currency prices fluctuate throughout the day in response to changing supply and demand conditions. Retail foreign-exchange transactions, in amounts under $1 million, carry an additional service charge and are thus made at a different exchange rate.

An exchange rate determined by free-market forces can and does change frequently. When the dollar price of pounds increases, for example, from $2 = £1 to $2.10 = £1, the dollar has *depreciated* relative to the pound. Currency **depreciation** means that it takes more units of a nation's currency to purchase a unit of some foreign currency. Conversely, when the dollar price of pounds decreases, say, from $2 = £1 to $1.90 = £1, the value of the dollar has *appreciated* relative to the pound. Currency **appreciation** means that it takes fewer units of a nation's currency to purchase a unit of some foreign currency.

In Table 11.3, look at the relation between columns 2 and 3 (In USD). Going forward in time from Tuesday (May 12) to Wednesday (May 13), we see that the dollar cost of a Japanese yen increased from $0.010377 to $0.010495; the dollar thus depreciated against the yen, and conversely, the yen appreciated against the dollar. To verify this conclusion, refer to columns 4 and 5 of the table (Per USD). Going forward in time from Tuesday to Wednesday, we see that the yen cost of the dollar decreased from 96.37 yen = $1 to 95.28 yen = $1. In similar fashion, we see that from Tuesday to Wednesday the dollar appreciated against Brazil's real from $0.4833 = 1 real to $0.4740 = 1 real; the real thus depreciated against the dollar, from 2.0691 real = $1 to 2.1097 real = $1.

Most tables of exchange-rate quotations express currency values relative to the U.S. dollar, regardless of the country where the quote is provided. Yet in many instances, the U.S. dollar is not part of a foreign-exchange transaction. In such cases, the people involved need to obtain an exchange quote between two non-dollar currencies. As an example, if a British importer needs francs to purchase Swiss watches, the exchange rate of interest is the Swiss franc relative to the British pound. The exchange rate between any two currencies (such as the franc and the pound) can be derived from the rates of these two currencies in terms of a third currency (the dollar). The resulting rate is called the **cross exchange rate**.

Referring again to Table 11.3, we see that, as of Wednesday, the dollar value of the U.K. pound is $1.5139 and the dollar value of the Swiss franc is $0.9029. We can then calculate the value of the U.K. pound relative to the Swiss franc as follows:

$$\frac{\$\text{Value of U.K. Pound}}{\$\text{Value of Swiss Franc}} = \frac{\$1.5139}{\$0.9029} = 1.6767$$

Thus, each U.K. pound buys about 1.68 Swiss francs; this is the cross exchange rate between the pound and the franc. In similar fashion, cross exchange rates can be calculated between any other two non-dollar currencies in Table 11.3.

Forward and Futures Markets

Foreign exchange can be bought and sold for delivery immediately (the **spot market**) or for future delivery (the **forward market**). Forward contracts are normally made by those who will receive or make payment in foreign exchange in the weeks or months ahead. As seen in Table 11.3, the New York foreign-exchange market is a spot market for most currencies of the world. However, regular forward markets exist only for the more widely traded currencies. Exporters and importers, whose foreign-exchange receipts and payments are in the future, are the primary participants in the forward market. The forward quotations for currencies such as the U.K. pound, Canadian dollar, Japanese yen, and Swiss franc are for delivery one month, three months, or six months from the date indicated in the table's caption (May 13, 2009).

Trading in foreign exchange can also be done in the **futures market**. In this market, contracting parties agree to future exchanges of currencies and set applicable exchange rates in advance. The futures market is distinguished from the forward market in that only a limited number of leading currencies are traded; moreover,

TABLE 11.4

FORWARD CONTRACT VERSUS FUTURES CONTRACT

	Forward Contract	**Futures Contract**
Issuer	Commercial bank	International Monetary Market (IMM) of the Chicago Mercantile Exchange and other foreign exchanges such as the Tokyo International Financial Futures Exchange
Trading	"Over the counter" by telephone	On the IMM's market floor
Contract size	Tailored to the needs of the exporter/importer/ investor; no set size	Standardized in round lots
Date of delivery	Negotiable	Only on particular dates
Contract costs	Based on the bid/offer spread	Brokerage fees for sell and buy orders
Settlement	On expiration date only, at prearranged price	Profits or losses paid daily at close of trading

trading takes place in standardized contract amounts and in a specific geographic location. Table 11.4 summarizes the major differences between the forward market and the futures market.

One such futures market is the **International Monetary Market (IMM)** of the Chicago Mercantile Exchange. Founded in 1972, the IMM is an extension of the commodity futures markets in which specific quantities of wheat, corn, and other commodities are bought and sold for future delivery at specific dates. The IMM provides trading facilities for the purchase and sale, for future delivery, of financial instruments (such as foreign currencies) and precious metals (such as gold). The IMM is especially popular with smaller banks and companies. Also, the IMM is one of the few places where individuals can speculate on changes in exchange rates.

Foreign-exchange trading on the IMM is limited to major currencies. Contracts are set for delivery on the third Wednesday of March, June, September, and December. Price quotations are in terms of U.S. dollars per unit of foreign currency, but futures contracts are for a fixed amount (for example, 62,500 U.K. pounds).

Here is how to read the IMM's futures prices as listed in Table 11.5.[3] The *size of each contract* is shown on the same line as the currency's name and country. For example, a contract for Japanese yen covers the right to purchase 12.5 million yen. Moving to the right of the size of the contract, we see the expression *$ per 100 yen.* The first column of the table shows the **maturity months** of the contract; using June as an example, the remaining columns yield the following information:

Open refers to the price at which the yen was first sold when the IMM opened on the morning of May 13, 2009. Depending on overnight events in the world, the opening price may not be identical to the closing price from the previous trading day. Because prices are expressed in terms of dollars per 100 yen, the 1.0381 implies that yen opened for sale at $1.0381 per 100 yen. Multiply this price by the size of a contract and you've calculated the full value of one contract at the open of trading for that day: ($1.0381 × 12.5 million)/100 = $129,762.50.

---

[3]This section is adapted from R. Wurman and others, *The Wall Street Journal: Guide to Understanding Money and Markets* (New York: Simon and Schuster, Inc., 1990).

TABLE 11.5

FOREIGN-CURRENCY FUTURES, MAY 13, 2009: SELECTED EXAMPLES

	Open	High	Low	Settle	Change	Open Interest
JAPAN YEN (CME)—12.5 million yen; $ per 100 yen						
June	1.0381	1.0516	1.0346	1.0475	.0097	84,457
Sept	1.0414	1.0521	1.0362	1.0485	.0095	1,126
CANADIAN DOLLAR (CME)—100,000 dlrs.; $ per Can $						
June	.8606	.8656	.8491	.8518	−.0092	76,347
Sept	.8640	.8659	.8498	.8524	−.0093	3,080

Source: From Chicago Mercantile Exchange, International Monetary Market, available at **http://www.cme.com/trading**.

The *high*, *low*, and *settle* columns indicate the contract's highest, lowest, and closing prices for the day. Viewed together, these figures provide an indication of how volatile the market for the yen was during the day. After opening at $1.0381 per 100 yen, yen for June delivery never sold for more than $1.0516 per 100 yen and never for less than $1.0346 per 100 yen; trading finally settled, or ended, at $1.0475 per 100 yen. Multiplying the size of the yen contract times the yen's settlement price gives the full value of a yen contract at the closing of the trading day: ($1.0475 × 12.5 million)/100 = $130,937.50.

Change compares today's closing price with the closing price as listed in the previous day's paper. A plus (+) sign means prices ended higher; a minus (−) means prices ended lower. In the yen's case, the yen for June delivery settled $0.0097 per 100 yen higher than it did the previous trading day.

Open interest refers to the total number of contracts outstanding; that is, those that have not been canceled by offsetting trades. It shows how much interest there is in trading a particular contract.

Foreign-Currency Options

During the 1980s, a new feature of the foreign-exchange market was developed: the option market. An **option** is simply an agreement between a holder (buyer) and a writer (seller) that gives the holder the *right*, but not the obligation, to buy or sell financial instruments at any time through a specified date. Although the holder is not obligated to buy or sell currency, the writer is obligated to fulfill a transaction. Having a throwaway feature, options are a unique type of financial contract in that you only use the contract if you want to do so. By contrast, forward contracts *obligate* a person to carry out a transaction at a specified price, even if the market has changed and the person would rather not.

Foreign-currency options provide an options holder the right to buy or sell a fixed amount of foreign currency at a prearranged price, within a few days or a couple of years. The options holder can choose the exchange rate he or she wants to guarantee, as well as the length of the contract. Foreign-currency options have been used by companies seeking to hedge against exchange-rate risk as well as by speculators in foreign currencies.

There are two types of foreign-currency options. A **call option** gives the holder the right to *buy* foreign currency at a specified price, whereas a **put option** gives the holder the right to *sell* foreign currency at a specified price. The price at which the option can be exercised (that is, the price at which the foreign currency is bought or sold) is called the **strike price**. The holder of a foreign-currency option has the right to exercise the contract but may choose not to do so if it turns out to be unprofitable. The writer of the options contract (for example, Bank of America, Citibank, Merrill Lynch) must deliver the foreign currency if called on by a call-holder or must buy foreign currency if it is put to them by a put-holder. For this obligation, the writer of the options contract receives a *premium*, or fee (the option price). Financial institutions have been willing to write foreign-currency options because they generate substantial premium income (the fee income on a $5 million deal can run to $100,000 or more). However, writing currency options is a risky business because the writer takes chances on tricky pricing. Foreign-currency options are traded in a variety of currencies in Europe and the United States. *The Wall Street Journal* publishes daily listings of foreign currency options contracts. It is left for more advanced textbooks to discuss the mechanics of trading foreign-currency options.

To see how exporters can use foreign-currency options to cope with exchange-rate risk, consider the case of Boeing, which submits a bid for the sale of jet planes to an airline company in Japan. Boeing must deal not only with the uncertainty of winning the bid but also with exchange-rate risk. If Boeing wins the bid, it will receive yen in the future. But what if the yen depreciates in the interim, from, say, 115 yen = $1 to 120 yen = $1? Boeing's yen holdings would convert into fewer dollars, thus eroding the profitability of the jet sale. Because Boeing wants to sell yen in exchange for dollars, it can offset this exchange-market risk by purchasing put options that give the company the right to sell yen for dollars at a specified price. Having obtained a put option, if Boeing wins the bid it has limited the exchange-rate risk. On the other hand, if the bid is lost, Boeing's losses are limited to the cost of the option. Foreign-currency options thus provide a worst-case rate of exchange for companies conducting international business. The maximum amount the company can lose by covering its exchange-rate risk is the amount of the option price.

Exchange-Rate Determination

What determines the equilibrium exchange rate in a free market? Let us consider the exchange rate from the perspective of the United States—in dollars per unit of foreign currency. Like other prices, the exchange rate in a free market is determined by both supply and demand conditions.

Demand for Foreign Exchange

A nation's *demand for foreign exchange* is a derived demand, driven by foreigner demand for domestic goods and assets such as bank accounts, stocks, bonds, and real property. It corresponds to the *debit* items on a country's balance of payments. For example, the U.S. demand for pounds may stem from its desire to import British goods and services, to make investments in Britain, or to make transfer payments to residents in Britain.

WEAK DOLLAR IS A BONANZA FOR EUROPEAN TOURISTS

As the dollar's exchange value depreciates, foreign tourists realize a good bargain on goods purchased in America, as seen in the following example.

Jackie Murphy, in a Nike store aisle piled high with boxes of shoes, held up a white pair of jogging shoes for her husband, Edward, to examine. She smiled when she saw the price tag.

"They're only $55!" said Murphy, a tourist from London, England, "Do you like them? Try them on."

Although Murphy is an experienced shopper—it is one of her favorite pastimes back home—she was shocked at her purchasing power on a vacation to Orlando in 2006. The power came primarily from a currency exchange rate that had the British pound approaching twice the value of the U.S. dollar. "The exchange rate is fantastic," said Edward Murphy, who sells electronics in London. "We couldn't have timed it better to come over on our vacation." In 2006, the dollar fell ten percent against the euro and about seven percent against the currencies of Australia, Brazil, Indonesia, Norway, Poland, and Sweden.

Many European and Canadian visitors followed the Murphy example, in part because of the inexpensive U.S. dollar. The American tourist industry was delighted about this situation. Because of the cheaper dollar, tourists could afford to stay longer, stay at nicer and more expensive hotels, take more tours, eat at more restaurants, and shop with bargain-basement enthusiasm. Adding to the bonanza for Europeans, air fares to and from the United States declined.

For example, the cheap dollar encouraged 15-year-old Molly Sanders of Liverpool, England, to purchase six heavy-metal T-shirts during a visit to Orlando, and her parents decided they could afford a road trip to Miami. The family booked hotel reservations and purchased theme park tickets in the United States rather than in Britain. By obtaining the tickets in dollars instead of pounds, they saved about $21 each day they went to the parks.

The exchange rate also led the British travel firm Virgin Holidays to renegotiate prices with the U.S. car rental companies and hotels that it uses. The new prices permitted the firm in 2006 to offer a package of airfare to Orlando, seven nights' accommodations, and a rental car for 399 pounds, or 130 pounds less than what it had previously offered. At the prevailing exchange rate, the discounted price was equal to $718, for about $234 in savings.

Source: "Foreign Travel Deals On a Weak Dollar," *The Wall Street Journal*, January 4, 2007, p. B7.

Like most demand schedules, the U.S. demand for pounds varies inversely with its price; that is, fewer pounds are demanded at higher prices than at lower prices. This relation is depicted by line D_0 in Figure 11.1. As the dollar depreciates against the pound (the dollar price of the pound rises), British goods and services become more expensive to U.S. importers. This is because more dollars are required to purchase each pound needed to finance the import purchases. The higher exchange rate reduces the number of imports bought, lowering the number of pounds demanded by U.S. residents. In like manner, an appreciation of the U.S. dollar relative to the pound would be expected to induce larger import purchases and more pounds demanded by U.S. residents.

Supply of Foreign Exchange

The *supply of foreign exchange* refers to the amount of foreign exchange that will be offered to the market at various exchange rates, all other factors held constant. The supply of pounds, for example, is generated by the desire of British residents and businesses to import U.S. goods and services, to lend funds and make investments

FIGURE 11.1

EXCHANGE-RATE DETERMINATION

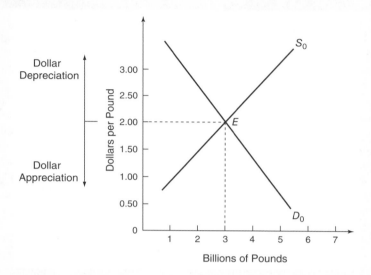

The equilibrium exchange rate is established at the point of intersection of the supply and demand schedules of foreign exchange. The demand for foreign exchange corresponds to the debit items on a nation's balance-of-payments statement; the supply of foreign exchange corresponds to the credit items.

in the United States, to repay debts owed to U.S. lenders, and to extend transfer payments to U.S. residents. In each of these cases, the British offer pounds in the foreign-exchange market to obtain the dollars they need to make payments to U.S. residents. Note that the supply of pounds results from transactions that appear on the *credit* side of the U.S. balance of payments; thus, one can make a connection between the balance of payments and the foreign-exchange market.

The supply of pounds is denoted by schedule S_0 in Figure 11.1. The schedule represents the number of pounds offered by the British to obtain dollars with which to buy U.S. goods, services, and assets. It is depicted in the figure as a positive function of the U.S. exchange rate. As the dollar depreciates against the pound (dollar price of the pound rises), the British will be inclined to buy more U.S. goods. The reason, of course, is that at higher and higher dollar prices of pounds, the British can get more U.S. dollars and hence more U.S. goods per British pound. American goods thus become cheaper to the British, who are induced to purchase additional quantities. As a result, more pounds are offered in the foreign-exchange market to buy dollars with which to pay U.S. exporters.

Equilibrium Rate of Exchange

As long as monetary authorities do not attempt to stabilize exchange rates or moderate their movements, the *equilibrium exchange rate* is determined by the market forces of supply and demand. In Figure 11.1, exchange-market equilibrium occurs

TABLE 11.6

ADVANTAGES AND DISADVANTAGES OF A STRENGTHENING AND WEAKENING DOLLAR

STRENGTHENING (APPRECIATING) DOLLAR

Advantages	Disadvantages
1. U.S. consumers see lower prices on foreign goods.	1. U.S. exporting firms find it harder to compete in foreign markets.
2. Lower prices on foreign goods help keep U.S. inflation low.	2. U.S. firms in import-competing markets find it harder to compete with lower-priced foreign goods.
3. U.S. consumers benefit when they travel to foreign countries.	3. Foreign tourists find it more expensive to visit the United States.

WEAKENING (DEPRECIATING) DOLLAR

Advantages	Disadvantages
1. U.S. exporting firms find it easier to sell goods on foreign markets.	1. U.S. consumers face higher prices foreign goods.
2. Firms in the United States have less competitive pressure to keep prices low.	2. Higher prices on foreign goods contribute to higher inflation in the United States.
3. More foreign tourists can afford to visit the United States.	3. U.S. consumers find traveling abroad more costly.

at point E, where S_0 and D_0 intersect. Three billion pounds will be traded at a price of $2 per pound. The foreign-exchange market is precisely cleared, leaving neither an excess supply nor an excess demand for pounds.

Given the supply and demand schedules of Figure 11.1, there is no reason for the exchange rate to deviate from the equilibrium level. But in practice, it is unlikely that the equilibrium exchange rate will remain very long at the existing level. This is because the forces that underlie the location of the supply and demand schedules tend to change over time, causing shifts in the schedules. Should the *demand* for pounds shift *rightward* (an increase in demand), the dollar will *depreciate* against the pound; *leftward* shifts in the demand for pounds (a decrease in demand) cause the dollar to *appreciate*. Conversely, a *rightward* shift in the *supply* of pounds (increase in supply) causes the dollar to *appreciate* against the pound; a *leftward* shift in the supply of pounds (decrease in supply) results in a *depreciation* of the dollar. The effects of an appreciating and depreciating dollar are summarized in Table 11.6.

Indexes of the Foreign-Exchange Value of the Dollar: Nominal and Real Exchange Rates

Since 1973, the value of the U.S. dollar in terms of foreign currencies has changed daily. In this environment of market-determined exchange rates, measuring the international value of the dollar is a confusing task. Financial pages of newspapers may be headlining a *depreciation* of the dollar relative to some currencies, while at the same time reporting its *appreciation* relative to others. Such events may leave the general public confused as to the actual value of the dollar.

Suppose the U.S. dollar appreciates ten percent relative to the yen and depreciates five percent against the pound. The change in the dollar's exchange value

TABLE 11.7

EXCHANGE RATE INDEXES OF THE U.S. DOLLAR
(MARCH 1973 = 100)*

Year	Nominal Exchange Rate Index	Real Exchange Rate Index
1973 (March)	100.0	100.0
1980	87.4	91.3
1984	138.3	117.7
1988	92.7	83.5
1992	86.6	81.8
1996	87.4	85.3
2000	98.3	103.1
2004	85.4	90.6
2008	80.7	88.5

*The "major currency index" includes the following nations and their trade weights with the United States: Canada, 30.3 percent; Euro area, 28.7 percent; Japan, 25.6 percent; United Kingdom, 8.0 percent; Switzerland, 3.2 percent; Australia, 2.6 percent; Sweden, 1.6 percent.

Source: From Federal Reserve, *Foreign Exchange Rates*, available at **http://www.federalreserve.gov/releases/H10/Summary/**. See also *Statistical Supplement to the Federal Reserve Bulletin*, various issues.

is some weighted average of the changes in these two bilateral exchange rates. Throughout the day, the value of the dollar may change relative to the values of any number of currencies under market-determined exchange rates. Direct comparison of the dollar's exchange rate over time thus requires a *weighted average* of all the bilateral changes. This average is referred to as the dollar's **exchange-rate index**; it is also known as the **effective exchange rate** or the **trade-weighted dollar**.

The exchange-rate index is a weighted average of the exchange rates between the domestic currency and the nation's most important trading partners, with weights given by relative importance of the nation's trade with each of these trade partners. One popular index of exchange rates is the so-called "major currency index," which is constructed by the U.S. Federal Reserve Board of Governors. This index reflects the impact of changes in the dollar's exchange rate on U.S. exports and imports with seven major trading partners of the United States. The base period of the index is March 1973.

Table 11.7 illustrates the **nominal exchange-rate index** of the U.S. dollar. This is the average value of the dollar, not adjusted for changes in prices levels, in the United States and its trading partners. An *increase* in the nominal exchange-rate index (from year to year) indicates a dollar *appreciation* relative to the currencies of the other nations in the index and a *loss* of competitiveness for the United States. Conversely, a *decrease* in the nominal exchange rate implies a dollar *depreciation* relative to the other currencies in the index and an *improvement* in U.S. international competitiveness. Simply put, the nominal exchange-rate index is based on **nominal exchange rates** that do not reflect changes in price levels in trading partners.

However, a problem arises when interpreting changes in the nominal exchange rate index when prices are not constant. When the prices of goods and services are changing in either the United States or a partner country (or both), one does not know the change in the relative price of foreign goods and services by simply looking at changes in the nominal exchange rate and failing to consider the new level of prices within both countries. For example, if the dollar appreciated against the peso by five percent, we would expect that, other things constant, U.S. goods would be five percent less competitive against Mexican goods in world markets than was previously the case. However, suppose that, at the same time that the dollar appreciated, U.S. goods prices increased more rapidly than Mexican goods prices. In this situation, the decrease in U.S. competitiveness against Mexican goods would be more than five percent, and the nominal five percent exchange-rate change would be misleading. Put simply, overall international competitiveness of U.S. manufactured goods depends not on the behavior of nominal exchange rates, but on movements in nominal exchange rates relative to prices.

As a result, economists calculate the **real exchange rate**, which embodies the changes in prices in the countries in the calculation. Simply put, the real exchange rate is the nominal exchange rate adjusted for relative price levels. To calculate the real exchange rate, we use the following formula:

$$\text{Real Exchange Rate} = \text{Nominal Exchange Rate} \times \frac{\text{Foreign country's price level}}{\text{Home country's price level}},$$

where both the nominal exchange rate and real exchange rate are measured in units of domestic currency per unit of foreign currency.

To illustrate, suppose that in 2005 the nominal exchange rate for the United States and Europe is 90 cents per euro; by 2007, the nominal exchange rate falls to 80 cents per euro. This is an 11 percent appreciation of the dollar against the euro $[(90 - 80)/90 = .11)]$, leading one to expect a substantial drop in competitiveness of U.S. goods relative to European goods. To calculate the real exchange rate, we must look at prices. Let us assume that the base year is 2005, at which consumer prices are set equal to 100. By 2007, however, U.S. consumer prices increase to a level of 108 while European consumer prices increase to a level of 102. The real exchange rate would then be calculated as follows:

$$\text{Real Exchange Rate}_{2007} = (80 \text{ cents} \times 102/108) = 75.6 \text{ cents per euro.}$$

In this example, the real exchange rate indicates that U.S. goods are *less* competitive on international markets than would be suggested by the nominal exchange rate. This result occurs because the dollar appreciates in nominal terms *and* U.S. prices increase *more* rapidly than European prices. In real terms, the dollar appreciates not by 11 percent (as with the nominal exchange rate) but by 16 percent $[(90 - 75.6)/90 = 0.16]$. Simply put, for variations in the exchange rate to have an effect on the composition of U.S. output, output growth, employment, and trade, there must be a change in the real exchange rate. That is, the change in the nominal exchange rate must alter the amount of goods and services that the dollar buys in foreign countries. Real exchange rates offer such a comparison and, therefore, provide a better gauge of international competitiveness than nominal exchange rates.

In addition to constructing a nominal exchange-rate index, economists construct a real exchange-rate index for a broad sample of U.S. trading partners. Table 11.7 also shows the **real exchange-rate index** of the U.S. dollar. This is the average value of the dollar based on real exchange rates. The index is constructed so that an appreciation of the dollar corresponds to higher index values. The importance that monetary authorities attach to the real exchange-rate index stems from economic theory, which states that a rise in the real exchange rate will tend to reduce the international competitiveness of U.S. firms; conversely, a fall in the real exchange rate tends to increase the international competitiveness of U.S. firms.[4]

Arbitrage

We have seen how the supply and demand for foreign exchange can set the market exchange rate. This analysis was from the perspective of the U.S. (New York) foreign-exchange market. But what about the relation between the exchange rate in

---

[4]For discussions of the nominal and real exchange rate indexes see "New Summary Measures of the Foreign Exchange Value of the Dollar," *Federal Reserve Bulletin*, October 1998, pp. 811–818 and "Real Exchange Rate Indexes for the Canadian Dollar," *Bank of Canada Review*, Autumn, 1999, pp. 19–28.

the U.S. market and that in other nations? When restrictions do not modify the ability of the foreign-exchange market to operate efficiently, normal market forces result in a consistent relation among the market exchange rates of all currencies. That is to say, if £1 = $2 in New York, then $1 = £0.5 in London. The prices for the same currency in different world locations will be identical.

The factor underlying the consistency of the exchange rates is called **exchange arbitrage**. Exchange arbitrage refers to the *simultaneous* purchase and sale of a currency in different foreign-exchange markets in order to profit from exchange-rate differentials in the two locations. This process brings about an identical price for the same currency in different locations and thus results in one market.

Suppose that the dollar/pound exchange rate is £1 = $2 in New York but £1 = $2.01 in London. Foreign-exchange traders would find it profitable to purchase pounds in New York at $2 per pound and immediately resell them in London for $2.01. A profit of 1 cent would be made on each pound sold, less the cost of the bank transfer and the interest charge on the money tied up during the arbitrage process. This return may appear to be insignificant, but on a $1 million arbitrage transaction it would generate a profit of approximately $5,000—not bad for a few minutes' work! As the demand for pounds increases in New York, the dollar price per pound will rise above $2; as the supply of pounds increases in London, the dollar price per pound will fall below $2.01. This arbitrage process will continue until the exchange rate between the dollar and the pound in New York is approximately the same as it is in London. Arbitrage between the two currencies thus unifies the foreign-exchange markets.

The preceding example illustrates **two-point arbitrage**, in which two currencies are traded between two financial centers. A more intricate form of arbitrage, involving three currencies and three financial centers, is known as **three-point arbitrage**, or triangular arbitrage. Three-point arbitrage involves switching funds among three currencies in order to profit from exchange-rate inconsistencies, as seen in the following example.

Consider three currencies—the U.S. dollar, the Swiss franc, and the British pound, all of which are traded in New York, Geneva, and London. Assume that the rates of exchange that prevail in all three financial centers are as follows: £1 = $1.50; £1 = 4 francs; and 1 franc = $0.50. Because the same exchange rates (prices) prevail in all three financial centers, two-point arbitrage is not profitable. However, these quoted exchange rates are mutually inconsistent. Thus, an arbitrager with $1.5 million could make a profit as follows:

1. Sell $1.5 million for £1 million.
2. Simultaneously, sell £1 million for 4 million francs.
3. At the same time, sell 4 million francs for $2 million.

The arbitrager has just made a risk-free profit of $500,000 ($2 million − $1.5 million) before transaction costs!

These transactions tend to cause shifts in all three exchange rates that bring them into proper alignment and eliminate the profitability of arbitrage. From a practical standpoint, opportunities for such profitable currency arbitrage have decreased in recent years, given the large number of currency traders—aided by sophisticated computer information systems—who monitor currency quotes in all financial markets. The result of this activity is that currency exchange rates tend to be consistent throughout the world, with only minimal deviations due to transaction costs.

The Forward Market

Foreign-exchange markets, as we have seen, may be spot or forward. In the *spot market*, currencies are bought and sold for immediate delivery (generally, two business days after the conclusion of the deal). In the *forward market*, currencies are bought and sold now for future delivery, typically one month, three months, or six months from the date of the transaction. The exchange rate is agreed on at the time of the contract, but payment is not made until the future delivery actually takes place. Only the most widely traded currencies are included in the regular forward market, but individual forward contracts can be negotiated for most national currencies.

Banks such as Citibank and Bank of America buy foreign-exchange forward agreements from some customers and sell foreign-exchange forward agreements to others. Banks provide this service to earn profits. The profit stems from purchasing the currency at one price (the bid price) and selling the currency at a slightly higher price (the offer price).

The Forward Rate

The rate of exchange used in the settlement of forward transactions is called the **forward rate**. This rate is quoted in the same way as the spot rate: the price of one currency in terms of another currency. Table 11.8 provides examples of forward

TABLE 11.8

FORWARD EXCHANGE RATES: SELECTED EXAMPLES

Exchange Rates   **May 13, 2009**

The foreign exchange rates below apply to trading among banks in amounts of $1 million and more, as quoted at 4:00 P.M. Eastern time by Reuters and other sources. Retail transactions provide fewer units of foreign currency per dollar.

Country/currency	In U.S. $		Per U.S. $	
	Wed.	**Tues.**	**Wed.**	**Tues.**
Canada dollar	.8506	.8605	1.1756	1.1621
1-month forward	.8507	.8607	1.1755	1.1618
3-months forward	.8511	.8611	1.1750	1.1613
6-months forward	.8517	.8619	1.1741	1.1602
Japan yen	.010495	.010377	95.28	96.37
1-month forward	.010499	.010381	95.25	96.33
3-months forward	.010506	.010389	95.18	96.26
6-months forward	.010519	.010403	95.07	96.13
Switzerland franc	.9029	.9044	1.1075	1.1057
1-month forward	.9032	.9047	1.1072	1.1053
3-months forward	.9041	.9057	1.1061	1.1041
6-months forward	.9054	.9071	1.1045	1.1024
UK pound	1.5139	1.5269	.6605	.6549
1-month forward	1.5137	1.5267	.6606	.6550
3-months forward	1.5134	1.5265	.6608	.6551
6-months forward	1.5131	1.5261	.6609	.6553

Source: Data taken from Table 11.3 on page 406 of this chapter.

rates as of May 13, 2009. Thus, under the Wednesday (May 13) quotations, the selling price of one-month forward U.K. pounds is $1.5137 per pound; the selling price of three-month forward pounds is $1.5134 per pound, and for six-month forward pounds it is $1.5131 per pound.

It is customary for a currency's forward rate to be stated in relation to its spot rate. When a foreign currency is worth more in the forward market than in the spot market, it is said to be at a **premium**; conversely, when the currency is worth less in the forward market than in the spot market, it is said to be at a **discount**. The per annum percentage premium (discount) in forward quotations is computed by the following formula:

$$\text{Premium (discount)} = \frac{\text{Forward Rate} - \text{Spot Rate}}{\text{Spot Rate}} \times \frac{12}{\text{Spot Rate No. of Months Forward}}$$

If the result is a negative forward premium, it means that the currency is at a forward discount.

According to Table 11.8, on Wednesday the one-month forward Swiss franc was selling at $0.9032, whereas the spot price of the franc was $0.9029. Because the forward price of the franc exceeded the spot price, the franc was at a one-month forward premium of 0.003 cents, or at a 0.4 percent forward premium per annum against the dollar:

$$\text{Premium} = \frac{\$0.9032 - \$0.9029}{\$0.9029} \times \frac{12}{1} = 0.0040$$

Similarly, the franc was at a three-month premium of 0.0012 cents, or at a 0.5 percent forward premium per annum against the dollar:

$$\text{Premium} = \frac{\$0.9041 - \$0.9029}{\$0.9029} \times \frac{12}{3} = 0.0053$$

Note that if the forward price of the franc is less than the spot price, the franc is at a forward discount and a negative sign would appear in front of the forward discount per annum against the dollar.

Relation Between the Forward Rate and Spot Rate

Referring to Table 11.8, we see that the one-month forward price of the Swiss franc is higher than the spot price; the same applies to the three-month forward price and the six-month forward price. Does this mean that traders in the market expect the spot price for the franc to increase in the future? That is a logical guess, but expectations have little to do with the relation between the forward rate and the spot rate. This relation is purely a mathematically driven calculation.

The forward rate is based on the prevailing spot rate plus (or minus) a premium (or discount) that is determined by the interest rate differential on comparable securities between the two countries involved. For example, if interest rates in Switzerland are *higher* than those of the United States, the franc shows a forward *discount*, which means the forward rate is less than the spot rate. Conversely, when Switzerland's interest rates are *lower* than those of the United States, the franc shows a forward *premium*, which means the forward rate is higher than the spot rate.

To illustrate, suppose that the interest rate on six-month Treasury bills is five percent in the United States and three percent in Switzerland; thus there is a two percent interest-rate differential in favor of the United States. Also assume that both the spot rate and forward rate between the dollar and the franc are identical. In this situation, Swiss investors will sell francs for dollars at the prevailing spot rate and use the dollars to purchase U.S. Treasury bills. To ensure that they will not lose money when dollars are converted back into francs when the Treasury bills reach maturity, they will obtain a six-month forward contract that allows francs to be bought with dollars at a guaranteed rate (the forward rate). When the investors sell francs for dollars in the spot market, and buy francs with dollars in the forward market, their actions will drive down the price of the franc on the spot market and drive the price of the franc up in the forward market. Thus, the franc moves to a premium in the forward market.[5] The flowchart below illustrates this process.

To profit from relatively high interest rates in the United States, Swiss investors will ➔➔➔ Sell francs for dollars in the spot market. / Buy francs with dollars in the forward market. ➔➔➔ Spot price of the franc falls. / Forward price of the franc rises. ➔➔➔ The franc moves to a premium in the forward market.

This is why currencies of countries whose interest rates are relatively low tend to sell at a premium over the spot rate in the forward market, and currencies of countries where interest rates are relatively high will tend to sell at a forward discount relative to the spot rate. It is also the reason that the dates on forward contracts are in regular intervals of one-month, three-months, and six-months—regularly traded securities have maturities with these intervals.

Managing Your Foreign Exchange Risk: Forward Foreign-Exchange Contract

Although spot transactions are popular, they leave the currency buyer exposed to potentially dangerous financial risks. Exchange rate fluctuations can effectively increase or decrease prices and can be a financial planning nightmare for companies and individuals. To illustrate exchange risks in spot transactions, assume a U.S. company orders machine tools from a company in Germany.

- The tools will be ready in six months and will cost 10 million euro.
- At the time of the order, the euro is trading at $1.40 per euro.
- The U.S. company budgets $14 million to be paid (in U.S. dollars) when it receives the tools (10,000,000 euro @ $1.40 per euro = $14,000,000).

There is no guarantee that the rate will remain the same six months later. Suppose the rate increases to $1.60 per euro. The cost in U.S. dollars would increase by $2,000,000 (10,000,000 euro @ $1.60 per euro = $16,000,000). Conversely, if the rate decreases to $1.20 per euro, the cost in U.S. dollars would decrease by $2,000,000 (10,000,000 euro @ $1.20 per euro = $12,000,000).

---

[5]This process will continue until the interest-rate differential between the two countries is exactly offset by a two percent forward premium for the pound. When this offset occurs, the Swiss will have no incentive to invest in the United States. It is left for more advanced textbooks to explain this point.

How can firms and individuals insulate themselves from volatile currency values? They can enter the forward market and engage in **hedging**, the process of avoiding or covering a foreign-exchange risk. Consider the following examples of hedging.

Case 1

A U.S. importer hedges against a dollar *depreciation*. Assume Sears, Roebuck and Co. owes 1 million francs to a Swiss watch manufacturer in three month's time. During this period, Sears is in an exposed or *uncovered* position. Sears bears the risk that the dollar price of the franc might rise in three months (the dollar might depreciate against the franc), say, from $0.60 to $0.70 per franc; if so, purchasing 1 million francs would require an extra $100,000.

To cover itself against this risk, Sears could immediately buy 1 million francs in the spot market, but this would immobilize its funds for three months. Alternatively, Sears could contract to purchase 1 million francs in the forward market, at today's forward rate, for delivery in three months. In three months, Sears would purchase francs with dollars at the contracted price and use the francs to pay the Swiss exporter. Sears has thus hedged against the possibility that francs will be more expensive than anticipated in three months. Note that hedging in the forward market does not require Sears to tie up its own funds when it purchases the forward contract. However, the contract is an obligation that can affect the company's credit. Sears's bank will want to be sure that it has an adequate balance or credit line so that it will be able to pay the necessary amount in three months. Note that Sears will not be able to benefit if the exchange rate moves in its favor as it has entered into a binding forward contract which it is obliged to fulfill.

Case 2

A U.S. exporter hedges against a dollar *appreciation*. Assume that Microsoft Corporation anticipates receiving 1 million francs in three months from its exports of computer software to a Swiss retailer. During this period, Microsoft is in an *uncovered* position. If the dollar price of the franc falls (the dollar appreciates against the franc), say, from $0.50 to $0.40 per franc, Microsoft's receipts will be worth $100,000 less when the 1 million francs are converted into dollars.

To avoid this foreign-exchange risk, Microsoft can contract to sell its expected franc receipts in the forward market at today's forward rate. By locking into a set forward-exchange rate, Microsoft is guaranteed that the value of its franc receipts will be maintained in terms of the dollar, even if the value of the franc should happen to fall.

The forward market thus eliminates the uncertainty of fluctuating spot rates from international transactions. Exporters can hedge against the possibility that the domestic currency will appreciate against the foreign currency, and importers can hedge against the possibility that the domestic currency will depreciate against the foreign currency. Hedging is not limited to exporters and importers. It applies to anyone who is obligated to make a foreign-currency payment or who will enjoy foreign-currency receipts at a future time. International investors, for example, also make use of the forward market for hedging purposes.

As our examples indicate, importers and exporters participate in the forward market to avoid the risk of fluctuations in foreign-exchange rates. Because they make forward transactions mainly through commercial banks, the foreign-exchange risk is transferred to those banks. Commercial banks can minimize foreign-exchange risk by matching forward purchases from exporters with forward sales to importers. However, because the supply of and demand for forward currency transactions by exporters and importers usually do not coincide, the banks may assume some of the risk.

Suppose that on a given day, a commercial bank's forward purchases do not match its forward sales for a given currency. The bank may then seek out other banks in the market that have offsetting positions. Thus, if Bank of America has an excess of 50 million euro in forward purchases over forward sales during the day, it will attempt to find another bank (or banks) that has an excess of forward sales over purchases. These banks can then enter forward contracts among themselves to eliminate any residual exchange risk that might exist.

How Markel Rides Foreign-Exchange Fluctuations

To corporate giants such as General Electric and Ford Motor Company, currency fluctuations are a fact of life for global production. But for tiny companies such as Markel Corporation, swings in the world currency market have major implications for its bottom line.[6] Markel Corporation is a family-owned tubing maker located in Plymouth Meeting, Pennsylvania. Its tubing and insulated lead wire are used in the appliance, automotive, and water-purification industries. About 40 percent of Markel's products are exported, mostly to Europe.

To shield itself from fluctuations in exchange rates, Markel purchases forward contracts through PNC Financial Services Group in Pittsburgh. Markel promises the bank, say, 50,000 euros in three months, and the bank guarantees a certain number of dollars no matter what happens to the exchange rate. When Markel's chief financial officer thinks the dollar is about to appreciate against the euro, the CFO might hedge his or her entire expected euro revenue stream with a forward contract. When the CFO thinks the dollar is going to depreciate, he or she will hedge perhaps half and take a chance that he or she will make more dollars by remaining exposed to currency fluctuations.

However, the CFO doesn't always guess right. In 2003, for example, Markel had to provide PNC with 50,000 euros from a contract the company purchased three months earlier. The bank paid $1.05 per euro, or $52,500. Had Markel waited, it could have sold at the going rate, $1.08, and made an additional $1,500.

To make matters worse, Markel reached an export deal with a German manufacturer in 1998 and set the sales price assuming the euro would be at $1.18 by 2003—about the level it was traded at when introduced officially in 1999. But the euro's exchange value sharply declined, bottoming out at 82 cents in 2000. That meant each euro Markel received for its products was worth far less in dollars than the company had anticipated. During 2000–2002, Markel realized more than $650,000 in currency losses, and the company posted overall losses.

Markel rode out its losses and by 2003 good times were beginning to return. Most of Markel's currency deals were written assuming that the euro would be valued between 90 and 95 cents. But when the euro soared to $1.08, aided by an imminent war with Iraq, nervous U.S. financial markets, and concerns about the U.S. trade deficit, Markel began to realize currency windfalls. Company executives estimated that

---

[6]Drawn from "Ship Those Boxes: Check the Euro," *The Wall Street Journal*, February 7, 2003, p. C1.

if the euro remained between $1.05 and $1.07, and the British pound stayed at about $1.60, Markel would realize $400,000 to $500,000 in currency gains in 2003: not enough to offset the currency losses of the three previous years, but at least a step in the right direction.

Volkswagen Hedges Against Foreign-Exchange Risk

Another example of hedging against foreign-exchange rate fluctuations is provided by Volkswagen, a German auto company. In 2005, Volkswagen announced that it was going to increase its hedging of foreign-exchange risk. Volkswagen was exposed to foreign-exchange risk because most of its operating costs, especially its labor costs, were denominated in euros, while a substantial share of its revenues were denominated in U.S. dollars. Thus, Volkswagen paid its workers in euros and received dollars for the cars it sold in the United States.

Between 2002 and 2004, the euro appreciated considerably relative to the dollar. That is, more dollars were required in order to purchase each euro. Since Volkswagen was unable or unwilling to change the price of cars sold in the United States enough to offset this swing in the exchange rate, the company's dollar revenues from sales in the United States lost substantial value in terms of euros. With costs holding steady and revenues falling, Volkswagen's profits on U.S. operations were reduced by an unfavorable change in the exchange rate between the euro and the dollar.

To avoid similar losses in the future, the company chose to combat the appreciating euro by increasing its hedging of foreign-exchange risk. Between 2004 and 2005, Volkswagen more than doubled its use of a variety of currency market contracts. In essence, this hedging strategy involved buying forward contracts for euros at a predetermined rate so that if the euro were to appreciate relative to the dollar and cause an unexpected reduction in dollar revenue, the company would receive an offsetting profit from its forward contract. If the euro were to depreciate and cause an unexpected increase in dollar revenue, the company would incur an offsetting loss from its foreign currency position. In this way, Volkswagen was able to shield its revenue flow from foreign exchange volatility for the duration of its futures contracts.

Volkswagen's strategy highlights the benefits of hedging against the currency risk posed by short-term fluctuations in exchange rates. When faced with a permanent shift in the exchange rate; however, companies operating in multiple currencies are forced to either change their prices, which are in one currency, or change their costs, which are in another. From 2005 to 2007, Volkswagen shifted some of its euro costs into dollar costs by expanding production facilities in the United States. This strategy was intended to permanently eliminate the currency mismatch between revenue and costs.[7]

Does Foreign-Currency Hedging Pay Off?

Although hedging is often used to offset foreign-exchange risk, some companies decide not to hedge. Let us see why.

---

[7]"Hedging Against Foreign-Exchange Rate Fluctuations," *Economic Report of the President*, 2007, p. 154.

As a firm that realizes more than half of its sales in profits in foreign currencies, Minnesota Mining & Manufacturing Co. (3M) is very sensitive to fluctuations in exchange rates. As the dollar appreciates against other currencies, 3M's profits decline; as the dollar depreciates, its profits increase. Indeed, when currency markets go wild, like they did during 1997–1998 when Asian currencies and the Russian ruble crashed relative to the dollar, deciding whether or not to hedge is a crucial business decision. Yet 3M didn't use hedges, such as the forward market or currency options market, to guard against currency fluctuations.[8]

In 1998, the producer of Scotch Tape and Post-Its announced that the appreciating dollar had cost the firm $330 million in profits and $1.8 billion in revenue during the previous three years. Indeed, 3M's no-hedging policy made investors nervous. Was 3M unwise in not hedging its currency risk? Not according to many analysts and other big firms that chose to hedge very little, if at all. Firms ranging from ExxonMobil to Deere to Kodak have maintained that currency fluctuations improve profits as often as they hurt them. In other words, although an appreciation of the dollar would detract from their profits, a dollar depreciation would add to them. As a result, hedging isn't necessary, as the ups and down of currencies even out over the long term.

The standard argument for hedging is increased stability of cash flows and earnings. Surveys of Corporate America's largest companies have found that one-third of them do some kind of foreign-currency hedging. For example, drug giant Merck and Co. hedges some of its foreign cash flows using the currency options market to sell the currencies for dollars at fixed rates. Merck maintains that it can protect against adverse currency moves by exercising its options or enjoy favorable moves by not exercising them. Either way, the firm aims to guarantee that cash flow from foreign sales remains stable so that it can sustain research spending in years when a strong dollar trims foreign earnings. According to Merck's chief financial officer, the firm pays money for insurance to dampen volatility from unknown events.

Yet many well-established companies see no need to pay for protection against currency risk. Instead, they often choose to cover the risks out of their own deep pockets. According to 3M officials, if you consider the cost of hedging over the entire cycle, the drain on your earnings is very high for purchasing that insurance. Indeed, foreign-currency hedging eats into profits. A simple forward contract that locks in an exchange rate costs up to half a percentage point per year of the revenue being hedged. Other techniques such as currency options are more costly. What's more, fluctuations in a firm's business can detract from the effectiveness of foreign-currency hedging.

Indeed, many companies have decided hedging is not worth the trouble. For example, in late 1993 Eastman Kodak concluded that the benefits of extensive use of foreign-currency hedging did not justify the costs because the ups and downs of currencies would even out over the long run. As a result, the firm switched from hedging its overall receipts and payments to hedging only a few specific contracts. Moreover, IBM reduced the impact of currency fluctuations without hedging by locating plants in many countries where it does business, so its costs are in the same currency as its revenues.

---

[8]"Perils of the Hedge Highwire," *Business Week*, October 26, 1998, pp. 74–76.

EXCHANGE-RATE RISK: THE HAZARD OF INVESTING ABROAD

TABLE 11.9

RETURN ON A THREE-MONTH GERMAN INVESTMENT

	Deutsche Mark Return*	Percentage Change in $/DM Exchange Rate	Dollar Return
May 27-August 26	2.4%	16.6%	19.0%
September 30-December 30	2.3	−12.5	−10.2

*In 2002, the euro replaced the deutsche mark as the currency of Germany.

Exchange-rate fluctuations can substantially change the returns on assets denominated in a foreign currency. A real-world demonstration follows.

Throughout 1992, short-term interest rates in Germany were significantly higher than those in the United States; however, an American choosing between a dollar-denominated and deutsche mark-denominated certificate of deposit (CD) with similar liquidities and default risks would not necessarily have earned a higher return on the German CD.

On May 27, 1992, an American saver with $10,000 to invest had the choice between a three-month CD with an annual interest rate of 3.85 percent from an American bank and a three-month CD with an annual interest rate of 9.65 percent (approximately 2.4 percent for three months) from a German bank. After three months, the U.S. CD was worth $10,096 and the German CD was worth $11,900 after exchanging the marks for dollars. As Table 11.9 shows, the substantially larger value of the German CD was due primarily to a 16.6 percent appreciation of the mark against the dollar from May 27 to August 26.

Now consider the choice facing our investor on September 30, 1992: a three-month U.S. CD offering an annual interest rate of 3.09 percent, and a comparable German investment offering an annual interest rate of 9.1 percent (approximately 2.3 percent for three months). After three months, the U.S. CD was worth $10,077. If the investor purchased the German CD, however, she would have had only $8,964 at the end of the three months—$1,036 less than the purchase price. This loss resulted from the 12.5 percent appreciation of the dollar against the mark between September and December 1992. With hindsight, the American saver would have preferred the U.S. CD to the German CD, even though the German interest rate was higher.

These examples provide a clear message. Even though interest rates play a key role in determining the relative attractiveness of assets denominated in domestic and foreign currencies, the effects of exchange-rate changes can swamp the effects of interest-rate differentials. Such large differences in returns illustrate why many investors choose to hedge against exchange-rate changes.

Source: Patricia S. Pollard, "Exchange-Rate Risk: The Hazard of Investing Abroad," *International Economic Conditions*, Federal Reserve Bank of St. Louis, February 1993, p. 1.

Interest Arbitrage

Investors make their financial decisions by comparing the rates of return of foreign investment with those of domestic investment. If rates of return from foreign investment are larger, they will desire to shift their funds abroad. **Interest arbitrage** refers to the process of moving funds into foreign currencies to take advantage of higher investment yields abroad. But investors assume a risk when they have foreign investments: When the investment's proceeds are converted back into the home currency, their value may fall because of a change in the exchange rate. Investors can eliminate this exchange risk by obtaining "cover" in the forward market.

Uncovered Interest Arbitrage

Uncovered interest arbitrage occurs when an investor does not obtain exchange-market cover to protect investment proceeds from foreign-currency fluctuations. Although this practice is rarely used, it is a good pedagogical starting point.

Suppose the interest rate on three-month Treasury bills is six percent (per annum) in New York and ten percent (per annum) in London, and the current spot rate is $2 per pound. A U.S. investor would seek to profit from this opportunity by exchanging dollars for pounds at the rate of $2 per pound and using these pounds to purchase three-month British Treasury bills in London. The investor would earn four percent more per year, or one percent more for the three months, than if the same dollars had been used to buy three-month Treasury bills in New York. These results are summarized in Table 11.10.

However, it is *not* necessarily true that our U.S. investor realizes an extra one percent rate of return (per three months) by moving funds to London. This amount will be realized only if the exchange value of the pound remains constant over the investment period. If the pound *depreciates* against the dollar, the investor makes *less*; if the pound *appreciates* against the dollar, the investor makes *more*!

Suppose our investor earns an extra one percent by purchasing three-month British Treasury bills rather than U.S. Treasury bills. Over the same period, suppose the dollar price of the pound falls from $2.00 to $1.99 (the pound *depreciates* against the dollar). When the proceeds are converted back into dollars, the investor *loses* 0.5 percent—($2 − $1.99)/$2 = .005. The investor thus earns only 0.5 percent more (1 percent − 0.5 percent) than if the funds had been placed in U.S. Treasury bills. The reader can verify that if the dollar price of the pound fell from $2 to $1.98 over the investment period, the U.S. investor would earn nothing extra by investing in British Treasury bills.

Alternatively, suppose that over the three-month period the pound rises from $2 to $2.02, a one percent *appreciation* against the dollar. This time, in addition to the extra one percent return on British Treasury bills, our investor realizes a return of one percent from the appreciation of the pound. The reason? When the investor bought pounds to finance his/her purchase of British Treasury bills, the investor paid $2 per pound; when the investor converted his or her investment proceeds back into dollars, the investor received $2.02 per pound—($2.02 − $2)/$2 = 0.01. Because the pound's appreciation adds to his or her investment's profitability, the investor earns two percent more than if the investor had purchased U.S. Treasury bills.

In summary, a U.S. investor's extra rate of return on an investment in the United Kingdom, as

TABLE 11.10

Uncovered Interest Arbitrage: An Example

	Rate per Year	Rate per 3 Months
U.K. 3-month Treasury bill interest rate	10%	2.5%
U.S. 3-month Treasury bill interest rate	6%	1.5%
Uncovered interest differential favoring the U.K.	4%	1.0%

compared to the United States, equals the interest-rate differential adjusted for any change in the value of the pound, as follows:

$$\text{Extra Return} = (\text{U.K. Interest Rate} - \text{U.S. Interest Rate})$$
$$- \text{ Percent Depreciation of the Pound}$$

or

$$\text{Extra Return} = (\text{U.K. Interest Rate} - \text{U.S. Interest Rate})$$
$$+ \text{ Percent Appreciation of the Pound}$$

Covered Interest Arbitrage

Investing funds in a foreign financial center involves an exchange-rate risk. Because investors typically desire to avoid this risk, interest arbitrage is usually *covered*.

Covered interest arbitrage involves two basic steps. First, an investor exchanges domestic currency for foreign currency, at the current spot rate, and uses the foreign currency to finance a foreign investment. At the same time, the investor contracts in the forward market to sell the amount of the foreign currency that will be received as the proceeds from the investment, with a delivery date to coincide with the maturity of the investment. It pays for the investor to make the foreign investment if the positive interest-rate differential in favor of the foreign investment more than offsets the cost of obtaining the forward cover.

Suppose the interest rate on three-month Treasury bills is 12 percent (per annum) in London and eight percent (per annum) in New York; the interest differential in favor of London is four percent per annum, or one percent for the three months. Suppose also that the current spot rate for the pound is $2, while the three-month forward pound sells for $1.99. This difference means that the three-month forward pound is at a 0.5 percent *discount*—($1.99 − $2)/$2 = −0.005.

By purchasing three-month Treasury bills in London, a U.S. investor could earn one percent more for the three months than if he bought three-month Treasury bills in New York. To eliminate the uncertainty over how many dollars will be received when the pounds are reconverted into dollars, the investor sells enough pounds on the three-month forward market to coincide with the anticipated proceeds of the investment. The cost of the forward cover equals the difference between the spot rate and the contracted three-month forward rate; this difference is the discount on the forward pound, or 0.5 percent. Subtracting this 0.5 percent from the interest-rate differential of 1 percent, the investor is able to realize a net rate of return that is 0.5 percent higher than if he or she had bought U.S. Treasury bills. These results are summarized in Table 11.11.

This investment opportunity will not last long, because the net profit margin will soon disappear. As U.S. investors purchase spot pounds, the spot rate will rise. Concurrently, the sale of forward pounds will push the forward rate downward. The result is a *widening* of the discount on the forward pounds, which means that the cost of covering the exchange-rate risk increases. This arbitraging process will continue until the forward discount on the pound widens to one percent, at which point the extra profitability of the foreign investment vanishes. The discount on the pound now equals the interest-rate differential between New York and London:

$$\text{Pound Forward Discount} = \text{U.K. Interest Rate} - \text{U.S. Interest Rate}$$

TABLE 11.11

Covered Interest Arbitrage: An Example

	Rate per Year	Rate per 3 Months
U.K. 3-month Treasury bill interest rate	12%	3%
U.S. 3-month Treasury bill interest rate	8%	2%
Uncovered interest—rate differential favoring the U.K.	4%	1%
Forward discount on the 3-month pound		−0.5%
Covered interest-rate differential favoring the U.K.		0.5%

In short, the theory of foreign exchange suggests that the forward discount or premium on one currency against another reflects the difference in the short-term interest rates between the two nations. The currency of the *higher*-interest-rate nation should be at a forward *discount* while the currency of the *lower*-interest-rate nation should be at a forward *premium*.

International differences in interest rates do exert a major influence on the relation between the spot and forward rates. But on any particular day, one would hardly expect the spread on short-term interest rates between financial centers to precisely equal the discount or premium on foreign exchange, for several reasons. First, changes in interest-rate differentials do not always induce an immediate investor response necessary to eliminate the investment profits. Second, investors sometimes transfer funds on an uncovered basis; such transfers do not have an effect on the forward rate. Third, factors such as governmental exchange controls and speculation may weaken the connection between the interest-rate differential and the spot and forward rates.

Foreign-Exchange Market Speculation

Besides being used for the financing of commercial transactions and investments, the foreign-exchange market is also used for exchange-rate speculation. **Speculation** is the attempt to profit by trading on expectations about prices in the future. Some speculators are traders acting for financial institutions or firms; others are individuals. In either case, speculators buy currencies that they expect to go up in value and sell currencies that they expect to go down in value. In the foreign-exchange market, speculators dominate: close to 90 percent of daily trading volume is speculative in nature.

Note the difference between arbitrage and speculation. With arbitrage, a currency trader *simultaneously* buys a currency at a low price and sells that currency at a high price, thus making a riskless profit. A speculator's goal is to buy a currency at one moment (such as today) and sell that currency at a higher price in the future (such as tomorrow). Speculation thus implies the deliberate assumption of exchange risk: If the price of the currency falls between today and tomorrow, the speculator loses money. An exchange-market speculator deliberately assumes foreign-exchange risk on the expectation of profiting from future changes in the spot exchange rate.

One of the greatest currency trades ever made was made in 1987 by 32 year old Andy Krieger, a currency trader at Bankers Trust Company in New York. Krieger was one of the most aggressive dealers in the world, with full approval of his bank.

While most of the bank's currency traders had an upper dealing limit of $50 million, Krieger's limit was about $700 million, a quarter of the bank's capital at the time. By using foreign currency options, Krieger could greatly leverage his exposure: $100,000 of currency options would buy control of $30 to $40 million in actual currency. In 1987, Krieger did this to launch a speculative attack on the New Zealand dollar.

Krieger was watching the currencies that were appreciating against the dollar following the October 19, 1987 crash in the stock markets around the world. As investors and companies rushed out of the U.S. dollar and into currencies that suffered less damage in the market crash, there were bound to be some currencies that would become overvalued, resulting in a good opportunity for speculative profit. Believing that the New Zealand dollar was overvalued, Krieger bet on its fall, selling hundreds of millions of New Zealand dollars at a time and pushing its value down five percent in a day. Krieger's profited by re-buying New Zealand dollars when its price bottomed out at 59 cents. Simply put, Krieger profited from a decline in the value of the New Zealand dollar between the sale and the repurchase, as he paid less to buy the dollars than he received on selling them. Krieger resigned from Bankers Trust the following year, apparently unhappy about his employers who had paid him a mere $3 million for his efforts that had netted the bank a profit of more than $300 million from the raid on the New Zealand dollar.

Currency speculation can exert either a stabilizing or a destabilizing influence on the foreign-exchange market. **Stabilizing speculation** goes against market forces by *moderating* or *reversing* a rise or fall in a currency's exchange rate. For example, it can occur when a speculator buys foreign currency with domestic currency when the domestic price of the foreign currency falls, or depreciates. The hope is that the domestic price of the foreign currency will soon increase, leading to a profit. Such purchases increase the demand for the foreign currency, which moderates its depreciation. Stabilizing speculation performs a useful function for bankers and businesspeople, who desire stable exchange rates.

Destabilizing speculation goes with market forces by *reinforcing* fluctuations in a currency's exchange rate. For example, it would occur when a speculator sells a foreign currency when it depreciates, on the expectation that it will depreciate further in the future. Such sales depress the foreign currency's value. Destabilizing speculation can disrupt international transactions in several ways. Because of the uncertainty of financing exports and imports, the cost of hedging may become so high that international trade is impeded. What is more, unstable exchange rates may disrupt international investment activity. This is because the cost of obtaining forward cover for international capital transactions may rise significantly as foreign-exchange risk intensifies.

To lessen the amount of destabilizing speculation, some government officials propose government regulation of foreign-currency markets. If foreign-currency markets are to be regulated by government, however, will such intervention be superior to the outcome that occurs in an unregulated market? Will government be able to identify better than markets what the "correct" exchange rate is? Many analysts contend that government would make even bigger mistakes. Moreover, markets are better than government in admitting their mistakes and reversing out of them. That is because, unlike governments, markets have no pride. Destabilizing speculation will be further discussed in Chapter 15. The techniques of foreign-exchange market speculation are contained in *Exploring Further 11.1*.

HOW TO PLAY THE FALLING (RISING) DOLLAR

KEY CURRENCY

When the dollar is expected to depreciate, U.S. investors may look to foreign markets for big returns. Why? A declining dollar makes foreign-denominated financial instruments worth more in dollar terms. However, those in the business emphasize that trading currency is "speculation," not investing. If the dollar rebounds, any foreign-denominated investment would provide lower returns. Simply put, big losses can easily occur if your bet is wrong.

The most direct way to play an anticipated drop in the dollar would be to stroll down to Bank of America and purchase $10,000 of euros, put the bills in your safe deposit box, and reconvert the currency to dollars in, say, six months. However, it's not an especially efficient way to do the job because of transaction costs.

Another way is to purchase bonds denominated in a foreign currency. A U.S. investor who anticipates that the yen's exchange value will significantly appreciate in the near future might purchase bonds issued by the Japanese government or corporations and expressed in yen. These bonds can be purchased from brokerage firms such as Charles Schwab and J.P. Morgan Chase & Co. The bonds are paid for in yen, which are purchased by converting dollars into yen at the prevailing spot rate. If the yen goes up, the speculator gets not only the accrued interest from the bond but also its appreciated value in dollars. The catch is that, in all likelihood, others have the same expectations. The overall demand for the bonds may be sufficient to force up the bond price, resulting in a lower interest rate. For the investor to win, the yen's appreciation must exceed the loss of interest income. In many cases, the exchange-rate changes are not large enough to make such investments worthwhile. Besides investing in a particular foreign bond, one can invest in a foreign-bond mutual fund, provided by brokerage firms like Merrill Lynch. Although you can own a foreign bond fund with

as little as $2,500, you generally must pony up $100,000 or more to own bonds directly.

Rather than investing in foreign bonds, some investors choose to purchase stocks of foreign corporations, denominated in foreign currencies. The investor in this case is trying to predict the trend of not only the foreign currency but also its stock market. The investor must be highly knowledgeable about both financial and economic affairs in the foreign country. Instead of purchasing individual stocks, an investor could put money in a foreign-stock mutual fund.

For investors who expect that the spot rate of a foreign currency will soon rise, the answer lies in a savings account denominated in a foreign currency. For example, a U.S. investor may contact a major Citibank or a U.S. branch of a foreign bank and take out an interest-bearing certificate of deposit expressed in a foreign currency. An advantage of such a savings account is that the investor is guaranteed a fixed interest rate. An investor who has guessed correctly also enjoys the gains stemming from the foreign currency's appreciation. However, the investor must be aware of the possibility that governments might tax or shut off such deposits or interfere with the investor's freedom to hold another nation's currency.

Finally, you can play the falling dollar by putting your money into a variety of currency derivatives, all of which are risky. For example, you can trade futures contracts at the Chicago Mercantile Exchange. Or trade currency directly by opening an account at a firm that specializes in that businesses, such as Saxo Bank (Danish) or CMC (British). The minimum lot is often $10,000, and you can leverage up to 95 percent. Thus, for a $100,000 trade, the typical size, you'd have to put only $5,000 down. For an appreciating dollar, the techniques of currency speculation would be the opposite.

Foreign Exchange Trading as a Career

As you complete this international economics course and approach graduating from your college or university, you might consider becoming a foreign exchange trader. You could gain employment from a bank or company dealing in foreign exchange or you might operate independently as a day trader.

Foreign Exchange Traders Hired by Commercial Banks, Companies, and Central Banks

Foreign exchange traders are hired by commercial banks, such as JP Morgan Chase and Bank of America, that make profits by trading and selling exchange from and to each other. Big companies, who have need of foreign currency in the way of doing trade, also hire currency traders. Another employer of currency traders are central banks, such as the Federal Reserve, who participate in the foreign exchange market to influence the value of their currencies.

A foreign exchange trader studies the various factors that affect local economies and rates of exchange, then takes advantage of any mis-valuations of currencies by buying and selling in different foreign exchange markets. Only those who are comfortable with a high degree of risk and uncertainty should look into this profession as a career. One decision can make you win or lose. Confidence along with guts are the core qualities required for foreign exchange trading.

A foreign exchange trader has to handle accounts, study various reports generated on each working day, and have an update of the leading economies around the world. Most of a foreign exchange trader's time is spent talking over the phone or working on a computer. The mode of communication in foreign exchange trading has to be extremely swift. Sharp reasoning skills are required to make fast decisions. Economics and mathematics majors have a distinct advantage in applying for positions as a foreign exchange trader. Accounting background is also helpful in keeping track of positions and profit and losses throughout frantic days. A bachelor's degree is required. Few people leave to get an advanced degree in this field.

Early in a foreign exchange trader's career, the trader typically specializes by following one currency and the underlying economy of that currency. As the trader gains experience and becomes confident in handling more than one currency, he or she can specialize in groups of geographically related countries, such as those who transact in Pacific Rim currencies.

Foreign exchange traders enjoy the adrenaline rush of participating in a hectic market. A trader must be on his toes every minute of the working day because any event around the world can influence the value of a currency and create an opportunity for profit. Indeed, most foreign exchange traders report that they are exhausted at every day's end. A primer on foreign-exchange trading is contained in *Exploring Further 11.2*.

Currency Markets Draw Day Traders

For decades, foreign-currency trading was practiced only by the biggest banks and firms like Deutsche Bank and General Electric. But then individual investors in Europe and Asia began trading currencies to pull speculative profits out of the market. By the first decade of the 2000s, many Americans were choosing to participate in this game of electronic poker. These traders range from rock stars and professional athletes to police officers, lawyers, doctors, and teachers.

Consider the case of Marc Coppola, the brother of actor Nicolas Cage and nephew of movie director Francis Ford Coppola. In 2005 he was reported to have won $1,400 on a $60,000 bet that the euro would appreciate against the dollar. Then he changed direction and gambled $40,000 that the euro would depreciate. When it dropped from $1.31 to $1.30, he cashed in half of his bet, then soon cashed in the remainder. However, Coppola noted that he was too cautious: He feared that the euro's exchange value would suddenly reverse its direction, and thus exited the trade too soon. Coppola wished that he had ridden the euro down to an exchange value of about $1.20, thus realizing additional speculative profits.

The foreign exchange market has become a speculative arena for individual traders. They establish online-trading accounts that, like the foreign-exchange market itself, operate 24 hours a day. Gain Capital Group, FX Solutions, Interbank FX, and Forex Capital Markets (FXCM) are some of the more popular firms that provide such accounts. To open an account, speculators need as little as $250, and they can borrow up to 400 times the value of the account, although 15 to 20 times leverage is more common.

Here's how it works. A ratio of 400-to-1 means a speculator can put up, say, $5,000 (referred to as the margin) to place a $2 million bet that the dollar will depreciate against the euro. The difference between the margin and the value of the bet is the leverage. The bet would win 200 for every 0.01 percentage point that the dollar depreciates against the euro. So if the dollar fell by 1 percent against the euro, the $2 million bet wins $20,000. However, losses can be large if the bet goes wrong.

Compared to other investment opportunities, foreign-exchange trading offers several advantages. The around-the-clock market allows speculators to place bets whenever they want, not just between 9:30 A.M. and 4 P.M. Eastern time, as with the U.S. stock market. Because transaction costs are smaller, currencies are also less expensive to trade than stocks. And trading is easier because only six pairs of currency (for example, the dollar versus euro) account for about 90 percent of trading volume, compared with thousands of stocks. Unlike stocks, there cannot be a bear market in foreign exchange: Because currencies are valued relative to one another, when some currencies depreciate others appreciate. Also, foreign-exchange trading may be less risky than investing in stocks because currencies often move in multiyear cycles, making it simpler to identify a trend.

However, professional traders caution against amateurs speculating in foreign currencies. They estimate that only 15 percent of day traders realize profits. Although the financial leverage that can be obtained by using an online account can help generate large profits if a speculator guesses correctly, it can result in huge losses if they guess things wrong. Simply put, currency speculation is a very risky business. It is recommended that you do not bet next semester's tuition on a possible depreciation or appreciation of the dollar.[9]

Summary

1. The foreign-exchange market provides the institutional framework within which individuals, businesses, and financial institutions purchase and sell foreign exchange. Three of the world's largest foreign-exchange markets are located in New York, Tokyo, and London.

2. The exchange rate is the price of one unit of foreign currency in terms of the domestic currency. From a U.S. viewpoint, the exchange rate might refer to the number of dollars necessary to buy a Swiss franc. A dollar depreciation (appreciation) is an increase (decrease) in the

---

[9]"Currency Markets Draw Speculation, Fraud," *The Wall Street Journal*, July 26, 2005, p. C1 and "Young Traders Run Currency Markets," *The Wall Street Journal*, November 5, 1987, p. A26.

number of dollars required to buy a unit of foreign exchange.

3. In the foreign-exchange market, currencies are traded around the clock and throughout the world. Most foreign-exchange trading is in the interbank market. Banks typically engage in three types of foreign-exchange transactions: spot, forward, and swap.

4. The equilibrium rate of exchange in a free market is determined by the intersection of the supply and demand schedules of foreign exchange. These schedules are derived from the credit and debit items in a nation's balance of payments.

5. Exchange arbitrage permits the rates of exchange in different parts of the world to be kept the same. This is achieved by selling a currency when its price is high and purchasing when the price is low.

6. Foreign traders and investors often deal in the forward market for protection from possible exchange-rate fluctuations. However, speculators also buy and sell currencies in the futures markets in anticipation of sizable profits. In general, interest arbitrage determines the relation between the spot rate and the forward rate.

7. Speculation in the foreign-exchange markets may be either stabilizing or destabilizing in nature.

Key Concepts & Terms

- Appreciation (p. 407)
- Bid rate (p. 404)
- Call option (p. 410)
- Covered interest arbitrage (p. 426)
- Cross exchange rate (p. 407)
- Currency swap (p. 402)
- Depreciation (p. 406)
- Destabilizing speculation (p. 428)
- Discount (p. 418)
- Effective exchange rate (p. 414)
- Exchange arbitrage (p. 416)
- Exchange rate (p. 405)
- Exchange-rate index (p. 414)
- Foreign-currency options (p. 409)
- Foreign-exchange market (p. 399)
- Forward market (p. 407)
- Forward rate (p. 417)
- Forward transaction (p. 402)
- Futures market (p. 407)
- Hedging (p. 420)
- Interbank market (p. 404)
- Interest arbitrage (p. 424)
- International Monetary Market (IMM) (p. 408)
- Maturity months (p. 408)
- Nominal exchange rates (p. 414)
- Nominal exchange-rate index (p. 414)
- Offer rate (p. 404)
- Option (p. 409)
- Premium (p. 418)
- Put option (p. 410)
- Real exchange rate (p. 414)
- Real exchange-rate index (p. 415)
- Speculation (p. 427)
- Spot market (p. 407)
- Spot transaction (p. 402)
- Spread (p. 404)
- Stabilizing speculation (p. 428)
- Strike price (p. 410)
- Three-point arbitrage (p. 416)
- Trade-weighted dollar (p. 414)
- Two-point arbitrage (p. 416)
- Uncovered interest arbitrage (p. 425)

Study Questions

1. You are given the following spot exchange rates: $1 = 3 francs, $1 = 4 schillings, and 1 franc = 2 schillings. Ignoring transaction costs, how much profit could a person make via three-point arbitrage?

2. Assume a speculator anticipates that the spot rate of the franc in three months will be lower than today's three-month forward rate of the franc, $0.50 = 1 franc.

a. How can this speculator use $1 million to speculate in the forward market?

b. What occurs if the franc's spot rate in three months is $0.40? $0.60? $0.50?

3. Suppose the spot rate of the pound today is $1.70 and the three-month forward rate is $1.75.

a. How can a U.S. importer who has to pay 20,000 pounds in three months hedge his or her foreign-exchange risk?

b. What occurs if the U.S. importer does not hedge and the spot rate of the pound in three months is $1.80?

4. Table 11.12 gives hypothetical dollar/franc exchange values for Wednesday, May 5, 2008.

TABLE 11.12

Dollar/Franc Exchange Values

	IN U.S. $		CURRENCY PER U.S. $	
	Wed.	Tues.	Wed.	Tues.
Switzerland (franc)	.5851	.5846		
30-Day Forward	.5853	.5848		
90-Day Forward	.5854	.5849		
180-Day Forward	.5851	.5847		

a. Fill in the last two columns of the table with the reciprocal price of the dollar in terms of the franc.

b. On Wednesday, the spot price of the two currencies was _____ dollars per franc, or _____ francs per dollar.

c. From Tuesday to Wednesday, in the spot market the dollar (appreciated/depreciated) against the franc; the franc (appreciated/depreciated) against the dollar.

d. In Wednesday's spot market, the cost of buying 100 francs was _____ dollars; the cost of buying 100 dollars was _____ francs.

e. On Wednesday, the 30-day forward franc was at a (premium/discount) of _____ dollars, which equaled _____ percent on an annual basis. What about the 90-day forward franc?

5. Suppose $1.69 = £1 in New York and $1.71 = £1 in London. How can foreign-exchange arbitragers profit from these exchange rates? Explain how foreign-exchange arbitrage results in the same dollar/pound exchange rate in New York and London.

6. Suppose the interest rate (on an annual basis) on three-month Treasury bills is ten percent in London and six percent in New York, and the spot rate of the pound is $2.

a. a. How can a U.S. investor profit from uncovered interest arbitrage?

b. If the price of the three-month forward pound is $1.99, will a U.S. investor benefit from covered interest arbitrage? If so, by how much?

7. Table 11.13 shows supply and demand schedules for the British pound. Assume that exchange rates are flexible.

TABLE 11.13

Supply and Demand of British Pounds

Quantity of Pounds Supplied	Dollars per Pound	Quantity of Pounds Demanded
50	$2.50	10
40	2.00	20
30	1.50	30
20	1.00	40
10	.50	50

a. The equilibrium exchange rate equals _____. At this exchange rate, how many pounds will be purchased, and at what cost in terms of dollars?

b. Suppose the exchange rate is $2 per pound. At this exchange rate, there is an excess (supply/demand) of pounds. This imbalance causes (an increase/a decrease) in the dollar price of the pound, which leads to (a/an) _____ in the quantity of pounds supplied and (a/an) _____ in the quantity of pounds demanded.

c. Suppose the exchange rate is $1 per pound. At this exchange rate, there is an excess (supply/demand) for pounds. This imbalance causes (an increase/a decrease) in the price of the pound, which leads to (a/an) _____ in the quantity of pounds supplied and (a/an) _____ in the quantity of pounds demanded.

8. Explain why exchange-rate quotations stated in different financial centers tend to be consistent with one another.

9. What is the strategy of speculating in the forward market? In what other ways can one speculate on exchange-rate changes?

10. Distinguish between stabilizing speculation and destabilizing speculation.

11. If the exchange rate changes from $1.70 = £1 to $1.68 = £1, what does this mean for the dollar? For the pound? What if the exchange rate changes from $1.70 = £1 to $1.72 = £1?

12. What is meant by the foreign-exchange market? Where is it located?

13. The supply and demand for foreign exchange are considered to be derived schedules. Explain.

14. What explains the relation between the spot rate and the forward rate?

15. What is meant by the forward market? How does it differ from the spot market?

16. Who are the participants in the forward-exchange market? What advantages does this market afford these participants?

Exploring Further 11.1

Techniques of Foreign-Exchange Market Speculation

Speculation in the foreign-exchange market can be conducted in the spot market and the forward market. Let us examine the techniques of speculating in these markets.

Speculating in the Spot Market

Imagine that you are a currency speculator in New York, willing to risk money on your opinion about future prices of a foreign currency—say, the Swiss franc. Consider the following scenarios.

Case 1:

Speculating on a Swiss franc appreciation.
GIVEN: Today's spot price is $0.40 per franc.
ASSUMPTION: In three months, the spot price of the franc will rise to $0.50.
PROCEDURE:

1. Purchase francs at today's spot price of $0.40 and deposit them in a bank to earn interest.
2. In three months, sell the francs at the prevailing spot price of $0.50 per franc.

OUTCOME: If assumption is right, profit = $0.10 per franc. If assumption is wrong and the spot price of the franc falls instead, you incur a loss, reselling francs at a price lower than the purchase price.

Case 2:

Speculating on a Swiss franc depreciation.
GIVEN: Today's spot price is $0.40 per franc.
ASSUMPTION: In three months, the spot price of the franc will fall to $0.25.
PROCEDURE:

1. Borrow francs today, exchange them for dollars at the prevailing spot price of $0.40 per franc, and deposit the dollars in a bank to earn interest.
2. In three months, buy francs at the prevailing spot price of $0.25 per franc and use them to pay back the loan.

OUTCOME: If assumption is right, profit = $0.15 per franc. (This return is reduced by the interest paid on borrowed money, but increased by the interest received on the bank savings account). If assumption is wrong and the spot price of the franc rises in three months instead, you incur a loss buying francs at a higher price than the initial selling price.

Speculating in the Forward Market

Although speculation on the spot market can lead to profits, it has a serious drawback: the speculator must have a large amount of idle cash or borrowing privileges, which require interest payments. However, speculation in the forward market does not require cash or credit facilities. All the speculator needs to do is sign a forward contract with a bank to either purchase or sell a specified amount of foreign currency at a specified date. The bank may impose a *margin requirement*, requiring the speculator to put up, say, ten percent of the value of the foreign contract as security. In practice, most speculation is done in the forward market.

Forward market speculation occurs when a speculator believes that a currency's spot price at some future date will differ from today's forward price for that same date. For example, suppose the 30-day forward pound is selling at a ten percent discount; this discount is the market's consensus (average expectation) that in 30 days the spot rate of the pound will be ten percent lower than it is today. However, as a speculator, you feel you have better information than the market. You believe that in 30 days the pound's spot rate will be only five percent lower (or maybe 15 percent higher) than it is today. You are willing to bet your money that the market consensus is wrong. Your gains or losses will equal the difference between the current forward rate and the spot rate 30 days from now. Consider the following scenarios.

Case 1:

Speculating that the spot rate of the Swiss franc in three months will be higher than its current three-month forward rate.

GIVEN: The current price of the three-month forward franc is $0.40.

ASSUMPTION: In three months, the prevailing spot price of the franc will be $0.50.

PROCEDURE:

1. Contract to purchase a specified amount of francs in the forward market, at $0.40 per franc, for a three-month delivery.
2. After receiving delivery of the francs in three months, resell them in the spot market at the prevailing price of $0.50 per franc.

OUTCOME: If assumption is right, profit = $0.10 per franc. If assumption is wrong and the prevailing spot price in three months is lower than $0.40 per franc, you incur a loss.

Case 2:

Speculating that the spot rate of the Swiss franc in three months will be lower than its current three-month forward rate.

GIVEN: The current price of the three-month forward franc is $0.40.

ASSUMPTION: In three months, the prevailing spot price of the franc will be $0.30.

PROCEDURE:

1. Contract to sell a specified amount of francs (which you do not currently have) for delivery in three months at the forward price of $0.40 per franc.
2. In three months, purchase an identical amount of francs in the spot market at $0.30 per franc and deliver them to fulfill the forward contract.

OUTCOME: If assumption is right, profit = $0.10 per franc. If assumption is wrong and the prevailing spot price in three months is higher than $0.40 per franc, you incur a loss.

When speculators purchase foreign currency on the spot or forward market with the anticipation of selling it at a higher future spot price, they are said to take a **long position** in the currency. But when speculators borrow or sell forward a foreign currency with the anticipation of purchasing it at a future lower price to repay the foreign-exchange loan or fulfill the forward sale contract, they are said to take a **short position** (that is, they are selling what they do not currently have).

Exploring Further 11.2

A Primer on Forex Trading

The foreign exchange market (forex or FX for short) is the "place" where currencies are traded. One characteristic of this market is that there is no central marketplace for foreign exchange. Rather, currency trading is conducted electronically *over the counter*, which means that all transactions occur via computer networks between traders around the world who negotiate directly with each other, rather than on one centralized exchange. The market is open 24 hours a day, five days a week, and currencies are traded worldwide. The main trading center is London, but New York, Tokyo, Hong Kong, and Singapore are all important centers as well.

What are you buying or selling in the forex market? The short answer is "nothing." No physical exchange of currencies takes place. All trades exist simply as computer entries and are netted out depending on the market price. For dollar-denominated accounts, all profits or losses are calculated in dollars and recorded as such on the trader's account.

Foreign exchange traders make money by purchasing currency at a low price and selling it later at a higher price, or, by anticipating the market is heading down, selling at a high price and buying back at a lower price later. Those with the most information, the best contacts, and strongest decision-making skills realize the most profit. Below are some of the principles that all forex traders need to understand.

Eight Major Currencies

Unlike the stock market, where investors have thousands of stocks to choose from, in the forex market there are only eight major currencies that need to be followed to determine the best overvalued or undervalued opportunities. The following eight currencies constitute most of the trade in the forex market:

1. U.S. dollar (USD)
2. Eurozone euro (EUR)
3. Japanese yen (JPY)
4. UK pound sterling (GBP)
5. Swiss franc (CHF)
6. Canadian dollar (CAD)
7. Australian dollar (AUD)
8. Hong Kong dollar (HKD)

Reading a Forex Quote: Currency Pairs

In the forex market, the value of a currency is determined by its comparison to another currency. The first currency of a currency pair is called the **base currency**, and the second currency is called the **quote currency**. The currency pair shows how much of the quote currency is needed to purchase one unit of the base currency.

For example the forex quote between the U.S. dollar and the Japanese yen (the currency pair) might look like this: USD/JPY = 119.510. The quote means that $1 = 119.51 Japanese yen. In other words, $1 can buy 119.51 Japanese yen.

There are two ways to quote a currency pair, either directly or indirectly. A **direct currency quote** is one in which the domestic currency is the base currency and the foreign currency is the quote currency. The forex quote shown above, USD/JPY = 119.51 is a direct currency quote if the U.S. dollar is the domestic currency and the Japanese yen is the foreign currency. Conversely, an **indirect currency quote** is a currency pair in which the foreign currency is the base currency and the domestic currency is the quote currency. An indirect quote would be JPY/USD and would be the reciprocal (1/119.51 = .0084) which means one Japanese yen will purchase $.0084.

The majority of forex traders focus on seven different currency pairs which include EUR/USD, USD/JPY, GBP/USD, USD/CHF, USD/CAD, AUD/USD, and NZD/USD. All other pairs are just different combinations of currencies, otherwise known as cross-currencies.

How Do Forex Traders Make a Profit? Bid Price and Ask Price

In the forex market, there are currency traders around the world who negotiate directly with each other. They do not charge commission. Instead, they make their money through the bid-ask spread.

Forex quotes always include a bid price and an ask price. The **bid price** is the price at which the trader is willing to buy a currency in exchange for another currency. This is one part of the bid with the other being the bid size, which details the amount of currency the trader is willing to purchase at the bid price. The opposite of the bid price is the **ask price**, which is the price at which the trader is willing to sell a currency in exchange for another currency. The difference between the bid and the ask price is referred to as the **spread**.

Consider the following forex quote between the U.S. dollar and the Canadian dollar:

$$USD/CAD = 1.2000/05$$
$$Bid = 1.2000$$
$$Ask = 1.2005$$

The quote before the slash is the bid price, and the two digits after the slash represent the ask price. Note that the bid price is always smaller than the ask price. If you wanted to *buy* this currency pair, this means that you intend to buy the base currency (U.S. dollar) and are therefore looking at the *ask* price to see how much in Canadian dollars the market will charge for a U.S. dollar. According to the ask price, you can buy one U.S. dollar with 1.2005 Canadian dollars. However, suppose you wanted to *sell* this currency pair which means sell the base currency (U.S. dollar) in exchange for the quoted currency (Canadian dollar). Thus, you would look for the *bid* price. It tells you that the market will buy US$1 (that is, you will be selling the U.S. dollar) for a price equivalent of 1.2000 Canadian dollars, which is the quoted price. The use of bid and ask is a basic characteristic of the market system, as it details the exact amount that you can buy or sell at any point in time. Remember that the current price is not the price for which you can purchase a currency, but the price at which the currency last traded hands. If you want to get an idea of the price for which you can buy a currency, you need to look at the bid and ask prices because they will often differ from the current price.

What is a Pip in Forex Trading?

Pip stands for *percentage in point* and is the smallest increment of trade in the forex market. Currency prices are quoted to the fourth decimal point, which is called 1 pip and is equal to 1/100th of 1 percent. Among the major currencies, the only exception to that rule is the Japanese yen whose quotation is only taken out to two decimal points—to 1/100th of yen, as opposed to 1/1000th with other major currencies. For example, in the EUR/USD currency pair, a movement from 0.8941 to 0.8942 is one pip, so a pip is 0.0001. In the USD/JPY currency pair, a movement from 130.45 to 130.46 is 1 pip, so a pip is 0.01.

What Do "Going Long" and "Going Short" Mean in Forex Trading?

Because currencies always trade in pairs (for example, dollars traded for euros), when a trader makes a trade he or she is always "long" in one currency and "short" in the other. For example, if a trader sells 100,000 units of EUR/USD, he or she would have exchanged euros for dollars and would now be "short" in euros and "long" in dollars.

To better understand this terminology, consider the following example. If you went to Office Max and bought a computer for $600, what would you be doing? You would be exchanging your dollars for a computer. You would basically be "short" $600 and "long" one computer. The store would be "long" $600 but "short" one computer in its inventory. The exact same principle applies to the forex market, except that no physical exchange of currency takes place.

We generally associate making profits in the foreign exchange market by initially buying a currency at a low price then selling it at a higher price later on; that is, "buy low and sell high." This is what you are doing when you are in a long position. However, you can also make a profit by being in a short position in which you initially sell currency at a high price then buy it back later on at a low price; that is, "sell high and buy low."

For example, assume that your expectation is that the dollar is going to become cheaper in terms of the Swiss franc in the future. To realize profit on this expectation, suppose that you move into a short position by initially selling $10,000 at the rate of 1.2025 francs per dollar and therefore realize 12,025 francs ($10,000 \times 1.2025 = 12,025$). Suppose that your expectation comes true and the price goes down to 1.2015 francs per dollar. Therefore, you use 12,015 of your francs to buy back $10,000 dollars ($10,000 \times 1.2015 = 12,015$) and realize a profit of 10 francs ($12,025 - 12,015 = 10$). Simply put, the key to making a profit in a short position is recognizing when the currency price will move down in your favor.

How Do Margin Trading and Leverage Work in the Forex Market?

Individual investors interested in trading in the forex market must first sign up with a broker who executes orders to buy or sell currencies on behalf of investors and charges them a commission.

Before the investor can place an order to buy or sell a currency, he must first deposit money into a **margin account**. The amount of money deposited depends on the margin percentage that is agreed upon by the investor and the broker. For accounts that will be trading in 100,000 currency units or more, the percentage is usually one or two percent. So, for an investor who wants to trade $100,000, this percentage means that 1,000 units needs to be deposited into the account. The remaining 99 percent, or 99,000 units, is provided by the broker. For the service of lending money to the investor, the broker charges interest.

When an investor uses a margin account, he or she is essentially borrowing to increase the possible return on his/her investment. The investor uses the **leverage** of borrowed money to control a larger

trading position than the amount he or she otherwise would be able to control with his/her own invested capital. The forex market offers tremendous leverage, often as high as 100:1 or even higher. This ratio means that an investor can control $100,000 worth of currency assets with as little as $1,000 worth of funds, which are placed in the investor's margin account. Leverage can be a double-edged sword: it can create massive profits when the investor is correct, but may also generate huge losses when the investor is wrong.

The purpose of the margin account is to cover against any currency-trading losses in the future. If the investor is losing money on his/her currency trades, the broker may initiate a margin call. When this call occurs, the broker instructs the investor to either deposit more money into the account or to close out the trading position to limit the risk to both parties.

Carry Trades as a Trading Strategy

One of the most popular trading techniques used by forex traders is the **carry trade**. It occurs when you borrow and pay interest in order to buy something else that has higher interest. For example, you might borrow from your broker in yen, where the interest rate is low, and use the proceeds to purchase U.S. dollar long-term securities, where the interest rate is high. Therefore, you must pay the interest on the currency that you have sold (yen), but you earn interest on the currency that you have bought (dollars).

Carry traders attempt to find two countries with a large difference in interest rates, and profit by buying the currency of the high interest-rate country and selling the currency of the low interest-rate country. For example, assume that the United Kingdom has an interest rate of six percent and that Canada has an interest rate of two percent; the interest rate differential thus equals four percent. So, if you purchase the British pound and sell the Canadian dollar (go long GBP/CAD), you will earn six percent in interest, but have to pay two percent, for a net return of four percent. As long as the exchange values of the currencies themselves do not change, you can capture the four percent spread equal to the interest rate differential.

The carry trade is appealing because of the type of returns it can earn, particularly if the proceeds are invested in bonds. These returns may not be huge, but they're steady and consistent, and so they appeal to money managers who want a steady income stream—for example, hedge fund managers with pension fund investors.

Carry traders hope to earn not only the interest rate differential between the two currencies, but they also look for their positions to appreciate in value as exchange rates change. During 2003–2004, for example, interest rates in Australia exceeded those in the United States by an average of 2.5 percent. A carry trader thus had the incentive to purchase Australian dollars and sell U.S. dollars (go long AUD/USD) and capture the interest rate spread of 2.5 percent. The return would become 25 percent with the use of 10:1 leverage. During that same period, the exchange value of the Australian dollar rose from 56 cents to almost 80 cents against the U.S. dollar, an appreciation of 42 percent. A carry trader in this currency trade would have not only earned the positive yield according to the interest rate differential, 2.5 percent, but also a capital gain of 42 percent on the underlying investment as the Australian dollar appreciated, for a total return of 44.5 percent. The key point is that a carry trader wants to choose trades that benefit not only from a positive and growing interest rate, but that also have the potential to appreciate in value.

The carry trade is a potentially lucrative way of trading and investing. However, it is not without considerable risks, especially when traded with a large amount of leverage. The biggest risk is generally that the exchange rate moves against you—the higher–interest rate currency rapidly depreciates, reducing the value of your assets relative to your borrowing. That's why these trades are often described as "picking up nickels in front of a steamroller."

Market Orders: Limit Order, Stop Order

Currency traders use orders to profit from market fluctuations when they are not in front of their computers. Recall that the forex market is open 24 hours a day. Fluctuations in the market are just as likely to take place when traders are asleep as when they are watching their screen. Traders routinely use market orders, limit orders, and stop orders to participate in the forex market without being there.

When conducting forex transactions, traders place a **market order** to buy or sell a currency at the current market price. When placing a market order, traders only have to specify the currency pair they want to buy or sell, say GBP/USD, and the amount of currency they are interested in buying or selling, say 100,000 units (one lot). The ask price is the price traders will pay when buying and the bid price is the price they will receive when selling.

In a **limit order**, traders not only specify the currency they want to buy or sell and the amount of the currency, but also at which price they want to do so; in other words, a limit is an order to buy or sell at a specified price or better. For example, suppose that traders place limit orders to buy one lot of GBP/USD at 1.9170. These orders mean that they can only be executed at a price equal to 1.9170 or lower (lower is always better for the buyer).

The **stop order** is an order that is activated when a currency reaches a specified price called the "stop." This order becomes a normal market order when the quoted prices reaches a specified level. Stop orders can be used to enter the market on momentum, like when a resistance or support level is broken, to limit the potential loss after establishing a position, and to protect the profit of an existing position that has moved favorably in price.

For example, consider how a stop order can protect an existing position. Suppose that forex traders buy lots of EUR/USD at 1.1355 in anticipation of an expected 80 pip rally in the euro. In order to control their risk, the traders place stop orders at

1.1335 (20 pips below the current price). If the price of the euro drops, traders' losses would be limited to 20 pips, or $200 (100,000 euro X .0020 = 200). Consider how a forex trader uses a stop order to buy on momentum. Suppose that the trader expects the U.S. dollar to appreciate against the Japanese yen, but does not want to buy yet because the USD/JPY is approaching a short-term resistance at 118.00. The trader instead places a buy stop order 10 pips above the resistance level. The stop is thus placed at 118.10. After this point, unless the USD/JPY goes to 118.10, the order won't be activated. By doing this, the trader is waiting for the resistance on the USD/JPY to be broken before entering the trade; that is, the trader is waiting for the upward momentum of the dollar to be confirmed before buying.

Currency Trading Selections: Fundamental Analysis and Technical Analysis

When forming a trading strategy, an important question that currency traders need to ask themselves is whether they desire to trade in short-term or long-term time periods? Generally, traders who prefer to base their trades on trends in the forex market will work on longer time horizons, because trends in the forex market develop over months rather than days. However, traders who look for quick changes in the market will usually operate on a much shorter time horizon, such as an hourly basis.

Once traders determine what time horizon is appropriate, the next question they must ask is what type of analysis should they use to make proper trade selections. No issues create more arguments on trading desks than the debate between fundamentalists and technicians.

Fundamental analysis involves examining the value of a country's currency based on economic news releases that reflect the strength or weakness of a country's economy. Fundamental traders follow these news announcements because they paint a picture of a currency's strength in relation to other countries. Among the variables that fundamental analysis considers are interest rates, trade balances, inflation rates, and gross domestic market. The general rule of thumb is that market fundamentals have a stronger impact on exchange rates over the long term and thus are more important to consider for longer-term trades. Although fundamental analysis may be an effective way to forecast overall economic conditions, it may not be a way to forecast exact market prices, especially in the short term.

Probably the most widely used method of making decisions and analyzing forex markets is **technical analysis**. This technique is concerned with studying patterns of exchange rate movements on charts in order to predict their short-term movements. Technical indicators use moving averages, oscillators, and momentum analysis to identify patterns that are repeatable. The goal of the technical analyst is to identify the signals exhibited in a current market by studying past market signals.

George Soros, Currency Speculator

Perhaps the most famous currency speculator of all time is George Soros. Born in Budapest, Hungary in 1930, Soros moved to England where he graduated from the London School of Economics in 1952. In 1956, he emigrated to the United States and became an investment banker. In 1973, Soros founded the investment company of Soros Fund Management, which eventually evolved into the highly successful Quantum Fund. When Soros retired in 2000, he was one of the world's wealthiest people. He became a substantial philanthropist, donating huge sums worldwide through his Open Society Foundation.

Concerning investment style, Soros was a master at translating economic trends into highly leveraged transactions in bonds and currencies. Soros was a short–term speculator who made large bets on the directions of financial markets. He maintained that financial markets were essentially chaotic. The prices of securities and currencies depend on human beings, or the traders who buy and sell assets. These persons' behaviors are often based on emotion, rather than logical considerations.

Soros also felt that market participants influenced one another and moved in herds. He said that most of the time he moved with the herd, but always watched for an opportunity to get out in front and "make a killing." How did Soros know when the time was right? He said that he had an instinctive physical reaction about when to buy and sell, and that emulating his strategy was difficult. Former Federal Reserve Chairman Paul Volcker noted that Soros made his mark as an enormously successful speculator, wise enough to withdraw when still way ahead of the game.

In September 1992, Soros became famous when his Quantum Fund made more than $1 billion by betting against the British pound. As background to this event, in 1990 Britain joined the European Exchange Rate Mechanism (ERM). This was a system intended to reduce exchange rate variability and achieve monetary stability in Europe, in preparation for the introduction of a single currency, the euro, which took place in 1999. The pound entered the ERM at an exchange rate of 2.95 marks to the pound. If the pound ever depreciated to the bottom of its permitted range, 2.778 marks per pound, the British government would be obliged to intervene. However, with British inflation at three times the rate of Germany's, the conditions for Britain's joining the ERM were not favorable at that time. Increasingly, speculators anticipated that the pound would depreciate against the mark to the extent that Britain would have to withdraw from the ERM.

Things reached a climax in September, 1992. The British government tried to prop up the sinking pound and withdrawal from the ERM was the last resort. The Bank of England raised interest rates from 10 percent to 15 percent in order to make the pound more attractive to foreign investors who were fleeing the pound. Also, the British government spent billions to buy up the pounds being frantically sold on the currency markets. However, these measures failed to prevent the pound from falling lower than its minimum level in the ERM.

In the meantime, Soros wondered how long the exchange rate band between the pound and mark could hold up against this market pressure. He began to take short positions against the pound. These positions meant that Soros borrowed huge sums of pounds and sold them on the forex market. He eventually returned the borrowed pounds by buying them back. Because the pound depreciated during this period (its price dropped), Soros bought pounds for less than he sold them, thus making a profit. Soros' bet paid off. The Bank of England was forced to withdraw from the ERM and to devalue the pound, and Soros earned an estimated $1.1 billion in the process. He was dubbed "the man who broke the Bank of England."

Soros is a controversial figure. Although he became extremely wealthy as an international investor and currency speculator, he freely acknowledges that the current system of financial speculation undermines healthy economic development in many countries. Also, critics point out that Soros played the currency markets through his Quantum Fund, registered in Curaçao, Netherlands Antilles, a Caribbean tax haven. By operating from Curaçao, Soros not only avoided paying taxes but also hid the nature of his investors and what he did with their money.

Source: Boris Schlossberg, "Forex Trading Guide," Investopedia, at http://www.investopedia.com/features/forex-trading-guide.aspx? See also Sam Cross, *All About the Foreign Exchange Market in the United States*, Federal Reserve Bank of New York, 1998 and Michael Archer and Jim Bickford, Getting Started in Currency Trading, *Hoboken, NJ: John Wiley and Sons, 2005.*

Exchange-Rate Determination

CHAPTER 12

Since the introduction of market-determined exchange rates by the major industrial nations in the 1970s, notable shifts in exchange rates have been observed. Although changes in long-term exchange rates have tended to undergo relatively gradual shifts, if we examine shorter intervals, we see that the exchange rate is very volatile. Indeed, exchange rates can fluctuate by several percentage points even during a single day. This chapter seeks to explain the forces that underlie fluctuations of exchange rates under a system of market-determined (floating) exchange rates.

What Determines Exchange Rates?

We have learned that foreign-exchange markets are highly competitive by nature. Large numbers of sellers and buyers meet in these markets, which are located in the major cities of the world and are connected electronically to form one worldwide market. Participants in the foreign-exchange market have excellent, up-to-the-minute information about the exchange rates between any two currencies. As a result, currency values are determined by the unregulated forces of supply and demand as long as central banks do not attempt to stabilize them. The supplies and demands for a currency come from private individuals, corporations, banks, and government agencies other than central banks. In a free market, the equilibrium exchange rate occurs at the point at which the quantity demanded of a foreign currency equals the quantity of that currency supplied.

To say that supply and demand determine exchange rates in a free market is at once to say everything and to say nothing. If we are to understand why some currencies depreciate and others appreciate, we must investigate the factors that cause the supply and demand schedules of currencies to change. These factors include **market fundamentals** (economic variables) such as productivity, inflation rates, real interest rates, consumer preferences, and government trade policy. They also include **market expectations** such as news about future market fundamentals and traders' opinions about future exchange rates.[1]

Because economists believe that the determinants of exchange-rate fluctuations are rather different in the short term (a few weeks or even days), interim (several months), and long term (one, two, or even five years), we will consider these time frames when analyzing exchange rates. In the *short term*, foreign-exchange transactions are dominated by transfers of assets (bank accounts, government securities) that respond to differences in real interest rates and to the shifting expectations of future exchange rates; such transactions have a major influence on short-term exchange rates. Over the *interim*, exchange rates are governed by cyclical factors such as fluctuations in economic activity. Over the *long term*, foreign-exchange transactions are dominated by flows of goods, services, and investment capital, which respond to forces such as inflation rates, investment profitability, consumer tastes, productivity, and government trade policy; because these factors tend to change slowly, their impact on the exchange rate occurs over the long term.

Note that day-to-day influences on foreign-exchange rates can cause the rate to move in the opposite direction from that indicated by longer-term fundamentals. Although today's exchange rate may be out of line with long-term fundamentals, this should not be construed as implying that it is necessarily inconsistent with short-term determinants—for example, interest-rate differentials, which are among the relevant fundamentals at the short end of the time dimension.

Figure 12.1 highlights the framework in which exchange rates are determined.[2] The figure views exchange rates as simultaneously determined by long-term structural, interim cyclical, and short-term speculative forces. The figure illustrates the idea that there exists some equilibrium level or path to which a currency will eventually gravitate. This path serves as a long-term magnet or anchor; it ensures that exchange rates will not fluctuate aimlessly without limit but rather will tend to gravitate over time toward the long-term equilibrium path.

Interim cyclical forces can induce fluctuations of a currency above and below its long-term equilibrium path. However, fundamental forces serve to push a currency toward its long-term equilibrium path. Note that interim cyclical fluctuations from a currency's long-term equilibrium path can be large at times, if economic disturbances induce significant changes in either trade flows or capital movements.

Longer-term structural forces and interim cyclical forces interact to establish a currency's equilibrium path. Exchange rates may sometimes move away from this path if short-term forces (for example, changing market expectations) induce fluctuations in exchange rates beyond those based on fundamental factors. Although such overshooting behavior can persist for significant periods, fundamental forces generally push the currency back into its long-term equilibrium path.

Unfortunately, predicting exchange-rate movements is a difficult job. That is because economic forces affect exchange rates through a variety of channels—some

---

[1]This approach to exchange-rate determination is known as the balance-of-payments approach. It emphasizes the flow of goods, services, and investment funds and their impact on foreign-exchange transactions and exchange rates. The approach predicts that exchange-rate depreciation (appreciation) tends to occur for a nation that spends more (less) abroad in combined purchases and investments than it acquires from abroad over a sustained period of time.

[2]This figure and its analysis are adapted from Michael Rosenberg, *Currency Forecasting* (Homewood, IL: Richard D. Irwin, 1996), pp. 3–5.

FIGURE 12.1

THE PATH OF THE YEN'S EXCHANGE RATE

This figure views the exchange value of a nation's currency as being determined by long-term structural, interim cyclical, and short-term speculative forces.

of which may induce negative impacts on a currency's value, others of which may exert positive impacts. Some of those channels may be more important in determining short-term tendencies, whereas other channels may be more important in explaining the long-term trend that a currency follows.

To simplify our analysis of exchange rates, we divide it into two parts. First, we consider how exchange rates are determined in the long term. Then we use our knowledge of the long-term determinants of the exchange rate to help us understand how they are determined in the short term.

To gain a better understanding of these determinants, you can refer to the "Forex View" column that appears daily in the *The Wall Street Journal*; it is usually located in the third section, "Money and Investing." The column typically discusses factors causing fluctuations in the dollar's exchange value.

Determining Long-Term Exchange Rates

Changes in the long-term value of the exchange rate are due to the reactions of traders in the foreign-exchange market to changes in four key factors: relative price levels, relative productivity levels, consumer preferences for domestic or foreign

TABLE 12.1

Determinants of the Dollar's Exchange Rate in the Long Term

Factor*	Change	Effect on the Dollar's Exchange Rate
U.S. price level	Increase	Depreciation
	Decrease	Appreciation
U.S. productivity	Increase	Appreciation
	Decrease	Depreciation
U.S. preferences	Increase	Depreciation
	Decrease	Appreciation
U.S. trade barriers	Increase	Appreciation
	Decrease	Depreciation

*Relative to other countries. The analysis for a change in one determinant assumes that the other determinants are unchanged.

goods, and trade barriers. Note that these factors underlie trade in domestic and foreign goods and thus changes in the demand for exports and imports. Table 12.1 summarizes the effects of these factors.

To illustrate the effects of these factors, refer to Figure 12.2, which shows the demand and supply schedules for pounds. Initially, the equilibrium exchange rate is $1.50 per pound. We will examine each factor by itself, assuming that all other factors remain constant.

Relative Price Levels

Referring to Figure 12.2(a), suppose the domestic price level increases rapidly in the United States and remains constant in the United Kingdom. This causes U.S. consumers to desire relatively low-priced UK goods. The demand for pounds thus increases to D_1 in the figure. Conversely, as the UK consumers purchase less relatively high-priced U.S. goods, the supply of pounds decreases to S_1. The increase in the demand for pounds and the decrease in the supply of pounds result in a depreciation of the dollar to $1.60 per pound. This analysis suggests that an increase in the U.S. price level relative to price levels in other countries causes the dollar to depreciate in the long term.

Relative Productivity Levels

Productivity growth measures the increase in a country's output for a given level of input. If one country becomes more productive than other countries, it can produce goods more cheaply than its foreign competitors can. If productivity gains are passed forward to domestic and foreign buyers in the form of lower prices, the nation's exports tend to increase and imports tend to decrease.

Referring to Figure 12.2(b), suppose U.S. productivity growth is faster than that of the United Kingdom. As U.S. goods become relatively less expensive, the UK demands more U.S. goods, which results in an increase in the supply of pounds to S_2. Also, Americans demand fewer UK goods, which become relatively more expensive, causing the demand for pounds to decrease to D_2. Therefore, the dollar appreciates to $1.40 per pound. Simply put, in the long term, as a country becomes more productive relative to other countries, its currency appreciates.

Preferences for Domestic or Foreign Goods

Referring to Figure 12.2(c), suppose that U.S. consumers develop stronger preferences for UK-manufactured goods such as automobiles and CD players. The stronger demand for UK goods results in Americans demanding more pounds to purchase these goods. As the demand for pounds rises to D_1, the dollar depreciates to $1.55 per pound. Conversely, if UK consumers demand additional American computer software, machinery, and apples, the dollar would tend to appreciate against the pound. We conclude that an increased demand for a country's exports

FIGURE 12.2

MARKET FUNDAMENTALS THAT AFFECT THE DOLLAR'S EXCHANGE RATE IN THE LONG TERM

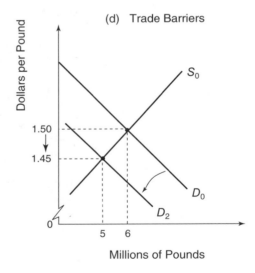

In the long term, the exchange rate between the dollar and the pound reflects relative price levels, relative productivity levels, preferences for domestic or foreign goods, and trade barriers.

causes its currency to appreciate in the long term; conversely, increased demand for imports results in a depreciation in the domestic currency.

Trade Barriers

Barriers to free trade also affect exchange rates. Suppose that the U.S. government imposes tariffs on British steel. By making steel imports more expensive than domestically-produced steel, the tariff discourages Americans from purchasing UK steel. In Figure 12.2 (d), this tariff causes the demand for pounds to decrease to D_2, which results in an appreciation of the dollar to $1.45 per pound. Simply put, trade barriers such as tariffs and quotas cause a currency appreciation in the long term for the country imposing the barriers.

Inflation Rates, Purchasing Power Parity, and Long-Term Exchange Rates

The determinants discussed earlier are helpful in understanding the long-term behavior of exchange rates. Let us now focus on the purchasing-power-parity approach and see how it builds on the relative price determinant of long-term exchange rates.

Law of One Price

The simplest concept of purchasing power parity is the **law of one price**. It asserts that identical goods should be sold everywhere at the same price when converted to a common currency, assuming that it is costless to ship the good between nations, there are no barriers to trade, and markets are competitive. It rests on the assumption that sellers will seek out the highest possible prices and buyers the lowest ones. Any differences that arise are quickly eliminated by arbitrage, the simultaneous buying at a low price and selling at a higher one.

The law of one price holds reasonably well for globally tradable commodities, such as oil, metals, chemicals, and some agricultural crops. However, the law does not appear to apply well to nontradable goods and services such as cab rides, housing, and personal services like haircuts. These products are largely insulated from global competition, and their prices can vary from place to place.

Before the costs of a good in different nations can be compared, its price must first be converted into a common currency. Once converted at the going market-exchange rate, the price of an identical good from any two nations should be identical. After converting francs into dollars, for example, machine tools purchased in Switzerland should cost the same as identical machine tools bought in the United States. This means that the purchasing power of the franc and the dollar is at parity and the law of one price prevails.

In theory, the pursuit of profits tends to equalize the price of an identical product in different nations. Assume that machine tools bought in Switzerland are cheaper than the same machine tools bought in the United States, after converting francs into dollars. Swiss exporters could realize a profit by purchasing machine tools in Switzerland at a low price and selling them in the United States at a high price. Such transactions would force prices up in Switzerland and force prices down in the

United States until the price of the machine tools would eventually become equal in both nations, whether prices are expressed in francs or dollars. As a result, the law of one price would prevail.

Although the law of one price seems reasonable enough, a look at actual examples points up why a single price might not apply in practice. First, it might not make much sense to buy cheap machine tools in Switzerland and ship them to the United States. It might cost too much to achieve the relatively more expensive prices after shipping the cheaper tools to the United States, setting up distribution networks to sell them, and so forth. These transaction costs might mean that price differences between the tools can persist. Similarly, the existence of U.S. tariffs on imported machine tools might drive a wedge between the prices of the tools in the United States and Switzerland.

The "Big Mac" Index and the Law of One Price

The Big Mac hamburger sandwich sold by McDonalds provides an example of the law of one price.

Big Macs are sold in more than 40 countries and have only negligible differences in the recipe. This hamburger sandwich comes close to being an "identical good" that applies to the law of one price. Other global products could be used as a prop in this exercise, such as Coca-Cola or Starbucks coffee, but over the years the Big Mac Index has been a quick guide to prices in many countries.

Since 1986, the *Economist* magazine each year publishes the Big Mac Index that is nothing more than an attempt to measure the true equilibrium value of a currency based on one product, a Big Mac. According to the law of one price, a Big Mac should cost the same in a given currency wherever it is purchased in the world, suggesting that the prevailing market-exchange rate is the true equilibrium rate. Does this always occur?

For example, the Big Mac Index suggests that the market-exchange rate between the dollar and the yen is in equilibrium when it equates the prices of Big Macs in the United States and Japan. Big Macs would thus cost the same in each country when the prices are converted to the dollar. If Big Macs do not cost the same, the law of one price breaks down. Thus, the yen is said to be overvalued or undervalued compared to the dollar. In this manner, the Big Mac Index can be used to determine the extent to which the market exchange rate differs from the true equilibrium exchange rate.

Table 12.2 shows what a Big Mac costs in different countries as of February 4, 2009. It turns out that in all of the countries surveyed the dollar price of the Big Mac was different from the U.S. level, thus violating the law of one price. In the table, the U.S. equivalent prices denote which currencies are overvalued and which are undervalued relative to the dollar. In the United States, a Big Mac cost $3.54. In Switzerland, the dollar-equivalent price of a Big Mac was $5.60. Compared to the dollar, the Swiss franc was *overvalued* by 58 percent ($5.60/$ 3.54 = 1.58). However, the Big Mac was a bargain in Hong Kong where the U.S. dollar equivalent price was $1.72; the Hong Kong dollar was *undervalued* by 52 percent ($1.72/$ 3.54 = 0.48).

Our Big Mac index shows that its prices were out of alignment with each other as of February 4, 2009. In theory, an arbitrageur could purchase Big Macs for the equivalent of $1.72 in, say Hong Kong, whose dollar was undervalued against the U.S. dollar, and sell them in Switzerland for $5.60, where the franc was overvalued

TABLE 12.2

BIG MAC INDEX

THE PRICE OF A BIG MAC, FEBRUARY 4, 2009

BIG MAC PRICES

Country/Currency	In Local Currency	In U.S. Dollars*	Local Currency Overvaluation (+), Undervaluation (−) (percent)
United States (dollar)	$3.54	$3.54	—
Switzerland (franc)	6.50	5.60	+58%
Sweden (krona)	38.0	4.58	+29
Eurozone (euro)	3.42	4.38	+24
Brazil (real)	8.02	3.45	−2
Canada (dollar)	4.16	3.36	−5
Japan (yen)	290	3.23	−9
Mexico (peso)	33.0	2.30	−35
Hong Kong (dollar)	13.3	1.72	−52

*At market exchange rate, February 4, 2009. The price of each country is based on the average of four cities.

Source: From "Big Mac Currencies," *The Economist*, available at **http://www.economist.com**.

against the U.S. dollar. This pursuit of profits would push prices up in Hong Kong and down in Switzerland until the price of Big Macs eventually equalized in the two countries. In practice, such arbitrage trading would not result in price equalization. Simply put, Big Mac prices show that the law of one price does not hold across countries.

Why do Big Mac prices vary from one nation to another, even when adjusted for exchange rates? One reason is the cost of moving goods across borders. The Big Mac itself is not tradable, but many of its ingredients are. Transportation costs for frozen beef patties, cooking oil, sesame-seed buns and other tradable Big Mac ingredients can create price gaps across countries. Also, the costs imposed by tariffs and other trade barriers can contribute to price disparities between countries because they drive a wedge between these prices. Finally, income disparities help explain why the Big Mac sells at different prices in different countries: prices tend to be higher in rich countries where people have a greater ability to pay higher prices.

To be sure, the Big Mac Index is primitive and has many flaws. However, it is widely understood by noneconomists and serves as an approximation of which currencies are too weak or strong, and by how much. Although the Big Mac Index was originally developed for fun, it has turned out to be a surprisingly useful predictor for exchange rate movements. It appears that those who were initially dubious of the validity of the Big Mac Index now realize that it might be something useful on which to chew.

Purchasing Power Parity

A prominent theory of how exchange rates move is the **purchasing-power-parity theory**. It says that exchange rates adjust to make goods and services cost the same everywhere and thus it is an application of the law of one price.

TABLE 12.3

THE LAW OF ONE PRICE APPLIED TO A SINGLE
PRODUCT, STEEL

According to the law of one price, if the yen price of steel
increases by ten percent and the dollar price of steel
remains constant, the yen will depreciate by ten percent
against the dollar to ensure that price is the same in both
countries.

Yen Price of a Ton of Steel	Dollar Price of a Ton of Steel	Exchange Rate: Yen per dollar
50,000 yen	$500	100
55,000	500	110

Our analysis of exchange rates begins by using the law of one price for a single good, steel, as seen in Table 12.3. Assume that the yen price of Japanese steel is 50,000 yen per ton and the dollar price of American steel is $500 per ton. Therefore, the law of one price says that the exchange rate between the yen and the dollar is 100 yen per dollar (50,000/500 = 100) to ensure that price is the same in both countries. Suppose that the yen price of Japanese steel increases ten percent, to 55,000 yen per ton, and the dollar price of American steel remains constant at $500 per ton. According to the law of one price, the exchange rate must increase to 110 yen per dollar (55,000/500 = 110), a ten percent depreciation of the yen. Applying the law of one price to the prices of steel in Japan and the United States, we conclude that if the Japanese price level increases by ten percent relative to the American price level, the yen will depreciate by ten percent against the dollar.

Although the law of one price can be applied to one good, economists are interested in how exchange rates are determined by looking at the prices of many goods, as measured by a nation's consumer price index or producer price index. The purchasing-power-parity theory provides a generalized explanation of exchange rates based on the prices of many goods. Therefore, the purchasing-power-parity theory is simply the application of the law of one price to national price levels.

According to the purchasing-power-parity theory, what is important are relative inflationary differences between one economy and the next. If the rate of inflation is much higher in one country, its money has lost purchasing power over domestic goods. We would expect that currency to depreciate, to restore parity with prices of goods abroad (the depreciation would make imported goods more expensive to domestic consumers while making domestic exports less expensive to foreigners). Thus, exports and imports of goods and services (trade flows) constitute the mechanism that makes a currency depreciate or appreciate, according to the purchasing-power-parity theory.

Going one step further, the purchasing-power-parity theory suggests that the *changes* in relative national price levels determine *changes* in exchange rates over the long term. The theory predicts that the foreign-exchange value of a currency tends to appreciate or depreciate at a rate equal to the difference between foreign and domestic inflation.[3]

Suppose we compare the consumer price indexes of the United States and Switzerland and find that U.S. inflation exceeds Switzerland's inflation by four percentage points per year. This difference means that the purchasing power of the dollar falls relative to the franc. The exchange value of the dollar against the franc should therefore depreciate four percent per year, according to the purchasing-power-parity theory.

---

[3]This chapter presents the so-called *relative version* of the purchasing-power-parity theory, which addresses changes in prices and exchange rates over a period of time. Another variant is the *absolute version*, which states that the equilibrium exchange rate will equal the ratio of domestic to foreign prices of an appropriate market basket of goods and services at a given point in time.

Conversely, the U.S. dollar should appreciate against the franc if U.S. inflation is less than Switzerland's inflation.

The purchasing-power-parity theory can be used to predict long-term exchange rates. We'll consider an example using the price indexes (P) of the United States and Switzerland. Letting zero be the base period and one represents period 1, the purchasing-power-parity theory is given in symbols as follows:

$$S_1 = S_0 \frac{P_{US_1}/P_{US_0}}{P_{S_1}/P_{S_0}}$$

where S_0 equals the equilibrium exchange rate existing in the base period and S_1 equals the estimated target at which the actual rate should be in the future.

For example, let the price indexes of the United States and Switzerland and the equilibrium exchange rate be as follows:

$$P_{US_0} = 100 \quad P_{S_0} = 100 \quad S_0 = \$0.50$$
$$P_{US_1} = 200 \quad P_{S_1} = 100$$

Putting these figures into the previous equation, we can determine the new equilibrium exchange rate for period 1:

$$S_1 = \$0.50 \left(\frac{200/100}{100/100}\right) = \$0.50(2) = \$1.00$$

Between one period and the next, the U.S. inflation rate rose 100 percent, whereas Switzerland's inflation rate remained unchanged. Maintaining purchasing power parity between the dollar and the franc requires the dollar to depreciate against the franc by an amount equal to the difference in the percentage rates of inflation in the United States and Switzerland. The dollar must depreciate by 100 percent, from $0.50 per franc to $1 per franc, to maintain its purchasing power parity. If the example assumed instead that Switzerland's inflation rate doubled while the U.S. inflation rate remained unchanged, the dollar would appreciate to a level of $0.25 per franc, according to the purchasing-power-parity theory.

Although the purchasing-power-parity theory can be helpful in forecasting appropriate levels to which currency values should be adjusted, it is not an infallible guide to exchange-rate determination. For instance, the theory overlooks the fact that exchange-rate movements may be influenced by investment flows. The theory also faces the problems of choosing the appropriate price index to be used in price calculations (for example, consumer prices or producer prices) and of determining the equilibrium period to use as a base. Moreover, government policy may interfere with the operation of the theory by implementing trade restrictions that disrupt the flow of exports and imports among nations.

The predictive power of the purchasing-power-parity theory is most evident in the long term. From 1973 to 2003, the UK price level increased about 99 percent relative to the U.S. price level, as seen in Figure 12.3. As the purchasing-power-parity theory forecasts, the pound depreciated against the dollar by about 73 percent during this period, although this amount is less than the 99 percent increase forecasted by the theory. Moreover, the figure shows that the purchasing-power-parity theory has negligible predictive power in the short term. From 1985 to 1988, for example, the British price level increased relative to the U.S. price level. Rather than depreciating, as the purchasing-power-parity theory predicts, the pound actually appreciated against the

FIGURE 12.3

This figure suggests that the predictive power of the purchasing-power-parity theory is most evident in the long term. In the short term, the theory has negligible predictive power.

Source: *Economic Report of the President* and *National Statistics Online* available at **http://www.statistics.gov.uk/**.

dollar. Simply put, the purchasing-power-parity theory is most appropriate for forecasting exchange rates in the long term; in the short term, it is a poor forecaster.

Determining Short-Term Exchange Rates: The Asset-Market Approach

We have seen that exchange-rate fluctuations in the long term stem from volatility in market fundamentals including relative price levels (purchasing power parity), relative productivity levels, preferences for domestic or foreign goods, and trade barriers. However, fluctuations in exchange rates are sometimes too large and too sudden to be explained solely by such factors. For example, exchange rates can change by two percentage points or more in a single day. But variations in the determinants usually do not occur frequently or significantly enough to fully account for such exchange-rate irascibility. Therefore, to understand why exchange rates can fluctuate sharply in a particular day or week, we must consider other factors besides relative price-level behavior, productivity trends, preferences, and trade barriers. We need to develop a framework that can demonstrate why exchange rates fluctuate in the short term.

To understand short-term exchange-rate behavior, it is important to recognize that foreign-exchange market activity is dominated by investors in assets such as Treasury securities, corporate bonds, bank accounts, stocks, and real property. Today, only about two percent of all foreign-exchange transactions are related to the financing of

INFLATION DIFFERENTIALS AND THE EXCHANGE RATE

FIGURE 12.4

INFLATION DIFFERENTIALS AND THE DOLLAR'S EXCHANGE VALUE

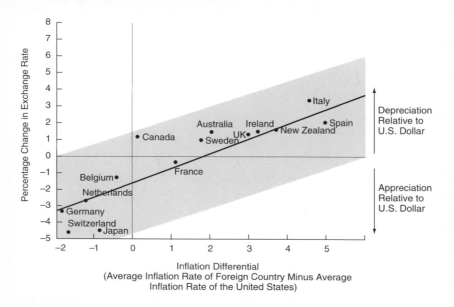

The purchasing-power-parity theory helps explain the behavior of a currency's exchange value. According to this theory, changes in relative national price levels determine changes in exchange rates over the long term. A currency is expected to depreciate by an amount equal to the excess of domestic inflation over foreign inflation; it appreciates by an amount equal to the excess of foreign inflation over domestic inflation.

Figure 12.4 shows the relation between inflation and the exchange rate for selected countries. The horizontal axis shows the country's average inflation minus the U.S. average inflation during the 1960–1997 period. The vertical axis shows the average percentage change in a country's exchange rate (foreign currency per dollar) over that period. Consistent with the predictions of the purchasing-power-parity theory, the figure shows that countries with relatively low inflation rates tend to have appreciating currencies, and countries with relatively high inflation tend to have depreciating currencies.

Source: From International Monetary Fund, IMF Financial Statistics, various issues.

exports and imports. This relation suggests that about 98 percent of foreign-exchange transactions are attributable to assets being traded in global markets. Because these markets are connected by sophisticated telecommunication systems and trading occurs on a 24-hour basis, investors in financial assets can trade rapidly and modify their

TABLE 12.4

DETERMINANTS OF THE DOLLAR'S EXCHANGE RATE AGAINST THE POUND IN THE SHORT TERM

Change in Determinant*	Repositioning of International Financial Investment	Effect on Dollar's Exchange Rate
U.S. Interest Rate		
Increase	Toward dollar-denominated assets	Appreciates
Decrease	Toward pound-denominated	Depreciates
British Interest Rate		
Increase	Toward pound-denominated assets	Depreciates
Decrease	Toward dollar-denominated assets	Appreciates
Expected Future Change in the Dollar's Exchange Rate		
Appreciate	Toward dollar-denominated assets	Appreciates
Depreciate	Toward pound-denominated assets	Depreciates

*The analysis for a change in one determinant assumes that the other determinants are unchanged.

outlooks of currency values almost instantaneously. Simply put, over short periods such as a month, decisions to hold domestic or foreign assets play a much greater role in exchange-rate determination than the demand for imports and exports does.

According to the **asset-market approach**, investors consider two key factors when deciding between domestic and foreign investments: relative levels of interest rates and expected changes in the exchange rate itself over the term of the investment. These factors, in turn, account for fluctuations in exchange rates that we observe in the short term. Table 12.4 summarizes the effects of these factors.

Relative Levels of Interest Rates

The level of the **nominal (money) interest rate** is a first approximation of the rate of return on assets that can be earned in a particular country. Thus, differences in the level of nominal interest rates between economies are likely to affect international investment flows, as investors seek the highest rate of return.

When interest rates in the United States are significantly higher than interest rates abroad, the foreign demand for U.S. securities and bank accounts will increase, which increases the demand for the dollars needed to buy those assets, thus causing the dollar to appreciate relative to foreign currencies. In contrast, if interest rates in the United States are on average lower than interest rates abroad, the demand for foreign securities and bank accounts strengthens and the demand for U.S. securities and bank accounts weakens. This weakness will cause the demand for foreign currencies needed to buy foreign assets to increase and the demand for the dollar to decrease, resulting in a depreciation of the dollar relative to foreign currencies.

To illustrate the effects of relative interest rates as a determinant of exchange rates, refer to Figure 12.5. It shows the demand and supply schedules for pounds. Initially, the equilibrium exchange rate is $1.50 per pound. Referring to Figure 12.5 (a), assume that an expansionary monetary policy of the U.S. Federal Reserve results in a fall in interest rates to three percent, while interest rates in the United Kingdom are at six percent. American investors will be attracted to the relatively high interest

FIGURE 12.5

FACTORS AFFECTING THE DOLLAR'S EXCHANGE RATE IN THE SHORT TERM

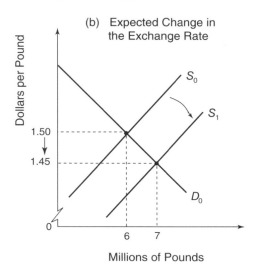

In the short term, the exchange rate between the dollar and the pound reflects relative interest rates and expected changes in the exchange rate.

rates in the United Kingdom and will demand more pounds to buy UK Treasury bills. The demand for pounds thus rises to D_1 in the figure. Concurrently, the UK investors will find investing in the United States less attractive than before, so fewer pounds will be offered to buy dollars for purchases of U.S. securities. The supply of pounds thus decreases to S_1 in the figure. The combined effect of these two shifts is to cause the dollar to depreciate to $1.60 per pound. Alternatively, if interest rates were lower in the United Kingdom than in the United States, the dollar would appreciate against the pound as Americans made fewer investments in the United Kingdom and the UK investors made more investments in the United States.

Things may not always be so simple, though, concerning the relation between interest rates, investment flows, and exchange rates. It is important to distinguish between the nominal interest rate and the **real interest rate** (the nominal interest rate minus the inflation rate).

$$\text{Real Interest rate} = \text{Nominal Interest Rate} - \text{Inflation Rate}$$

For international investors, it is the relative changes in the real interest rate that matter.

If a rise in the nominal interest rate in the United States is accompanied by an equal rise in the U.S. inflation rate, the real interest rate remains constant. In this case, higher nominal interest rates do not make dollar-denominated securities more attractive to UK investors. This is because rising U.S. inflation will encourage U.S. buyers to seek out low-priced UK goods, which will increase the demand for pounds

TABLE 12.5

SHORT-TERM NOMINAL AND REAL INTEREST
RATES, 2007

Country	Nominal Interest Rate* (Percent)	Inflation Rate** (Percent)	Real Interest Rate (Percent)
Canada	4.2	−3.8	8.0
France	3.9	2.5	1.4
Germany	3.8	1.8	2.0
Japan	0.8	0.6	0.2
Netherlands	3.9	1.2	2.7
South Korea	3.3	1.2	2.1
Mexico	7.7	4.7	3.0
United States	4.4	2.7	1.7

*Rates are for three-month treasury bills.
**Measured by the GDP deflator.

Source: From *International Financial Statistics*, December, 2008 and World Bank, *Data and Statistics*, available at **www.worldbank.org**.

and cause the dollar to depreciate. British investors will expect the exchange rate of the dollar, in terms of the pound, to depreciate along with the declining purchasing power of the dollar. The higher nominal return on U.S. securities will thus be offset by the expectation of a lower future exchange rate, leaving the motivation for increased UK investment in the United States unaffected. Only if higher nominal interest rates in the United States signal an increase in the real interest rate will the dollar appreciate; if they signal rising inflationary expectations and a falling real interest rate, the dollar will depreciate. Table 12.5 provides examples of short-term real interest rates for various nations.

Movements in real interest rates help explain the behavior of the dollar during 1974–2006, as seen in Figure 12.6. In the late 1970s, real interest rates in the United States were at low levels, as was the trade-weighted value of the dollar. By the early 1980s, U.S. real interest rates were increasing. This movement

FIGURE 12.6

INTEREST RATE DIFFERENTIALS AND EXCHANGE RATES

An increase in the U.S. real interest rate increases the expected return on dollar assets, such as Treasury bills and certificates of deposit. This increase encourages flows of foreign investment into the United States, thus causing the dollar's exchange value to appreciate. Conversely, a decrease in the U.S. real interest rate reduces the expected profitability on dollar assets, which promotes a depreciation of the dollar's exchange value.

attracted investment funds to the United States that caused the dollar's exchange value to rise. After 1985, U.S. real interest rates declined and the dollar's value weakened. The positive relation between the real interest rate and the dollar's exchange rate broke down after 1995: While U.S. real interest rates remained unchanged, the dollar appreciated. This appreciation was due to a booming U.S. stock market in the late 1990s that attracted foreign investment inflows and pushed up the dollar's exchange value, even though U.S. real interest rates remained constant. Following 2002, the U.S. real interest rate declined and the dollar's exchange value depreciated at the same time, repeating the experience of the late 1980s. Simply put, we expect to see appreciating currencies in countries whose real interest rates are higher than abroad because these countries will attract investment funds from all over the world. Countries that experience relatively low real interest rates tend to find their currencies depreciating.

Expected Change in the Exchange Rate

Differences in interest rates may not be all investors need to know to guide their decisions. They must also consider that the return actually realized from an investment is paid out over some future period. This time frame means that the realized value of that future payment can be altered by changes in the exchange rate itself over the term of the investment. Simply put, investors must think about possible gains or losses on foreign currency transactions in addition to interest rates on assets.

Expectations about the future path of the exchange rate itself will figure prominently in the investor's calculation of what he or she will actually earn from an investment denominated in another currency. Even a high interest rate would not be attractive if one expects the denominating currency to depreciate at a similar or greater rate and erase all economic gain. Conversely, if the denominating currency is expected to appreciate, the realized gain would be greater than what the interest rate alone would suggest, and the asset appears more lucrative.

Figure 12.5(b) illustrates the effects of investor expectations of changes in exchange rates over the term of an investment. Assume that the equilibrium exchange rate is initially $1.50 per pound. Suppose that UK investors expect that in three months the exchange value of the dollar will appreciate against the pound. Thus, by investing in three-month U.S. Treasury bills, UK investors can anticipate a foreign currency gain: today, selling pounds for dollars when dollars are relatively cheap, and, in three months, purchasing pounds with dollars when dollars are more valuable (pounds are cheap). The expectation of foreign currency gain will make U.S. Treasury bills seem more attractive, and the UK investors will purchase more of them. In the figure, the supply of pounds in the foreign-exchange market shifts rightward from S_0 to S_1 and the dollar appreciates to $1.45 per pound today. In this way, future expectations of an appreciation of the dollar can be self-fulfilling for today's value of the dollar.

Referring to the previous example, UK investors expect that the dollar will appreciate against the pound in three months. What triggers these expectations? The answer lies in the long-term determinants of exchange rates discussed earlier in this chapter. The dollar will be expected to appreciate if there are expectations that the U.S. price level will decrease relative to the UK price level, U.S. productivity will increase relative to UK productivity, U.S. tariffs will increase, the U.S. demand for imports will decrease, or the UK demand for U.S. exports will increase. Given anticipated gains resulting from an appreciating dollar, UK investment will flow to the United States, which causes an increase in today's value of the dollar in terms of the pound, as seen in the following flowchart:

| Long-run determinants of the dollar's exchange rate | → | Expected appreciation of the dollar in 3 months | → | Expected foreign-exchange gain for UK investors | → | UK invest-ment flows to the United States today | → | The dollar appreciates against the pound today |

Simply put, any long-term factor that causes the expected future value of the dollar to appreciate will cause the dollar to appreciate today.

Diversification, Safe Havens, and Investment Flows

Although relative levels of interest rates between countries and expected changes in exchange rates tend to be strong forces directing investment flows among economies, other factors can also affect these flows. For example, the size of the stock of assets denominated in a particular currency in investor portfolios can induce a change in investor preferences. Why? Investors know that it is prudent to have an appropriate degree of *diversification* across asset types, including the currencies in which they are denominated. Thus, even though dollar-denominated Treasury securities may provide a high relative return, if the accumulation has been large, at some point foreign investors, considering both risk and reward, will decide that their portfolio's share of U.S. securities is large enough. To improve the diversity of their portfolios, investors will slow or halt their purchases of U.S. securities.

There is also likely to be a significant *safe-haven* effect behind some investment flows. Some investors may be willing to sacrifice a significant amount of return if an economy offers them an especially low-risk repository for their funds. In recent decades, the United States, with a long history of stable government, steady economic growth, and large and efficient financial markets, can be expected to draw foreign investment for this reason.

The Ups and Downs of the Dollar

Let us now apply the determinants of exchange rates to the path of the U.S. dollar since the 1980s. During this period, the dollar has experienced sustained appreciations and depreciations several times, but for different reasons. Let us examine the forces causing the ups and downs of the dollar.

The 1980s

During the 1980s, the dollar's exchange value followed a path of appreciation and then depreciation. The dollar actually began its ascent in 1979 in response to a sharp tightening of monetary policy, which pushed up domestic interest rates. The Federal Reserve's objective at this time was not dollar appreciation, but to reign in double-digit inflation, which plagued the economy. Nevertheless, as investors became convinced of the Federal Reserve's determination to fight inflation and the likely dual prospect of steadily increasing interest rates and decelerating inflation, the United

States became an attractive destination for foreign investment. Also, the Reagan administration enacted sizable tax cuts along with increased government spending, which resulted in large federal budget deficits. Borrowing due to these deficits increased the demand for a shrinking pool of domestic saving and added to the upward pressure on interest rates. Investment flowed into the United States and the dollar climbed higher. The dollar peaked in 1985, about 50 percent above its level in 1979.

The latter half of the 1980s witnessed a depreciation of the dollar of similar magnitude. What caused the change? One factor was a turn in the speculative belief that the dollar would continue to appreciate. At this point, a large number of investors apparently felt that the dollar was far above a sustainable level and now was more likely to depreciate than appreciate. These investor expectations were reinforced by sizable currency interventions by the United States and other major economies aimed at weakening an overvalued dollar. Investors thus developed expectations that the government wanted the dollar to depreciate and that changes in macroeconomic policy would support that desire. The Federal Reserve enacted an expansionary monetary policy that forced interest rates down. Fiscal policy began to reduce the size of budget deficits, which also fostered lower interest rates. Both factors contributed to investment outflows and a weakening dollar.

On balance, the 1980s illustrated that fluctuations in the dollar's exchange value were not haphazard, but were broadly predictable responses to changes in economic fundamentals that influenced the expected rate of return on dollar-denominated assets. Also, those fluctuations were significantly caused by changes in macroeconomic policy, including monetary policy and fiscal policy.

The 1990s

The 1990s began in economic weakness for the United States. The pace of economic growth slowed sharply and the economy fell into recession in 1991. In response to the weakening economy, monetary policy turned to a more expansionary stance, and the federal budget deficit grew as fiscal policy increased government spending and dampened tax receipts. Interest rates in the United States fell. In contrast, economic activity abroad was moving relatively briskly. In this environment, the demand for dollar-denominated assets declined, and the dollar depreciated about 15 percent on average against the currencies of its major trading partners.

By the mid-1990s, however, the U.S. economy was growing rapidly. What underlaid the acceleration of growth was a sharp increase in the pace of investment spending by business and a market acceleration in productivity growth. The combination of strong consumer demand, deregulation, trade liberalization, and a rush to include computers in the production process propelled investment spending up at a record pace. But even with the federal budget's move towards a surplus, the flow of domestic saving could not keep pace with investment, and interest rates edged up. Also, the United States witnessed a declining rate of inflation, while the economies of other nations such as Japan and Europe were sluggish. These factors resulted in the United States becoming an attractive destination for foreign investors. An increase in the foreign demand for dollar-denominated assets pushed the dollar steadily higher, rising over 30 percent on average against the currencies of its trading partners from 1995 through 2001.

This time, the dollar's sharp appreciation was propelled by the private sector. Economic policy moved in conflicting directions, probably making its net impact on the dollar a minor one. The government's move toward budget surpluses certainly added to national saving and lessened the dollar's appreciation. However, the Federal Reserve implemented a steadily more contractionary monetary policy that increased interest rates; this may have added to the dollar's upward momentum. But the Federal Reserve was not the main force behind the appreciation of the dollar.

The First Decade of the 2000s

A rising dollar and the large flow of investment into the United States that pushed the currency higher could not be sustained. Borrowers and lenders alike tend to find sound reasons to reduce the size of the investment inflow. For lenders, rising risk and the imperative of adequate portfolio diversification can prompt a diminished willingness to acquire dollar-denominated assets. For the borrower, a rising burden of debt service may reduce the desire to borrow.

The depreciation of the dollar in 2002–2004 reflected a weakening of the demand for dollar-denominated assets on the part of foreign investors. Recession in the United States in 2001, a declining stock market, uncertainty about corporate accounting practices, and a steady decline in interest rates to levels not seen in over 30 years (and decreasing significantly more than foreign interest rates) all pointed to a likely deterioration of the attractiveness of the investment climate in the United States. Add to this the inevitable elevation of uncertainty due to the ongoing war on terrorism and the war with Iraq, and a depreciation of the dollar was not surprising.

By 2005, the dollar had reversed its course and began to appreciate against other currencies. This was the consequence of the current and prospective strong performance of the U.S. economy that raised the incentive of foreign lenders to invest in dollar assets. Also, a restrictive monetary policy by the Federal Reserve pushed U.S. interest rates above those of its major trading partners, like Europe and Japan, which attracted foreign investment to higher-yielding U.S. assets. During 2006–2007, the dollar was again weakening with some slackening of private investment flows to the United States. By 2008, however, the dollar realized renewed strength as the status of the United States as a safe haven resulted in investment inflows during the economic crisis of 2007–2008 only to be followed by a return to weakness in 2009. It remains to be seen how the value of the dollar will fluctuate in the years ahead.

Exchange-Rate Overshooting

Changes in expected future values of market fundamentals contribute to exchange-rate volatility in the short term. For example, announcements by the Federal Reserve of changes in monetary-growth targets or by the president and Congress of changes in tax or spending programs cause changes in expectations of future exchange rates that can lead to immediate changes in equilibrium exchange rates. In this manner, frequent changes in policy contribute to volatile exchange rates in a system of market-determined exchange rates.

The volatility of exchange rates is further intensified by the phenomenon of **overshooting**. An exchange rate is said to overshoot when its short-term response

FIGURE 12.7

SHORT-TERM/LONG-TERM EQUILIBRIUM EXCHANGE RATES: OVERSHOOTING

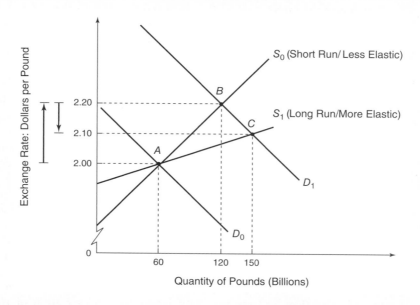

Given the short-term supply of pounds (S_0), if the demand for pounds increases from D_0 to D_1, then the dollar depreciates from $2 per pound to a short-term equilibrium of $2.20 per pound. In the long term, the supply of pounds is more elastic (S_1), and the equilibrium exchange rate is lower, at $2.10 per pound. Because of the difference in these elasticities, the short-term depreciation of the dollar overshoots its long-term depreciation.

(depreciation or appreciation) to a change in market fundamentals is *greater* than its long-term response. Changes in market fundamentals thus exert a disproportionately large *short-term* impact on exchange rates. Exchange-rate overshooting is an important phenomenon because it helps explain why exchange rates depreciate or appreciate so sharply from day to day.

Exchange-rate overshooting can be explained by the tendency of elasticities to be smaller in the short term than in the long term. Referring to Figure 12.7, the short-term supply schedule and demand schedule of the UK pound are denoted by S_0 and D_0, respectively, and the equilibrium exchange rate is $2 per pound. If the demand for pounds increases to D_1, the dollar depreciates to $2.20 per pound in the short term. However, because of the dollar depreciation, the UK price of U.S. exports decreases, the quantity of U.S. exports demanded increases, and thus the quantity of pounds supplied increases. The longer the time period, the greater the rise in the quantity of exports is likely to be, and the greater the rise in the quantity of pounds supplied will be. The long-term supply schedule of pounds is thus more elastic than the short-term supply schedule, as shown by S_1 in the figure. Following the increase in the demand for pounds to D_1, the long-term equilibrium exchange rate is $2.10 per pound, as compared to the short-term equilibrium exchange rate of $2.20

per pound. Because of differences in these elasticities, the dollar's depreciation in the short term overshoots its long-term depreciation.

Overshooting can also be explained by the fact that exchange rates tend to be more flexible than many other prices. Many prices are written into long-term contracts (for example, workers' wages) and do not respond immediately to changes in market fundamentals. However, exchange rates tend to be highly sensitive to current demand and supply conditions. Exchange rates often depreciate or appreciate more in the short term than in the long term so as to compensate for other prices that are slower to adjust to their long-term equilibrium levels. As the general price level slowly gravitates to its new equilibrium level, the amount of exchange-rate overshooting dissipates, and the exchange rate moves toward its long-term equilibrium level.

Forecasting Foreign-Exchange Rates

Previous sections of this chapter have examined various factors that determine exchange-rate movements. But even a clear understanding of how factors influence exchange rates does not guarantee that we can forecast how exchange rates will change. Not only do exchange-rate determinants often point in the opposite direction, but predicting how these determinants will change is also difficult. Simply put, **forecasting exchange rates** is very tricky, especially in the short term.

Nevertheless, exchange-rate forecasts are necessary for exporters, importers, investors, bankers, and foreign-exchange dealers. For example, corporations often have for brief periods large amounts of cash, used to make bank deposits in various currencies. Choosing a currency in which to make deposits requires some idea of what the currency's exchange rate will be in the future. Long-term corporate planning, especially concerning decisions about foreign investment, necessitates an awareness of where exchange rates will move over an extended time period—hence the need for long-term forecasts. For multinational enterprises, short-term forecasting tends to be more widespread than long-term forecasting. Most corporations revise their currency forecasts at least every quarter.

The need of business and investors for exchange-rate forecasts has resulted in the emergence of consulting firms, including Global Insights and Goldman Sachs. In addition, large banks such as JP Morgan Chase and Bank of America provide free currency forecasts to corporate clients. Customers of consulting firms often pay fees ranging up to $100,000 per year or more for expert opinions. Consulting firms provide forecast services ranging from video screens to "listening-post" interviews with forecast service employees who provide their predictions of exchange-rate movements and respond to specific questions from the client.

Most exchange-rate forecasting methods use accepted economic relations to formulate a model that is then refined through statistical analysis of past data. The forecasts generated by the models are usually tempered by the additional insights or reasoning of the forecaster before being offered to the final user.

In the current system of market-determined exchange rates, currency values fluctuate almost instantaneously in response to new information regarding changes in interest rates, inflation rates, money supplies, trade balances, and the like. To successfully forecast exchange-rate movements, it is necessary to estimate the future values of these economic variables and determine the relation between them and

TABLE 12.6

EXCHANGE-RATE FORECASTERS

Forecasting Organization	Methodology	Horizon
Global Insights	Econometric	24 months
JP Morgan Chase	Judgmental	Under 12 months
	Econometric	Over 12 months
Bank of America	Econometric	Over 12 months
	Technical	Under 12 months
Goldman Sachs	Technical	Under 12 months
	Econometric	Over 12 months
UBS Global Asset Management	Judgmental	8 months
	Econometric	12 months

Source: Data collected by author.

future exchange rates. However, even the most sophisticated analysis can be rendered worthless by unexpected changes in government policy, market psychology, and so forth. Indeed, people who deal in the currency markets on a daily basis have come to feel that market psychology is a dominant influence on future exchange rates.

Despite these problems, exchange-rate forecasters are currently in demand. Their forecasting approaches are classified as judgmental, technical, or fundamental. Table 12.6 provides examples of exchange-rate forecasting organizations and their methods.[4]

Judgmental Forecasts

Judgmental forecasts are sometimes known as *subjective* or *common sense models*. They require the gathering of a wide array of political and economic data and the interpretation of these data in terms of the timing, direction, and magnitude of exchange-rate changes. Judgmental forecasters formulate projections based on a thorough examination of individual nations. They consider economic indicators, such as inflation rates and trade data; political factors, such as a future national election; technical factors, such as potential intervention by a central bank in the foreign-exchange market; and psychological factors that relate to one's "feel for the market."

Technical Forecasts

Technical analysis involves the use of historical exchange-rate data to estimate future values. This approach is technical in that it extrapolates from past exchange-rate trends and then projects them into the future to generate forecasts, while ignoring economic

---

[4]This section is drawn from Sam Cross, *The Foreign-Exchange Market in the United States*, Federal Reserve Bank of New York, 1998, pp. 113–115.

and political determinants of exchange-rate movements. Technical analysts look for specific exchange-rate patterns. Once the beginning of a particular pattern has been determined, it automatically implies what the short-term behavior of the exchange rate will be. Therefore, the technological approach is founded on the idea that history repeats itself.

Technical analysis encompasses a variety of charting techniques involving a currency's price, cycles, or volatility. A common starting point for technical analysis is a chart that plots a trading period's opening, high, low, and closing prices. These charts most often plot one trading day's range of prices, but also are created on a weekly, monthly, and yearly basis. Traders watch for new highs and lows, broken trend lines, and patterns that are thought to predict price targets and movement.

To illustrate technical analysis, assume you have formed an opinion about the yen's exchange value against the dollar based on your analysis of economic fundamentals. Now you want to look at what the markets can tell you; you're looking for price trends, and you can use charts to do it. As shown in Figure 12.8 you might want to look at the relative highs and lows of the yen for the past several months; the trend lines in the figure connect the higher highs and the lower lows for the yen. If the yen's exchange rate moves substantially above or below the trend lines, it might signal that a trend is changing. Changes in trends help you decide when to purchase or sell yen in the foreign-exchange market.

FIGURE 12.8

Technical Analysis of the Yen's Exchange Value

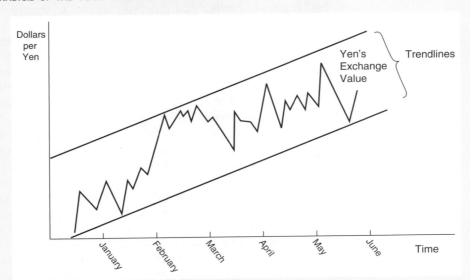

When forecasting exchange rates, technical analysts watch for new highs and lows, broken trend lines, and patterns that are thought to predict price targets and movement.

Because technical analysis follows the market closely, it is used to forecast exchange-rate movements in the short term. However, determining an exchange-rate pattern is useful only as long as the market continues to consistently follow that pattern. However, no pattern can be relied on to continue more than a few days, or perhaps weeks. A client must therefore respond quickly to a technical recommendation to buy or sell a currency. Clients require immediate communication of technical recommendations, so as to make timely financial decisions.

Although fundamental-based models can often provide only a long-term forecast of exchange rate movements, technical analysis is the main method of analyzing shorter-term movements in an exchange rate. The results of technical analysis are used to predict the market direction of an exchange rate and to generate signals to a currency trader regarding when to buy or sell a currency. It is not surprising that most foreign-exchange dealers use some technical model input to help them formulate a trading strategy for currencies, especially for intraday and one-week horizons.

Fundamental Analysis

Fundamental analysis is the opposite of technical analysis. It involves consideration of economic variables that are likely to affect the supply and demand of a currency, and thus its exchange value. Fundamental analysis uses computer-based econometric models, which are statistical estimations of economic theories. To generate forecasts, econometricians develop models for individual nations that attempt to incorporate the fundamental variables that underlie exchange-rate movements: interest rates, balance of trade, productivity, inflation rates, and the like. If you take an econometric course at your university, you might consider preparing an exchange-rate forecast as your class project. *Exploring Further 12.1* gives you an idea of the types of variables you might include in your econometric model.

However, econometric models used to forecast exchange rates face limitations. They often rely on predictions of key economic variables, such as inflation rates or interest rates, and obtaining reliable information can be difficult. Moreover, there are always factors affecting exchange rates that cannot easily be quantified (such as intervention by a country's central bank in currency markets). Also, the precise timing of a factor's effect on a currency's exchange rate may be unclear. For example, inflation-rate changes may not have their full impact on a currency's value until three or six months in the future. Thus, econometric models are best suited for forecasting long-term trends in the movement of an exchange rate. However, they do not generally provide foreign currency traders precise price information regarding when to purchase or sell a particular currency. Thus, currency traders generally prefer technical analysis to fundamental analysis when forming a trading strategy. In spite of the appeal of technical analysis, most forecasters tend to use a combination of fundamental, technical, and judgmental analysis, with the emphasis on each shifting as conditions change. They form a general view about whether a particular currency is over- or undervalued in a longer-term sense. Within that framework, they assess all current economic forecasts, news events, political developments, statistical releases, rumors, and changes in sentiment, while also carefully studying the charts and technical analysis.

INTERNATIONAL COMPARISONS OF GDP: PURCHASING POWER PARITY

GLOBALIZATION

TABLE 12.7

COMPARING GDPs INTERNATIONALLY, 2008: TOP 8 COUNTRIES (BILLIONS OF DOLLARS)

GDP Based on Purchasing Country	Power Parity	GDP Based on Market Exchange Country	Rate
United States	$14,204	United States	$14,204
China	7,903	Japan	4,904
Japan	4,355	China	3,859
India	3,388	Germany	3,652
Germany	2,925	France	2,853
Russian Federation	2,288	United Kingdom	2,646
United Kingdom	2,176	Italy	2,293
France	2,112	Brazil	1,613

Source: World Bank, *Data and Statistics*, at **www.worldbank.org/data.**

When economists calculate a country's gross domestic product (GDP), they add up the market values of the goods and services its economy produces and get a total—in dollars for the United States and yuan for China. To compare countries' GDPs, there are two methods to convert each country's output into dollars.

The simplest way to do this is to use market exchange rates. In 2008, for example, China produced 26,664 billion yuan worth of goods and services. Using the market exchange rate of 6.91 yuan to the dollar, China's GDP equaled $3,859 billion (26,664/6.91 = 3,859). However, that number is too low. For one thing, many goods in developing economies such as China are much cheaper than they are in countries such as the United States. Moreover, China holds its yuan at a rate to keep it less expensive than the dollar. As a result, it is cheaper to produce goods in China, which also makes consumer items cheaper to buy. Therefore, it is not fair to compare China's output in dollar terms without taking its cheaper currency into account.

One problem with simply using market exchange rates to convert China's GDP into dollars is that not all goods and services are bought and sold in a world market. Haircuts and plumbing services do not get exchanged across countries. If all goods and services were traded in world markets without any frictions, such as tariffs or transport costs, prices would be the same everywhere after correcting for the exchange rate. However, in practice many goods and services are not traded. As a result, using market exchange rates to convert China's GDP from yuan into dollars can give a misleading result: Exchange rates *overstate* the size of economies with relatively

high price levels and *understate* the size of economies with relatively low price levels. Also, exchange rates are often subject to sizable fluctuations. These fluctuations means that countries may appear to become suddenly "richer" or "poorer" even though in reality there has been little or no change in the relative volume of goods and services produced.

Purchasing power parity addresses these problems by taking into account the relative cost of living and the inflation rates of different countries, rather than just a comparison of GDPs based on market exchange rates. Therefore, GDPs of countries converted into a common currency using purchasing power parities are valued at a uniform price level and thus reflect only differences in the volumes of goods and services produced in countries.

Today, organizations such as the World Bank, International Monetary Fund, and Central Intelligence Agency accept the purchasing power parity method as a more realistic method of making international comparisons of GDPs than the market exchange rate method. They present international statistics on each country's GDP relative to every other's based on purchasing power parity relative to the U.S. dollar. Referring to Table 12.7, notice that in 2008 China had the third largest GDP in the world ($3,859 billion) when measured at market exchange rates, but it had the second largest GDP ($7,903 billion) when measured at purchasing power parity.

Source: Organisation for Economic Cooperation and Development, "International Comparisons of GDP," *PPP Methodological Manual*, Paris, France, June 30, 2005, Chapter 1.

TRADE CONFLICTS

COMERCIAL MEXICANA GETS BURNED BY SPECULATION

Although speculators like George Soros can pull huge profits out of the foreign exchange market, sometimes their currency bets backfire. Consider the case of Controladora Comercial Mexicana SAB (Comercial Mexicana), the owner of supermarkets and Costco stores in Mexico.

One day in October 2008, Comercial Mexicana was prospering as Mexico's third largest retailer and a competitor of discount giant Wal-Mart. But a few days later, the family-owned chain went bankrupt, decimated by foreign currency losses that resulted in the firm losing almost half its value. Why did this occur?

Comercial Mexicana and other Mexican firms made bad bets using currency contracts, obtained from big banks such as J.P. Morgan Chase & Co, that were linked to the dollar/peso exchange rate. Their bets were based on expectations of a stronger peso. However, the world credit crisis of 2008 threw the peso into a tailspin. Mexico's central bank, seeing the risk to its economy, sold billions of dollars from its reserves to purchase the weakening peso and thus prop up its value. The central bank burned through about 13 percent of its international currency reserves in this strategy that turned out to be futile: Mexico's peso plummeted 24 percent in October of 2008 as risk-averse investors yanked money from the country.

Under the currency deal, J.P. Morgan Chase & Co. offered Comercial Mexicana financing and currency trades at favorable rates. But there was a hitch. If the dollar strengthened (the peso depreciated) beyond a certain threshold, then the firm would have to sell dollars at a loss. In some cases, the contracts had triggers that doubled the number of dollars the firm sold.

When Comercial Mexicana purchased the currency contracts, the deals were initially profitable. But soon things deteriorated as investors panicked over the global financial crisis and began pulling money out of Mexico. As the peso depreciated, Comercial Mexicana encountered losses of $1.4 billion. Being unable to pay its debt, the firm filed for bankruptcy.

Rather than sticking to its business of selling tomatoes and digital cameras to Mexican shoppers, Comercial Mexicana tried to make money on the dollar/peso exchange rate. However, the firm was unprepared for the destabilizing effects of the global financial crisis of 2008.

Source: William Freebairn, "Comercial Mexicana Drops 44 Percent After Saying Debt Rose," Bloomberg.com, October 24, 2008 and "Big Currency Bets Backfire," *The Wall Street Journal*, October 22, 2008, p. A1.

Summary

1. In a free market, exchange rates are determined by market fundamentals and market expectations. The former includes real interest rates, consumer preferences for domestic or foreign products, productivity, investment profitability, product availability, monetary and fiscal policy, and government trade policy. Economists generally agree that the major determinants of exchange-rate fluctuations are different in the long term than in the short term.

2. The determinants of long-term exchange rates differ from the determinants of short-term exchange rates. In the long term, exchange rates are determined by four key factors: relative price levels, relative productivity levels, consumer preferences for domestic or foreign goods, and trade barriers. These factors underlie trade in domestic and foreign goods and thus changes in the demand for exports and imports.

3. In the long term, a nation's currency tends to appreciate when the nation has relatively low levels of inflation, relatively high levels of productivity, relatively strong demand for its export products, and relatively high barriers to trade.

4. According to the purchasing-power-parity theory, changes in relative national price levels determine changes in exchange rates over the long term. A currency maintains its purchasing power parity

if it depreciates (appreciates) by an amount equal to the excess of domestic (foreign) inflation over foreign (domestic) inflation.

5. Over short periods of time, decisions to hold domestic or foreign financial assets play a much greater role in exchange-rate determination than the demand for imports and exports does. According to the asset market approach to exchange rate determination, investors consider two key factors when deciding between domestic and foreign investments: relative interest rates and expected changes in exchange rates. Changes in these factors, in turn, account for fluctuations in exchange rates that we observe in the short term.

6. Short-term interest-rate differentials between any two nations are important determinants of international investment flows and short-term exchange rates. A nation that has relatively high (low) interest rates tends to find its currency's exchange value appreciating (depreciating) in the short term.

7. In the short term, market expectations also influence exchange-rate movements. Future expectations of rapid domestic economic growth, falling domestic interest rates, and high domestic inflation rates tend to cause the domestic currency to depreciate.

8. Exchange-rate volatility is intensified by the phenomenon of overshooting. An exchange rate is said to overshoot when its short-term response to a change in market fundamentals is greater than its long-term response.

9. Currency forecasters use several methods to predict future exchange-rate movements: (a) judgmental forecasts, (b) technical analysis, and (c) fundamental analysis.

Key Concepts & Terms

- Asset-market approach (p. 455)
- Forecasting exchange rates (p. 463)
- Fundamental analysis (p. 466)
- Judgmental forecasts (p. 464)

- Law of one price (p. 448)
- Market expectations (p. 444)
- Market fundamentals (p. 443)
- Nominal (money) interest rate (p. 455)
- Overshooting (p. 461)

- Purchasing-power-parity theory (p. 450)
- Real interest rate (p. 456)
- Technical analysis (p. 464)

Study Questions

1. Suppose that the nominal interest rate on three-month Treasury bills is 8 percent in the United States and 6 percent in the United Kingdom, and the rate of inflation is 10 percent in the United States and 4 percent in the United Kingdom.
   a. What is the real interest rate in each nation?
   b. In which direction would international investment flow in response to these real interest rates?
   c. What impact would these investment flows have on the dollar's exchange value?

2. Explain how the following factors affect the dollar's exchange rate under a system of market-determined exchange rates: (a) a rise in the U.S. price level, with the foreign price level held constant; (b) tariffs and quotas placed on U.S. imports; (c) increased demand for U.S. exports and decreased U.S. demand for imports; (d) rising productivity in the United States relative to other countries; (e) rising real interest rates overseas, relative to U.S. rates; (f) an increase in U.S. money growth; and (g) an increase in U.S. money demand.

3. Suppose the dollar/franc exchange rate equals $0.50 per franc. According to the purchasing-power-parity theory, what will happen to the dollar's exchange value under each of the following circumstances?

a. The U.S. price level increases by 10 percent and the price level in Switzerland stays constant.
b. The U.S. price level increases by 10 percent and the price level in Switzerland increases by 20 percent.
c. The U.S. price level decreases by 10 percent and the price level in Switzerland increases by 5 percent.
d. The U.S. price level decreases by 10 percent and the price level in Switzerland decreases by 15 percent.

4. What factors underlie changes in a currency's value in the short term?
5. The appreciation in the dollar's exchange value from 1980 to 1985 made U.S. products (less/more) expensive and foreign products (less/more) expensive, (decreased, increased) U.S. imports, and (decreased, increased) U.S. exports.
6. Identify the factors that account for changes in a currency's value over the long term.
7. Explain why you agree or disagree with each of the following statements:
   a. "A nation's currency will depreciate if its inflation rate is less than that of its trading partners."
   b. "A nation whose interest rate falls more rapidly than that of other nations can expect the exchange value of its currency to depreciate."
   c. "A nation that experiences higher growth rates in productivity than its trading partners can expect the exchange value of its currency to appreciate."
8. If a currency becomes overvalued in the foreign-exchange market, what will be the likely impact on the home country's trade balance? What if the home currency becomes undervalued?
9. Assuming market-determined exchange rates, use supply and demand schedules for pounds to analyze the effect on the exchange rate (dollars per pound) between the U.S. dollar and the UK pound under each of the following circumstances:

a. Voter polls suggest that the UK's conservative government will be replaced by radicals who pledge to nationalize all foreign-owned assets.
b. Both the UK and U.S. economies slide into recession, but the UK recession is less severe than the U.S. recession.
c. The Federal Reserve adopts a tight monetary policy that dramatically increases U.S. interest rates.
d. Britain's oil production in the North Sea decreases, and exports to the United States fall.
e. The United States unilaterally reduces tariffs on UK products.
f. Britain encounters severe inflation, while price stability exists in the United States.
g. Fears of terrorism reduce U.S. tourism in the United Kingdom.
h. The British government invites U.S. firms to invest in British oil fields.
i. The rate of productivity growth in Britain decreases sharply.
j. An economic boom occurs in the United Kingdom, which induces the UK consumers to purchase more U.S.-made autos, trucks, and computers.
k. Ten-percent inflation occurs in both the United Kingdom and the United States.
10. What predictions does the purchasing-power-parity theory make concerning the impact of domestic inflation on the home country's exchange rate? What are some limitations of the purchasing-power-parity theory?
11. What methods do currency forecasters use to predict future changes in exchange rates?
12. Why are international investors especially concerned about the real interest rate as opposed to the nominal rate?
13. What is meant by exchange-rate overshooting? Why does it occur?
14. In a free market, what factors underlie currency exchange values? Which factors best apply to long- and short-term exchange rates?

Exploring Further 12.1

Fundamental Forecasting Regression Analysis

Recall that fundamental forecasting involves estimating an exchange rate's response to changes in economic factors. By determining how these factors have influenced exchange-rate fluctuations in the past, one can gain insight about the future course of the exchange rate. Regression analysis is often used to make such an assessment. Forecasting organizations, such as Global Insight, construct regression models based on 20 or more economic determinants of exchange rates.

Generating forecasts using fundamental analysis involves three steps: construction of a regression equation to determine the numerical values for the model's coefficients; estimation of future values of the regression equation's independent variables such as inflation rate differentials between two countries; and substituting the estimated values of the independent variables into the estimated regression equation to generate the exchange rate forecast.

For example, suppose we wish to forecast the percentage change in the Swiss franc's exchange value against the dollar in the next quarter. For simplicity, assume that our forecast for the franc is dependent on only two factors that influence the franc's exchange value: the inflation-rate differential between the United States and Switzerland; and the income-growth differential, measured as a percentage change, between the United States and Switzerland. Assume also that these factors have a lagged effect on the franc's exchange rate. A regression model can be constructed as follows:

$$Y_t = b_0 + b_1 X1_{t-n} + b_2 X2_{t-n} + u_t,$$

wherein the dependent variable, the quarterly percentage change in the franc's exchange value (Y) is related to quarterly percentage changes in the two independent variables, the U.S./Swiss inflation differential ($X1$) and the U.S./Swiss income growth differential ($X2$). In the model, b_0 is a constant, b_1 indicates the sensitivity of the franc's exchange value to changes in the inflation differential between the United States and Switzerland, b_2 indicates the

sensitivity of the franc's exchange value to changes in the income growth differential between the United States and Switzerland, t stands for the time period, n indicates the number of quarters lagged, and u_t is an error term with all assumed statistical properties.

Once the regression model is constructed, a set of historical data must be compiled for quarterly changes in the franc's exchange rate, the U.S./Swiss inflation differential, and the U.S./Swiss income-growth differential. A large time-series database is desirable, generally consisting of 30 or more quarters of information. Using these data, suppose our model estimates the following regression coefficients:

$$b_1 = 0.6$$
$$and$$
$$b_2 = 0.4.$$

The regression coefficient $b_1 = 0.6$ implies that for every one-unit percentage change in the U.S./Swiss inflation differential, the predicted percentage change in the franc's exchange value is 0.6 percent, the income-growth differential remaining constant. Underlying this positive relation is the tendency for relatively high inflation in the United States to cause a rise (appreciation) in the franc's value against the dollar, and vice versa. The regression coefficient $b_2 = 0.4$ suggests that for each one-unit percentage change in the U.S./Swiss income-growth differential, the predicted percentage change in the franc's exchange value is 0.4 percent, the inflation-rate differential remaining constant. The positive relation suggests that relatively high income growth in the United States leads to an appreciation in the franc against the dollar, and vice versa. Once the regression coefficients have been estimated, and any potential statistical problems have been corrected, the coefficients can be tested to determine if they are statistically significant. If these coefficients are constant over time and they capture the true relation between exchange rates and fundamentals, the model will predict future currency values. If the coefficients vary from time to time, or if the coefficient estimates are seriously biased, the model may yield incorrect results.

If we have a forecast of the economic fundamentals, we can now project the future exchange rate. Suppose that for the next year the U.S. inflation rate is forecasted to exceed the Swiss inflation rate by three percentage points and that the U.S. income-growth rate is forecasted to exceed the Swiss income-growth rate by one percentage point. Combining these data with the estimated regression coefficients, the forecast for the franc's exchange value is as follows:

$$
\begin{aligned}
Y_t &= b_0 + b_1 X1_{t-n} + b_2 X2_{t-n} + u_t \\
&= 0.01 + 0.6(3\%) + 0.4(1\%) \\
&= 1\% + 1.8\% + 0.4\% \\
&= 3.2\%.
\end{aligned}
$$

Our forecast is that the franc will appreciate by about 3.2 percent against the dollar.

In practice, using regression analysis to forecast exchange rates is more difficult than our simplified model suggests. Recall that our model was based on the impact of inflation differentials and income-growth differentials on trade flows and their effects on foreign-exchange market trading. In reality, most foreign-exchange market trading is related to investment flows and speculation, which requires that other variables be included in our model, such as relative interest rates and future expectations. Also, other exchange-rate determinants, such as labor strikes, are difficult to measure and cannot be included in our model. As a result of these limitations, even the most sophisticated regression models cannot produce consistently accurate exchange-rate forecasts. Forecasters typically modify the results of regression models with their own commonsense judgments.

Mechanisms of International Adjustment

In Chapter 10, we learned about the meaning of the balance of payments. Recall that, owing to double-entry bookkeeping, total inpayments (credits) always equal total outpayments (debits) when all balance-of-payments accounts are considered. A deficit refers to an excess of outpayments over inpayments for selected accounts grouped along functional lines. For example, a current account deficit suggests an excess of imports over exports of goods, services, income flows, and unilateral transfers. A current account surplus implies the opposite.

A nation finances or covers a current account deficit out of its international reserves or by attracting investment (such as purchases of factories) or borrowing from other nations. The capacity of a deficit nation to cover the excess of outpayments over inpayments is limited by its stocks of international reserves and the willingness of other nations to invest in, or lend to, the deficit nation. For a surplus nation, once it believes that its stocks of international reserves or overseas investments are adequate—although history shows that this belief may be a long time in coming—it will be reluctant to run prolonged surpluses. In general, the incentive for reducing a current-account surplus is not as direct and immediate as that for reducing a current-account deficit.

The **adjustment mechanism** works for the return to equilibrium after the initial equilibrium has been disrupted. The process of current-account adjustment takes two different forms. First, under certain conditions, there are adjustment factors that automatically promote equilibrium. Second, should the automatic adjustments be unable to restore equilibrium, discretionary government policies may be adopted to achieve this objective.

This chapter emphasizes the **automatic adjustment** of the current-account that occurs under a fixed exchange-rate system.[1] The adjustment variables that we will

---

[1] Under a fixed exchange-rate system, the supply of and demand for foreign exchange reflect credit and debit transactions in the balance of payments. However, these forces of supply and demand are not permitted to determine the exchange rate. Instead, government officials peg, or fix, the exchange rate at a stipulated level by intervening in the foreign-exchange markets to purchase and sell currencies. This topic is examined further in the next chapter.

emphasize include prices and income. The influence of interest rates on a country's capital and financial account will also be discussed. Subsequent chapters discuss the adjustment mechanism under flexible exchange rates and the role of government policy in promoting current-account adjustment.

Although the various automatic adjustment approaches have their contemporary advocates, each was formulated during a particular period and reflects a different philosophical climate. The idea that the current account can be adjusted by prices stemmed from the *classical* economic thinking of the 1800s and early 1900s. The classical approach was geared toward the existing gold standard associated with fixed exchange rates. That income changes could promote current-account adjustments reflected the *Keynesian* theory of income determination, which grew out of the Great Depression of the 1930s.

Price Adjustments

The original theory of current-account adjustment is credited to David Hume (1711–1776), the English philosopher and economist.[2] Hume's theory arose from his concern with the prevailing mercantilist view that advocated government controls to ensure a continuous current-account surplus. According to Hume, this strategy was self-defeating over the long term because a nation's current account tends to move toward equilibrium *automatically*. Hume's theory stresses the role that adjustments in national *price levels* play in promoting current-account equilibrium.

Gold Standard

The classical **gold standard** that existed from the late 1800s to the early 1900s was characterized by three conditions. First, each member nation's money supply consisted of gold or paper money backed by gold. Second, each member nation defined the official price of gold in terms of its national currency and was prepared to buy and sell gold at that price. Third, the free import and export of gold were permitted by member nations. Under these conditions, a nation's money supply was directly tied to its current account. A nation with a current-account surplus would acquire gold, directly expanding its money supply. Conversely, the money supply of a deficit nation would decline as the result of a gold outflow.

The current account can also be tied directly to a nation's money supply under a modified gold standard, requiring that the nation's stock of money be fractionally backed by gold at a constant ratio. It would also apply to a fixed exchange-rate system in which current-account disequilibriums are financed by some acceptable international reserve asset, assuming that a constant ratio between the nation's international reserves and its money supply are maintained.

Quantity Theory of Money

The essence of the classical **price-adjustment mechanism** is embodied in the **quantity theory of money**. Consider the following *equation of exchange*:

---

[2]David Hume, "Of the Balance of Trade." Reprinted in Richard N. Cooper, ed., *International Finance: Selected Readings* (Harmondsworth, England: Penguin Books, 1969), Chapter 1.

$$MV = PQ,$$

where M refers to a nation's money supply. The V refers to the velocity of money—that is, the number of times per year the average currency unit is spent on final goods. The expression MV corresponds to the aggregate demand, or total monetary expenditures on final goods. Alternatively, the monetary expenditures on any year's output can be interpreted as the physical volume of all final goods produced (Q) multiplied by the average price at which each of the final goods is sold (P). As a result, $MV = PQ$.

This equation is an identity. It says that total monetary expenditures on final goods equals the monetary value of the final goods sold; the amount spent on final goods equals the amount received from selling them.

Classical economists made two additional assumptions. First, they took the volume of the final output (Q) to be fixed at the full employment level in the long term. Second, they assumed that the velocity of money (V) was constant, depending on institutional, structural, and physical factors that rarely changed. With V and Q relatively stable, a change in M must induce a *direct and proportionate change* in P. The model linking changes in M to changes in P became known as the quantity theory of money.

Current-Account Adjustment

The preceding analysis showed how, under the classical gold standard, the current account is linked to a nation's money supply, which is linked to its domestic price level. Let us consider how the price level is linked to the current account.

Suppose that, under the classical gold standard, a nation realized a current-account deficit. The deficit nation would experience a gold outflow, which would reduce its money supply and thus its price level. The nation's international competitiveness would be enhanced, so that its exports would rise and its imports fall. This process would continue until its price level had fallen to the point where current-account equilibrium was restored. Conversely, a nation with a current-account surplus would realize gold inflows and an increase in its money supply. This process would continue until its price level had risen to the point where current-account equilibrium was restored. Thus, the opposite price-adjustment process would occur at the same time in each trading partner.

The price-adjustment mechanism as devised by Hume illustrated the impossibility of the mercantilist notion of maintaining a continuous current-account surplus. The linkages (current account—money supply—price level—current account) demonstrated to Hume that, over time, current-account equilibrium tends to be achieved automatically.

With the advent of Hume's price-adjustment mechanism, classical economists had a very powerful and influential theory. It was not until the Keynesian revolution in economic thinking during the 1930s that this theory was effectively challenged. Even today, the price-adjustment mechanism is a hotly debated issue. A brief discussion of some of the major criticisms against the price-adjustment mechanism is in order.

The classical linkage between changes in a nation's gold supply and changes in its money supply no longer holds. Central bankers can easily offset a gold outflow (or inflow) by adopting an expansionary (or contractionary) monetary policy. The experience of the gold standard of the late 1800s and early 1900s indicates that these offsetting monetary policies often occurred. The classical view that full employment always exists has also been challenged. When an economy is far below its full employment level, there is a smaller chance that prices in general will rise in response to an increase in the money supply than if the economy is at full employment. It has also been pointed out that, in a modern industrial world, prices and wages are inflexible in a downward direction. If prices are inflexible downward, then changes in M will affect not P but rather Q. A deficit nation's falling money supply will bring about a fall in output and employment. Furthermore, the stability and predictability of V have been questioned. Should a gold inflow that results in an increase in M be offset by a decline in V, total spending (MV) and PQ would remain unchanged.

These issues are part of the current debate over the price-adjustment mechanism's relevance. They have caused sufficient doubts among economists to warrant a search for additional adjustment explanations. The most notable include the effect of interest-rate changes on capital movements and the effect of changing incomes on trade flows.

Financial Flows and Interest-Rate Differentials

Although the classical economists emphasized the price adjustment mechanism's impact on a country's current account, they were aware of the impact of changes in interest rates on international investment (capital) movements. With national financial systems greatly interdependent today, it is recognized that interest-rate fluctuations can induce significant changes in a nation's capital and financial account, as discussed in Chapter 10.

Recall that capital and financial transactions include all international purchases or sales of assets, such as real estate, corporate stocks and bonds, commercial bank deposits, and government securities. The vast majority of transactions appearing in the capital and financial account come from financial transactions. The most important factor that causes financial assets to move across national borders is interest rates in domestic and foreign markets. However, other factors are important too, such as investment profitability, national tax policies, and political stability.

Figure 13.1 shows the hypothetical capital and financial account schedules for the United States. Capital and financial account *surpluses* and *deficits* are measured on the vertical axis. In particular, financial flows between the United States and the rest of the world are assumed to respond to *interest-rate differentials* between the two areas (U.S. interest rate minus foreign interest rate) for a particular set of economic conditions in the United States and abroad.

Referring to schedule CFA_0, the U.S. capital and financial account is in *balance* at point A, where the U.S. interest rate is equal to that abroad. Should the United States reduce its monetary growth, the scarcity of money would tend to raise interest rates in the United States compared with the rest of the world. Suppose U.S. interest rates rise one percent above those overseas. Investors, seeing higher U.S. interest rates, will tend to sell foreign securities to purchase U.S. securities that offer a higher yield. The one percent interest-rate differential leads to *net financial inflows* of $5 billion for the United States, which thus moves to point B on schedule CFA_0. Conversely, should foreign interest rates rise above those in the United States, the United States will face *net financial outflows* as investors sell U.S. securities to purchase foreign securities offering a higher yield.

CAPITAL AND FINANCIAL ACCOUNT SCHEDULE FOR THE UNITED STATES

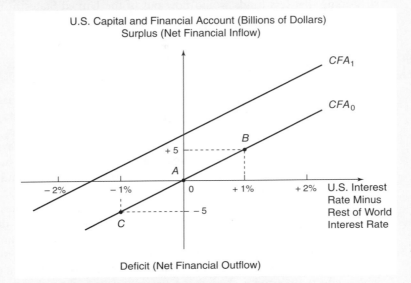

Interest-rate differentials between the United States and the rest of the world induce movements along the U.S. capital and financial account schedule. Relatively high (low) U.S. interest rates trigger net financial inflows (outflows) and an upward (downward) movement along the capital and financial account schedule. The schedule shifts upward/downward in response to changes in noninterest rate determinants such as investment profitability, tax policies, and political stability.

Figure 13.1 assumes that interest-rate differentials are the basic determinant of financial flows for the United States. That is, movements along schedule CFA_0 are caused by changes in the interest rate in the United States relative to that in the rest of the world. However, certain determinants other than interest-rate differentials might cause the United States to import (or export) more or less assets at each possible interest-rate differential and thereby change the location of schedule CFA_0.

To illustrate, assume that the United States is located along schedule CFA_0 at point A. Suppose that rising U.S. income leads to higher sales and increased profits. Direct investment (in an auto-assembly plant, for example) becomes more profitable in the United States. Nations such as Japan will invest more in their U.S. subsidiaries, whereas General Motors will invest less overseas. The higher profitability of direct investment leads to a greater flow of funds into the United States at each possible interest-rate differential and an upward shift in the schedule to CFA_1.

Suppose the U.S. government levies an *interest equalization tax*, as it did from 1964 to 1974. This tax was intended to help reverse the large financial outflows that the United States faced when European interest rates exceeded those in the United States. By taxing U.S. investors on dividend and interest income from foreign securities, the tax reduced the net profitability (that is, the after-tax yield) of foreign securities. At the same time, the U.S. government enacted a foreign-credit-restraint program, which placed direct restrictions on foreign lending by U.S. banks and financial institutions and later on foreign lending of nonfinancial corporations. By discouraging flows of funds from the United States to Europe, these policies resulted in an upward shift in the U.S. capital and financial account schedule in Figure 13.1, suggesting that less funds would flow out of the United States in response to higher interest rates overseas.

Income Adjustments

When the classical economists considered mechanisms of international adjustment, they emphasized automatic price changes to promote adjustments in a nation's current account. A weakness of the classical economists was that they neglected the role of income adjustments on the current account. John Maynard Keynes addressed this weakness by formulating his **income adjustment mechanism** in the 1930s.[3] This theory focuses on automatic changes in income to bring about adjustment in a nation's current account.

Keynes asserted that under a system of fixed exchange rates, the influence of income changes in nations with current-account surpluses and deficits would help restore equilibrium automatically. Given a persistent current-account surplus, a nation will experience rising income, and its imports will increase. Conversely, a current-account deficit nation will experience a fall in income, resulting in a decline in imports. These effects of income changes on import levels will reverse the disequilibrium in the current account. The income adjustment mechanism is more fully discussed in *Exploring Further 13.1*.

The preceding income-adjustment analysis needs to be modified to include the impact that changes in domestic expenditures and income levels have on foreign economies. This process is referred to as the **foreign repercussion effect**.

Assume a two-country world, the United States and Canada, in which there initially exists a current-account equilibrium. Owing to changing consumer preferences, suppose the United States faces an autonomous increase in imports from Canada. This increase results in an increase in Canada's exports. The result is a decrease in U.S. income, and an increase in Canada's income. The fall in U.S. income induces a fall in the level of U.S. imports (and a fall in Canada's exports). At the same time, the rise in Canada's income induces a rise in Canada's imports (and a rise in U.S. exports). This feedback process is repeated again and again.

The consequence of this process is that both the rise in income of the surplus nation (Canada) and the fall in income of the deficit nation (United States) are dampened. This is because the autonomous increase in U.S. imports (and Canadian exports) will cause the U.S. income to decrease as imports are substituted for home-produced goods. The decline in U.S. income will generate a reduction in its imports. Because U.S. imports are Canada's exports, the rise in Canada's income will be moderated. From the perspective of the United States, the decline in its income will be cushioned by an increase in exports to Canada stemming from a rise in Canada's income.

The importance of the foreign repercussion effect depends in part on the economic size of a country as far as international trade is concerned. A small nation

---

[3]John Maynard Keynes, *The General Theory of Employment, Interest, and Money* (London: Macmillan, 1936).

that increases its imports from a large nation will have little impact on the large nation's income level. But for major trading nations, the foreign repercussion effect is likely to be significant and must be taken into account when the income-adjustment mechanism is being considered.

Disadvantages of Automatic Adjustment Mechanisms

The preceding sections have considered automatic balance-of-payments adjustment mechanisms under a system of fixed exchange rates. According to the classical economists, automatic price changes promote adjustment in the current account. Keynesian theory emphasized another adjustment process, the effect of changes in national income on a nation's current account.

Although elements of price and income adjustments may operate in the real world, these adjustment mechanisms have a major shortcoming. The problem is that an efficient adjustment mechanism requires central bankers to forgo their use of monetary policy to promote the goal of full employment without inflation; each nation must be willing to accept inflation or recession when current-account adjustment requires it. Take the case of a nation that faces a current-account deficit caused by an autonomous increase in imports or decrease in exports. For income adjustments to reverse the deficit, monetary authorities must permit domestic income to decrease and not undertake policies to offset its decline. The opposite applies equally to a nation with a current-account surplus. Simply put, modern nations are reluctant to make significant internal sacrifices for the sake of external equilibrium. The result is that the reliance on an automatic payments-adjustment process tends to be politically unacceptable.

Monetary Adjustments

The previous sections have examined how changes in national price, interest rate, and income levels serve as international adjustment mechanisms. During the 1960s, a new theory emerged, called the *monetary approach to the balance of payments*.[4] The central notion of the monetary approach is that the balance of payments is affected by discrepancies between the amount of money people desire to hold and the amount supplied by the central bank. For example, if Americans demand more money than is being supplied by the Federal Reserve, then the excess demand for money will be fulfilled by inflows of money from another country, say China. Conversely, if the Federal Reserve is supplying more money than demanded, the excess supply of money is eliminated by outflows of money to China. Therefore, the monetary approach focuses attention on the determinants of money demand and money supply and their impact on the balance of payments. It is left for more advanced textbooks to consider the monetary approach to the balance of payments.

---

[4]The monetary approach to the balance of payments developed its intellectual background at the University of Chicago. It originated with Robert Mundell, *International Economics* (New York: Macmillan, 1968) and Harry Johnson, "The Monetary Approach to Balance-of-Payments Theory," *Journal of Financial and Quantitative Analysis*, March 1972.

Summary

1. Because persistent current-account disequilibrium—whether surplus or deficit—tends to have adverse economic consequences, there exists a need for adjustment.
2. Current-account adjustment can be classified as automatic or discretionary. Under a system of fixed exchange rates, automatic adjustments can occur through variations in prices and incomes. The demand for and supply of money can also influence the payments position of a country.
3. David Hume's theory provided an explanation of the automatic adjustment process that occurred under the gold standard. Starting from a condition of current-account balance, any surplus or deficit would automatically be eliminated by changes in domestic price levels. Hume's theory relied heavily on the quantity theory of money.
4. With the advent of Keynesian economics during the 1930s, greater emphasis was put on the income effects of trade in explaining adjustment.
5. The foreign repercussion effect refers to a situation in which a change in one nation's macroeconomic variables relative to another nation will induce a chain reaction in both nations' economies.
6. An automatic current-account adjustment mechanism has several disadvantages. Nations must be willing to accept adverse changes in the domestic economy when required for current-account adjustment. Policymakers must forgo using discretionary economic policy to promote domestic equilibrium.

Key Concepts & Terms

- Adjustment mechanism (p. 473)
- Automatic adjustment (p. 473)
- Foreign repercussion effect (p. 478)
- Gold standard (p. 474)
- Income adjustment mechanism (p. 478)
- Price-adjustment mechanism (p. 474)
- Quantity theory of money (p. 474)

Study Questions

1. Keynesian theory suggests that under a system of fixed exchange rates, the influence of income changes in surplus and deficit nations helps promote current-account equilibrium. Explain.
2. How do adjustments in domestic interest rates help affect international investment flows?
3. What are some major disadvantages of the automatic adjustment mechanism under a system of fixed exchange rates?
4. When analyzing the income-adjustment mechanism, one must account for the foreign repercussion effect. Explain.
5. What is meant by the quantity theory of money? How did it relate to the classical price-adjustment mechanism?
6. What is meant by the term *mechanisms of international adjustment*? Why does a deficit nation have an incentive to undergo adjustment? What about a surplus nation?
7. Under a fixed exchange-rate system, what automatic adjustments promote current-account equilibrium?

Exploring Further 13.1

Income Adjustment Mechanism

The income adjustment mechanism of John Maynard Keynes was developed in the 1930s to show the process by which changes in national income promote equilibrium in the balance of payments. To illustrate this principle, let us first assume a *closed economy* with no foreign trade, with price and interest-rate levels constant. In this simple Keynesian model, national income (Y) is the sum of consumption expenditures (C) plus savings (S):

$$Y = C + S.$$

Total expenditures on the national product are C plus business investment (I). This relation is given as follows:

$$Y = C + I.$$

Figure EF 13.1 represents the familiar income-determination model found in introductory economics textbooks. Referring to Figure EF 13.1(a), consumption is assumed to be functionally dependent on income, whereas investment spending is autonomous—that is, independent of the level of income. The economy is in equilibrium when the level of planned expenditures equals income. This equilibrium occurs at Y_E, where the 45-degree line intersects the $(C + I)$ schedule. At any level of income lower (or higher) than Y_E, planned expenditure exceeds (or falls below) income and income rises (or falls).

Combining these relations yields the following:

$$Y = C + S = C + I.$$

FIGURE EF 13.1

INCOME DETERMINATION IN A CLOSED ECONOMY

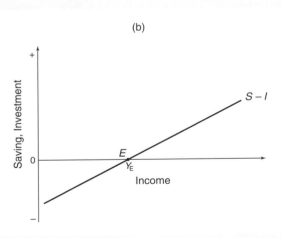

In an economy not exposed to international trade, equilibrium income occurs where the level of planned expenditures (consumption plus investment) equals income: $Y = C + I$. An equivalent condition for equilibrium income is planned saving equals planned investment: $S = I$, or $S - I = 0$.

The basic equilibrium condition can thus be stated as:

$$S = I$$

or

$$S - I = 0.$$

This equivalent condition for equilibrium income is illustrated in Figure EF 13.1(b). Like consumption, saving is assumed to be functionally related to income. Given a constant level of investment, the $(S - I)$ schedule is upward sloping. Savings can be regarded as a leakage from the income stream, whereas investment is an injection into the income stream. At income levels below Y_E, I exceeds S, and the level of income rises. The opposite holds equally true. The economy is thus in equilibrium where $S = I$ (or $S - I = 0$). Figure EF 13.1(b) illustrates income determination in an open economy.

Suppose an economy that is initially in equilibrium experiences some disturbance, say, an increase in investment spending. This increase would bid up the level of equilibrium income. This result comes about through a **multiplier process**; that is, the initial investment sets off a chain reaction that results in greater levels of spending, so that income increases by some multiple of the initial investment. Given an autonomous injection of investment spending into the economy, the induced increase in income is given by:

$$\Delta Y = k\Delta I,$$

where k represents some multiplier.

Let's see how the multiplier is derived for a closed economy. First, remember that in equilibrium, an economy will find planned saving equal to planned investment. It follows that any I must be matched by an equivalent S if the economy is to remain in balance. Because it has been assumed that saving is functionally dependent on income, changes in saving will be related to changes in income. If we use s to represent the marginal propensity to save out of additional income levels, then $S=sY$. Given an autonomous increase in investment, the equilibrium condition suggests that:

$$\Delta I = \Delta S = s\Delta Y.$$

From the preceding expression, the multiplier can be derived as:

$$\Delta Y = \frac{1}{S}\Delta I.$$

Suppose, for example, a nation finds that its marginal propensity to save (s) is 0.25, and there occurs an autonomous increase in investment of $100. According to the multiplier principle, the induced change in income stemming from the initial increase in investment spending equals the increase in investment spending times the multiplier (k). Because the s is assumed to equal 0.25, $k = 1/s = 1/0.25 = 4$. The $100 increase in investment expenditure ultimately results in a $400 increase in the level of income.

Income Determination in an Open Economy

Now assume an *open economy* subject to international trade. The condition for equilibrium income, as well as the formulation of the spending multiplier, must both be modified. In an open economy, imports (M), like savings, constitute a leakage out of the income stream, whereas exports (X), like investment, represent an injection into the stream of national income. The condition for equilibrium income, which relates leakages to injections in an open economy's income stream, becomes:

$$S + M = I + X.$$

Rearranging terms, this becomes:

$$S - I = X - M.$$

Assume that exports are unrelated to the level of domestic income. Also assume that imports are functionally dependent on domestic income; that is,

$$\Delta M = m\Delta Y,$$

where m represents the marginal propensity to import. We are now in a position to derive what is known as the **foreign-trade multiplier**.

First, let the injections into and leakages from the income stream rise by the same amount, so that the induced change in income will be of equilibrium magnitude. This yields:

$$\Delta S + \Delta M = \Delta I + \Delta X.$$

Given that

$$\Delta S = s\Delta Y$$

and

$$\Delta M = m\Delta Y,$$

the induced change in income stemming from the changes in injections and leakages can be shown as follows:

$$(s + m)\Delta Y = \Delta I + \Delta X.$$

Holding exports constant ($\Delta X = 0$), the induced change in income is equal to the change in investment times the foreign trade multiplier, or

$$\Delta Y = \left(\frac{1}{S + m}\right) \times \Delta I.$$

The preceding expression states that *the foreign-trade multiplier equals the reciprocal of the sum of the marginal propensities to save and to import.* In this formulation, an autonomous change in exports, with investment remaining fixed, would have an impact on domestic income identical to that of an equivalent change in investment.

Implications of the Foreign-Trade Multiplier

To show the adjustment implications of the foreign-trade multiplier, we construct a diagram based on the framework of Figure EF 13.1. Remember that the $(S - I)$ schedule is positively sloped. This is because changes in savings are assumed to be directly related to changes in income, investment being unaffected. Subtracting investment from saving yields an upward-sloping $(S - I)$ schedule, as shown in Figure EF 13.2. Similarly, it has been assumed that changes in imports are

directly related to changes in income, exports remaining constant. When imports are subtracted from exports, the result is a downward-sloping $(X - M)$ schedule. As before, the equilibrium condition of an open economy with no government is $(X - M) = (S - I)$.

Starting at equilibrium income level $1,000 in Figure EF 13.2, suppose a disturbance results in an autonomous increase in exports by, say, $200. This is shown by shifting the $(X - M)$ schedule upward by $200, resulting in the new schedule $(X' - M)$. The level of income rises, generating increases in imports and savings. Domestic equilibrium is established at income level $1,400, where $(S - I) = (X' - M)$. The trade account is no longer in balance; there is a trade surplus of $100. This trade surplus is less than the initial $200 rise in exports because part of the surplus is offset by increases in imports induced by the rise in income from $1,000 to $1,400.

In this example, we can use the concept of a foreign-trade multiplier to determine the effect of the increase in exports on the home economy. Inspection of the $(S - I)$ schedule in Figure EF 13.2 reveals that the slope of the schedule, which represents the marginal propensity to save, equals 0.25. The slope of the $(X - M)$ schedule indicates that the marginal propensity to import also equals 0.25. The foreign-trade multiplier is the reciprocal of the sum of the marginal propensities to save and to import; that is, 1/0.50 or 2. An autonomous increase in exports of $200 thus generates a twofold increase in domestic income, and equilibrium income rises from $1,000 to $1,400.

As for the trade account effect, the $400 rise in domestic income induces a $100 increase in imports, given a marginal propensity to import of 0.25. Part of the initial export-led surplus is neutralized, lowering it from $200 to $100. Over time, the increase in imports generated by increased domestic expenditures will tend to reduce the trade surplus, but not enough to restore the balance-of-payments equilibrium.

Consider another case that illustrates the national-income and balance-of-payments effects

FIGURE EF 13.2

DOMESTIC INCOME AND TRADE-BALANCE EFFECTS OF AN INCREASE IN EXPORTS AND AN INCREASE IN INVESTMENT.

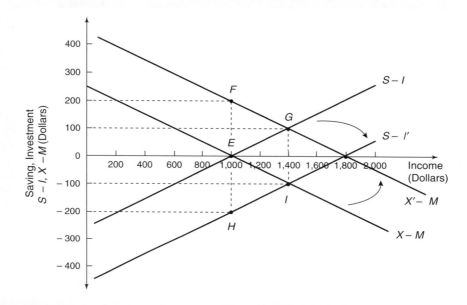

Starting at equilibrium income, an autonomous increase in domestic exports leads to a rise in domestic income, which promotes an increase in imports and savings. Because of the multiplier effect, the induced increase in income tends to be larger than the initial increase in exports. The trade account moves into surplus because the induced increase in imports tends to be less than the initial increase in exports. Again starting at equilibrium income, an autonomous increase in domestic investment generates an increase in income, which promotes additional savings and imports. Because of the multiplier effect, the increase in investment generates a magnified increase in income. As the increase in income induces a rise in imports, a trade deficit appears.

of a change in expenditures. Assume that, owing to improved profit expectations, domestic investment rises autonomously by $200. Starting at equilibrium level $1,000 in Figure EF 13.2, the increase in investment will displace the $(S - I)$ schedule downward by $200 because the negative term is increased. This increase gives us the new schedule $(S - I')$. Domestic income rises from $1,000 to $1,400, which stimulates a rise in imports, producing a trade deficit of $100. Unlike the previous case of export-led expansion, an autonomous increase in domestic investment spending (or government expenditures) increases domestic income but at the expense of a balance-of-payments deficit. This deficit should serve as a reminder to economic policy makers that under a system of fixed exchange rates, the impact of domestic policies on the balance of payments cannot be overlooked.

Exchange-Rate Adjustments and the Balance of Payments

The previous chapter demonstrated that disequilibrium in the balance of trade tends to be reversed by automatic adjustments in prices, interest rates, and incomes. However, if these adjustments are allowed to operate, reversing trade imbalances may come at the expense of domestic recession or price inflation. The cure may be perceived as worse than the disease.

Instead of relying on adjustments in prices, interest rates, and incomes to counteract trade imbalances, governments permit alterations in exchange rates. By adopting a floating exchange-rate system, a nation permits its currency to depreciate or appreciate in a free market in response to shifts in either the demand for or supply of the currency.

Under a fixed exchange-rate system, rates are set by the government in the short term. However, if the official exchange rate becomes overvalued over a period of time, a government may initiate policies to *devalue* its currency. Currency devaluation causes a depreciation of a currency's exchange value; it is initiated by government policy rather than by the free-market forces of supply and demand. When a nation's currency is undervalued, it may be *revalued* by the government; this policy causes the currency's exchange value to appreciate. Currency devaluation and revaluation will be discussed further in the next chapter.

In this chapter, we examine the impact of exchange-rate adjustments on the balance of trade. We will learn under what conditions currency depreciation (appreciation) will improve (worsen) a nation's trade position.

Effects of Exchange-Rate Changes on Costs and Prices

Industries that compete with foreign producers, or that rely on imported inputs in production, can be noticeably affected by exchange-rate fluctuations. Changing exchange rates influence the international competitiveness of a nation's industries through their influence on relative costs. How do exchange-rate fluctuations affect relative costs? The answer depends on the extent to which a firm's costs are denominated in terms of the home currency or foreign currency.

Case 1

No foreign sourcing—all costs are denominated in dollars.
Table 14.1 illustrates the hypothetical production costs of Nucor, a U.S. steel manufacturer. Assume that in its production of steel, Nucor utilizes U.S. labor, coal, iron, and other inputs whose costs are denominated in dollars. In period 1, the exchange value of the dollar is assumed to be 50 cents per Swiss franc (2 francs per dollar). Assume that the firm's cost of producing a ton of steel is $500, which is equivalent to 1,000 francs at this exchange rate.

Suppose that in period 2, because of changing market conditions, the dollar's exchange value *appreciates* from 50 cents per franc to 25 cents per franc, a 100 percent appreciation (the franc depreciates from 2 to 4 francs per dollar). With the dollar appreciation, Nucor's labor, iron, coal, and other input costs remain constant in dollar terms. However, in terms of the franc, these costs rise from 1,000 francs to 2,000 francs per ton, a 100 percent increase. The 100 percent dollar appreciation induces a 100 percent increase in Nucor's franc-denominated production cost. The international competitiveness of Nucor is thus reduced.

This example assumes that all of a firm's inputs are acquired domestically and that their costs are denominated in the domestic currency. But, in many industries, some of a firm's inputs are purchased in foreign markets (foreign sourcing), and these input costs are denominated in a foreign currency. What impact does a change in the home-currency's exchange value have on a firm's costs in this situation?

Case 2

Foreign sourcing—some costs denominated in dollars and some costs denominated in francs.
Table 14.2 again illustrates the hypothetical production costs of Nucor, whose costs of labor, iron, coal, and certain other inputs are assumed to be denominated in dollars. However, suppose Nucor acquires scrap iron from Swiss suppliers (foreign sourcing), and these costs are denominated in francs. Once again, assume the dollar's

TABLE 14.1

EFFECTS OF A DOLLAR APPRECIATION ON A U.S. STEEL FIRM'S PRODUCTION COSTS WHEN ALL COSTS ARE DOLLAR-DENOMINATED

| | COST OF PRODUCING A TON OF STEEL | | | |
| | PERIOD 1 $0.50 PER FRANC (2 FRANCS = $1) | | PERIOD 2 $0.25 PER FRANC (4 FRANCS = $1) | |
	Dollar Cost	Franc Equivalent	Dollar Cost	Franc Equivalent
Labor Materials (iron/coal)	$160	320 francs	$160	640 francs
	300	600	300	1,200
Other costs (energy)	40	80	40	160
Total	$500	1,000 francs	$500	2,000 francs
Percentage change	—	—	—	100%

TABLE 14.2

EFFECTS OF A DOLLAR APPRECIATION ON A U.S. STEEL FIRM'S PRODUCTION COSTS WHEN SOME COSTS ARE DOLLAR-DENOMINATED AND OTHER COSTS ARE FRANC-DENOMINATED

| | COST OF PRODUCING A TON OF STEEL | | | |
| | PERIOD 1 $.50 PER FRANC (2 FRANCS = $1) | | PERIOD 2 $.25 PER FRANC (4 FRANCS = $1) | |
	Dollar Cost	Franc Equivalent	Dollar Cost	Franc Equivalent
Labor	$160	320 francs	$160	640 francs
Materials				
$ denominated (iron/coal)	$120	240 francs	$120	480 francs
Franc denominated (scrap iron)	$180	360 francs	$ 90	360 francs
Total	$300	600 francs	$210	840 francs
Other costs (energy)	$ 40	80 francs	$ 40	160 francs
Total cost	$500	1,000 francs	$410	1,640 francs
Percentage change	—	—	−18%	+64%

exchange value appreciates from 50 cents per franc to 25 cents per franc. As before, the cost in francs of Nucor's labor, iron, coal, and certain other inputs rise by 100 percent following the dollar appreciation; however, the franc cost of scrap iron remains constant. As can be seen in the table, Nucor's franc cost per ton of steel rises from 1,000 francs to 1,640 francs—a large increase of 64 percent. Thus, the dollar appreciation worsens Nucor's international competitiveness, but not as much as in the previous example.

In addition to influencing Nucor's franc-denominated cost of steel, a dollar appreciation affects a firm's dollar cost when franc-denominated inputs are involved. Because scrap-iron costs are denominated in francs, they remain at 360 francs after the dollar appreciation; however, the dollar-equivalent scrap-iron cost falls from $180 to $90. Because the costs of Nucor's other inputs are denominated in dollars and do not change following the dollar appreciation, the firm's total dollar cost falls from $500 to $410 per ton—a decrease of 18 percent. This cost reduction offsets some of the cost disadvantage that Nucor incurs relative to Swiss exporters as a result of the dollar appreciation (franc depreciation).

The preceding examples suggest the following generalization: As franc-denominated costs become a larger portion of Nucor's total costs, a dollar appreciation (depreciation) leads to a smaller increase (decrease) in the franc cost of Nucor steel and a larger decrease (increase) in the dollar cost of Nucor steel compared to the cost changes that occur when all input costs are dollar-denominated. As franc-denominated costs become a smaller portion of total costs, the opposite conclusions apply. These conclusions have been especially significant for the world trading system during the 1980s to 2000s as industries—e.g., autos and computers—have become increasingly internationalized and utilize increasing amounts of imported inputs in the production process.

Changes in relative costs because of exchange-rate fluctuations also influence relative prices and the volume of goods traded among nations. By increasing relative

JAPANESE FIRMS OUTSOURCE PRODUCTION TO LIMIT EFFECTS OF STRONG YEN

Facing a strong yen in recent years, Japanese exporters have realized that a more costly yen results in smaller profits if they convert their dollar profits back into yen. How can they protect their profits? By moving production to the United States and thus lessening the amount of money they convert from dollars to yen.

During the 1990s, executives at Toyota, Toshiba, and other Japanese firms were apprehensive about an appreciating yen that made their exports more expensive. By 2003, however, the harm caused by an appreciating yen was not nearly as great for these firms due to their increasing efforts to locate production in the United States and other offshore markets. Although the yen's appreciation hindered Japan's companies, it did not stop them in their tracks.

For example, Toshiba exported about $6 billion more in goods than it imported in 1996. This level meant that the firm's sales could theoretically decline by 6 billion yen ($54 million) each time the yen appreciated against the dollar by one yen. Since then, Japan's largest semiconductor producer has succeeded in slashing its net dollar exposure by locating manufacturing abroad and increasing

dollar-based imports of parts. In 1996, Toshiba started up a plant in Indonesia to manufacture color-TV sets; it also opened a factory in the Philippines to produce hard-disk and optical-disk drives. Other factories in Asia followed, including a personal-computer plant in China. By 2003, Toshiba produced more than 30 percent of its goods abroad, compared with 17 percent in 1995; and it exported only $1 billion of goods more than it imported.

Moving production to the United States and other countries helps Japan's electronics and auto firms to escape much of the dollar/yen problem and sell their products to foreigners. However, it contributes to the excess capacity of manufacturing plants in Japan and results in job losses for Japanese workers. Simply put, a continually strong yen can promote a hollowing out of Japan's economy, as some have feared.

Sources: "Japanese Firms Practice Yen Damage Control," *The Wall Street Journal*, September 26, 2003, p. A7 and "The Strong Yen and Toyota's Choice," *The Wall Street Journal*, December 20, 1994, p. A11.

U.S. production costs, a dollar *appreciation* tends to *raise* U.S. export prices in foreign-currency terms, which induces a decrease in the quantity of U.S. goods sold abroad; similarly, the dollar appreciation leads to an increase in U.S. imports. By decreasing relative U.S. production costs, a dollar *depreciation* tends to *lower* U.S. export prices in foreign-currency terms, which induces an increase in the quantity of U.S. goods sold abroad; similarly, the dollar depreciation leads to a decrease in U.S. imports.

Several factors govern the extent by which exchange-rate movements lead to relative price changes among nations. Some U.S. exporters may be able to offset the price-increasing effects of an appreciation in the dollar's exchange value by reducing profit margins to maintain competitiveness. Perceptions concerning long-term trends in exchange rates also promote price rigidity: U.S. exporters may be less willing to raise prices if the dollar's appreciation is viewed as temporary. The extent to which industries implement pricing strategies depends significantly on the substitutability of their product: the greater the degree of product differentiation (as in quality or service), the greater control producers can exercise over prices; the pricing policies of such producers are somewhat insulated from exchange-rate movements.

Is there any way in which companies can offset the impact of currency swings on their competitiveness? Suppose the exchange value of the Japanese yen appreciates against other currencies, which causes Japanese goods to become less competitive in world markets. To insulate themselves from the squeeze on profits caused by the rising yen, Japanese companies could move production to affiliates located in countries whose currencies have depreciated against the yen. This strategy would be most likely to occur if the yen's appreciation is sizable and is regarded as being permanent. Even if the yen's appreciation is not permanent, shifting production offshore can help reduce the uncertainties associated with currency swings. Indeed, Japanese companies have resorted to offshore production to protect themselves from an appreciating yen.

Cost-Cutting Strategies of Manufacturers in Response to Currency Appreciation

For years, manufacturers have watched with dismay as the home currency surges to new heights, making it harder for them to wring profits out of exports. This situation tests their ingenuity to become more efficient in order to remain competitive on world markets. Let us consider how Japanese and American manufacturers responded to appreciations of their home currencies.

Appreciation of the Yen: Japanese Manufacturers

From 1990 to 1996, the value of the Japanese yen relative to the U.S. dollar increased by almost 40 percent. In other words, if the yen and dollar prices in the two nations had remained unchanged, Japanese products in 1996 would have been roughly 40 percent more expensive, compared with U.S. products, than they were in 1990. How then did Japanese manufacturers respond to a development that could have had disastrous consequences for their competitiveness in world markets?

Japanese firms remained competitive by using the yen's strength to cheaply establish integrated manufacturing bases in the United States and in dollar-linked Asia. This strategy allowed Japanese firms to play both sides of the fluctuations in the yen/dollar exchange rate: using cheaper dollar-denominated parts and materials to offset higher yen-related costs. While they maintained their U.S. markets, many Japanese companies also used the strong yen to purchase cheaper components from around the world and ship them home for assembly. That action provided a competitive edge in Japan for these firms.

Consider the Japanese electronics manufacturer Hitachi whose TV sets were a global production effort in the mid-1990s, as shown in Figure 14.1. The small tubes that projected information onto Hitachi TV screens came from a subsidiary in South Carolina, while the TV chassis and circuitry were manufactured by an affiliate in Malaysia. From Japan came only computer chips and lenses, which amounted to 30 percent of the value of the parts used. By sourcing TV production in countries whose currencies had fallen against the yen, Hitachi was able to hold down the dollar price of its TV sets in spite of the rising yen.

To limit their vulnerability to a rising yen, Japanese exporters also shifted production from commodity-type goods to high-value products. The demand for commodities—for example, metals and textiles—is quite sensitive to price changes because these goods are largely indistinguishable, except by price. Customers, therefore, could easily switch to non-Japanese suppliers if an increase in the yen shoved

FIGURE 14.1

COPING WITH THE YEN'S APPRECIATION: HITACHI'S GEOGRAPHIC DIVERSIFICATION
AS A MANUFACTURER OF TELEVISION SETS

From Japan, Hitachi procured semiconductors and lenses. Thus, only 30 percent of the value of the parts used was yen denominated.

The small tubes that project information onto the screen came from Hitachi Electric Devices U.S.A. in South Carolina. Denominated in dollars.

The chassis, including circuit board, came from another Hitachi subsidiary, Consumer Products Malaysia, in Selangor, Malaysia. Denominated in dollars.

Hitachi Consumer Product de Mexico assembled the TVs in Tijuana. Peso-denominated costs such as labor decreased in yen terms as the dollar depreciated against the yen and the peso depreciated against the dollar.

Hitachi's global diversification permitted it to sell TVs in the United States without raising prices as the yen appreciated against the dollar.

the dollar price of Japanese exports higher. In contrast, more sophisticated, high-value products—for example, transportation equipment and electrical machinery—are less sensitive to price increases. For these goods, factors such as embedded advanced technology and high-quality standards work to neutralize the effect on demand if prices are driven up by an appreciating yen. Shifting production from commodity-type products to high-value products from 1990 to 1996 enhanced the competitiveness of Japanese firms.

Then, there's the Japanese auto industry. To offset the rising yen, Japanese automakers cut the yen prices of their autos and thus realized falling unit-profit margins. They also reduced manufacturing costs by increasing worker productivity, importing materials and parts whose prices were denominated in currencies that had depreciated against the yen, and outsourcing larger amounts of a vehicle's production to transplant factories in countries whose currencies had depreciated against the yen.

In 1994, Toyota Motor Corporation announced that its competitiveness had been eroded by as much as 20 percent as a result of the yen's recent appreciation. Toyota therefore convinced its subcontractors to cut part prices by 15 percent over three years. By using common parts in various vehicles and shortening the time needed to design, test, and commercialize automobiles, Toyota was also able to cut costs. Moreover, Toyota pressured Japanese steelmakers to produce less costly galvanized sheet steel for use in its vehicles. Also, Toyota reintroduced less expensive models with fewer options in an effort to reduce costs and prices and thus recapture sales in the midsize-family-car segment of the market.

Foreign-made parts, once rejected by Japanese automakers as inferior to domestically produced parts, became much less alien to them in the 1990s. Foreign parts steadily made their way into Japanese autos, helped by both the strong yen and Japanese automakers' urgency to slash costs. Moreover, Japanese auto-parts makers set up manufacturing operations in Southeast Asia and South America to cut costs; these parts were then exported to Japan for assembly into autos.

Appreciation of the Dollar: U.S. Manufacturers

From 1996 to 2002, U.S. manufacturers were alarmed as the dollar appreciated by 22 percent on average against the currencies of major U.S. trading partners. This appreciation resulted in U.S. manufacturers seeking ways to tap overseas markets and defend their home turf.

Take American Feed Co., a Napoleon, Ohio company that makes machinery used in auto plants. In 2001, the firm reached a deal with a similar manufacturing company in Spain. Both companies produce machines that car factories use to unroll giant coils of steel and feed them through presses to make parts. According to the pact, when orders come in, management of the two companies meet to decide which plant should make which parts, in essence divvying up the work to keep both factories operating. As a result, American Feed can share in the benefits of having a European production base without having to take on the risks of building its own factory there. Also, the company redesigned its machines to make them more efficient and less expensive to build. These efforts chopped about 20 percent off the machines' production costs.

Then, there's Sipco Molding Technologies, a Meadville, Pennsylvania tool-and-die maker that also had to cut costs to survive the dollar's appreciation. For years, Sipco had a partnership with an Austrian company, which designed a special line of tools that Sipco once built in the United States. However, because of the strong dollar, the Austrian company assumed the responsibility of designing and making the tools, while Sipco simply resold them. Although these efforts helped the firm cut costs, it resulted in a loss of jobs for 30 percent of its employees.

Will Currency Depreciation Reduce a Trade Deficit? The Elasticity Approach

We have seen that currency depreciation tends to improve a nation's competitiveness by reducing its costs and prices, while currency appreciation implies the opposite. Under what circumstances will currency depreciation reduce a trade deficit?

Several aspects of currency depreciation must be considered, and each of them will be dealt with in a separate section. The **elasticity approach** emphasizes the relative *price effects* of depreciation and suggests that depreciation works best when demand elasticities are high. The **absorption approach** deals with the *income effects* of depreciation; the implication is that a decrease in domestic expenditure relative to income must occur for depreciation to promote trade equilibrium. The **monetary approach** stresses the effects depreciation has on the *purchasing power of money* and the resulting impact on domestic expenditure levels. Let us begin by considering the elasticity approach.

Currency depreciation affects a country's balance of trade through changes in the relative prices of goods and services internationally. A trade-deficit nation may be able to reverse its imbalance by lowering its relative prices, so that exports increase and imports decrease. The nation can lower its relative prices by permitting its exchange rate to depreciate in a free market or by formally devaluing its currency under a system of fixed exchange rates. The ultimate outcome of currency depreciation depends on the price elasticity of demand for a nation's imports and the price elasticity of demand for its exports.

Recall that *elasticity of demand* refers to the responsiveness of buyers to changes in price. It indicates the percentage change in the quantity demanded stemming from a one percent change in price. Mathematically, elasticity is the ratio of the percentage change in the quantity demanded to the percentage change in price. This ratio can be symbolized as follows:

$$Elasticity = \frac{\Delta Q}{Q} \div \frac{\Delta P}{P}$$

The elasticity coefficient is stated numerically, without regard to the algebraic sign. If the preceding ratio exceeds one, a given percentage change in price results in a larger percentage change in quantity demanded; this is referred to as relatively *elastic* demand. If the ratio is less than one, demand is said to be relatively *inelastic*, because the percentage change in quantity demanded is less than the percentage change in price. A ratio precisely equal to one denotes *unitary elastic* demand, meaning that the percentage change in quantity demanded just matches the percentage change in price.

Next, we investigate the effects of a currency depreciation on a nation's balance of trade—that is, the value of its exports minus imports. Suppose the UK pound depreciates by ten percent against the dollar. Whether the UK trade balance will be improved depends on what happens to the dollar inpayments for the United Kingdom's exports as opposed to the dollar outpayments for its imports. This balance, in turn, depends on whether the U.S. demand for UK exports is elastic or inelastic and whether the UK demand for imports is elastic or inelastic.

Depending on the size of the demand elasticities for UK exports and imports, the United Kingdom's trade balance may improve, worsen, or remain unchanged in response to the pound depreciation. The general rule that determines the actual outcome is the so-called **Marshall-Lerner condition**. The Marshall-Lerner condition states: (1) Depreciation will *improve* the trade balance if the currency-depreciating nation's demand elasticity for imports plus the foreign demand elasticity for the nation's exports exceeds one. (2) If the sum of the demand elasticities is less than one, depreciation will *worsen* the trade balance. (3) The trade balance will be *neither helped nor hurt* if the sum of the demand elasticities equals one. The Marshall-Lerner condition may be stated in terms of the currency of either the nation undergoing a depreciation or its trading partner. Our discussion is confined to the currency of the currency-depreciating country, the United Kingdom.

Case 1
Improved trade balance
Table 14.3 illustrates the effect of a depreciation of the pound on the UK trade balance. Referring to Table 14.3(*a*), assume that the UK demand elasticity for imports equals 2.5 and the U.S. demand elasticity for UK exports equals 1.5; the sum of the elasticities is 4.0. Suppose the pound depreciates by ten percent against the dollar. An assessment of the overall impact of the depreciation on the United Kingdom's payments position requires identification of the depreciation's impact on import expenditures and export receipts.

TABLE 14.3

EFFECT OF POUND DEPRECIATION ON THE TRADE BALANCE OF THE UNITED KINGDOM

(A) IMPROVED TRADE BALANCE

Sector	Change in Pound Price (%)	Change in Quantity Demanded (%)	Net Effect (in pounds)
Import	+10	−25	−15% outpayments
Export	0	+15	+15% inpayments

Assumptions:

UK demand elasticity for imports = 2.5

Demand elasticity for UK exports = 1.5 Sum = 4.0

Pound depreciation = 10%

(B) WORSENED TRADE-BALANCE

Sector	Change in Pound Price (%)	Change in Quantity Demanded (%)	Net Effect (in pounds)
Import	+10	−2	+8% outpayments
Export	0	+1	+1% inpayments

Assumptions:

UK demand elasticity for imports = 0.2

U.S. demand elasticity for UK exports = 0.1 Sum = 0.3

Pound depreciation = 10%

If prices of imports remain constant in terms of foreign currency, then a depreciation increases the home-currency price of goods imported. Because of the depreciation, the pound price of UK imports rises ten percent. British consumers would thus be expected to reduce their purchases from abroad. Given an import demand elasticity of 2.5, the depreciation triggers a 25 percent decline in the quantity of imports demanded. The ten percent price increase in conjunction with a 25 percent quantity reduction results in approximately a 15 percent decrease in UK outpayments in pounds. This cutback in import purchases actually reduces import expenditures, which reduces the UK deficit.

How about UK export receipts? The pound price of the exports remains constant, but after depreciation of the pound, consumers in the United States find UK exports costing ten percent less in terms of dollars. Given a U.S. demand elasticity of 1.5 for UK exports, the ten percent UK depreciation will stimulate foreign sales by 15 percent, so that export receipts in pounds will increase by approximately 15 percent. This increase strengthens the UK payments position. The 15 percent reduction in import expenditures coupled with a 15 percent rise in export receipts means that the pound depreciation will reduce the UK payments deficit. *With the sum of the elasticities exceeding one, the depreciation strengthens the United Kingdom's trade position.*

Case 2
Worsened trade balance

In Table 14.3(*b*), the UK demand elasticity for imports is 0.2 and the U.S. demand elasticity for UK exports is 0.1; the sum of the elasticities is 0.3. The ten percent pound depreciation raises the pound price of imports by ten percent, inducing a two percent reduction in the quantity of imports demanded. In contrast to the previous case, under relatively inelastic conditions the depreciation contributes to an *increase*, rather than a decrease, in import expenditures of some eight percent. As before, the pound price of UK exports is unaffected by the depreciation, whereas the dollar price of exports falls ten percent. American purchases from abroad increase by one percent, resulting in an increase in pound receipts of about one percent. With expenditures on imports rising eight percent while export receipts increase only one percent, the UK deficit will tend to *worsen*. As stated in the Marshall-Lerner condition, *if the sum of the elasticities is less than one, currency depreciation will cause a deterioration in a nation's trade position.* The reader is left to verify that a nation's trade balance remains unaffected by depreciation if the sum of the demand elasticities equals one.

Although the Marshall-Lerner condition provides a general rule as to when a currency depreciation will be successful in restoring payments equilibrium, it depends on some simplifying assumptions. For one, it is assumed that a nation's trade balance is in equilibrium when the depreciation occurs. If there is initially a very large trade deficit, with imports exceeding exports, then a depreciation might cause import expenditures to change more than export receipts, even though the sum of the demand elasticities exceeds one. The analysis also assumes no change in the sellers' prices in their own currency. But this may not always be true. To protect their competitive position, foreign sellers may lower their prices in response to a depreciation of the home country's currency; domestic sellers may raise home-currency prices so that the depreciation's effects are not fully transmitted into lower foreign-exchange prices for their goods. However, neither of these assumptions invalidates the Marshall-Lerner condition's spirit, which suggests that currency depreciations work best when demand elasticities are high.

Simply put, the Marshall-Lerner condition illustrates the price effects of currency depreciation on the home-country's trade balance. The extent to which price changes affect the volume of goods traded depends on the elasticity of demand for imports and exports. If the elasticities were known in advance, it would be possible to determine the proper exchange-rate policy to restore payments equilibrium. Table 14.4 shows estimated price elasticities of demand for total imports and exports by country.

TABLE 14.4

LONG-TERM PRICE ELASTICITIES OF DEMAND FOR TOTAL IMPORTS AND EXPORTS OF SELECTED COUNTRIES

Country	Import Price Elasticity	Export Price Elasticity	Sum of Import and Export Elasticities
Canada	0.9	0.9	1.8
France	0.4	0.2	0.6
Germany	0.1	0.3	0.4
Italy	0.4	0.9	1.3
Japan	0.3	0.1	0.4
United Kingdom	0.6	1.6	1.2
United States	0.3	1.5	1.8

Source: From Peter Hooper, Karen Johnson, and Jaime Marquez, "Trade Elasticities for the G-7 Countries," *Princeton Studies in International Economics*, No. 87, August 2000, p. 9.

J-Curve Effect: Time Path of Depreciation

Empirical estimates of price elasticities in international trade suggest that, according to the Marshall-Lerner condition, currency depreciation will often improve a nation's trade balance. However, a problem in measuring world price elasticities is that there tends to be a *time lag* between changes in exchange rates and their ultimate effect on real trade. One popular description of the time path of trade flows is the so-called **J-curve effect**. This view suggests that in the very short term, a currency depreciation will lead to a worsening of a nation's trade balance. But as time passes, the trade balance will likely improve. This is because it takes time for new information about the price effects of depreciation to be disseminated throughout the economy and for economic units to adjust their behavior accordingly.

A currency depreciation affects a nation's trade balance through its net impact on export receipts and import expenditures. Export receipts and import expenditures are calculated by multiplying the commodity's per-unit price times the quantity being demanded. Figure 14.2 illustrates the process by which depreciation influences export receipts and import expenditures.

The immediate effect of depreciation is a change in relative prices. If a nation's currency depreciates ten percent, it means that import prices initially increase ten percent in terms of the home currency. The quantity of imports demanded will then fall according to home demand elasticities. At the same time, exporters will initially receive ten percent more in home currency for each unit of foreign currency they earn. This means they can become more competitive and lower their export prices measured in terms of foreign currencies. Export sales will then rise in accordance with foreign demand elasticities. The problem with this process is that for depreciation to take effect, time is required for the pricing mechanism to induce changes in the volume of exports and imports.

The time path of the response of trade flows to a currency's depreciation can be described in terms of the J-curve effect, so called because the trade balance continues to get worse for awhile after depreciation (sliding down the hook of the J) and then gets better (moving up the stem of the J). This effect occurs because the initial effect of depreciation is an increase in import expenditures: the home-currency price of imports has risen, but the volume is unchanged owing to prior commitments. As time passes, the quantity adjustment effect becomes relevant: import volume is depressed, whereas exports become more attractive to foreign buyers.

Advocates of the J-curve effect cite the experience of the U.S. balance of trade during the 1980s and 1990s. As seen in Figure 14.3, between 1980 and 1987 the U.S. trade deficit expanded at a very rapid rate. The deficit decreased substantially between 1988 and 1991. The rapid increase in the trade deficit that took place during the early 1980s occurred mainly because of the appreciation of the dollar at the time, which resulted in a

FIGURE 14.2

DEPRECIATION FLOWCHART

FIGURE 14.3

TIME PATH OF U.S. BALANCE OF TRADE (IN BILLIONS OF DOLLARS) IN RESPONSE TO
DOLLAR APPRECIATION AND DEPRECIATION

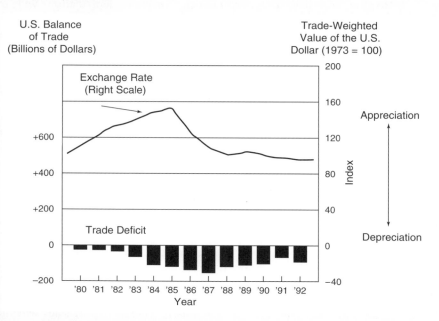

Between 1980 and 1987, the U.S. merchandise trade deficit expanded at a rapid rate. The trade deficit decreased substantially between 1988 and 1991. The rapid increase in the trade deficit that took place during the early 1980s occurred mainly because of the appreciation of the dollar at the time, which resulted in a steady increase in imports and a drop in U.S. exports. The depreciation of the dollar that began in 1985 led to a boom in exports in 1988 and a drop in the trade deficit through 1991.

steady increase in imports and a drop in U.S. exports. The depreciation of the dollar that began in 1985 led to a boom in exports in 1988 and a drop in the trade deficit through 1991.

What factors might explain the time lags in a currency depreciation's adjustment process? The types of lags that may occur between changes in relative prices and the quantities of goods traded include the following:

- *Recognition lags* of changing competitive conditions
- *Decision lags* in forming new business connections and placing new orders
- *Delivery lags* between the time new orders are placed and their impact on trade and payment flows is felt
- *Replacement lags* in using up inventories and wearing out existing machinery before placing new orders
- *Production lags* involved in increasing the output of commodities for which demand has increased

Empirical evidence suggests that the trade-balance effects of currency depreciation do not materialize until years afterward. Adjustment lags may be four years or more, although the major portion of adjustment takes place in about two years.[1]

Exchange Rate Pass-Through

The J-curve analysis assumes that a given change in the exchange rate brings about a proportionate change in import prices. In practice, this relation may be less than proportionate, thus weakening the influence of a change in the exchange rate on the volume of trade.

The extent to which changing currency values lead to changes in import and export prices is known as the **exchange rate pass-through** relation. Pass-through is important because buyers have incentives to alter their purchases of foreign goods only to the extent that the prices of these goods change in terms of their domestic currency following a change in the exchange rate. This change depends in part on the willingness of exporters to permit the change in the exchange rate to affect the prices they charge for their goods, measured in terms of the buyer's currency.

Assume that Toyota of Japan exports autos to the United States and that the prices of Toyota are fixed in terms of the yen. Suppose the dollar's value depreciates ten percent relative to the yen. Assuming no offsetting actions by Toyota, U.S. import prices will rise ten percent. This is because ten percent more dollars are needed to purchase the yen than are used to pay for the import purchases. Complete pass-through thus exists: import prices in dollars rise by the full proportion of the dollar depreciation.

To illustrate the calculation of complete currency pass-through, assume that Caterpillar charges $50,000 for a tractor exported to Japan. If the exchange rate is 150 yen per U.S. dollar, the price paid by the Japanese buyer will be 7,500,000 yen. Assuming the dollar price of the tractor remains constant, a ten percent appreciation in the dollar's exchange value will increase the tractor's yen price ten percent, to 8,250,000 yen ($165 \times 50,000 = 8,250,000$). Conversely, if the dollar depreciates by ten percent, the yen price of the tractor will fall by ten percent, to 6,750,000. So long as Caterpillar keeps the dollar price of its tractor constant, changes in the dollar's exchange rate will be fully reflected in changes in the foreign-currency price of exports. The ratio of changes in the foreign-currency price to changes in the exchange rate will be 100 percent, implying complete currency pass-through.

Partial Exchange Rate Pass-Through

Although complete exchange rate pass-through is a possibility, in practice the relation tends to be partial. Table 14.5 presents estimates of average exchange rate pass-through rates for the United States and other advanced countries over the 1975–2003 period. For example, the exchange rate pass-through for the United States over this period was 0.42. This rate means that a one percent change in the dollar's exchange rate produced a 0.42 percent change in U.S. import prices. Because the percentage change in import prices was less than the percentage change in the exchange rate,

---

[1]Helen Junz and Rudolf R. Rhomberg, "Price Competitiveness in Export Trade among Industrial Countries," *American Economic Review*, May 1973, pp. 412–419.

EXCHANGE RATE PASS-THROUGH INTO
IMPORT PRICES AFTER ONE YEAR

Country	Pass Through Rate (For every one percent a currency depreciates/appreciates, the price of imports for the country increases/decreases by)*
OECD** average	0.64%
United States	0.42
Euro area	0.81
Japan	0.57 – 1.0
Other advanced countries	0.60

*Estimates are based on data from 1973 to 2003.

**The organization for Economic Cooperation and Development consists of Australia, Austria, Belgium, Canada, Czech Republic, Denmark, Finland, France, Germany, Greece, Hungary, Iceland, Ireland, Italy, Republic of Korea, Japan, Luxembourg, Mexico, the Netherlands, New Zealand, Norway, Poland, Portugal, Spain, Sweden, Switzerland, Turkey, the UK, and the United States.

Sources: Jose Campa and Linda Goldberg, "Exchange Rate Pass-Through Into Import Prices," *Review of Economics and Statistics*, November 2005, pp. 984–985 and Hamid Faruquee, "Exchange Rate Pass-Through in the Euro Area," *IMF Staff Papers*, April 2006, pp. 63–88.

exchange rate pass-through was "partial" for the United States. Similar conclusions apply to other countries included in the table. When exchange rate pass-through is partial at home and abroad, the effect of changes in the exchange rate on trade volume is lessened, as it forestalls movement in relative trade prices.

Why does exchange rate pass-through tend to be partial? The answer appears to lie in invoicing practices, market-share considerations, and distribution costs.[2]

Invoice Practices

Businesses involved in international trade can select the currency they want to use to express the price of their exports. They can invoice their exports in their own home currency or in the currency of their customers. Evidence on import and export invoicing in recent years reveals that the dollar is the dominant currency of invoicing across non-European countries, as seen in Table 14.6. For example, 93 percent of U.S. imports and 99 percent of U.S. exports were priced in dollars during the first decade of the 2000s.

The dominant use of dollars in invoicing U.S. trade helps explain the partial pass-through of changes in the dollar's exchange rate to U.S. import prices. When foreign producers invoice their exports to the United States in dollars, the price of these goods remains fixed in terms of the dollar if the dollar depreciates against other currencies. The exchange rate movements affect only the foreign producers' profits and will not increase the dollar price paid by U.S. importers. After a time, of course, foreign producers may choose to adjust their prices in response to the exchange rate.

Market Share Considerations

Another factor that contributes to partial exchange rate pass-through for a period following a dollar depreciation is the desire of foreign producers to preserve market share for goods sold in the United States. In practice, many goods and services are produced in imperfectly competitive markets. In terms of prices for these goods, firms are able to make a profit margin over costs. Firms may choose not to pass on the full change in costs brought about by changing exchange rates and instead choose to change their profit margins, thus reducing the sensitivity of consumer prices to the exchange rate. Therefore, exporters to the United States may accept a lower profit margin when their currency appreciates in order to keep their dollar prices constant against American competitors. This is especially pertinent for the

---

[2]This section is drawn from Linda Goldberg and Elanor Wiske Dillon, "Why a Dollar Depreciation May Not Close the U.S. Trade Deficit," *Current Issues in Economics and Finance*, Federal Reserve Bank of New York, June 2007.

TABLE 14.6

USE OF THE U.S. DOLLAR IN EXPORT AND IMPORT INVOICING, 2002–2004

Country	Dollar Share in Export Financing	Dollar Share in Import Financing	U.S. Share in Exports
United States	99.8%	92.8%	
Japan	48.0	68.7	24.8%
South Korea	83.2	79.6	17.0
Malaysia	90.0	90.0	20.5
Thailand	84.4	76.0	17.0
Australia	69.6	50.5	8.1
United Kingdom	26.0	37.0	15.5
Euro area	30.4	38.0	14.2
EU Accession countries*	17.5	23.9	3.2

*Bulgaria, Czech Republic, Estonia, Hungary, and Poland.

Sources: Linda Goldberg and Cedric Tille, "The International Role of the Dollar and Trade Balance Adjustment." *The Group of Thirty Occasional Paper No. 71*, 2006 and Annette Kamps, "The Determinants of Currency Invoicing in International Trade," *European Central Bank Working Paper No. 665*, August 2006.

United States that has a very large market and where imports command a lower share of consumption than they do in smaller markets. Because American consumers can generally substitute domestic goods for imports, foreign exporters are reluctant to pass all of the exchange rate movement into prices because of fear of losing market share. Simply put, relatively strong domestic competition for imported goods in the United States tends to lessen the extent of exchange rate pass-through into import prices.

For example, Kellwood Co., a major U.S. marketer of garments such as Calvin Klein, noted that some of its Asian suppliers, such as sewing factories and fabric mills, inquired about increasing their prices as the dollar depreciated against their currencies in the first decade of the 2000s. But these suppliers knew that if they increased their prices, Kellwood could purchase inputs from other competing suppliers. To maintain Kellwood as a customer, these suppliers cut their profit margins and thus refrained from raising their prices, which allowed Kellwood's prices on Calvin Klein garments to remain unchanged.

Distribution Costs

Thus far we have considered the transmission of exchange rates into the prices of imports arriving at a country's borders. However, other costs occur between the time a good arrives at the border and the time it is sold to the consumer. These are the costs of distributing the imported good to the final consumer, which include transportation, marketing, wholesaling, and retailing costs. For example, in 1996, a Barbie doll shipped from China to the United States cost about $2, where it sold for about $10. The manufacturer, Mattel, earned about $1 of profit on this doll. The remaining $7 represented payments for transportation in the United States and other marketing and distribution costs. For the United States, distribution costs

WHY A DOLLAR DEPRECIATION MAY NOT CLOSE THE U.S. TRADE DEFICIT

Partial exchange rate pass-through has implications for the trade deficit of the United States. With the U.S. trade deficit at high levels during the first decade of the 2000s, many looked to a dollar depreciation to reduce the U.S. appetite for foreign goods by pushing up the cost of imports and reducing the price of U.S. exports for consumers overseas.

However, others argued that three factors carry particular force for the United States (as explained in this chapter): the near-exclusive use of the dollar in invoicing U.S. trade, the market share strategies of foreign exporters, and sizable U.S. distribution costs added to U.S. imports. These factors reduce the pass-through of the currency depreciation to U.S. import prices and consumer prices, resulting in partial exchange rate pass-through. With import prices and consumer prices rising only modestly from their pre-depreciation levels, U.S. consumers would have little incentive to significantly decrease their demand for imports or to seek out comparable domestic goods.

The unresponsiveness of U.S. import and consumer prices to a dollar depreciation suggests that any substantial trade balance adjustment achieved through exchange-rate changes must come instead from a reduction in U.S. export prices. However, this would be asking a lot of the export sector. For example, in 2006, the U.S. trade deficit stood at $759 billion. If imports remained constant, exports would have to grow 52 percent to single-handedly close this gap. This growth appeared to be more than the U.S. export sector could deliver.

Thus, other developments would have to be included to reduce the U.S. trade deficit. One development might be an increase in U.S. public or private saving, with related reductions in U.S. consumption of all goods. Another development might be an increase in the global demand for U.S. exports driven by economic growth abroad or increased market access for U.S. exporters. Simply put, it appeared unlikely that a weaker dollar by itself could close the U.S. trade deficit.

Source: Linda Goldberg and Eleanor Wiske Dillon, "Why a Dollar Depreciation May Not Close the U.S. Trade Deficit," *Current Issues in Economics and Finance*, Federal Reserve Bank of New York, June 2007.

average about 40 percent of overall U.S. consumer prices.[3] Because domestic distribution services are not traded internationally, their costs are not affected by fluctuations in the dollar's exchange rate. Therefore, as distribution costs become a large percentage of the consumer price, the sensitivity of the consumer price to exchange-rate fluctuations is reduced. The effects of exchange rate pass-through are more fully discussed in *Exploring Further 14.1.*

The Absorption Approach to Currency Depreciation

According to the elasticities approach, currency depreciation offers a price incentive to reduce imports and increase exports. But even if elasticity conditions are favorable, whether the home country's trade balance will actually improve may depend on how the economy reacts to the depreciation. The absorption approach provides insights into this question by considering the impact of depreciation on the spending

---

[3]Sidney S. Alexander, "Effects of a Devaluation on a Trade Balance," *IMF Staff Papers*, April 1952, pp. 263–278.

behavior of the domestic economy and the influence of domestic spending on the trade balance.[4]

The absorption approach starts with the idea that the value of total domestic output (Y) equals the level of total spending. Total spending consists of consumption (C), investment (I), government expenditures (G), and net exports ($X - M$). This relation can be written as follows:

$$Y = C + I + G + (X - M).$$

The absorption approach then consolidates $C + I + G$ into a single term A, which is referred to as absorption, and designates net exports ($X - M$) as B. Total domestic output thus equals the sum of absorption plus net exports:

$$Y = A + B.$$

This can be rewritten as follows:

$$B = Y - A.$$

This expression suggests that the balance of trade (B) equals the difference between total domestic output (Y) and the level of absorption (A). If national output exceeds domestic absorption, the economy's trade balance will be positive. Conversely, a negative trade balance suggests that an economy is spending beyond its ability to produce.

The absorption approach predicts that a currency depreciation will improve an economy's trade balance only if national output rises relative to absorption. This relation means that a country must increase its total output, reduce its absorption, or do some combination of the two. The following examples illustrate these possibilities.

Assume that an economy faces *unemployment* as well as a *trade deficit*. With the economy operating below maximum capacity, the price incentives of depreciation would tend to direct idle resources into the production of goods for export, in addition to diverting spending away from imports to domestically produced substitutes. The impact of the depreciation is thus to expand domestic output as well as to improve the trade balance. It is no wonder that policymakers tend to view currency depreciation as an effective tool when an economy faces unemployment with a trade deficit.

However, in the case of an economy operating at *full employment*, no unutilized resources are available for additional production. National output is at a fixed level. The only way in which currency depreciation can improve the trade balance is for the economy to somehow cut domestic absorption, freeing resources needed to produce additional export goods and import substitutes. For example, domestic policy-makers could decrease absorption by adopting restrictive fiscal and monetary policies in the face of higher prices resulting from the depreciation. But this decrease would result in sacrifice on the part of those who bear the burden of such measures. Currency depreciation may thus be considered inappropriate when an economy is operating at maximum capacity.

The absorption approach goes beyond the elasticity approach, which views the economy's trade balance as distinct from the rest of the economy. Instead, currency

---

[4]See Donald S. Kemp, "A Monetary View of the Balance of Payments," *Review*, Federal Reserve Bank of St. Louis, April 1975, pp. 14–22; and Thomas M. Humphrey, "The Monetary Approach to Exchange Rates: Its Historical Evolution and Role in Policy Debates," *Economic Review*, Federal Reserve Bank of Richmond, July-August 1978, pp. 2–9.

depreciation is viewed in relation to the economy's utilization of its resources and level of production. The two approaches are therefore complementary.

The Monetary Approach to Currency Depreciation

A survey of the traditional approaches to currency depreciation reveals a major shortcoming. According to the elasticities and absorption approaches, monetary consequences are not associated with balance-of-payments adjustment; or, to the extent that such consequences exist, they can be neutralized by domestic monetary authorities. The elasticities and absorption approaches apply only to the trade account of the balance of payments, neglecting the implications of capital movements. The *monetary approach* to depreciation addresses this shortcoming.[5] According to the monetary approach, currency depreciation may induce a *temporary* improvement in a nation's balance-of-payments position. For example, assume that equilibrium initially exists in the home country's money market. A depreciation of the home currency would increase the price level; that is, the domestic-currency prices of potential imports and exports. This increase would increase the demand for money, because larger amounts of money are needed for transactions. If that increased demand is not fulfilled from domestic sources, an inflow of money from overseas occurs. This inflow results in a balance-of-payments surplus and a rise in international reserves. But the surplus does not last forever. By adding to the international component of the home-country money supply, the currency depreciation leads to an increase in spending (absorption), which reduces the surplus. The surplus eventually disappears when equilibrium is restored in the home country's money market. The effects of depreciation on real economic variables are thus temporary. *Over the long run, currency depreciation merely raises the domestic price level.*

Summary

1. Currency depreciation (devaluation) may affect a nation's trade position through its impact on relative prices, incomes, and the purchasing power of money balances.

2. When all of a firm's inputs are acquired domestically and their costs are denominated in the domestic currency, an appreciation in the domestic currency's exchange value tends to increase the firm's costs by the same proportion, in terms of the foreign currency. Conversely, a depreciation of the domestic currency's exchange value tends to reduce the firm's costs by the same proportion in terms of the foreign currency.

3. Manufacturers often obtain inputs from abroad (foreign sourcing) whose costs are denominated in terms of a foreign currency. As foreign-currency-denominated costs become a larger portion of a producer's total costs, an appreciation of the domestic currency's exchange value leads to a smaller increase in the foreign-currency cost of the firm's output and a larger decrease in the domestic cost of the firm's output—compared to the cost changes that occur when all input costs are denominated in the domestic currency. The opposite applies for currency depreciation.

---

[5]Giovanni Olivei, "Exchange Rates and the Prices of Manufacturing Products Imported into the United States," *New England Economic Review*, First Quarter 2002, pp. 4–6.

4. By increasing (decreasing) relative U.S. production costs, a dollar appreciation (depreciation) tends to raise (lower) U.S. export prices in terms of a foreign currency, which induces a decrease (increase) in the quantity of U.S. goods sold abroad; similarly, a dollar appreciation (depreciation) tends to raise (lower) the amount of U.S. imports.

5. According to the elasticities approach, currency depreciation leads to the greatest improvement in a country's trade position when demand elasticities are high. Recent empirical studies indicate that the estimated demand elasticities for most nations are quite high.

6. The time path of currency depreciation can be explained in terms of the J-curve effect. According to this concept, the response of trade flows to changes in relative prices increases with the passage of time. Currency depreciation tends to worsen a country's trade balance in the short term, only to be followed by an improvement in the long term (assuming favorable elasticities).

7. The extent to which exchange-rate changes lead to changes in import prices and export prices is known as the pass-through relation. Complete (partial) pass-through occurs when a change in the exchange rate brings about a proportionate (less than proportionate) change in export prices and import prices. Empirical evidence suggests that pass-through tends to be partial rather than complete. Partial pass-through is explained by currency invoicing, market share strategies, and sizable distribution costs.

8. The absorption approach emphasizes the income effects of currency depreciation. According to this view, a depreciation may initially stimulate a nation's exports and production of import-competing goods. But this stimulus will promote excess domestic spending unless real output can be expanded or domestic absorption reduced. The result would be a return to a payments deficit.

9. The monetary approach to depreciation emphasizes the effect that depreciation has on the purchasing power of money balances and the resulting impacts on domestic expenditures and import levels. According to the monetary approach, the influence of currency depreciation on real output is temporary; over the long term, depreciation merely raises the domestic price level.

Key Concepts & Terms

- Absorption approach (p. 491)
- Elasticity approach (p. 491)
- Exchange rate pass-through (p. 497)
- J-curve effect (p. 495)
- Marshall-Lerner condition (p. 492)
- Monetary approach (p. 491)

Study Questions

1. Assume the United States exports 1,000 computers at a price of $3,000 each and imports 150 UK autos at a price of £10,000 each. Assume that the dollar/pound exchange rate is $2 per pound.
   a. Calculate, in dollar terms, the U.S. export receipts, import payments, and trade balance prior to a depreciation of the dollar's exchange value.
   b. Suppose the dollar's exchange value depreciates by 10 percent. Assuming that the price elasticity of demand for U.S. exports equals 3.0 and the price elasticity of demand for U.S. imports equals 2.0, does the dollar depreciation improve or worsen the U.S. trade balance? Why?
   c. Now assume that the price elasticity of demand for U.S. exports equals 0.3 and the price elasticity of demand for U.S. imports equals 0.2. Does this change the outcome? Why?

2. How does the J-curve effect relate to the time path of currency depreciation?

3. Suppose ABC Inc., a U.S. auto manufacturer, obtains some of its auto components in Mexico and that the costs of these components are denominated in pesos; the costs of the remaining components are denominated in dollars. Assume the dollar's exchange value appreciates by 50 percent against the peso. Compared to your answer in study question 8, what impact will the dollar appreciation have on the firm's international competitiveness? What about a dollar depreciation?

4. What implications does currency pass-through have for a nation whose currency depreciates?

5. How can currency depreciation-induced changes in household money balances promote payments equilibrium?

6. What is meant by the Marshall-Lerner condition? Do recent empirical studies suggest that world elasticity conditions are sufficiently high to permit successful depreciations?

7. Suppose ABC Inc., a U.S. auto manufacturer, obtains all of its auto components in the United States and that its costs are denominated in dollars. Assume the dollar's exchange value appreciates by 50 percent against the Mexican peso. What impact does the dollar appreciation have on the firm's international competitiveness? What about a dollar depreciation?

8. Three major approaches to analyzing the economic impact of currency depreciation are (a) the elasticities approach, (b) the absorption approach, and (c) the monetary approach. Distinguish among the three.

9. According to the absorption approach, does it make any difference whether a nation's currency depreciates when the economy is operating at less than full capacity versus at full capacity?

10. How does a currency depreciation affect a nation's balance of trade?

Exploring Further   14.1

Exchange Rate Pass-Through

Exchange rate pass-through denotes the impact of a change in the exchange rate between exporting and importing countries on local-currency prices of imports. Among the factors that determine the extent of pass-through are the responsiveness of markups to competitive conditions and the degree of returns to scale in the production of the imported good.

Our assumption that Toyota's costs in dollars decline by the same percentage of the dollar appreciation implies that the change in the exchange rate has no impact on the Japanese price of inputs used in the production of Toyotas. This is a reasonable approximation for labor inputs, but it is an unrealistic assumption when Toyota relies heavily on imported raw materials and energy. In this case, a dollar appreciation would raise Toyota's price of imported raw materials and energy. Allowing for this effect would lower the extent of exchange rate pass-through, other things equal.

If the typical foreign firm sets the price of a good exported to the United States as a constant markup over marginal cost (with price and marginal cost measured in U.S. dollars), then complete pass-through occurs when returns to scale are constant, implying constant marginal cost. In this situation, a dollar appreciation of, say, ten percent lowers the foreign firm's marginal cost measured in USD by the same amount. With a constant markup, the dollar price of the imported good must then decline by ten percent.

Pass-through will be less than complete (partial) when returns to scale are decreasing, implying increasing marginal cost. Again assume that the foreign firm sets the price of a good exported to the United States as a constant markup over marginal cost. The increase in U.S. demand for the imported good brought by a dollar appreciation now puts upward pressure on the foreign firm's marginal cost. Thus when measured in dollars, marginal cost declines by less than ten percent in response to a ten percent dollar appreciation.

Because the markup is constant, this leads to partial pass-through; that is, a decline in the dollar price of the imported good is less than ten percent. The reader can verify that the opposite result occurs in the presence of increasing returns to scale (declining marginal cost), where a change in the exchange rate is more than fully passed through in the import price.

A constant markup of price over cost is typical of industries with a very large number of firms, where the impact of any individual firm's price changes on the industry price is negligible. In the limiting case of a perfectly competitive industry, the markup will be constant at zero. In a setting with monopolistic competition, the markup will be positive but constant, because a firm's market share is relatively small. However, in an oligopoly setting, the markup will usually depend on the good's dollar price and the dollar price of competing goods, as well as the strength of demand for both the imported and competing goods.

To illustrate how the markup may respond to changes in the dollar price of the imported good, let us consider an example in which a monopolist foreign firm, say, Toyota, sells all of its output to the United States. We assume that the demand curve D depicted in Figure EF 14.1(a) represents the U.S. demand for Toyotas as a function of the dollar price of Toyotas. Profit maximization requires equalization of marginal revenue and marginal cost, both expressed in dollars, which occurs at the intersection of the schedules MR and MC_0. Note that the marginal cost schedule is horizontal, implying constant returns to scale. Toyota sets the profit-maximizing price P_0 as a markup over marginal cost, with Q_0 denoting the quantity of Toyotas demanded at price P_0.

Figure EF 14.1(b) illustrates how a dollar appreciation affects the dollar price of Toyotas. The appreciation lowers the dollar cost of producing Toyotas, and thus the marginal cost schedule shifts down by the same proportion of the appreciation.

FIGURE EF 14.1

EXCHANGE RATE PASS-THROUGH WITH A MONOPOLISTIC FOREIGN FIRM (TOYOTA)

The graph shows that at the new equilibrium the difference between the dollar price of Toyotas, P_1, and marginal cost, MC_1, is larger than at the old equilibrium. This new equilibrium signals that the foreign firm charges a higher markup (in dollars) over production cost. The graph also shows that as a consequence of the higher markup, the decline in the dollar price of Toyotas is smaller than the dollar appreciation, implying partial pass-through.

Figure EF 14.1(c) illustrates the opposite case of a dollar depreciation. The depreciation raises the dollar cost of producing Toyotas; thus, the marginal cost curve shifts up. At the new equilibrium, the dollar price of Toyotas increases by less than the increase in marginal cost resulting from the depreciation. This smaller increase implies that the firm charges a lower markup (in dollars) over production cost, implying partial pass-through.

The example in Figure EF 14.1 shows that exchange rate pass-through can be less than complete even in the presence of constant returns to scale. As the reader can verify, increasing marginal cost (that is, decreasing returns to scale) would lower the extent of exchange rate pass-through. Conversely, decreasing marginal cost (increasing returns to scale) would increase the extent of pass-through.

To summarize, the two determinants of exchange rate pass-through, the responsiveness of markups to competitive conditions and the degree of return to scale in production, can interact in different ways to produce different outcomes.

Exchange-Rate Systems and Currency Crises

Previous chapters have discussed the determination of exchange rates and their effects on the balance of payments. This chapter surveys the exchange-rate practices that are currently being used. The discussion focuses on the nature and operation of actual exchange-rate systems and identifies economic factors that influence the choice of alternative exchange-rate systems. The chapter also discusses the operation and effects of currency crises.

Exchange-Rate Practices

In choosing an exchange-rate system, a nation must decide whether to allow its currency to be determined by market forces (floating rate) or to be fixed (pegged) against some standard of value. If a nation adopts a floating rate, it must decide whether to float independently, to float in unison with a group of other currencies, or to crawl according to a predetermined formula such as relative inflation rates. The decision to anchor a currency includes the options of anchoring to a single currency, to a basket of currencies, or to gold. However, since 1971, the technique of expressing official exchange rates in terms of gold has not been used; gold has been phased out of the international monetary system. The role of gold in the international monetary system will be further discussed in Chapter 17.

Members of the International Monetary Fund (IMF) have been free to follow any exchange-rate policy that conforms to three principles: Exchange rates should not be manipulated to prevent effective balance-of-payments adjustments or to gain unfair competitive advantage over other members. Members should act to counter short-term disorderly conditions in exchange markets. When members intervene in exchange markets, they should take into account the interests of other members. Table 15.1 summarizes the exchange-rate practices used by IMF member countries.

What characteristics make a country more suited for fixed rather than flexible exchange rates? Among these characteristics are the size of the nation, openness to

TABLE 15.1

EXCHANGE-RATE ARRANGEMENTS OF
IMF MEMBERS, 2008

Exchange Arrangement	Number of Countries
Exchange arrangements with no separate legal tender*	10
Currency-board arrangements	13
Conventional pegged (fixed) exchange rates	68
Pegged exchange rates within horizontal bands	3
Crawling pegged exchange rates	8
Crawling band	2
Managed floating exchange rates	44
Independently floating exchange rates	40
	188

*The currency of another country circulates as the sole legal tender, or the member belongs to a monetary or currency union in which the same legal tender is shared by the members of the union.

Source: International Monetary Fund, *Classification of Exchange Rate Arrangements and Monetary Policy Frameworks*, April 31, 2008, available at **http://www.imf.org/**. See also *International Financial Statistics*, various issues.

trade, the degree of labor mobility, and the availability of fiscal policy to cushion downturns. Table 15.2 summarizes the usage of these factors. The important point is that no single currency system is right for all countries or at all times. The choice of an exchange-rate system should depend on the particular circumstances facing the country in question.

Choosing an Exchange Rate System: Constraints Imposed by Free Capital Flows

The choice of an exchange rate system depends on many variables including the freedom of capital to flow in to and out of a country. One consequence of allowing free capital flows is that it constrains a country's choice of an exchange-rate system and its ability to operate an independent monetary policy. For reasons related to the tendency for capital to flow to where returns are the highest, a country can maintain only two of the following three policies—free capital flows, a fixed exchange rate, and an independent monetary policy. This tendency is illustrated in Figure 15.1. Countries must choose to be on one side of the triangle,

TABLE 15.2

CHOOSING AN EXCHANGE-RATE SYSTEM

Characteristics of Economy	Implication for the Desired Degree of Exchange-Rate Flexibility
Size and openness of the economy	If trade is a large share of national output, then the costs of currency fluctuations can be high. This suggests that small, open economies may best be served by fixed exchange rates.
Inflation rate	If a country has much higher inflation than its trading partners, its exchange rate needs to be flexible to prevent its goods from becoming uncompetitive in world markets. If inflation differentials are more modest, a fixed rate is less troublesome.
Labor-market flexibility	The more rigid wages are, the greater the need for a flexible exchange rate to help the economy respond to an external shock.
Degree of financial development	In developing countries with immature financial markets, a freely floating exchange rate may not be sensible because a small number of foreign-exchange trades can cause big swings in currencies.
Credibility of policymakers	The weaker the reputation of the central bank, the stronger the case for pegging the exchange rate to build confidence that inflation will be controlled.
Capital mobility	The more open an economy to international capital, the harder it is to sustain a fixed rate.

FIGURE 15.1

THE IMPOSSIBLE TRINITY

Countries can adopt only two of the following three policies: free capital flows, a fixed exchange rate, and an independent monetary policy.

adopting the policies at each end, but forgoing the policy on the opposite corner. Economists refer to this restriction as the **impossible trinity**.[1]

The easiest way to understand this restriction is through specific examples. The United States allows free capital flows and has an independent monetary policy, but it has a flexible exchange rate. To combat inflation, suppose the Federal Reserve increases its target interest rate relative to foreign interest rates, thus inducing capital to flow into the United States. By increasing the demand for dollars relative to other currencies, these capital inflows cause the dollar to appreciate against other currencies. Conversely, if the Federal Reserve reduces its target interest rate, net capital outflows decrease the demand for dollars, thus causing the dollar to depreciate against other currencies. Therefore, the United States, by not having a fixed exchange rate, can maintain both an independent monetary policy and free capital flows.

In contrast, Hong Kong essentially fixes the value of its currency to the U.S. dollar and allows free capital flows. The trade-off is that Hong Kong sacrifices the ability to use monetary policy to influence domestic interest rates. Unlike the United States, Hong Kong cannot decrease interest rates to stimulate a weak economy. If Hong Kong's interest rates were to diverge from world rates, capital would flow in to or out of the Hong Kong economy, just as in the U.S. case above. Under a flexible exchange rate, these flows would cause the exchange value of the Hong Kong dollar to change relative to that of other currencies. However, under a fixed exchange rate, the monetary authority must offset these capital flows by purchasing domestic or

[1]See Robert Mundell, "The Appropriate Use of Monetary and Fiscal Policy for Internal and External Stability," *IMF Staff Papers*, March 1962 and "Capital Mobility and Stabilization Policy under Fixed and Flexible Exchange Rates," *Canadian Journal of Economics*, November 1963.

foreign currency in order to keep the supply and demand for its currency fixed, and thus the exchange rate constant. Simply put, Hong Kong loses the ability to have an independent monetary policy if it allows free capital flows and maintains a fixed exchange rate.

Similar to the case of Hong Kong, until 2005 China tied its exchange rate to the U.S. dollar. However, China could conduct an independent monetary policy, because it sets restrictions on capital flows. In China's case, world and domestic interest rates could differ, because controls on the transfer of funds in to and out of the country limited the resulting changes in the money supply and the corresponding pressures on the exchange rate. As these three examples show, if a country chooses to allow capital to flow freely, it must also choose between having an independent monetary policy or a fixed exchange rate.

How does a country decide whether to give up a fixed exchange rate, an independent monetary policy, or free capital movements? The answer largely depends on global economic trends. For example, the post-World War II era saw substantial interdependence of markets and increasing international trade. Countries such as the United States wanted to facilitate this increase in trade by eliminating the risk of exchange-rate fluctuations. In 1944, representatives from major industrial countries designed and implemented a plan that encouraged fixed exchange rates for the dollar and other currencies while maintaining independent monetary policies. Just as with the systems described above, something had to be given up—the free movement of capital flows. Participating countries imposed ceilings on the interest rates that banks could offer to depositors and restrictions on the types of assets in which banks could invest. Moreover, governments intervened in financial markets to direct capital toward strategic domestic sectors. Although none of these controls alone prevented international capital flows, in combination they allowed governments to reduce the amount of international capital transactions.[2]

Fixed Exchange-Rate System

Few nations have allowed their currencies' exchange values to be determined solely by the forces of supply and demand in a free market. Until the industrialized nations adopted managed floating exchange rates in the 1970s, the practice generally was to maintain a pattern of relatively **fixed exchange rates** among national currencies. Changes in national exchange rates presumably were initiated by domestic monetary authorities when long-term market forces warranted it.

Use of Fixed Exchange Rates

Fixed exchange rates tend to be used primarily by small, developing nations whose currencies are anchored to a **key currency**, such as the U.S. dollar. A key currency is widely traded on world money markets, has demonstrated relatively stable values over time, and has been widely accepted as a means of international settlement. Table 15.3 identifies the major key currencies of the world. Instead of anchoring the value of the domestic currency to another currency, a country could fix its currency's value to a commodity such as gold, a key feature of the gold standard described in Chapter 17.

---

[2]See *Economic Report of the President*, 2004, Chapters 13–14.

TABLE 15.3

KEY CURRENCIES: CURRENCY COMPOSITION OF
OFFICIAL FOREIGN EXCHANGE RESERVES OF THE
MEMBER COUNTRIES OF THE INTERNATIONAL
MONETARY FUND, 2008

Key Currency	Composition of Official Foreign Exchange Reserves
U.S. Dollar	64.0%
Euro	26.5
British Pound	4.1
Japanese Yen	3.2
Other	2.2
	100.0%

Source: From Currency Composition of Official Foreign Exchange
Reserves (COFER), International Monetary Fund, 2008, available at
http://www.imf.org.

One reason why developing nations choose to anchor their currencies to a key currency is that it is used as a means of international settlement. Consider a Norwegian importer who wants to purchase Argentinean beef over the next year. If the Argentine exporter is unsure of what the Norwegian krone will purchase in one year, he might reject the krone in settlement. Similarly, the Norwegian importer might doubt the value of Argentina's peso. One solution is for the contract to be written in terms of a key currency. Generally speaking, smaller nations with relatively undiversified economies and large foreign-trade sectors have been inclined to anchor their currencies to one of the key currencies.

Maintaining an anchor to a key currency provides several benefits for developing nations. First, the prices of the traded products of many developing nations are determined primarily in the markets of industrialized nations such as the United States; by anchoring, say, to the dollar, these nations can stabilize the domestic-currency prices of their imports and exports. Second, many nations with high inflation have anchored to the dollar (the United States has relatively low inflation) in order to exert restraint on domestic policies and reduce inflation. By making the commitment to stabilize their exchange rates against the dollar, governments hope to convince their citizens that they are willing to adopt the responsible monetary policies necessary to achieve low inflation. Anchoring the exchange rate may thus lessen inflationary expectations, leading to lower interest rates, a lessening of the loss of output due to disinflation, and a moderation of price pressures.

In maintaining fixed exchange rates, nations must decide whether to anchor their currencies to another currency or a currency basket. Anchoring to a *single currency* is generally done by developing nations whose trade and financial relations are mainly with a single industrial-country partner. Therefore, the developing country anchors its currency to the currency of its dominant trading partner.

Developing nations with more than one major trading partner often anchor their currencies to a group or *basket of currencies*. The basket is composed of prescribed quantities of foreign currencies in proportion to the amount of trade done with the nation anchoring its currency. Once the basket has been selected, the currency value of the nation is computed using the exchange rates of the foreign currencies in the basket. Anchoring the domestic-currency value of the basket enables a nation to average out fluctuations in export or import prices caused by exchange-rate movements. The effects of exchange-rate changes on the domestic economy are thus reduced. Rather than constructing their own currency basket, some nations anchor the value of their currencies to the **special drawing right (SDR)**, a basket of four currencies established by the IMF, as discussed in Chapter 17.

Par Value and Official Exchange Rate

Under a fixed exchange-rate system, governments have assigned their currencies a **par value** in terms of gold or other key currencies. By comparing the par values of two currencies, we can determine their **official exchange rate**. Under the gold standard, the official exchange rate between the U.S. dollar and the UK pound was, for example, $2.80 = £1 as long as the United States bought and sold gold at a fixed price of $35 per ounce and the United Kingdom bought and sold gold at £12.50 per ounce ($35.00/£12.50 = $2.80 per pound). The major industrial nations set their currencies' par values in terms of gold until gold was phased out of the international monetary system in the early 1970s.

Rather than defining the par value of a currency in terms of a commodity, countries may anchor their currencies against another key currency. Developing nations often set the values of their currencies to that of a large, low-inflation country like the United States. For example, the monetary authority of Bolivia may define its official exchange rate as 20 pesos per dollar.

Exchange-Rate Stabilization

We have learned that a first requirement for a nation adopting a fixed exchange-rate system is to define the official exchange rate of its currency. The next step is to set up an **exchange-stabilization fund** to defend the official rate. Through purchases and sales of foreign currencies, the exchange-stabilization fund attempts to ensure that the market exchange rate does not move above or below the official exchange rate.

In Figure 15.2, assume that the market exchange rate equals $2.80 per pound, seen at the intersection of the demand and supply schedules of UK pounds, D_0 and S_0. Also assume that the official exchange rate is defined as $2.80 per pound. Now suppose that rising interest rates in the United Kingdom cause U.S. investors to demand additional pounds to finance the purchase of UK securities; let the demand for pounds rise from D_0 to D_1 in Figure 15.2(a). Under free-market conditions, the dollar would depreciate from $2.80 per pound to $2.90 per pound. But under a fixed exchange-rate system, the monetary authority will attempt to defend the official rate of $2.80 per pound. At this rate, there exists an excess demand for pounds equal to £40 billion; this means that the United Kingdom faces an excess supply of dollars in the same amount. To keep the market exchange rate from depreciating beyond $2.80 per pound, the U.S. exchange-stabilization fund would purchase the excess supply of dollars with pounds. The supply of pounds thus rises from S_0 to S_1, resulting in a stabilization of the market exchange rate at $2.80 per pound.

Conversely, suppose that increased prosperity in the United Kingdom leads to rising imports from the United States; the supply of pounds thus increases from, say, S_0 to S_1 in Figure 15.2(b). At the official exchange rate of $2.80 per pound, there exists an excess supply of pounds equal to £40 billion. To keep the dollar from appreciating against the pound, the U.S. stabilization fund would purchase the excess supply of pounds with dollars. The demand for pounds thus increases from D_0 to D_1, resulting in a stabilization of the market exchange rate at $2.80 per pound.

This example illustrates how an exchange-stabilization fund undertakes its pegging operations to offset short-term fluctuations in the market exchange rate. However, over the long term, the official exchange rate and the market exchange rate may move apart, reflecting changes in fundamental economic conditions—income levels, tastes and preferences, and technological factors. In the case of a **fundamental disequilibrium**, the cost of defending the existing official rate may become prohibitive.

Consider the case of a deficit nation that finds its currency weakening. Maintaining the official rate may require the exchange-stabilization fund to purchase sizable quantities of its currency with foreign currencies or other reserve assets.

FIGURE 15.2

EXCHANGE-RATE STABILIZATION UNDER A FIXED EXCHANGE-RATE SYSTEM

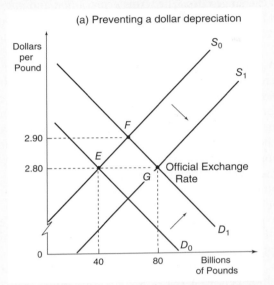

(a) Preventing a dollar depreciation

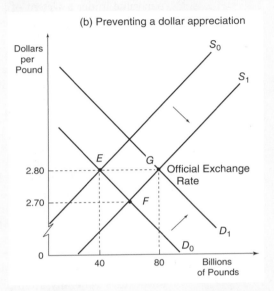

(b) Preventing a dollar appreciation

To defend the official exchange rate of $2.80 per pound, the central bank must supply all of the nation's currency that is demanded at the official rate and demand all of the nation's currency that is supplied to it at the official rate. To prevent a dollar depreciation, the central bank must purchase the excess supply of dollars with an equivalent amount of pounds. To prevent a dollar appreciation, the central bank must purchase the excess supply of pounds with an equivalent amount of dollars.

These purchases may impose a severe drain on the deficit nation's stock of international reserves. Although the deficit nation may be able to borrow reserves from other nations or from the IMF to continue the defense of its exchange rate, such borrowing privileges are generally of limited magnitude. At the same time, the deficit nation will be undergoing internal adjustments to curb the disequilibrium. These measures will likely be aimed at controlling inflationary pressures and raising interest rates to promote capital inflows and discourage imports. If the imbalance is persistent, the deficit nation may view such internal adjustments as too costly in terms of falling income and employment levels. Rather than continually resorting to such measures, the deficit nation may decide that the reversal of the disequilibrium calls for an adjustment in the exchange rate itself. Under a system of fixed exchange rates, a chronic imbalance may be counteracted by a currency devaluation or revaluation.

Devaluation and Revaluation

Under a fixed exchange-rate system, a nation's monetary authority may decide to pursue a balance-of-payments equilibrium by devaluing or revaluing its currency. The purpose of **devaluation** is to cause the home currency's exchange value to *depreciate*, thus counteracting a payments *deficit*. The purpose of currency **revaluation** is to cause the home currency's exchange value to *appreciate*, thus counteracting a payments *surplus*.

The terms *devaluation* and *revaluation* refer to a legal redefinition of a currency's par value under a system of fixed exchange rates. The terms *depreciation* and *appreciation* refer to the actual impact on the market exchange rate caused by a redefinition of a par value or to changes in an exchange rate stemming from changes in the supply of or demand for foreign exchange.

Devaluation and revaluation policies work on relative prices to divert domestic and foreign expenditures between domestic and foreign goods. By raising the home price of the foreign currency, a devaluation makes the home country's exports cheaper to foreigners in terms of the foreign currency, while making the home country's imports more expensive in terms of the home currency. Expenditures are diverted from foreign to home goods as home exports rise and imports fall. In like manner, a revaluation discourages the home country's exports and encourages its imports, diverting expenditures from home goods to foreign goods.

Before implementing a devaluation or revaluation, the monetary authority must decide (1) if an adjustment in the official exchange rate is necessary to correct a payments disequilibrium, (2) when the adjustment will occur, and (3) how large the adjustment should be. Exchange-rate decisions of government officials may be incorrect; that is, ill-timed and of improper magnitude.

In making the decision to undergo a devaluation or revaluation, monetary authorities generally attempt to hide behind a veil of secrecy. Just hours before the decision is to become effective, public denials of any such policies by official government representatives are common. This is to discourage currency speculators, who try to profit by shifting funds from a currency falling in value to one rising in value. Given the destabilizing impact that massive speculation can exert on financial markets, it is hard to criticize monetary authorities for being secretive in their actions. However, the need for devaluation tends to be obvious to outsiders as well as to government officials and in the past has nearly always resulted in heavy speculative pressures. Table 15.4 summarizes the advantages and disadvantages of fixed exchange rates.

TABLE 15.4

ADVANTAGES AND DISADVANTAGES OF FIXED EXCHANGE RATES AND FLOATING EXCHANGE RATES

	Advantages	Disadvantages
Fixed exchange rates	Simplicity and clarity of exchange-rate target	Loss of independent monetary policy
	Automatic rule for the conduct of monetary policy	Vulnerable to speculative attacks
	Keeps inflation under control	
Floating exchange rates	Continuous adjustment in the balance of payments	Conducive to price inflation
	Operate under simplified institutional arrangements	Disorderly exchange markets can disrupt trade and investment patterns
	Allow governments to set independent monetary and fiscal policies	Encourage reckless financial policies on the part of government

Bretton Woods System of Fixed Exchange Rates

An example of fixed exchange rates is the **Bretton Woods system**. In 1944, delegates from 44 member nations of the United Nations met at Bretton Woods, New Hampshire to create a new international monetary system. They were aware of the unsatisfactory monetary experience of the 1930s, during which the international gold standard collapsed as the result of the economic and financial crises of the Great Depression, and nations experimented unsuccessfully with floating exchange rates and exchange controls. The delegates wanted to establish international monetary order and avoid the instability and nationalistic practices that had been in effect until 1944.

The international monetary system that was created became known as the Bretton Woods system. The founders felt that neither completely fixed exchange rates nor floating rates were optimal; instead, they adopted a kind of semi-fixed exchange-rate system known as **adjustable pegged exchange rates**. The Bretton Woods system lasted from 1946 until 1973.

The main feature of the adjustable peg system was that currencies were tied to each other to provide stable exchange rates for commercial and financial transactions. However, when the balance of payments moved away from its long-term equilibrium position, a nation could repeg its exchange rate via devaluation or revaluation policies. Member nations agreed in principle to defend existing par values as long as possible in times of balance-of-payments disequilibrium. They were expected to use fiscal and monetary policies first to correct payments imbalances. But if reversing a persistent payments imbalance meant a severe disruption to the domestic economy in terms of inflation or unemployment, member nations could correct this *fundamental disequilibrium* by repegging their currencies up to ten percent without permission from the IMF and by greater than ten percent with the fund's permission.

Under the Bretton Woods system, each member nation set the par value of its currency in terms of gold or, alternatively, the gold content of the U.S. dollar in 1944. Market exchange rates were almost but not completely fixed, being kept within a band of one percent on either side of parity for a total spread of two percent. National exchange-stabilization funds were used to maintain the band limits. In 1971, the exchange-support margins were widened to 2.25 percent on either side of parity to eliminate payments imbalances by setting in motion corrective trade and capital movements. Devaluations or revaluations could be used to adjust the par value of a currency when it became overvalued or undervalued.

Although adjustable pegged rates are intended to promote a viable balance-of-payments adjustment mechanism, they have been plagued with operational problems. In the Bretton Woods system, adjustments in prices and incomes often conflicted with domestic-stabilization objectives. Also, currency devaluation was considered undesirable because it seemed to indicate a failure of domestic policies and a loss of international prestige. Conversely, revaluations were unacceptable to exporters, whose livelihoods were vulnerable to such policies. Repegging exchange rates only as a last resort often meant that when adjustments did occur, they were sizable. Moreover, adjustable pegged rates posed difficulties in estimating the equilibrium rate to which a currency should be repegged. Also, once the market exchange rate reached the margin of the permissible band around parity, it in effect became a rigid fixed rate that presented speculators with a one-way bet. Given persistent weakening pressure, for example, at the band's outer limit, speculators had the incentive to move out of a weakening currency that was expected to depreciate further in value as the result of official devaluation.

IS CHINA A CURRENCY MANIPULATOR?

Trade tensions between the United States and China have run high during the first decade of the 2000s. In 2009, U.S. Treasury Secretary Timothy Geithner restated a long-held American accusation that China's desire to manipulate its currency hurts the U.S. economy. He noted that to prevent the yuan from appreciating, the People's Bank of China has massively intervened by selling yuan and purchasing dollar-denominated assets such as U.S. Treasury securities.

As the argument goes, China's currency policy has resulted in its yuan being significantly undervalued relative to the dollar, giving the Chinese an unfair competitive advantage. An undervalued yuan makes U.S. exports to China more expensive than they would be if exchange rates were determined by market forces. This undervaluation harms U.S. production and employment in manufacturing industries such as textiles, apparel, and furniture that have to compete against artificially low-cost goods from China. An undervalued yuan also makes Chinese goods cheaper for American consumers, encouraging them to import more goods from China. As a result, China takes jobs away from Americans. If the dollar–yuan exchange rate was set by market forces instead of being manipulated by the People's Bank of China, the yuan would appreciate sharply, increasing the price of Chinese exports and taking pressure off U.S. manufacturing industries. China's huge trade surplus with the United States and its large accumulation of dollar reserves are cited as evidence that China has manipulated the value of its currency relative to the dollar for competitive advantage. For the sake of stability in the economies of the United States and China, and also the global economy, action needs to be taken to allow market forces to determine the dollar–yuan exchange rate.

However, other analysts contend that there is little or no connection between the yuan and the health of U.S. manufacturing. They note that the transition away from manufacturing in the United States is a long-term trend that goes far beyond competition from Chinese exports. Jobs have been slashed because technological improvements have made each worker more productive.

Moreover, if the United States wants to make its workers more competitive with those in China, it should reform its educational system rather than rely on illusory gains from changes in exchange rates.

Also, there is a good economic rationale for China's desire to maintain a stable value against the dollar. As long as this fixed rate is credible, it serves as an effective monetary anchor for China's internal price level. After inflation skyrocketed to more than 20 percent per year during 1993–1995, the fixed rate anchor helped China regain price-level stability.

Moreover, China's currency intervention yields positive results for the U.S. economy. China has maintained large investments in U.S. debt, which helps keep U.S. interest rates low, allowing American firms to make investments that would be unattractive at a higher cost of borrowing. Such investments increase the amount of capital available and thus increase the size of the economy. An undervalued yuan also promotes a lower inflation rate in the United States.

Also, China argues that its currency peg policy is not intended to favor exports over imports, but rather to foster economic stability. Chinese officials note that many developing countries, including China, tie their currencies to the dollar at a fixed rate to promote economic stability. Chinese leaders fear that abandoning the peg could induce an economic crisis in China and would especially damage its export sectors at a time when painful economic reforms, such as shutting down inefficient state-owned businesses and restructuring the banking system, are being implemented. Simply put, Chinese officials view economic stability as crucial to maintaining political stability. They are concerned that an appreciating yuan would reduce employment and decrease wages in several industries and thus cause worker unrest.

Source: Morris Goldstein and Nicholas Lardy, editors, *Debating China's Exchange Rate Policy*, Peterson Institute for International Economics, Washington, D.C., 2008.

These problems reached a climax in the early 1970s. Faced with continuing and growing balance-of-payments deficits, the United States suspended the dollar's convertibility into gold in August 1971. This suspension terminated the U.S. commitment to exchange gold for dollars at $35 per ounce—a commitment that had existed for 37 years. This policy abolished the tie between gold and the international value of the dollar, thus floating the dollar and permitting its exchange rate to be set by market forces. The floating of the dollar terminated U.S. support of the Bretton Woods system of fixed exchange rates and led to the demise of that system.

Floating Exchange Rates

Instead of adopting fixed exchange rates, some nations allow their currencies to float in the foreign-exchange market. By **floating** (or flexible) **exchange rates**, we mean currency prices that are established daily in the foreign-exchange market, without restrictions imposed by government policy on the extent to which the prices can move. With floating rates, there is an equilibrium exchange rate that equates the demand for and supply of the home currency. Changes in the exchange rate will ideally correct a payments imbalance by bringing about shifts in imports and exports of goods, services, and short-term capital movements. The exchange rate depends on relative productivity levels, interest rates, inflation rates, and other factors discussed in Chapter 12.

Unlike fixed exchange rates, floating exchange rates are not characterized by par values and official exchange rates; they are determined by market supply and demand conditions rather than central bankers. Although floating rates do not have an exchange-stabilization fund to maintain existing rates, it does not necessarily follow that floating rates must fluctuate erratically. They will do so if the underlying market forces become unstable. Because there is no exchange-stabilization fund under floating rates, any holdings of international reserves serve as working balances rather than to maintain a given exchange rate for any currency.

Achieving Market Equilibrium

How do floating exchange rates promote payments equilibrium for a nation? Consider Figure 15.3, which illustrates the foreign-exchange market in Swiss francs in the United States. The intersection of supply schedule S_0 and demand schedule D_0 determines the equilibrium exchange rate of $0.50 per franc.

Referring to Figure 15.3(a), suppose a rise in real income causes U.S. residents to demand more Swiss cheese and watches, and therefore more francs; let the demand for francs rise from D_0 to D_1. Initially the market is in disequilibrium, because the quantity of francs demanded (60 francs) exceeds the quantity supplied (40 francs) at the exchange rate of $0.50 per franc. The excess demand for francs leads to an increase in the exchange rate from $0.50 to $0.55 per franc; the dollar thus falls in value, or depreciates, against the franc, while the franc rises in value, or appreciates, against the dollar. The higher value of the franc prompts Swiss residents to increase the quantity of francs supplied on the foreign-exchange market to purchase more U.S. goods, which are now cheaper in terms of the franc; at the same time, it dampens U.S. demand for more expensive Swiss goods. Market equilibrium is restored at the exchange rate of $0.55 per franc, at which the quantities of francs supplied and demanded are equal.

FIGURE 15.3

MARKET ADJUSTMENT UNDER FLOATING EXCHANGE RATES

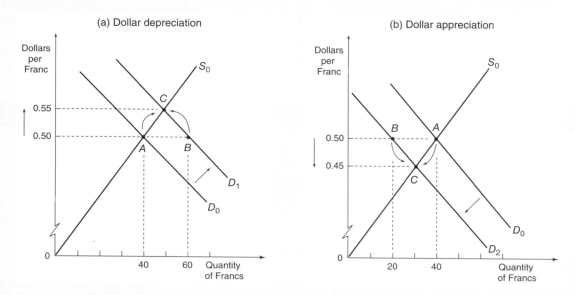

Under a floating exchange-rate system, continuous changes in currency values restore payments equilibrium at which the quantity supplied and quantity demanded of a currency are equal. Starting at equilibrium point A, an increase in the demand for francs leads to a depreciation of the dollar against the franc; conversely, a decrease in the demand for francs leads to an appreciation of the dollar against the franc.

Suppose instead that real income in the United States falls, which causes U.S. residents to demand less Swiss cheese and watches, and therefore fewer francs. In Figure 15.3(b), let the demand for francs fall from D_0 to D_2. The market is initially in disequilibrium because the quantity of francs supplied (40 francs) exceeds the quantity demanded (20 francs) at the exchange rate of $0.50 per franc. The excess supply of francs causes the exchange rate to fall from $0.50 to $0.45 per franc; the dollar thus appreciates against the franc, while the franc depreciates against the dollar. Market equilibrium is restored at the exchange rate of $0.45 per franc, at which the quantities of francs supplied and demanded are equal.

This example illustrates one argument in favor of floating rates: When the exchange rate is permitted to adjust freely in response to market forces, market equilibrium will be established at a point where the quantities of foreign exchange supplied and demanded are equal. If the exchange rate promotes market equilibrium, monetary authorities will not need international reserves for the purpose of intervening in the market to maintain exchange rates at their par value. Presumably, these resources can be used more productively elsewhere in the economy.

Trade Restrictions, Jobs, and Floating Exchange Rates

During economic downturns, labor unions often lobby for import restrictions in order to save jobs for domestic workers. Do import restrictions lead to rising total employment in the economy?

As long as the United States maintains a floating exchange rate, the implementation of import restrictions to help one industry will gradually shift jobs from other industries in the economy to the protected industry, with no significant impact on aggregate employment. Short-term employment gains in the protected industry will be offset by long-term employment losses in other industries.

Suppose the United States increases tariffs on autos imported from Japan. This policy would reduce auto imports, causing a decrease in the U.S. demand for yen to pay for imported vehicles. With floating exchange rates, the yen would depreciate against the dollar (the dollar would appreciate against the yen) until balance in international transactions is attained. The change in the exchange rate would encourage Americans to purchase more goods from Japan and the Japanese to purchase fewer goods from the United States. Sales and jobs would therefore be lost in other U.S. industries. Trade restrictions thus result in a zero-sum game within the United States. Job increases in Detroit are offset by job decreases in Los Angeles and Portland, with exchange-rate changes imposing costs on unprotected workers in the U.S. economy.

Arguments for and Against Floating Rates

One advantage claimed for floating rates is their simplicity. Floating rates allegedly respond quickly to changing supply and demand conditions, clearing the market of shortages or surpluses of a given currency. Instead of having formal rules of conduct among central bankers governing exchange-rate movements, floating rates are market determined. They operate under simplified institutional arrangements that are relatively easy to enact.

Because floating rates fluctuate throughout the day, they permit continuous adjustment in the balance of payments. The adverse effects of prolonged disequilibriums that tend to occur under fixed exchange rates are minimized under floating rates. It is also argued that floating rates partially insulate the home economy from external forces. This insulation means that governments will not have to restore payments equilibrium through painful inflationary or deflationary adjustment policies. Switching to floating rates frees a nation from having to adopt policies that perpetuate domestic disequilibrium as the price of maintaining a satisfactory balance-of-payments position. Nations thus have greater freedom to pursue policies that promote domestic balance than they do under fixed exchange rates.

Although there are strong arguments in favor of floating exchange rates, this system is often considered to be of limited usefulness for bankers and business people. Critics of floating rates maintain that an unregulated market may lead to wide fluctuations in currency values, discouraging foreign trade and investment. Although traders and investors may be able to hedge exchange-rate risk by dealing in the forward market, the cost of hedging may become prohibitively high.

Floating rates in theory are supposed to allow governments to set independent monetary and fiscal policies. But this flexibility may cause another sort of problem: *inflationary bias.* Under a system of floating rates, monetary authorities may lack the financial discipline required by a fixed exchange-rate system. Suppose a nation faces relatively high rates of inflation compared with the rest of the world. This domestic inflation will have no negative impact on the nation's trade balance under floating rates because its currency will automatically depreciate in the exchange market. However, a protracted depreciation of the currency would result in persistently increasing import prices and a rising price level, making inflation self-perpetuating and the depreciation continuous. Because there is greater freedom for domestic financial management under floating rates, there may be less resistance to overspending and to its subsequent pressure on wages and prices. Table 15.4 (on page 514) summarizes the advantages and disadvantages of floating exchange rates.

Managed Floating Rates

The adoption of managed floating exchange rates by the United States and other industrial nations in 1973 followed the breakdown of the international monetary system based on fixed rates. Before the 1970s, only a handful of economists gave serious consideration to a general system of floating rates. However, because of defects in the decision-making process caused by procedural difficulties and political biases, adjustments of par values under the Bretton Woods system were often delayed and discontinuous. It was recognized that exchange rates should be adjusted more promptly and in small but continuous amounts in response to evolving market forces. In 1973, a **managed floating system** was adopted, under which informal guidelines were established by the IMF for coordination of national exchange-rate policies.

The motivation for the formulation of guidelines for floating arose from two concerns. The first was that nations might intervene in the exchange markets to avoid exchange-rate alterations that would weaken their competitive position. When the United States suspended its gold-convertibility pledge and allowed its overvalued dollar to float in the exchange markets, it hoped that a free-market adjustment would result in a depreciation of the dollar against other, undervalued currencies. Rather than permitting a **clean float** (a market solution) to occur, foreign central banks refused to permit the dollar depreciation by intervening in the exchange market. The United States considered this a **dirty float**, because the free-market forces of supply and demand were not allowed to achieve their equilibrating role. A second motivation for guidelines was the concern that floats over time might lead to disorderly markets with erratic fluctuations in exchange rates. Such destabilizing activity could create an uncertain business climate and reduce the level of world trade.

Under managed floating, a nation can alter the degree to which it intervenes in the foreign-exchange market. Heavier intervention moves the nation nearer to a fixed exchange-rate status, whereas less intervention moves the nation nearer to a floating exchange-rate status. Concerning day-to-day and week-to-week exchange-rate movements, a main objective of the floating guidelines has been to prevent the emergence of erratic fluctuations. Member nations should intervene in the foreign-exchange market as necessary to prevent sharp and disruptive exchange-rate fluctuations from day to day and week to week. Such a policy is known as **leaning against the wind**—intervening to reduce short-term fluctuations in exchange rates without attempting to adhere to any particular rate over the long term. Members should also not act aggressively with respect to their currency exchange rates; that is, they should not enhance the value when it is appreciating or depress the value when it is depreciating.

Under the managed float, some nations choose **target exchange rates** and intervene to support them. Target exchange rates are intended to reflect long-term economic forces that underlie exchange-rate movements. One way for managed floaters to estimate a target exchange rate is to follow statistical indicators that respond to the same economic forces as the exchange-rate trend. Then, when the values of indicators change, the exchange-rate target can be adjusted accordingly. Among these indicators are rates of inflation in different nations, levels of official foreign reserves, and persistent imbalances in international payments accounts. In practice, defining a target exchange rate can be difficult in a market based on volatile economic conditions.

Managed Floating Rates in the Short and Long Terms

Managed floating exchange rates attempt to combine market-determined exchange rates with foreign-exchange market intervention in order to take advantage of the best features of floating exchange rates and fixed exchange rates. Under a managed float, market intervention is used to stabilize exchange rates in the short term; in the long term, a managed float allows market forces to determine exchange rates.

Figure 15.4 illustrates the theory of a managed float in a two-country framework, Switzerland and the United States. The supply and demand schedules for francs are denoted by S_0 and D_0; the equilibrium exchange rate, at which the quantity of francs supplied equals the quantity demanded, is $0.50 per franc.

Suppose there occurs a permanent increase in U.S. real income, as a result of which U.S. residents demand additional francs to purchase more Swiss chocolate. Let the demand for francs rise from D_0 to D_1, as shown in Figure 15.4(a). Because

FIGURE 15.4

MANAGED FLOATING EXCHANGE RATES

Under this system, central bank intervention is used to stabilize exchange rates in the short term; in the long term, market forces are permitted to determine exchange rates.

this increase in demand is the result of long-term market forces, a managed float permits supply and demand conditions to determine the exchange rate. With the increase in demand for francs, the quantity of francs demanded (180 francs) exceeds the quantity supplied (100 francs) at the exchange rate of $0.50 per franc. The excess demand results in a rise in the exchange rate to $0.60 per franc at which the quantity of francs supplied and the quantity demanded are equal. In this manner, long-term movements in exchange rates are determined by the supply and demand for various currencies.

Figure 15.4(b) illustrates the case of a short-term increase in the demand for francs. Suppose U.S. investors demand additional francs to finance purchases of Swiss securities, which pay relatively high interest rates; again, let the demand for francs rise from D_0 to D_1. In a few weeks, suppose Swiss interest rates fall, causing the U.S. demand for francs to revert to its original level, D_0. Under floating rates, the dollar price of the franc would rise from $0.50 per franc to $0.60 per franc and then fall back to $0.50 per franc. This type of exchange-rate irascibility is widely considered to be a disadvantage of floating rates because it leads to uncertainty regarding the profitability of international trade and financial transactions; as a result, the pattern of trade and finance may be disrupted.

Under managed floating rates, the response to this temporary disturbance is exchange-rate intervention by the Federal Reserve to keep the exchange rate at its long-term equilibrium level of $0.50 per franc. During the time period in which demand is at D_1, the central bank will sell francs to meet the excess demand. As soon as the disturbance is over, and demand reverts back to D_0, exchange-market intervention will no longer be needed. In short, central bank intervention is used to offset temporary fluctuations in exchange rates that contribute to uncertainty in carrying out transactions in international trade and finance.

Since the advent of managed floating rates in 1973, the frequency and size of U.S. foreign-exchange interventions have varied. Intervention was substantial from 1977 to 1979, when the dollar's exchange value was considered to be unacceptably low. American stabilization operations were minimal during the Reagan administration's first term, consistent with its goal of limiting government interference in markets; they were directed at offsetting short-term market disruptions. Intervention was again substantial in 1985, when the dollar's exchange value was deemed unacceptably high, hurting the competitiveness of U.S. producers. The most extensive U.S. intervention operations took place after the Louvre Accord of 1987, when the major industrial nations reached informal understandings about the limits of tolerance for exchange-rate fluctuations.

Exchange-Rate Stabilization and Monetary Policy

We have seen how central banks can buy and sell foreign currencies to stabilize their values under a system of managed floating exchange rates. Another stabilization technique involves a nation's *monetary policy*. As we shall see, stabilizing a currency's exchange value requires the central bank to adopt (1) an *expansionary* monetary policy to offset currency *appreciation*, and (2) a *contractionary* monetary policy to offset currency *depreciation*.

Figure 15.5 illustrates the foreign-exchange market for the United States. Assume the supply schedule of UK pounds is denoted by S_0 and the demand schedule of pounds is denoted by D_0. The equilibrium exchange rate, at which the quantity of pounds supplied and the quantity demanded are equalized, is $2 per pound.

FIGURE 15.5

EXCHANGE-RATE STABILIZATION AND MONETARY POLICY

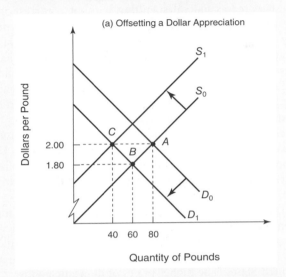

(a) Offsetting a Dollar Appreciation

(b) Offsetting a Dollar Depreciation

In the absence of international policy coordination, stabilizing a currency's exchange value requires a central bank to initiate (a) an expansionary monetary policy to offset an appreciation of its currency, and (b) a contractionary monetary policy to offset a depreciation of its currency.

Suppose that as a result of production shutdowns in the United Kingdom, caused by labor strikes, U.S. residents purchase fewer UK products and therefore demand fewer pounds. Let the demand for pounds decrease from D_0 to D_1 in Figure 15.5(a). In the absence of central-bank intervention, the dollar price of the pound falls from $2 to $1.80; the dollar thus appreciates against the pound.

To offset the appreciation of the dollar, the Federal Reserve can increase the supply of money in the United States, which will decrease domestic interest rates in the short term. The reduced interest rates will cause the foreign demand for U.S. securities to decline. Fewer pounds will thus be supplied to the foreign-exchange market to buy dollars with which to purchase U.S. securities. As the supply of pounds shifts leftward to S_1, the dollar's exchange value reverts to $2 per pound. In this manner, the expansionary monetary policy has offset the dollar's appreciation.

Referring now to Figure 15.5(b), suppose a temporary surge in UK interest rates causes U.S. investors to demand additional pounds with which to purchase additional UK securities. Let the demand for pounds rise from D_0 to D_1. In the absence of central-bank intervention, the dollar's exchange value would rise from $2 to $2.20 per pound; the dollar has depreciated against the pound.

To offset this dollar depreciation, the Federal Reserve can decrease the supply of money in the United States, which will increase domestic interest rates and attract UK investment. More pounds will thus be supplied to the foreign-exchange market to purchase dollars with which to buy U.S. securities. As the supply of pounds increases from S_0 to S_1, the dollar's exchange value reverts to $2 per pound. The contractionary monetary policy thus helps offset the dollar depreciation.

These examples illustrate how domestic monetary policies can be used to stabilize currency values. However, such policies are not without costs, as seen in the following example.

Suppose the U.S. government increases federal spending without a corresponding increase in taxes. To finance the resulting budget deficit, assume the government borrows funds from the money market, which raises domestic interest rates. High U.S. interest rates enhance the attractiveness of dollar-denominated securities, leading to increased foreign purchases of these assets, an increased demand for dollars, and an appreciation in the dollar's exchange value. The appreciating dollar makes U.S. goods more expensive overseas and foreign goods less expensive in the United States, thus causing the U.S. trade account to fall into deficit.

Now suppose the Federal Reserve intervenes and adopts an expansionary monetary policy. The resulting increase in the supply of money dampens the rise in U.S. interest rates and the dollar's appreciation. By restraining the increase in the dollar's exchange value, the expansionary monetary policy enhances the competitiveness of U.S. businesses and keeps the U.S. trade account in balance.

However, the favorable effects of the expansionary monetary policy on the domestic economy are temporary. When pursued indefinitely (over the long term), a policy of increasing the domestic money supply leads to a *weakening* in the U.S. trade position, because the monetary expansion required to offset the dollar's appreciation eventually promotes higher prices in the United States. The higher prices of domestic goods offset the benefits of U.S. competitiveness that initially occur under the monetary expansion. American spending eventually shifts back to foreign products and away from domestically produced goods, causing the U.S. trade account to fall into deficit.

This example shows how monetary policy can be used to stabilize the dollar's exchange value in the short term. But when monetary expansion occurs on a sustained, long-term basis, it brings with it eventual price increases that nullify the initial gains in domestic competitiveness. The long-term effectiveness of using monetary policy to stabilize the dollar's exchange value is limited, because the increase in the money supply to offset the dollar's appreciation does not permanently correct the underlying cause of the trade deficit—the increase in domestic spending.

Attempting to stabilize both the domestic economy and the dollar's exchange value can be difficult for the Federal Reserve. In early 1995, for example, the dollar was taking a nosedive against the yen, and the U.S. economy showed signs of slowing. To boost the dollar's exchange value would have required the Federal Reserve to adopt a restrictive monetary policy, which would have led to higher interest rates and net investment inflows. However, further increases in domestic interest rates would heighten the danger that the U.S. economy would be pushed into a recession by the next year. The Federal Reserve thus had to choose between supporting domestic economic expansion or the dollar's exchange value. In this case, the Federal Reserve adopted a policy of lower interest rates, thus appearing to respond to U.S. domestic needs.

Is Exchange-Rate Stabilization Effective?

Many governments have intervened in foreign-exchange markets to try to dampen volatility and to slow or reverse currency movements.[3] Their concern is that excessive

---

[3]This section is drawn from Michael Hutchinson, "Is Official Foreign Exchange Intervention Effective?" *Economic Letter*, Federal Reserve Bank of San Francisco, July 18, 2003.

short-term volatility and longer-term swings in exchange rates that "overshoot" values justified by fundamental conditions may hurt their economies, particularly sectors heavily involved in international trade. And, the foreign-exchange market can be volatile. For example, one euro cost about $1.15 in January 1999, then dropped to $0.85 by the end of 2000, only to climb to over $1.18 in June 2003. Over this same period, one U.S. dollar bought as much as 133 yen and as little as 102 yen, a 30 percent fluctuation. Many other currencies have also experienced similarly large price swings in recent years.

Many central banks intervene in foreign-exchange markets. The largest player is Japan. Between 1991 and 2000, for example, the Bank of Japan bought U.S. dollars on 168 occasions for a cumulative amount of $304 billion and sold U.S. dollars on 33 occasions for a cumulative amount of $38 billion. A typical case: On April 3, 2000, the Bank of Japan purchased $13.2 billion in the foreign-exchange market in an attempt to stop the more than four percent depreciation of the dollar against the yen that had occurred during the previous week. Japan's intervention magnitudes dwarf all other countries' official intervention in the foreign-exchange market. For example, it exceeded U.S. intervention in the 1991–2000 period by a factor of more than 30. However, compared to overall market transactions in the foreign-exchange market, the magnitude of Japan's interventions has been quite small.

Not surprisingly, intervention supported by central bank interest rate changes tends to have an even larger impact on exchange rates than intervention alone. Moreover, cases where intervention was coordinated between two central banks, such as the Federal Reserve and the Bank of Japan, had a larger impact on exchange rates than unilateral foreign-exchange operations. However, episodes of coordinated intervention are rather rare.

Academic researchers have often questioned the usefulness of official foreign-exchange intervention. However, proponents of foreign-exchange intervention note that it may be useful when the exchange rate is under speculative attack; that is, when a change in the exchange rate is not justified by fundamentals. It may also be helpful in coordinating private-sector expectations. Recent research provides some support for the short-term effectiveness of intervention. However, this should not be interpreted as a rationale for intervention as a long-term management tool.[4]

The Crawling Peg

Instead of adopting fixed or floating rates, why not try a compromise approach, the **crawling peg**. This system has been used by nations including Bolivia, Brazil, Costa Rica, Nicaragua, Solomon Islands, and Peru. The crawling-peg system means that a nation makes small, frequent changes in the par value of its currency to correct balance-of-payments disequilibriums. Deficit and surplus nations both keep adjusting until the desired exchange-rate level is attained. The term *crawling peg* implies that par-value changes are implemented in a large number of small steps, making the process of exchange-rate adjustment continuous for all practical purposes. The peg thus crawls from one par value to another.

---

[4]Michael Hutchinson, "Intervention and Exchange Rate Stabilization Policy in Developing Countries," *International Finance* 6, 2003, pp. 41–59.

The crawling-peg mechanism has been used primarily by nations having high inflation rates. Some developing nations, mostly South American, have recognized that a pegging system can operate in an inflationary environment only if there is provision for frequent changes in the par values. Associating national inflation rates with international competitiveness, these nations have generally used price indicators as a basis for adjusting crawling pegged rates. In these nations, the primary concern is the criterion that governs exchange-rate movements, rather than the currency or basket of currencies against which the peg is defined.

The crawling peg differs from the system of adjustable pegged rates. Under the adjustable peg, currencies are tied to a par value that changes infrequently (perhaps once every several years) but suddenly, usually in large jumps. The idea behind the crawling peg is that a nation can make small, frequent changes in par values, perhaps several times a year, so that they creep along slowly in response to evolving market conditions.

Supporters of the crawling peg argue that the system combines the flexibility of floating rates with the stability usually associated with fixed rates. They contend that a system providing continuous, steady adjustments is more responsive to changing competitive conditions and avoids a main problem of adjustable pegged rates—that changes in par values are frequently wide of the mark. Moreover, small, frequent changes in par values made at random intervals frustrate speculators with their irregularity.

In recent years, the crawling-peg formula has been used by developing nations facing rapid and persistent inflation. However, the IMF has generally contended that such a system would not be in the best interests of nations such as the United States or Germany, which bear the responsibility for international currency levels. The IMF has felt that it would be hard to apply such a system to the industrialized nations, whose currencies serve as a source of international liquidity. Although even the most ardent proponents of the crawling peg admit that the time for its widespread adoption has not yet come, the debate over its potential merits is bound to continue.

Currency Crises

A shortcoming of the international monetary system is that major currency crises have been a common occurrence in recent years. A **currency crisis**, also called a **speculative attack**, is a situation in which a weak currency experiences heavy selling pressure. There are several possible indications of selling pressure. One is sizable losses in the foreign reserves held by a country's central bank. Another is depreciating exchange rates in the forward market, where buyers and sellers promise to exchange currency at some future date rather than immediately. Finally, in extreme cases where inflation is running rampant, selling pressure consists of widespread flight out of domestic currency into foreign currency or into goods that people think will retain value, such as gold or real estate. Experience shows that currency crises can decrease the growth of a country's gross domestic product by six percent, or more. That is like losing one or two years of economic growth in most countries. Table 15.5 provides examples of currency crises.

A currency crisis ends when selling pressure stops. One way to end pressure is to devalue, that is, establish a new exchange rate at a sufficiently depreciated level. For example, Mexico's central bank might stop exchanging pesos for dollars at the previous rate of 10 pesos per dollar and set a new level of 20 pesos per dollar.

TABLE 15.5

EXAMPLES OF CURRENCY CRISES

- **Mexico, December 1994–1995**. Mexico's central bank maintained the value of the peso within a band that depreciated four percent a year against the U.S. dollar. In order to reduce interest rates on its debt, the Mexican government in April 1994 began issuing debt linked to the dollar. The amount of this debt soon exceeded the central bank's falling foreign-exchange reserves. Unrest in the province of Chiapas led to a speculative attack on the peso. Although the government devalued the peso by 15 percent by widening the band, the crisis continued. The government then let the peso float; it depreciated from 3.46 per dollar before the crisis to more than 7 per dollar. To end the crisis, Mexico received pledges for $49 billion in loans from the U.S. government and the IMF. Mexico's economy suffered a depression and banking problem that led to government rescues.

- **Russia, 1998**. The Russian government was paying high interest rates on its short-term debt. Falling prices for oil, a major export, and a weak economy also contributed to speculative attacks against the ruble, which had an official crawling band with the U.S. dollar. Although the IMF approved loans for Russia of about $11 billion and the Russian government widened the band for the ruble by 35 percent, the crisis continued. This crisis led to the floating of the ruble and its depreciation against the dollar by about 20 percent. Russia went into recession and experienced a burst of inflation. Many banks became insolvent. The government defaulted on its ruble-denominated debt and imposed a moratorium on private-sector payments of foreign debt.

- **Turkey, 2001**. The Turkish lira had an IMF-designed official crawling peg against the U.S. dollar. In November 2000, rumors about a criminal investigation into ten government-run banks led to a speculative attack on the lira. Interbank interest rates rose to 2,000 percent. The central bank then intervened. Eight banks became insolvent and were taken over by the government. The central bank's intervention had violated Turkey's agreement with the IMF, yet the IMF lent Turkey $10 billion. In February 2001, a public dispute between the president and prime minister caused investors to lose confidence in the stability of Turkey's coalition government. Interbank interest rates rose to 7,500 percent. Thus, the government let the lira float. The lira depreciated from 668,000 per dollar before the crisis to 1.6 million per dollar by October 2001. The economy of Turkey stagnated and inflation skyrocketed to 60 percent.

Source: From Kurt Schuler, *Why Currency Crises Happen*, Joint Economic Committee, U.S. Congress, January 2002.

Another way to end selling pressure is to adopt a floating exchange rate. Floating permits the exchange rate to "find its own level," which is almost always depreciated compared to the previous pegged rate. Devaluation and allowing depreciation make foreign currency and foreign goods more costly in terms of domestic currency, which tends to decrease demand for foreign currency, ending the imbalance that triggered selling pressure. However, in some cases, especially when confidence in the currency is low, the crisis continues, and further rounds of devaluation or depreciation occur.

Currency crises that end in devaluations or accelerated depreciations are sometimes called **currency crashes**. Not all crises end in crashes. A way of trying to end the selling pressure of a crisis without suffering a crash is to impose restrictions on the ability of people to buy and sell foreign currency. However, these controls create profit opportunities for people who discover how to evade them, so over time controls lose effectiveness unless enforced by an intrusive bureaucracy. Another way to end selling pressure is to obtain a loan to bolster the foreign reserves of the monetary authority. Countries that wish to bolster their foreign reserves often ask the IMF for loans. Although the loan can help temporarily, it may just delay rather than end selling pressure. The final way to end selling pressure is to restore confidence in the existing exchange rate, such as by announcing appropriate and credible changes in monetary policy.

Sources of Currency Crises

Why do currency crises occur?[5] A popular explanation is that big currency speculators instigate the crises for their own profit. The world's best-known currency speculator, George Soros, made $2 billion in 1992 by speculating against European currencies. However, speculation can also result in substantial losses. George Soros retired in 2000 after suffering the effects of losing almost $2 billion as the result of unsuccessful speculations. However, currency speculation is not just an activity of big speculators. Millions of ordinary people also speculate in the form of holding foreign currency in their wallets, under their mattresses, and the like. Millions of small speculators can move markets like the big speculators do. Simply put, currency crises are not simply caused by big currency speculators who arise out of nowhere. There must be an underlying reason for a currency crisis to occur.

One source for a currency crisis is budget deficits financed by inflation. If the government cannot easily finance its budget deficits by raising taxes or borrowing, it may pressure the central bank to finance them by creating money. Creating money can increase the supply of money faster than demand is growing, thus causing inflation. Budget deficits financed by inflation seemed to capture the essentials of many currency crises up through the 1980s. By the 1990s, however, this explanation appeared to be lacking. During the currency crises in Europe in 1992–1993, budget deficits in most adversely affected countries were small and sustainable. Moreover, most East Asian countries affected by the currency crisis of 1997–1998 were running budget surpluses and realizing strong economic growth. Economists have thus looked for other explanations for currency crises.

Currency crises may also be caused by weak financial systems. Weak banks can trigger speculative attacks if people think the central bank will rescue the banks even at the cost of spending much of its foreign reserves to do so. The explicit or implicit promise to rescue the banks is a form of moral hazard—a situation in which people do not pay the full cost of their own mistakes. As people become apprehensive about the future value of the local currency, they sell it to obtain more stable foreign currencies.

Some of the major currency crises of the last 20 years have occurred in countries that had recently deregulated their financial systems. Many governments formerly used financial regulations to channel investment into politically favored outlets. In return, they restricted competition among banks, life insurance companies, and the like. Profits from restricted competition subsidized unprofitable government-directed investments. Deregulation altered the picture by reducing the government direction of investments and allowing more competition among institutions. However, governments failed to ensure that in the new environment of greater freedom to reap the rewards of success, financial institutions also bore greater responsibility for failure. Therefore, financial institutions made mistakes in the unfamiliar environment of deregulation, failed, and were rescued at public expense. This rescue resulted in public fears about the future value of the local currency and the selling of it to obtain more stable foreign currencies.

A weak economy can trigger a currency crisis by creating doubt about the determination of the government and the central bank to continue with the current

---

[5]Kurt Schuler, *Why Currency Crises Happen*, Joint Economic Committee, U.S. Congress, January 2002.

monetary policy if weakness continues. A weak economy is characterized by falling GDP growth per person, a rising unemployment rate, a falling stock market, and falling export growth. If the public expects the central bank to increase the money supply to stimulate the economy, it may become apprehensive about the future value of the local currency and begin selling it on currency markets.

Political factors can also cause currency crises. Developing countries have historically been more prone to currency crises than developed countries because they tend to have a weaker rule of law, governments more prone to being overthrown by force, central banks that are not politically independent, and other characteristics that create political uncertainty about monetary policy.

External factors can be another source for a currency crisis. For example, an increase in interest rates in major international currencies can trigger a currency crisis if a central bank resists increasing the interest rate it charges. Funds may flow out of the local currency into foreign currency, decreasing the central bank's reserves to unacceptably low levels and therefore putting pressure on the government to devalue its currency if the currency is pegged. Moreover, a big external shock that disrupts the economy, such as war or a spike in the price of imported oil, can likewise trigger a currency crisis. External shocks have been key features in many currency crises historically.

Also, the choice of an exchange-rate system affects whether and how currency crises occur. In recent years, fixing the value of the domestic currency to that of a large, low-inflation country has become popular. It helps to keep inflation under control by linking the inflation rate for internationally traded goods to that found in the anchor country. For example, prior to 2002, the exchange rate for the Argentine peso was pegged at one peso per U.S. dollar. Therefore, a bushel of corn sold on the world market at $4 had its price set at 4 pesos. If the public expects this exchange rate to be unchangeable, then the fixed rate has the extra advantage of anchoring inflation expectations for Argentina to the inflation rate in the United States, a relatively low-inflation country.

In spite of the advantage of promoting relatively low inflation, a fixed exchange-rate system makes countries vulnerable to speculative attacks on their currencies. Recall that preservation of fixed exchange rates requires the government to purchase or sell domestic currency for foreign currency at the target rate of exchange. This requirement forces the central bank to maintain a sufficient quantity of international reserves in order to fulfill the demand by the public to sell domestic currency for foreign currency at the fixed exchange rate. If the public thinks that the central bank's supply of international reserves has decreased to the level where the ability to fulfill the demand to sell domestic currency for foreign currency at a fixed exchange rate is doubted, then a devaluation of the domestic currency is anticipated. This anticipation can result in a speculative attack on the central bank's remaining holdings of international reserves. The attack consists of huge sales of domestic currency for foreign currency so that the decrease in international reserves is expedited, and devaluation results from the decline in reserves. It is no wonder that the most important recent currency crises have happened to countries having fixed exchange rates but demonstrating a lack of political will to correct previous economic problems.

Next, we will examine how the speculative attacks on East Asian currencies contributed to a major currency crisis.

Speculators Attack East Asian Currencies

After more than a decade of maintaining the Thai baht's peg to the U.S. dollar, Thai authorities abandoned the peg in July 1997.[6] By October, market forces had led the baht to depreciate by 60 percent against the dollar. The depreciation triggered a wave of speculation against other Southeast Asian currencies. Over the same period, the Indonesian rupiah, Malaysia ringgit, Philippine peso, and South Korean won abandoned links to the dollar and depreciated 47, 35, 34, and 16 percent, respectively. This episode reopened one of the oldest debates in economics: whether a currency should have a fixed or floating exchange rate. Consider the case of Thailand.

Although Thailand was widely regarded as one of Southeast Asia's outstanding performers throughout the 1980s and 1990s, it relied heavily on inflows of short-term foreign capital, attracted both by the stable baht and by Thai interest rates, which were much higher than comparable interest rates elsewhere. The capital inflow supported a broad-based economic boom that was especially visible in the real estate market.

However, by 1996, Thailand's economic boom had fizzled. As a result, both local and foreign investors grew nervous and began withdrawing funds from Thailand's financial system, which put downward pressure on the baht. However, the Thai government resisted the depreciation pressure by purchasing baht with dollars in the foreign-exchange market and also raising interest rates, which increased the attractiveness of the baht. But the purchases of the baht greatly depleted Thailand's reserves of hard currency. Moreover, raising interest rates adversely affected an already weak financial sector by dampening economic activity. These factors ultimately contributed to the abandonment of the baht's link to the dollar.

Although Thailand and other Southeast Asian countries abandoned fixed exchange rates in 1997, some economists questioned whether such a policy would be in their best interest in the long term. Their reasoning was that these economies were relatively small and wide open to international trade and investment flows. Moreover, inflation rates were modest by the standards of a developing country, and labor markets were relatively flexible. In other words, floating exchange rates were probably not the best long-term option. Indeed, these economists maintained that unless the Southeast Asian governments anchored their currencies to something, their currencies might drift into a vicious cycle of depreciation and higher inflation. There was certainly a concern that central banks in the region lacked the credibility to enforce tough monetary policies without the external constraint of a fixed exchange rate. Simply put, neither fixed exchange rates nor floating exchange rates offer a magical solution. What really makes a difference to a country's prospects is the quality of its overall economic policies.

Capital Controls

Because capital flows have often been an important element in currency crises, controls on capital movements have been established to support fixed exchange rates and thus avoid speculative attacks on currencies. **Capital controls**, also known as

---

[6]Ramon Moreno, "Lessons from Thailand," *Economic Letter*, Federal Reserve Bank of San Francisco, November 7, 1997.

exchange controls, are government-imposed barriers to foreign savers investing in domestic assets (for example, government securities, stock, or bank deposits) or to domestic savers investing in foreign assets. At one extreme, a government may seek to gain control over its payments position by directly circumventing market forces through the imposition of direct controls on international transactions. For example, a government that has a virtual monopoly over foreign-exchange dealings may require that all foreign-exchange earnings be turned over to authorized dealers. The government then allocates foreign exchange among domestic traders and investors at government-set prices.

The advantage of such a system is that the government can influence its payments position by regulating the amount of foreign exchange allocated to imports or capital outflows, limiting the extent of these transactions. Capital controls also permit the government to encourage or discourage certain transactions by offering different rates for foreign currency for different purposes. Furthermore, capital controls can give domestic monetary and fiscal policies greater freedom in their stabilization roles. By controlling the balance of payments through capital controls, a government can pursue its domestic economic policies without fear of balance-of-payments repercussions.

Speculative attacks in Mexico and East Asia were fueled in part by large changes in capital outflows and inflows. As a result, some economists and politicians argued for restrictions on capital mobility in developing countries. For example, Malaysian Prime Minister Mahathir imposed limits on capital outflows in 1998 to help his economy regain financial stability.

Although restrictions on capital outflows may seem attractive, they suffer from several problems. Evidence suggests that capital outflows may further increase after the controls are implemented, because confidence in the government is weakened. Also, restrictions on capital outflows often result in evasion, as government officials get paid to ignore domestic residents who shift funds overseas. Finally, capital controls may provide government officials the false sense of security that they do not have to reform their financial systems to ameliorate the crisis.

Although economists are generally dubious of controls on capital outflows, controls on capital inflows often receive more support. Supporters contend that if speculative capital cannot enter a country, then it cannot suddenly leave and create a crisis. They note that the financial crisis in East Asia in 1997–1998 illustrated how capital inflows can result in a lending boom, excessive risk taking by domestic banks, and ultimately financial collapse. However, restrictions on the inflow of capital are problematic because they can prevent funds that would be used to finance productive investment opportunities from entering a country. Also, limits on capital inflows are seldom effective because the private sector finds ways to evade them and move funds into the country.[7]

Should Foreign-Exchange Transactions Be Taxed?

The 1997–1998 financial crises in East Asia, in which several nations were forced to abandon their fixed exchange-rate regimes, produced demands for more stability and

[7]Sebastian Edwards, "How Effective Are Capital Controls?" *Journal of Economic Perspective*, Winter 2000, Vol. 13, No. 4, pp. 65–84.

government regulation in the foreign-exchange markets. Indeed, market volatility was blamed for much of the trouble sweeping the region.

Economists generally argue that the free market is the best device for determining how money should be invested. Global capital markets provide needy countries with funds to grow, while permitting foreign investors to diversify their portfolios. If capital is allowed to flow freely, they contend, markets will reward countries that pursue sound economic policies and will pressure the rest to do the same. Indeed, most countries welcome and even encourage capital inflows such as foreign direct investment in factories and businesses, which represent long-lasting commitments. But some have become skeptical of financial instruments such as stocks and bonds, bank deposits, and short-term debt securities, which can be pulled out of a country with a stroke of a computer key. That's what occurred in East Asia in 1997, in Mexico in 1994 and 1995, and in the United Kingdom and Italy in 1992 and 1993.

To prevent international financial crises, several notable economists have called for sand to be thrown in the wheels of international finance by imposing a tax on foreign-exchange transactions. The idea is that a tax would increase the cost of these transactions, which would discourage massive responses to minor changes in information about the economic situation and thus dampen volatility in exchange rates. Proponents argue that such a tax would give traders an incentive to look at long-term economic trends, not short-term hunches, when buying and selling foreign exchange and securities. Traders would pay a small tax, say, 0.1 percent for every transaction, so they would not buy or sell unless expected returns justified the additional expense. Fewer transactions suggest less volatility and more stable exchange rates.

Proponents of a tax may well contend that they are not trying to interfere with free markets, but only to prevent excess volatility. However, we do not know how much volatility is excessive or irrational. It's true that economists cannot explain all exchange-rate volatility in terms of changes in the economic fundamentals of nations, but it does not follow from this that we should seek to regulate such fluctuations. Indeed, some of the volatility may be produced by uncertainty about government policies.

There are other drawbacks to the idea of taxing foreign-exchange transactions. Such a tax could impose a burden on countries that are quite rationally borrowing overseas. By raising the cost of capital for these countries, it would discourage investment and hinder their development. Also, a tax on foreign-exchange transactions would be difficult to implement. Foreign-exchange trading can be conducted almost anywhere in the world, and a universal agreement to impose such a tax seems extremely unlikely. Those countries that refused to implement the tax would become centers for foreign-exchange trading.

Increasing the Credibility of Fixed Exchange Rates

As we have learned, when speculators feel that a central bank is unable to defend the exchange rate for a weakening currency, they will sell the local currency to obtain more stable foreign currencies. Are there ways to convince speculators that the exchange rate is unchangeable? Currency boards and dollarization are explicitly intended to maintain fixed exchange rates and thus prevent currency crises.

Currency Board

A **currency board** is a monetary authority that issues notes and coins convertible into a foreign anchor currency at a *fixed* exchange rate. The anchor currency is a currency chosen for its expected stability and international acceptability. For most currency boards, the U.S. dollar or the UK pound has been the anchor currency. Also, a few currency boards have used gold as the anchor. Usually, the fixed exchange rate is set by law, making changes to the exchange rate very costly for governments. Put simply, currency boards offer the strongest form of a fixed exchange rate that is possible short of full currency union.

The commitment to exchange domestic currency for foreign currency at a fixed exchange rate requires that the currency board have sufficient foreign exchange to honor this commitment. This condition means that its holdings of foreign exchange must at least equal 100 percent of its notes and coins in circulation, as set by law. A currency board can operate in place of a central bank or as a parallel issuer alongside an existing central bank. Usually, a currency board takes over the role of a central bank in strengthening the currency of a developing country.

By design, a currency board has no discretionary powers. Its operations are completely passive and automatic. The sole function of a currency board is to exchange its notes and coins for the anchor at a fixed rate. Unlike a central bank, a currency board does not lend to the domestic government, to domestic companies, or to domestic banks. In a currency-board system, the government can finance its spending only by taxing or borrowing, not by printing money and thereby creating inflation. This limitation results from the stipulation that the backing of the domestic currency must be at least 100 percent.

A country that adopts a currency board thus puts its monetary policy on autopilot. It is as if the chairman of the board of governors of the Federal Reserve System were replaced by a personal computer. When the anchor currency flows in, the board issues more domestic currency and interest rates fall; when the anchor currency flows out, interest rates rise. The government sits back and watches, even if interest rates skyrocket and a recession ensues.

Many economists maintain that, especially in the developing world, central banks are incapable of retaining nonpolitical independence and thus instill less confidence than is necessary for the smooth functioning of a monetary system. They are answerable to the prerogatives of populism or dictatorship and are at the beck and call of political changes. The bottom line is that central banks should not be given the onerous responsibility of maintaining the value of currencies. This job should be left to an independent body whose sole mandate is to issue currency against a strict and unalterable set of guidelines that require a fixed amount of foreign exchange or gold to be deposited for each unit of domestic currency issued.

Currency boards can confer considerable credibility on fixed exchange-rate regimes. The most vital contribution a currency board can make to exchange-rate stability is by imposing discipline on the process of money creation. This discipline results in the greater stability of domestic prices, which, in turn, stabilizes the value of the domestic currency. In short, the major benefits of the currency-board system are as follows:

- Making a nation's currency and exchange-rate regimes more rule-bound and predictable
- Placing an upper bound on the nation's base money supply

- Arresting any tendencies in an economy toward inflation
- Forcing the government to restrict its borrowing to what foreign and domestic lenders are willing to lend it at market interest rates
- Engendering confidence in the soundness of the nation's money, thus assuring citizens and foreign investors that the domestic currency can always be exchanged for some other strong currency
- Creating confidence and promoting trade, investment, and economic growth

Proponents cite Hong Kong as a country that has benefited from a currency board. In the early 1980s, Hong Kong had a floating exchange rate. The immediate cause of Hong Kong's economic problems was uncertainty about its political future. In 1982, the United Kingdom and China began talks about the fate of Hong Kong following the expiration of the United Kingdom's lease on the territory in 1997. Fear that China would abandon Hong Kong's capitalist system sent Hong Kong's stock market down by 50 percent. Hong Kong's real estate market weakened also, and small banks with heavy exposure in real estate suffered runs. The result was a 16 percent depreciation in the Hong Kong dollar against the U.S. dollar. With this loss of confidence, many merchants refused to accept Hong Kong dollars and quoted prices in U.S. dollars instead. Panic buying of vegetable oil, rice, and other staples emptied merchants' shelves.

In 1983, the government of Hong Kong ended its economic crises by announcing that Hong Kong would adopt a currency-board system. It pegged its exchange rate at HK$7.8 = US $1. The currency reform immediately reversed the loss of confidence about Hong Kong's economy despite continuing troubles in the U.K.-China discussions. A stable currency provided the basis for Hong Kong to continue its rapid economic growth.

By maintaining a legal commitment to exchange domestic currency for a foreign currency at a fixed exchange rate, and a commitment to issue currency only if it is backed by foreign reserves, a currency board can be a good way to restore confidence in a country gripped by economic chaos. Although a currency board cannot solve all of a country's economic problems, it may achieve more financial credibility than a domestic central bank can.

Although currency boards help discipline government spending, therefore reducing a major source of inflation in developing countries, there are concerns about currency boards. Perhaps the most common objection is that a currency board prevents a country from pursuing a discretionary monetary policy and thus reduces its economic independence. Also, it is sometimes said that a currency-board system is susceptible to financial panics because it lacks a lender of last resort. Another objection is that a currency-board system creates a colonial relation with the anchor currency. Critics cite the experiences of British colonies, which operated under currency-board systems in the early 1900s.

It is possible for a nation's monetary system to be orderly and disciplined under either a currency board or a central banking system. But neither system by itself guarantees either order or discipline. The effectiveness of both systems depends on other factors, such as fiscal discipline and a sound banking system. In other words, it is a whole network of responsible and mutually supporting policies and institutions that make for sound money and stable exchange rates. No monetary regime, however well conceived, can bear the entire burden alone.

For Argentina, No Panacea in a Currency Board

For much of the post-World War II era, when the financial press focused on Argentina, it was to highlight bouts of very high inflation and failed stabilization efforts. Hyperinflation was rampant in the 1970s and 1980s, and prices increased by more than 1,000 percent in both 1989 and 1990.

In 1991, to tame its tendency to finance public spending by printing pesos, Argentina introduced convertibility of its peso into dollars at a fixed one-to-one exchange rate. To control the issuance of money, the Argentines abandoned their central bank-based monetary regime, which they felt lacked credibility, and established a currency board. Under this arrangement, currency could be issued only if the currency board had an equivalent amount of dollars.

The fixed exchange rate and the currency board were designed to ensure that Argentina would have a low inflation rate, one similar to that in the United States. At first, this program appeared to work: By 1995, prices were rising at less than two percent per year.

However, during the late 1990s, the Argentine economy was hit with four external shocks: the appreciation of the dollar, which had the same negative effect on Argentine export- and import-competing industries that it had on similar industries in the United States; rising U.S. interest rates that spilled over into the Argentine economy, resulting in a decrease in spending on capital goods; falling commodity prices on world markets, which significantly harmed Argentina's commodity-exporting industries; and the depreciation of Brazil's real, which made Brazil's goods relatively cheaper in Argentina and Argentina's goods relatively more expensive in Brazil. These external shocks had a major deflationary effect on the Argentine economy, resulting in falling output and rising unemployment.

Argentina dealt with its problems by spending much more than it collected in taxes to bolster its economy. To finance its budget deficits, Argentina borrowed dollars on the international market. When further borrowing became impossible in 2001, Argentina defaulted, ended convertibility of pesos into dollars, and froze most deposits at banks. Violence and other protests erupted as Argentineans voiced their displeasure with politicians.

Some economists have questioned whether the establishment of a currency board was a mistake for Argentina. They note that although Argentina tied itself to the American currency area as if it were Utah or Massachusetts, it did not benefit from adjustment mechanisms that enable the American currency area to work smoothly in the face of negative external shocks. For example, when unemployment rose in Argentina, its people could not move to the United States where jobs were relatively plentiful. Also, Federal Reserve policy was geared to the conditions of the United States rather than to Argentina. Moreover, the U.S. Congress did not target American fiscal policy on problem areas in Argentina. As a result, the negative shocks to the Argentine economy were dealt with by wage and price deflation. It was a consequence of having fixed its currency rigidly to the dollar.

Dollarization

Instead of using a currency board to maintain fixed exchange rates, why not "dollarize" an economy? **Dollarization** occurs when residents of, say, Ecuador, use the U.S.

dollar alongside or instead of the sucre. Partial dollarization occurs when Ecuadoreans hold dollar-denominated bank deposits or Federal Reserve notes to protect against high inflation in the sucre. Partial dollarization has existed for years in many Latin American and Caribbean countries, where the United States is a major trading partner and a major source of foreign investment.

Full dollarization means the elimination of the Ecuadorean sucre and its complete replacement with the U.S. dollar. The monetary base of Ecuador, which initially consisted entirely of sucre-denominated currency, would be converted into U.S. Federal Reserve notes. To replace its currency, Ecuador would sell foreign reserves (mostly U.S. Treasury securities) to buy dollars and exchange all outstanding sucre notes for dollar notes. The U.S. dollar would be the sole legal tender and sole unit of account in Ecuador. Full dollarization has occurred in the U.S. Virgin Islands, the Marshall Islands, Puerto Rico, Guam, Ecuador, and other Latin American countries.

Full dollarization is rare today because of the symbolism countries attach to a national currency and the political impact of a perceived loss of sovereignty associated with the adoption of another country's unit of account and currency. When it does occur, it is principally implemented by small countries or territories that are closely associated politically, geographically, and/or through extensive economic and trade ties with the country whose currency is adopted.

Why Dollarize?

Why would a small country want to dollarize its economy? Benefits to the dollarizing country include the credibility and policy discipline that is derived from the implicit irrevocability of dollarization. Behind this lies the promise of lower interest and inflation rates, greater financial stability, and increased economic activity. Countries with a history of high inflation and financial instability often find the potential offered by dollarization to be quite attractive. Dollarization is considered to be one way of avoiding the capital outflows that often precede or accompany an embattled currency situation.

A major benefit of dollarization is the decrease in transaction costs as a result of a common currency. The elimination of currency risk and hedging allows for more trade and more investment within the unified currency zone to occur. Another benefit is in the area of inflation. The choice of another currency necessarily means that the rate of inflation in the dollarized economy will be tied to that of the issuing country. To the extent that a more accepted, stable, recognized currency is chosen, lower inflation now and in the future can be expected to result from dollarization. Also, greater openness results from a system where exchange controls are unnecessary and balance-of-payments crises are minimized. Dollarization will not assure an absence of balance-of-payments difficulties, but it does ensure that such crises will be handled in a way that forces a government to deal with events in an open manner, rather than by printing money and contributing to inflation.

Effects of Dollarization

A convenient way to think about any country that plans to adopt the dollar as its official currency is to treat it as one would treat any of the 50 states in the United States. Thus, in discussions about monetary policy in the United States, it is assumed that the Federal Reserve conducts monetary policy with reference to national economic conditions rather than the economic conditions in an individual state or region, even though economic conditions are not uniform throughout the country. The reason for this is that monetary policy works through interest rates on credit markets that are national in scope. Thus, monetary policy cannot be tailored to deal with business conditions in an individual state or region that is different from the national economy. When Ecuador dollarized its economy, it essentially accepted the monetary policy of the Federal Reserve.

With dollarization in Ecuador, U.S. monetary policy would presumably be carried out as it is now. If Ecuadorean business cycles do not coincide with those in the United States, Ecuador cannot count on the Federal Reserve to come to its rescue, just as any state in the United States cannot count on the Federal Reserve to come to its rescue. This limitation may be a major downside for the Ecuadoreans. Despite this, Ecuador might still be better off without the supposed safety valve of an independent monetary policy.

Another limitation facing the Ecuadoreans is that the Federal Reserve is not their lender of last resort as it is for Americans. That is, if the U.S. financial system should come under stress, the Federal Reserve could use its various monetary powers to aid these institutions and contain possible failures. Without the consent of the U.S. Congress, the Federal Reserve could not perform this function for Ecuador or for any other country that decided to adopt the dollar officially as its currency.

A third limitation arising from the adoption of the dollar as the official currency is that Ecuador could no longer get any **seigniorage** from its monetary system. This cost for Ecuador stems from the loss of the foreign reserves (mainly U.S. Treasury securities) that it can sell in exchange for dollars. These reserves bear interest and, therefore, are a source of income for Ecuador. This income is called seigniorage. But once Ecuador's reserves are replaced by dollar bills, this source of income disappears.

With dollarization, Ecuador enjoys the same freedom that the 50 states in the United States enjoy as to how to spend its tax dollars. Ecuador state expenditures for education, police protection, social insurance, and the like are not affected by its use of the U.S. dollar. Also, Ecuador can establish its own tariffs, subsidies, and other trade policies. Therefore, Ecuador's sovereignty is not compromised in these areas. However, there is an overall constraint on Ecuadorean fiscal policy: Ecuador does not have the recourse of printing more sucre to finance budget deficits and thus has to exercise caution in its spending policies.

Official dollarization of Ecuador's economy also has implications for the United States. First, when Ecuadoreans acquire dollars they surrender goods and services to Americans. Therefore, for each dollar sent abroad, Americans enjoy a one-time increase in the amount of goods and services they are able to consume. Second, by opting to hold dollars rather than the interest-bearing debt of the United States, the United States, in effect, gets an interest-free loan from Ecuador. The interest that does not have to be paid is a measure of seigniorage that accrues on an annual basis to the United States. On the other hand, use of U.S. currency abroad might hinder the formulation and execution of monetary policy by the Federal Reserve. Also, by making Ecuador more dependent on U.S. monetary policy, dollarization could result in more pressure on the Federal Reserve to conduct policy according to the interests of Ecuador rather than those of the United States.

Economic crises tend to occur sporadically virtually every decade and in various countries ranging from Sweden to Argentina, from Russia to Korea, and from Japan to the United States. Each crisis is unique, yet each bears some resemblance to others. In general, economic crises have been caused by factors such as an overshooting of markets, excessive leveraging of debt, credit booms, miscalculations of risk, rapid outflows of capital from a country, and unsustainable macroeconomic policies.

Concerning the global economic crisis of 2007–2009, what began as a bursting of the U.S. housing market bubble and an increase in foreclosures ballooned into a global financial and economic crisis. Some of the largest and most venerable banks, investment houses, and insurance companies either declared bankruptcy or had to be rescued financially. In the automobile industry, General Motors and Chrysler declared bankruptcy and were nationalized by the U.S. government. Many blamed the United States for the crisis and saw it as an example of the excesses of a country that did not practice sound principles of finance.

The global economic crisis brought home an important point: the United States is a major center of the financial world. Regional financial crises, such as the Asian financial crisis of 1997–1998, can occur without seriously infecting the rest of the global financial system. But when the U.S. financial system stumbles, it tends to bring major parts of the rest of the world down with it. The reason is that the United States is the main guarantor of the international financial system, the provider of dollars widely used as currency reserves and as an international medium of exchange, and a contributor to much of the financial capital that sloshes around the world seeking higher yields. The rest of the world may not appreciate it, but a financial crisis in the United States often takes on a global aspect.

The financial crisis that began in the United States quickly spread to other industrial countries and also to emerging market and developing economies. Investors pulled capital from countries, even those with small levels of perceived risk, and caused values of stocks and domestic currencies to plunge. Also, slumping exports and commodity prices added to the woes, pushing economies worldwide into either recession or into a period of slow economic growth. As economies throughout the world deteriorated, it became clear that the United States and other countries could not export their way out of recession: There was no major economy that could play the role of an economic engine to pull other countries out of their economic doldrums.

The global crisis played out at two levels. The first was among the industrialized nations of the world where most of the losses from subprime mortgage debt, excessive leveraging of investments, and inadequate capital backing financial institutions have occurred. The second level of the crisis was among emerging market and other economies who were innocent bystanders to the crisis but who had weak economies that could be whipsawed by activities in global markets. These nations had insufficient sources of capital and thus had to turn to help from the International Monetary Fund, World Bank, and capital surplus nations such as Japan.

To cope with the global financial crisis, the United States and other countries attempted to control the contagion, minimize losses to society, restore confidence in financial institutions and instruments, and lubricate the wheels of the economy in order for it to return to full operation. To achieve these goals, countries such as the United States, China, South Korea, Spain, Sweden, and Germany enacted a variety of measures such as:

- Injecting capital through loans or stock purchases to prevent bankruptcy of financial institutions.
- Increasing deposit insurance limits in order to limit withdrawals from banks.
- Purchasing toxic debt of financial institutions on the verge of failure so that they would start lending again.
- Coordinating interest-rate reductions by central banks to inject liquidity into the economy.
- Enacting stimulative fiscal policies to bolster sagging aggregate demand.

At the G-20 Summit on Financial Markets and the World Economy in November of 2008, participating countries generally recognized that economic crisis was not merely an aberration that could be fixed by tweaking the system: Also, there appeared to be no international mechanism capable of coping with and preventing global crises from erupting. The countries concluded that major changes are needed in the global financial system to reduce risk, provide oversight, and to establish an early warning system of impending financial crises. However, needed reforms will be successful only if they are grounded in a commitment to free market principles. The extent to which the United States and other countries are willing to alter their financial systems remains to be seen.

Source: Dick Nanto, *The Global Financial Crisis: Analysis and Policy Implications*, April 3, 2009, Congressional Research Service, U.S. Library of Congress, Washington. D.C., U.S. Government Printing Office.

Summary

1. Most nations maintain neither completely fixed nor floating exchange rates. Contemporary exchange-rate systems generally embody some features of each of these standards.

2. Small, developing nations often anchor their currencies to a single currency or a currency basket. Anchoring to a single currency is generally used by small nations whose trade and financial relations are mainly with a single trading partner. Small nations with more than one major trading partner often anchor their currencies to a basket of currencies.

3. The special drawing right is a currency basket composed of the four key currencies of IMF members. The basket-valuation technique attempts to make the SDR's value more stable than the foreign-currency value of any single currency in the basket. Developing nations often choose to anchor their exchange rates to the SDR.

4. Under a fixed exchange-rate system, a government defines the official exchange rate for its currency. It then establishes an exchange-stabilization fund, which buys and sells foreign currencies to prevent the market exchange rate from moving above or below the official rate. Nations may officially devalue/revalue their currencies to restore trade equilibrium.

5. With floating exchange rates, market forces of supply and demand determine currency values. Among the major arguments for floating rates are (a) simplicity, (b) continuous adjustment, (c) independent domestic policies, and (d) reduced need for international reserves. Arguments against floating rates stress (a) disorderly exchange markets, (b) reckless financial policies on the part of governments, and (c) conduciveness to price inflation.

6. With the breakdown of the Bretton Woods system of fixed exchange rates, major industrial nations adopted a system of managed floating exchange rates. Under this system, central-bank intervention in the foreign-exchange market is intended to prevent disorderly market conditions in the short term. In the long term, exchange rates are permitted to float in accordance with changing supply and demand.

7. To offset a depreciation in the home currency's exchange value, a central bank can (a) use its international reserves to purchase quantities of that currency on the foreign-exchange market; or (b) initiate a contractionary monetary policy, which leads to higher domestic interest rates, increased investment inflows, and increased demand for the home currency. To offset an appreciation in the home currency's exchange value, a central bank can sell additional quantities of its currency on the foreign-exchange market or initiate an expansionary monetary policy.

8. Under a crawling-peg exchange-rate system, a nation makes frequent devaluations (or revaluations) of its currency to restore payments balance. Developing nations suffering from high inflation rates have been major users of this mechanism.

9. A currency crisis, also called a *speculative attack*, is a situation in which a weak currency experiences heavy selling pressure. Among the causes of currency crises are budget deficits financed by inflation, weak financial systems, political uncertainty, and changes in interest rates on world markets. Although a fixed exchange-rate system has the advantage of promoting low inflation, it is especially vulnerable to speculative attacks.

10. Capital controls are sometimes used by governments in an attempt to support fixed exchange rates and prevent speculative attacks on currencies. However, capital controls are hindered by the private sector's finding ways to evade them and move funds into or out of a country.

11. Currency boards and dollarization are explicitly intended to maintain fixed exchange rates and thus prevent currency crises. A currency board is a monetary authority that issues notes and coins convertible into a foreign currency at a fixed exchange rate. The most vital contribution a currency board can make to exchange-rate stability is to impose discipline on the process of money creation. This discipline results in greater stability in domestic prices which, in turn, stabilizes the value of the domestic currency. Dollarization occurs when residents of a country use the U.S. dollar alongside or instead of their own

currency. Dollarization is seen as a way to protect a country's growth and prosperity from bouts of inflation, currency depreciation, and speculative attacks against the local currency.

Key Concepts & Terms

- Adjustable pegged exchange rates (p. 515)
- Bretton Woods system (p. 515)
- Capital controls (p. 530)
- Clean float (p. 520)
- Crawling peg (p. 525)
- Currency board (p. 533)
- Currency crashes (p. 527)
- Currency crisis (p. 526)
- Devaluation (p. 513)
- Dirty float (p. 520)
- Dollarization (p. 535)
- Exchange controls (p. 531)
- Exchange rates (p. 517)
- Exchange-stabilization fund (p. 512)
- Fixed exchange rates (p. 510)
- Floating exchange rates (p. 517)
- Fundamental disequilibrium (p. 512)
- Impossible trinity (p. 509)
- Key currency (p. 510)
- Leaning against the wind (p. 520)
- Managed floating system (p. 520)
- Official exchange rate (p. 511)
- Par value (p. 511)
- Revaluation (p. 513)
- Seigniorage (p. 537)
- Special drawing right (SDR) (p. 511)
- Speculative attack (p. 526)
- Target exchange rates (p. 521)

Study Questions

1. What is the purpose of capital controls?
2. What is the purpose of a currency devaluation? What about a currency revaluation?
3. Why do nations use a crawling-peg-exchange-rate system?
4. What techniques can a central bank use to stabilize the exchange value of its currency?
5. Discuss the philosophy and operation of the Bretton Woods system of adjustable pegged exchange rates.
6. Present the case for and the case against a system of floating exchange rates.
7. Why do some developing countries adopt currency boards? Why do others dollarize their monetary systems?
8. What advantage does the SDR offer to small nations seeking to peg their exchange rates?
9. How do managed floating exchange rates operate? Why were they adopted by the industrialized nations in 1973?
10. Why do small nations adopt currency baskets against which they peg their exchange rates?
11. What factors underlie a nation's decision to adopt floating exchange rates or fixed exchange rates?
12. What factors contribute to currency crises?

Macroeconomic Policy in an Open Economy

Since the Great Depression of the 1930s, governments have actively pursued the goal of a fully employed economy with price stability. They have used fiscal and monetary policies to achieve this goal. A nation that has a closed economy (one that is not exposed to international trade and financial flows) could use these policies in view of its own goals. However, with an open economy, the nation finds that the success of these policies depends on factors such as its exports and imports of goods and services, the international mobility of financial capital, and the flexibility of its exchange rate. These factors can support or detract from the ability of monetary and fiscal policy to achieve full employment with price stability.

This chapter considers macroeconomic policy in an open economy. The chapter first examines the way in which monetary and fiscal policy are supposed to operate in a closed economy. The chapter then describes the effect of an open economy on monetary and fiscal policy.

Economic Objectives of Nations

What are the objectives of macroeconomic policy? Since the Great Depression of the 1930s, governments have actively pursued the goal of economic stability at full employment. Known as **internal balance**, this goal has two dimensions: a fully employed economy and no inflation; or, more realistically, a reasonable amount of inflation. Nations traditionally have considered internal balance to be of primary importance and have formulated economic policies to attain this goal. Policymakers are also aware of a nation's current-account position. A nation is said to be in **external balance** when it realizes neither deficits nor surpluses in its current account. And, an economy realizes **overall balance** when it attains internal balance and external balance.

Besides pursuing internal and external balance, nations have other economic goals such as long-term economic growth and a reasonably equitable distribution of national income. Although these and other commitments may influence macroeconomic policy, the discussion in this chapter is confined to the pursuit of internal and external balance.

Policy Instruments

To attain external and internal balance, policymakers enact expenditure-changing policies, expenditure-switching policies, and direct controls.

Expenditure-changing policies alter the level of total spending (aggregate demand) for goods and services, including those produced domestically and those imported. They include **fiscal policy**, which refers to changes in government spending and taxes, and **monetary policy**, which refers to changes in the money supply and interest rates by a nation's central bank (such as the Federal Reserve). Depending on the direction of change, expenditure-changing policies are either expenditure increasing or reducing.

Expenditure-switching policies modify the direction of demand, shifting it between domestic output and imports. Under a system of fixed exchange rates, a nation with a trade deficit could devalue its currency to increase the international competitiveness of its firms, thus diverting spending from foreign-produced goods to domestically produced goods. To increase its competitiveness under a managed floating exchange-rate system, a nation could purchase other currencies with its currency, thereby causing its currency's exchange value to depreciate. The success of these policies in promoting trade balance largely depends on switching demand in the proper direction and amount, as well as on the capacity of the home economy to meet the additional demand by supplying more goods.

Direct controls consist of government restrictions on the market economy. They are selective expenditure-switching policies whose objective is to control particular items in the current account. Direct controls, such as tariffs, are levied on imports in an attempt to switch domestic spending away from foreign-produced goods to domestically-produced goods. Direct controls may also be used to restrain capital outflows or to stimulate capital inflows.

The formation of macroeconomic policy is subject to constraints that involve considerations of fairness and equity. Policymakers are aware of the needs of groups they represent, such as labor and business, especially when pursuing conflicting economic objectives. For example, to what extent should the domestic interest rate rise in order to eliminate a deficit in the capital account? The outcry of adversely affected groups within the nation, that suffer from a high interest rate, may be more than sufficient to convince policymakers not to pursue capital account balance. Reflecting perceptions of fairness and equity, policy formation tends to be characterized by negotiation and compromise.

Aggregate Demand and Aggregate Supply: A Brief Review

In your principles of macroeconomics course, you learned about a model that can be used to analyze the output and price level of an economy in the short term. This model is called the aggregate demand-aggregate supply model. Using the framework of Figure 16.1, let us review the main characteristics of this model as applied to Canada.

MONETARY AND FISCAL POLICY RESPOND TO FINANCIAL TURMOIL IN THE ECONOMY

TRADE CONFLICTS

Following six consecutive years of expansion, the U.S. economy peaked in December 2007, beginning a recession that continued throughout 2008 and 2009. This was triggered by breakdowns in key credit markets that posed great risk to the financial system and the broader economy.

The Federal Reserve responded with unprecedented measures to unclog credit markets and free up the financial flows vital to a well-functioning economy. Besides lowering the federal funds rate target to virtually zero, the Federal Reserve expanded its role as lender of last resort by providing credit to banks and other financial institutions as well as businesses that were unable to secure adequate credit accommodations from banking institutions.

To provide additional stimulus to the weakening economy, the U.S. government enacted the Economic Stimulus Act of 2008. It was designed to provide temporary (one-time) tax rebates to those lower- and middle-income individuals and households who would immediately spend it. About $113 billion was dispensed, which amounted to about 0.8 percent of GDP. The government hoped that the tax rebates would burn such a hole in peoples' pockets that they would not be able to resist

spending it, therefore adding to aggregate demand. However, this optimism was unwarranted. It turned out that only 10–20 percent of the tax rebate dollars were spent: most of the money went into household saving or for paying down past debt such as credit card bills, neither of which directly expanded the economy.

When Barack Obama became president in 2009, he inherited an economy that was falling deeper into recession. Obama noted that decreases in consumption and investment spending continued to drag the economy downward. The result was a fiscal stimulus program of $789 billion, the most expansive unleashing of the government's fiscal firepower in the face of a recession since World War II. The stimulus included $507 billion in spending programs and $282 billion in tax relief, designed to increase aggregate demand. If more goods and services are being bought, whether cement for a new highway or groceries paid for with a household tax cut, there is less chance of decreasing demand resulting in companies laying off workers, which would result in greater declines in demand and a deeper downturn. At the writing of this text, the effects of these stimulus programs remained to be seen.

In Figure 16.1, the aggregate demand curve (*AD*) shows the level of real output (real gross domestic product) that Canadians will purchase at alternative price levels during a given year. Aggregate demand consists of spending by domestic consumers, by businesses, by government, and by foreign buyers (net exports). As the price level falls, the quantity of real output demanded increases.

Figure 16.1 also shows the economy's aggregate supply curve (*AS*). This curve shows the relation between the level of prices and amount of real output that will be produced by the economy during a given year. The aggregate supply curve is generally upward sloping because per-unit production costs, and therefore the prices that firms must receive, increase as real output increases.[1] The economy is in

---

[1]The aggregate supply curve actually has three distinct regions. First, when the economy is in deep recession or depression, the aggregate supply curve is horizontal. Because excess capacity in the economy places no upward pressure on prices, changes in aggregate demand cause changes in real output, but no change in the price level. Second, as the economy approaches full employment, scarcities in resource markets develop. Increasing aggregate demand places upward pressure on resource prices, thus bidding up unit production costs and causing the aggregate supply curve to slope upward: More output is produced only at a higher price level. Finally, the aggregate supply curve becomes vertical when the economy is at full employment.

FIGURE 16.1

MACROECONOMIC EQUILIBRIUM: THE AGGREGATE
DEMAND-AGGREGATE SUPPLY MODEL

The economy is in equilibrium where the aggregate
demand curve intersects the aggregate supply curve.
This intersection determines the equilibrium price level
and output for the economy. Increases (decreases) in
aggregate demand or aggregate supply result in
rightward (leftward) shifts in these curves.

equilibrium when aggregate demand equals aggregate
supply. This is where the two lines intersect in the
figure.

An increase (decrease) in aggregate demand is
depicted by a rightward (leftward) shift in the aggregate demand curve. Shifts in aggregate demand are
caused by changes in the determinants of aggregate
demand: consumption, investment, government purchases, or net exports. Similarly, an increase (decrease)
in aggregate supply is depicted by a rightward (leftward)
shift in the aggregate supply curve. Shifts in the aggregate
supply curve occur in response to changes in the price
of resources, technology, business expectations, and the
like. Next, we will use the aggregate demand-aggregate
supply framework to analyze the effects of fiscal and
monetary policy.

Monetary and Fiscal Policy in a Closed Economy

Monetary policy and fiscal policy are the main macroeconomic tools by which government can influence
the performance of an economy. If aggregate output
is too low and unemployment is too high, the tradi-
tional policy solution is for government to increase aggregate demand for real output through expansionary monetary or fiscal policies. This solution results in an
increase in the country's real GDP. Conversely, if inflation is troublesome, it's source
tends to be a level of aggregate demand that exceeds the rate of output that can be
supported by the economy's resources at constant prices. The solution in this situation is for the government to reduce the level of aggregate demand through contractionary monetary or fiscal policy. As the aggregate demand curve decreases, the
upward pressure on prices caused by excess aggregate demand is softened and inflation moderates.

Figure 16.2(a) illustrates the effects of an expansionary monetary or fiscal policy
in a closed Canadian economy. For simplicity, let us assume that Canada's aggregate
supply curve is horizontal until the full employment level of real GDP is attained at
$800 trillion; at this point, the aggregate supply curve becomes vertical. Also assume
that the economy's equilibrium real GDP equals $500 trillion, shown by the intersec-
tion of AD_0 and AS_0. The economy thus suffers from recession because its equilibrium output lies below the full employment level. To combat the recession, suppose
that an expansionary monetary or fiscal policy is implemented that increases aggregate demand to AD_1. Equilibrium real GDP would rise from $500 trillion to $700
trillion and unemployment would decline in the economy.

To expand aggregate demand, the Bank of Canada (as well as central banks of other
countries) would usually increase the money supply through purchasing securities

FIGURE 16.2

EFFECT OF AN EXPANSIONARY MONETARY OR FISCAL POLICY ON EQUILIBRIUM REAL GDP

(a) Expansionary Monetary Policy or Fiscal Policy in a Closed Economy

(b) Expansionary Monetary Policy or Fiscal Policy in an Open Economy

(1) The policy's initial and secondary
effects reinforce each other.

(2) The policy's initial and secondary
effects conflict with each other.

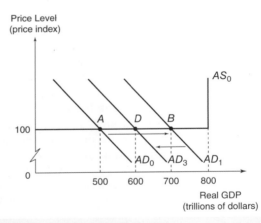

(a) Expansionary monetary or fiscal policy in a closed economy. (b) Expansionary monetary policy or fiscal policy in an open economy. (1) The policy's initial and secondary effects reinforce each other. (2) The policy's initial and secondary effects conflict with each other.

in the open market.[2] Increasing the money supply reduces the interest rate within the country and this, in turn, increases consumption and investment spending. The resulting increase in aggregate demand generates a multiple increase in real GDP.[3] To offset inflation, the Bank of Canada would decrease the money supply by selling securities in the open market, and the interest rate would rise. The increase in the interest rate reduces consumption and investment spending, thus decreasing aggregate demand. This decrease lowers any excess demand pressure on prices.

Instead of using monetary policy to stabilize the economy, Canada could use fiscal policy that operates either through changes in government spending or taxes. Because government spending is a component of aggregate demand, the Canadian government can directly affect aggregate demand by altering its own spending. To combat recession, for example, the government could increase its spending so as to raise aggregate demand, which results in a multiple increase in equilibrium real GDP. Instead, the government could combat recession by lowering income taxes, which would increase the amount of disposable income in the hands of households. This increase results in a rise in consumption spending, an increase in aggregate demand, and a multiple increase in equilibrium real GDP. A contractionary fiscal policy works in the opposite direction.

Monetary and Fiscal Policy in an Open Economy

The previous section examined how monetary policy and fiscal policy can be used as economic stabilization tools in a closed economy. Next we will consider the effects of these policies in an open economy. The key question is whether an expansionary monetary policy or fiscal policy in an open economy is more or less effective in increasing real GDP than it is in a closed economy.[4]

The answer to this question is influenced by a country's decision to adopt either a system of fixed or floating exchange rates, as discussed below. Note that in practice, many countries maintain neither rigidly fixed exchange rates nor freely floating exchange rates. Rather, they maintain managed floating exchange rates in which a central bank buys or sells currencies in an attempt to prevent exchange-rate movements from becoming disorderly. Heavier exchange-rate intervention moves a country closer to our fixed exchange-rate conclusion for monetary and fiscal policy; less intervention moves a country closer to our floating exchange-rate conclusion.

---

[2]Open market operations are the most important monetary tool of the Federal Reserve (Fed). They consist of the purchase or sale of securities by the Fed; this transaction is made with a bank or some other business or individual. Open market purchases result in an increase in bank reserves and the money supply. Open market sales cause bank reserves and the money supply to decrease. Other tools of monetary policy include changes in the discount rate, the interest rate that the Federal Reserve charges banks to borrow reserves; and changes in the required reserve ratio, the percentage of their deposits that banks are required to hold as reserves.

[3]Fiscal and monetary policies are based on the multiplier effect. According to this principle, changes in aggregate demand are multiplied into larger changes in equilibrium output and income. This process results from households receiving income and then spending it, which generates income for others, and so on.

[4]This chapter considers solely the effects of expansionary monetary and fiscal policy. A contractionary monetary and fiscal policy tends to have the opposite effects.

DOES CROWDING OCCUR IN AN OPEN ECONOMY?

TRADE CONFLICTS

In your principles of macroeconomics course, you learned about "crowding out" in the domestic economy. Crowding out refers to private consumption or investment spending decreasing as a result of increased government expenditures and the subsequent budget deficits. The source of the decline in private spending is higher interest rates caused by budget deficits.

For example, suppose that the government enacts an expansionary fiscal policy, say, an increase in defense spending. The policy must be financed either by increased taxes or through the borrowing of funds to permit the enlarged federal deficit. If the government borrows funds, the total demand for funds will increase as the government competes with the private sector to borrow the available supply of funds. The additional government borrowing thus increases the total demand for funds and pushes up interest rates. Because of higher interest rates, businesses will delay or cancel purchases of machinery and equipment, residential housing construction will be postponed, and consumers will refrain from buying interest-sensitive goods, such as major appliances and automobiles. Therefore, the higher interest rates caused by government borrowing squeeze out private-sector borrowing. Crowding out lessens the effectiveness of an expansionary fiscal policy.

Although economists tend to accept the logic of the crowding-out argument, they recognize that government deficits don't necessarily squeeze out private spending. In recessions, the main problem is that people are not spending all of the available funds. Typically, consumers are saving more than businesses intend to invest. Such a shortage of spending is the main motivation for increased government spending. In this recessionary situation, deficit-financed government spending doesn't crowd out private spending.

Moreover, the extent of crowding out tends also to be lessened in an open economy with capital flows. This is because inflows of capital from abroad tend to keep interest rates lower than they otherwise would have been. The government can borrow more money without forcing up interest rates that crowd private borrowers out of the market.

The experience of the United States during the first decade of the 2000s casts doubt on the crowding-out hypothesis. In spite of growing federal budget deficits, interest rates remained low in the United States as foreigners were content to purchase huge amounts of securities issued by the government. Analysts noted that if not for the inflow of foreign capital, U.S. interest rates would be about 1.5 percentage points higher. However, skeptics noted that the free spending policy would eventually have to cease if foreigners begin to doubt the ability of the United States to repay its debt with sound currency. This doubt would cause foreign investors to demand higher interest rates if they were to keep lending the United States the money it needs, or they might simply stop lending to the United States, thus making the crowding out more likely.

Note that our conclusions depend on the expansionary or contractionary effects that monetary policy or fiscal policy have on aggregate demand. In a closed economy, an expansionary monetary or fiscal policy has a single effect on aggregate demand: it causes aggregate demand to expand by increasing domestic consumption, investment, or government spending. In an open economy, the policy has a second effect on aggregate demand: it causes aggregate demand to increase or decrease by changing net exports and other determinants of aggregate demand. If the initial and secondary effects of the policy result in increases in aggregate demand, the expansionary effect of the policy is strengthened. But if the initial and secondary effects have conflicting impacts on aggregate demand, the expansionary effect of the policy is weakened. The examples below clarify this point.

Let us begin by assuming that the mobility of international investment (capital) is high for Canada. This high mobility suggests that a small change in the relative interest rate across nations induces a large international flow of investment. This assumption is consistent with investment movements among many nations, such as the United States, Japan, and Germany, and the conclusions of many analysts that investment mobility increases as national financial markets become globalized.

Effect of Fiscal and Monetary Policy Under Fixed Exchange Rates

Consider first the effects of an expansionary fiscal policy or monetary policy under a system of fixed exchange rates. The conclusion that will emerge from our discussion is that an expansionary fiscal policy is more successful in stimulating the economy, and an expansionary monetary policy is less successful, than they are in a closed economy. This conclusion is summarized in Table 16.1.[5]

Fiscal Policy Is Strengthened Under Fixed Exchange Rates

Referring to Figure 16.2(b-1), assume that Canada operates under a fixed exchange-rate system and that its government initially has a balanced budget in which government spending equals government taxes. To combat a recession, suppose the government adopts an expansionary fiscal policy, say, an increase in its spending on goods and services. The initial effect of a rise in government spending is to increase aggregate demand from AD_0 to AD_1, the same amount that occurs in our example of expansionary fiscal policy in a closed economy. This increase causes equilibrium real GDP to expand from $500 trillion to $700 trillion.

The second effect of the expansionary fiscal policy is that increased spending causes the Canadian government's budget to go into deficit. As the government demands more money to finance its excess spending, the domestic interest rate rises. A higher interest rate attracts an inflow of investment from foreigners, which results in an increased demand for Canadian dollars in the foreign-exchange market. The dollar's exchange rate is thus under pressure to appreciate. However, appreciation cannot occur because Canada has a fixed exchange-rate system. To prevent its dollar from appreciating, the Canadian government must intervene in the foreign-exchange market and purchase foreign currency with dollars. This purchase results

TABLE 16.1

The Effectiveness of Monetary and Fiscal Policy in Promoting Internal Balance for an Economy with a High Degree of Capital Mobility

Exchange-Rate Regime	Monetary Policy	Fiscal Policy
Floating exchange rates	Strengthened	Weakened
Fixed exchange rates	Weakened	Strengthened

[5]This analysis originated with R. Mundell, "The Appropriate Use of Monetary and Fiscal Policy for Internal and External Stability," *IMF Staff Papers*, March 1961, pp. 70–77 and J. M. Flemming, "Domestic Financial Policies Under Fixed and Under Flexible Exchange Rates," *IMF Staff Papers*, 1962, pp. 369–379.

in an increase in the domestic money supply. The effect of the rise in the money supply is to increase the amount of loanable funds available in the economy. As these funds are channeled into domestic spending, aggregate demand increases again, from AD_1 to AD_2, and equilibrium real GDP increases to $800 trillion.

Because the initial and secondary effects of the expansionary fiscal policy reinforce each other, real GDP increases by a greater amount than in the example of expansionary fiscal policy in a closed economy. Simply put, the effect of an expansionary fiscal policy is more pronounced in an economy with capital mobility and fixed exchange rates than it is in a closed economy.

Monetary Policy Is Weakened Under Fixed Exchange Rates

Contrast this outcome with monetary policy. As we will learn, in an open economy with capital mobility and fixed exchange rates, an expansionary monetary policy is less effective in increasing real GDP than it is in a closed economy.

Referring to Figure 16.2(b-2), again assume that Canada suffers from recession. To combat the recession, suppose the Bank of Canada implements an expansionary monetary policy. The initial effect of the monetary expansion is to reduce the domestic interest rate, resulting in increased consumption and investment that expand aggregate demand from AD_0 to AD_1. This expansion causes equilibrium real GDP to rise from $500 trillion to $700 trillion.

The second effect of the monetary expansion is that a lower Canadian interest rate discourages foreign investors from placing their funds in Canadian capital markets. As the demand for Canadian dollars decreases, its exchange value is under pressure to depreciate. To maintain a fixed exchange rate, the Bank of Canada intervenes in the foreign-exchange market and purchases dollars with foreign currency. This purchase causes the domestic money supply to decrease as well as the availability of loanable funds in the economy. The resulting decrease in domestic spending leads to a decrease in aggregate demand from AD_1 to AD_3 that causes equilibrium real GDP to decline from $700 trillion to $600 trillion. This contraction in aggregate demand counteracts the initial expansion that was intended to stimulate the economy. Hence, an expansionary monetary policy is weakened when its initial and secondary effects conflict with each other. Simply put, under a system of fixed exchange rates and capital mobility, monetary policy is less effective in stimulating the economy than it is in a closed economy.

Effect of Fiscal and Monetary Policy Under Floating Exchange Rates

We will now modify our example by replacing Canada's fixed exchange-rate system with a system of floating exchange rates. The conclusion that emerges from this discussion is that with high capital mobility and floating exchange rates, an expansionary monetary policy is more successful in stimulating the economy, and an expansionary fiscal policy is less successful, than they are in a closed economy.

Monetary Policy Is Strengthened Under Floating Exchange Rates

Again assume that Canada suffers from recession. To stimulate its economy, suppose that the Bank of Canada adopts an expansionary monetary policy. As in a closed economy, an increase in the supply of money results in a lower domestic interest rate that initially generates more spending on consumption and investment and causes aggregate demand to increase. Referring to Figure 16.2(b-1), as aggregate demand increases from AD_0 to AD_1, equilibrium real GDP rises from $500 trillion to $700 trillion.

The second effect of the expansionary monetary policy is that because investment is highly mobile between countries, the decreasing Canadian interest rate induces investors to place their funds in foreign capital markets. As Canadian investors sell dollars to purchase foreign currency that is used to facilitate foreign investments, the dollar depreciates. This depreciation results in an increase in exports, a decrease in imports, and an improvement in Canada's current account. The improving current account provides an extra boost to aggregate demand which expands from AD_1 to AD_2. This expansion causes equilibrium real GDP to increase from $700 trillion to $800 trillion.

Because the initial and secondary effects of the expansionary monetary policy are complementary, the policy is strengthened by increasing Canada's output and employment. Simply put, in an economy with capital mobility and floating exchange rates, an expansionary monetary policy is more effective in stimulating the economy than it is in a closed economy.

Fiscal Policy Is Weakened Under Floating Exchange Rates

The result is different if the Canadian government uses fiscal policy to combat recession. Referring to Figure 16.2(b-2), the initial effect of a rise in government spending is to increase aggregate demand from AD_0 to AD_1 that causes equilibrium real GDP to increase from $500 trillion to $700 trillion. Secondly, as the increased government spending causes the government's budget to go into deficit, the Canadian interest rate rises. A higher interest rate causes an inflow of investment from foreigners, which results in an increase in the demand for Canadian dollars in the foreign-exchange market. The exchange value of the dollar thus appreciates, which results in falling exports, rising imports, and a deterioration of Canada's current account. As the current account worsens, aggregate demand decreases from AD_1 to AD_3 and equilibrium real GDP contracts from $700 trillion to $600 trillion. Because the initial and secondary effects of the fiscal policy are conflicting, the policy's expansionary effect is weakened. Therefore, an expansionary fiscal policy in an economy with capital mobility and floating exchange rates is less effective in stimulating the economy than it is in a closed economy.

Macroeconomic Stability and the Current Account: Policy Agreement Versus Policy Conflict

So far we have assumed that the goal of fiscal and monetary policy is to promote internal balance in Canada: that is, full employment without inflation. Besides desiring internal balance, suppose that Canadians want their economy to achieve current-account (external) balance whereby its exports equal its imports. This balance suggests that Canada prefers to "finance its own way" in international trade by earning from its exports an amount of money necessary to pay for its imports. Will Canadian policymakers be able to achieve both internal and external balance at the same time? Or will conflict develop between these two objectives?

Again, let's assume that the Canadian economy suffers from recession. Suppose also that Canada's current account realizes a deficit in which imports exceed exports, so that Canada is a net borrowing country from the rest of the world. Given a system of floating exchange rates, recall that an expansionary monetary policy for Canada results in a depreciation of its dollar and therefore a rise in its exports and a fall in its imports. This rise in net exports serves to reduce the deficit in Canada's current account. The conclusion is that an expansionary monetary policy, which is appropriate for combating Canada's recession, is also compatible with the objective of reducing Canada's current-account deficit. Simply put, a single economic policy promotes overall balance for Canada.

Instead, let's assume that Canada suffers from inflation and a current-account deficit. When adopting a contractionary monetary policy to combat inflation, the Bank of Canada causes the domestic interest rate to increase, which results in an appreciation of its dollar. This appreciation results in a fall in Canada's exports, a rise in its imports, and a larger current-account deficit. The conclusion is that Canada's contractionary monetary policy to combat inflation conflicts with its objective of promoting balance in its current account. Policy conflict thus prevails for the monetary policy. However, if Canada initially had a current-account surplus, an expansionary monetary policy would help reduce it.

Simply put, when Canada finds itself in a policy-conflict zone, monetary policy (or fiscal policy) alone will not restore both internal and external balance. A combination of policies is needed. Suppose, for example, that Canada experiences recession with a current-account deficit. An expansionary monetary policy to combat recession might be accompanied by tariffs or quotas, to reduce imports and improve the current account. Each economic objective is matched with an appropriate policy instrument so that both objectives can be attained at the same time. It is left for more advanced texts to further analyze this topic.

Inflation With Unemployment

This analysis so far has looked at the economy under special circumstances. It has been assumed that as the economy advances to full employment, domestic prices remain unchanged until full employment is reached. Once the nation's capacity to produce has been achieved, further increases in aggregate demand pull prices upward. This type of inflation is known as **demand-pull inflation**. Under these conditions, internal balance (full employment with stable prices) can be viewed as a single target that requires but one policy instrument: a reduction in aggregate demand via monetary policy or fiscal policy.

A more troublesome problem is the appropriate policy to implement when a nation experiences *inflation with unemployment*. Here the problem is that internal balance cannot be achieved just by manipulating aggregate demand. To decrease inflation, a reduction in aggregate demand is required; to decrease unemployment, an expansion in aggregate demand is required. Thus, the objectives of full employment and stable prices cannot be considered as one and the same target; rather, they are two independent targets, requiring two distinct policy instruments.

Achieving overall balance thus involves three separate targets: current-account equilibrium, full employment, and price stability. To ensure that all three objectives can be achieved simultaneously, monetary and fiscal policy may not be enough; direct controls may also be needed.

Inflation with unemployment has been a problem for the United States. In 1971, for example, the U.S. economy experienced inflation with recession and a current-account deficit. Increasing aggregate demand to achieve full employment would presumably intensify inflationary pressures. The president therefore implemented a comprehensive system of **wage and price controls** to remove the inflationary constraint. Later the same year, the United States entered into exchange-rate realignments that resulted in a depreciation of the dollar's exchange value by 12 percent against the trade-weighted value of other major currencies. The dollar depreciation was intended to help the United States reverse its current-account deficit. In short, it was the president's view that the internal and external problems of the United States could not be eliminated through expenditure-changing policies alone.

International Economic-Policy Coordination

Policymakers have long been aware that the welfare of their economies is linked to that of the world economy. Because of the international mobility of goods, services, capital, and labor, economic policies of one nation have spillover effects on others. Recognizing these spillover effects, governments have often made attempts to coordinate their economic policies.

Economic relations among nations can be visualized along a spectrum, illustrated in Figure 16.3, ranging from open *conflict* to *integration*, where nations implement policies jointly in a supranational forum to which they have ceded a large degree of authority, such as the European Union. At the spectrum's midpoint lies policy *independence*: Nations take the actions of other nations as a given; they do not attempt to influence those actions or be influenced by them. Between independence and integration lie various forms of policy coordination and cooperation.

Cooperative policymaking can take many forms, but in general it occurs whenever officials from different nations meet to evaluate world economic conditions. During these meetings, policymakers may present briefings on their individual economies and discuss current policies. Such meetings represent a simple form of cooperation. A more involved format might consist of economists' studies on a particular subject, combined with an in-depth discussion of possible solutions. However,

FIGURE 16.3

Relations Among National Governments

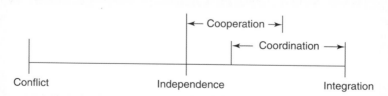

Relations among national governments can be visualized along a spectrum ranging from policy conflict to policy interdependence. Between these extremes are a variety of forms of cooperation and coordination.

G-20 AGREES TO COOPERATE ON GLOBAL ECONOMIC POLICY: INTERNATIONAL POLICY COORDINATION

TRADE CONFLICTS

For decades the world economy has been out of balance with the United States, on one side, accounting for most of the global current-account deficit and a more variable group—China, Japan, and Germany—accounting for most of the global surplus. This state of affairs has meant that the United States has consumed more than it has produced and invested more than it has saved in the first decade of the 2000s. Moreover, U.S. trading partners, some of whom are very poor on a per capita basis, have lent the United States, a wealthy country, the funds needed to import the resources to fill the gap. Although the U.S. consumer has served as the engine of economic growth for foreign exporting countries, if the United States were a developing country, such behavior would have triggered a crisis long ago.

Responding to this imbalance, in 2009 the Group of 20 (G-20) nations agreed to implement an elaborate structure to coordinate macroeconomic policies to foster balanced economic growth. The G-20 plan to boost growth came at a time when U.S. consumers were anticipated to save more and spend less, thus decreasing global demand. Among the policy changes envisioned: China and Japan would rely less on exports and more on domestic consumption; the United States would curtail its budget deficit; and Europe would make difficult structural reforms to increase business investment. According to the G-20 leaders, the world would face sluggish growth if adjustments in one part of the global economy are not matched by offsetting adjustments in other parts.

Reaching a strong agreement on international economic policy coordination was a priority for the G-20 as the group sought to establish itself as the coordinating body for the world's largest economies and developing countries. Under the former system, international economic cooperation was dominated only by the largest advanced countries, the G-8. The new system includes not only advanced nations but also fast-growing emerging economies such as China, Brazil, and India. Under the G-20 plan, members will need periodically to review each nation's policies and see that they are making necessary adjustments: the group will act by moral suasion, not sanctions.

Critics say the plan is likely to deteriorate into a talkfest, as have other similar international efforts to get countries to enact economic changes. The International Labor Organization, for example, operates mainly by consensus on its labor standards and is criticized as ineffective. However, the G-20 officials said they don't need sanctions to force them to act on economic issues because the depth of the recession of 2007–2009 and the need for change is apparent to all.

If the G-20's rebalancing process is to be successful, it will depend on the willingness of the United States to carry through on its commitments first, such as sharply cutting government spending or increasing taxes in order to move toward a balanced federal budget. Otherwise, other nations will dismiss the effort as inconsequential. At the writing of this textbook, it was not clear if this plan will work. However, the odds are that containment of large imbalances will not happen quickly for the G-20.

true policy coordination goes beyond these two forms of cooperation; policy coordination is a formal agreement among nations to initiate particular policies.

International economic policy coordination is the attempt to significantly modify national policies—monetary policy, fiscal policy, exchange-rate policy—in recognition of international economic interdependence. Policy coordination does not necessarily imply that nations give precedence to international concerns over domestic concerns. It does recognize, however, that the policies of one nation can spill over to influence the objectives of others; nations should therefore communicate with one another and attempt to coordinate their policies so as to take these linkages into account. Presumably, they will be better off than if they had acted independently.

To facilitate policy coordination, economic officials of the major governments talk with one another frequently in the context of the International Monetary Fund and the Organization for Economic Cooperation and Development. Also, central-bank senior officials meet monthly at the Bank for International Settlements.

Policy Coordination in Theory

If economic policies in each of two nations affect the other, then the case for policy coordination would appear to be obvious. Policy coordination is considered important in the modern world because economic disruptions are transmitted rapidly from one nation to another. Without policy coordination, national economic policies can destabilize other economies. The logic of policy coordination is illustrated in the following basketball spectator problem.

Suppose you are attending a professional basketball game between the Los Angeles Lakers and the Chicago Bulls. If everyone is sitting, someone who stands has a superior view. Spectators usually can see well if everyone sits or if everyone stands. Sitting in seats is more comfortable than standing. When there is no cooperation, everyone stands; each spectator does what is best for herself/himself given the actions of other spectators. If all spectators sit, someone, taking what the others will do as a given, will stand. If all spectators are standing, then it is best to remain standing. With spectator cooperation, the solution is for everyone to sit. The problem is that each spectator may be tempted to get a better view by standing. The cooperative solution will not be attained, therefore, without an outright agreement on coordination—in this situation, everyone remains seated.

Consider the following economic example. Suppose the world consists of just two nations, Germany and Japan. Although these nations trade goods with each other, they desire to pursue their own domestic economic priorities. Germany wants to avoid trade deficits with Japan, while achieving full employment for its economy; Japan desires full employment for its economy, while avoiding trade deficits with Germany. Assume that both nations achieve balanced trade with each other, but each nation's economy operates below full employment. Germany and Japan contemplate enacting expansionary government spending policies that would stimulate demand, output, and employment. But each nation rejects the idea, recognizing the policy's adverse impact on the trade balance. Germany and Japan realize that bolstering domestic income to increase jobs has the side effect of stimulating the demand for imports, thus pushing the trade account into deficit.

The preceding situation is favorable for successful policy coordination. If Germany and Japan agree to simultaneously expand their government spending, then output, employment, and incomes will rise concurrently. While higher German income promotes increased imports from Japan, higher Japanese income promotes increased imports from Germany. An appropriate increase in government spending results in each nation's increased demand for imports being offset by an increased demand for exports, which leads to balanced trade between Germany and Japan. In our example of mutual implementation of expansionary fiscal policies, policy coordination permits each nation to achieve full employment and balanced trade.

This is an optimistic portrayal of international economic policy coordination. The synchronization of policies appears simple because there are only two economies and two objectives. However, in the real world, policy coordination generally involves many countries and many diverse objectives, such as low inflation, high employment, economic growth, and trade balance.

If the benefits of international economic policy coordination are really so obvious, it may seem odd that agreements do not occur more often than they do. Several obstacles hinder successful policy coordination. Even if national economic objectives are harmonious, there is no guarantee that governments can design and implement coordinated policies. Policymakers in the real world do not always have sufficient information to understand the nature of the economic problem or how their policies will affect economies. Implementing appropriate policies when governments disagree about economic fundamentals is difficult for several reasons.

- Some nations give higher priority to price stability, for instance, or to full employment, than others.
- Some nations have a stronger legislature, or weaker trade unions, than others.
- The party pendulums in different nations, for example, shift with elections occurring in different years.
- One nation may experience economic recession while another nation experiences rapid inflation.

Although the theoretical advantages of international economic policy coordination are clearly established, attempts to quantify their gains are rare. Skeptics point out that in practice, the gains from policy coordination are smaller than what is often suggested. Let us consider some examples of international economic policy coordination.

Does Policy Coordination Work?

Does coordination of economic policies improve the performance of nations? Proponents of policy coordination cite the examples of the Plaza Agreement of 1985 and the Louvre Accord of 1987.

The deterioration of the U.S. trade balance was a disturbing feature of the economic recovery of the United States in the early 1980s. This deterioration was influenced by a dramatic appreciation of the dollar that overwhelmed the other determinants of international cost competitiveness. Between 1980 and 1985, the dollar's appreciation boosted the ratio of U.S. unit labor costs to foreign unit labor costs by 39 percent, thus detracting from the international competitiveness of U.S. manufacturers. American net exports of goods and services declined, resulting in large trade deficits. As the U.S. economic recovery slowed, protectionist pressures increased in Congress.

Fearing a disaster in the world trading system, government officials of the **Group of Five (G-5)** nations—the United States, Japan, Germany, Great Britain, and France—met at New York's Plaza Hotel in 1985. There was widespread agreement that the dollar was overvalued and that the twin U.S. deficits (trade and federal budget) were too large. Each country made specific pledges on macroeconomic policy and also agreed to initiate coordinated sales of the dollar to shove its exchange value downward. By 1986, the dollar had dramatically depreciated, especially against the German mark and the Japanese yen.

However, the sharp decline in the dollar's exchange value set off a new concern: an uncontrolled dollar plunge. So in 1987 another round of policy coordination occurred to put the brakes on the dollar's decline. The G-5 financial ministers met in Paris and agreed in the Louvre Accord to pursue intervention policies curbing the pace of the dollar's depreciation, to be accompanied by other macroeconomic adjustments.

Although the episodes of the Plaza Agreement and Louvre Accord point to the success of policy coordination, by the first decade of the 2000s government officials were showing less enthusiasm for it. They felt that coordinating policy had become much more difficult because of the way policy is made, especially given the rise of independent central banks. Back in the 1980s, the governments of Japan and Germany could dictate what their central banks would do. Since that time the Bank of Japan and the European Central Bank have become more independent and see themselves as protectors of discipline against high-spending government officials. That role makes domestic fiscal and monetary coordination difficult, and international efforts to coordinate policies even more difficult. Also, the huge growth in global financial markets has made currency intervention much less effective.

An example of unsuccessful international policy coordination occurred in 2000. At that time, the **Group of Seven (G-7)** industrial nations—the United States, Canada, Japan, the United Kingdom, Germany, France, and Italy—launched coordinated purchases of the euro to boost its value. Although the euro was launched in 1999, at an exchange value of $1.17 per euro, by mid-2000 its value had dropped to $0.84 per euro. Many economists feared that continued speculative attacks against the euro might result in a free fall of its value, which could destabilize the international financial system. To prevent this from happening, the G-7 nations enacted a coordinated intervention by purchasing euros with their currencies in the foreign exchange market. The added demand for the euro helped boost its value to more than $0.88 per euro. However, the success of the intervention was short-lived. Within two weeks following the intervention, the euro's value slid to an all-time low. Most economists considered the coordinated intervention to be a failure.

Summary

1. International economic policy refers to various government activities that influence trade patterns among nations, including (a) monetary and fiscal policies, (b) exchange-rate adjustments, (c) tariff and nontariff trade barriers, (d) foreign-exchange controls and investment controls, and (e) export-promotion measures.

2. Since the 1930s, nations have actively pursued internal balance (full employment without inflation) as a primary economic objective. Nations also consider external balance (current-account equilibrium) as an economic objective. A nation realizes overall balance when it attains both internal and external balance.

3. To achieve overall balance, nations implement expenditure-changing policies (monetary and fiscal policies), expenditure-switching policies (exchange-rate adjustments), and direct controls (price and wage controls).

4. For an open economy with a fixed exchange-rate system and high capital mobility, fiscal policy is more successful, and monetary policy is less successful, in promoting internal balance than it is in a closed economy. If the open economy has a floating exchange-rate system, monetary policy is more successful, and fiscal policy is less successful, in promoting internal balance than they are in a closed economy.

5. When a nation experiences inflation with unemployment, achieving overall balance involves three separate targets: Current-account equilibrium, full employment, and price stability. Three policy instruments may be needed to achieve these targets.

6. International economic policy coordination is the attempt to significantly modify national policies in recognition of international economic interdependence. Nations regularly consult with each other in the context of the International Monetary Fund, Organization for Economic Cooperation and Development, Bank for International Settlements, and Group of Seven. The Plaza Agreement and Louvre Accord are examples of international economic policy coordination.

7. Several problems confront international economic-policy coordination: (a) different national economic objectives, (b) different national institutions, (c) different national political climates, and (d) different phases in the business cycle. Moreover, there is no guarantee that governments can design and implement policies that are capable of achieving the intended results.

Key Concepts & Terms

- Demand-pull inflation (p. 551)
- Direct controls (p. 542)
- Expenditure-changing policies (p. 542)
- Expenditure-switching policies (p. 542)
- External balance (p. 541)
- Fiscal policy (p. 542)
- Group of Five (G-5) (p. 555)
- Group of Seven (G-7) (p. 556)
- Internal balance (p. 541)
- International economic policy coordination (p. 553)
- Monetary policy (p. 542)
- Overall balance (p. 541)
- Wage and price controls (p. 552)

Study Questions

1. What are the most important instruments of international economic policy?
2. What institutional constraints bear on the formation of economic policies?
3. What are some obstacles to successful international economic policy coordination?
4. What is meant by the terms *expenditure-changing policy* and *expenditure-switching policy*? Give some examples of each.
5. What is meant by the terms *policy agreement* and *policy conflict*?
6. Under a system of fixed exchange rates and high capital mobility, is monetary policy or fiscal policy better suited for promoting internal balance? Why?
7. Distinguish among external balance, internal balance, and overall balance.

International Banking: Reserves, Debt, and Risk

The world's banking system plays a vital role in facilitating international transactions and maintaining economic prosperity. Commercial banks, such as Citicorp, help finance trade and investment and provide loans to international borrowers. Central banks, such as the Federal Reserve, serve as a lender of last resort to commercial banks and sometimes intervene in foreign-currency markets to stabilize currency values. Also, the International Monetary Fund (IMF) serves as a lender to nations having deficits in their balance of payments. This chapter concentrates on the role that banks play in world financial markets, the risks associated with international banking, and strategies employed to deal with these risks.

We'll begin with an investigation of the nature of international reserves and their importance for the world financial system. This is followed by a discussion of banks as international lenders and the problems associated with international debt.

Nature of International Reserves

The need for a central bank, such as the Bank of England, for international reserves is similar to an individual's desire to hold cash balances (currency and checkable deposits). At both levels, monetary reserves are intended to bridge the gap between monetary receipts and monetary payments.

Suppose that an individual receives income in equal installments every minute of the day and that expenditures for goods and services are likewise evenly spaced over time. The individual will require only a minimum cash reserve to finance purchases, because no significant imbalances between cash receipts and cash disbursements will arise. In reality, however, individuals purchase goods and services on a fairly regular basis from day to day, but receive paychecks only at weekly or longer intervals. A certain amount of cash is therefore required to finance the discrepancy that arises between monetary receipts and payments.

When an individual initially receives a paycheck, cash balances are high. But as time progresses, these holdings of cash may fall to virtually zero just before the next paycheck is received. Individuals are thus concerned with the amount of cash balances that, on average, are necessary to keep them going until the next paycheck arrives.

Although individuals desire cash balances primarily to fill the gap between monetary receipts and payments, this desire is influenced by a number of other factors. The need for cash balances may become more acute if the absolute dollar volume of transactions increases, because larger imbalances may result between receipts and payments. Conversely, to the extent that individuals can finance their transactions on credit, they require less cash in hand.

Just as an individual desires to hold cash balances, national governments have a need for **international reserves**. The chief purpose of international reserves is to enable nations to finance disequilibrium in their balance-of-payments positions. When a nation finds its monetary receipts falling short of its monetary payments, the deficit is settled with international reserves. Eventually, the deficit must be eliminated, because central banks tend to have limited stocks of reserves.

From a policy perspective, the advantage of international reserves is that they enable nations to sustain *temporary* balance-of-payments deficits until acceptable adjustment measures can operate to correct the disequilibrium. Holdings of international reserves facilitate effective policy formation because corrective adjustment measures need not be implemented prematurely. However, should a deficit nation possess abundant stocks of reserve balances, it may be able to resist unpopular adjustment measures, making eventual adjustments even more troublesome.

Demand for International Reserves

When a nation's international monetary payments exceed its international monetary receipts, some means of settlement is required to finance its payments deficit. Settlement ultimately consists of transfers of international reserves among nations. Both the magnitude and the longevity of a balance-of-payments deficit that can be sustained in the absence of equilibrating adjustments are limited by a nation's stock of international reserves.

On a global basis, the **demand for international reserves** depends on two related factors: the monetary value of international transactions and the disequilibrium that can arise in balance-of-payments positions. The demand for international reserves is also contingent on such things as the speed and strength of the balance-of-payments adjustment mechanism and the overall institutional framework of the world economy.

Exchange-Rate Flexibility

One determinant of the demand for international reserves is the *degree of exchange-rate flexibility* in the international monetary system. This is because exchange-rate flexibility in part underlies the efficiency of the balance-of-payments adjustment process.

Figure 17.1 represents the exchange-market position of the United States in trade with the United Kingdom. Starting at equilibrium point E, suppose that an increase in imports increases the U.S. demand for pounds from D_0 to D_1. The prevailing

FIGURE 17.1

THE DEMAND FOR INTERNATIONAL RESERVES AND EXCHANGE-RATE FLEXIBILITY

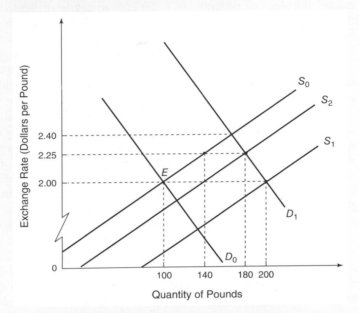

When exchange rates are fixed (pegged) by monetary authorities, international reserves are necessary for the financing of payment imbalances and the stabilization of exchange rates. With floating exchange rates, payment imbalances tend to be corrected by market-induced fluctuations in the exchange rate; the need for exchange-rate stabilization and international reserves then disappears.

exchange-rate system will determine the quantity of international reserves needed to bridge the gap between the number of pounds demanded and the number supplied.

If exchange rates are fixed or pegged by the monetary authorities, international reserves play a crucial role in the exchange-rate stabilization process. In Figure 17.1, suppose the exchange rate is pegged at $2 per pound. Given a rise in the demand for pounds from D_0 to D_1, the United States would face an excess demand for pounds equal to £100 at the pegged rate. If the U.S. dollar is not to depreciate beyond the pegged rate, the monetary authorities—that is, the Federal Reserve—must enter the market to supply pounds, in exchange for dollars, in the amount necessary to eliminate the disequilibrium. In the figure, the pegged rate of $2 per pound can be maintained if the monetary authorities supply £100 to the market. Coupled with the existing supply schedule S_0, the added supply will result in a new supply schedule at S_1. Market equilibrium is restored at the pegged rate.

Rather than operating under a rigidly pegged system, suppose a nation makes an agreement to foster some automatic adjustments by allowing market rates to float within a narrow band around the official exchange rate. This limited exchange-rate flexibility would be aimed at correcting minor payments imbalances, whereas large and persistent disequilibrium would require other adjustment measures.

Referring to Figure 17.1, assume that the U.S. official exchange rate is $2 per pound, but with a band of permissible exchange-rate fluctuations whose upper limit is set at $2.25 per pound. Given a rise in the U.S. demand for pounds, the value of the dollar will begin to decline. Once the exchange rate depreciates to $2.25 per pound, domestic monetary authorities will need to supply £40 on the market to defend the band's outer limit. This supply will have the effect of shifting the market supply schedule from S_0 to S_2. Under a system of limited exchange-rate flexibility, then, movements in the exchange rate serve to reduce the payments disequilibrium. Smaller amounts of international reserves are required for exchange-rate stabilization purposes under this system than if exchange rates are rigidly fixed.

A fundamental purpose of international reserves is to facilitate government intervention in exchange markets to stabilize currency values. The more active a government's stabilization activities, the greater is the need for reserves. Most exchange-rate standards today involve some stabilization operations and require international reserves. However, if exchange rates were allowed to float freely without government interference, theoretically there would be no need for reserves. This is because a floating rate would serve to eliminate an incipient payments imbalance, negating the need for stabilization operations. Referring again to Figure 17.1, suppose the exchange market is initially in equilibrium at a rate of $2 per pound. Given an increase in the demand for foreign exchange from D_0 to D_1, the home currency would begin to depreciate. It would continue to weaken until it reached an exchange value of $2.50 per pound, at which point market equilibrium would be restored. The need for international reserves would thus be nonexistent under freely floating rates.

Other Determinants

The lesson of the previous section is that changes in the degree of exchange-rate flexibility are inversely related to changes in the quantity of international reserves demanded. In other words, a monetary system characterized by more rapid and flexible exchange-rate adjustments requires smaller reserves, and vice versa.

In addition to the degree of exchange-rate flexibility, several other factors underlie the demand for international reserves, including (1) automatic adjustment mechanisms that respond to payments disequilibrium, (2) economic policies used to bring about payments equilibrium, and (3) the international coordination of economic policies.

Our earlier analysis has shown that adjustment mechanisms involving prices, interest rates, incomes, and monetary flows automatically tend to correct balance-of-payments disequilibrium. A payments deficit or surplus initiates changes in each of these variables. The more efficient each of these adjustment mechanisms is, the smaller and more short-lived market imbalances will be and the fewer reserves will be needed. The demand for international reserves therefore tends to be smaller with speedier and more complete automatic adjustment mechanisms.

The demand for international reserves is also influenced by the choice and effectiveness of government policies adopted to correct payments imbalances. Unlike automatic adjustment mechanisms, which rely on the free market to identify industries and labor groups that must bear the adjustment burden, the use of government policies involves political decisions. All else being equal, the greater a nation's propensity to apply commercial policies (including tariffs, quotas, and subsidies) to key sectors, the less will be its need for international reserves. This lower need assumes, of course, that the policies are effective in reducing payments disequilibrium.

Because of uncertainties about the nature and timing of payments disturbances, however, nations are often slow to initiate such trade policies and find themselves requiring international reserves to weather periods of payments disequilibrium.

The international coordination of economic policies is another determinant of the demand for international reserves. A primary goal of economic cooperation among finance ministers is to reduce the frequency and extent of payment imbalances and hence the demand for international reserves. Since the end of World War II, nations have moved toward the harmonization of national economic objectives by establishing programs through such organizations as the IMF Fund and the Organization for Economic Cooperation and Development. Another example of international economic organization has been the European Union, whose goal is to achieve a common macroeconomic policy and full monetary union. By reducing the intensity of disturbances to payments balance, such policy coordination reduces the need for international reserves.

Other factors influence the demand for international reserves. The quantity demanded is positively related to the level of world prices and income. One would expect rising price levels to inflate the market value of international transactions and, therefore, to increase the potential demand for reserves. The need for reserves would also tend to rise with the level of global income and trade activity.

In summary, central banks need international reserves to cover possible or expected excess payments to other nations at some future time. The quantity of international reserves demanded is directly related to the size and duration of these payment gaps. If a nation with a payments deficit is willing and able to initiate quick actions to increase receipts or decrease payments, the amount of reserves needed will be relatively small. Conversely, the demand for reserves will be relatively large if nations initiate no actions to correct payments imbalances or adopt policies that prolong such disequilibrium.

Supply of International Reserves

The analysis so far has emphasized the demand for international reserves. But what about the **supply of international reserves**?

The total supply of international reserves consists of two distinct categories: *owned reserves* and *borrowed reserves*. Reserve assets such as gold, acceptable foreign currencies, and special drawing rights (SDRs) are generally considered to be directly owned by the holding nations. But if nations with payments deficits find their stocks of owned reserves falling to unacceptably low levels, they may be able to borrow international reserves as a cushioning device. Lenders may be foreign nations with excess reserves, foreign financial institutions, or international agencies such as the IMF.

Foreign Currencies

International reserves are a means of payment used in financing foreign transactions. One such asset is holdings of *national currencies* (foreign exchange). As seen in Table 17.1, the largest share of international reserves today consists of holdings of national currencies.

SHOULD SDRS REPLACE THE DOLLAR AS THE WORLD'S RESERVE CURRENCY?

The United States dollar is the main reserve currency in the world today. Dollars are used throughout the world as a medium of exchange, unit of account, and store of value, and many nations keep wealth in dollar-denominated assets such as U.S. Treasury securities. According to a 2007 survey, about 64 percent of the world's official foreign exchange reserves are held in dollars, while about 86 percent of daily foreign exchange trades involve dollars. The euro, the second most important reserve currency, lags far behind the dollar, followed by the British pound and Japanese yen. The dollar's popularity is supported by a strong and sophisticated U.S. economy and its safe-haven attractiveness for international investors. However, the widening trade deficits and expanding foreign debt that the United States has incurred in recent decades have weakened the prestige of the dollar.

As more and more people have used dollars in international transactions in the post World War II era, the efficiencies in using dollars in exchange increased, thus solidifying the dollar's place as the world's premier currency. Some have compared the dollar's popularity to that of the Microsoft Windows operating system. Computer users may feel that substitute software is easier to use, but the convenience of being able to transfer files around the world to anyone using Microsoft enhances the system's popularity. In the dollar's case, widespread use of the dollar makes dealing in the currency easier and less expensive than any other: The more countries that transact in dollars, the cheaper it is for them all to transact in dollars. Therefore, any one country would hesitate to stop dealing in dollars, even if it desired to use a different currency unless it knew that other countries would do the same. This reluctance may be a key reason why the dollar is so difficult to displace as the world's main reserve currency.

The United States realizes substantial benefits from the dollar serving as the main reserve currency of the world. First, Americans can purchase products at a marginally cheaper rate than other nations, which must exchange their currency with each purchase and pay a transaction cost. Also, Americans can borrow at lower interest rates for homes and automobiles and the U.S. government can finance larger deficits longer and at lower interest rates. Moreover, the United States can issue debt (securities) in its own currency, thus pushing exchange rate risk onto foreign lenders. This risk means that foreigners face the possibility that a fall in the dollar's exchange value could wipe out the returns on their investments in the United States.

For example, if a Chinese investor realizes a return of five percent on his or her holdings of U.S. Treasury securities, and if the dollar depreciates five percent against China's yuan, the investor would realize no gain. With holdings of dollar-denominated assets of about $1 trillion dollars in 2009, China has been especially concerned about the possibility of losing purchasing power in the event of substantial dollar depreciation.

In spite of the widespread appeal of the dollar, there is increasing concern about its continuing role as the world's main reserve currency. Countries such as China fear that the United States is digging a hole with an economy based on huge deficits and massive borrowing that cloud the dollar's future. They worry about the volatility of the dollar and the destabilizing effect that it can have on international trade and finance. Simply put, critics claim that a credit-based reserve currency such as the dollar is inherently risky, facilitates global imbalances, and promotes the spread of financial crises. As a result, they argue that the dollar should no longer serve as the world's reserve currency.

Before the dollar is displaced as a reserve currency, there must be a new contender for the throne. Not the British pound, whose best days are in the past, nor the Chinese yuan whose reserve currency status is decades in the future, if it ever occurs. As for the euro, the improved liquidity and breadth of Europe's financial markets have eroded some of the advantages that have historically supported the preeminence of the dollar as a reserve currency. Nevertheless, the dollar has kept it place as the dominant reserve currency, supported by the edge that U.S. financial markets still have over European markets in terms of size, credit quality, and liquidity, as well as inertia in the use of international currencies.

In 2009, officials at the central bank of China proposed an overhaul of the international monetary system in which the Special Drawing Right (SDR) would eventually replace the dollar as the world's main reserve currency. Their goal was to adopt a reserve currency that is disconnected from a single country (the United States) and would remain stable in the long term, therefore lessening the financial risks caused by the volatility of the dollar. To accomplish this objective, the Chinese advocated a new world reserve currency based on a basket of currencies instead of just the dollar. This currency basket would be fulfilled by the SDR whose value is currently based on the euro, yen, pound, and dollar in accordance with the relative importance of each currency in international trade and finance. Moreover, China proposed that the size of the currency basket be expanded to include all major currencies such as the Chinese yuan and the Russian ruble. The SDR would be managed by the International Monetary Fund.

Several steps would have to be taken to broaden the SDR's use so it could fulfill IMF member countries' demands for a reserve currency. A settlement system between the SDR and other currencies would have to be established so the SDR would be widely accepted in world trade and financial transactions. Currently, the SDR is only used as a unit of account by the IMF and other international organizations. Also, the SDR would have to be actively promoted for use in trade, commodities pricing, investment, and corporate bookkeeping. Moreover, financial assets (securities), which are denominated in SDRs, would have to be created to increase the attractiveness of the SDR. Achieving these results would require a significant amount of time.

Proponents maintain that allowing the SDR to serve as the world's reserve currency would provide several benefits. For the Chinese, it would cushion any depreciation in the dollar's exchange value because the dollar would only be a portion of a basket of several currencies. This would help stabilize the value of China's holdings of U.S. Treasury securities. Also, a basket reserve currency would help support aggregate demand in the world by decreasing the fear of currency volatility. Such fear served as a motivation for countries like China to save large amounts of reserves to guard against losses due to international currency volatility. Moreover, the economic welfare of the world should not depend on the behavior of a single currency, namely the dollar. Currency risk would be diversified through a basket reserve unit, thus enhancing stability and confidence throughout the world. Also, there is the issue of equity. Because the dollar is the main reserve currency, where investors flee to safety during economic strife, the United States can attract the savings of other countries even when the interest rates it pays are very low.

However, there are potential pitfalls of using the SDR as a reserve currency. One problem is that the SDR is backed by nothing other than the good faith and credit of the IMF; that is, the IMF produces nothing to support the value of the SDR. In contrast, the dollar is backed by the goods and services produced by Americans and their willingness to exchange those goods and services for dollars. Also, who would determine the "right price" of the SDR, the IMF? Would the IMF succumb to political pressure to change the SDR's currency weightings in favor of particular nations? Moreover, the use of the SDR would add another step to each international transaction, as buyers and sellers would have to convert their local currency into SDRs. This conversion would increase the cost of doing business for companies, investors, and so on.

For the United States, a loss in its reserve currency position would entail several costs. First, Americans would have to pay more for imported goods as the dollar depreciates when foreigners no longer buy dollars as they previously did when the dollar served as the reserve currency. Also, interest rates on both private and governmental debt would increase. Next, the increased private cost of borrowing could result in weaker consumption, decreased investment, and slower growth. Simply put, the economic supremacy of the United States would be lessened if the dollar lost its reserve currency position. Indeed, the United States has expressed strong reservations concerning the proposal to replace the dollar with the SDR as the reserve currency.

Adopting the SDR as a reserve currency might be technically possible and it could occur if the United States followed persistently bad economic policy in the form of deficit spending, high inflation, and currency depreciation. If foreigners expect that the costs of holding dollars (in terms of lost purchasing power) exceeded the benefits of transacting in dollars, they might opt for an alternative reserve currency. However, replacing the dollar with the SDR as the reserve currency will likely not occur soon because people still realize sizable efficiencies from conducting international transactions in dollars. Until the SDR matches these benefits, it will not replace the dollar as the world's premier currency.

TABLE 17.1

INTERNATIONAL RESERVES, 2006, ALL COUNTRIES
(IN BILLIONS OF SDRs*)

Item	Amount	Percentage
Foreign exchange	4,434.9	98.5%
IMF reserve positions	15.0	0.3
Gold**	33.4	0.7
SDRs	18.9	0.5
Total	4,502.2	100.0%

*For 2008, 1 SDR = $1.53.
**At 35 SDRs per ounce.

Source: From International Monetary Fund, *International Financial Statistics*, March 2009.

Over the course of the 1800s–1900s, two national currencies in particular have gained prominence as means of financing international transactions. These currencies, the U.S. dollar and the UK pound, have been considered *reserve currencies* (or *key currencies*), because trading nations have traditionally been willing to hold them as international reserve assets. Since World War II, the U.S. dollar has been the dominant reserve currency. Other reserve currencies are the Japanese yen and a few other currencies that are acceptable in payment for international transactions.

The role of the pound as a reserve currency is largely due to circumstances of the late 1800s and early 1900s. Not only did Britain (now the United Kingdom) at that time play a dominant role in world trade, but the efficiency of London as an international money market was also widely recognized. This was the golden age of the gold standard, and the pound was freely convertible into gold. Traders and investors felt confident in financing their transactions with pounds. With the demise of the gold standard and the onset of the Great Depression during the 1930s, Britain's commercial and financial status began to deteriorate, and the pound lost some of its international luster. Today, the pound still serves as an important international reserve asset, but it is no longer the most prestigious reserve currency.

The emergence of the U.S. dollar as a reserve currency stems from a different set of circumstances. Emerging from World War II, the U.S. economy was not only unharmed but actually stronger. Because of the vast inflows of gold into the United States during the 1930s and 1940s, the dollar was in a better position than the pound to assume the role of a reserve currency.

The mechanism that supplied the world with dollar balances was the balance-of-payments deficits of the United States. These deficits stemmed largely from U.S. foreign aid granted to Europe immediately after World War II, as well as from the flow of private investment funds abroad from U.S. residents. The early 1950s were characterized as a *dollar-shortage era*, when the massive development programs of the European nations resulted in an excess demand for the dollars used to finance such efforts. As the United States began to run modest payments deficits during the early 1950s, the dollar outflow was appreciated by the recipient nations.

By the late 1950s, the U.S. payments deficits had become larger. As foreign nations began to accumulate larger dollar balances than they were accustomed to, the dollar-shortage era gave way to a *dollar glut*. Throughout the 1960s, the United States continued to provide reserves to the world through its payments deficits. However, the persistently weak position of the U.S. balance of payments increasingly led foreigners to question the soundness of the dollar as a reserve currency. By 1970, the amount of dollar liabilities in the hands of foreigners was several times as large as U.S. reserve assets. Lack of confidence in the soundness of the dollar inspired several European nations to exercise their rights to demand that the U.S. Treasury convert their dollar holdings into gold, which in turn led the United States to suspend its gold convertibility pledge to the rest of the world in 1971.

Using the dollar as a reserve currency meant that the supply of international reserves varied with the payments position of the United States. During the 1960s, this situation gave rise to the so-called **liquidity problem**. To preserve confidence in the dollar as a reserve currency, the United States had to strengthen its payments position by eliminating its deficits. But correction of the U.S. deficits would mean elimination of additional dollars as a source of reserves for the international monetary system. The creation in 1970 of SDRs as reserve assets and their subsequent allocations have been intended as a solution for this problem.

Gold

The historical importance of gold as an international reserve asset should not be underemphasized. At one time, gold served as the key monetary asset of the international payments mechanism; it also constituted the basis of the money supplies of many nations.

As an international money, gold fulfilled several important functions. Under the historic **gold standard**, gold served directly as an international means of payments. It also provided a unit of account against which commodity prices as well as the parities of national currencies were quoted. Although gold holdings do not yield interest income, gold has generally served as a viable store of value despite inflation, wars, and revolutions. Perhaps the greatest advantage of gold as a monetary asset is its overall acceptability, especially when compared with other forms of international monies.

Today, the role of gold as an international reserve asset has declined. Over the past 30 years, gold has fallen from nearly 70 percent to less than 3 percent of world reserves. Private individuals rarely use gold as a medium of payment and virtually never as a unit of account. Nor do central banks currently use gold as an official unit of account for stating the parities of national currencies. The monetary role of gold is currently recognized by only a few nations, mostly in the Middle East. In most nations outside the United States, private residents have long been able to buy and sell gold as they would any other commodity. On December 31, 1974, the U.S. government revoked a 41-year ban on U.S. citizens' ownership of gold. The monetary role of gold today is only that of a glittering ghost haunting efforts to reform the international monetary system.

International Gold Standard

Under the international gold standard, whose golden age was about 1880 to 1914, the values of most national currencies were anchored in gold. Gold coins circulated within these countries as well as across national boundaries as generally accepted means of payment. Monetary authorities were concerned about maintaining the public's confidence in the paper currencies that supplemented gold's role as money. To maintain the integrity of paper currencies, governments agreed to convert them into gold at a fixed rate. This requirement was supposed to prevent monetary authorities from producing excessive amounts of paper money. The so-called *discipline* of the gold standard was achieved by having the money supply bear a fixed relation to the monetary stock of gold. Given the cost of producing gold relative to the cost of other commodities, a monetary price of gold could be established to produce growth in monetary gold—and thus in the money supply—at a rate that corresponded to the growth in real national output.

Over the course of the gold standard's era, the importance of gold began to decline, whereas both paper money and demand deposits showed marked increases. From 1815 to 1913, gold as a share of the aggregate money supply of the United States, France, and Britain fell from about 33 to 10 percent. At the same time, the proportion of bank deposits skyrocketed from a modest 6 percent to about 68 percent. By 1913, paper monies plus demand deposits accounted for approximately 90 percent of the U.S. money supply.

After World War I, popular sentiment favored a return to the discipline of the gold standard, in part because of the inflation that gripped many economies during the war years. The United States was the first to return to the gold standard, followed by several European nations. However, efforts to restore the prewar gold standard ended in complete collapse during the 1930s. In response to the economic strains of the Great Depression, nations one by one announced that they could no longer maintain the gold standard.

In the United States, the Great Depression brought an important modification of the gold standard. In 1934, the Gold Reserve Act gave the U.S. government title to all monetary gold and required citizens to turn in their private holdings to the U.S. Treasury. This was done to end the pressure on U.S. commercial banks to convert their liabilities into gold. The U.S. dollar was also devalued in 1934, when the official price of gold was raised from $20.67 to $35 per ounce. The dollar devaluation was not specifically aimed at defending the U.S. trade balance. The rationale was that a rise in the domestic price of gold would encourage gold production, adding to the money supply and the level of economic activity. The Great Depression would be solved! In retrospect, the devaluation may have had some minor economic effects, but there is no indication that it did anything to lift the economy out of its depressed condition.

Gold Exchange Standard

Emerging from the discussions among the world powers during World War II was a new international monetary organization, the International Monetary Fund. A main objective of the IMF was to reestablish a system of fixed exchange rates, with gold serving as the primary reserve asset. Gold became an international unit of account when member nations officially agreed to state the par values of their currencies in terms of gold or, alternatively, the gold content of the U.S. dollar.

The post-World War II international monetary system as formulated by the fund nations was nominally a **gold exchange standard**. The idea was to economize on monetary gold stocks as international reserves, because they could not expand as fast as international trade was growing. This growth required the United States, which emerged from the war with a dominant economy in terms of productive capacity and national wealth, to assume the role of world banker. The dollar was to become the chief reserve currency of the international monetary system. The coexistence of both dollars and gold as international reserve assets led to this system's being dubbed the *dollar-gold system*.

As a world banker, the United States assumed responsibility for buying and selling gold at a fixed price to foreign official holders of dollars. The dollar was the only currency that was made convertible into gold; other national currencies were pegged to the dollar. The dollar was therefore regarded as a reserve currency that was as good as gold because it was thought that the dollar would retain its value relative to other currencies and remain convertible into gold.

As long as the monetary gold stocks of the United States were large relative to outstanding dollar liabilities abroad, confidence in the dollar as a viable reserve currency remained intact. Immediately following World War II, the U.S. monetary gold stocks peaked at $24 billion, about two-thirds of the world total. But as time passed, the amount of foreign dollar holdings rose significantly because of the U.S. payments deficits, whereas the U.S. monetary gold stock dwindled as some of the dollars were turned back to the U.S. Treasury for gold. By 1965, the total supply of foreign-held dollars exceeded the U.S. stock of monetary gold. With the United States unable to redeem all outstanding dollars for gold at $35 per ounce, its ability as a world banker to deliver on demand was questioned.

These circumstances led to speculation that the United States might attempt to solve its gold-shortage problem by devaluing the dollar. By increasing the official price of gold, a dollar devaluation would lead to a rise in the value of U.S. monetary gold stocks. To prevent speculative profits from any rise in the official price of gold, the United States along with several other nations in 1968 established a *two-tier gold system*. This system consisted of an *official tier*, in which central banks could buy and sell gold for monetary purposes at the official price of $35 per ounce, and a *private market*, where gold as a commodity could be traded at the free-market price. By separating the official gold market from the private gold market, the two-tier system was a step toward the complete demonetization of gold.

Demonetization of Gold

The formation of the two-tier gold system was a remedy that could only delay the inevitable collapse of the gold exchange standard. By 1971, the U.S. stock of monetary gold had declined to $11 billion, only a fraction of U.S. dollar liabilities to foreign central banks. The U.S. balance-of-payments position was also deteriorating. In August 1971, President Richard Nixon announced that the United States was suspending its commitment to buy and sell gold at $35 per ounce. The closing of the gold window to foreign official holders brought an end to the gold exchange standard, and the last functional link between the dollar and monetary gold was severed.

It took several years for the world's monetary authorities to formalize the **demonetization of gold** as an international reserve asset. On January 1, 1975, the official price of gold was abolished as the unit of account for the international monetary system. National monetary authorities could enter into gold transactions at market-determined prices, and the use of gold was terminated by the IMF. It was agreed that one-sixth of the fund's gold would be auctioned at prevailing prices and the profits distributed to the developing nations.

As for the United States, the 41-year ban on gold ownership for U.S. residents was ended on January 1, 1975. Within a few weeks, the U.S. Treasury was auctioning a portion of its gold on the commodity markets. These actions were a signal by the United States that it would treat gold in the same way that it treats any other commodity.

Special Drawing Rights

The liquidity and confidence problems of the gold exchange standard that resulted from reliance on the dollar and gold as international monies led in 1970 to the creation by the IMF of a new reserve asset, termed **special drawing rights**. The objective was to introduce into the payments mechanism a new type of international money, in addition to the dollar and gold, that could be transferred among participating nations in settlement of payments deficits. With the IMF managing the stock of SDRs, world reserves would presumably grow in line with world commerce.

Under the Bretton Woods system of fixed exchange rates, a participating country needed official reserves—government or central bank holdings of gold and widely accepted foreign currencies—that could be used to purchase the domestic currency in world foreign exchange markets, as required to maintain its exchange rate. But the international supply of two key reserve assets—gold and the U.S. dollar—proved inadequate for supporting the expansion of world trade and financial development that was occurring. Thus, the international community decided to create a new international reserve asset under the auspices of the IMF. However, by the early 1970s, the Bretton Woods system had collapsed and the major currencies shifted to a floating exchange rate regime. Also, the growth in international capital markets facilitated borrowing by creditworthy governments. Both of these developments lessened the need for SDRs.

Today, the SDR has only limited use as a reserve asset, and its main function is to serve as the unit of account of the IMF and some other international organizations. Also, some of the IMF's member nations peg their currency values to the SDR. Rather than being an international currency, the SDR is a potential claim on the freely usable currencies of IMF members. Holders of SDRs can obtain these currencies in exchange for their SDRs.

The value of the SDR is defined as a basket of currencies that includes the U.S. dollar, Japanese yen, UK pound, and the euro. The weights of the currencies reflect the amount of exports and imports of these countries during the previous five years. As of 2009, the weights in the basket were: the U.S. dollar = 44 percent, the euro = 34 percent, the yen = 11 percent, and the pound = 11 percent. The SDR's basket composition is reviewed every five years to ensure that it reflects the relative importance of currencies in the world's trading and financial systems. The latest value of the SDR can be found on the IMF's Web site, which is updated daily.

The SDR interest provides the basis for calculating the interest charged to members on IMF loans, the interest paid and charged to members on the SDR holdings, and the interest paid to members on a portion of their quota subscriptions. The SDR interest rate is determined weekly and is based on a weighted average of representative interest rates on short-term debt in the money markets of the SDR basket currencies.

Facilities for Borrowing Reserves

The discussion so far has considered the different types of *owned reserves*—national currencies, gold, and SDRs. Various facilities for *borrowing reserves* have also been implemented for nations with weak balance-of-payments positions. Borrowed reserves do not eliminate the need for owned reserves, but they do add to the flexibility of the international monetary system by increasing the time available for nations to correct payments disequilibrium. Let's examine the major forms of international credit.

IMF Drawings

One of the original purposes of the IMF was to help member nations finance balance-of-payments deficits. The fund has furnished a pool of revolving credit for nations in need of reserves. Temporary loans of foreign currency are made to deficit nations, which are expected to repay them within a stipulated timeframe. The transactions by which the fund makes foreign-currency loans available are called **IMF drawings**.

Deficit nations do not borrow from the fund. Instead, they purchase with their own currency the foreign currency required to help finance deficits. When the nation's balance-of-payments position improves, it is expected to reverse the transaction and make repayment by repurchasing its currency from the fund. The fund currently allows members to purchase other currencies at their own option up to the first 50 percent of their fund quotas, which are based on the nation's economic size. Special permission must be granted by the fund if a nation is to purchase foreign currencies in excess of this figure. The fund extends such permission once it is convinced that the deficit nation has enacted reasonable measures to restore payments equilibrium.

Since the early 1950s, the fund has also fostered liberal exchange-rate policies by entering into *standby arrangements* with interested member nations. These agreements guarantee that a member nation may draw specified amounts of foreign currencies from the fund over given time periods. The advantage is that participating nations can count on credit from the fund should it be needed. It also saves the drawing nation from administrative time delays when the loans are actually made.

General Arrangements to Borrow

During the early 1960s, the question was raised whether the IMF had sufficient amounts of foreign currencies to meet the exchange-stabilization needs of its deficit member nations. Owing to the possibility that large drawings by major nations might exhaust the fund's stocks of foreign currencies, the **General Arrangements to Borrow** were initiated in 1962. Ten leading industrial nations, called the Group of Ten, originally agreed to lend the fund up to a maximum of $6 billion. In 1964, the Group of Ten expanded when Switzerland joined the group. By serving as an intermediary and guarantor, the fund could use these reserves to offer compensatory financial assistance to one or more of the participating nations. Such credit arrangements were expected to be used only when the deficit nation's borrowing needs exceeded the amount of assistance that could be provided under the fund's own drawing facilities.

The General Arrangements to Borrow do *not* provide a permanent increase in the supply of world reserves once the loans are repaid and world reserves revert back to their original levels. However, these arrangements have made world reserves more flexible and adaptable to the needs of deficit nations.

Swap Arrangements

During the early 1960s, a wave of speculative attacks occurred against the U.S. dollar, based on expectations that it would be devalued in terms of other currencies. To help offset the flow of short-term capital out of the dollar into stronger foreign currencies, the U.S. Federal Reserve agreed with several central banks in 1962 to initiate reciprocal currency arrangements, commonly referred to as **swap arrangements**. Today, the swap network on which the United States depends to finance its interventions in the foreign-exchange market includes the central banks of Canada and Mexico.[1]

Swap arrangements are bilateral agreements between central banks. Each government provides for an exchange, or swap, of currencies to help finance temporary payments disequilibrium. If Mexico, for example, is short of dollars, it can ask the Federal Reserve to supply them in exchange for pesos. A drawing on the swap network is usually initiated by telephone, followed by an exchange of wire messages specifying terms and conditions. The actual swap is in the form of a foreign-exchange contract calling for the sale of dollars by the Federal Reserve for the currency of a foreign central bank. The nation requesting the swap is expected to use the funds to help ease its payments deficits and discourage speculative capital outflows. Swaps are to be repaid (reversed) within a stipulated period of time, normally within 3 to 12 months.

International Lending Risk

In many respects, the principles that apply to international lending are similar to those of domestic lending: the lender needs to determine the credit risk of whether the borrower will default. However, when making international loans, bankers face two additional risks: country risk and currency risk.

Credit risk is financial and refers to the probability that part or all of the interest or principal of a loan will not be repaid. The larger the potential for default on a loan, the higher the interest rate that the bank must charge the borrower.

Assessing credit risk on international loans tends to be more difficult than on domestic loans. American banks are often less familiar with foreign business practices and economic conditions than those in the United States. Obtaining reliable information to evaluate foreign credit risk can be time consuming and costly. Many U.S. banks, therefore, confine their international lending to major multinational corporations and financial institutions. To attract lending by U.S. banks, a foreign government may provide assurances against default by a local private borrower, thus reducing the credit risk of the loan.

Country risk is political and is closely related to political developments in a country, especially the government's views concerning international investments and loans. Some governments encourage the inflow of foreign funds to foster domestic economic development. Fearing loss of national sovereignty, other governments may discourage such inflows by enacting additional taxes, profit restrictions, and

---

[1]Because of the formation of the European Central Bank and in light of 15 years of disuse, the bilateral swap arrangements of the Federal Reserve with many European central banks, such as Austria, Germany, and Belgium, were jointly deemed no longer necessary in view of the well-established, present-day arrangements for international monetary cooperation. Accordingly, the respective parties to the arrangements mutually agreed to allow them to lapse in 1998.

wage/price controls that can hinder the ability of local borrowers to repay loans. In the extreme, foreign governments can expropriate the assets of foreign investors or make foreign loan repayments illegal.

Currency risk is economic and is associated with currency depreciations and appreciations as well as exchange controls. Some loans by U.S. banks are denominated in foreign currency instead of dollars. If the currency in which the loan is made depreciates against the dollar during the period of the loan, the repayment will be worth fewer dollars. If the foreign currency has a well-developed forward market, the loan may be hedged. But many foreign currencies, especially of the developing nations, do not have such markets, and loans denominated in these currencies cannot always be hedged to decrease this type of currency risk. Another type of currency risk arises from exchange controls, which are common in developing nations. Exchange controls restrict the movement of funds across national borders or limit a currency's convertibility into dollars for repayment, thus adding to the risk of international lenders.

When lending overseas, bankers must evaluate credit risk, country risk, and currency risk. Evaluating risks in foreign lending often results in detailed analyses, compiled by a bank's research department, that are based on a nation's financial, economic, and political conditions. When international lenders consider detailed analyses to be too expensive, they often use reports and statistical indicators to help them determine the risk of lending.

The Problem of International Debt

Much concern has been voiced over the volume of international lending in recent years. At times, the concern has been that international lending was insufficient. Such was the case after the oil shocks in 1974–1975 and 1979–1980, when it was feared that some oil-importing developing nations might not be able to obtain loans to finance trade deficits resulting from the huge increases in the price of oil. It so happened that many oil-importing nations were able to borrow dollars from commercial banks. They paid the dollars to OPEC nations that redeposited the money in commercial banks, which then re-lent the money to oil importers, and so on. In the 1970s, the banks were part of the solution; if they had not lent large sums to the developing nations, the oil shocks would have done far more damage to the world economy.

By the 1980s, however, commercial banks were viewed as part of an international debt problem because they had lent so much to developing nations. Flush with OPEC money after the oil price increases of the 1970s, the banks actively sought borrowers and had no trouble finding them among the developing nations. Some nations borrowed to prop up consumption because their living standards were already low and hard hit by oil-price hikes. Most nations borrowed to avoid cuts in development programs and to invest in energy projects. It was generally recognized that banks were successful in recycling their OPEC deposits to developing nations following the first round of oil-price hikes in 1974 and 1975. But the international lending mechanism encountered increasing difficulties beginning with the global recession of the early 1980s. In particular, some developing nations were unable to pay their external debts on schedule.

Another indicator of debt burden is the **debt service/export ratio**, which refers to scheduled interest and principal payments as a percentage of export earnings. The debt service/export ratio permits one to focus on two key indicators of whether a reduction in the debt burden is possible in the short term: the interest rate that the nation pays on its external debt and the growth in its exports of goods and services. All else being constant, a rise in the interest rate increases the debt service/export ratio, while a rise in exports decreases the ratio. It is a well-known rule of international finance that a nation's debt burden rises if the interest rate on the debt exceeds the rate of growth of exports.

Dealing with Debt-Servicing Difficulties

A nation may experience debt-servicing problems for a number of reasons: (1) It may have pursued improper macroeconomic policies that contribute to large balance-of-payments deficits, (2) it may have borrowed excessively or on unfavorable terms, or (3) it may have been affected by adverse economic events that it could not control.

Several options are available to a nation facing debt-servicing difficulties. First, it can cease repayments on its debt. However, such an action undermines confidence in the nation, making it difficult (if not impossible) for it to borrow in the future. Furthermore, the nation might be declared in default, in which case its assets (such as ships and aircraft) might be confiscated and sold to discharge the debt. As a group, however, developing nations in debt may have considerable leverage in winning concessions from their lenders.

A second option is for the nation to try to service its debt at all costs. To do so may require the restriction of other foreign-exchange expenditures, a step that may be viewed as socially unacceptable.

Also, a nation may seek debt rescheduling, which generally involves stretching out the original payment schedule of the debt. There is a cost because the debtor nation must pay interest on the amount outstanding until the debt has been repaid.

When a nation faces debt-servicing problems, its creditors seek to reduce their exposure by collecting all interest and principal payments as they come due, while granting no new credit. But there is an old adage that goes as follows: When a man owes a bank $1,000, the bank owns him; but when a man owes the bank $1 million, he owns the bank. Banks with large amounts of international loans find it in their best interest to help the debtor recover financially. To deal with debt-servicing problems, therefore, debtor nations and their creditors generally attempt to negotiate rescheduling agreements. That is, creditors agree to lengthen the time period for repayment of the principal and sometimes part of the interest on existing loans. Banks have little option but to accommodate demands for debt rescheduling because they do not want the debtor to officially default on the loan. With default, the bank's assets become nonperforming and subject to markdowns by government regulators. These actions could lead to possible withdrawals of deposits and bank insolvency.

Besides rescheduling debt with commercial banks, developing nations may obtain emergency loans from the IMF. The IMF provides loans to nations experiencing balance-of-payments difficulties provided that the borrowers initiate programs to correct these difficulties. By insisting on **conditionality**, the IMF asks borrowers to adopt austerity programs to shore up economies and put muddled finances in order. Such measures have resulted in the slashing of public expenditures, private consumption, and, in some cases, capital investment. Borrowers must also cut imports and expand exports. The IMF views austerity programs as a necessity because with a sovereign debtor, there is no other way to make it pay back its loans. The IMF faces a difficult situation in deciding how tough to get with borrowers. If it goes soft and offers money on easier terms, it sets a precedent for other debtor nations. But if it miscalculates and requires excessive austerity measures, it risks triggering political turmoil and possibly a declaration of default.

The IMF has been criticized, notably by developing nations, for demanding austerity policies that excessively emphasize short-term improvements in the balance of payments rather than fostering long-term economic growth. Developing nations also contend that the IMF austerity programs promote downward pressure on economic activity in nations that are already exposed to recessionary forces. The crucial issue faced by the IMF is how to resolve the economic problems of the debtor nations in a manner most advantageous to them, to their creditors, and to the world as a whole. The mutually advantageous solution is one that enables these nations to achieve sustainable, noninflationary economic growth, thus assuring creditors of repayment and benefiting the world economy through expansion of trade and economic activity.

Reducing Bank Exposure to Developing-Nation Debt

When developing nations cannot meet their debt obligations to foreign banks, the stability of the international financial system is threatened. Banks may react to this threat by increasing their capital base, setting aside reserves to cover losses, and reducing new loans to debtor nations.

Banks have additional means to improve their financial position. One method is to liquidate developing-nation debt by engaging in outright *loan sales* to other banks in the secondary market. But if there occurs an unexpected increase in the default risk of such loans, their market value will be less than their face value. The selling bank thus absorbs costs because its loans must be sold at a discount. Following the sale, the bank must adjust its balance sheet to take account of any previously unrecorded difference between the face value of the loans and their market value. Many small and medium-sized U.S. banks, eager to dump their bad loans in the 1980s, were willing to sell them in the secondary market at discounts as high as 70 percent, or 30 cents on the dollar. But many banks could not afford such huge discounts. Even worse, if the banks all rushed to sell bad loans at once, prices would fall further. Sales of loans in the secondary market were often viewed as a last-resort measure.

Another debt-reduction technique is the *debt buyback*, in which the government of the debtor nation buys the loans from the commercial bank at a discount. Banks have also engaged in *debt-for-debt swaps*, in which a bank exchanges its loans for securities issued by the debtor nation's government at a lower interest rate or discount.

Cutting losses on developing-nation loans has sometimes involved banks in **debt/equity swaps**. Under this approach, a commercial bank sells its loans at a discount to the developing-nation government for local currency, which it then uses to finance an equity investment in the debtor nation.

To see how a debt/equity swap works, suppose that Brazil owes Manufacturers Hanover Trust (of New York) $1 billion. Manufacturers Hanover decides to swap some of the debt for ownership shares in Companhia Suzano del Papel e Celulose, a pulp-and-paper company. Here is what occurs:

- Manufacturers Hanover takes $115 million in Brazilian government-guaranteed loans to a Brazilian broker. The broker takes the loans to the Brazilian central bank's monthly debt auction, where they are valued at an average of 87 cents on the dollar.
- Through the broker, Manufacturers Hanover exchanges the loans at the central bank for $100 million worth of Brazilian cruzados. The broker is paid a commission, and the central bank retires the loans.
- With its cruzados, Manufacturers Hanover purchases 12 percent of Suzano's stock, and Suzano uses the bank's funds to increase capacity and exports.

Although debt/equity swaps enhance a bank's chances of selling developing-nation debt, they do not necessarily decrease its risk. Some equity investments in developing nations may be just as risky as the loans that were swapped for local factories or land. Moreover, banks that acquire an equity interest in developing-nation assets may not have the knowledge to manage those assets. Debtor nations also worry that debt/equity swaps will allow major companies to fall into foreign hands.

Debt Reduction and Debt Forgiveness

Another method of coping with developing-nation debt involves programs enacted for debt reduction and debt forgiveness. **Debt reduction** refers to any voluntary scheme that lessens the burden on the debtor nation to service its external debt. Debt reduction is accomplished through two main approaches. The first is the use of negotiated modifications in the terms and conditions of the contracted debt, such as debt reschedulings, retiming of interest payments, and improved borrowing terms. Debt reduction may also be achieved through measures such as debt/equity swaps and debt buybacks. The purpose of debt reduction is to foster comprehensive policies for economic growth by easing the ability of the debtor nation to service its debt, thus freeing resources that will be used for investment.

Some proponents of debt relief maintain that the lending nations should permit **debt forgiveness**. Debt forgiveness refers to any arrangement that reduces the value of contractual obligations of the debtor nation; it includes schemes such as markdowns or write-offs of developing-nation debt or the abrogation of existing obligations to pay interest.

Debt-forgiveness advocates maintain that the most heavily indebted developing nations are unable to service their external debt and maintain an acceptable rate of per capita income growth because their debt burden is overwhelming. They contend that if some of this debt were forgiven, a debtor nation could use the freed-up foreign-exchange resources to increase its imports and invest domestically, thus increasing domestic economic growth rates. The release of the limitation on foreign exchange would provide the debtor nation additional incentive to invest because it would not have to share as much of the benefits of its increased growth and investment with its creditors in the form of interest payments. Moreover, debt forgiveness would allow the debtor nation to service its debt more easily; this would reduce the debt-load burden of a debtor nation and could potentially lead to greater inflows of foreign investment.

Debt-forgiveness critics question whether the amount of debt is a major limitation on developing-nation growth and whether that growth would in fact resume if a large portion of that debt were forgiven. They contend that nations such as Indonesia and South Korea have experienced large amounts of external debt relative to national output but have not faced debt-servicing problems. Also, debt forgiveness does not guarantee that the freed-up foreign-exchange resources will be used productively—that is, invested in sectors that will ultimately generate additional foreign exchange.

The Eurodollar Market

One of the most widely misunderstood topics in international finance is the nature and operation of the **eurodollar market**, also called the eurocurrency market. This market operates as a financial intermediary, bringing together lenders and borrowers. Originally, eurodollars were held almost exclusively in Europe, and thus the name eurodollars. Most of these deposits are still held by commercial banks in London, Paris, and other European cities; but they also are held in such places as the Bahamas, Bahrain, Hong Kong, Japan, Panama, and Singapore. Regardless of where they are held, such deposits are referred to as eurodollars. The size of the eurodollar market has increased from about $1 billion in the 1950s to more than $5 trillion in the first decade of the 2000s.

Eurodollars are bank deposit liabilities, such as time deposits, denominated in U.S. dollars and other foreign currencies in banks outside the United States, including foreign branches of U.S. banks. Transactions in dollars constitute about three-fourths of the volume of transactions. Eurodollar deposits in turn may be redeposited in other foreign banks, lent to business enterprises, invested, or retained to improve reserves or overall liquidity. The average deposit is in the millions and has a maturity of less than six months. Thus, the eurodollar market is out of reach for all but the most wealthy. The only way for most individuals to invest in this market is indirectly through a money market fund.

Eurodollar deposits are practically free of regulation by the host country, including U.S. regulatory agencies. For example, they are not subject to the reserve requirements mandated by the Federal Reserve and to fees of the Federal Deposit Insurance Corporation. Because eurodollars are subject to less regulation than similar deposits within the United States, banks issuing eurodollar deposits can operate on narrower margins or spreads between dollar borrowing and lending rates than can domestic U.S. banks. This gives eurodollar deposits a competitive advantage relative to deposits issued by domestic U.S. banks. Thus, banks issuing eurodollar deposits can compete effectively with domestic U.S. banks for loans and deposits.

The eurodollar market has grown rapidly since the 1950s, due in part to the U.S. banking regulations that prevented U.S. banks from paying competitive interest rates on savings accounts (Regulation Q), which have increased the costs of lending for U.S. banks. Also, continuing deficits in the U.S. current account have increased the dollar holdings for foreigners, as did the sharp increase in oil prices that resulted in enormous wealth in the oil-exporting countries. These factors, combined with the relative freedom allowed foreign currency banking in many countries, resulted in the rapid growth of the market.

As a type of international money, eurodollars increase the efficiency of international trade and finance. They provide an internationally accepted medium of exchange, store of value, and standard of value. Because eurodollars eliminate the risks and costs associated with converting from one currency to another, they permit savers to search the world more easily for the highest returns and borrowers to scan out the lowest cost of funds. Thus, they are a link among various regional capital markets, helping to create a worldwide market for capital.[2]

Summary

1. The purpose of international reserves is to permit nations to bridge the gap between monetary receipts and payments. Deficit nations can use international reserves to buy time in order to postpone adjustment measures.

2. The demand for international reserves depends on two major factors: (a) the monetary value of international transactions and (b) the size and duration of the balance-of-payments disequilibrium.

3. The need for international reserves tends to become less acute under a system of floating exchange rates than under a system of fixed rates. The more efficient the international adjustment mechanism and the greater the extent of international policy coordination, the smaller the need for international reserves.

4. The supply of international reserves consists of owned and borrowed reserves. Among the major sources of reserves are (a) foreign currencies, (b) monetary gold stocks, (c) special drawing rights, (d) IMF drawing positions, (e) the General Arrangements to Borrow, and (f) swap arrangements.

5. When making international loans, bankers face credit risk, country risk, and currency risk.

6. Among the indicators used to analyze a nation's external debt position are its debt-to-export ratio and debt service/export ratio.

7. A nation experiencing debt-servicing difficulties has several options: (a) cease repayment on its debt, (b) service its debt at all costs, or (c) reschedule its debt. Debt rescheduling has been widely used by borrowing nations in recent years.

8. A bank can reduce its exposure to developing-nation debt through outright loan sales in the secondary market, debt buybacks, debt-for-debt swaps, and debt/equity swaps.

9. Eurodollars are deposits, denominated and payable in dollars and other foreign currencies, in banks outside the United States. The eurodollar market operates as a financial intermediary, bringing together lenders and borrowers.

Key Concepts & Terms

- Conditionality (p. 574)
- Country risk (p. 572)
- Credit risk (p. 572)
- Currency risk (p. 573)
- Debt/equity swap (p. 575)
- Debt forgiveness (p. 576)
- Debt reduction (p. 576)
- Debt service/export ratio (p. 574)
- Demand for international reserves (p. 560)
- Demonetization of gold (p. 569)
- Eurodollar market (p. 577)
- General Arrangements to Borrow (p. 571)
- Gold exchange standard (p. 568)
- Gold standard (p. 567)
- IMF drawings (p. 571)
- International reserves (p. 560)
- Liquidity problem (p. 567)
- Special drawing rights (p. 570)
- Supply of international reserves (p. 563)
- Swap arrangements (p. 572)

---

[2]See Charles J. Woelfel, "Eurodollars," *Encyclopedia of Banking and Finance*, 10th edition, London, UK: Fitzroy Dearborn Publishers, 1995.

Study Questions

1. What advantages does a gold exchange standard have over a pure gold standard?

2. What is meant by a reserve currency? Historically, which currencies have assumed this role?

3. What options are available to a nation experiencing debt-servicing difficulties? What limitations apply to each option?

4. How can debt/equity swaps help banks reduce losses on developing-nation loans?

5. What are special drawing rights? Why were they created? How is their value determined?

6. Distinguish between debt-to-export ratio and debt service/export ratio.

7. What caused the international debt problem of the developing nations in the 1980s? Why did this debt problem threaten the stability of the international banking system?

8. In terms of volume, which component of world reserves is currently most important? Which is currently least important?

9. What is a eurodollar? How did the eurodollar market develop?

10. The total supply of international reserves consists of two categories: (a) owned reserves and (b) borrowed reserves. What do these categories include?

11. What is the current role of gold in the international monetary system?

12. What methods do banks use to reduce their exposure to developing-nation debt?

13. A nation's need for international reserves is similar to an individual's desire to hold cash balances. Explain.

14. What risks do bankers assume when making loans to foreign borrowers?

15. What are the major factors that determine a nation's demand for international reserves?

16. What facilities exist for trading nations that wish to borrow international reserves?

A

absorption approach an approach to currency depreciation that deals with the income effects of depreciation; a decrease in domestic expenditures relative to income must occur for depreciation to promote payments equilibrium, according to the absorption approach

adjustable pegged exchange rates a system of semifixed exchange rates where it is understood that the par value of the currency will be changed occasionally in response to changing economic conditions

adjustment mechanism a mechanism that works to return a balance of payments to equilibrium after the initial equilibrium has been disrupted; the process takes two different forms: automatic (economic processes) and discretionary (government policies)

ad valorem tariff a tariff expressed as a fixed percentage of the value of the imported product

advanced nations include those of North America and Western Europe, plus Australia, New Zealand, and Japan

agglomeration economies a rich country specializes in manufacturing niches and gains productivity through groups of firms clustered together, some producing the same product and others connected by vertical linkages

antidumping duty a duty levied against commodities a home nation believes are being dumped into its markets from abroad

appreciation (as applied to currency markets) when, over time, it takes fewer units of a nation's currency to purchase one unit of a foreign currency

Asia-Pacific Economic Cooperation (APEC) includes Australia, Brunei, Canada, Chile, China, Indonesia, Japan, Malaysia, Mexico, New Zealand, Paupua New Guinea, the Phillippines, Peru, Russia, Singapore, South Korea, Taiwan, Thailand, the United States, and Vietnam; in 1993, leaders of the APEC countries put forth their vision of an Asia-Pacific economic community in which barriers to trade and investment in the region would be eliminated by the year 2020

ask price the price at which the trader is willing to sell a currency in exchange for another currency

asset-market approach a method of determining short-term exchange rates where investors consider two key factors when deciding between domestic and foreign investments; relative levels of interest rates and expected changes in the exchange rate itself over the term of the investment

autarky a case of national self-sufficiency or absence of trade

automatic adjustment (of the balance-of-payments process) a mechanism that works to return a balance of payments to equilibrium automatically through the adjustments in economic variables

B

balance of international indebtedness a statement that summarizes a country's stock of assets and liabilities against the rest of the world at a fixed point in time

balance of payments a record of the flow of economic transactions between the residents of one country and the rest of the world

basis for trade why nations export and import certain products

beggar-thy-neighbor policy the practice of imposing protectionist policies to achieve gains from trade at the expense of other nations

Benelux a cusoms union formed in 1948 that includes Belgium, the Netherlands, and Luxembourg

bid rate the price that the bank is willing to pay for a unit of foreign currency

bonded warehouse a storage facility operated under the lock and key of (in the case of the United States) the U.S. Customs Service

brain drain emigration of highly educated and skilled people from developing nations to industrial nations

Bretton Woods system a new international monetary system created in 1944 by delegates from 44 member nations of the United Nations that met at Bretton Woods, New Hampshire

buffer stock supplies of a commodity financed and held by a producers' association; used to limit commodity price swings

buy-national policies when a home nation's government, through explicit laws, openly discriminates against foreign suppliers in its purchasing decisions

C

call option gives the holder the right to buy foreign currency at a specified price

capital and financial account the net result of both private-sector and official capital and financial transactions

capital controls government-imposed barriers to foreign savers investing in domestic assets or to domestic savers investing in foreign assets; also known as *exchange controls*

capital/labor ratio a country's ratio of capital inputs to labor inputs

carry trade It occurs when you borrow and pay interest in order to buy something else that has higher interest

cartel a group of firms or nations that attempts to support prices higher than would exist under more competitive conditions

clean float when free-market forces of supply and demand are allowed to determine the exchange value of a currency

Commodity Credit Corporation (CCC) a government-owned corporation administered by the U.S. Department of Agriculture

commodity terms of trade measures the relation between the prices a nation gets for its exports and the prices it pays for its imports

common agricultural policy members of the European Union agree to maintain identical governmental agricultural policies to support farmers

common market a group of trading nations that permits the free movement of goods and services among member nations, the initiation of common external trade restrictions against non-members, and the free movement of factors of production across national borders within the economic bloc

community indifference curve the indifference curve that represents the tastes and preferences of all of the households of a nation

complete specialization a situation in which a country produces only one good

compound tariff a tariff that is a combination of a specific tariff and an ad valorem tariff

conditionality the standards imposed by the IMF on borrowing countries to qualify for a loan, which can include requirements that the borrowers initiate programs to correct economic difficulties, adopt austerity programs to shore up their economies, and put their muddled finances in order

conglomerate diversification in the case of an MNE, diversification into nonrelated markets

constant opportunity costs a constant rate of sacrifice of one good for another as a nation slides along its production possibilities schedule

consumer surplus the difference between the amount that buyers would be willing and able to pay for a good and the actual amount they do pay

consumption effect a trade restriction's loss of welfare that occurs because of increased prices and lower consumption

consumption gains post-trade consumption points outside a nation's production possibilities schedule

convergence criteria economic standards required of all nations in a monetary union; in the instance of the Maastricht Treaty, these standards included price stability, low long-term interest rates, stable exchange rates, and sound public finances

corporate average fuel economy standards (CAFE) fuel economy standards imposed by the U.S. government on automobile manufacturers

cost-based definition of dumping a method of calculating the fair market value of a product in dumping cases; the U.S. Commerce Department "constructs" fair market value equal to the sum of (1) the cost of manufacturing the merchandise, (2) general expenses, (3) profit on home-market sales, and (4) the cost of packaging the merchandise for shipment to the United States

cost-insurance-freight (CIF) valuation when ad valorem tariffs are levied as a percentage of the imported commodity's total value as it arrives at its final destination

countervailing duty a levy imposed by importing countries to counteract foreign export subsidies; the size of the duty is limited to the amount of the export subsidy

country risk risk associated with political developments in a country, especially the government's views concerning international investments and loans

country risk analysis a process that multinational corporations and banks carry out to help them decide whether to do business abroad

covered interest arbitrage the process of moving funds into foreign currencies to take advantage of higher investment yields abroad, while avoiding exchange rate risk

crawling peg a system in which a nation makes small, frequent changes in the par value of its currency to correct balance-of-payments disequilibriums

credit risk   the probability that part or all of the interest or principal of a loan will not be repaid

credit transaction   a balance of payments transaction that results in a receipt of a payment from foreigners

cross exchange rate   the resulting rate derived when the exchange rate between any two currencies can be derived from the rates of these two currencies in terms of a third currency

currency board   a monetary authority that issues notes and coins convertible into a foreign anchor currency at a fixed exchange rate

currency crashes   financial crises that often end in currency devaluations or accelerated depreciations

currency crisis   a situation in which a weak currency experiences heavy selling pressure, also called a *speculative attack*

currency risk   investment risk associated with currency depreciations and appreciations as well as exchange controls

currency swap   the conversion of one currency to another currency at one point in time, with an agreement to reconvert it to the original currency at a specified time in the future

current account   the net value of monetary flows associated with transactions in goods and services, investment income, employee compensation, and unilateral transfers

customs union   an agreement among two or more trading partners to remove all tariff and nontariff trade barriers among themselves; each member nation imposes identical trade restrictions against nonparticipants

customs valuation   the process of determining the value of an imported product

D

deadweight loss   the net loss of economic benefits to a domestic economy due the protective effect and the consumption effect of a trade barrier

debit transaction   a balance of payments transaction that leads to a payment to foreigners

debt/equity swap   when a commercial bank sells its loans at a discount to the debtor-nation's government for local currency, which it then uses to finance an equity investment in the debtor nation

debt forgiveness   any arrangement that reduces the value of contractual obligations of the debtor nation

debt reduction   any voluntary scheme that lessens the burden on the debtor nation to service its external debt

debt service/export ratio   the scheduled interest and principal payments as a percentage of export earnings

demand for international reserves the requirement for international reserves; depends on two related factors: (1) the monetary value of international transactions and (2) the disequilibrium that can arise in balance-of-payments positions; the requirements for international reserves include assets such as key foreign currencies, special drawing rights, and drawing rights at the International Monetary Fund

demand-pull inflation   when a nation's capacity to produce has been achieved, and further increases in aggregate demand pull prices upward

demonetization of gold   occurred in the 1970s when the official price of gold was abolished as the unit of account for the international monetary system

depreciation   (as applies to currency markets) when, over time, it takes more units of a nation's currency to purchase one unit of a foreign currency

destabilizing speculation   speculation that occurs when speculators expect a current trend in exchange rates to continue and their transactions accelerate the rise or fall of the target currency's value

devaluation   an official change in a currency's par value, which causes the currency's exchange value to depreciate

developing nations   most nations in Africa, Asia, Latin America, and the Middle East

direct controls   consist of government restrictions on the market economy

direct currency quote   one in which the domestic currency is the base currency and the foreign currency is the quote currency

dirty float   a condition under a managed floating system when free-market forces of supply and demand are not allowed to achieve their equilibrating role; countries may manage their exchange rates to improve the competitiveness of their producers

discount   the valuation of a currency when it is worth less in the forward market than in the spot market

distribution of income   the distribution of wages earned across a country

dollarization   occurs when residents of a foreign country use the U.S. dollar alongside or instead of their domestic currency

domestic content requirements requirements that stipulate the minimum percentage of a product's total value that must be produced domestically if the product is to qualify for zero tariff rates

domestic production subsidy   a subsidy that is sometimes granted to producers of import-competing goods

domestic revenue effect   the amount of tariff revenue shifted from domestic consumers to the tariff-levying government

double-entry accounting   a system of accounting in which each credit entry is balanced by a debit entry, and vice versa, so that the recording of any transaction leads to two offsetting entries

dumping   when foreign buyers are charged lower prices than domestic buyers for an identical product, after allowing for transportation costs and tariff duties

dynamic comparative advantage   a changing pattern in comparative advantage; governments can establish policies to promote opportunities for changes in comparative advantage over time

dynamic effects of economic integration   effects that relate to member nations' long-term rates of growth, which include economies of scale, greater competition, and investment stimulus

dynamic gains from international trade   the effect of trade on the country's growth rate and thus on the volume of additional resources made available to, or utilized by, the trading country

E

economic integration   a process of eliminating restrictions on international trade, payments, and factor mobility

economic interdependence   all aspects of a nation's economy are linked to the economies of its trading partners

economic sanctions   government-mandated limitations placed on customary trade or financial relations among nations

economic union   where national, social, taxation, and fiscal policies are harmonized and administered by a supranational institution

economies of scale   when increasing all inputs by the same proportion results in a greater proportion of total output

effective exchange rate   a weighted average of the exchange rates between a

domestic currency and that nation's most important trading partners, with weights given by relative importance of the nation's trade with each trade partner

effective tariff rate   measures the total increase in domestic production that a tariff makes possible, compared to free trade

elasticity approach   an approach to currency depreciation that emphasizes the relative price effects of depreciation and suggests that depreciation works best when demand elasticities for a nation's imports and exports are high

escape clause   allows the president to temporarily terminate or make modifications in trade concessions granted foreign nations and to temporarily levy restrictions on surging imports

euro   the official currency of the EMU

eurodollar market   a market that operates as a financial intermediary, bringing together lenders and borrowers; also called the eurocurrency market

European Monetary Union (EMU) the countries of Europe that in 1999 abolished their national currencies and central banks and replaced them with the euro and the European Central Bank

European Union (EU)   a trading bloc that replaced the European Community following ratification of the Maastricht Treaty by the 12 member countries of the European Community

exchange arbitrage   the simultaneous purchase and sale of a currency in different foreign-exchange markets in order to profit from exchange-rate differentials in the two locations

exchange controls   government-imposed barriers to foreign savers investing in domestic assets (for example, government securities, stock,

or bank deposits) or to domestic savers investing in foreign assets

exchange rate   the price of one currency in terms of another

exchange rate pass-through (relation)   the extent to which changing currency values lead to changes in import and export prices

exchange-rate index   a weighted average of the exchange rates between a domestic currency and that nation's most important trading partners, with weights given by relative importance of the nation's trade with each trade partner

exchange-stabilization fund   a government entity that attempts to ensure that the market exchange rate does not move above or below the official exchange rate through purchases and sales of foreign currencies

exit barriers   cost conditions that make lengthy industry exit a rational response by companies

expenditure-changing policies policies that alter the level of aggregate demand for goods and services, including those produced domestically and those imported

expenditure-switching policies policies that modify the direction of demand, shifting it between domestic output and imports

export controls   enacted to stabilize export revenues, these measures offset a decrease in the market demand for the primary commodity by assigning cutbacks in the market supply

export quotas   limitations on export sales administered by one or more exporting nations or industries

export subsidy   a subsidy paid to exporters so they can sell goods abroad at the lower world price but still receive the higher support price

Export-Import Bank (Eximbank)   an independent agency of the U.S.

government established to encourage the exports of U.S. businesses

export-led growth   involves promoting economic growth through the export of manufactured goods—trade controls are either nonexistent or very low, in the sense that any disincentives to export resulting from import barriers are counterbalanced by export subsidies export-oriented policy see export-led growth

external balance   when a nation realizes neither balance-of-payments deficits nor balance-of-payments surpluses

external economies of scale   for a firm relate to the size of an entire industry within a particular geographic area

F

factor-endowment theory   asserts that a country exports those goods that use its abundant factor more intensively

factor-price equalization   free trade's tendency to cause cheap factors of production to become more expensive, and the expensive factors of production to become cheaper

fast-track authority   devised in 1974, this provision commits the U.S. Congress to consider trade agreements without amendment; in return, the president must adhere to a specified timetable and several other procedures

fiscal policy   refers to changes in government spending and taxes

fixed exchange rates   a system used primarily by small developing nations whose currencies are anchored to a key currency, such as the U.S. dollar

floating exchange rates   when a nation allows its currency to fluctuate according to the free-market forces of supply and demand

flying-geese pattern of economic growth   where countries gradually move up in technological development by following in the pattern of countries ahead of them in the development process

forecasting exchange rates   attempts to predict future rates of exchange

foreign direct investment   foreign acquisition of a controlling interest in an overseas company or facility

foreign repercussion effect   the impact that changes in domestic expenditures and income levels have on foreign economies; a rise in domestic income stimulates imports, causing a foreign expansion that in turn raises demand for domestic exports

foreign-currency options   provide an options holder the right to buy or sell a fixed amount of foreign currency at a prearranged price, within a few days or several years

foreign-exchange market   the organizational setting within which individuals, businesses, governments, and banks buy and sell foreign currencies and other debt instruments

foreign-trade multiplier   when an increase in exports sets off a chain reaction that results in greater levels of spending so that domestic income increases by some multiple of the export increase

foreign-trade zone (FTZ)   special zones that enlarge the benefits of a bonded warehouse by eliminating the restrictive aspects of customs surveillance and by offering more suitable manufacturing facilities; FTZs are intended to stimulate international trade, attract industry, and create jobs by providing an area that gives users tariff and tax breaks

forward market   where foreign exchange can be traded for future delivery

forward rate   the rate of exchange used in the settlement of forward transactions

forward transaction   an outright purchase and sale of foreign currency at a fixed exchange rate but with payment or delivery of the foreign currency at a future date

free trade   a system of open markets between countries in which nations concentrate their production on goods they can make most cheaply, with all the consequent benefits of the division of labor

free trade area   an association of trading nations whose members agree to remove all tariff and nontariff barriers among themselves

free-on-board (FOB)   valuation when a tariff is applied to a product's value as it leaves the exporting country

free-trade argument   if each nation produces what it does best and permits trade, over the long term each party will enjoy lower prices and higher levels of output, income, and consumption than could be achieved in isolation

free-trade-biased sector   generally comprises exporting companies, their workers, and their suppliers; it also consists of consumers, including wholesalers and retail merchants of imported goods

fundamental analysis   the opposite of technical analysis; involves consideration of economic variables that are likely to affect a currency's value

fundamental disequilibrium   when the official exchange rate and the market exchange rate may move apart, reflecting changes in fundamental economic conditions—income levels, tastes and preferences, and technological factors

futures market   a market in which contracting parties agree to future exchanges of currencies and set applicable exchange rates in advance; distinguished from the forward market in that only a limited number of leading currencies are traded; trading takes place in standardized contract amounts and in a specific geographic location

G

gains from international trade   gains trading partners simultaneously enjoy due to specialization and the division of labor

General Agreement on Tariffs and Trade (GATT)   signed in 1947, GATT was crafted as an agreement among contracting parties, the member nations, to decrease trade barriers and to place all nations on an equal footing in trading relations; GATT was never intended to become an organization; instead it was a set of bilateral agreements among countries around the world to reduce trade barriers

General Arrangements to Borrow   initiated in 1962, 10 leading industrial nations, called the Group of Ten, originally agreed to lend the fund up to a maximum of $6 billion; in 1964, the Group of Ten expanded when Switzerland joined the group; by serving as an intermediary and guarantor, the fund could use these reserves to offer compensatory financial assistance to one or more of the participating nations

generalized system of preferences (GSP)   a system in which industrialized nations attempt to promote economic development in developing countries through lower tariffs and increased trade, rather than foreign aid

globalization   the process of greater interdependence among countries and their citizens

global quota   a technique permitting a specified number of goods to be imported each year, but does not specify where the product is shipped from or who is permitted to import

gold exchange standard   a system of fixed exchange rates, with gold serving as the primary reserve asset; member nations officially agreed to state the par values of their currencies in terms of gold or, alternatively, the gold content of the U.S. dollar

gold standard   a monetary system in which each member nation's money supply consisted of gold or paper money backed by gold, where each member nation defined the official price of gold in terms of its national currency and was prepared to buy and sell gold at that price; free import and export of gold was permitted by member nations

goods and services balance   the result of combining the balance of trade in services and the merchandise trade balance

Group of Five (G-5)   five industrial nations—the United States, Japan, Germany, the United Kingdom, and France—that sent officials to a world trade meeting at New York's Plaza Hotel in 1985 to try to correct the overvalued dollar and the twin U.S. deficits

Group of Seven (G-7)   seven industrial nations—the United states, Canada, Japan, the United Kingdom, Germany, France, and Italy—that launched coordinated purchases of the euro to boost its value

guest workers   foreign workers, when needed, allowed to immigrate on a temporary basis

H

Heckscher–Ohlin theory   differences in relative factor endowments among nations that underlie the basis for trade

hedging   the process of avoiding or covering a foreign-exchange risk

home market effect   countries will specialize in products for which there is large domestic demand

horizontal diversification   in the case of an MNE, occurs when a parent company producing a commodity in the source country sets up a subsidiary to produce the identical product in the host country

I

IMF drawings   the transactions by which the fund makes foreign-currency loans available

importance of being unimportant   when one trading nation is significantly larger than the other, the larger nation attains fewer gains from trade while the smaller nation attains most of the gains from trade

import license   used to administer an import quota; a license specifying the volume of imports allowed

import quota   a physical restriction on the quantity of goods that may be imported during a specific time period

import substitution   a policy that involves extensive use of trade barriers to protect domestic industries from import competition

impossible trinity   a restriction whereby a country can maintain only two of the following three policies— free capital flows, a fixed exchange rate, and an independent monetary policy

income adjustment mechanism   in 1930s, John Maynard Keynes formulated this theory that focuses on automatic changes in income to bring about adjustment in a nation's current account

increasing opportunity costs   when each additional unit of one good produced requires the sacrifice of increasing amounts of the other good

increasing returns to scale   when increasing all inputs by the same proportion results in a total output to increase by a greater proportion

indifference curve   a curve depicting the various combinations of two commodities that are equally preferred in the eyes of the consumer

indirect currency quote   a currency pair is one in which foreign currency is the base currency and the domestic currency is the quote currency

industrial policy government policy that is actively involved in creating comparative advantage

infant-industry argument a tariff that temporarily shields newly developing industries from foreign competition

intellectual property rights (IPRs) the exclusive rights to use an invention, idea, product, or process for a given time awarded to the inventor (or author) through registration with the government of that invention, idea, product, or process

interbank market bank transactions with other banks

interest arbitrage the process of moving funds into foreign currencies to take advantage of higher investment yields abroad

interindustry specialization when each nation specializes in a particular industry in which it enjoys a comparative advantage

interindustry trade the exchange between nations of products of different industries

internal balance the goal of economic stability at full employment

international commodity agreements (ICAs) agreements between leading, producing and consuming nations of commodities about matters such as stabilizing prices, assuring adequate supplies to consumers, and promoting the economic development of producers

international economic-policy coordination the attempt to coordinate national policies—monetary, fiscal, or exchange-rate policy—in recognition of international economic interdependence

international joint ventures an example of multinational enterprise in which a business organization

established by two or more companies combines their skills and assets

International Monetary Fund (IMF) headquartered in Washington, and consisting of 184 nations, the IMF can be thought of as a bank for the central banks of member nations

International Monetary Market (IMM) an extension of the commodity futures markets in which specific quantities of wheat, corn, and other commodities are bought and sold for future delivery at specific dates; the IMM provides trading facilities for the purchase and sale for future delivery of financial instruments (such as foreign currencies) and precious metals (such as gold)

international reserves assets held to enable nations to finance disequilibrium in their balance-of-payments positions

intra-industry specialization the focus on the production of particular products or groups of products within a given industry

intra-industry trade two-way trade in a similar commodity

J

J-curve effect a popular description of the time path of trade flows that suggests that in the very short term, a currency depreciation will lead to a worsening of the nation's trade balance, but as time passes, the trade balance will likely improve

judgmental forecasts subjective or common-sense exchange rate forecasts based on economic, political, and other data for a country

K

Kennedy Round round of trade negotiations named after U.S. President John F. Kennedy between GATT members during the period 1964–1967

key currency a currency that is widely traded on world money markets, has demonstrated relatively stable values over time, and has been widely accepted as a means of international settlement

L

labor mobility a measure of how labor migration responds to wage differentials

labor theory of value the cost or price of a good depends exclusively upon the amount of labor required to produce it

large nation an importing nation that is large enough so that changes in the quantity of its imports, by means of tariff policy, influence the world price of the product

law of comparative advantage when each nation specializes in the production of that good in which it has a relative advantage, the total output of each good increases; thus, all countries can realize welfare gains

law of one price part of the purchasing-power-parity approach to determining exchange rates; asserts that identical goods should cost the same in all nations, assuming that it is costless to ship goods between nations and there are no barriers to trade

leaning against the wind intervening to reduce short-term fluctuations in exchange rates without attempting to adhere to any particular rate over the long term

Leontief paradox the phenomenon of exports being less capital intensive than import-competing goods

level playing field a condition in which domestic and foreign producers can compete on equal terms

license on demand allocation a system in which licenses are required to import at the within-quota tariff

limit order an order to buy or sell at a specified price or better

liquidity problem when a government or central bank runs short of needed international reserves

long position the position speculators take when they purchase foreign currency on the spot or forward market with the anticipation of selling it at a higher future spot price

M

Maastricht Treaty signed in 1991, this agreement set 2002 as the date for completing the process of replacing the EU countries' central banks with a European Central Bank and replacing their national currencies with a single European currency

magnification effect an extension of the Stolper-Samuelson theorem, which suggests that the change in the price of a resource is greater than the change in the price of the good that uses the resources relatively intensively in its production process

managed floating system an exchange-rate system in which the rate is usually allowed to be determined by the free-market forces of supply and demand, while sometimes entailing some degree of government (central bank) intervention

margin of dumping the amount by which the domestic price of a firm's product exceeds its foreign price, or the amount by which the foreign price of a firm's product is less than the cost of producing it

marginal rate of transformation (MRT) the slope of the production possibilities schedule that shows the amount of one product a nation must sacrifice to get one additional unit of the other product

market economy where the commercial decisions of independent buyers and sellers acting in their own interest govern both domestic and international trade

market expectations examples include news about future market fundamentals and traders' opinions about future exchange rates

market fundamentals economic variables such as productivity, inflation rates, real interest rates, consumer preferences, and government trade policy

market order to buy or sell a currency at the current market price

Marshall-Lerner condition a general rule that states: (1) Depreciation will improve the trade balance if the currency-depreciating nation's demand elasticity for imports plus the foreign demand elasticity for the nation's exports exceeds one. (2) If the sum of the demand elasticities is less than one, depreciation will worsen the trade balance. (3) The trade balance will be neither helped nor hurt if the sum of the demand elasticities equals one

maturity months the months of a given year when the futures contract matures

mercantilists an advocate or practitioner of mercantilism; a national economic system in which a nation could regulate its domestic and international affairs so as to promote its own interests through a strong foreign-trade sector

merchandise trade balance the result of combining the dollar value of merchandise exports recorded as a plus (credit) and the dollar value of merchandise imports recorded as a minus (debit)

migration moving from one country to settle in another

Ministry of Economy, Trade, and Industry (METI) created by the Japanese government to implement its industrial policies in manufacturing

monetary approach an approach to currency depreciation that stresses the effects depreciation has on the purchasing power of money and the

resulting impact on domestic expenditure levels

monetary policy refers to changes in the money supply by a nation's central bank

monetary union the unification of national monetary policies and the acceptance of a common currency administered by a supranational monetary authority

most-favored nation (MFN) clause an agreement between two nations to apply tariffs to each other at rates as low as those applied to any other nation

Multifiber Arrangement (MFA) a system of rules negotiated by the United States and Europe to restrict competition from developing exporting countries employing low-cost labor

multilateral contract contract that stipulates a minimum price at which importers will purchase guaranteed quantities from the producing nations and a maximum price at which producing nations will sell guaranteed amounts to importers

multinational enterprise (MNE) an enterprise that cuts across national borders and is often directed from a company planning center that is distant from the host country

multiplier process when an initial increase in investment spending sets off a chain reaction that results in greater levels of spending, so that income increases by some multiple of the initial investment increase

N

net creditor the status of a nation when that country's claims on foreigners exceed foreign claims on that country at a particular time

net debtor the status of a nation when foreign claims on a country exceed that country's claims on foreigners at a particular time

net foreign investment in national income accounting, is synonymous with the current account balance

nominal exchange rate exchange-rate quotes published in newspapers that are not adjusted inflation rates in trading partners

nominal exchange-rate index the average value of a currency, not adjusted for changes in price levels of that country and its trading partners

nominal interest rate the rate of return on assets that can be earned in a particular country, not adjusted for the rate of inflation

nominal tariff rate the tariff rate published in a country's tariff schedule

nonmarket economy where state planning and control govern foreign and sometimes domestic trade

nonrestrained suppliers a trading partner that is not restrained by a voluntary export agreement

nontariff trade barriers (NTBs) policies other than tariffs that restrict international trade

normal trade relations the U.S. government's replacement for the term most-favored nation

North American Free Trade Agreement (NAFTA) a trade agreement between Canada, Mexico, and the United States, which went into effect in 1994

no-trade boundary the terms-of-trade limit at which a country will cease to export a good

O

offer rate the price at which the bank is willing to sell a unit of foreign currency

official exchange rate the exchange rate determined by comparing the par values of two currencies

official reserve assets holding key foreign currencies, special drawing rights, and reserve positions in the IMF by official monetary institutions

official settlements transactions the movement of financial assets among official holders; these financial assets fall into two categories: official reserve assets and liabilities to foreign official agencies

offshore-assembly provision (OAP) when import duties apply only to the value added in the foreign assembly process, provided that domestically made components are used by overseas companies in their assembly operations

openness the ratio of a nation's exports and imports as a percentage of its gross domestic product (GDP)

optimum currency area a region in which it is economically preferable to have a single official currency rather than multiple official currencies

optimum tariff a tariff rate at which the positive difference between the gain of improving terms of trade and the loss of declining import volume is maximized

option an agreement between a holder (buyer) and a writer (seller) that gives the holder the right, but not the obligation, to buy or sell financial instruments at any time through a specified date

Organization of Petroleum Exporting Countries (OPEC) a group of nations that sells petroleum on the world market and attempts to support prices higher than would exist under more competitive conditions to maximize member-nation profits

outer limits for the equilibrium terms of trade defined by the domestic cost ratios of trading nations

outsourcing when certain aspects of a product's manufacture are performed in more than one country

overall balance when an economy attains internal and external balance

overshooting an instance of an exchange rate's short-term response to a change in market fundamentals is greater than its long-term response

P

par value a central value in terms of a key currency that governments participating in a fixed-exchange rate system set their currencies

partial specialization when a country specializes only partially in the production of the good in which it has a comparative advantage

persistent dumping when a producer consistently sells products abroad at lower prices than at home

pip stands for *percentage in point* and is the smallest increment of trade in the forex market

predatory dumping when a producer temporarily reduces the prices charged abroad to drive foreign competitors out of business

premium the valuation of a currency when it is worth more in the forward market than in the spot market

price adjustment mechanism see quantity of money theory

price-based definition of dumping a method of calculating fair market value in dumping cases; dumping occurs when a company sells a product in its home market at a price above that for which the same product sells in the foreign market

price-specie-flow doctrine David Hume's theory that a favorable trade balance was possible only in the short term, and that over time, it would automatically be eliminated via changes in product prices

primary products agricultural goods, raw materials, and fuels

principle of absolute advantage in a two-nation, two-product world, international specialization and trade will be beneficial when one nation has an absolute cost advantage in one good and the other nation has an absolute cost advantage in the other good

principle of comparative advantage ability to produce a good or service at a lower opportunity cost than others can produce it

producer surplus the revenue producers receive over and above the minimum amount required to induce them to supply the good

product life cycle theory many manufactured goods undergo a predictable trade cycle; during this cycle, the home country initially is an exporter, then loses its competitive advantage vis-à-vis its trading partners, and eventually may become an importer of the commodity

production controls artificial curtailments in the production of a commodity

production gains increases in production resulting from specialization in the product of comparative advantage

production possibilities schedule a schedule that shows various alternative combinations of two goods that a nation can produce when all of its factor inputs are used in their most efficient manner

protection-biased sector generally consists of import-competing companies, the labor unions representing workers in that industry, and the suppliers to the companies in the industry

protective effect a tariff's loss to the domestic economy resulting from wasted resources when less efficient domestic production is substituted for more efficient foreign production

protective tariff a tariff designed to insulate import-competing producers from foreign competition

purchasing-power-parity theory a method of determining the equilibrium exchange rate by means of the price levels and their variations in different nations

put option gives the holder the right to sell foreign currency at a specified price

Q

quantity theory of money states that increases in the money supply lead directly to an increase in overall prices, and a shrinking money supply causes overall prices to fall

R

real exchange rate the nominal exchange rate adjusted for changes in relative price levels

real exchange-rate index the average value of a currency based on real exchange rates

real interest rate the nominal interest rate minus the inflation rate

Reciprocal Trade Agreements Act an act passed in Congress in 1934 which set the stage for a wave of trade liberalization through negotiating authority and generalized reductions

redistributive effect with a tariff, the transfer of consumer surplus, in monetary terms, to the domestic producers of the import-competing product

region of mutually beneficial trade the area that is bounded by the cost ratios of the two trading countries

regional trading arrangement where member nations agree to impose lower barriers to trade within the group than to trade with nonmember nations

revaluation an official change in a currency's par value, which causes the currency's exchange value to appreciate

revenue effect represents the government's collections of tariff revenue; found by multiplying the number of imports times the tariff

revenue tariff a tariff imposed for the purpose of generating tax revenues and may be placed on either exports or imports

S

safeguards relief provided by the escape clause to U.S. firms and workers who are substantially injured from surges in imports that are fairly traded

scientific tariff a tariff that eliminates foreign cost advantages over domestic firms

Section 301 section of the Trade Act of 1974 that gives the U.S. trade representative (USTR) authority, subject to the approval of the president, and means to respond to unfair trading practices by foreign nations

seigniorage profit from issuing money

selective quota an import quota allocated to specific countries

short position the position speculators take when they borrow or sell forward a foreign currency with the anticipation of purchasing it at a future lower price to repay the foreign-exchange loan or fulfill the forward sale contract

small nation a nation whose imports constitute a very small portion of the world market supply

Smoot-Hawley Act act passed in 1930 under which U.S. average tariffs were raised to 53 percent on protected imports

social regulation governmental attempts to correct a variety of undesirable side effects in an economy that relate to health, safety, and the environment

special drawing right (SDR) an artificial currency unit based on a basket of four currencies established by the IMF

specific factor   factor that cannot move easily from one industry to another

specific tariff   a tariff expressed in terms of a fixed amount of money per unit of the imported product

specific-factors theory   considers the income-distribution effects of trade when factor inputs are immobile among industries in the short term

speculation   the attempt to profit by trading on expectations about prices in the future

speculative attack   see currency crisis

sporadic dumping   (distress dumping) when a firm disposes of excess inventories on foreign markets by selling abroad at lower prices than at home

spot market   where foreign exchange can be traded for immediate delivery

spot transaction   an outright purchase and sale of foreign currency for cash settlement not more than two business days after the date of the transaction

spread   the difference between the bid and the ask prices

stabilizing speculation   occurs when speculators expect a current trend in an exchange rate's movement to change and their purchase or sale of the currency moderates movements of the exchange rate

static effects of economic integration include the trade-creation effect and the trade-diversion effect

statistical discrepancy   a correcting entry inserted into the balance-of-payments statement to make the sum of the credits and debits equal

Stolper-Samuelson theorem   an extension of the theory of factor-price equalization, which states that the export of the product that embodies large amounts of the relatively cheap, abundant resource makes this resource more scarce in the domestic market

stop order   an order that is activated when a currency reaches a specified price called the "stop"

strategic trade policy   the policy that government can assist domestic companies in capturing economic profits from foreign competitors

strike price   the price at which an option can be exercised

subsidies   granted by governments to domestic producers to improve their trade competitiveness; include outright cash disbursements, tax concessions, insurance arrangements, and loans at below-market interest rates

supply of international reserves includes owned reserves, such as key currencies and special drawing rights, and borrowed reserves, which can come from the IMF and other official arrangements or can be obtained from major commercial banks

swap arrangements   bilateral agreements between central banks where each government provides for an exchange, or swap, of currencies to help finance temporary payments disequilibrium

T

target exchange rates   desired exchange rates for a currency set by the host country and supported by intervention

tariff   a tax levied on a product when it crosses national boundaries

tariff avoidance   the legal utilization of the tariff system to one's own advantage in order to reduce the amount of tariff that is payable by means that are within the law

tariff escalation   occurs when tariff structures of industrialized nations are characterized by rising rates that give greater protection to intermediate and finished products than to primary commodities

tariff evasion   when individuals or firms evade tariffs by illegal means such as smuggling imported goods into a country

tariff-rate quota   a device that allows a specified number of goods to be imported at one tariff rate (the within-quota rate), and any imports above that specified number to be imported at a higher tariff rate (the over-quota rate)

technical analysis   a method of exchange-rate forecasting that involves the use of historical exchange-rate data to estimate future values

technology transfer   the transfer to other nations of knowledge and skills applied to how goods are produced

terms of trade   the relative prices at which two products are traded in the marketplace

terms-of-trade effect   the tariff revenue extracted from foreign producers in the form of a lower supply price

theory of overlapping demands nations with similar per capita incomes will have overlapping demand structures and will likely consume similar types of manufactured goods; wealthy nations will likely trade with other wealthy nations, and poor nations will likely trade with other poor nations

theory of reciprocal demand   relative demand conditions determine what the actual terms of trade will be within the outer limits of the terms of trade

three-point arbitrage   a more intricate form of arbitrage, involving three currencies and three financial centers; also called triangular arbitrage

Tokyo Round   round of talks between GATT members from 1973–1979, in which signatory nations agreed to tariff cuts that took the across-the-board form initiated in the Kennedy Round

trade adjustment assistance   government assistance granted to domestic workers displaced by increased imports

trade balance derived by computing the net exports (imports) in the merchandise accounts; also called merchandise trade balance

trade promotion authority (also known as *fast-track authority*) devised in 1974, this provision commits the U.S. Congress to consider trade agreements without amendment; in return, the president must adhere to a specified timetable and several other procedures

trade remedy laws laws designed to produce a fair trading environment for all parties engaging in international business; these laws include the escape clause, countervailing duties, antidumping duties, and unfair trading practices

trade triangle an area in a production possibilities diagram showing a country's exports, imports, and equilibrium terms of trade

trade-creation effect a welfare gain resulting from increasing trade caused by the formation of a regional trade bloc

trade-diversion effect a welfare loss resulting from the formation of a regional trade bloc; it occurs when imports from a low-cost supplier outside the trade bloc are replaced by purchases from a higher-cost supplier within the trade bloc

trade-weighted dollar a weighted average of the exchange rates between a domestic currency and the currencies of the nation's most important trading partners, with weights given by relative importance of the nation's trade with each trade partner

trading possibilities line a line in a production possibilities diagram representing the equilibrium terms-of-trade ratio

transfer pricing a technique where an MNE reports most of its profits in a low-tax country, even though the profits are earned in a high-tax country

transition economies national economies making the transition from a centrally planned economy to a market economy

transplants the assembly plants of Japanese companies that produce automobiles in the United States

transportation costs the costs of moving goods from one nation to another

two-point arbitrage the simultaneous purchase and sale of a currency in two foreign-exchange markets in order to profit from exchange-rate differentials in different locations

U

uncovered interest arbitrage when an investor does not obtain exchange-market cover to protect investment proceeds from foreign-currency fluctuations

unilateral transfers include transfers of goods and services (gifts in kind) or financial assets (money gifts) between the United States and the rest of the world

Uruguay Round round of talks between GATT members from 1986–1993 in which across-the-board tariff

cuts for industrial countries averaged 40 percent

V

variable levies an import tariff that increases or decreases as domestic or world prices change to guarantee that the price of the imported product after payment of duty will equal a predetermined price

vertical diversification in the case of an MNE, occurs when the parent MNE decides to establish foreign subsidiaries to produce intermediate goods or inputs that go into the production of the finished good

W

wage and price controls intervention by the government to set price and wage levels

wage insurance after finding new jobs, a temporary government subsidy of wages granted to domestic workers displaced by foreign trade and increased imports

World Bank an international organization that provides loans to developing countries aimed toward poverty reduction and economic development

World Trade Organization (WTO) organization that embodies the main provisions of GATT, but its role was expanded to include a mechanism intended to improve GATT's process for resolving trade disputes among member nations

Index

The Economic Report of the President

http://www.gpoaccess.gov/index.html

Description: Information about the U.S. and world economies, as well as recent and historical international trade statistics.

The U.S. Census Bureau

http://www.census.gov/ftp/pub/foreign-trade/www

Description: Extensive, recent, and historical data on U.S. exports, imports, and trade balances with individual countries. The U.S. Census Bureau has also developed a profile of U.S. exporting companies.

The World Bank Group

http://www1.worldbank.org

Description: One of the world's largest sources of developmental assistance. This site provides economic briefs and data for countries by region.

United Nations Statistics

http://unstats.un.org/unsd/

Description: International data from the United Nations' home page covering a wide range of variables.

World Trade Organization

http://www.wto.org/

Description: Includes a brief biographical sketch of David Ricardo, information on recent world trade and output growth, and a summary of arguments in favor of free trade.

The Institute for International Economics

http://www.iie.com/

Description: Sources of information relevant to international equilibrium, including essays and working papers.

The Penn World Dataset

http://www.bized.co.uk/dataserv/penndata/pennhome.htm

Description: Statistics on 28 key economic variables for the world's major economies from 1950 to 1992, including GDP per capita adjusted for changes in terms of trade.

U.S. Department of Commerce/International Trade Administration

http://www.ita.doc.gov/td/industry/otea/

Description: Trade statistics for the United States by world, region, or country.

Bureau of Labor Statistics/Foreign Labor Statistics

http://www.bls.gov/home.htm

Description: Comparison of the hourly compensation of U.S. workers in manufacturing to that of workers in other countries.

International Trade Commission

http://www.usitc.gov/

Description: Information about U.S. tariffs as well as many documents that address contemporary issues in international economics.

Bureau of Industry and Security/U.S. Department of Commerce

http://www.bis.doc.gov/

Description: Information on U.S. export controls, including restrictions on exports of nuclear weapons and financial services encryption products.

Office of the United States Trade Representative (OUSTR)

http://www.ustr.gov/

Description: Reports issued by the OUSTR and related entities including the National Trade Estimate Report on Foreign Trade Barriers.

European Union/Sectoral and Trade Barriers Database

http://mkaccdb.eu.int/

Description: Sectoral and Trade Barriers Database of selected countries prepared by the European Union.

The Department of State

http://www.state.gov

Description: Reports on the history, politics, and economic and trade policies of the regions and countries with which the United States regularly trades.

The Export-Import Bank

http://www.exim.gov/

Description: Information and services from the government-held corporation that encourages the sale of U.S. goods in foreign markets.

National Science Foundation

http://www.nsf.gov/sbe/srs/fedfunds/start.htm

Description: Information on R&D expenditures and the extent of government support in the United States.

United Nations Conference on Trade and Development (UNCTAD)

http://www.unctad.org

Description: UNCTAD is an organization that helps developing nations compete in world markets.

CIA's Handbook of International Economic Statistics

http://www.cia.gov

Description: Comprehensive information on most countries and territories, including geography, natural resources, demographics, government, and economic statistics.

Free Trade Area of the Americas

http://www.alca-ftaa.org/
Description: Information about the plan to integrate the economies of North and South America.

Asia-Pacific Economic Cooperation

http://www.apecsec.org/
Description: Regional organization of 18 countries that promotes free trade and economic coordination.

European Union

http://europa.eu.int/
Description: Information and news items related to the European Union.

Association of Southeast Asian Nations (ASEAN)

http://www.aseansec.org/home.htm
Description: Information and news items about ASEAN's role in promoting economic growth, social progress, and cultural development of ten Southeast Asian nations.

U.S. Citizenship and Immigration Services

http://uscis.gov/graphics/
Description: Comprehensive statistics on U.S. immigration.

Bureau of Economic Analysis

http://www.bea.gov/
Description: Information on the U.S. balance of payments, U.S. exports and imports, and the international investment position of the United States.

White House Briefing Room

http://www.whitehouse.gov/
Description: Summary statistics on international aspects of the economy.

Federal Reserve Bank of St. Louis

http://www.stlouisfed.org/
Description: Provides historical information on exchange rates.

Pacific Rate Exchange Service

http://fx.sauder.ubc.ca/
Description: Provides information on current and past daily exchange rates, as well as exchange-rate forecasts for the Canadian dollar relative to five other major currencies.

Asian Development Bank

http://www.adb.org/
Description: Promotes the economic and social progress of its developing member countries. It has extensive reports and statistics on a number of Asian countries.

U.S. Department of Agriculture/Foreign Agricultural Service

http://www.fas.usda.gov/
Description: Detailed look at various countries' exports and imports of agricultural products to and from the U.S.

Council on Foreign Relations

http://www.cfr.org/
Description: National organization that is committed to the study and debate of America's global role. Site includes some of their recent studies on international finance and trade.

Federal Reserve Bank of New York

http://www.ny.frb.org/
Description: Go to News Items and Foreign Exchange, which includes regular reports on the Fed's intervention in foreign-exchange markets.

Bank for International Settlements/Central Banks

http://www.bis.org/cbanks.htm
Description: Links to numerous central banks around the world.

The International Monetary Fund (IMF)

http://www.imf.org/
Description: International Monetary Fund provides loans, technical assistance, and policy guidance to developing members in order to reduce poverty, improve living standards, and safeguard the stability of the international monetary system.

Bank for International Settlements

http://www.bis.org/
Description: News, publications, and services of the Bank for International Settlements, which facilitates international policy coordination through its monthly meetings of central bank officials.

Organisation for Economic Cooperation and Development (OECD)

http://www.oecd.org/
Description: Paris-based organization of 29 countries. Its goal is to develop compatible, wide-ranging policies that boost prosperity.

National Bureau of Economic Research (NBER)

http://www.nber.org/
Description: Provides online data and summaries of research studies relating to international finance, trade, and investment.

European Central Bank

http://www.ecb.int/
Description: Information on Eurocurrency, including pictures of its design and a discussion of the changeover process.